EDEN Annual Conference 2025

Shaping the Future of Education in the Age of AI: Empowering Inclusion, Innovation and Ethical Growth

Full Papers

Bologna, Italy
15 - 17 June 2025

Editor:

Elena Trepulė

ISBN: 979-8-3313-2645-6

Printed from e-media with permission by:

Curran Associates, Inc.
57 Morehouse Lane
Red Hook, NY 12571

Some format issues inherent in the e-media version may also appear in this print version.

European Distance and E-Learning Network (EDEN)
Budapest University of Technology & Economics
H-1111 Budapest, Egry J. u.1.
Hungary

Phone: +36 1 463 1628
Fax: +36 1 463 1858

secretariat@eden-online.org

Additional copies of this publication are available from:

Curran Associates, Inc.
57 Morehouse Lane
Red Hook, NY 12571 USA
Phone: 845-758-0400
Fax: 845-758-2633
Email: curran@proceedings.com
Web: www.proceedings.com

EDEN Annual Conference Proceedings

Shaping the Future of Education in the Age of AI: Empowering Inclusion, Innovation and Ethical Growth

EDEN 2025 Annual Conference

hosted by

University of Bologna, Bologna, Italy

15-17 June 2025

Edited by

Elena Trepulė

on behalf of EDEN Digital Learning Europe

EDEN Annual Conference Proceedings

2025 Annual Conference | Bologna, 15-17 June 2025

ISSN: 2707-2819

Published by EDEN Digital Learning Europe

Editor:

Elena Trepulė

Editorial co-ordination:

Gabija Morozovienė

EDEN DLE Secretariat

Kuklase tn 16-12, 13423, Tallinn, Estonia

E-mail: secretariat@eden-europe.eu

https://eden-europe.eu/

Co-funded by the European Union

Funded by the European Union. Views and opinions expressed are however those of the author(s) only and do not necessarily reflect those of the European Union or the European Education and Culture Executive Agency (EACEA). Neither the European Union nor EACEA can be held responsible for them.

Acknowledgement and thanks are given to the Conference Scientific Committee:

Wim E.A. Van Petegem, EDEN President, Belgium; Chair

Antonella Poce, EDEN DLE Management Board, Italy; Chair

Pier Cesare Rivoltella, Bologna University, Italy; Chair

Airina Volungevičienė, Lithuania

Alfredo Soeiro, Portugal

Chiara Panciroli, Bologna University, Italy

Denise Whitelock, The Open University, UK

Elena Trepulė, EDEN / Vytautas Magnus University, Lithuania

Giuliana Benvenuti, Bologna University, Italy

Josep M. Duart, UOC, Spain

Mart Laanpere, Tallinn University, Estonia

Maurizio Gabbrielli, Bologna University, Italy

Maurizio Sobrero, Bologna University, Italy

Polona Baloh Kremavc, Slovenia

Rebecca Montanari, Bologna University, Italy

Roberto Vecchi, Bologna University, Italy

Sandra Kučina Softić, University of Zagreb University Computing Centre, Croatia

Simone Martini, Bologna University, Italy

Simona Tondelli, Bologna University, Italy

Vlad Mihăescu, UPT, Romania

TABLE OF CONTENTS

Universal Design for Learning to integrate Artificial Intelligence and Bologna Principles in Higher Education

Martha Lorena Obermeier[1]

[1] Escuela de Lenguas, Campus Tapachula, Universidad Autónoma de Chiapas, México; lorena.obermeier@gmail.com

Correspondence: Martha Lorena Obermeier: lorena.obermeier@gmail.com

Abstract:

The Bologna Process principles promote equality and inclusion in Education, regardless of the regional contexts. At the same time, every country has different contexts and resources. Including Artificial Intelligence in education could be considered a tool to reduce those inequalities. On the other hand, using AI promotes more inequalities as it demands access to devices and connectivity. This literature review presents these topics and the ethical considerations needed to foster equality and quality of education.

Keywords: Artificial Intelligence, Higher Education, Universal Design for Learning, Inclusion.

Introduction

Higher Education Institutions face a challenge in today's society as their pertinence is being continually questioned. The Bologna Process states principles to give accessibility to students to educational programs equivalent in many countries. This offers them access to job positions in different countries. To offer high-quality education, institutions will need to improve the quality of their programs. Due to the inequalities between countries and the number of students, institutions need to carefully consider how to take advantage of Artificial Intelligence to improve the quality of their programs.

A literature review was conducted to answer the research question: how can Artificial Intelligence be effectibly introduced in Higher Education Institutions to follow the Bologna Process Principles? The review included articles and book chapters related to the Bologna Process, and Artificial Intelligence integration in education.

The Bologna Process

Educational plans are traditionally designed to face local challenges, even if graduates are going to face global challenges (Fejes, 2006). In some countries, educational reforms are based on traditional beliefs facing the past, not the future. The traditional curriculum is being challenged by today's needs: flexibility, employability, and mobility. Karseth (2006) states that The Bologna Declaration is a commitment to create a space that enhances the employability and mobility of citizens and increases their competitiveness. The action lines consider several factors as: the adoption of a system to allow degrees' equivalences for undergraduate and graduate cycles; a system of credits in educational programs; mobility opportunities for students and faculty; quality assurance, and a broader dimension in Higher Education.

The Bologna process is considered a standardization process to prepare graduates to compete in the job market with knowledge and highly developed competencies. This process aims at the fact that all citizens become employable and mobile. A mobile subject will have more chances to perform a job in any other country. Those who do not want to develop skills or use technology reduce their mobility and job opportunities. The adoption of the Bologna Process principles allows students to not lag behind students from other countries.

The Principles suggests that Higher Education should be designed considering the national and global context, as it is affected by the context at the same time that it influences it (Orr, 2020). Candidates searching for employment will need to develop soft skills to succeed in the digital world. They will also need to develop a mindset to embrace innovation and digitalization. The Bologna Process proposes changes to ensure that all universities are connected and it removes barriers (Isaacs, 2020). This initiative will allow students to freely circulate between universities and their degrees will be valid in different countries. The objective is to create compatible studies, which can be attained by having a high level of commitment and openness to change. To be compatible, programs need to have the same basic structure with credits as a measure of learning. Universities will need to offer short training opportunities with alternative credentials for the accomplishment of certain skills that need to be constantly updated.

According to West et al. (2020), educational institutions have traditionally awarded credentials to back up alumni skills, knowledge, and qualities. These credentials remain important, but there is a need for alternative credentials for the informal or online development of skills and knowledge. These alternative credentials are digital certificates such as micro-diplomas, nanodegrees, or digital badges. These digital versions are embedded with data explaining the criteria for earning it. They represent the achievement of a discrete accomplishment or skill and they are more easily managed. Micro credentials and digital badges can be considered as a stimulus, which improves confidence and self-regulated learning, and as complementary to formal university degrees.

Inequality

Every country in the European Union has a different concept of what inclusive education is, and this makes it difficult to achieve (Galkiene & Monkeviciene, 2021). Inclusive Education has been considered as an important topic in educational policies. It is not limited to students with disabilities, but also to students from different cultural or social backgrounds. Policies on inclusive education state that efforts should be made to eliminate barriers related to social background, religion, or economic status.

According to Castillo et al. (2022), to achieve Sustainable Development Goals, countries need to reduce inequalities in education. Even if some countries have made initiatives to reduce inequalities with scholarships and other initiatives, they persist. There is a need of trained teachers in some countries, as well as a need for a long term vision in policies.

Many countries have a debt with students in conditions of vulnerability as they have the lowest opportunities of access to education and lower levels of learning (Schmelkes et al., 2022). These students access educational institutions with deficiencies in infrastructure, educational tools, and technological equipment. Most of the times, the teachers in these institutions do not have the appropriate training. To have equality in education, learning opportunities need to be accessible and affordable.

Frameworks to Ensure Quality in Education

In today's society, a person needs to be a lifelong learner. Even if the person obtained a degree, the job market continually needs employees with certain skills. These short trainings need commitment and self-regulated learning from the student. Banihashem et al. (2024) state that studies on self-regulated learning are mostly developed in North America, Europe, and Asia. Studies from South America and Africa lack representation, which may be due to funding reasons and a lack of international collaboration. There is a need for studies on self-regulated learning from several parts of the world, which could help identify students at risk of dropping out. These results could also help to design interventions to develop self-regulated learners.

As students learn in a more self-regulated way, any online course needs to have structure (van Dorresteijn et al., 2024). Dropout rates in online courses and programs are high mostly due to a poor sense of community, lack of interaction, feelings of isolation, and inadequate support. Self-regulation skills and digital literacy are also contributors to its efficiency. The literature on the topic also mentions time management, critical thinking, and metacognition as conditions for good performance in online contexts. Students who feel confident have better performance and increased chances of completing the course.

The student is an aspect of the educational process, but the course needs to be well-designed, especially in online contexts. There are several frameworks and principles in the literature to ensure quality in online training. The first one is the Community of Inquiry framework, which has three components to ensure the quality of online or blended learning experiences. Social presence, cognitive presence, and teaching presence overlap and give deep and meaningful learning as a result (Oyarzun & Martin, 2023). Instructional design is a time-intensive process, in which instructors assume different roles as subject expert, course designer, developer, facilitator, evaluator, technology expert, and lifelong learner. Even if it is a time consuming complicated process, the result can help to improve learners' confidence and reduce dropout rates.

The second one is the principles of Universal Design for Learning (UDL), which provides multiple means for learner engagement, motivation for learning, and goal orientation. Westine et al. (2019) state that this framework was developed to optimize learning based on scientific knowledge of how knowledge occurs. It promotes accessibility and successful learning. It considers three main principles:

- Multiple means of representation: use of textbooks, videos, simulations, concept maps, and animations. The what of learning.
- Multiple means of engagement in learning: guided inquiry and problem-based learning. The why of learning.
- Multiple means of expression: demonstration of knowledge creating films, exhibitions, models, or projects. The how of learning.

UDL as a Framework for an Inclusive Higher Education

Inclusion means offering access opportunities to higher education to people from diverse contexts. Inclusion should not only focus on minorities but also on students with disabilities (Benade, 2019). The curricular design of a program or course is the first approach to promoting inclusion. Participation from different agents like faculty, chairs, administrative staff, and students should be encouraged to improve conditions for inclusion (McMahon & Walker, 2019). At the same time, inclusion fosters community building and offers access to education using diverse technologies. A student who feels like a part of a community has more probability of obtaining a degree.

The United Nations Educational, Scientific and Cultural Organization (UNESCO, 2009) states that inclusion should be fostered in education and access should be granted to all persons giving them the same opportunities. According to Dalton et al. (2019), inclusive education should gather students with disabilities or with different needs in the same classroom or learning environment. In some countries, students do not have access to education as educational institutions do not have access to facilities or faculty is not trained to teach students with special needs.

The UDL conceptual framework is a guideline to promote flexible educational practices to reduce barriers to education. At the same time, it improves inclusion possibilities for students with disabilities, from minority groups, or unprivileged contexts (Estes et al., 2020). Educational institutions face many challenges to foster inclusive education. Some of them are the lack of trained faculty, the lack of technological support, and the lack of an inclusive culture in the administrative areas of the institutions. Negative attitudes toward students with disabilities are commonly perceived, as well as stereotypes, lack of access to facilities, and lack of support.

McKenzie and Dalton (2020) consider that the UDL framework places the teacher at the center of the learning process. This is the reason why it demands continual updates, flexible institutional policies, and adaptation to unexpected needs or situations. Inclusive education is time-consuming in the design process, but it reduces barriers, fosters continual updates, and uses students' diversity as a learning resource (Roski et al., 2021). The developers of the UDL approach emphasize the necessity to eliminate barriers. They followed Vygotsky's theory and developed principles of learning to learn. This framework improves teaching and learning, as it builds learner' self-efficacy. As every student is unique, schools must be prepared to provide education regardless their characteristics and needs. For this approach, diversity in learning styles, abilities, and interests is a natural phenomenon. Applying this framework empowers learners. It presents information in various ways, increases satisfaction and fosters engagement in the learning process.

In any classroom, students are diverse in ethnicity, gender, culture, mental and physical ability, and academic needs. This model is centered on the learner usually related with the use of technology as it emphasizes the importance of considering differences in the instructional design. This model makes education accessible to all students regarding their needs as it provides an enriched learning experience with flexibility to access information (Bhan & Panshikar, 2023). Applying this approach means reconceptualising the existing educational system.

AI in Educational Contexts

The manifesto by Bozkurt et al. (2024) presents both positive and negative aspects of using AI in educational contexts. One of the positive aspects is that AI can automate administrative time-consuming tasks. It can also personalize instruction as it generates lesson plans or educational materials, improving opportunities to facilitate knowledge. As it integrates knowledge from diverse knowledge domains, it encourages system thinking to critically evaluate materials.

The negative aspects of AI are related to unequal access and how it widens the gap between those with access and those without it. This gap marginalizes minority groups that are not considered in the data gathered. The use of data for decision-making raises concerns about transparency and privacy issues. Another threat perceived is related to integrity as it can be used for plagiarism and cheating, as a result, superficial learning and knowledge retention become a concern. The outputs may lack accuracy spreading misinformation. The same attributes that make AI integration into education positive, make it negative at the same time. As it can generate lesson plans, it cannot replicate mentoring, emotional connections, or understanding individual needs. At the moment, there is still a lack of governance as there are insufficient regulations and policies, which could lead to loss of privacy and intrusive surveillance. As AI is the new instructional technology to be incorporated into education, educators will need training to implement it in class.

Even if it raises many concerns, it has been found that AI can enhance engagement and alleviate monotony. AI tools also enhance interactivity, engagement, and motivation. At the same time, it is considered that it develops a more positive attitude towards academic challenges. In a study on the use of AI for academic writing, there were concerns about language comprehension, fears of compromising authenticity, and possible negative impact on academic performance. There is also a concern that relying upon this tool can improve dependence on its use. Another concern is the authenticity of the writing, even if it can save time editing texts. This tool should be seen as a way to reduce time for performing some tasks instead of considering it a replacement for performing them.

Concerns About AI

Digital technology causes many changes in several areas and one of the most influenced areas is open and distance education. The integration of AI into education has caused diverse reactions. While some think that it can improve access to education, others consider that it enhances inequalities. AI fosters engagement and collaboration in multimodal environments as it allows text, image, and audio to create an interactive learning experience. There is still a need to study AI's effects on education to develop a supportive culture and improve resources.

There are different conditions and concerns about its use all over the world as it is stated in an ICDE (2024) Report on Higher Education with AI. In Asia, the main concern is privacy issues and a lack of technical support. Hong Kong universities focus on training their staff on AI literacy, but they need to work on pedagogy and curricular redesign. Africa still has many challenges related to infrastructure and skills gaps. In North America, universities have mainly started to introduce the use of chatbots. Latin America mainly faces the challenges of the digital divide. As AI is critical and contributes to advancing the UN Sustainable Development Goals, some countries lack electricity and internet connection. The need to innovate faces the attachment to traditional pedagogical practices. In this case, AI inclusion in education demands a shift of mindsets to design activities, and assessment tools and transform teaching roles. This technology can also develop competency-based training programs for specific skills or knowledge, which can be assessed with micro-credentials.

Conclusions

Literature in online learning is abundant, but some of the aspects not highlighted in online learning are inclusion, diversity, and equity of access. Even if online learning and AI integration can offer training opportunities to students with disabilities, learners may need expensive technological gadgets as screen readers, alternative keyboards, or assistive software. These devices also need high-speed internet connection and access can be limited to learners from some marginalized or ethnic groups. At the beginning of this article, the Bologna Process was mentioned as principles to attain equality in Higher Education Institutions in the European Union. This equality would give the same access to alumni from different institutions in different countries. UDL framework is aligned with the Bologna Process statement on providing inclusive opportunities. Then, the inequalities that AI can present were mentioned. Some policies on the use of AI should be stated to reduce the inequalities that it can produce and secure equal access to high-quality education in different countries, regardless of their conditions.

The research question of the study was about the best way to integrate Artificial Intelligence in Higher Education Institutions to follow the Bologna Process Principles. After conducting a literature review, it was found that the Universal Design for Learning is a framework that can help to integrate AI that reduce inequalities as it is aligned with the Bologna Process Principles.

Competing interests

The author(s) has/have no competing interests to declare.

References

Bhan, S. & Panshikar, A. (2023). Training in UDL for Teacher Educators in Developing Countries. In K. Koreeda, M. Tsuge, S. Ikuta, E. Dalton, & L. Ewe (Eds.), Developing Inclusive Environments in Education: Global Practices and Curricula (pp. 1-13). IGI Global Scientific Publishing. https://doi.org/10.4018/979-8-3693-0664-2.ch001

Banihashem, S.K., Bond, M., Bergdahl, N., Khosravi, H., & Noroozi, O. (2024). A Systematic Mapping Review at the Intersection of Artificial Intelligence and Self-Regulated Learning: A call for increased theoretical grounding, focus on motivation and diversifying context. Pre-print. http://dx.doi.org/10.13140/RG.2.2.13057.47207

Benade, L. (2019). Flexible Learning Spaces: Incusive by Design? New Zealand Journal of Education Studies, 54, 53-68.

Bozkurt, A., Xiao, J., Farrow, R., Bai, J. Y. H., Nerantzi, C., Moore, S., Dron, J., Stracke, C. M., Singh, L., Crompton, H., Koutropoulos, A., Terentev, E., Pazurek, A., Nichols, M., Sidorkin, A. M., Costello, E., Watson, S., Mulligan, D., Honeychurch, S., ... & Asino, T. I. (2024). The Manifesto for Teaching and Learning in a Time of Generative AI: A Critical Collective Stance to Better Navigate the Future. Open Praxis, 16(4), pp. 487–513. https://doi.org/10.55982/openpraxis.16.4.777

Castillo, N.M., Adam, T., & Hafler, B. (2022). Improving the Impact of Educational Technologies on Learning Within Low-income Contexts. In D.A. Wagner, N.M. Castillo, & L.S. Grant (eds.). Learning, Marginalization, and improving the quality of education in low-income countries. Open Book Publishers.

Dalton, E.M., Lyner-Cleophas, M., Ferguson, B.T., McKenzie, J. (2019). Inclusion, universal design and universal design for learning in higher education: South Africa and the United states. African Journal of Disability, 8(0), 1-7.

van Dorresteijn, C., Fajardo-Tovar, D., Pareja Roblin, N., Cornelissen, F., Meij, M., Voogt, J., & Volman, M. (2024) What Factors Contribute to Effective Online Higher Education? A Meta-Review. Tech Know Learn. https://doi.org/10.1007/s10758-024-09750-5

Estes, M.D., Beverly, C.L., & Castillo, M. (2020). Designing for accessibility: the intersection of instructional design and disability. In M.J. Bishop, E. Boiling, J. Elen, & V. Svihla (Eds.), Handbook of Research in Educational Communications and Technology. Learning Design (pp. 205-227). Springer.

Fejes, A. (2006). The Bologna Process- Governing Higher Education in Europe through standardization. Revista Española de Educación Comparada, 12. 203-231.

Galkiene, A., & Monkeviciene, O. (2021). Preconditions of Transforming the Educational Process by Applying Inclusive Education Strategies: Theoretical Background. In A. Galkiene and O. Monkeviciene (Eds.) Improving Inclusive Education Through Universal design for Learning. Springer International Publishing AG.

International Council for Open and Distance Education. (2024). Navigating the future of Higher Education with AI (2024 ICDE Leadership Summit Policy Dialogue Report). Globethics Publications.

Isaacs, A.K. (2020). A new concept for the future EHEA. In A. Curaj, L. Deca, & R. Pricopie, European Higher Education Area: Challenges for a new decade (pp.503-515). Springer International Publishing AG.

Karseth, B. (2006). Curriculum restructuring in Higher Education after the Bologna Process: a new pedagogic regime? Revista Española de Educación Comparada, 12. 255-284.

McKenzie, J.A., & Dalton, E.M. (2020). Universal design for learning in inclusive education policy in South Africa. African Journal of Disability, 9(0), 1-8.

McMahon, D.D., & Walker, Z. (2019). Leveraging emerging technology to design an inclusive future with universal design for learning. Center for Educational Policy Studies Journal, 9(3), 75-93.

Orr, D. (2020). Bologna process in the Global Higher Education arena. Going digital ? In A. Curaj, L. Deca, & R. Pricopie, European Higher Education Area: Challenges for a new decade (pp. 503-515). Springer International Publishing AG.

Oyarzun, B., & Martin, F. (2023). A systematic review of research on online learner collaboration from 2012-21 : Collaboration technologies, design, facilitation, and outcomes. Online Learning, 27(1), 71-106. http://10.24059/olj.v27i1.3407

Roski, M., Walkowiak, M., & Nehring, A. (2021). Universal design for learning: the more, the better? Educ. Sci., 11(164), 1-25.

Schmelkes del Valle, S., Robles Vásquez, H., & Santos del Real, A. (2022). Mexico: Education and Learning at the Bottom of the Pyramid. In D.A. Wagner, N.M. Castillo, & L.S. Grant (eds.). Learning, Marginalization, and improving the quality of education in low-income countries. Open Book Publishers.

UNESCO. (2009). Policy guidelines on inclusion in education. https://unesdoc.unesco.org/ark:/48223/pf0000177849

West, R.E., Newby, T., Cheng, Z., Erickson, A., Clemens, K. (2020). Acknowledging all learning: alternative micro, and open credentials. In M.J. Bishop et al. (Eds), Handbook of Research in Educational Communications and Technology (593-613). Springer Nature Switzerland.

Smart Decision-Making: The Role of Digital Twins, Retrieval-Augmented Generation-Enhanced AI, and Learning Analytics

Neven Vrček[1], Nina Begičević Ređep[2], Barbara Šlibar[3], Darko Grabar[4]

[1] Department of Information Systems Development, University of Zagreb Faculty of organization and Informatics, Croatia; nvrcek@foi.unizg.hr
[2] Department of Organization, University of Zagreb Faculty of organization and Informatics, Croatia; nbegicev@foi.unizg.hr
[3] Department of Organization, University of Zagreb Faculty of organization and Informatics, Croatia; bslibar@foi.unizg.hr
[4] Application Development Centre, University of Zagreb Faculty of organization and Informatics, Croatia; darko.grabar@foi.unizg.hr

Correspondence: Barbara Šlibar: bslibar@foi.unizg.hr

Abstract:

Decision-making in higher education institutions faces complex challenges due to increasing data, regulatory demands, resource management, and changing educational needs. Effective decisions require accurate, timely insights into institutional processes. This study introduces an integrated decision-support approach consisting of Learning Analytics, Digital Twins, and Generative Artificial Intelligence (AI) with Retrieval-Augmented Generation (RAG). The objective is to enhance decision accuracy and operational efficiency in higher education. Learning Analytics provide insights into student performance, teaching effectiveness, and curriculum efficiency. Generative AI with RAG facilitates rapid retrieval and synthesis of institutional documentation and regulatory framework, enhancing decision accuracy. Digital Twins simulate institutional operations, enabling predictive resource planning and infrastructure modeling. Preliminary results indicate significant improvements in strategic planning and resource management by using an integrated decision support approach. Collectively, these technologies transform strategic decision-making and efficiency in higher education, enabling an agile and smart approach, offering a robust solution to contemporary challenges.

Keywords: Decision-making, Agile Approach, Learning Analytics, Generative AI, Retrieval-Augmented Generation, Digital Twins, Higher education

Introduction

Decision-making in higher education institutions (HEIs) has become increasingly complex, driven by rapid growth in data volumes, shifting regulatory landscapes, and dynamic educational environments. Accurate, informed decisions significantly impact institutional effectiveness, student achievement, resource optimization, and sustainable development.

Currently, institutions rely on diverse technologies such as learning management systems (LMSs), student information systems, and business Intelligence tools. While these systems support data collection and routine administrative processes, they typically lack comprehensive predictive capabilities and integrated insights essential for strategic data-driven decision-making. Consequently, there is an urgent need for innovative solutions capable of offering deeper analytics, predictive modeling, and proactive support for institutional decisions.

Decision-making styles in higher education (HE) vary from intuitive to experience-based approaches. While intuition-based decisions draw from accumulated knowledge and experience, they often lack scalability and transparency. Conversely, data-driven decision-making approaches utilize quantitative analyses to support evidence-based strategies, enhancing accountability, precision, and strategic planning capabilities. However, traditional data-driven methods may still struggle with predictive accuracy, real-time adaptability, and integrated institutional planning.

To bridge these gaps, this paper proposes an advanced integrated approach utilizing Learning Analytics (LA), Generative Artificial Intelligence (AI) with Retrieval-Augmented Generation (RAG), and Digital Twins (DTs). Learning Analytics enable institutions to capture and analyze student behavior data comprehensively, thereby supporting targeted interventions and refining educational strategies. Generative AI enhanced with RAG technology rapidly synthesizes relevant institutional and external information, facilitating efficient administrative processes and agile decision-making. Digital Twins create virtual simulations of institutional processes, facilities, and resources, thus offering predictive insights and enabling proactive resource allocation and infrastructure management. Together, these integrated technologies can substantially improve strategic planning and decision-making capabilities, agile responsiveness, and overall operational effectiveness, addressing the evolving complexities in the HE sector.

Agile Decision-Making in Higher Education Institutions

In the contemporary landscape of HE, marked by rapid technological advancements, the imperative for agile decision-making has never been more important. Agile decision-making, characterized by responsiveness, adaptability, and data-driven insights, is thus crucial for HEIs to remain competitive and relevant.

The agile approach, initially developed in information technology (IT) for flexible software development (Beck et al., 2021), has gained relevance across various fields, including HEIs (Anifa et al., 2024; Philbin, 2015). HEIs, operating in a dynamic environment, face challenges like financial constraints, regulatory pressures, and evolving student preferences demanding agile adaptation (Ivetić & Ilić, 2020; Menon & Suresh, 2020). The emergence of technologies like AI further underscores the need for agility. Agile principles, emphasizing collaboration, adaptability, responsiveness, and iterative improvement, are crucial for HEIs to navigate these challenges (Prejean et al., 2019). However, bureaucratic structures and traditional leadership often obstruct agile adoption (Barrett-Maitland et al., 2024).

Agile decision-making in HEIs necessitates a shift from traditional, rigid approaches to more flexible and responsive strategies. Currently, **strategic planning** in HEIs is often tied to 4-5 year accreditation cycles, which limits adaptability. To enhance agility, annual revisions of strategies and action plans are recommended, allowing for timely adjustments to changing priorities and external pressures. **Collaboration**, while generally strong within HEIs, must be optimized to streamline processes and prevent delays caused by extensive stakeholder involvement. Promoting agile teamwork and fostering transparent communication are crucial. The **decision-making style** in HEIs, although collaborative, can be time-consuming due to its democratic nature. To align with agile principles, HEI management should encourage shared decision-making, situational leadership, data-driven approaches, and transformational leadership. **Change management** in HEIs is often reactive, caused by outside factors. HEIs should adopt a proactive, structured approach to change, raising awareness about its importance and moving beyond crisis-driven adaptations. The **lean approach** can be effectively applied at smaller unit levels. HEI leadership should encourage the identification and elimination of non-value-added activities, such as unnecessary paperwork and redundant meetings. Finally, **continuous improvement** initiatives, currently focused on quality assurance, should be expanded. HEIs should support agile teams to identify improvement opportunities, foster knowledge sharing and collect stakeholder feedback.

To effectively implement agile decision-making, HEIs can leverage the transformative potential of emerging technologies, including LA, Generative AI with RAG, and DTs. By integrating these technologies, HEIs can create a dynamic and responsive ecosystem for agile decision-making, ultimately enhancing the quality of education.

Transformative approach for smart decision-making

The confluence of LA, AI enhanced with RAG, and DTs presents a transformative paradigm for enhancing agile decision-making within HEIs. This integrated approach fosters a data-driven culture, enabling HEIs to swiftly adapt to dynamic environments, optimize resource allocation, and ultimately enhance educational quality.

Learning Analytics

A widely accepted definition of Learning Analytics (LA) is "the measurement, collection, analysis and reporting of data about learners and their contexts, for purposes of understanding and optimising learning and the environments in which it occurs" (Society for Learning Analytics Research (SoLAR), 2011). This professional and scientific discipline encompasses tracking student performance, monitoring teaching effectiveness, and assessing curriculum design. Institutions utilize learning analytics to proactively identify at-risk students, tailor instructional strategies, and refine educational programs, enhancing overall academic success and student retention. Numerous studies have demonstrated learning analytics' capacity to improve student engagement and institutional effectiveness, making it an indispensable tool for modern educational management (Foster & Francis, 2019; Qazdar et al., 2023; Ramaswami et al., 2023). Advanced analytical techniques, such as machine learning and predictive modeling, are employed to forecast student outcomes and identify potential challenges before they arise. By integrating these insights into decision-making processes, institutions can implement targeted interventions, such as personalized learning plans and support services, to address individual student needs.

Furthermore, LA facilitate continuous improvement in teaching practices and curriculum design. Educators can use data-driven feedback to adapt their instructional methods, ensuring they meet diverse student needs and learning styles (Osakwe et al., 2022). This iterative process fosters a culture of evidence-based practice, where decisions are grounded in empirical dana.

The adoption of LA empowers educational institutions with data-driven decision-making, allowing for the identification of trends, evaluation of educational programs, and the optimization of learning outcomes based on empirical evidence (Qazdar et al., 2023). Stakeholders can access real-time data on institutional performance, fostering a collaborative environment focused on achieving shared goals. As a result, LA not only enhance academic success but also contribute to the overall operational efficiency and strategic planning of HEIs.

Generative AI using Retrieval-Augmented Generation

Generative AI with Retrieval-Augmented Generation represents a sophisticated method combining generative AI models with advanced information retrieval systems (Khairi et al., 2024). RAG technology retrieves relevant documents from extensive databases based on a given query, then generates coherent and contextually accurate responses by synthesizing the retrieved content. Within HE, RAG significantly enhances administrative efficiency by rapidly providing precise answers to queries about institutional policies, regulations, accreditation requirements, and prior practices. Institutions leveraging RAG technology achieve greater responsiveness, improved compliance accuracy, and streamlined administrative decision-making processes (Arslan et al., 2024).

It integrates the strengths of generative AI and information retrieval to offer a powerful tool for HEIs. Generative AI models, such as GPT-4, are capable of producing human-like text based on input data, while retrieval systems ensure that the generated content is grounded in accurate and relevant information. This combination allows institutions to access a wealth of knowledge quickly and efficiently, supporting informed decision-making across various administrative functions.

In addition to enhancing administrative efficiency, RAG technology contributes to improved compliance and regulatory adherence. By providing precise and up-to-date information on accreditation standards, institutional policies, and legal requirements, RAG helps institutions maintain compliance with external regulations. This reduces the risk of non-compliance and associated penalties, ensuring that institutions operate within the legal framework.

The implementation of RAG technology also fosters a culture of transparency and accountability. It not only enhances administrative processes but also supports the overall strategic planning and decision making of HEIs.

Digital Twins

Digital Twins are sophisticated virtual models that replicate physical entities, systems, or processes in a digital environment, facilitating real-time monitoring, simulation, and predictive analytics (Kartashova et al., 2020; Yan et al., 2021). Within HEIs, DTs offer transformative opportunities for enhancing management, strategic planning and decision making, and resource allocation. By creating detailed digital representations of campus infrastructure, academic programs, and administrative operations, institutions can explore scenarios and outcomes through simulation without disrupting actual processes.

DTs enable higher education administrators to perform comprehensive predictive analyses for enrollment patterns, facility usage, and service demands (Han et al., 2022). For example, through simulation of academic scheduling, institutions can proactively adjust faculty assignments and classroom allocations to optimize resource utilization and minimize operational costs. Additionally, infrastructure modeling via DTs supports strategic planning for future campus expansions, renovations, or emergency preparedness by virtually testing various scenarios and assessing potential impacts. By anticipating issues before they occur, institutions can significantly enhance their resilience and responsiveness, promoting sustainability and efficiency across institutional operations.

Furthermore, DTs facilitate continuous improvement in campus management and academic program development. By integrating real-time data from various sources, such as IoT sensors and administrative systems, DTs provide a comprehensive view of institutional operations. This enables administrators to make informed decisions based on accurate and up-to-date information, enhancing overall operational efficiency.

The implementation of Digital Twin technology also promotes collaboration and transparency within HEIs. Stakeholders can access detailed simulations and predictive analyses, fostering a collaborative environment focused on achieving shared goals. As a result, DTs not only enhance operational management but also support strategic planning, decision making and resource allocation, contributing to the overall effectiveness and sustainability of HEIs.

Innovative Practices for Enhanced Smart Decision Making

The proposed integration of LA, RAG with AI, and DTs constitutes an innovative approach because it transcends the traditional isolated application of these technologies, emphasizing their synergistic potential in decision-making support for HEIs. Implementing such a comprehensive framework requires careful strategic planning, collaboration across departments, and systematic change management.

A successful integration strategy begins with establishing a centralized data infrastructure, ensuring interoperability between Learning Analytics platforms, Digital Twin systems, and Generative AI solutions. This infrastructure should enable real-time data sharing and analysis, enhancing the accuracy and responsiveness of institutional decision-making. Additionally, institutions must clearly define goals and performance indicators to measure the effectiveness of the integrated system, aligning them with strategic objectives like improving student outcomes, optimizing resource allocation, and increasing operational efficiency.

The initial steps toward implementation include comprehensive stakeholder engagement to communicate the value and benefits of adopting this integrated framework. Institutional leaders, faculty members, administrative staff, and IT professionals must collaborate to identify specific decision-making processes that will benefit most from these technologies. Pilot projects in select departments or programs can provide valuable insights into the practical application and fine-tuning of the integrated system, allowing iterative improvements and demonstrating early successes to foster broader institutional buy-in.

Given the complexity of integrating these advanced technologies, institutions may face several barriers, including resistance to change, technological compatibility challenges, data privacy concerns, and the need for significant investments in infrastructure and training. Effective mitigation tactics involve robust change management strategies, clear communication of the benefits and anticipated outcomes, targeted professional development and training programs, and careful attention to privacy and ethical considerations, ensuring adherence to regulatory requirements.

Overall, this integrated decision-support approach offers a groundbreaking pathway to enhance the strategic agility and resilience of HEIs, empowering them to proactively respond to emerging challenges and dynamically shape their future directions.

In the following sections, we demonstrate the application of innovative practices in HEIs for smart decision-making by showcasing an implemented example for each component of the transformative approach. These examples are further elaborated as case studies.

Case Study: Higher Education Learning Analytics Capability Maturity Model

To illustrate a LA case study, this section presents the development and structure of the Higher Education Learning Analytics Capability Maturity Model (HELA-CMM), a framework designed to facilitate the strategic implementation of LA for agile decision-making within HEIs (Šimić et al., 2025). The HELA-CMM is specifically tailored to address the complexities of LA adoption, providing a roadmap for HEIs to enhance their capacity for data-driven, agile decision-making.

The development of the HELA-CMM adhered to a design science research paradigm. The proposed HELA-CMM comprises 28 capabilities organized into eight key categories, each critical for the effective implementation of LA and the promotion of agile decision-making:

- Teaching / Learning / Assessment: Focuses on the integration of LA into pedagogical practices to enhance student engagement and learning outcomes.

- Data Management & Analytics: Addresses the infrastructure and processes necessary for collecting, storing, and analyzing educational data.
- Ethics, Privacy, Legal Issues: Emphasizes the importance of responsible data handling and adherence to ethical and legal standards.
- People Competences: Highlights the need for developing the skills and knowledge required to effectively utilize LA tools and interpret data.
- Management / Leadership: Underscores the role of institutional leadership in championing LA initiatives and fostering a data-driven culture.
- Culture: Focuses on cultivating an organizational culture that values data-driven decision-making and continuous improvement.
- Infrastructure: Addresses the technological and organizational infrastructure required to support LA implementation.
- Quality Assurance: Emphasizes the use of LA to monitor and enhance the quality of educational programs and services.

Each of these categories encompasses specific capabilities that enable HEIs to assess their current maturity level and identify areas for improvement. Figure 1 illustrates the HELA-CMM categories positioned in the Generic Capability Reference Model (Šimić et al., 2025).

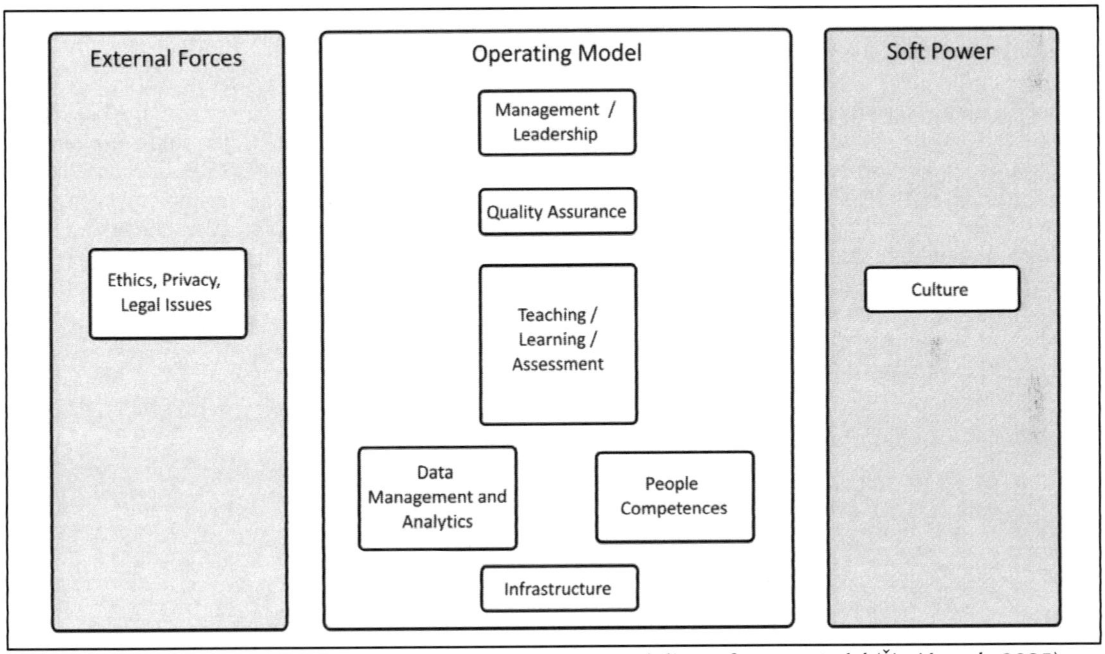

Figure 1: HELA-CMM categories positioned in the Generic Capability Reference Model (Šimić et al., 2025).

The HELA-CMM is designed to empower HEIs to leverage LA for agile decision-making. By providing a structured framework for assessing and improving LA capabilities, institutions can:

- Identify areas for strategic intervention: The model enables institutions to pinpoint specific areas where improvements in LA capabilities can lead to enhanced decision-making.
- Facilitate data-driven adaptation: By utilizing LA insights, institutions can respond rapidly to emerging trends and student needs, promoting agility and responsiveness.
- Enhance resource allocation: LA can provide valuable insights into the effectiveness of various programs and initiatives, enabling institutions to allocate resources more efficiently.

- Improve student success: By leveraging data to personalize learning experiences and provide timely interventions, institutions can enhance student engagement and success rates.
- Benchmarking and continuous improvement: The HELA-CMM provides a tool for benchmarking against other institutions and for tracking progress over time, facilitating continuous improvement.

Case Study: RAG-Enhanced AI for Smart Document Management in Higher Education

The developed Document Management System (DMS) is designed to simplify and streamline document handling within organizations and was developed at the University of Zagreb Faculty of Organization and Informatics (Center for Software Development) with a particular focus on the needs of higher education institutions. Key functionalities include the upload of all relevant documents, automatic metadata generation (e.g., title, summary, type, and category), advanced document search using filters and metadata, as well as interactive retrieval through chatbot-based queries. The system is currently undergoing real-world testing with initial users to validate performance and usability.

Technically, the system is built upon the RAG paradigm, ensuring efficient document retrieval and intelligent response generation. The backend is implemented using PHP (Symfony) or Python, while data storage and vector search capabilities are supported by a PostgreSQL vector database. The system leverages OpenAI's Large Language Models (LLMs) for natural language processing. The frontend is developed using modern JavaScript and associated web frameworks. The entire solution is predominantly based on open-source technologies, promoting transparency, flexibility, and sustainability.

The developed DMS featuring automatic metadata generation and advanced search capabilities, directly supports data-driven decision-making in HEIs.

By enabling quick and precise retrieval of relevant documents through metadata filters and chatbot-based queries, management and researchers can efficiently access critical information for informed strategic planning and operational adjustments. Leveraging the RAG paradigm and OpenAI's LLMs, the DMS ensures intelligent and contextually relevant document retrieval, facilitating agile decision-making. This technology empowers HEIs to rapidly respond to evolving needs by providing instant access to needed data, thus enhancing their ability to adapt and innovate in a dynamic educational landscape. It supports data-driven decision-making by enabling comprehensive data analysis and trend identification, crucial for strategic resource allocation and policy development in HEIs. Figure 2 illustrates the end-user interface for query-based document retrieval and interpretation within the developed DMS system and Figure 3 illustrates administration interface – LLM prompt definitions of the DMS system.

Figure 2: End user interface of the DMS – query base document retrieval and interpretation.

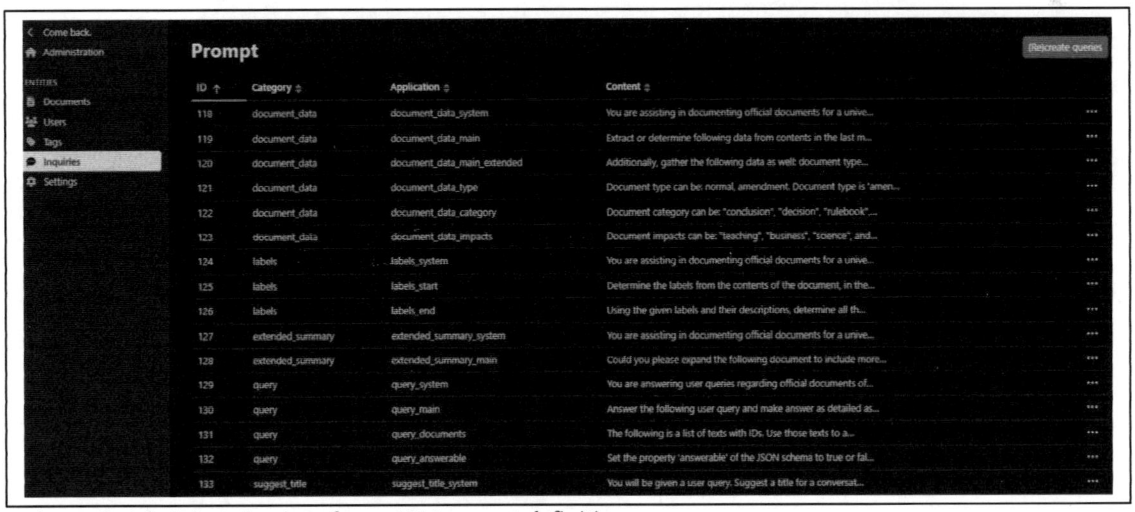

Figure 3: Administration interface – LLM prompt definitions.

Case Study: Digital Twin for Dynamic Class Scheduling

In our illustrative case study, a medium-sized university implemented a DT system to enhance its decision-making processes regarding course scheduling and delivery formats. The DT integrated real-time data collection from multiple sources, including student attendance tracking systems (both physical classroom presence and online platform activity), along with strategic data from the university's student information system such as historical attendance patterns, student academic performance, and course completion rates.

The system monitored real-time attendance trends, providing instant visibility into how many students attended classes physically versus those joining online. Simultaneously, predictive analytics were applied to historical data to evaluate the impact of attendance mode (physical vs. online) on student academic success. This predictive component identified correlations between attendance patterns and academic outcomes, enabling administrators to anticipate potential performance issues and intervene proactively.

Additionally, the DT allowed administrators to simulate various class-scheduling scenarios, considering different ratios of physical and online attendance. These simulations provided insights into optimal resource allocation, helping the institution decide whether to scale classroom infrastructure or invest further in online teaching platforms. As a result, the university optimized its resource utilization, improved student academic performance, and demonstrated increased flexibility and responsiveness to shifting student attendance behaviors.

Figure 4 illustrates the end-user interface for Dynamic Class Scheduling developed at the University of Zagreb Faculty of Organization and Informatics (Center for Software Development). The system enables the collection of data on students attending classes in person as well as those attending online; it plans and records classes by subject and by teacher; exam dates, teacher office hours, generates various reports, and schedules the classes of faculty staff.

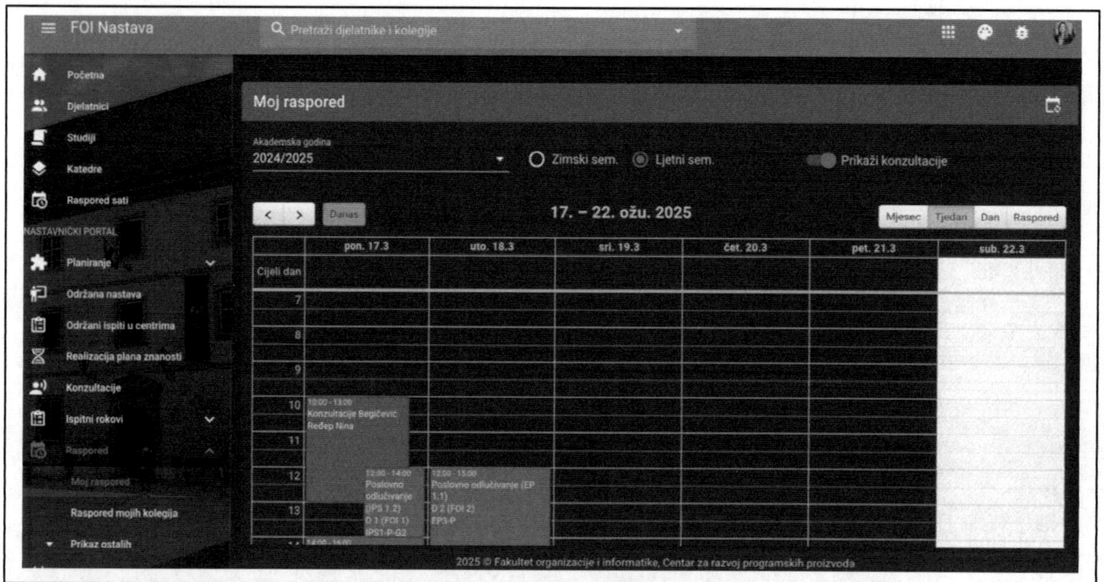

Figure 4: End user interface of the Digital Twin – Dynamic Class Scheduling.

Conclusion

The integration of LA, AI enhanced with RAG, and DTs represents a transformative approach to decision-making in HEIs. This integrated framework addresses existing gaps in institutional effectiveness, offering advanced predictive capabilities, real-time decision support, and comprehensive insights across various operational dimensions. Learning Analytics enhances educational outcomes through precise analysis and targeted interventions, Digital Twins offer robust simulations for strategic resource planning, while Generative AI with RAG streamlines administrative decision-making by efficiently synthesizing essential institutional knowledge.

The collective implementation of these technologies significantly elevates institutions' capacity to proactively respond to dynamic educational landscapes, changing regulatory environments, and evolving student needs. As a result, institutions can achieve greater strategic agility, operational efficiency and improved educational quality.

Despite the notable advantages, successful implementation requires careful planning, strong organizational commitment, and continuous adaptation to technological advances and ethical considerations. Institutions must address potential barriers such as technological complexity, initial resource investment, resistance to change, and ethical concerns related to data privacy and AI decision-making processes. Future research should explore further refinements to the integration of these technologies, addressing ongoing challenges and continually enhancing their practical application within HE settings.

Competing interests

The authors have no competing interests to declare.

Acknowledgements

This work has been fully funded by the Croatian Science Foundation under the grant IP-2020-02-5071.

References

Anifa, M., Ramakrishnan, S., Kabiraj, S., & Joghee, S. (2024). Systematic Review of Literature on Agile Approach. NMIMS Management Review, 32(2), 84–105. https://doi.org/10.1177/09711023241272294

Arslan, M., Ghanem, H., Munawar, S., & Cruz, C. (2024). A Survey on RAG with LLMs. Procedia Computer Science, 246, 3781–3790. https://doi.org/10.1016/j.procs.2024.09.178

Barrett-Maitland, N., Williams-Shakespeare, E., Allen, D., & Edwards-Braham, S. (2024). From tradition to innovation: Proposing agile leadership as the new paradigm for a higher education institution in a developing country. Power and Education, 17577438241307310. https://doi.org/10.1177/17577438241307310

Beck, K., Beedle, M., van Bennekum, A., Cockburn, A., Cunningham, W., Fowler, M., Grenning, J., Highsmith, J., Hunt, A., Jeffries, R., Kern, J., Marick, B., Martin, R. C., Mellor, S., Schwaber, K., Sutherland, J., & Thomas, D. (2021). Manifesto for Agile Software Development. https://agilemanifesto.org/

Foster, C., & Francis, P. (2019). A systematic review on the deployment and effectiveness of data analytics in higher education to improve student outcomes. Assessment & Evaluation in Higher Education, 45(6), 822–841. https://doi.org/10.1080/02602938.2019.1696945

Han, X., Yu, H., You, W., Huang, C., Tan, B., Zhou, X., & Xiong, N. N. (2022). Intelligent Campus System Design Based on Digital Twin. Electronics, 11(21), Article 21. https://doi.org/10.3390/electronics11213437

Ivetić, P., & Ilić, J. (2020). REINVENTING UNIVERSITIES: AGILE PROJECT MANAGEMENT IN HIGHER EDUCATION. European Project Management Journal, 10(1), 64–68.

Kartashova, L. A., Gurzhii, A. M., Zaichuk, V. O., Sorochan, T. M., & Zhuravlev, F. M. (2020). Digital twin of an educational institution: An innovative concept of blended learning. Proceedings of the Symposium on Advances in Educational Technology, Aet.

Khairi, A., Fuadi, W., & Afrillia, Y. (2024). Strategic Framework for Implementing Retrieval-Augmented Generation (RAG) and Large Language Models (LLMs) for Personalized AI in Informatics Engineering: A Case Study of Malikussaleh University. Proceedings of International Conference on Multidisciplinary Engineering (ICOMDEN), 2, 00083–00083.

Menon, S., & Suresh, M. (2020). Factors influencing organizational agility in higher education. Benchmarking: An International Journal, 28(1), 307–332. https://doi.org/10.1108/BIJ-04-2020-0151

Osakwe, J., Iyawa, G., Ujakpa, M., & Ankome, T. (2022). Learning Analytics Tools for Enhancing Students' Performance: A Global Perspective. 2022 IST-Africa Conference (IST-Africa), 1–12. https://doi.org/10.23919/IST-Africa56635.2022.9845553

Philbin, S. P. (2015). Exploring the application of agile management practices to higher education institutions. Proceedings of the International Annual Conference of the American Society for Engineering Management., 1–1. https://openresearch.lsbu.ac.uk/item/875xx

Prejean, E. A., Kilcoyne, M. S., Liao, W., & Parker, C. (2019). Is Higher Education Talking and Walking Agile Management: A Review of the Literature. American International Journal of Business Management, 2(7), 8–18.

Qazdar, A., Hasidi, O., Qassimi, S., & Abdelwahed, E. H. (2023). Newly Proposed Student Performance Indicators Based on Learning Analytics for Continuous Monitoring in Learning Management Systems. International Journal of Online and Biomedical Engineering (iJOE), 19(11), Article 11. https://doi.org/10.3991/ijoe.v19i11.39471

Ramaswami, G., Susnjak, T., & Mathrani, A. (2023). Effectiveness of a Learning Analytics Dashboard for Increasing Student Engagement Levels. Journal of Learning Analytics, 10(3), Article 3. https://doi.org/10.18608/jla.2023.7935

Šimić, D., Begičević Ređep, N., Rako, S., Kadoić, N., Van Petegem, W., Rienties, B., Cabrera Lanzo, N., Eichhorn, M., Guàrdia Ortiz, L., Kučina Softić, S., & Tillmann, A. (2025). HELA-CMM: Capability maturity model for adoption of learning analytics in higher education. International Journal of Educational Technology in Higher Education, (In press).

Society for Learning Analytics Research (SoLAR). (2011). What is Learning Analytics? https://www.solaresearch.org/about/what-is-learning-analytics/

Yan, M.-R., Hong, L.-Y., & Warren, K. (2021). Integrated knowledge visualization and the enterprise digital twin system for supporting strategic management decision. Management Decision, 60(4), 1095–1115. https://doi.org/10.1108/MD-02-2021-0182

Using AI-based chatbots for individualized teacher professional development: An empirical study of the in-service training programme at the University College of Teacher Education Burgenland

Thomas Leitgeb[1], Michael Leitgeb[2]

[1] Centre for Digital Education and STEAM, University College of Teacher Education, Austria; thomas.leitgeb@ph-burgenland.at
[2] Centre for Digital Education and STEAM, University College of Teacher Education, Austria; michael.leitgeb@ph-burgenland.at

Correspondence: Thomas Leitgeb: thomas.leitgeb@ph-burgenland.at

Abstract:

This research paper investigates the potential of AI-based chatbots to support teachers in identifying professional development (PD) opportunities tailored to subject-specific, pedagogical, and technological requirements. Drawing on the Technological, Pedagogical, and Content Knowledge (TPACK) framework, Self-Determination Theory (SDT), and reflexivity, we conducted a six-week field study with 1,125 teachers at the University College of Teacher Education Burgenland (Austria). A mixed-methods design was employed, integrating quantitative approaches (logistic regression, correlation) and qualitative techniques (content and sentiment analysis) to capture the breadth and depth of teacher–chatbot interactions. Results show a moderate positive correlation ($\rho = 0.36$, $p < 0.05$) between the specificity of user queries and user satisfaction, while targeted keywords (e.g., "digital didactics") increased the likelihood of positive feedback by a factor of 2.05 ($p < 0.01$). Qualitative findings reveal that teachers have a pronounced interest in digital competencies, artificial intelligence, and inclusion, with 85% of user feedback on chatbot performance being positive. These findings suggest that AI-based chatbots can facilitate a more individualized, context-sensitive search for PD opportunities, thereby promoting teacher autonomy, competence, and relatedness. The paper discusses methodological and practical implications in the context of the EDEN Digital Learning Europe Annual Conference 2025 theme, "Empowering Inclusion, Innovation and Ethical Growth," highlighting how AI-enabled PD tools align with broader European policy initiatives.

Keywords: AI-based chatbots, Teacher professional development (PD), TPACK (Technological, Pedagogical, and Content Knowledge), Self-Determination Theory (SDT), Individualized/Personalized learning

1. Introduction

The future of education in the age of artificial intelligence (AI) entails both promising opportunities and complex challenges. The capacity of AI to personalize learning and training—whether for students or in-service teachers—demands careful consideration of ethical, pedagogical, and technological factors (Adiguzel et al., 2023). Within teacher education, professional development (PD) is widely considered a cornerstone for advancing teaching quality (Day & Leitch, 2007; Garet et al., 2001). Yet finding suitable PD that resonates with a teacher's subject area, pedagogical style, and technological readiness often proves difficult due to the abundance of available courses (Desimone, 2009).

In response to these complexities, AI-based chatbots have emerged as potential tools to assist teachers in the initial discovery of relevant PD offerings (Kasneci et al., 2023). Whereas adaptive learning and recommendation systems have received considerable attention in higher education (Holmes et al., 2019), the application of chatbots for teacher PD selection remains relatively unexplored. Grounded in the Technological, Pedagogical, and Content Knowledge (TPACK) framework (Mishra & Koehler, 2006), reflexivity theory (Mezirow, 1997), and Self-Determination Theory (SDT) (Deci & Ryan, 1985), the present study investigates how AI-based chatbots can increase relevance, autonomy, and motivation in teacher PD.

At the policy level, the Bologna Process has spurred the harmonization of higher education standards across Europe, placing increasing emphasis on digital competencies, innovation, and inclusivity (Leitgeb et al., 2024). In keeping with the EDEN Digital Learning Europe Annual Conference 2025 theme of "Empowering Inclusion, Innovation and Ethical Growth," this paper addresses how AI-driven teacher PD initiatives can align with continental policy goals. Specifically, it explores how chatbots could help ensure equitable access to teacher training opportunities, mitigate biases, and further ethical awareness of AI technologies in education.

This paper is structured as follows. First, we situate our research within the theoretical frameworks of TPACK and SDT to elucidate the significance of tailoring PD to specific subject matter, pedagogical approaches, and technology readiness levels. Second, we outline our mixed-methods research design, describing how quantitative (e.g., logistic regression, correlations) and qualitative (e.g., content and sentiment analysis) methods were integrated. Next, we present our findings and discuss how they illuminate the viability of chatbot systems in fostering individualized professional learning. We then address methodological implications, ethical considerations, and directions for future research, concluding with an overview of how AI-based chatbots can be harnessed to further "Empowering Inclusion, Innovation and Ethical Growth" in teacher education and beyond.

2. Theoretical Framework

2.1 TPACK and Reflexivity

The Technological, Pedagogical, and Content Knowledge (TPACK) framework (Mishra & Koehler, 2006) underscores the need for teachers to synthesize three core domains:

1. **Content Knowledge (CK):** Mastery of the subject area.
2. **Pedagogical Knowledge (PK):** Instructional methods, curriculum design, and student engagement strategies.
3. **Technological Knowledge (TK):** Proficiency in digital tools and platforms.

As technology moves further into the educational sphere, the TPACK model highlights the importance of context-specific alignment among these domains (Voogt et al., 2013). However, teachers often encounter numerous technology-related PD options without clear guidance on how these offerings integrate with disciplinary content or specific pedagogical goals (Cherner & Smith, 2016). Reflexivity (Mezirow, 1997) further stresses that professional development should engage teachers as active participants who question their assumptions, consider new teaching paradigms, and adapt these insights to unique classroom realities. An AI-based chatbot can prompt reflection—for example, by asking teachers what they wish to improve in their lessons—while simultaneously recommending relevant PD opportunities.

2.2 Self-Determination Theory (SDT)

Alongside TPACK and reflexivity, teacher motivation plays a pivotal role in sustained professional growth (Deci & Ryan, 1985). Self-Determination Theory (SDT) posits that people are more intrinsically motivated when their basic psychological needs for autonomy, competence, and relatedness are satisfied (Biesta et al., 2015). Traditional PD systems often limit teachers to predefined courses, compromising autonomy and diminishing active engagement (Garet et al., 2001). By contrast, an AI-driven chatbot that offers flexible, personalized PD paths can fortify teacher autonomy, while the system's focus on context-relevant, competence-boosting recommendations aligns with teachers' need to feel effective. Finally, the inclusion of peer-based features—

such as discussion forums—could foster relatedness, although our study focuses primarily on individual chatbot interactions.

3. Methodology

3.1 Study Design

We employed a mixed-methods approach (Creswell & Plano Clark, 2018) to examine how AI-based chatbots facilitate teacher PD selection. This design integrates quantitative metrics (e.g., user satisfaction, query specificity) and qualitative insights (e.g., user feedback comments, thematic interests) to produce a holistic understanding of the phenomenon.

- **Quantitative Phase:**
  - **Interaction Logging:** We recorded every teacher–chatbot interaction, including timestamps, hashed user IDs, and optional user feedback (thumbs up/down plus comments).
  - **Descriptive Statistics:** Used to track frequency of queries, daily usage fluctuations, and query specificity.
  - **Inferential Statistics:** Spearman's rank correlation measured the association between query specificity (coded on a 0–2 scale) and user satisfaction. Logistic regression tested whether the presence of targeted keywords (e.g., "digital didactics," "AI-based language learning") predicted positive user feedback.
- **Qualitative Phase:**
  - **Content Analysis:** Adopted an inductive–deductive approach (Mayring, 2000) to categorize user queries into thematic clusters (e.g., digital tools, AI, inclusive education).
  - **Sentiment Analysis:** Manually classified user comments (positive, neutral, negative) to capture emotional reactions to chatbot responses.

3.2 Sample and Context

The AI-based chatbot was integrated into the ongoing PD offerings at the University College of Teacher Education Burgenland. A recruitment email was sent to approximately 4,000 teachers affiliated with the institution, 1,125 of whom voluntarily opted to test the chatbot. Over a six-week observation period (15 April to 31 May 2024), these teachers generated 2,060 recorded interactions, of which 2,030 were deemed valid after data cleaning. Roughly 28% of eligible teachers participated, indicating a substantial minority but leaving open questions about representativeness and potential self-selection biases.

3.3 Data Collection Procedures

- **Platform Integration:** Teachers accessed the chatbot via a secure web portal or personalized email link.
- **Logging Mechanism:** Each user query, system response, and feedback indicator was stored in a relational database with standardized fields (timestamp, query content, output, user feedback).
- **Data Quality Assurance:** We removed incomplete, duplicate, or malformed entries, preserving 2,030 valid interactions for analysis.

3.4 Measurement of Key Variables

1. **Query Specificity:**

    - Queries were coded on a three-point scale: 0 = low specificity (e.g., "I need a course"), 1 = moderate specificity ("What training is available for language teaching?"), and 2 = high specificity ("I want a fully online seminar on AI-based reading strategies for secondary school English classes").

    - Two independent coders achieved an intercoder reliability (Cohen's Kappa) above 0.80.

2. **User Satisfaction:**

    - Operationalized as a binary variable: 1 = thumbs up, 0 = thumbs down.

    - Interactions lacking user feedback were excluded from binary satisfaction analysis.

3. **Targeted Keywords:**

    - Queries were automatically scanned for critical terms (e.g., "online seminar," "digital didactics," "inclusion"). Presence/absence of these terms served as predictors in the logistic regression model.

3.5 Data Analysis

1. **Descriptive Statistics:**

    - Examined frequencies (e.g., daily request counts), means, medians, and standard deviations to identify usage trends.

    - Generated time-series plots to visualize query volume fluctuations.

2. **Inferential Statistics:**

    - **Spearman's Rank Correlation (ρ):** Assessed the link between query specificity (ordinal) and user satisfaction.

    - **Logistic Regression:** Examined how targeted keywords affected the likelihood of positive feedback, while controlling for query specificity and other confounders. Model fit was evaluated via McFadden's R^2 and the Hosmer–Lemeshow test.

3. **Qualitative Content Analysis (Mayring, 2000):**

    - Explored recurring PD topics (e.g., AI in education, digital competencies, inclusive teaching methods).

    - Coded user suggestions for system improvement.

4. **Sentiment Analysis:**

    - Two researchers manually labeled feedback comments as positive, neutral, or negative, achieving an intercoder reliability > 0.80.

4. Results

4.1 Usage Trends and Query Patterns

Over the six-week observation period, 1,125 teachers recorded 2,060 total chatbot interactions ($M = 1.69$ queries per user, $SD = 0.95$). Daily request frequencies fluctuated considerably. Peaks emerged on 16 and 18 April (205 and 331 queries, respectively), possibly coinciding with institutional announcements about upcoming PD sessions. After mid-April, usage dropped and later exhibited minor surges before culminating in a high (232 queries) on 31 May, the final day of the pilot.

A large proportion of queries (approximately 60%) referenced online formats (e.g., "online seminar," "webinar"). The most frequently used search terms included "online" (262 mentions) and "online seminar" (192), suggesting a pronounced interest in flexible, digital learning formats. Many user questions explicitly addressed "What online seminars are there on...?" or "Which courses fit ...?"—indicating that teachers aimed to find targeted offerings rather than general PD information.

4.2 Quantitative Findings

We found a moderate positive correlation between query specificity and user satisfaction ($\rho = 0.36$, $p < 0.05$). Teachers posing highly detailed questions (e.g., specifying content area, grade level, and format) were more likely to rate the chatbot's suggestions positively. This correlation aligns with TPACK, where contextual alignment of technology, pedagogy, and subject area is pivotal. A logistic regression model tested whether targeted keywords in a user's query predicted positive feedback. The final model (McFadden's $R^2 = 0.24$) showed that the presence of terms like "digital didactics" increased the odds of a thumbs-up by a factor of 2.05 (95% CI [1.35, 3.10], $p < 0.01$). The Hosmer–Lemeshow test indicated good fit ($p = 0.45$), and variance inflation factors (VIF) were below 2.0, suggesting no serious multicollinearity. These findings indicate that thematically explicit queries—for instance, queries focusing on AI, digital skills, or inclusion—resulted in more favorable user ratings. Of the 2,060 chatbot responses, 85.6% ($n = 1,765$) correctly matched relevant PD recommendations, while 14.4% yielded generic or irrelevant content. The main causes of irrelevancy were ambiguous user inputs (e.g., "I need a course" without further details) or requests outside the system's database scope.

4.3 Qualitative Insights

Figure-like analyses (cumulative frequency counts) reveal a strong interest in digital competence (65 mentions), AI-based teaching (87), inclusion (52), and language support (34). Additional topics included differentiation, psychosocial health, sustainability, gifted-and-talented education, and gender issues—albeit at lower frequencies. This distribution underscores a growing demand for technologically oriented and diversity-sensitive PD that aligns with contemporary educational challenges. Overall, 85% of written feedback on chatbot recommendations was positive, 10% neutral, and 5% negative. Positive comments commended the chatbot's speed and contextual relevance. Negative feedback typically centered on unhelpful or off-topic suggestions, often due to minimal user query detail. In SDT terms, the chatbot appears to have bolstered teacher autonomy (customizable PD pathways) and competence (context-relevant suggestions), though further enhancements might improve the social or collaborative dimension of PD (relatedness). Qualitative content analysis revealed user calls for more refined filtering mechanisms (e.g., subject area, grade level, digital competence level) and for additional chat prompts clarifying the scope of recommended courses. Some users requested better integration with institutional e-learning platforms to streamline direct enrollment. Others suggested adding a peer-feedback forum to encourage collaborative sense-making of PD outcomes.

5. Discussion

The findings indicate that AI-based chatbots can serve as effective, individualized filters in a crowded PD landscape. In line with TPACK, teachers who provided precise content and pedagogical details received more tailored, technology-oriented solutions, thereby increasing satisfaction and perceived usefulness. These results reinforce prior research on the importance of context-specific scaffolding in teacher PD (Borko, 2004; Voogt et al., 2013).

From an SDT perspective, teachers benefited from autonomy (selecting PD options aligned with personal interests), competence (locating relevant, high-quality resources), and, to a lesser extent, relatedness. While the chatbot did not explicitly facilitate peer interactions, some users requested expansion toward group-based PD forums—a potential way to strengthen relatedness. Indeed, an expanded or integrated design might connect teachers seeking similar PD themes, fostering online learning communities in line with the EDEN conference themes of Innovation and Inclusion (Vangrieken et al., 2017).

The methodological approach illustrates how mixed methods can capture large-scale trends (e.g., correlation between specificity and satisfaction) as well as the nuanced reasons for user sentiment (positive or negative). Triangulating usage data, logistic regression, and content analysis strengthens the validity of the conclusion that query specificity significantly influences perceived chatbot value.

5.1 Ethical and Practical Considerations

Ethical Dimensions:

- **Data Privacy:** We employed hashing and pseudonymization to comply with GDPR, but further institutional frameworks may be needed to assure participants that sensitive information (e.g., subject area deficits) is protected (Drachsler & Greller, 2016).
- **Algorithmic Bias:** Institutions must guard against biases in training data that might skew PD recommendations (Buolamwini & Gebru, 2018). Periodic bias audits and transparency about how recommendations are generated are crucial.

Practical Recommendations:

1. **Adaptive Prompts:** Include guided question templates in the chatbot interface, prompting teachers to clarify subject area, grade level, and technology readiness.
2. **Hybrid Integration:** Embed the chatbot within broader PD ecosystems, where user insights feed into peer mentoring programs and professional learning communities.
3. **Expansion of Keyword Database:** Regularly update recognized keywords to reflect emerging trends (e.g., AI, sustainability, mental health).
4. **Extended Feedback Instruments:** Move beyond thumbs up/down to more nuanced survey items, interviews, or reflection logs.

5.2 Implications for European Policy

The findings resonate with the Bologna Process objective of improving quality and accessibility in higher education. By systematically embedding AI-based chatbots, teacher education institutions can scale up targeted, inclusive PD offerings (Leitgeb et al., 2024). Such tools can also foster cross-border collaborations if the chatbot databases incorporate PD courses from multiple European institutions, potentially accelerating a common framework for digital literacy and AI competencies in teacher training.

6. Conclusion and Outlook

This study provides empirical evidence that AI-based chatbots can support teachers in identifying individualized PD opportunities, thus promoting autonomy, competence, and motivation. Guided by TPACK and SDT, we found that specificity and thematically targeted keywords lead to significantly higher user satisfaction, with 85% positive sentiment overall. Recurrent interests in digital competence, AI, and inclusion highlight the evolving demands of contemporary teacher development.

These results are encouraging but come with caveats. First, the six-week observation period offers only a snapshot, leaving long-term adoption and impact on classroom practice untested. Second, demographic data (e.g., digital literacy level, subject area, teaching experience) were not collected, limiting our capacity to differentiate the chatbot's effectiveness across subgroups. Future work should adopt longitudinal designs and incorporate broader metrics (e.g., actual PD enrollment, classroom implementation, student outcomes) to assess sustainability.

Nevertheless, this research aligns strongly with the EDEN Digital Learning Europe Annual Conference 2025 theme, "Empowering Inclusion, Innovation and Ethical Growth." By integrating advanced AI-driven solutions into PD ecosystems, educational institutions can more effectively address the Bologna Process goals of harmonizing quality standards, ensuring equitable access, and fostering continuous innovation in teacher training. The next steps involve refining chatbot algorithms to minimize irrelevant outputs, incorporating robust bias mitigation strategies, and embedding collaborative features that enhance peer-to-peer learning. As digital transformation accelerates worldwide, responsibly designed AI solutions hold great potential to facilitate the personalized, inclusive, and ethically minded professional development that teachers—and their students—both need and deserve.

References:

Biesta, G., Priestley, M., & Robinson, S. (2015). The role of beliefs in teacher agency. Teachers and Teaching, 21(6), 624–640.

Borko, H. (2004). Professional development and teacher learning: Mapping the terrain. Educational Researcher, 33(8), 3–15.

Buolamwini, J., & Gebru, T. (2018). Gender Shades: Intersectional accuracy disparities in commercial gender classification. Proceedings of Machine Learning Research, 81, 77–91.

Cherner, T., & Smith, D. (2016). Reconceptualizing TPACK to meet the needs of twenty-first-century education. The New Educator, 13(4), 329–349.

Creswell, J. W., & Plano Clark, V. L. (2018). Designing and conducting mixed methods research (3rd ed.). SAGE.

Day, C., & Leitch, R. (2007). The continuing professional development of teachers: Issues of coherence, cohesion, and effectiveness. In T. Townsend (Ed.), International Handbook of School Effectiveness and Improvement (pp. 703–725). Springer.

Deci, E. L., & Ryan, R. M. (1985). Intrinsic motivation and self-determination in human behavior. Springer.

Desimone, L. M. (2009). Improving impact studies of teachers' professional development: Toward better conceptualizations and measures. Educational Researcher, 38(3), 181–199.

Drachsler, H., & Greller, W. (2016). Privacy and analytics: It's a DELICATE issue – A checklist for trusted learning analytics. In Proceedings of the Sixth International Conference on Learning Analytics & Knowledge (LAK '16) (pp. 89–98). ACM.

Garet, M. S., Porter, A. C., Desimone, L., Birman, B. F., & Yoon, K. S. (2001). What makes professional development effective? Results from a national sample of teachers. American Educational Research Journal, 38(4), 915–945.

Holmes, W., Bialik, M., & Fadel, C. (2019). Artificial intelligence in education: Promises and implications for teaching and learning. Center for Curriculum Redesign.

Kasneci, E., Sessler, K., Kasneci, G., & Seidel, T. (2023). ChatGPT for good? On opportunities and challenges of large language models for education. Learning and Individual Differences, 103, 102274.

Leitgeb, T., Maitz, K., Sitter, G., Matischek-Jauk, M., Knaus, M., et al. (2024). KI-Leitlinien für den PH-Verbund Süd-Ost – Leitlinien für die Nutzung von Künstlicher Intelligenz in der Hochschule. University College of Teacher Education Burgenland.

Mayring, P. (2000). Qualitative content analysis. Forum: Qualitative Social Research, 1(2).

Mezirow, J. (1997). Transformative learning: Theory to practice. New Directions for Adult and Continuing Education, 74, 5–12.

Mishra, P., & Koehler, M. J. (2006). Technological pedagogical content knowledge: A new framework for teacher knowledge. Teachers College Record, 108(6), 1017–1054.

Voogt, J., Fisser, P., Roblin, N. P., Tondeur, J., & van Braak, J. (2013). Technological pedagogical content knowledge – a review of the literature. Journal of Computer Assisted Learning, 29(2), 109–121.

Vangrieken, K., Meredith, C., Packer, T., & Kyndt, E. (2017). Teacher communities as a context for professional development: A systematic review. Teaching and Teacher Education, 61, 47–59.

Artificial Intelligence in Vocational Education and Training: A Micro, Meso and Macro Perspective From the AI Pioneers Project

Lisa Meyne[1], Frieda Klaus[2], Dr. Christine Siemer[3], Dr. Ludger Deitmer[4], Prof. Dr. Dr. h.c. Michael Gessler[5]

[1] Institute Technology and Education (ITB), University of Bremen, Germany: lmeyne@uni-bremen.de
[2] Institute Technology and Education (ITB), University of Bremen, Germany: fklaus@uni-bremen.de
[3] Institute Technology and Education (ITB), University of Bremen, Germany: chsiemer@uni-bremen.de
[4] Institute Technology and Education (ITB), University of Bremen, Germany: deitmer@uni-bremen.de
[5] Institute Technology and Education (ITB), University of Bremen, Germany: mgessler@uni-bremen.de

Correspondence: Lisa Meyne, lmeyne@uni-bremen.de

Abstract:

Vocational education and training (VET) is facing new challenges as a result of the digital transformation, particularly with regard to the use of artificial intelligence (AI). Various funding programmes have been set up to provide support: One of these is the Erasmus+ funding programme, which funds the AI Pioneers project. A central aim of AI Pioneers is to research, promote and evaluate the use of AI in adult and vocational education. This includes establishing an interdisciplinary, international network and communities of practice.

Various research methods were used in the project to generate findings at the three levels of VET: Macro, meso and micro. At the micro level, practical use cases for the application of AI in vocational schools were investigated. The meso level includes an egocentric social network analysis of the funded project partners and their networks. In addition, a European survey was conducted at the macro level. This survey aimed to expand the European Commission's digital competence framework for competences for educators (DigCompEdu) to include AI competences.

The results show that ethical aspects play a crucial role in the implementation and utilisation of AI. It also demonstrates that the establishment of a sustainable network requires the involvement of all relevant stakeholders, as AI is an interdisciplinary issue. This holistic perspective facilitates a comprehensive identification of both the challenges and opportunities of AI in VET and ensures knowledge transfer.

Keywords: Artificial Intelligence, Vocational Education and Training, VET, Community of Practice, AI Competences, Social Network Analysis

1 Introduction

Discussions on artificial intelligence (AI) in education have been lively in recent years due to a variety of developments in the field. Furthermore, there have been a large number of strategy papers and funding programmes, particularly at international level, to support the use of AI in educational settings, for example through the announcement by the European Commission regarding the Artificial Intelligence Act (AI Act) or the Digital Education Action Plan 2021-2027. In addition to a range of risks, the use of AI nevertheless offers a wide variety of potential in educational settings, especially in vocational education and training (VET) (De Witt, 2024; Roppertz, 2021). UNESCO (2024), for example, emphasises that the use of AI in education opens up new possibilities for teaching and learning methods as well as for education management, as AI has the potential to improve learning experiences and support the tasks of teachers. In line with recent developments, the integration of AI skills into schools and apprenticeships, teaching and universities is of particular importance (CEDEFOP, 2023). According to Seufert (2023), the use of AI is accompanied regarding teaching and learning processes by new learning objectives, methods and learning environments. AI competences will be required in the context of learning objectives, and new forms of collaboration will also become indispensable. Learning environments will develop into pedagogically smart agents (Seufert, 2023), with AI-based digital media and data science supporting educational processes. A study from 2021 recommended stimulating didactically orientated innovation processes and creating spaces for experimentation (mmb Institut, 2021). Since AI can be used at different levels (mmb Institut, 2021), practical applications, the development of AI competences and the networking of stakeholders are crucial.

However, in order to be able to use new AI technologies effectively, basic knowledge and application expertise is required (Rampelt et al., 2025). Most recently UNESCO presented the AI competency framework for teachers (Cukurova et al., 2024), although in the last few years, there have been diverse approaches to formulating competences in dealing with AI. Therefore, Mikeladze et al. (2024) point out that there is a general lack of clear frameworks for educators to acquire AI skills. They distinguish between specific AI skills and general digital and basic skills such as problem solving and contextual reflection.

The benefits of the learners are central to the promotion of AI competences for VET teachers. This is reflected in the European Commission's digital framework for competences for educators (DigCompEdu), as well as professional engagement and professional collaboration (Punie & Redecker, 2017). Accordingly, tailored to the six areas of competence, an expansion to include AI competences in VET is necessary.

When developing skills, it is also essential to consider the aspect of mutual learning in networks, especially from an international perspective, as there is plenty of potentials to share lessons learned. Accordingly, it should be emphasised that cooperation is instrumental in developing AI competences (Rampelt et al., 2025), which highlights the relevance of networks in this discourse on AI. In particular, the European Union's funding efforts within the Erasmus+ programme not only promote the implementation of AI in VET and competency development, but above all the establishment of cooperation and international networks and project alliances (European Commission, 2025; Meyne & Siemer, 2024).

In the course of this paper, the issues of AI competences, practical use cases and networking will be addressed in the AI debate from the perspective of an international project network within the Erasmus+ funding line. The Erasmus+ project AI Pioneers (funding period 2023-2025) promotes the use and teaching of AI in adult education and VET and, among others, deals with the topic of AI competences. A central component of the project is the network formation of a European reference network of AI pioneers in adult and vocational education. In the following, an experience paper based on the project results and its innovative practice is presented.

2 Project Context and Theoretical Framework

Before we go into the theoretical framework and the empirical findings, we would like to explain the AI Pioneers project in more detail. The aim of the project is researching, promoting and evaluating the use of AI in adult and VET. Therefore, the project wants to create a supportive ecosystem for AI integration in VET and adult learning through collaboration with stakeholders, policymakers, vocational schools and companies whose individuals want to deal with the topic of AI as a leader in their institutions or as a newcomer. The term Pioneer is drawn from the DigCompEdu Framework of the European Commission, in which "pioneers" describe people who question digital and pedagogical practices and drive innovation. They experiment with new technologies and/or develop innovative teaching approaches and are rare innovators who serve as a role model for younger teachers (Punie & Redecker, 2017).

The project wants to support network members with knowledge and resources to establish them as reference points for the use of AI in education. These include individuals with an affinity for AI who are already using it or want to integrate it in the future. Members are thus associate partners of the project, but also individuals who can be reached through dissemination activities. Furthermore, with a total of 10 project partners from seven different EU countries involved in the project network (Germany, Greece, Portugal, Italy, Spain, Cyprus, Estonia), the project wants to develop a community of practice (CoP) in the use of AI in the European partner countries by promoting network formation with a diverse range of networking activities and events. Additionally, the project addresses further topics regarding the use of AI in VET focussing on policy recommendations and AI toolkits with practical examples of implementation. Recognizing the potential risks associated with AI technologies, the project also aims to develop guidelines for the ethical use of AI in education. Therefore, the development of an evaluation schema for AI in education on e.g., data privacy, ethics, algorithmic bias, equitable access to AI technology and EU values could already be completed. Key project-related publications to date relate to the evaluation schema for AI in education on data, privacy, ethics, and EU values (Roman Etxebarrieta et al., 2025) and the supplement of the DigCompEdu Framework with regard to AI competences (Bekiaridis & Attwell, 2023; see in detail Chapter 3.1).

The main research questions of the AI Pioneers project among others are the following:

- To what extent is AI already being used in adult and vocational training in European countries?
- What impact does the application of AI have on data protection, ethics and European values?
- Which AI competences can be identified from the perspective of European stakeholders in VET and adult education across different competence areas?
- How can the long-term development of a network of AI Pioneers be achieved effectively with regard to the use of AI in the teaching/learning process of vocational school teachers and trainers?

As a conceptual basis for this paper, we refer to the different levels within a VET system and thus address with this paper micro, meso and macro perspectives (Pilz, 2017, 2022) of the research conducted within the AI Pioneers project. The macro level includes the institutional structure of VET systems, but also economic, social and political framework conditions, for example the EU AI Act. Concepts and models for the organisational, didactic and methodological design of VET are located at the meso level. These include elements such as curricula, institutions, certification and teaching staff. On the micro level, specific teaching and learning processes are included, for example the practice of learning, which also encompasses the specific design of the teaching and learning processes mentioned above (Pilz, 2017, 2022).

3. Empirical Findings From the AI Pioneers Project

The AI Pioneers project has already generated a variety of empirical findings. In the following, three central findings will be presented that can be assigned to the micro, meso and macro levels (Pilz, 2017, 2022). The first is the micro-level, which deals with the concrete practical application of AI in vocational schools by identifying use cases (Deitmer et al., 2024). This is followed by the meso-level, in which an egocentric social network survey to examine social networks is explained (Meyne & Siemer, 2024, in press). Finally, the results of a European study are presented, which have contributed to a supplement of the DigCompEdu framework and thus represent the macro level (Bekiaridis & Attwell, 2023).

3.1 Micro Level - Practical AI Use Cases in VET Schools

VET must continuously adapt to changing requirements, particularly in the context of digital transformation. The application and use of AI play a central role here, especially in the practice of vocational schools at the micro level. Technological progress, specifically the development of AI systems, is shaping this change and requires professionals, apprentices and VET personnel to develop advanced skills in the form of action- and design-oriented competences (Roppertz, 2021; Rott & Schmidt-Hertha, 2024). AI can not only enhance digital learning environments and improve the quality of educational offerings (Attwell et al., 2021), but can also be used as a learning tool, for example through chatbots and personalized offerings. In VET, the focus is on both school-based and vocational learning (Attwell et al., 2023), making AI increasingly important as a cross-curricular topic.

In a recent study, Deitmer et al. (2024)[1] analysed homepages of vocational schools in northern and western Germany to identify those with an AI affinity. A total of 220 schools were identified that had an affinity for AI in the spectrum of robotics, industry 4.0 innovations and beyond regular courses. Through additional workshops with schools and vocational teachers as well as separate expert interviews with vocational teachers, N=15 vocational schools with explicit AI activities were identified on the northern part of Germany. In the following, seven specific use cases in German vocational schools are presented that were identified by the methodological approach and in the context of further workshops and the expansion of the AI Pioneers network, in order to demonstrate the application of AI in VET (Deitmer et al., 2024).

A digital robotics laboratory has been set up at a technical vocational school in Osnabrück, where mechatronics apprentices in particular programme collaborative robots (cobots). With the help of audiovisual glasses, they learn to control the robot, for example, to check whether it is packaging the right objects. The focus of the teaching is, among other things, on questions such as ‘what is machine learning?’, ‘how do neural networks work?’ and ‘how are neural networks trained?’ (Deitmer et al., 2024).

In a technical vocational school in Emden, the integration of robotics and AI in training and teaching is being researched, with a focus on machine learning. In one project, Raspberry Pies are assembled on a system with

[1] This paper was written as part of the AI Pioneers project and appeared in: Ubiquity Proceedings, 4 (1), 21.

robots, where the cases are refined and labelled. A cobot handles the components and works together with the apprentices (Deitmer et al., 2024). Furthermore, at a technical vocational school in Bremen, mechatronics engineering apprentices in their second year of training are working on an AI-related project. Over a period of two semesters and with the support of their teachers, they are developing an autonomous vehicle for warehouse logistics that uses an ultrasonic sensor to detect obstacles and follow a lane. To support its teaching, a technical vocational school in Neustadt am Rübenberge uses a fully automated production plant with transport and handling systems and industrial robots. The school also operates an assembly plant in which cobots (UR3) use AI-based image processing to monitor the material stores and detect errors (Deitmer et al., 2024).

Moreover, a technical vocational school in Hildesheim uses the tool 'Moral Machines' in ethics classes to discuss moral dilemmas in road traffic. As part of the 'Autonomous Driving/Firefight Challenge', apprentices learn the basics of data processing systems. From simple tasks such as changing direction between two obstacles to the more complex challenge of finding and extinguishing a candle, they work with microcontroller technology. AI supports both the creation and optimisation of source codes as well as risk assessment and forecasting of future developments. Furthermore, a technical vocational school in Wolfsburg is using its experience with digital learning environments to automate processes so that mechatronics apprentices can deepen their knowledge through practical projects. The apprentices are working on an AI-supported energy management project for buildings, in which consumption data is analysed to determine potential savings in heating and electricity. A machine learning module recognises unusual fluctuations in consumption and sends warning messages. A Python software with ChatGPT integration also provides recommendations for action (Deitmer et al., 2024).

Finally, AI is being integrated both passively and actively in a technical vocational school in Verden. Passive integration means that AI is used as a tool without being directly part of the teaching. Active integration involves using AI to develop specific skills and reflect on experiences. Reflection on the tools used is important for competence-oriented learning processe, where the entry point is often a real-world problem, such as 3D printing, in which where students use ChatGPT to research topics and reflect on the results.

These practical AI use cases show the wide variety of AI application examples and potentials in VET. The potential to learn from each other e.g., via cooperation projects can be emphasised based on the experiences among these practical scenarios of AI integration in educational settings.

3.2 Meso Level - An Egocentered Social Network Survey of AI Pioneers

Within the internationalisation of VET, the importance of stakeholders and organisations as well as cooperation structures between them in the context of various research efforts is given high priority (Gessler, 2019; Röhrer et al., 2021). The same applies to networking at European level, for example through the Erasmus+ programme for the promotion of innovative projects within international project networks (European Commission, 2024). However, there has hardly been a systematic and empirical survey of network structures within innovation projects with regard to VET (Meyne & Siemer, 2024, in press)2. The research by Meyne and Siemer (2024) approaches this from a meso level perspective and looks at the funded partners of the Erasmus+ project AI Pioneers. Furthermore, the established network structures within the European Reference Networks of AI Pioneers and the country-specific CoPs of the individual project partners are analysed. In this respect, the social capital that is built up through project-related network activities with regard to the use of AI in VET within the network structures is important. This capital will be further developed and strengthened during the project period as part of the Erasmus+ funding. In their study, Meyne and Siemer (2024, in press) refer to social capital according to Bourdieu (1983), which can be outlined as the combination of resources related to the existence of lasting relationships that can be institutionalised in different ways.

From a network theory perspective, the theoretical framework of the study is based on the work of Granovetter (1973) and Marsden and Campbell (2012), as well as other approaches from psychology, sociology and economics. To collect the data, an egocentric network analysis was conducted with the funded project partners of the AI Pioneers project. The egocentric network structures of N=10 egos were collected using a fully structured interview questionnaire and a semi-structured interview guide. According to Marsden and Campbell (2012, p. 18), egocentric networks can be defined as follows:

[2] This paper was developed in the context of the AI Pioneers project and will be published in the International Journal for Research in Vocational Education and Training.

> "Egocentric network data describe the local social environments surrounding individual actors in a network – usually comprising one or more of each focal actor's direct contacts ('alters') and certain qualities of the dyadic relationships between that actor ('ego') and the alters."

The results of the study show that the 10 egocentric networks of the funded AI Pioneers partners consisted of a total of 74 relationships at the time of data collection (summer 2024), with most of the alteri recorded coming from the education sector and specifically from the area of technical vocational education (Meyne & Siemer, in press). The majority of the relationships analysed already existed before the start of the AI Pioneers project (n = 57), meaning that they were continued during the project period with a focus on the application of AI in VET. At the same time, new relationships were also established in the project context, creating new social capital (n = 17; Meyne & Siemer, in press). The aspect of trust between ego and alter is of particular importance for the continuation and implementation of new relationships, whereby the duration of the relationship and thus the shared experiences within it come to the fore (Meyne & Siemer, in press):

> "I don't think that it's the quantity of institutions that you have a network with, it's about the quality. It's about the relationship. It's always better to have three good connections and then you can extend your network, when someone starts trusting, building the trust, (...)." (E05, 131)

It also shows that the analysed alteri in the AI Pioneers network primarily contribute their expertise and their networking knowledge to the egocentric networks. Due to the innovative nature of the project, a high level of interest in the project and a willingness to support the project can be considered as established (Meyne & Siemer, in press).

3.3 Macro Level - An European Survey for the Supplement of the DigCompEdu Framework

Various developments in the field of AI have led to transformations in teaching and learning processes in recent years and their innovative changes are having an impact on all levels of education. Accordingly, it is necessary to address and promote AI skills in educational settings in schools, at the workplace and in teaching and training so that various target groups are able to use the potential of AI by applying new technologies (CEDEFOP, 2023; Rampelt et al., 2025). Therefore, at the macro level, there is a requirement to create competence frameworks for the use of AI in education for the creation of general conditions for the micro level of teaching and learning. Mikeladze et al. (2024) emphasise that there has so far been a lack of sophisticated AI competence frameworks in which the learner perspective is placed at the forefront. This is precisely the perspective adopted by the European Commission's Joint Research Centre (JRC) in its digital competence framework for educators (Punie & Redecker, 2017). In this regard, the following six competence areas are addressed with overall 22 competence descriptions: 1) professional engagement, 2) digital resources, 3) teaching and learning, 4) assessment, 5) empowering learners, and 6) facilitating learners' digital competence. For educators, an extension of the DigCompEdu to AI competences is necessary, which is why the framework was expanded for the context of vocational and adult education as part of the AI Pioneers project (Bekiaridis & Attwell, 2023)3. Bekiaridis and Attwell (2023) emphasise that teaching AI skills in adult and vocational education is becoming increasingly important as AI is already used in many areas. As a result, curricula should not only cover the basics and applications of AI, but also ethical issues such as bias and data protection, as well as critical thinking. Furthermore, digital skills are essential to understand and use AI systems. In addition to the application of AI tools, their critical evaluation is also coming into focus in order to prepare learners for a future in which AI is commonplace.

In order to expand the existing DigCompEdu framework on AI competences, an examination of recent and relevant research was first carried out, followed by an EU-wide online survey of teachers and trainers, as well as expert interviews and discussions with key stakeholders (N=14) in the AI Pioneers project. A total of N=310 teachers and trainers took part in the online survey (data collection between June and October 2023). Of these, 265 came from EU countries and 45 from countries outside the EU (Bekiaridis & Attwell, 2023). Most of the respondents were from the fields of general education and adult education as well as VET and teacher training (Bekiaridis & Attwell, 2023). A selection of the empirical findings is presented below.

The results of the online survey show that the majority of respondents' organisations did not have a specific AI policy at institutional level (meso level) at the time of data collection. Furthermore, participants were also asked about their views on challenges in using AI technologies in education. Fundamental challenges in dealing with AI were identified with regard to technical complexity, ethical issues, limited access and adoption, lack of data, resistance to change as well as bias and fairness. With regard to AI skills, the teachers and trainers

---

[3] This document was created as part of the AI Pioneers project.

were asked in the survey which skills they believe are necessary to incorporate AI into their teaching practices (Bekiaridis & Attwell, 2023). Particular focus was places on competences in the areas of data literacy, computational thinking, ethical considerations and reflection, collaboration and communication, technical skills, as well as to curriculum development and pedagogical approaches to AI integration. Apart from some deviations, the respondents largely agree that the promotion of AI competences in all competence areas of the DigCompEdu framework is useful, desirable and necessary (Bekiaridis & Attwell, 2023).

Moreover, the expert interviews also emphasised that the integration of AI and the promotion of associated skills is crucial in educational settings. In addition to challenges and concerns, the interviewees particularly underlined that AI has the potential to pursue highly personalised and adaptive learning approaches and thus adapt teaching and learning processes to the needs of learners. Furthermore, AI can automate administrative tasks in educational settings, giving teachers more capacity to interact with learners. At the same time, the interviewees emphasise the importance of a responsible and ethical approach to AI in order to protect the rights and data of students. Furthermore, continuous monitoring, research, and collaboration among important actors are crucial because AI can foster collaborative networks. It connects educators worldwide with like-minded individuals and experts, facilitating the exchange of ideas, best practices and innovative teaching strategies (Bekiaridis & Attwell, 2023).

4 Discussion of the Findings

The results outlined show that all levels of VET offer both development needs and potential. At the micro level, it is crucial to provide scope for testing and further developing AI applications in vocational teaching. An analysis of explicit AI projects at vocational schools has shown that AI has already been implemented in some schools, which underlines the importance of networking and exchanging experiences on AI applications (Rampelt et al., 2025). The aim of the AI Pioneers project is to foster a network of AI pioneersthat serves as a community of practice (CoP). Since exchange is crucial both nationally and internationally, CoPs have already been established in the project partner countries to enable transnational learning and mutual knowledge transfer, so that all participants can benefit from the experiences of others. In this context, the identification of specific use cases plays a significant role, because it revealed that the commitment of individual stakeholders and VET institutions is a crucial factor for AI implementation, so that the analysed individuals and VET schools can be considered pioneers (Punie & Redecker, 2017).

The analysis of network data at the meso level highlights the necessity of providing resources for establishing a sustainable network. In particular, in an international context, the long-term implementation of networking activities by actors at the meso level is difficult without the support of the macro level. This results in the urgency that the creation of social capital and international networking in VET requires capacity and resources to enable successful professional collaboration and the exchange of best practices in the use of AI to meet the social and political challenges in this area and to learn from each other.

Focusing on the macro level and the development of AI competences, outsourcing routine tasks to AI offers opportunities for teachers and trainers. In the near future, the role of the teachers and trainers will increasingly become more of a learning facilitator. The results at the macro level emphasise that, in addition to the explicit promotion of AI skills, the focus should continue to be on tasks that cannot be performed with the support of AI. In this respect, new paths need to be explored, particularly with a focus on assessment, in order to enable comprehensive skills development. Mikeladze et al. (2024) also emphasises the need for interdisciplinary discussions between experts and teachers regarding the development of appropriate AI competences, as the fields of AI expertise develop, interdisciplinary exchange between experts and subject teachers is essential. This requires the further development and implementation of AI competency frameworks so that educators can acquire a balanced combination of pedagogical knowledge, subject matter expertise, digital literacy, and AI skills. This will enable them to provide their students with a technologically enriched education (Mikeladze et al, 2024).

As AI technologies are continuously changing, the underlying competency frameworks must also be regularly reviewed and adapted. There cannot be a universal solution for all educational institutions, as the competences required depend heavily on the respective implementation. Instead, a basic framework should serve as a guide that can be flexibly adapted to specific needs. Particularly in VET, the focus in future should be on the differentiated use of AI and the corresponding expertise within individual sectors in order to enable targeted competence development. Interdisciplinary networks would particularly benefit from this differentiation, as they enable the targeted exchange of proven methods and specialised knowledge. At the same time, the challenge remains that specific user knowledge about the underlying technology, e.g., about algorithms and neural networks, is required. Only in this way can critical reflection on the use of AI in educational processes take place.

In order to sustainably anchor AI competences in VET, it is crucial to integrate them into policy instruments and curricula. This will enable institutional framework conditions to be created and lifelong learning to be promoted so that all stakeholders in VET can benefit long-term from the potential of AI.

5 Conclusion and Outlook

Despite the progress achieved at micro, meso and macro level in the AI debate as presented above, it is evident that ethical issues also play a crucial role and need to be considered when implementing AI in (vocational) educational institutions. As briefly introduced, AI Pioneers has therefore developed an evaluation schema that serves as a guideline for the implementation of AI in VET institutions (Roman Etxebarrieta et al., 2025). This schema comprehensively addresses ethical aspects and questions that arise. Further research in this area is desirable and necessary to advance the AI debate in education.

Due to the interdisciplinary nature of AI, it is essential to involve all relevant stakeholders at different levels in the implementation process. This is the only way to ensure a holistic view of the challenges and opportunities of AI in education, especially in VET. In this respect, as well, further (quantitative) empirical research would be of great benefit to science and practice.

In conclusion, the results and discussion have shown the importance of further research in the field of AI in VET, especially with a focus on AI competences and the development of AI concepts and strategies at a political level. For example, a follow-up project to AI Pioneers can focus on self-assessment so that teachers and trainers can independently assess themselves in terms of AI competences and check their own level of knowledge (micro level). By designing AI Labs, the scope for testing AI can be established for both teachers and students (micro level). In addition, the development of Continuous Professional Development Courses (CPD) can be helpful in promoting AI competences on the basis of the DigCompEdu framework (meso level). At the macro level, as the discussion has already shown, clear concepts for AI policies and strategies for school development are also required and would be beneficial for VET practice.

Competing interests

The authors have no competing interests to declare.

Acknowledgements

We would like to thank the AI Pioneers project partners as well as the associated and network members for their contribution, their participation in research and networking as well as the active dialogue and critical debate.

Funding Information

This article is based on the Erasmus+ project "AI and the future of Education" (acronym: AI Pioneers) [Project number: 101087261] which is funded by the European Union. Views and opinions expressed are however those of the authors only and do not necessarily reflect those of the European Union or the European Education and Culture Executive Agency (EACEA). Neither the European Union nor EACEA can be held responsible for them.

References

Attwell, G., Deitmer, L., & Bekiaridis, G. (2023). AI pioneers: Developing a community of practice for artificial intelligence (AI) and vocational education and training. In V. Tūtlys, L. Vaitkutė & C. Nägele (Eds.), Vocational Education and Training Transformations for Digital, Sustainable and Socially Fair Future. Proceedings of the 5th Crossing Boundaries Conference in Vocational Education and Training, Kaunas, 25. – 26. May (pp. 30–37). European Research Network on Vocational Education and Training, VETNET, Vytautas Magnus University Education Academy, Institute of Educational Science. https://doi.org/10.5281/zenodo.7808076

Attwell, G., Roppertz, S., Deitmer, L. (2021). MOOC and artificial intelligence. Potentials for the Professional Development of VET Teachers and Trainers. In C. Nägele, B. E. Stalder & M. Weich (Eds.), Pathways in Vocational Education and Training and Lifelong Learning. Proceedings of the 4th Crossing Boundaries Conference in Vocational Education and Training, Mutenz and Bern online, 8.–9. April (pp. 67–72). European Research Network on Vocational Education and Training, VETNET, University of Applied Sciences and Arts Northwestern Switzerland and Bern University of Teacher Education. https://doi.org/10.5281/zenodo.4602924

Bekiaridis, G., & Attwell, G. (2023). Supplement to the DigCompEDU Framework: Outlining the Skills and Competences of Educators Related to AI in Education. Bremen, Germany: University of Bremen, Institute Technology and Education. https://doi.org/10.26092/elib/2708

Bourdieu, P. (1983). Ökonomisches Kapital, kulturelles Kapital, soziales Kapital. In R. Kreckel (Ed.), Soziale Ungleichheiten (pp. 183–198). Schwartz.

Cukurova, M., Miao, F., & UNESCO (2024). AI competency framework for teachers. UNESCO Publishing. https://doi.org/10.54675/ZJTE2084

De Witt, C. (2024). Künstliche Intelligenz in der Berufsbildung. Technologische Entwicklungen, didaktische Potenziale und notwendige ethische Standards. BWP, 53(1), 8–12. https://www.bwp-zeitschrift.de/dienst/publikationen/de/19416

Deitmer, L., Dersch, I., Meyne, L., & Siemer, C. (2024). How do technical vocational school teachers deal with artificial intelligence in the classroom? An attempt to analyze AI use at German VET Schools. Ubiquity Proceedings, 4(1), 21. https://doi.org/10.5334/uproc.143

European Commission. (2024). Erasmus+ Program Guide (Version 1: 28-11-2023). https://erasmus-plus.ec.europa.eu/sites/default/files/2023-11/2024-Erasmus%2BProgramme-Guide_EN.pdf

European Commission. (2025). Erasmus+ Program Guide (Version 2: 20-01-2025). https://erasmus-plus.ec.europa.eu/sites/default/files/2025-01/erasmus-programme-guide-v2.2025_en.pdf

Gessler, M. (2019). Promotoren der Innovation im transnationalen Berufsbildungstransfer: Eine Fallstudie. In M. Gessler, M. Fuchs & M. Pilz (Eds.), Konzepte und Wirkungen des Transfers dualer Berufsbildung (pp. 231–279). Springer Fachmedien. https://doi.org/10.1007/978-3-658-23185-9

Granovetter, M. S. (1973). The strength of weak ties. American Journal of Sociology, 78(6), 1360–1380. https://doi.org/10.1086/225469

Marsden, P. V., & Campbell, K. E. (2012). Reflections on conceptualizing and measuring tie strength. Social Forces, 91(1), 17–23. https://doi.org/10.1093/sf/sos112

Meyne, L., & Siemer, C. (2024). Social capital of actors in VET: An egocentric case study based on the AI Pioneers project. In C. Nägele, B. Esmond, N. Kersh & B. E. Stalder (Eds.), Trends in vocational education and training research, vol. VII. Proceedings of the European Conference on Educational Research (ECER), Vocational Education and Training Network (VETNET) (pp. 75–81). VETNET. https://doi.org/10.5281/zenodo.13236742

Meyne, L., & Siemer, C. (in press). Mapping Emerging Social Capital in a European VET Innovation Project Through Multi-Perspective Egocentric Social Network Analysis. International Journal for Research in Vocational Education and Training.

Mikeladze, T., Meijer, P. C., & Verhoeff, R. P. (2024). A comprehensive exploration of artificial intelligence competence frameworks for educators: A critical review. European Journal of Education, 59(3). https://doi.org/10.1111/ejed.12663

mmb Institut. (2021) (Eds.). KI@Bildung: Lehren und Lernen in der Schule mit Werkzeugen Künstlicher Intelligenz. Schlussbericht. https://www.telekom-stiftung.de/sites/default/files/files/media/publications/KI%20Bildung%20Schlussbericht.pdf

Pilz, M. (2017). Policy borrowing in vocational education and training (VET)—VET system typologies and the "6P strategy" for transfer analysis. In P. Matthias (Ed.), Vocational education and training in times of economic crisis: Lessons from around the world (pp. 473–490). Springer International.

Pilz, M. (2022). Ansätze und Methoden der international vergleichenden Berufsbildungsforschung. In P. Grollmann, D. Frommberger, T. Deißinger, U. Lauterbach, M. Pilz, T. Schröder & G. Spöttl (Eds), Vergleichende Berufsbildungsforschung – Ergebnisse und Perspektiven aus Theorie und Empirie. Jubiläumsaufgabe des Internationalen Handbuchs der Berufsbildung (pp. 77–95). Bundesinstititut für Berufsbildung.

Punie, Y., & Redecker, C., (2017). European Framework for the Digital Competence of Educators: DigCompEdu. Publications Office of the European Union. https://doi.org/10.2760/178382

Rampelt, F., Klier, J., Kirchherr, J., & Ruppert, R. (2025). KI-Kompetenzen in deutschen Unternehmen. Schlüssel zu einer Jahrhundertchance für Deutschland. Stifterverband.

Röhrer, N., Vogelsang, B., & Fuchs, M. (2021). The region matters—for whom? The regional actor network for vocational education and training in tourism of Cancún (Mexico). International Journal of Training and Development, 25, 244–258. https://doi.org/10.1111/ijtd.12217

Roman Etxebarrieta, G., Orcasitas-Vicandi, M., & Antzaka, A. (2025). Evaluation schema for AI in education on data, privacy, ethics, and EU values. AI Pioneers. https://aipioneers.org/evaluation-schema-for-ai-in-education-on-data-privacy-ethics-and-eu-values-wp5/

Roppertz, S. (2021). Die Rolle und Bedeutung von Künstlicher Intelligenz in der Berufsausbildung – Implikationen für angehende Berufs- und Wirtschaftspädagog*innen. bwp@ Berufs- und Wirtschaftspädagogik – online, 40, 1–23. https://www.bwpat.de/ausgabe40/roppertz_bwpat40.pdf

Rott, K. J., & Schmidt-Hertha, B. (2024). KI in der Berufsbildung implementieren – Bedarfe und Anforderungen von Auszubildenden und Lehrpersonal. Berufsbildung in Wissenschaft und Praxis, 1, 24–27. https://lit.bibb.de/vufind/Record/DS-782046/Preview

Seufert, S. (2023). KI-basierte Anwendungsfälle für die Lernortkooperation. Gestaltung eines digitalen Ökosystems in der Berufsbildung. Zeitschrift für Berufs- und Wirtschaftspädagogik, 119 (2), 208–235. https://doi.org/10.25162/zbw-2023-0009

Generation of personalised e-learning path in adaptive e-learning

Olga Ovtsarenko[1,2]

[1] Department of Information Technologies, Vilnius Tech, PhD student, Lithuania; olga.ovtsarenko@vilniustech.lt
[2] Centre for Sciences TTK UAS, senior lecturer, Estonia; olga.ovtsarenko@tktk.ee

Correspondence: Olga Ovtsarenko: olga.ovtsarenko@tktk.ee

Abstract:

Over the past two decades, e-learning has transformed traditional educational methods by allowing learners to access content anytime and anywhere.

The rise in popularity of e-learning is due to:

- widespread internet connectivity, powerful computing devices, and software platforms that have opened up digital education to a broader audience,
- cost-effectiveness and reduced costs associated with physical infrastructure, travel, and printed materials,
- scalability of digital platforms that allow for the delivery of education to large numbers of learners without geographic limitations,
- diverse content, including videos, interactive tests, simulations, and games catering to different learners.

The research focuses on developing an automated system for creating a personalized e-learning path in an adaptive learning environment.

The research's target audience is students of vocational and higher education institutions, both first-year and experienced learners with different goals and experiences.

It is planned to use machine learning algorithms for personalization based on existing data from the e-learning platform and learning management systems (LMS) and integrate with existing e-learning platforms for practical application and visualization.

The research objectives are to adapt and organize existing content for personalization using student data and ensure the necessary privacy.

Keywords: adaptive learning; attributes; personalization; machine learning; data processing; optimization; visualization.

Introduction

The achievements of modern technologies make it possible to use contemporary education tracking and rapid analysis of updated data from online resources to generate a student's path in independent online learning.

Online education has become one of the innovations that has changed the dynamics of education worldwide (Sahni, 2023). Modern technologies make it possible to use tracking of students' learning activity on e-course platforms and rapid analysis of updated data from online resources to form and optimize the student's path in independent online learning. Thus, e-learning becomes individual with the ability to take into account the variability of data - the updated student knowledge portfolio and the use of additional learning resources. When interacting with the e-course activity log, the adaptive learning environment evaluates academic performance, takes into account student preferences and, after checking and comparing data with the planned results, selects the most appropriate educational materials from available resources to improve student performance (Kabudi et al., 2021). Students prefer digital environments where modern technologies take into account their expectations and abilities, providing recommendations and providing access to the necessary high-quality educational resources (Green and Donovan, 2028). An adaptive learning system must be intelligent in order to dynamically adapt educational content to individual needs. Real-time learning needs such as optimal learner states (e.g. engagement, performance, workload, responsiveness, etc.) must be achieved and maintained to optimize the overall learning process (Ming, and Cali, 2016).

When interacting with online resources, an adaptive learning environment feels academic performance, can take into account students' preferences, and, following the success of testing, selects the most suitable educational materials objects from the available educational materials to improve student performance. Students like digital environments, where current technologies shape their expectations and abilities to access, acquire, manipulate, construct, create and communicate information. An adaptive learning system should be intelligent enough to adapt the learning content to fit individuals dynamically. Real-time learning needs such as optimal learner states (e.g. engagement, performance, workload, reacting, etc.) are attained and maintained, and the entire learning experience is optimised.

The research focuses on developing an automated system for creating a personalized e-learning path within an adaptive learning environment. The target audience of the research is students from vocational and higher education institutions, both freshmen and experienced learners with different goals and experiences.

It is planned to use machine learning algorithms for personalization based on available data from the e-course platform and learning management systems (LMS), as well as integration with existing e-learning platforms for practical application. The research focuses on adapting and organizing existing content for personalization using student data and ensuring the necessary privacy.

Related works

This section discusses the known and used methods of personalization and optimization in learning systems and their design (Ovtšarenko, 2023). Known methods in learning theory that define learning and curriculum requirements taking into account the analysis/registration of a student's skill/knowledge portfolio and, based on this, student access to additional materials/sequences (Nigenda et al., 2018), organized educational resources (Johnson & Wang, 2019), with a hierarchical structure of competencies (Lee & Kim, 2021), can be supplemented by modern information systems (Garcia & Santos, 2020). Methods based on the principles of interpreting learning requirements depending on students' learning styles and the ability of the learning environment to take into account user experience (Miller & Davis, 2018) with different types of content adaptation and navigation for different students, using concept and query map algorithms (Zhang & Patel, 2022), EEG signals (Thompson & Robertson, 2021; Zhang et al., 2021), and user behavior analysis (Hernandez & Xu, 2019) are also used. Using student attributes such as student age, education level, gender or other characteristics (Vagale et al., 2020; White & Adams, 2020) to compare and exploit similarities between student characteristics and learning paths (Kumar & Chen, 2021) and to develop a recommender system given the ontological structure of student characteristics (Nelson & Parker, 2022) is also a well-known group of methods.

Using student knowledge and time level to filter/teach content based on changes in student knowledge portfolio (Singh & Zhang, 2020) and performance (Williams & Lee, 2019), course time limits with maximum student performance scores (Jiang et al., 2022) and training datasets to develop student models (Nabizadeh et al., 2020) has applications in learning analytics. Using intelligent tutoring system and virtual tutor to automatically generate sequential and pedagogically progressive learning paths on open educational resources (Minn, 2022) is popular due to its similarity to the involvement of a real teacher in the learning process. Known methods for automating learning paths can be divided into main groups, the first of which are methods based on artificial intelligence (AI), including data mining using an adapted clustering approach, creating learning path models with independent learning path calculation algorithms (Smith & Brown, 2020), with a differential evolution algorithm, student behavior analytics, using artificial intelligence technologies with the theory of educational psychology and with recommendations for learning paths based on a knowledge graph (Johnson, 2019; Lee, 2021; Gonzalez, 2021). The second group of methods is based on the creation or personalization of a learning path based on rules not created by artificial intelligence. It includes taking into account and labeling the main learning styles of students, tracking topics based on criteria and over time, including pedagogical agents in the learning process (Carter & Murphy, 2018), analyzing the difference between the current and required set of student skills (Kim & Rodriguez, 2020), a multidisciplinary approach based on ontology (Singh & Zhang, 2020) and the use of concept maps for adaptive learning systems with clustering technology (Chang, 2020). Most studies use AI solutions to collect intermediate modeling data or implement solutions. However, when developing a learning path, the possibility of using other methods should be considered and analyzed if they are more effective in a particular domain.

The novelty of this study on the development of an automatic learning path in an adaptive learning environment is the use of a multi-criteria approach or selection of methods to find the most effective solution for automating and optimizing the student's learning path. When developing an independent learning path, the possibility of using different methods should be considered and analyzed if they are more effective in obtaining a better result.

Research

According to a review of research on adaptive learning and self-creation of a learning path, the use of various criteria to provide a dynamic adaptive learning environment to create a learner's learning path is appropriate and very promising, as it will maximise the use of the most appropriate processing methods for different stages in the study of e-course topics. When designing the structure of the educational material with planning its adaptability, it is necessary to consider what skills, knowledge and competencies the student should acquire, and to correctly determine the order and connection of the topics of the entire course. The structure of competencies based on the hierarchy can be used for adaptive learning and personalized electronic assessment.

AI is effective for automated collection and processing of metadata. Methods of collecting and processing information with the participation of educational environment administrators and creators of educational materials and using available data from student activity logs on the Moodle platform make it possible to track student activity (Ovtsarenko, 2024).

The modified formulas with normalization coefficients and scaling were used to update the data, which in turn were used to visualize and build a 3D model of the course structureon the data-based in the preview research (Ovtsarenko and Safiulina, 2025). Through data visualization, insights and patterns in data can be easily interpreted (Ovtsarenko, 2025: Collection_2: dataset_6)
Using data obtained when calculating competence with dynamic change of assessment allows to evaluate the educational trajectory offered by the teacher when changing the level of the evaluation. This requires visualization of the data obtained during the calculation and analysis of the three-dimensional model of competencies with a minimal grading score of 0.1 (Fig. 1).

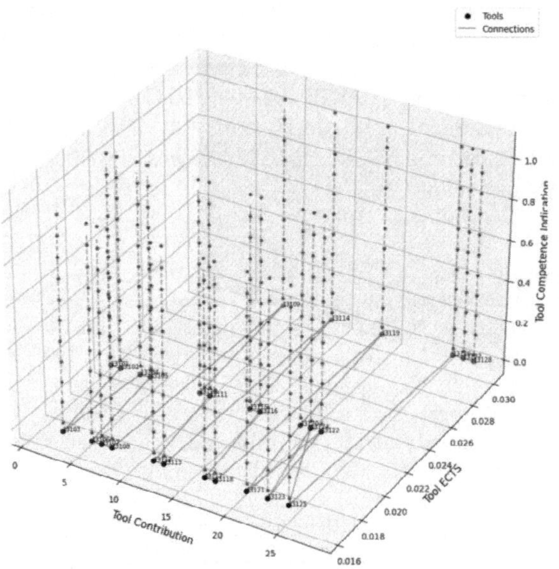

a b

Figure 1. E-course 3 ECTS structure visualization with assessment - e-course tools connected structure with base grading level.

The method involves a combination of data processing, mathematical modelling and 3D visualization:

1. Processing data from an Excel file using the Pandas library. The input Excel file contains rows representing tools with corresponding attributes (Tool_Code, Tool_Contribution, Tool_ECTS) (Ovtšarenko, 2024. Collection_2: code_6).
2. Calculating a dynamic tool competency score based on static weights representing the importance of each parameter. The evaluation scores vary dynamically from 0.1 to 1 (Ovtšarenko, 2024. Collection_2: 131_dataset).
   The static component (base_competence) is calculated using the tool contribution and the ECTS values.
   A dynamic adjustment based on the square of the score is added and scaled by the score weight, allowing for the dynamic change in the competency score for each tool to be assessed as the score changes.
3. Using the matplotlib library for 3D plotting (Ovtšarenko, 2024. Collection_2: Data_visualization):
   - X-axis: dynamic evaluation scores.
   - Y-axis: tool contribution.
   - Z-axis: calculated competency score.

Each tool is visualized as a line in 3D space connecting its competency values across all assessment points. Vertical lines are added at the first and last points of each tool line, highlighting the range of competency. Each tool is labelled with its Tool_Code.

The visualization represents the dynamic changes in competency scores and assessments.

By displaying multiple tools in the same 3D space, it becomes easy to compare their change in competency.

This approach provides numerical data (via calculations) and visual interpretations (via 3D graphs) for the dynamic relationship between tool parameters and assessment-based competency.

The visualizations (Fig.1) represent dynamic evaluation of tools using three parameters (axes):

- X-axis: Dynamic evaluation scores (measuring evaluation points over time or different assessments).
- Y-axis: Tool contribution (quantifies how much each tool contributed to a specific outcome).
- Z-axis: Calculated competency score (measured competency based on assessments or tools).

Each tool is represented as a line in 3D space, showing how its competency score (Z-axis) changes dynamically (along with the X-axis) relative to its contribution (Y-axis).

In Fig. 1 (a), tools are represented as black dots (base points) with vertical red lines connecting. The lines emphasize the range of competency scores (Z-axis) for a tool at the first and last assessment points.
Labels 13103, 13109, 13122, etc., correspond to Tool_Codes.

This visualization combines numerical calculations with visual interpretation, allowing users –teachers and students to see the dynamic relationship between tool parameters and competency outcomes. The clear labelling of tools and trajectories makes it easier to:

- comparing tools,
- identifying tools with the most significant competency changes,
- interpreting how contributions and evaluations affect competency scores over time.

Results and Discussion

Students and teachers can use visualization to optimize learning paths using insights from the dynamic relationships between assessments, tool contributions, and competency development.

Recommendations for teachers:

- Tools with growth in competency scores (Z-axis) indicate positive and practical contributions.
- Teachers can focus on these tools to improve student learning outcomes.
- Tools with flat or declining competency trajectories (lines along the Z-axis) signal areas where tools may be less effective or require adjustment.
- The graph shows how tools perform across different assessment criteria (red and blue lines in the right graph).
- Teachers can tailor assessment strategies based on which assessment scale best reflects meaningful changes in competency.
- By observing tools that work better for some students or in specific contexts, teachers can personalize teaching approaches for different students.
- The range of competency scores (highlighted by vertical lines) provides insight into progress over time. Teachers can measure whether interventions are improving students' skills or stagnating.

Opportunities for students:

- Students can visually track their improvement in competencies by understanding which tools or activities are leading to meaningful progress (steeper upward trajectories along the z-axis)
- Tools with high contributions (y-axis) and consistently improving competency scores deserve priority in their learning efforts.
- Tools with flat or unstable competency scores may indicate methods that are not working for them. Students can focus on alternative tools or teaching strategies showing more promising results.
- The differences in the red (0.01 score) and blue (0.03 score) lines help students understand how detailed assessment affects their performance. They can focus on areas that help them excel in specific grading systems.
- Students can set achievable learning goals by analyzing competency score ranges (vertical lines) and effectively measuring their progress.
- This visualization enables real-time feedback: teachers can adjust teaching strategies, and students can adapt teaching methods with the ability to track how these changes dynamically impact competency scores.
- Using information about course learning resources improves the analysis of their use, learning paths and assessment of student competence. Competency indicators are organized into graduated sub-levels, and students are expected to have developed specific skills at a previous stage of learning. The purpose of competence indicators is to help understand student development.

The research findings indicate that implementing adaptive learning systems with self-creation of learning paths enhances the effectiveness of e-learning. The hierarchical structure of educational materials allows for personalized electronic assessment and ensures a structured approach to competency development. Based on student performance and test results, the calculated efficiency index provides insight into training success and allows for personalized recommendations for further learning.

The study confirms that data-driven adaptive learning models can optimize the selection of educational resources, aligning with student learning styles and progress. AI-based analysis of student activity in an e-learning system enables the recommendation of appropriate learning materials, enhancing knowledge retention and engagement. Furthermore, incorporating virtual mentors fosters independent learning and maintains student motivation, improving the learning experience.

Evaluating student feedback highlights the importance of measuring user satisfaction and teaching quality.

The research emphasizes the significance of structuring educational material using a hierarchical competency model. By aligning topics with revised Bloom's taxonomy, students can develop knowledge progressively, reinforcing their understanding at different cognitive levels.

However, the integration of human expertise remains essential. Administrators and educational content creators must supplement AI-driven methods with qualitative insights to refine and validate adaptive learning recommendations.

A crucial aspect of adaptive learning is continuously monitoring student performance and emotional states. The study highlights that real-time feedback from virtual tutors contributes significantly to student engagement. The system ensures adaptive recommendations align with student needs by leveraging AI for automated data collection and analysis. However, additional research is needed to enhance the balance between automated adaptation and human intervention in personalized education.

Summary

The research is aimed at solving an effective problem: increasing adaptability and personalization in e-learning systems. It includes data analysis, the use of artificial intelligence methods, and research activities to find the best solution (Ovcharenko, 2023).

The study used the method of weighted attribute values in the formula for calculating the competency indicator with a dynamic evaluation parameter, with normalization and scaling coefficients of weighted parameters for updating the data. The calculations allow data visualisation in a three-dimensional coordinate system for a more understandable assessment and decision-making.

Visualization of the resulting calculated data transforms complex data into an understandable, practically applicable format. Students can better focus on areas for improvement and independently plan their learning path. At the same time, teachers can personalize learning and improve the curriculum. Together, they can continuously optimize the learning path to maximize the development of competencies. Using this visualization iteratively, students and teachers can ensure that learning is effective, targeted and adaptive. 3D visualization gives students and teachers a dynamic tool for monitoring and optimizing learning outcomes.

For students, visualization serves as a self-assessment tool to track progress, identify problem areas, and prioritize efforts on tools or concepts that demonstrate the most significant learning gaps. For educators, it enables data-driven decisions to evaluate the effectiveness of tools or assessments and improve e-course design. The ability to compare multiple tools in a single 3D space enhances the overall learning experience and facilitates collaborative optimization between students and educators, improving student achievement.

The generalized structure of one topic of an e-course, consistent with the hierarchical structure of competencies, presents the sequence of the student's use of the educational material and the use of variable and measurable data used to adapt the educational material and generate recommendations. Adaptation provided by AI occurs both in the learning process and in the feedback process, including for assessing the quality of the educational material.

A review of the available research results revealed the possible use and potential of applying a multi-criteria approach to creating learning paths. Adapting the learning environment using advanced machine learning techniques and AI as adaptive logic based on the changing knowledge level of the learner is set to enable a new level of modern personalized learning.

The study highlights the potential of using streaming data from e-learning interactions to personalize the learning experience and improve educational outcomes. Using data collected from the Moodle e-learning system, this approach highlights the importance of real-time data processing and machine learning algorithms to create customized recommendations that meet the individual needs of learners. Going forward, the implementation of personalized real-time recommendations offers promising advances in adaptive learning, contributing to a more effective and engaging learning environment.

Personalized learning paths, based on AI-based analysis and student feedback, optimize the delivery of educational content and support independent learning. The proposed methodology enables dynamic adaptation, improving students' overall learning experience.

Competing interests

The author has/have no competing interests to declare.

References

Becker, P., & Stewart, R. (2022). Artificial intelligence in education psychology and personalized learning paths. AI in Education, 20(1), 55-73.

Carter, H., & Murphy, S. (2018). Intelligent tutoring systems and virtual tutors in online education. Journal of Educational Technology, 29(4), 188-204.

Chang, W., & Lin, K. (2020). Concept maps and clustering technology in adaptive learning systems. IEEE Transactions on Educational Technology, 19(2), 135-151.

Garcia, P., & Santos, L. (2020). Modern information systems and adaptive learning technologies. IEEE Transactions on Learning Technologies, 13(2), 87-102.

Hernandez, F., & Xu, L. (2019). User behaviour analysis in adaptive e-learning platforms. Journal of Interactive Learning, 36(2), 45-61.

Jiang, B., Li, X., Yang, S., Kong, Y., Cheng, W., Hao, C., & Lin, Q. (2022). Data-Driven Personalized Learning Path Planning Based on Cognitive Diagnostic Assessments in MOOCs, Appl. Sci., 12, 3982. https://doi.org/10.3390/app12083982

Johnson, R., & Wang, T. (2019). Organizing educational resources for adaptive learning. Journal of Online Education, 27(3), 55-72.

Kim, J., & Rodriguez, T. (2020). Training datasets for student modeling and predictive learning analytics. AI & Education Review, 10(3), 205-220.

Kumar, P., & Chen, H. (2021). Differential evolution algorithms in adaptive learning path optimization. Computational Intelligence in Education, 11(4), 150-167.

Lee, M., & Kim, H. (2021). Hierarchical structures of competencies in e-learning systems. Computers & Education, 159, 104023.

Miller, C., & Davis, B. (2018). Personalized learning environments and user experience adaptation. Educational Review, 45(5), 233-249.

Minn, S. (2022). AI-assisted knowledge assessment techniques for adaptive learning environments. Computers and Education: Artificial Intelligence, 3, 2022, 100050. https://doi.org/10.1016/j.caeai.2022.100050

Nabizadeh, A. H., Gonçalves, D., Gama, S., Jorge, J., & H. Rafsanjani (2020). Adaptive learning path recommender approach using auxiliary learning objects. Computers & Education, 147, 103777. https://doi.org/10.1016/j.compedu.2019.103777

Nelson, S., & Parker, J. (2022). Ontology-based recommender systems for personalized learning. Expert Systems with Applications, 91, 113408.

Nigenda, R. S., Padrón, C. M., Martínez-Salazar, I., & Torres-Guerrero, F. (2018). Design and evaluation of planning and mathematical models for generating learning paths, Computational Intelligence, 34:821–838. https://doi.org/10.1111/coin.12134

Ovtšarenko, O. (2023). Generation of a learning path in e-learning environments: literature review. New Trends in Computer Sciences, 1(1), 32–50.

Ovtšarenko, O. (2024). Opportunities of machine learning algorithms for education. Discover Education, 3, 209. https://doi.org/10.1007/s44217-024-00313-5.

Ovtsarenko, Olga (2024). Collection_2. figshare. Collection. https://doi.org/10.6084/m9.figshare.c.7588160

Ovtšarenko, O., & Safiulina, E. (2025). Computer-Driven Assessment of Weighted Attributes for E-Learning Optimization. Computers, 14(4), 116. https://doi.org/10.3390/computers14040116

Ramanauskaite, S., & Slotkiene, A. (2019). Hierarchy-Based Competency Structure and Its Application in E-Evaluation, MDPI, Appl. Sci., 9(17), 3478. https://doi.org/10.3390/app9173478

Singh, A., & Zhang, L. (2020). Filtering and teaching content based on student knowledge portfolios. Learning Analytics Review, 7(2), 32-48.

Smith, J., & Brown, A. (2020). Adaptive learning and skill portfolio analysis. Educational Technology Journal, 35(4), 112-130.

Thompson, E., & Robertson, J. (2021). EEG signals in personalized education and cognitive analysis. Journal of Learning Sciences, 14(6), 89-105.

White, D., & Adams, R. (2020). Student attributes and demographic-based learning customization. Journal of Educational Data Science, 8(3), 79-96.

Williams, B., & Lee, D. (2019). Performance-driven adaptive learning models and analytics. Journal of Adaptive Learning Systems, 24(1), 99-115.

Zhang, Y., & Patel, K. (2022). Concept and query map algorithms for adaptive learning systems. AI in Education Journal, 18(1), 12-28.

EDUard: A Cutting-Edge Software for supporting and enhancing learning with AI and Gamification

Carolina Mele[1,2], Luigi Iovino[2], Lucia Miranda[1] and Angelo Rega[1,2]

[1] Pegaso Telematic University, 80143 Naples, Italy
[2] Garage94 s.r.l., 80044 Ottaviano, Italy

Correspondence: Carolina Mele: carolina.mele@unipegaso.it

Abstract:
This article examines the integration of Artificial Intelligence (AI) and Gamification in educational tools, focusing on EDUard, a cross-platform software designed to support and enhance the learning of school subjects for primary and secondary school students. EDUard stands out as an inclusive and highly adaptable solution, designed to improve learning through gamification while adjusting to the individual needs of each student. By combining engaging game mechanics with personalized learning paths, the software not only promotes the improvement of fundamental skills such as reading, writing, and mathematics but also addresses the learning needs of students with special educational needs (SEN). The article highlights EDUard's innovative approach, its ability to stimulate student motivation and improve academic outcomes, as well as its potential to transform the educational landscape by creating more inclusive, dynamic, and personalized learning opportunities.

Keywords: learning, gamification, inclusive education, personalized learning, educational technology, inclusion

Introduction

In recent years, technological advances have radically transformed the educational landscape, generating significant impacts on the way teaching and learning are conceived and implemented.

Recent research highlights how the adoption of advanced technologies, and in particular Artificial Intelligence (AI), has opened up new perspectives for education, creating opportunities to personalise learning and improve the effectiveness of educational strategies (Zawacki-Richter et al., 2019).

Indeed, the introduction of AI has emerged as an innovative solution capable of overcoming the limitations of traditional educational systems, which are often based on standardised and rigid approaches, unable to adequately respond to the specific needs of students and their individual learning styles.

In this context, the use of Artificial Intelligence has enabled the development of personalised and adaptive learning models, in which learning content is shaped in real time to respond to the individual needs and preferences of students (Holmes et al., 2019).

The main goal of such approaches is to maximise the potential of each student and address educational challenges more effectively, while improving educational outcomes (Liriwati, 2023). The integration of AI in the educational context has therefore led to a fundamental revision in the conception and practice of teaching, shifting the focus towards more dynamic and targeted solutions.

Indeed, personalised and adaptive approaches promote education that evolves according to each student's progress and difficulties, improving engagement and reducing the risk of dropping out (Johnson & Lester, 2018).

Furthermore, such solutions help promote equity in access to educational resources, ensuring more inclusive and accessible learning opportunities (Luckin et al., 2016).

A key aspect of educational innovation concerns the introduction and adoption of Gamification, which involves the integration of playful elements, typical of games and video games, in contexts that are not themselves playful, such as learning.

Gamification is based on the integration of game mechanics (e.g. scores, challenges and prizes) with the intention of stimulating students' motivation, interest and active participation (Deterding et al., 2011; Nappo et al., 2022).

Numerous studies have highlighted the effectiveness of Gamification in fostering more dynamic and interactive learning, improving not only engagement but also students' academic performance (Hamari & Koivisto, 2014). Integrating game elements into educational processes has been shown to increase students' intrinsic motivation, reducing the perception of learning as an obligation and making the educational experience more stimulating (Sailer & Homner, 2020). Furthermore, Gamification fosters the development of crucial soft skills such as problem solving, collaboration and time management, skills that are crucial for academic and professional success (Subhash & Cudney, 2018).

In the context of digital learning, the adoption of Gamification in educational software has made it possible to create highly interactive and adaptive learning environments, capable of modulating the difficulty level of exercises according to students' skills, while providing immediate and personalised feedback.

Systematically, then, the integration of Gamification into educational technology tools offers several concrete benefits for learning, such as:

- Increased motivation: students are naturally attracted and motivated by the dynamics of play, and this motivation can be channelled towards achieving educational goals. Play provides immediate gratification that helps students remain focused and engaged for longer periods of time (Hamari & Koivisto, 2014);

- Active learning: unlike traditional teaching methods, gamification directly involves the learner, transforming them from passive spectators to active participants. This makes learning an integral part of the game, where each exercise represents a fun and stimulating challenge (Dichev & Dicheva, 2017);

- Reduction of performance anxiety: gamification creates an environment in which error is considered part of the learning process, turning mistakes into opportunities for improvement rather than moments of frustration, thus promoting a positive attitude towards studying (Apostol et al., 2013);

- Personalisation of the learning process: the tiered structure, typical of gamification, allows learning to be adapted to the individual capabilities of each learner, offering personalised paths that respect the time and manner of each one (as highlighted in the Journal of Education, 2022);

- Greater emotional involvement: the playful elements typical of Gamification, can make learning a more interactive and engaging experience, increasing students' interest and participation (Gee, 2003);

- Co-operative learning: activities developed with Gamification can be structured to promote co-operation between students, improving not only their academic skills, but also social skills such as teamwork and communication (Dacre et al., 2021).

The integration of Gamification in educational tools represents an effective strategy to improve the learning experience, making it more dynamic, personalised and in line with students' needs (Rega, 2011)

Starting from this background, therefore, in this study we will delve into the architecture and use of EDUard, a state-of-the-art educational software developed to support and enhance the learning of school subjects in primary and secondary schools, which significantly integrates Gamification and Artificial Intelligence approaches.

Software's Description

EDUard is a cross-platform software (Windows, Android, iOS) designed to support and enhance the learning of school subjects, both for typically developing students and students with special educational needs (SEN). Precisely because of this characteristic, EDUard is considered an inclusive tool, as it allows its use by the entire class group, including students with disabilities in all the various activities.

EDUard was designed for primary and secondary school students, with the aim of supporting and enhancing the learning of school subjects and instrumental skills.

The software was developed from the didactic methodology of Gamification, making use of a number of cardinal principles, which manifest themselves in various aspects:

- **Design**: each activity's graphic interface features a cartoon style, with the aim of making the experience playful and engaging;

- **Mechanics**: activities are structured in the form of interactive games, which can lead to students competing against each other within the class group, thus fostering social interaction and cooperative learning. In addition, immediate feedback on student performance is provided for each activity;

- **Components**: the activities are designed to be highly customisable, allowing the learning experience to be tailored to the specific needs of each student in order to optimise the learning process.

The integration of these gamification elements is aimed at improving engagement, motivation and learning effectiveness, making the educational experience more stimulating and accessible for all students.

EDUard software is divided into three different sessions, each focusing on specific areas of competence development.

1. **Training of instrumental skills:** This session focuses on strengthening the basic skills necessary for learning, such as reading, writing, math skills and executive functions. The activities proposed in this section are designed to strengthen the basic skills that form the foundation for the acquisition of competences in the various school subjects.

   The exercises included within this section are aimed at improving reading, writing and calculation skills as well as executive functions such as attention, working memory, planning, inhibition and cognitive flexibility. These skills are essential for optimal management of the educational process, as they support the regulation of cognitive behaviour and effective functioning in complex learning contexts (Nappo et al., 2021).

   Each activity in this section is highly customisable, allowing the exercises to be adapted to the specific needs of each student. In this way, this section serves as a digital 'compensatory' tool, offering targeted support to optimise learning and meet the different cognitive needs of students.

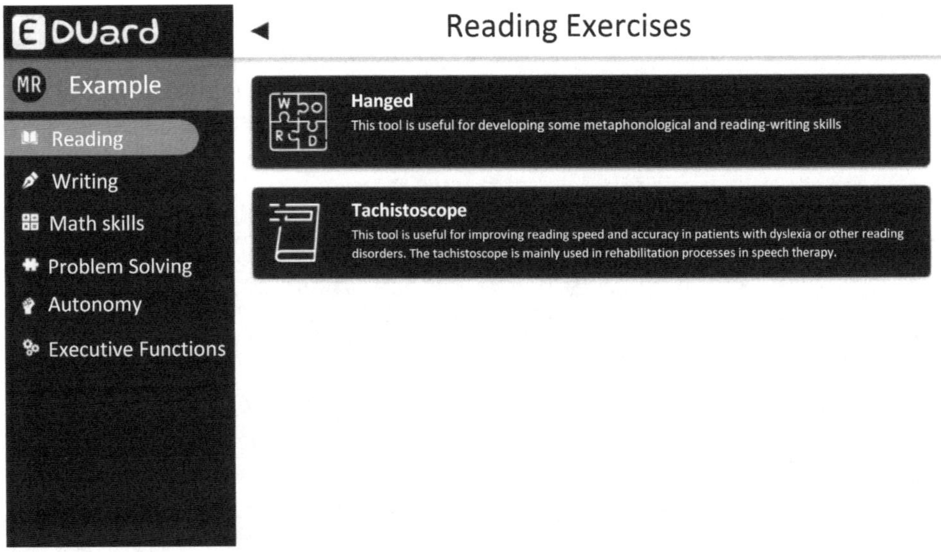

Figure 1: Instrumental skills training section.

2. **Training of school disciplines**: This section is dedicated to training in the main academic disciplines, including mathematics, Italian, science, history, geography, foreign languages (English, French and Spanish), geometry and art.

   EDUard has been designed for primary and secondary school students, and for this reason includes a filtering system that allows the selection of exercises according to school grade. It should be specified, however, that although there are specific indications regarding the destination of the exercises for each level, students still have the possibility of accessing exercises from a different school year or grade (lower or higher), should it be deemed necessary.

   Each exercise has been designed in accordance with the indications of the ministerial teaching programme and focuses on deepening and achieving the objectives and educational goals set for each school year and grade considered.

   EDUard's teaching approach integrates theory with practice, aiming to reinforce discipline-specific knowledge. The activities are structured to favour a progressive and personalised acquisition of skills, adapting to the pace and needs of the students.

   A fundamental feature of EDUard is the option to use a 'prompt', a suggestion that the student can activate and use when he or she is having difficulty performing an exercise independently. The introduction of the prompt aims to prevent frustration on the part of the student, supporting learning without interrupting the cognitive flow. This element is crucial in digital educational tools, as it allows students to continue the activity in a constructive manner.

   At the end of each activity, EDUard provides immediate feedback, allowing the teacher, as much as the student, to monitor results and identify any strengths and weaknesses. This functionality allows progress to be tracked in real time and future learning activities to be adapted.

   A further innovative aspect of EDUard is the "Lesson worksheets" section, present for each subject, where the teacher can use pre-prepared worksheets for each school year and for each subject, as a verification tool at the end of the explanation of a specific topic. The innovative benefits of the worksheets are many. Firstly, the use of the worksheets, in a Gamification context, transforms the traditional moment of assessment into a more serene and engaging opportunity for students, reducing the performance anxiety linked to the time of tests. A further benefit stems from the availability of a large database of worksheets, which allows teachers to easily select the verification activities best suited to their teaching needs. Finally, a further benefit of the worksheets also derives from the possibility of obtaining immediate feedback on the execution of the worksheets, eliminating the need for the teacher to manually correct student activities.

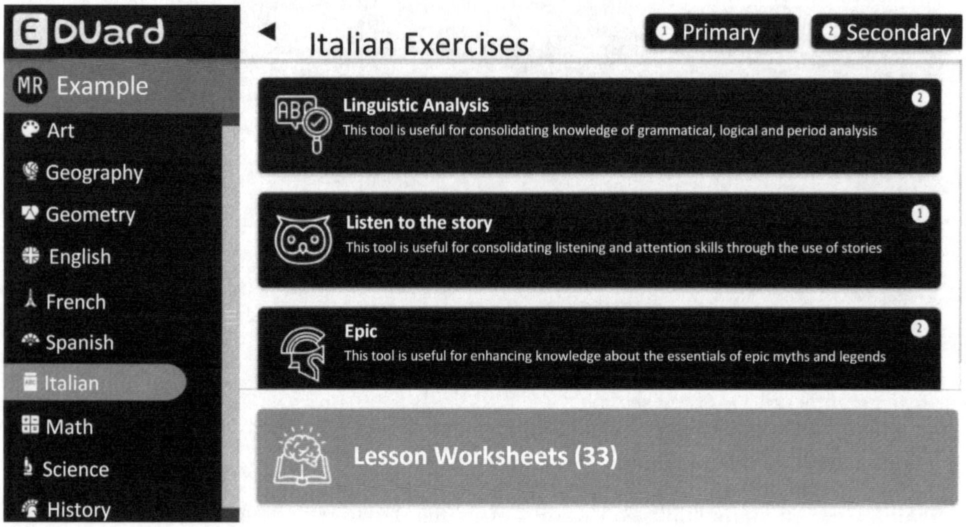

Figure 2: School discipline training section.

3. **Assessment of learning style:** The third and final section is dedicated to the evaluation of the student's learning style, conducted through the completion of a questionnaire structured according to the model proposed by Mariani (2000). Upon completion of the questionnaire, the software provides a detailed assessment of the student's learning style, identifying their preferred ways of acquiring and processing information. This section offers teachers a useful tool for better understanding the cognitive and teaching characteristics of students, enabling them to adapt their teaching in a targeted and more effective manner. Furthermore, based on the results obtained from the questionnaire, the software employs Artificial Intelligence technologies to generate customised teaching material, which can be integrated into lessons to respond more specifically to the individual needs of each student. This approach makes it possible to create individualised learning paths, optimising the educational process and improving teaching effectiveness.

In addition to the three main sections described above, EDUard offers an additional section called 'Tools'. This section includes two specific tools designed to support the teacher in organising and customising the learning experience:

- **Conceptual maps:** Through this tool, the teacher has the possibility of creating, or having students create, digital concept maps. These maps will have the characteristic of being highly customisable, so as to respond to the individual cognitive and teaching needs of the students. Moreover, all the concept maps generated are saved in the teacher's profile, allowing them to be retrieved and reused at any time.

- **SmartBook Editor:** This tool is designed to allow teachers to generate QRcodes associated with specific videos and teaching documents that they want to share with their students. QRcodes allow students to quickly access the teaching materials proposed by teachers, making access to them quicker and more effective. This functionality optimises the management of educational resources, promoting quick and convenient access to the multimedia content proposed by teachers.

EDUard is therefore a powerful and versatile learning support tool, capable not only of fostering the development of fundamental skills, but also of offering an in-depth analysis of each student's learning style. Thanks to the distinguishing features of this software, the educational experience becomes unique and tailored, and able to address individual needs and enhance every potential.

EDUard not only makes learning more engaging for students, but also supports teachers by providing tools that make it easier for them to manage lessons and assessment, saving valuable time and allowing them to build more focused teaching.

In a world where education is evolving at an increasingly fast pace, EDUard is not just a piece of software, but stands out as a true ally for teachers and students, to build a future where every student fully expresses his or her abilities and achieve academic success in an authentic and lasting way, approaching learning not as an obligation, but as an enjoyable experience.

Through its ability to personalise learning and make it engaging, it is opening the door to a more inclusive, motivating and successful educational future.

In future prospects, it is planned to initiate targeted data collection in order to obtain solid statistical support to objectively quantify the benefits of the application. This step is a priority objective to further consolidate and validate the effectiveness of the EDUard software.

Competing interests

The author(s) has/have no competing interests to declare.

References

Apostol, S., Zaharescu, L., & Alexe, I. (2013). GAMIFICATION OF LEARNING AND EDUCATIONAL GAMES. Elearning & Software For Education, (2).

Dacre, N., Gkogkidis, V., & Jenkins, P. (2021). Co-creation of innovative gamification based learning: A case of synchronous partnership. arXiv preprint arXiv:2103.13273.

Deterding, S., Sicart, M., Nacke, L., O'hara, K., & Dixon, D. (2011). Gamification. using game-design elements in non-gaming contexts. In CHI'11 extended abstracts on human factors in computing systems (pp. 2425-2428).

Diario della Formazione. (2022). Guida alla Gamification: metodologia per aumentare la motivazione.

Dichev, C., & Dicheva, D. (2017). Gamifying education: what is known, what is believed and what remains uncertain: a critical review. International journal of educational technology in higher education, 14, 1-36.

Gee, J. P. (2003). What video games have to teach us about learning and literacy. Computers in entertainment (CIE), 1(1), 20-20.

Hamari, J., & Koivisto, J. (2014). Measuring flow in gamification: Dispositional flow scale-2. Computers in human behavior, 40, 133-143.

Holmes, W., Bialik, M., & Fadel, C. (2019). Artificial Intelligence in Education: Promises and Implications for Teaching and Learning. Center for Curriculum Redesign.

Johnson, W. L., & Lester, J. C. (2018). The power of personalized learning: How adaptive technologies are shaping education outcomes. Journal of Learning Analytics, 5(2), 22-40.

Liriwati, I. (2023). Adaptive Learning through Artificial Intelligence: A Comprehensive Approach. International Journal of Learning Technologies, 9(1), 15-34.

Luckin, R., Holmes, W., Griffiths, M., & Forcier, L. B. (2016). Intelligence Unleashed: An Argument for AI in Education. Pearson Education.

Mariani, L. (2000). Portfolio: strumenti per documentare e valutare cosa si impara e 17. come si impara. Guida per l'insegnante. Zanichelli.

Nappo, R., Crisci, G., Ciaramella, F., Boccia, V., Carillo, C., Giugliano, M., ... & Rega, A. (2021). Assessment and training of executive functions in children through a game-based software: preliminary usability data from therapists' perspective. Proceedings http://ceur-ws.org ISSN, 1613, 0073.

Nappo, R., Cerasuolo, M., Ciaramella, F., Simeoli, R., & Rega, A. (2022). Framework guidelines to design and develop game-based cognitive training. In INTED2022 Proceedings (pp. 6897-6902). IATED.

Rega, A. (2011). Nuovi modi di giocare. La tecnologia a servizio dell'apprendimento nei contesti ludici. Ricerca di Senso, 9, 407-412.

Sailer, M., & Homner, L. (2020). The gamification of learning: A meta-analysis. Educational psychology review, 32(1), 77-112.

Subhash, S., & Cudney, E. A. (2018). Gamified learning in higher education: A systematic review of the literature. Computers in human behavior, 87, 192-206.

Zawacki-Richter, O., Marín, V. I., Bond, M., & Gouverneur, F. (2019). Systematic review of research on artificial intelligence applications in higher education – Where are the educators? International Journal of Educational Technology in Higher Education, 16(1), 1-27.

IA-CREATE: Bridging AI and Inclusion to foster Personalized Education paths

Lucia Miranda[1,2], Mariangela Cerasuolo[3], Carolina Mele[1] and Angelo Rega[1]

[1] Pegaso Telematic Unniversity, Napoli, Italy
[2] Neapolisanit S.R.L., Rehabilitation Center, Ottaviano Italy
[3] Associazione Italiana per l'Assistenza Spastici Onlus Sez Di Cicciano, Cicciano, Italy

Correspondence: Lucia Miranda: lucia.miranda@unipegaso.it

Abstract:

School inclusion is crucial to ensure equal opportunities for all students, including those with Special Educational Needs (SEN). To support teachers in inclusive teaching, the European Erasmus+ project IA-ME (2022-1-IT02- KA220-SCH-000087877) has developed IA-CREATE, an innovative digital platform. IA-CREATE helps teachers to design customized educational paths thanks to the CREATE+ questionnaire, based on international diagnostic models such as DSM-5 and ICF-CY. This tool analyses students' cognitive, language, motor and social skills, automatically generating targeted educational plans with inclusive strategies and technologies.

The platform, which can be accessed on PCs and tablets, allows students' progress to be monitored in real time and fosters collaboration between teachers, families and specialists. With the support of artificial intelligence and a multilingual interface, IA-CREATE makes teaching more effective and accessible, contributing to the digital transformation of education and the promotion of a more inclusive school.

Keywords: Inclusive Education; Special Educational Needs (SEN); Artificial Intelligence in Educatio; Personalized Learning; Educational Technology; Teacher Support Tools

Introduction

School inclusion is a fundamental pillar of modern education systems, conceived as a process through which all schools must strive to adequately respond to the Special Educational Needs (SEN) of students, favouring equal learning opportunities for all, regardless of individual difficulties. As mentioned in Ministerial Decree no. 153 of 1 August 2023 (Ministero dell'Istruzione e del Merito, 2023), inclusion is an essential principle for guaranteeing the right to study and the full participation of every pupil in the school environment. This concept implies the creation of school environments capable of welcoming and valuing diversity, responding in an inclusive manner to a wide variety of needs. To achieve effective inclusion, it is crucial that teachers possess not only general pedagogical skills, but also adequate training in inclusive methodologies, the use of educational technologies and the management of complex classroom dynamics, which characterise inclusiveness (Ainscow, 2020).

Teachers play a central role not only as key players in the educational process, but also as the first to deal with diversity within the classroom. To perform this task effectively, it is essential to have targeted training, specialised skills and innovative tools to promote authentic inclusion. Traditional training is not sufficient to provide teachers with the necessary resources to deal with the challenges associated with students with cognitive, physical, emotional or language difficulties (ISTAT, 2022). Improving teachers' teaching skills must involve a change in methodologies, classroom management and the use of technology. The introduction of innovative tools, such as those based on artificial intelligence, offers teachers the possibility of personalising teaching, responding more precisely to the individual needs of students (Valditara, 2024). These tools facilitate the identification of pupils' strengths and difficulties, enabling the creation of personalised educational plans and improving learning opportunities for each student (Selwyn, 2021).

Several research studies show that the integration of advanced technological tools, especially those based on AI, can significantly improve teaching practices and foster more effective inclusion (Kamalov et al., 2023). The increasing diffusion of educational technologies, supported by digital innovation policies, opens up new possibilities for supporting students with SEN, offering digital tools that facilitate the personalisation of teaching and the early identification of effective teaching strategies. However, in order for these technologies to be effectively implemented, it is necessary that teachers receive specific and continuous training, enabling them to make the most of the potential offered by AI and other advanced technologies.

In this perspective, the European Erasmus+ project IA-ME (2022-1-IT02-KA220-SCH-000087877) represents an innovative initiative aimed at enhancing teachers' competences and promoting inclusive education, with a special focus on students with SEN. IA-ME aligns with the priorities of the Digital Education Action Plan 2021-2027, contributing to the creation of an accessible digital educational ecosystem, capable of adapting to the needs of each student. The project's distinctive element lies in the use of artificial intelligence (AI) as a key tool to personalise teaching, automate the assessment of student difficulties and improve classroom management. AI makes it possible to develop targeted teaching strategies, facilitating teachers' work and offering SEN students support tailored to their educational needs. In parallel, IA-ME responds to the need for a digital transformation of the education system, accelerated by the pandemic of COVID-19, which has highlighted gaps in teachers' digital skills (Ghomi & Redecker, 2019). The project aims to fill this gap through innovative AI-based tools, facilitating the adoption of effective teaching methodologies for quality education in digital contexts.

IA-ME is structured around three main objectives

- Raising awareness among educational institutions and teachers on the importance of more inclusive technologies for education;
- Providing advanced digital tools to support teachers in managing students with SEN;
- Strengthen their professional competences, improving skills in the management of inclusive classrooms.

The project is aimed directly at primary and secondary school teachers, both support and curricular, who are at the forefront of implementing inclusive practices. However, the benefits of the initiative also extend to indirect recipients, including students with SEN, their families and the entire school community, who will benefit from a more equitable and effective educational approach.

IA-ME envisages the achievement of four main outcomes:

- A manual containing guidelines for teachers on the use of ICT in inclusive education;
- A multilingual AI-based web application for assessing student needs and generating personalised educational plans;
- A MOOC (Massive Open Online Course) for the continuous professional development of teachers;
- A project synthesis manual, which will collect best practices and recommendations for further dissemination of the acquired knowledge.

Through a combination of state-of-the-art technologies, innovative training and evidence-based methodologies, IA-ME represents a concrete opportunity to transform inclusive education. The project aims to reduce inequalities, improve teachers' digital skills and ensure that every student, regardless of their difficulties, has the opportunity to develop their potential within a fair and accessible school environment.

IA-CREATE Description

One of the main products of the IA-ME project, designed to support teachers in the educational management of students with Special Educational Needs (SEN), is the IA-CREATE (Innovative Application - Customized Resources for Educational Achievement and Tailored Experiences) platform. This innovative solution is designed to simplify and enhance the process of personalised learning, a crucial aspect of educational inclusion that not only improves the quality of teaching, but also ensures greater equity in access to education for all students, regardless of their difficulties or specific needs.

IA-CREATE enables teachers to create tailor-made learning paths, taking into account the specific needs of each student, and advises teachers on inclusive educational strategies and technologies aimed at fostering the success of all pupils, regardless of their individual difficulties. The process of personalising learning has, in fact, as its primary objective the enhancement of each student's potential, helping to improve not only their cognitive skills, but also their emotional and social skills, which are fundamental for integrated and inclusive learning (Matucci, 2021).

The software simplifies the customisation process through a detailed analysis of students' individual skills and needs. The platform is distinguished by its ability to collect and analyse a wide range of data on different aspects of student development and behaviour, thus providing a complete picture of the student's educational needs. This approach helps optimise the educational experience, making teaching more focused, inclusive and effective. IA-CREATE is free, accessible on tablets and PCs at no extra cost, and its intuitive interface is also suitable for those with limited technological skills. Moreover, available in six languages, it is ideal for multicultural contexts, promoting global inclusion.

At the heart of IA-CREATE is the CREATE+ questionnaire, an advanced tool for collecting detailed information on each student's strengths and difficulties. Teachers fill in the questionnaire, which then automatically draws up a customised educational path, highlighting the educational objectives to be achieved and suggesting the most appropriate teaching methods and technologies to support learning and achieve the set objectives.

CREATE+ was developed through an interdisciplinary approach involving experts in pedagogy, psychology and technology, ensuring an accurate assessment of students' special educational needs. Furthermore, this tool benefits from a solid theoretical and methodological basis, enabling the creation of educational paths that are not only effective but also scientifically validated.

The questionnaire is structured on a sound pedagogical framework, supported by academic research and contributions from focus groups conducted in several European countries, including Greece, Spain, Hungary, Italy and Turkey (Miranda et al., 2024). These focus groups made it possible to enrich and adapt the questionnaire to different school and cultural realities, ensuring that the proposed solutions are relevant and applicable in various educational contexts. The multicultural and interdisciplinary approach of the project ensures that the students' educational needs are understood and comprehensively addressed, taking into account the specificities of each school context. Furthermore, the questionnaire ensures that the information collected is relevant and useful for the definition of educational needs, drawing inspiration from international diagnostic tools:

- DSM-5 (American Psychiatric Association, 2013)
- ICF-CY (World Health Organization, 2007)
- VALUTAZIONE CRITERIALE DELLE ABILITA' (Guazzo, 2013)
- VB-MAPP (Sundberg, 2008)
- VINELAND ADAPTIVE BEHAVIOR SCALES-2 (Sparrow, 2011)
- ASSESSMENT OF BASIC LANGUAGE AND LEARNING SKILLS-REVISED (Rispoli, 2013)
- DENVER CHECKLIST (Rogers & Dawson, 2010)

The CREATE+ questionnaire is a dynamic and innovative tool, developed with the aim of gathering detailed information on each individual student's educational journey. Its design was geared towards ensuring an in-depth assessment of individual needs, while maintaining a user-friendly structure for teachers. In this way, CREATE+ aims to facilitate the process of personalising learning, enabling effective guidance towards educational success for all students, regardless of their difficulties.

The evaluation process has two distinct but complementary levels:

1. The first level focuses on identifying special educational needs, exploring aspects such as disabilities, temporary impairments, and socio-cultural or linguistic disadvantages. This makes it possible to exclude irrelevant questions and focus on the specific needs of the students so that the educational pathway can be adapted more precisely.
2. The second level, on the other hand, delves into students' general abilities, examining skills such as motor, language and cognitive skills.

This two-level approach provides a comprehensive picture of educational needs, which is essential for targeted and effective instructional design.

After the initial screening process, the core of the CREATE+ questionnaire develops along four fundamental educational dimensions, each of which explores in depth specific areas of development and learning:

1. cognitive, neuropsychological and learning
2. communicative and linguistic
3. autonomy and orientation
4. relational, interactive and social

The cognitive, neuropsychological and learning dimension focuses on the assessment of the learner's general cognitive abilities, as well as his or her ability to cope with complex learning tasks. The communicative and linguistic dimension aims at analysing language competence, examining both comprehension and verbal and non-verbal expression skills. The autonomy and orientation dimension focuses on assessing the learner's independence, motor skills, and spatial orientation abilities. Finally, the relational, interactional and social dimension explores emotional and social dynamics, focusing on the skills of interaction, collaboration with others, and emotional regulation.

Each dimension is broken down into specific sub-domains, thus ensuring an even more precise assessment of the various skills and difficulties. The answers to the questionnaire are provided on a Likert scale:

- Score 0 - Skill not present: The student shows no evidence of possessing the skill
- Score 1 - Emerging skill: The student shows initial awareness or can perform the skill with significant support
- Score 2 - Well mastered skill: The student consistently performs the skill independently and proficiently
- Not applicable: The skill has not been introduced or taught to the individual yet

This scoring system is crucial for the creation of customised learning pathways, as it allows for the precise identification of areas of intervention. A score of 1 on a given item, for example, signals a short-term educational goal, thus providing immediate guidance for teachers on which skills to focus on to foster student growth and learning in a targeted manner.

Another of the innovative aspects of IA-CREATE is the ability to monitor student progress in real time. The platform allows teachers to plan and calendar objectives and activities, continuously adapting educational paths to emerging needs. This approach enables formative assessment, where the learning process is constantly updated and optimised according to student progress.

Furthermore, a further section of IA-CREATE is 'community' which facilitates continuous and transparent communication between teachers, families, and other professionals involved in educational support, creating a shared and coordinated learning environment. This communication element is crucial to the success of an inclusive approach, as it fosters synergetic work between all educational actors, ensuring that the student's needs are followed in a cohesive and multidisciplinary manner.

To access the IA-CREATE platform, users can visit the project's official website at www.ia-me.eu/ia-create/ or consult the resources section on the IA-ME platform (www.ia-me.eu). Thanks to its free access and ease of use, IA-CREATE represents a fundamental resource for educational inclusion, making the personalisation of learning a process that is not only easier, but also more effective, guaranteeing each student a tailor-made education that meets his or her specific needs.

In conclusion, IA-CREATE represents a powerful resource for the personalisation of learning, offering an innovative and easy-to-use tool that supports teachers in the creation of inclusive educational pathways. Free access, the possibility to monitor progress and the focus on cultural and educational diversity make IA-CREATE a pillar for inclusive education, helping to reduce inequalities and promote quality learning for every student. Moreover, the systemic and integrated approach that characterises IA-CREATE is bound to make a difference in inclusive education, helping teachers to address educational challenges in an innovative and efficient way, thus ensuring that all students have the same opportunities for educational success.

Competing interests

The author(s) has/have no competing interests to declare.

References

American Psychiatric Association. (2013). Diagnostic and statistical manual of mental disorders (5th ed.). American Psychiatric Publishing.

Ainscow, M. (2020). Inclusion and equity in education: Making sense of global challenges. Prospects, 49(3), 123-134. https://doi.org/10.1007/s11125-020-09450-1

European Commission. (2020). Digital Education Action Plan 2021-2027. https://eur-lex.europa.eu/legal-content/EN/TXT/?uri=CELEX%3A52020DC0624

Ghomi, M., & Redecker, C. (2019, May). Digital competence of educators (DigCompEdu): Development and evaluation of a self-assessment instrument for teachers' digital competence. In CSEDU (1) (pp. 541-548).

Guazzo, A. (2013). Valutazione criteriale delle abilità. Vannini.

ISTAT. (2022, December). Alunni con disabilità, Anno scolastico 2021-2022. Istituto Nazionale di Statistica.

Kamalov, F., Santandreu Calong, D., & Gurrib, I. (2023). New era of artificial intelligence in education: Towards a sustainable multifaceted revolution. https://arxiv.org/abs/2303.10230

Ministero dell'Istruzione e del Merito. (2023). Decreto Ministeriale n. 153 del 1 agosto 2023.

Matucci, G. (2021). Personalizzazione degli apprendimenti, eguaglianza, capacità. Diritto costituzionale: rivista quadrimestrale, 3, 87-109.

Miranda, L., Cerasuolo, M., Mele, C., & Rega, A. (2024). Teachers' perspectives and challenges in inclusive education: Insights from IA-ME project focus groups. ISYDE 2024 - Lifelong Digital Learning and Education: promoting flexibility, inclusion, critical thinking, and international exchange, 164-165.

Rispoli, M. (2013). Assessment of Basic Language and Learning Skills-Revised (ABLLS-R). Behavior Analysts, Inc.

Rogers, S. J., & Dawson, G. (2010). Early Start Denver Model for young children with autism: Promoting language, learning, and engagement. The Guilford Press.

Selwyn, N. (2021). Education and technology: Key issues and debates. Bloomsbury Publishing.

Sparrow, S. S., Cicchetti, D. V., & Balla, D. A. (2011). Vineland adaptive behavior scales (2nd ed.). Pearson.
Sundberg, M. L. (2008). VB-MAPP: Verbal behavior milestones assessment and placement program. AVB Press.

Valditara, A. (2024). Intelligenza artificiale a scuola: Come personalizzare la didattica. Tecnica della Scuola.

World Health Organization. (2007). International classification of functioning, disability and health: Children & youth version: ICF-CY. World Health Organization.

Empowering Teachers in AI-TPACK: The Critical Role of Institutional Support

Amera Alharbi[1], Ashwaq Althowibi[2]

[1]English Language and Translation Department, College of Science and Theoretical Studies, Saudi Electronic University, Dammam, KSA, aa.alharbi@seu.edu.sa

[2]English language institute princess Noura bint Abdulrahman university, KSA afalthowibi@pnu.edu.sa

Correspondence: Amera Alharbi: aa.alharbi@seu.edu.sa

Abstract:
Artificial Intelligence (AI) is transforming the pedagogical practices in education; however, its effective adoption requires more than the technological development. The technological pedagogical content knowledge (TPACK) is also influenced by teachers' readiness to incorporate AI in their teaching, which in turn depends on the institutional support in the form of professional development, resources, and administrative encouragement. This paper explores how institutional support influences teachers' AI-TPACK readiness. To conduct this research, a quantitative research design was applied, and English language educators were surveyed to determine the relationship between institutional support and the adoption of AI. The results show that institutional support improves teachers' AI-TPACK abilities in specific areas, for example, TPK and TCK. However, concerns such as AI ethics, and overreliance on tools persist, thus requiring thorough preparation for AI-focused professional training. The study further suggests that long-term, dynamic professional training programs should address not only the technical aspects of AI but also the theoretical underpinning of using AI in teaching and learning and ethical issues in AI. In the context of the rising influence of AI on education, institutions need to establish clear policies and programs for the rational emergence of AI in classrooms. The findings of this study therefore are significant in helping policymakers, educators, and institutional administrators to improve the integration of AI in education.

Keywords: AI in Education, AI-TPACK, Institutional Support, Teacher Readiness, AI Professional Development, Ethical AI Integration.

Introduction

The integration of Artificial Intelligence (AI) in education has revolutionized teaching and learning processes, offering educators new tools to enhance pedagogical practices (Celik, 2023). AI applications such as ChatGPT have gained significant attention for their ability to support instructional design and personalized learning (Agbong-Coates, 2024). However, successful AI integration into teaching requires more than just technological accessibility; it demands teacher readiness, institutional support, and targeted professional development (Tondeur et al., 2017). While AI integration in education has been widely studied, limited research has examined how institutional support directly influences AI-TPACK adoption among English language teachers. This study fills that gap by investigating the relationship between institutional support and teachers' AI-TPACK readiness.

Literature Review

AI-TPACK Framework

The Technological, Pedagogical and Content Knowledge (TPACK) framework provides a starting point for teachers to incorporate technology into teaching. Based on Shulman's (1986) idea of Pedagogical Content Knowledge (PCK), Mishra and Koehler (2006) extended the framework to include technological aspect to the previous components (content knowledge and pedagogical knowledge). As artificial intelligence is changing the world of education, the AI-TPACK framework has emerged to include the specific skills related to AI within the classic model (Celik, 2023; Ning, 2024). The AI-TPACK framework goes beyond the conventional concepts by requiring teachers to acquire and exhibit:

- ***AI-Technological Knowledge***: Understanding of the functions, limitations, and opportunities of AI in education.
- ***AI-Technological Pedagogical Knowledge***: Using AI-enabled resources to provide feedback, engage learners, and manage learning pathways.
- ***AI-Technological Content Knowledge:*** Using AI for general learning, for example, using natural language processing tools for language learning.

This integration emphasizes the evolving interaction between technology and pedagogy which offers new possibilities for personalized learning while reconsidering traditional teaching paradigms (Karataş & Yüce, 2024; Casal-Otero et al., 2023). However, the AI-TPACK framework raises concerns on the ethical issues such as bias, privacy, and access (Deng & Zhang, 2023; Wang, 2024). The existence of effective AI integration requires strong institutional backing to address these issues.

Institutional Support and AI-TPACK Readiness

Research highlights the critical role of teacher readiness to employ AI literacy using TPACK framework. Yue et al. (2024), for example, explored K–12 teachers' readiness and attitudes toward AI education and provide strategies for professional development. Although the AI-TPACK model is presented as a potential solution, research concludes that institutional support is critical for the effective implementation of the model (Wang et al., 2021). Such support can take many forms, from practical strategies learned in workshops to the availability of advanced educational materials to regularly scheduled professional development sessions, or administrative requirement (Koehler & Mishra, 2009). Teachers may understand the concept of AI-TPACK, but they may not have the necessary ethical knowledge and readiness to incorporate AI into their teaching. The researchers established that desire to use AI is not always accompanied by appropriate usage in the classroom because of ignorance of the benefits of AI in education and ethical issues (Karataş & Aksu Atac, 2024; Güneyli et al., 2024). Without institutional support and a clear framework for ethical training in AI, teachers may inadvertently subject students to biased AI content, data security threats, and an overdependence on AI technologies, which may be detrimental to learning (Alnasib, 2023). This justifies the need for systematic institutional support in the form of AI literacy programs, ethical guidelines, and professional development.

AI-TPACK and Teacher Readiness

Despite the optimistic views on the application of AI technologies in education, successful implementation in the classroom is difficult due to a noticeable gap between practice and theory (Velander et al., 2023). Although the AI technologies provide the personal and interesting approach to learning, they require a clear pedagogical direction (Yue et al., 2024). Educators understand the potential of AI, but they fail to apply the theory in practice because of lack of skills and ethical perception (Mishra et al., 2023). Conventional professional learning lacks the ability to address integration issues (Dogan et al., 2025). According to the latter, AI-PD involve dual focus, first: teaching teachers about the potentials and dangers of AI, and the ethical issues associated with it. Second, teaching them how to incorporate AI into the pedagogical process, assessment, and instructional design. It is essential to have ongoing mentoring, shared professional learning, and extended professional learning cycles to support the sustainable uptake of the new pedagogy (Dogan et al., 2025). Cukurova et al. (2024) have shown that one off AI workshops are massively lacking. A more systematic and prolonged training was suggested instead, to ensure that teachers develop technical literacy, understand the theory of education, and know how to use AI responsibly. In addition, algorithmic bias, data privacy risks, and potential inequalities continue to pose a significant ethical challenge to the integration of AI in education (Wang, 2021, 2024; Deng & Zhang, 2023). However, without institutional support, educators may lack the resources and preparedness to implement AI effectively (Deng & Zhang, 2023; Wang, 2021, 2024). The current research contributes to this debate by exploring how institutional support can be used to enhance teachers' AI-TPACK preparedness.

Research Methodology

Study Design

A quantitative approach was adopted in the research design which explored English language teachers' opinions on how institutional supports enhance AI technological pedagogical content knowledge (AI TPACK) through intensive ChatGPT use in education. The researchers looked at the correlation between Institutional Support as a determinant of professional development in the integration of AI-TPACK. A survey collected quantitative data to measure how institutional Support influence teacher readiness to implement AI into their classrooms. As the main focus of the study was to explore the measurable relationships between institutional support and AI integration, a quantitative survey was chosen to efficiently capture trends across a broad sample (Creswell, 2014). Future research could complement these findings with qualitative methods to explore deeper contextual factors.

Participants

The current study was approved by the institutional review board. There are numerous ways of recruiting participants for a survey, all of which have their strengths and weaknesses. One way that is often employed is purposive sampling because it enables the researcher to choose the kind of people they want to include in their study. It can be a relatively quicker method of identifying participants as the researcher does not have to wade through a multitude of subjects. Lastly, purposive sampling can assist in making sure that the survey participants are so chosen that they are reasonably representative of the population of interest (Ames et al., 2019). However, like any other method, the purposive sampling method is not without its limitations. For instance, it takes more time to recruit participants using purposive sampling than probability methods such as simple randomization because the researchers have to look for specific individuals within the population (Etikan et al., 2016). In order to avoid such limitations, we explicitly followed strict inclusion and exclusion criteria for selecting the participants. The participants were one hundred English language teachers from Saudi Arabian universities. Purposive sampling was used to select participants who had previously used AI tools like ChatGPT and were currently engaged in university teaching. Purposive sampling provided participants who gave details about the employment of AI in educational contexts. Also, an attempt was made to include a variety of participants in terms of age, teaching experience, and gender to increase the data richness. To ensure that participants had previous experience with AI tools, purposive sampling was used, in line with the study's objective of looking for informed perspectives (Etikan et al., 2016). The use of this approach limits the generalizability of the findings, but it increases the relevance of the findings by providing insights from educators who are actually using AI. PLS-SEM is suitable for application to small-to-medium sample sizes, and Hair et al. (2017) recommend that model estimation should be considered reliable for between 50 and 100 cases.

Instrument

This research employs a quantitative approach to explore the critical role of institutional support in influencing teachers' readiness to incorporate AI in teaching. Participants provided ratings on the survey items on a 5-point rating scale with the response options being 1 = Strongly Disagree, 2 = Disagree, 3 = Neither Agree nor Disagree, 4 = Agree, and 5 = Strongly Agree. The measurement items AI TPACK Readiness and Institutional Support were developed based on validated instruments. AI TPACK Readiness is modified from Celik (2023) to measure the dependent variable. To find out whether teachers were willing and ready to use AI tools in teaching, we asked them questions about their knowledge and competence. The research is adopted institutional support measurement from Tondeur et al. (2017) to determine the role of institutional policies, resource allocation, and teacher training on technology integration. Pilot testing with ten participants also confirmed content clarity and reliability. Cronbach's alpha, composite reliability, and AVE scores were used to assess reliability and validity to further ensure construct robustness.

Data Collection Procedures

Ethics approval was obtained from the Institutional Review Board (IRB) prior to performing the study in order to uphold research guidelines. The email invitation contained detailed information on the study's purpose, scope, objectives, informed consent, and a secure survey link. Responses were on average completed in 10 to 15 minutes. The participants of this study included 100 English teachers in Saudi Arabia who applied AI tools. Participants were selected through purposive sampling methods based on their fulfilment of the teachers' inclusion criteria for those working in English language education. The survey was available to respondents for two weeks, with weekly email reminders to facilitate response. Appearing in the form, was the voluntary nature of the study where participants had control over their anonymity and could withdraw with no consequences. To comply with ethical guidelines, all collected data was anonymized, and participant identifiers shifted to coded labels to ensure confidentiality. Survey results were analyzed through Partial Least Squares Structural Equation Modeling (PLS-SEM) using Smart PLS software. This was done using descriptive statistics as an overview of the data. The researchers tested the reliability and validity of the measurement model. Finally, a path analytic approach tested the hypothesis, investigating if and how institutional support influences teachers' readiness for AI integration.

Results

Demographic Data

The demographic data of the respondents is provided in Table 2 below.

Table 1: Demographic Information

Demographic Variable	Category	Percentage (%)
Gender	Male	58%
	Female	40%
	I prefer not to respond	2%
Age group	20 - 25	20%
	26 - 30	50%
	31 - 35	20%
	36 and above	10%
Teaching Experience	1-5 years	30%
	6-10 years	40%
	11-15 years	20%
	16 and above	10%
Education Level	Bachelor's Level	25%
	Master's Level	60%
	PhD Level	10%
	Other	5%
Familiarity with AI Tools	Low	20%
	Moderate	50%
	High	30%

Based on Table 1, males made up of 58% (n = 168), while female counts n = 114, which represented 40%, and 2% did not say anything about their gender. 50% of the overall responses came from participants aged between 26-30 years old, followed by 20% for the age group of 20-25, and age group of 31-35 years old respectively while the age group above 36 years old was 10%.

The data includes mostly English language teachers with 6-10 years (40%) and 1-5 years (30%) of teaching experience, and there are only 20% of teachers with experience from 11-15 years old and 10% of 16 years of experience or more. 60% of the participants were Masters degree holders, 25% were Bachelors degree holders,

10% were doctorate degree holders, and 5% held other qualifications. 50% of the respondents reported moderate familiarity with AI tools, while the other half split evenly between high and low experience reporting.

Assessment of the measurement model

A causal-predictive SEM analysis using Smart PLS 4 was performed to evaluate the relationships between the model variables. PLS-SEM is more appropriate for complex structural models including second-order models, small sample sizes and is less stringent on data normality.

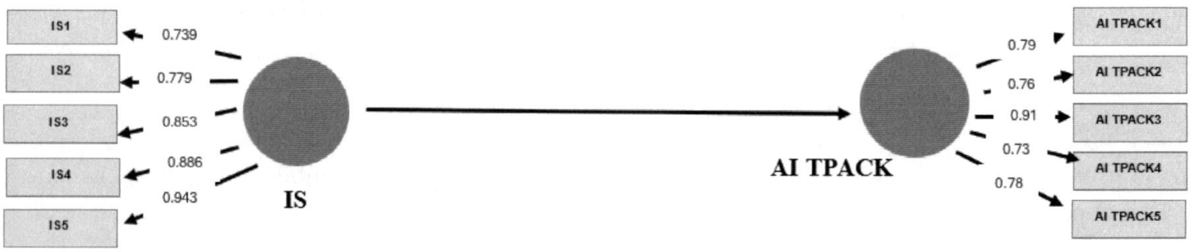

Figure 1: Item loadings

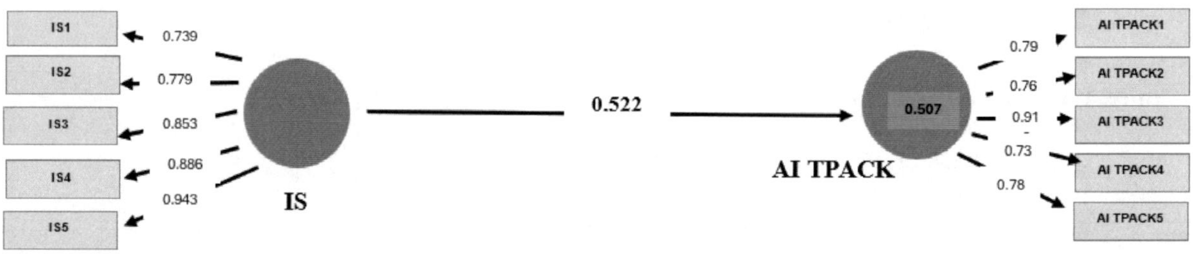

Figure 2: Path coefficients and R-square

Figure 1 shows the loadings of items from different scales as well as R2 for each variable in inner model. The significance levels of outer model items and the inner model relationships can be seen in figure 2. The loadings of the various items of the respective scales from above are shown in Figure 1 with the associated p-values being depicted in Figure 2 above. Also, Table 2 indicates that Cronbach's alpha (α) > 0.70, composite reliability (CR) > 0.70, and average variance extracted (AVE) > 0.50, thus confirming the reliability in the measurements carried out. Further, as depicted in Table 3, the Fornell–Larcker criterion is satisfied as the square of the variance captured in each variable is higher than the inter-correlations.

Table 2. Convergent validity of the tested variables

Instruments	α	CR	rho	AVE	R^2
Institutional Supports	0.864	0.867	0.891	0.506	-
AI TPACK	0.712	0.830	0.823	0.608	**0.507**

Table 3. Divergent validity based on the Fornell–Larcker approach

Measures	1	2
Institutional Supports	**0.671**	
AI TPACK	0.719	**0.735**

Table 4 shows the coefficient estimates of the structural model. Institutional support had a positive and direct effect on AI TAPCK integration (β=0.507, ρ = 0.00), and the R^2 of the model also high, meaning the model explains the variance that is 0.507. Falk and Miller (1992) offered some benchmarks for R^2, stating that the lowest recommended value is 0.10. As a result, institutional support justifies the variations in teachers' Incorporation of AI TAPCK since all the Two paths of the path analysis had substantial path coefficients indicating that supportive institutional Support reinforces the preparedness of teachers to integrate AI into all components of TAPCK (CK, PK, TK). The implication for AI adoption in education: supportive environments are key. These results highlight the need for not only fostering positive attitudes and technical comfort with respect to teachers themselves, but also for institutions to provide the resources, training, and encouragement needed by teachers to successfully onboard AI as an educational tool.

Table 4. Direct and interaction effects

Relationships	β	T	ρ
Institutional support-> AI TAPCK	0.522	9.046	0.000

Note: β, beta value; ρ, ρ-value; T, T-value

Discussion, Conclusion and Implications

This study also established that institutional support is a leading factor that determines teachers' willingness to incorporate AI in teaching. Institutional support acts as both an implementer of AI adoption and a solver of implementation issues. The results supported the AI-TPACK framework because institutional support enhances Technological Pedagogical Knowledge (TPK) and Technological Content Knowledge (TCK) both directly and indirectly. However, some educators still have doubts about the significance of AI in education, which is in line with Karataş and Yüce (2024) who found that faculty resist AI adoption due to ethical issues and fear of additional workload. In addition, teacher perceptions of AI and their technical literacy were also found to be significant predictors of AI adoption, as previous research has suggested that institutional support is a critical enabler of technology integration in education (Tondeur et al., 2017; Celik, 2023). This study also established a very strong relationship between institutional support and AI-TPACK readiness (β = 0.507, ρ = 0.00), which supports the argument that provision of resources, training, and enabling policies are necessary to overcome the barriers to the integration of AI.

The study's structural model identified that institutional support is multi-dimensional, it goes beyond just the provision of physical resources to include motivational and professional support. Teachers who perceive strong leadership and structured training programs are more likely to use AI tools, as does the wider AI-PD and institutional support for teacher training literature (Dogan et al., 2025). Professional learning must be continuous and have to be step by step and relevant to the needs of teachers. This result suggests that the current conventional PD models are insufficient for AI training, as pointed out by Cukurova et al. (2024). To enhance the pedagogical value of AI, PD programs should graduate from the basic level of tool knowledge to the understanding of ethical issues, subject matter applications, and long-term integration of AI in the curriculum.

The research also revealed several challenges to the implementation of AI including over reliance on AI, ethical issues and student autonomy. As pointed out in previous research, dependency on AI reduces the level of critical and creative thinking of students (Su, 2023). To this end, institutions should work towards ensuring that there is a balance between the integration of AI in learning as well as making sure that AI does not take away the thinking skills that are supposed to be learned. The development of ethical frameworks and pedagogical guidelines is crucial in the alignment of the use of AI in classrooms. This study is in line with Wang et al. (2021) and Alnasib (2023) who argued that there is a need for institutional support to address ethical issues and prepare teachers for AI. Future work should explore how curriculum integration strategies can be used to achieve the maximum possible benefits of AI with the minimum possible drawbacks. Owing to the ubiquity of AI, it is important for educational institutions to have policies on the use of AI. Longitudinal research should examine the impact of PD programs focused on AI on teaching effectiveness over time, in line with Dogan et al. (2025) on the importance of continuous professional learning. Furthermore, future work should investigate the role of AI ethics, student motivation, and teacher AI literacy programs to guarantee that AI is applied properly and equally in education. Furthermore, the training of the teachers should not only be on the operational aspects of AI but also on the ethical and academic aspects of AI. Pre-service training should include scenarios involving AI, best and worst practices of using AI, and AI-based assessment tasks. The implementation of AI in education should be holistic to ensure that it improves instead of complicating education processes.

References

Agbong-Coates, I. (2024). Chatgpt integration significantly boosts personalized learning outcomes: a philippine study. International Journal of Educational Management and Development Studies, 5(2), 165-186. https://doi.org/10.53378/353067

Alnasib, B. (2023). Factors affecting faculty members' readiness to integrate artificial intelligence into their teaching practices: a study from the saudi higher education context. International Journal of Learning Teaching and Educational Research, 22(8), 465-491. https://doi.org/10.26803/ijlter.22.8.24

Ames, H., Glenton, C., & Lewin, S. (2019). Purposive sampling in a qualitative evidence synthesis: A worked example from a synthesis on parental perceptions of vaccination communication. BMC medical research methodology, 19, 1-9.

Casal-Otero, L., Catala, A., Fernández-Morante, C., Taboada, M., Cebreiro, B., & Barro, S. (2023). AI literacy in K-12: a systematic literature review. International Journal of STEM Education, 10(1). https://doi.org/10.1186/s40594-023-00418-7

Celik, I. (2023). Towards Intelligent-TPACK: An empirical study on teachers' professional knowledge to ethically integrate artificial intelligence (AI)-based tools into education. Computers in Human Behavior, 138, 107468. https://doi.org/10.1016/j.chb.2022.107468

Creswell, J. W. (2014). Research Design: Qualitative, Quantitative and Mixed Methods Approaches (4th ed.). Thousand Oaks, CA: Sage

Cukurova, M., Kralj, L., Hertz, B., & Saltidou, E. (2024). Professional Development for Teachers in the Age of AI.

Deng, G., & Zhang, J. (2023). Technological pedagogical content ethical knowledge (TPCEK): The development of an assessment instrument for pre-service teachers. Computers & Education, 197, 104740. https://doi.org/10.1016/j.compedu.2023.104740

Dogan, S., Nalbantoglu, U. Y., Celik, I., & Agacli Dogan, N. (2025). Artificial intelligence professional development: a systematic review of TPACK, designs, and effects for teacher learning. Professional Development in Education, 1-28.

Etikan, I., Musa, S. A., & Alkassim, R. S. (2016). Comparison of convenience sampling and purposive sampling. American journal of theoretical and applied statistics, 5(1), 1-4.

Falk, R. F., & Miller, N. B. (1992). A primer for soft modeling. University of Akron Press.

Güneyli, A., Burgul, N., Dericioğlu, S., Cenkova, N., Becan, S., Şimşek, Ş., ... & Güneralp, H. (2024). Exploring teacher awareness of artificial intelligence in education: a case study from northern cyprus. European Journal of Investigation in Health Psychology and Education, 14(8), 2358-2376. https://doi.org/10.3390/ejihpe14080156

Hair Jr, J. F., Matthews, L. M., Matthews, R. L., & Sarstedt, M. (2017). PLS-SEM or CB-SEM: updated guidelines on which method to use. International Journal of Multivariate Data Analysis, 1(2), 107-123.

Karataş, F., & Yüce, E. (2024). AI and the future of teaching: Preservice teachers' reflections on the use of artificial intelligence in open and distributed learning. International Review of Research in Open and Distributed Learning, 25(3), 304-325.

Koehler, M., & Mishra, P. (2009). What is technological pedagogical content knowledge (TPACK)? Contemporary Issues in Technology and Teacher Education, 9(1), 60–70. https://www.learntechlib.org/primary/p/29544/.

Mishra, P., & Koehler, M. J. (2006). Technological pedagogical content knowledge: A framework for teacher knowledge. Teachers College Record, 108(6), 1017–1054.

Mishra, P., Warr, M., & Islam, R. (2023). TPACK in the age of ChatGPT and Generative AI. Journal of Digital Learning in Teacher Education, 39(4), 235–251. https://doi.org/10.1080/21532974.2023.2247480

Ning, Y. (2024). Teachers' AI-TPACK: Exploring the relationship between knowledge elements. Sustain- ability, 16(3), 978. https://doi.org/10.3390/su16030978

Shulman, L. (1986). Those who understand: Knowledge growth in teaching. Educational Researcher, 15(2), 4–14. https://doi.org/10.3102/0013189X015002004

Tondeur, J., Scherer, R., Siddiq, F., & Baran, E. (2017). A comprehensive investigation of TPACK within pre-service teachers' ICT profiles: Mind the gap!. Australasian Journal of educational technology, 33(3).

Velander, J., Taiye, M., Otero, N., & Milrad, M. (2023). Artificial intelligence in k-12 education: Electing and reflecting on Swedish teachers' understanding of ai and its implications for teaching & learning. Education and Information Technologies, 29(4), 4085–4105. https://doi.org/10.1007/s10639-023-11990-4

Wang, K. (2024). Pre-Service Teachers' GenAI Anxiety, Technology Self-Efficacy, and TPACK: Their structural relations with behavioral intention to design GenAI-Assisted teaching. Behavioral Sci- ences, 14(5), 373. https://doi.org/10.3390/bs14050373

Wang, L., Zhang, Y., Wang, D., Tong, X., Liu, T., Zhang, S., ... & Clarke, M. (2021). Artificial intelligence for COVID-19: a systematic review. Frontiers in medicine, 8, 704256.

Yue, M., Jong, M. S. Y., & Ng, D. T. K. (2024). Understanding K-12 teachers' technological pedagogical content knowledge readiness and attitudes toward artificial intelligence education. Education and Information Technologies. https://doi.org/10.1007/s10639-024-12621-2

Beyond scenario creation: Human and GenAI synergy in situational judgment test response development

Dafna Avidov[1], Orit Ezra[1], Guy Cohen[1], Anat Cohen[1], Alla Bronshtein[2]

[1] School of Education, Tel Aviv University, Israel; dafnavidav@mail.tau.ac.il
[1] School of Education, Tel Aviv University, Israel; oezra1@gmail.com
[1] School of Education, Tel Aviv University, Israel; guycohen@mail.tau.ac.il
[1] School of Education, Tel Aviv University, Israel; anatco@tauex.tau.ac.il
[2] Faculty of Medical & Health Sciences, Tel Aviv University, Israel; allab@tauex.tau.ac.il

Correspondence: Anat Cohen; anatco@tauex.tau.ac.il

Abstract

Self-regulated learning (SRL) is required for learners of all ages and disciplines. There is a need for a variety of assessment tools to assess the professional knowledge of teachers in SRL and self-regulated teaching (SRT). Situational judgment tests (SJT) can serve as a measurable assessment tool for evaluating teachers' SRL and SRT knowledge. This research constitutes the second stage in the development of such an SJT tool dealing with the formulation of responses to scenarios created in the previous stage. Additionally, the introduction of GenAI-assisted evaluation poses the need to explore the still understudied human-GenAI interaction during assessment tools development. This study used thematic analysis for exploring the responses generated by GenAI (ChatGPT) and researchers for the previously formulated scenarios to examine the contribution of both agents in the tool development process. A main theme – standardization and patterning (GenAI) versus flexibility and openness (researchers) was found. The study highlights the potential of combining GenAI and researchers in developing assessment tools and the contribution of each.

Keywords: Generative artificial intelligence; Situational judgment tests; Self-regulated learning; human-machine interaction.

Introduction

Research on self-regulated learning (SRL) has grown significantly in recent years, especially in light of the development of online learning environments (Luo & Zhou, 2024) and emergency and crisis situations (Pelikan et al, 2021). SRL skills are important for learners of all ages and disciplines (Panadero, 2017). SRL is a process in which learners actively manage their own learning and involves the use of cognitive and metacognitive strategies, motivational and behavioral strategies (Pintrich, 1999; Zimmerman, 1986). This subject receives a lot of attention in teaching training programs in universities and colleges due to the significant role of teachers in developing these skills among their students (Ortube et al., 2024). Teachers have a dual role regarding SRL, both as independent learners during their professional development and as promoters of independent learning among their students (Karlen et al., 2020). Considering this, it is important to develop SRL skills among teachers and ways in which they can be applied in the classroom, which is termed in the literature as SRT - self-regulated teaching (Kramarski & Heaysman, 2021).

There appears to be a great deal of research on SRL and interventions to promote it (Ortube et al., 2024). A common limitation in these studies is the heavy reliance on self-report questionnaires and even their use as a single measurement tool, which may make it difficult to gain a deeper understanding of the processes occurring in the learning processes (Zepeda et al., 2019), therefore there is a need for additional assessment methods.

Furthermore, a measurement tool is needed to assess how teachers are self-regulated learners and how they promote self- regulated learning in their classroom.

Situational judgment tests (SJT), which are used in various fields such as medicine (Schubert et al., 2008), retail (Weekley & Jones, 1999), and in education (Nadmilail & Matore, 2021), can serve as a measurable assessment tool among teachers for the application and teaching of skills. These tests present authentic scenarios to the examinees, and they are required to choose or rate effective responses to assess their ability and judge professional behavior related to their field of occupation (Chao et al., 2020). It is important to note that the process of developing situational judgment tests (SJTs) is complex and requires significant resources of cognitive effort and time (Avidov et al., 2024). Initially, goals for professional behavior should be defined using literature and content experts. Relevant scenarios are then collected in a way that tests the knowledge required for the field. The next step involves creating responses on a continuum that represents different levels of knowledge in their content area, and the final step involves developing a scoring key for the responses (Aldrup et al., 2020; Schubert et al., 2008). Figure 1 shows the key steps in developing the SJT test.

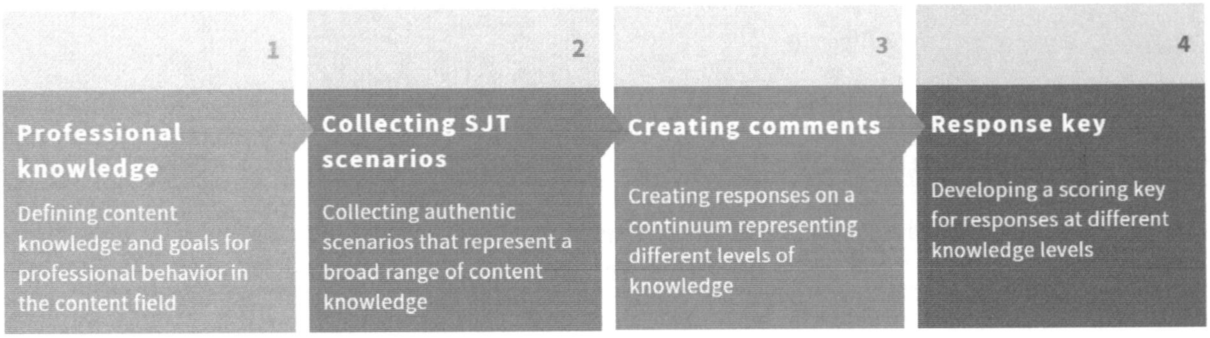

Figure 1: SJT test development stages

Interaction between humans and Generative artificial intelligence (GenAI), based on large language models (LLM), can advance complex development processes of assessment tools, saving time and human resources while producing optimal results (Xia et al., 2024). Alongside the contribution of this interaction, there are also risks such as: overreliance, which could lead to unsafe use and delegating essential decisions to artificial intelligence, which could result in a loss of skills and autonomy (Slattery, et al., 2024). Given that there is little research dealing with the interaction between researchers and artificial intelligence in the development of assessment tools in general and SJT in particular, it is important to examine it. In the context of SJT, artificial intelligence has been used to test the accuracy and response consistency of these tests (Borchert et al., 2023; Sareen, 2023). Previous research (Avidov et al., 2024) explored the development of scenarios for the SJT test to assess teachers' knowledge of SRL-PS. The current study goes one step further and examines the contribution of interaction between researchers and artificial intelligence to the further development of the tool.

The current research

Research objective and questions

The present study is a qualitative study aimed at examining the interaction process between researchers and artificial intelligence in developing an SJT assessment tool for measuring professional knowledge related to SRL-SRT. The development of an SJT test consists of 4 stages: defining content knowledge and goals; collecting authentic scenarios; creating responses; and developing a scoring key for responses. This study focuses on the stage of generating possible responses to the scenarios in the SJT test. These responses are positioned along a continuum representing different levels of teachers' knowledge regarding SRL-SRT.

The research question guiding this study is: What are the differences between researcher-generated responses and AI-generated responses (under researcher guidance) for SJT tests related to SRL-SRT? Additionally, what are the key themes emerging from the interaction between researchers and AI?

Method

The research process involves a sequence of actions carried out by the researchers with the assistance of artificial intelligence (ChatGPT) to examine the nature of this interaction in the tool's development. In the first stage, two SJT scenarios were selected from a preliminary study (Avidov et al., 2024). The first scenario focuses on the teacher and describes a situation in which the teacher lacks information about students' progress. The second scenario focuses on the student and describes difficulties in time management while completing a homework assignment.

Scenario 1 - lack of information about student progress

Teacher Yasmin is implementing the problem-solving method using the checklist and videos. However, she does not know how each student is progressing in the learning process. What should Yasmin do?

Scenario 2 - homework scheduling

Parents told Teacher Hamoudi that they really like the new problem-solving method and recognize its importance. However, they noted that their children still rely on them to plan and manage their time. What should Hamoudi do?

In the second stage, possible responses to the scenarios were formulated by both the researchers and ChatGPT. The researchers' responses were based on an index (attached in Table 1) that is theory-driven (Pintrich, 2000) and grounded in previous studies (Cohen et al., 2022; Assi & Cohen, 2023). For each scenario, multiple responses were generated according to SRL-SRT skills, structured along a continuum representing different levels of knowledge.

The AI-generated responses were created through a structured, step-by-step dialogue, which included:

1. Clarifying knowledge about SRL-PS, the cognitive, motivational, and behavioral strategies outlined in the index.
2. An inquiry was conducted on distinguishing between SRL and SRT, as well as understanding SJT.
3. Only after these clarifications were made, ChatGPT was instructed to propose three responses for each strategy, corresponding to high, medium, and low levels of knowledge.

The full dialogue with ChatGPT is documented in the following link: https://chatgpt.com/share/67a0d0d9-3e8c-800d-ba08-a178118af852

Table 1. Index for Assessing Teachers' Knowledge of SRL-PS

Teachers' SRL and SRT		
Problem-solving cognitive strategies	**Problem-solving Motivation strategies**	**Problem-solving Behavioral strategies**
• **Problem definition** (problem comprehension, criterions, rules, general questions) • **Problem exploration** (previous knowledge, operational questions) • **Providing and selecting solutions** (based on criterions and rules). • **Solution evaluation** (feedback, improvements) • **Feedback during monitoring** • **Time planning and management**	• Goals • Interest & value • Expectancy • Affect • Attribution	• Self-observati on • Help-seeking • Increase/decr ease effort • Persist

In the third stage, the researchers' responses and ChatGPT-generated responses were analyzed to identify emerging themes. Thematic Analysis, a widely used approach in qualitative research, enables the identification, examination, and interpretation of patterns and insights within the data (Kiger et al., 2020).

In this study, the thematic development process facilitated an examination of the interaction between researchers and artificial intelligence in generating responses to SJT scenarios. Figure 2 illustrates the research process.

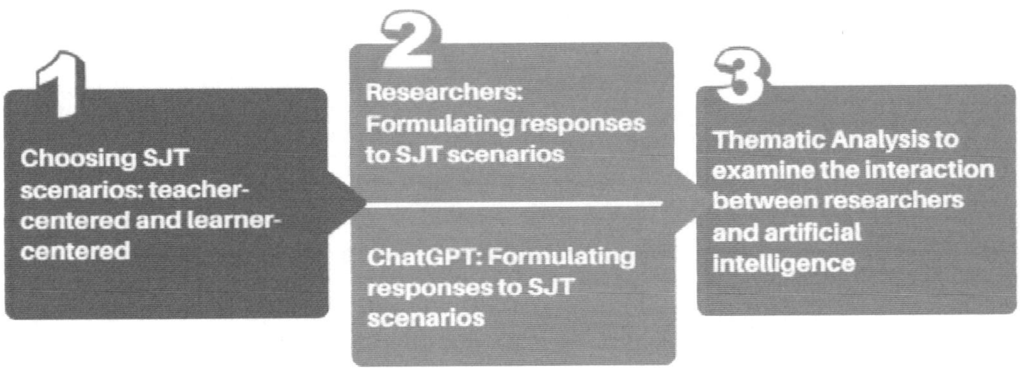

Figure 2. Research course

Findings and discussion

This chapter presents and discusses the research findings, which are the product of the process of generating responses to SJT scenarios for the assessment of SRL-SRT knowledge. These responses were formulated by researchers and GenAI. The findings represent the comparative qualitative analysis between responses formulated by the researchers and the responses generated following the interaction between the researchers and the ChatGPT. This analysis led to the creation of an overarching theme – standardization and patterning versus flexibility and openness, which includes several subthemes that conceptualize the characteristics of the interaction between researchers and GenAI in the context of SJT:

Subtheme 1 – fixed pattern (GenAI) versus variable pattern (researchers)

ChatGPT presents responses at three levels of knowledge that express **the use and non-use** of SRL or SRT strategies. For example, in the scenario "lack of information about student progress" the following pattern can be seen in responses relating to knowledge of cognitive strategies related to coming up with ideas and choosing a solution: at the high level the response represents choosing a solution from a set of options, while at the low levels the response represents not choosing a solution from a set of options.

Researchers, on the other hand, occasionally present responses at three levels of knowledge that reflect **different levels of usage** of SRT-SRL strategies. For example, in the scenario "lack of information about student progress," the following pattern can be seen in responses related to knowledge of behavioral strategies of increasing/decreasing effort: at the high level, the response represents writing a monitoring plan that includes increasing/decreasing effort in a diary, at the medium level, the response represents defining a monitoring plan in general without reference to a diary, and at the low level, the response represents defining points in time for increasing effort.

These findings demonstrate the templated GenAI responses, which are generated according to a fixed pattern. Using a fixed pattern is an advantage, especially when it comes to an assessment tool (standardization). In contrast, the responses written by the researchers are variable and not dichotomous and are more considerate of nuances. This corresponds with dilemmas that arise when developing tests and questionnaires, dealing with the balance between a standard pattern on the one hand and different patterns on the other (Rattray & Jones2007), which are particularly significant in the development of SJT assessment tools (Lievens & Sackett, 2007).

Subtheme 2 – systematic coverage (GenAI) versus deepening (researchers)

ChatGPT presents responses with **systematic and complete coverage** of all knowledge levels and all strategies (cognitive and metacognitive, motivational, and behavioral) in the "Lack of information on student progress" scenario and the "homework scheduling" scenario. These responses were obtained easily and in a short time.

The researchers, however, only **present responses to some of the SRL-SRT strategies**. For example, in the scenario "homework scheduling," the researchers formulated responses that relate to the cognitive strategy of time management, but there is no representation for the other cognitive strategies, such as problem definition and problem exploration, nor for some of the motivational and behavioral strategies.

Additionally, the researchers **do not present full coverage of the different levels of knowledge** regarding usage of SRL-SRT strategies. For example, in the scenario "lack of information about student progress" in the motivational strategy of increasing the teacher's value and interest in the task, coverage was found: at a high level of use of SRL strategies – writing a list of benefits for tracking students; and at a medium level of use – clarifying the value of tracking students, but there is no representation at the low level.

However, the researchers **focused on a particular strategy and created responses to it based on teachers' difficulties from previous research**, which found that teachers have difficulty planning time as learners and as teachers who provide this strategy to their students (Cohen & Cohen, 2024). In addition, the researchers drew on prior knowledge indicating the importance of parents helping their children plan their time. For example, in the scenario "homework scheduling", a response indicating knowledge about the cognitive strategy of time management includes directing the attention of parents and students to planning time for a task.

These findings show that the process of generating responses through the interaction of researchers and GenAI requires little time resources and cognitive effort to systematically cover the strategies and knowledge levels of SRL-SRT. In contrast, researchers will require increased time resources and effort to reach the same result. At the same time, the researchers' formulated responses reflect deepening. It should be noted that such deepening can also be achieved with GenAI through complex, long, and iterative discourse (Svendsen & Garvey, 2023).

Subtheme 3 - Autonomy (AI) versus contextuality (researchers)

ChatGPT presents responses, in some cases, in inaccurate contexts. For example, in the scenario "lack of information on student progress" in responses to the motivational strategy Goal orientations, the responses given by ChatGPT are tailored to the cognitive strategy Goal setting. Its high-level response is to formulate a clear goal for monitoring the progress of each student.

Lack of context in ChatGPT responses can also be found in the same scenario in the behavioral strategy of increasing/decreasing effort. In this strategy in the context of SRL-SRT, the intention is to determine when to invest more and when to invest less in order to regulate effort. In the high-level response, ChatGPT's suggestion is to invest more effort and not regulate effort.

Researchers, on the other hand, make appropriate connections to SRL-SRT strategies while combining cognitive and behavioral strategies. For example, in the cognitive strategy of time management, there is an integration of a behavioral strategy that is expressed in the use of the tool. Researchers present a high-level response, setting a date in a diary for the solution. In order to develop an SJT tool, it is important to maintain the connection to the SRL research literature, and to link strategies (Ezra et al., 2024).

Conclusions

This study examined the contribution of the interaction between human expertise and GenAI (such as ChatGPT) in the development of situational judgment test (SJT) to assess teachers' professional knowledge in SRL-SRT. This study used thematic analysis of the GenAI and researchers' responses to authentic SJT scenarios. The thematic analysis of the interaction demonstrates a significant contribution of each of the agents to the development of the tool: standardization and patterns application of the GenAI versus flexibility and openness of the researchers. The theme and the subthemes that construct an overall typology are described in Figure 3.

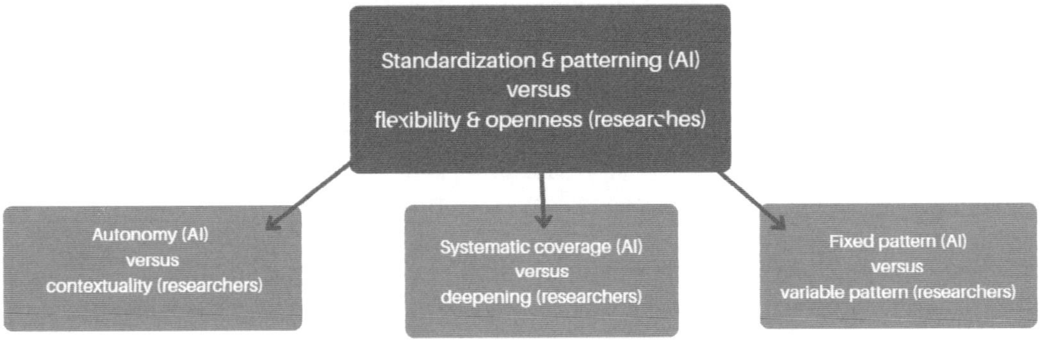

Figure 3: Typology of GenAI- researchers interaction

The study proposes an initial topology for analyzing and interpreting the output of human – AI interaction concerning the creation of SJT tools and evaluation tools in general. The typology deals with major issues in test construction such as the desire to construct standardized tests for better validity and reliability, while renewing and expanding the number of responses in a way that prevents the tests takers from answering automatically. The typology could be used and further enhanced in future studies analyzing other interactions between researchers and AI.

The interaction highlights the potential of combining human experts with GenAI and the contribution of each agent to the development of the tool: GenAI operates according to defined patterns, while researchers operate in a way that varies depending on the circumstances. In addition, GenAI generates responses to all strategies and all levels of responses (high, medium, and low levels of SRL-SRT knowledge), while researchers focus on relevant aspects based on previous research. Furthermore, GenAI does not always connect SRL strategies and does not always maintain conceptual accuracy in the context of the SRL content domain, while researchers bring a deeper understanding of these elements. This study adds to previous studies that have shown how the interaction of humans and GenAI allows for the expansion of the capabilities of each agent (Drori et al., 2023). While GenAI helps accelerate the development processes of the assessment tool and overcome the required cognitive load, the expertise of the researchers ensures the required accuracy, focus, and contextuality.

Acknowledgement

This research is supported by the Chief Scientist office of the Israeli Ministry of Education and by the Science and Technology Education Center (SATEC) at Tel-Aviv University.

References

Aldrup, K., Carstensen, B., Köller, M. M., & Klusmann, U. (2020). Measuring teachers' social-emotional competence: Development and validation of a situational judgment test. Frontiers in psychology, 11, 892.

Assi, A., & Cohen, A. (2023, September). Video-based SRL program for teachers and students. In Proceedings of the 15th International Conference on Education Technology and Computers (pp. 175-182).

Avidov, D., Ezra, O., Cohen, A., & Bronshtein, A. (2024). Generative AI in the service of situational judgment tests (SJT) for self-regulation learning during problem solving (SRL-PS). Paper for The EDEN 2024 Annual Conference, University of Graz, Graz, Austria. Best paper award.

Borchert, R. J., Hickman, C. R., Pepys, J., & Sadler, T. J. (2023). Performance of ChatGPT on the situational judgement test—A professional Dilemmas–based examination for doctors in the United Kingdom. JMIR Medical Education, 9(1), e48978.

Cohen, G., Assi, A., Cohen, A., Bronshtein, A., Glick, D., Gabbay, H., & Ezra, O. (2022). Video-Assisted Self-Regulated Learning (SRL) Training: COVID-19 Edition. In: Hilliger, I., Muñoz-Merino, P.J., De Laet, T., Ortega Arranz, A., Farrell, T. (eds) Educating for a New Future: Making Sense of Technology-Enhanced Learning Adoption. EC-TEL 2022. Lecture Notes in Computer Science, (p.p. 59-73). Springer, Cham.

Cohen, G., & Cohen, A. (June 2023) Mapping Difficulties in Problem-Solving Process During Video-Assisted Self-Regulated Learning Training for Students: Introducing thePS-SOS MAP 2023 Ubiquity Proceedings, 3(1): 289-296.

Chao, T. Y., Sung, Y. T., & Huang, J. L. (2020). Construction of the situational judgment tests for teachers. Asia-Pacific Journal of Teacher Education, 48(4), 355-374.

Drori, I., Zhang, S. J., Shuttleworth, R., Zhang, S., Tyser, K., Chin, Z., Lantigua, P., Surbehera, S., Hunter, G., Austin, D., Tang, L., Hicke, Y., Simhon, S., Karnik, S., Granberry, D., & Udell, M. (2023). From human days to machine seconds: Automatically answering and generating machine learning final exams. In KDD '23: Proceedings of the 29th ACM SIGKDD Conference on Knowledge Discovery and Data Mining (pp. 3947-3955). ACM. https://doi.org/10.1145/3580305.3599827

Ezra. O., cohen. A., Shany. D., (2024) Human experts and Generative AI interaction: From real-world and real-life language learning diary-research app to a diary-learning app. Paper for The EDEN 2024 Annual Conference, University of Graz, Graz, Austria.

Karlen, Y., Hertel, S., & Hirt, C. N. (2020). Teachers' Professional Competences in Self-Regulated Learning: An Approach to Integrate Teachers' Competences as Self-Regulated Learners and as Agents of Self-Regulated Learning in a Holistic Manner. Frontiers in Education, 5, 159. https://doi.org/10.3389/feduc.2020.00159

Kiger, M. E., & Varpio, L. (2020). Thematic analysis of qualitative data: AMEE Guide No. 131. Medical teacher, 42(8), 846-854.

Kramarski, B., & Heaysman, O. (2021). A conceptual framework and a professional development model for supporting teachers' "triple SRL–SRT processes" and promoting students' academic outcomes. Educational Psychologist, 56(4), 298–311. https://doi.org/10.1080/00461520.2021.1985502

Lievens, F., & Sackett, P. R. (2007). Situational judgment tests in high-stakes settings: Issues and strategies with generating alternate forms. Journal of Applied Psychology, 92(4), 1043.

Luo, R. Z., & Zhou, Y. L. (2024). The effectiveness of self-regulated learning strategies in higher education blended learning: A five years systematic review. Journal of Computer Assisted Learning, 40(6), 3005-3029.

Nadmilail, A. I., & Matore, M. E. E. M. (2021). Trend of using situational judgement test on school teachers: A systematic literature review. The journal of contemporary issues in business and government, 27(2), 6117-6141.

Ortube, A. F., Panadero, E., & Dignath, C. (2024). Self-regulated learning interventions for pre-service teachers: A systematic review. Educational Psychology Review, 36(4), 113.

Pelikan, E. R., Lüftenegger, M., Holzer, J., Korlat, S., Spiel, C., & Schober, B. (2021). Learning during COVID-19: the role of self-regulated learning, motivation, and procrastination for perceived competence. Zeitschrift für Erziehungswissenschaft, 24(2), 393-418

Pintrich, P. R. (1999). The role of motivation in promoting and sustaining self-regulated learning. International Journal of Educational Research, 31(6), 459–470. https://doi.org/10.1016/S0883-0355(99)00015-4

Pintrich, P. R. (2000). The role of goal orientation in self-regulated learning. In Handbook of self-regulation (pp. 451-502). Academic Press.

Rattray, J., & Jones, M. C. (2007). Essential elements of questionnaire design and development. Journal of clinical nursing, 16(2), 234-243.

Sareen, K. (2023). Assessing the ethical capabilities of Chat GPT in healthcare: A study on its proficiency in situational judgement test. Innovations in Education and Teaching International, 1-11.

Slattery, P., Saeri, A. K., Grundy, E. A., Graham, J., Noetel, M., Uuk, R., ... & Thompson, N. (2024). The ai risk repository: A comprehensive meta-review, database, and taxonomy of risks from artificial intelligence. arXiv preprint arXiv:2408.12622. https://airisk.mit.edu/

Schubert, S., Ortwein, H., Dumitsch, A., Schwantes, U., Wilhelm, O., Kiessling, C., ... & Kiessling, C. (2008). A situational judgement test of professional behaviour: development and validation. Medical teacher, 30(5), 528-533.

Svendsen, A., & Garvey, B. (2023). An outline for an interrogative/prompt library to help improve output quality from Generative-AI datasets (A white paper). Analytic Research Consortium. http://dx.doi.org/10.2139/ssrn.4495319

Weekley, J. A., & Jones, C. (1999). Further studies of situational tests. Personnel Psychology, 52(3), 679-700.

Xia, Q., Weng, X., Ouyang, F., Lin, T. J., & Chiu, T. K. F. (2024). A scoping review on how generative artificial intelligence transforms assessment in higher education. International Journal of Educational Technology in Higher Education, 21, 40. https://doi.org/10.1186/s41239-024-00468-z

Zepeda, C. D., Hlutkowsky, C. O., Partika, A. C., & Nokes-Malach, T. J. (2019). Identifying teachers' supports of metacognition through classroom talk and its relation to growth in conceptual learning. Journal of Educational Psychology, 111(3), 522–541.

Zimmerman, B. J. (1986). Becoming a self-regulated learner: Which are the key subprocesses? Contemporary Educational Psychology, 11(4), 307–313. https://doi.org/10.1016/0361-476X(86)90027-5

Artificial Intelligence in Teaching and Learning. Analysis and Evaluation of AI Use Cases in German Higher Education

Klaus Wannemacher[1], Elke Bosse[1], Maren Lübcke[1]

[1] University Management Division, HIS Institute for Higher Education Development e. V., Germany; wannemacher@his-he.de, bosse@his-he.de, luebcke@his-he.de

Correspondence: Klaus Wannemacher: wannemacher@his-he.de

Abstract:

Generative AI applications are increasingly being used in higher education to support teachers and students as well as to take on tasks in the area of teaching support and administration. However, little is known about the specific use and institutional framework conditions in individual cases. The HIS Institute for Higher Education Development (HIS-HE) has therefore investigated the use of AI tools in teaching and learning as part of an exploratory study commissioned by the „University Forum on Digitalisation“ (Hochschulforum Digitalisierung). As part of a call for contributions, 77 use cases from 51 German universities were identified. This article provides an overview of the results of the analysis and evaluation of these tried-and-tested use cases, describes trends in the current use of AI in teaching and learning and gives an insight into the added value and conditions for success of AI use.

Keywords: Artificial intelligence, teaching and learning, qualitative survey, use cases, didactic added value, German higher education

Introduction

A recent quantitative study on the use of AI at universities in the United States (Robert & MacCormack, 2025) identified a broad spectrum of fields of application for AI in teaching and learning. According to the results of the „EDUCAUSE AI Landscape Study 2025“, AI tools at the US universities surveyed frequently influence the area of academic integrity (74%), homework and project work in courses (65%), assessment practice (54%) and curriculum design (Robert & MacCormack, 2025). The other areas surveyed that achieved approval ratings below 50% include, for example, digital skills training, support services for students and laboratory work. According to the findings of the „EDUCAUSE AI Landscape Study“, teaching and learning is the functional area of universities in which there is the most pronounced reaction to the use of generative AI through students and other user groups at higher education institutions. Previous studies on AI use in teaching and learning had shown evidence of similar trends (e.g. Arbeitsgruppe Digitale Medien, 2024; Salden & Leschke, 2024; Wannemacher & Bodmann, 2021; de Witt et al., 2023). However, little is known about the actual use of AI tools in teaching and learning at German universities. The present study therefore aimed to analyse the specific use of AI applications as broadly as possible and to gain an insight into the current areas of application in German higher education.

Methods

In order to capture the broadest possible spectrum of use cases for the use of AI in teaching and learning, a call for use cases was issued in November 2024 by the HIS Institute for Higher Education Development (HIS-HE) via the „University Forum on Digitalisation“ (Hochschulforum Digitalisierung) and relevant networks. Use cases were sought in which generative AI tools have been used profitably by lecturers, students – or in the areas of teaching support and administration at German universities. This call for contributions was guided by a theoretical framework that distinguishes key application areas (e.g. planning, implementation, evaluation), users (i.e. lecturers, students, support staff) and AI tools used (e.g. text-generating, multimodal).

The cases could be submitted online using a standardised template that was closely aligned with the theoretical framework. In addition to a detailed description of the use cases, the submitters were asked to evaluate their use case themselves based on a selection of quality features (e.g. transferability, degree of innovation, maturity level).

The call led to a sample of 77 use cases from 51 different German universities, which were collected through a survey instrument with open questions. For the evaluation, both a statistical analysis and a thematic analysis were used. All submissions were reviewed by several experts and classified on the basis of nine guiding categories (subject area, degree programme or other area; teaching format/teaching concept; name and type of tool(s); (teaching) objectives pursued with the use of AI; use of the AI tool for planning, implementing and evaluating teaching, learning and testing; reason or initial situation for the use of AI; concrete approach to the use of AI; challenges in the use of AI; added value of the use of AI for the submitter personally or for the students; recommendations for the use of AI in teaching and learning).

Findings

Overall trends in the use of AI in teaching and learning

With regard to the trends in AI use, the statistical analysis of all 77 submitted use cases shows that a slightly larger proportion of them come from universities of applied sciences (52%) than from universities (45%), which deviates only slightly from the actual distribution of these types of higher education institutions in Germany. In terms of subject groups, the engineering sciences are particularly well represented, with the study area of computer science being the most prevalent. This is followed by law, economics and social sciences as well as a slightly lower number of use cases from the humanities and other subject groups. The types of courses in which the AI tools were primarily used include seminars and, to a lesser extent, lectures and exercises. In particular, text-generating AI tools are applied in the use cases. In addition, there is a wide range of areas of application with a focus on content transfer or the activation of students by lecturers (Wannemacher et al., 2025; cf. Hochschulforum Digitalisierung, 2025).

Spectrum of application fields

The thematic analysis of the 77 submitted use cases was guided by the theoretical framework, and the results obtained revealed a very broad spectrum of current AI use in teaching and learning. In particular, five distinct fields of application were identified: In the field of teaching, the submitted use cases range from practice-oriented teaching scenarios to the testing of AI tools in the teaching of subject-specific scientific working methods. A further distinction can be made between the use of AI for learning support and exam preparation, the either interdisciplinary or subject-specific promotion of AI skills and the use of AI in the area of student advisory services. The following section reports the results using anchor examples, which were selected – in line with the aforementioned theoretical framework of AI use in teaching and learning – in order to illustrate the various areas of AI use and their different user groups in more detail.

Teaching scenarios

Both the use cases submitted as part of this study and an additional study on AI use in higher education indicate that teaching and learning is currently the field of application in which AI tools are particularly widespread. A thorough review of the cases submitted shows that the use of AI can extend across all phases of the teaching process and can therefore hardly be separated into the planning, implementation and evaluation of teaching. Rather, it makes sense to differentiate between the extent to which the use of AI concentrates on individual elements of traditional teaching formats or serves the development of new, practical teaching scenarios.

Many use cases illustrate how new teaching scenarios can be developed with the help of AI. The professional context may vary greatly from case to case, but the use of AI seems to benefit the practical promotion of profession-specific skills.

- An experience-oriented AI use case was designed at the University of Applied Sciences Hamburg (HAW Hamburg), where AI-based conversation simulations are used in the field of personnel psychology to strengthen practical skills in the field of de-escalating communication and to gain experience in escalating communication situations.
- Another anchor example is a use case at Stuttgart Media University, which is committed to research-based and explorative learning. Here, students in the project seminar "AI Media Products" work on a case study and develop a consulting concept for a fictitious media group that is planning to use generative AI, develop a media strategy, an economically viable business plan, new AI-based or AI-

supported media or TV and online formats, implement these prototypically with the help of AI tools and carry out accompanying acceptance research.

A subject-specific focus can be seen in the submitted use cases insofar as several cases can be assigned to professionalisation in the field of teacher training.

- At Hamburg University of Technology, for example, students are trained to use AI tools independently for everyday work tasks and school-specific educational areas, to critically reflect on the use of AI tools in school education and to independently derive further fields of application as part of a seminar in industrial-technical sciences, special needs education and craft/design/technology.
- AI is also integrated into practice-oriented industrial-technical teaching training at the University of Paderborn, where teaching students develop learning scenarios for vocational training in a seminar in the Master of Education programme and then implement and reflect on them with real school classes.

Subject-specific scientific work

Another area of AI use that also affects teaching is the testing of AI tools to support subject-specific academic working methods. Even if fundamental scientific working methods should continue to be taught and learned intensively, students can use AI tools to support them in selected areas, such as research, translations, outline suggestions for qualification papers, etc. As the following examples illustrate, the use of AI in the submitted use cases is often geared towards the specific requirements of certain disciplines.

- At the University of Passau, University of Erlangen-Nuremberg and the University of Applied Sciences for the Public Service in Bavaria (HföD), for example, AI-based assistance systems are being researched and developed on an interdisciplinary basis to promote writing and argumentation skills in law and business (research project "DeepWrite").
- Another subject-specific focus is shown by a use case at Kiel University. Here, students in a seminar on medieval history were able to explore the potential uses of AI for the term paper process. Through guided experimentation under the supervision of specially trained tutors and involving educational videos, they were able to examine and discuss the potential added value of using AI in comparison with a conventional arrangement of the process of term paper writing.

Learning support and exam preparation

In addition to the use of AI in teaching, the submitted use cases include numerous examples of learning and examination-related support services. AI tools are used to support the learning process, taking into account different learning situations and enabling students to be offered individualised learning tasks or to provide personalised feedback even in large groups. AI-based learning assistance, tutoring or mentoring systems are often used.

- An example of this is a use case from the Technical University of Ingolstadt, which is based on the project "THI Success AI – Study success through AI-generated learning paths". An AI-based lecturer dashboard gives teachers an overview of the students' level of knowledge and allows better planning of the attendance phases of the lecture. A chatbot enables students to generate exercises independently and have their questions answered. On the online platform, the recommended learning process is aligned with the students' current level of knowledge and individual learning preferences.
- Another use case for AI-supported formative assessment and feedback was developed in language education at the Humboldt University of Berlin for language didactics modules and courses. An AI-supported tool was used to evaluate formative assessments and generate formative feedback. The aim was to relieve the burden on teachers and enable formative feedback not only for individual students, but for all students. The human-in-the-loop approach, in which teachers checked the AI-based feedback that students received in advance, made it possible to deliberately avoid purely automated assessment.

In some of the use cases evaluated, approaches to individualised exam preparation are also pursued with the help of AI applications.

- At Kempten University of Applied Sciences, for example, an AI tool, which is primarily designed for personalised learning and can be used in various teaching formats, is used for formative self-assessment, automated and individual feedback in exercises and tutorials. In the exercises of the "Software Engineering" module, it enables students to check their learning progress by automatically classifying and evaluating student answers and providing immediate feedback on the quality of the solution.

- At the private CBS International Business School in Cologne, students are also supported by an AI-based "mentor bot", which helps them prepare for exercises and train independently with AI applications. The mentor bot offers an examination mode that can be used by students as a training and feedback unit.

Promotion of AI skills

In view of the increasing use of AI in professional life and other societal areas, there is a need for the purposeful promotion of AI skills, in which universities in particular can play a major role. As the submitted use cases show, many universities already offer their students opportunities to engage with AI tools in a protected form and to test both their benefits and their limitations, i.e. to practice a reflective approach to AI. In addition, the submitted use cases include various examples that are geared towards either interdisciplinary or subject-specific training in the use of AI tools. Some of the evaluated use cases focus on the development or provision of AI infrastructure.

- At the HAWK University of Applied Sciences and Arts Hildesheim/Holzminden/Göttingen and 40 other universities in Germany, for example, the AI platform HAWKI is used as an open source offering, which was developed in the HAWK Interaction Design Lab as part of research-based learning and creative exploration of the potential of AI models such as ChatGPT. As an interface to AI models, HAWKI offers university members the opportunity to deal specifically with AI models and their effects in the context of their own research and teaching.

Other use cases illustrate how students are taught AI skills across disciplines in more or less extensive workshop formats.

- At the University of Hildesheim, AI tools are used to guide students in a 90-minute seminar unit "Via prompt-battle to the Declaration of having written a term paper independently": In several rounds, students develop and test prompts that focus on scientific aspects such as research, independence, critical thinking, and scientific rigor. Particularly successful prompts are documented and discussed.
- At the Rosenheim University of Applied Sciences, AI certificates can be earned as part of the digi.peer+ certificate programme. The teaching format is a certificate programme with individual workshops that focus on digital collaborative tools and generative AI in a scientific context. These workshops provide students with application-oriented knowledge on the use of modern technologies in academic practice.

In addition to interdisciplinary training courses, there are also various examples among the use cases that provide for the subject-specific teaching of AI skills.

- At Munich University of Applied Sciences, students without programming knowledge in a STEM degree programme (e.g., computer science and design) develop their own chatbot on a project-related basis. The students receive a working example chatbot, use prompts to adapt the chatbot's character to their own ideas, and can make simple programming extensions. This offering provides a motivating introduction to the degree programme and, in turn, allows lecturers to work with motivated students who can test current technologies early in their studies.

Advisory services for students

Many of the submitted use cases arose from specific problem areas at universities, including pronounced counseling needs, rising dropout rates, the heterogeneity of the student body, and others, for which universities are also seeking AI-supported solutions. The relevant examples are primarily related to the area of support services, particularly student counseling.

- At the Lübeck University of Applied Sciences, for example, the DiSEA dashboard is provided, which can help students better monitor their academic progress and identify challenges early on. An AI-based self-study course, using different personas, provides academic advisors with insights into how they can best support students using the dashboard or specifically encourage them to actively integrate the dashboard into their daily learning routine, thereby increasing their self-organisation and motivation.
- At Cologne University of Applied Sciences (TH Köln), a „StudiCoachBot" is being used as an AI-based chatbot to coach students specifically on the topic of test anxiety. The chatbot is not offered in a specific course, but rather serves as a mental health counseling service. The StudiCoachBot is based on a systemic coaching approach that asks solution- and resource-oriented questions to stimulate self-reflection processes among students on the topic of test anxiety.

Conclusion: Manifold scenarios of AI tool use with varying didactic added value

The use of AI systems in education and teaching has gained significant momentum compared to the situation prior to the release of generative AI tools in 2022 (cf. Wannemacher & Bodmann, 2021). Many of the use cases have emerged in response to specific challenges encountered in various areas of teaching and learning, comprising the employment of AI tools for the planning, implementation, and evaluation of teaching, including exam preparation, or for the provision of support, advice, and mentoring services for students. The use of AI tools in teaching and learning is designed to enhance didactically planned teaching practices and to augment the flexibility and personalisation of teaching and learning. Various cases explore the subject-specific application potential of AI and teach AI-based scientific working techniques. In many of the submitted cases, the objectives pursued include promoting AI-related professional competence and practising reflective use of AI. The development of AI competence is often a process that teachers and students undertake collaboratively. Previous approaches to using AI tools as chatbot-based learning process facilitators or feedback providers have therefore been expanded and differentiated.

The findings of the present study are therefore in line with Robert & McCormack's (2025) results for the US higher education system, namely that teaching and learning is the functional area of universities in which the use of AI is most strongly responded to, for example, in order to ensure academic integrity, through using AI in didactically targeted teaching, and in assessments and examinations. Furthermore, the evaluated use cases reveal in more detail the didactic added value that can be realised through the use of AI. Based on the examined use cases, productive approaches include, among many others:

- Using AI tools for the design of experience-based and practice-oriented courses.
- The training of conversation strategies using an AI-based simulator.
- The testing of different types of AI tools for handling subject-specific tasks.
- Facilitation of learning effectiveness through automated feedback on individual learning activities or through mentoring tools for exam preparation.

In addition, the findings indicate that the implementation of specific approaches can significantly enhance teaching quality, address individual learning challenges, and ensure continuous and effective learning processes. These approaches encompass skills training facilitated by AI tutorials or certificate courses as well as needs-based preparation and provision of teaching materials.

As a limitation of the present study it must be acknowledged that the selected use cases are "young" innovations whose evaluation and integration into standard teaching and learning practices are still pending in most cases. In addition, the rapid advancements in AI systems imply that the present exploratory study can only offer a snapshot of application examples for the winter semester of 2024/2025. Consequently, there is a necessity for further investigation into the impact and prevalence of AI use, employing case studies to broaden the present findings and to use them as a foundation for more extensive quantitative surveys.

Even if more detailed investigations are still pending, it can be deduced from the results presented for practical use at higher education institutions that

- the didactic added value of using AI applications in teaching and learning should be actively explored at higher education institutions and possibilities for the AI-supported development of learning media should be examined,
- initial experiences with AI-supported teaching should be passed on within universities as part of teaching-related transfer formats,
- universities should make use of new opportunities for more intensive and personalised support for students in their studies and teaching, e.g. through AI-based chatbots and learning assistants,
- the ability of students to use AI tools independently should be specifically promoted as part of discipline-related methods training,
- faculties and departments should work towards a medium-term, conventional or AI-supported adaptation of curricula to AI-related changes in professional requirement profiles,
- resources should be provided for legally unobjectionable AI infrastructures, and active testing of AI applications by lecturers and students should be made possible, and

- that universities, in their efforts to create AI-promoting framework conditions, should promote a critical understanding and a reflective approach to AI technologies among students and strive for a balance between the advantages of generative AI and the promotion of student independence.

Competing interests

The authors have no competing interests to declare.

References

Arbeitsgruppe Digitale Medien und Hochschuldidaktik der dghd in Kooperation mit der GMW (2024). Didaktische Handreichung zur praktischen Nutzung von KI in der Lehre. https://www.gmw-online.de/wp-content/uploads/2024/10/KI-Handreichung-dghd_GMW_V01_21102024.pdf

Hochschulforum Digitalisierung (2025). KI-Use-Case-Katalog. Eine Übersicht zu KI-Use-Cases in Studium, Lehre und Support. https://ki-use.hochschulforumdigitalisierung.de

Robert, J., McCormack, M. (2025). 2025 EDUCAUSE AI Landscape Study: Into the Digital AI Divide. Research report. Boulder, CO: EDUCAUSE, February 2025. https://www.educause.edu/content/2025/2025-educause-ai-landscape-study/introduction-and-key-findings

Salden, P., Leschke, J. (2024). Learning Analytics und Künstliche Intelligenz in Studium und Lehre. Erfahrungen und Schlussfolgerungen aus einer hochschulweiten Erprobung. Springer VS.

Wannemacher, K., Bodmann, L. (2021). Künstliche Intelligenz an den Hochschulen. Potenziale und Herausforderungen in Forschung, Studium und Lehre sowie Curriculumentwicklung. Berlin: Hochschulforum Digitalisierung. https://hochschulforumdigitalisierung.de/sites/default/files/dateien/HFD_AP_59_Kuenstliche_Intelligenz_Hochschulen_HIS-HE.pdf

Wannemacher, K., Bosse, E., Lübcke, M., Kaemena, A. (2025): Wie KI Studium und Lehre verändert. Anwendungsfelder, Use-Cases und Gelingensbedingungen. Berlin: Hochschulforum Digitalisierung. https://hochschulforumdigitalisierung.de/wp-content/uploads/2025/04/HFD_AP_87_Wie_KI_Studium_und_Lehre_veraendert_final.pdf

de Witt, C., Gloerfeld, C., Wrede, S. E. (ed.) (2023). Künstliche Intelligenz in der Bildung. Berlin: Springer Nature.

Holding a lead, or the tail wagging the dog? Exploring educator influence over the behaviour of AI Digital Assistants

Tim Coughlan[1], Bart Rienties[1], John Domingue[2], Christothea Herodotou[1], Thomas Ullmann[1], Duygu Bektik[1], Chris Edwards[1], Denise Whitelock[1], Emily Coughlan[1] & Felipe Tessarolo[1]

[1] Institute of Educational Technology, The Open University, UK; tim.coughlan@open.ac.uk; bart.rienties@open.ac.uk; christothea.herodotou@open.ac.uk; thomas.ullmann@open.ac.uk; duygu.bektik@open.ac.uk; chris.edwards@open.ac.uk; denise.whitelock@open.ac.uk; emily.coughlan@open.ac.uk; felipe.tessarolo@open.ac.uk
[2] Knowledge Media Institute, The Open University, UK; john.domingue@open.ac.uk

Correspondence: Tim Coughlan: tim.coughlan@open.ac.uk

Abstract:

As GenAI tools become more pervasive in learning, the ways in which educators can influence the behaviour of these systems should be a focus for research and innovation. As part of designing and trialling an institutional AI digital assistant for study, we are exploring where and how educators' technological, pedagogical and content expertise could be brought to bear in the way in which the assistant behaves. In this paper, we draw on feedback from 20 educators and education researchers who took part in a trial of a prototype of the system and reflect on the process of designing the system to be embedded into the study of online courses. We highlight six methods through which educators can exert influence over the behaviour of such assistants and reflect on the alignment, possibilities and limitations of these to meet educator goals. This contributes to opening up a space for educators to think strategically and creatively about teaching with AI.

Keywords: Artificial intelligence, Virtual assistants, AI tutors, learning design

Introduction

As GenAI tools proliferate, a key focus for educators should be how to influence the behaviour of these systems. However, research on teacher roles in relation to GenAI is limited (Zhai, 2024) and there is evidence of an erosion of trust between students and teachers (Luo, 2024). Educators need new ways to maintain influence over the quality of the education they provide, and online teaching practices are likely to change significantly (e.g. Ullmann et al., 2024). Building effective strategies requires articulation of issues and approaches that are positive for educators and students. To support this, it is necessary to understand how educators wish to influence the behaviour of GenAI tools and identify methods through which they can achieve this.

Most research on the educational impacts of GenAI has used generic assistant tools such as ChatGPT (Deng et al., 2025). However, our research explores the potential for institutionally-owned AI Digital Assistants (i-AIDA), and has found evidence of a preference for these among students (Rienties et al., 2024; Rienties et al., 2025). The concept of an i-AIDA opens up space for more creative and strategic thinking about how educational institutions create innovative and valuable learning experiences for the future. Alongside work to understand student perspectives and use of an initial version of AIDA, this research seeks to answer the following questions:

1) What do educators view as desirable roles and behaviours for an i-AIDA?

2) What methods exist for educators to influence interactions between students and an i-AIDA?

Background

Current research suggests GenAI has potential to support learning but also highlights concerns and salient gaps in understanding of how it can fulfil this potential. A systematic review of 69 studies (Deng et al., 2025) suggests GenAI tools could be effective in improving academic performance, motivation and higher-order thinking. However, amongst other limitations, almost all of these studies were classroom based, with no distance learning studies. Around the world, many students and educators have high awareness of GenAI and expect to continue using it, but have concerns around its ethical use, particularly in relation to academic integrity (Yusuf et al., 2024). Findings also suggest that students could become dependent on GenAI tools which deliver short term gains without enhancing intrinsic motivation or broader knowledge, suggesting careful consideration of where and how these tools are used is needed (Fan et al., 2024).

There is also concern that increased use of GenAI leaves educators with minimal or passive roles in teaching. However, research suggests that both teachers and students perceive there to be qualities that make teachers irreplaceable (Chan & Tsai, 2024). Reviewing strengths and limitations of GenAI, Mishra et al. (2023) argue we should neither expect a complete transformation of education, or only resistance to change. Instead, they note that the technology itself lacks agency and will be given meaning within the structures and systems that exist in education. Educators need to understand the opportunities and problems that this technology presents for learning, and for society, and reimagine how they make use of their technological, pedagogical, content and contextual knowledge.

Researchers have conceptualised how educators could work with GenAI. Molenaar (2022) propose six levels of automation, ranging from full teacher control, through various degrees of support or autonomy where AI technologies undertake tasks while monitored by teachers, through to technology controlling teaching automatically. Zhai (2024) suggests that many are passively observing GenAI while building awareness or scepticism, while others are innovators setting examples that will shape the future of GenAI in education.

Further research identifies potential roles and relationships between educators, students and GenAI tools. Exploring the erosion of trust between students and teachers around GenAI, Luo (2024) suggests the importance of transparency and personal connections: that teachers should know their students well enough to be confident of their knowledge and skills, and the negative impacts of teachers using AI without transparency while restricting use of it by their students. There is evidence that proactive efforts can be fruitful, for example by developing clear frameworks for students to understand where and how GenAI can be used (Furze et al., 2024).

Researchers have defined specific pedagogical roles that these systems can play (Sharples, 2023: Mollick & Mollick, 2023), such as a Socratic opponent or storyteller. Sharples (2023) argues that to succeed in such roles, AI-based systems will require recognition of limitations, and to understand and respect the perspectives of teachers.

There remains more to understand about how GenAI could support or hinder learning, and how educators work could change as a result. Drawing on the above, we can identify a wide range of roles that an i-AIDA could play, and that educators should be able to influence the behaviour and use by their students. Creating the means to enable this influence became a focus of our design work.

Methodology

To answer the research questions we draw on data from a Design-Based Research project to create and evaluate an i-AIDA (see figure 1). The i-AIDA was embedded into a virtual learning environment and supports dialogue, quizzes and other interactive elements linked to the current page of content and the wider course. It draws on course materials and selected additional resources in its responses. It can take on different roles (e.g. as a Socratic Tutor or Study Buddy). Additional features and design improvements are being made as the project progresses.

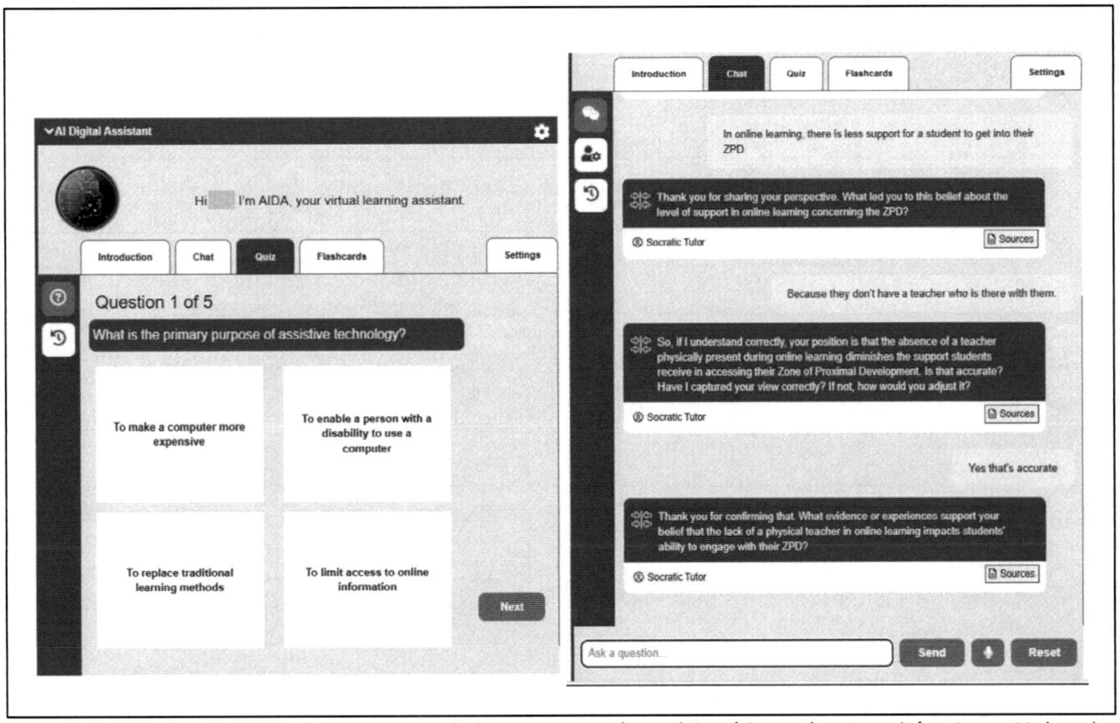

Figure 1: Screenshots from the version of the i-AIDA evaluated in this study. Copyright Open University (2025).

This paper focuses on two activities from the project:

1) A study in which educators and educational researchers interacted with a prototype AIDA. 20 educators and educational researchers at the institution took part in recorded sessions where they were guided to use the assistant and asked to think aloud to provide their feedback, alongside pre and post surveys. Data was subject to a thematic analysis to identify areas where participants discussed ways in which they wanted AIDA to behave and its ideal roles in relation to students and educators.

2) **Reflecting on the process of creating an i-AIDA and embedding it into courses.** We identify how, during the project, the interdisciplinary team have engaged with educators, identified issues and devised methods to enable influence over the assistant.

Educator perspectives on an AI Digital Assistant

Table 1 presents a summary of themes identified in think-aloud data which reflect issues in the i-AIDA's behaviour and expectations of ways that the participants should be able to influence it.

Table 1: Thematic analysis

Theme	**Definition**	**Example quotes**
Clarifying roles and processes	Making clear the roles for AI and for educators	"I would hope the tutor and the AI also talk to each other. Otherwise there would be a broken chain somewhere."
Supporting assessment processes	Appropriate ways to involve educators and AI in assessment	"it's as much about undertaking the process of being assessed and the process of receiving and managing feedback as it is actually finding out how well you know the material."

Fairness in assessment	Assessment by AI can be considered unfair so educators need to have oversight.	"I thought my answer is quite limited for that mark and I probably wouldn't necessarily have thought it would come up with a mark."
Providing nuanced feedback	The feedback given by the assistant needs further depth of understanding.	"The answer might be close to the correct one, but ... just didn't capture the information in the same way the student wrote it down. I would be slightly less emphatic about the correctness"
Providing personalised feedback	Areas where feedback needs to be given with an understanding of the student	"as far as I'm concerned I gave an answer that's relevant to me. What I've got (in feedback) is generic... if it's not personalised it's not worth spending any time on it"
Giving encouragement	Teaching entails listening and being proactive in prompting the student.	"(if) you're a tutor, or (in a similar role)...You ask them a question that enables you to find out something about them... have you finished this week's study? Did you enjoy it? What did you think of it? I'm really interested in hearing about your reactions"
Holding rich discussions	Teaching should involve rich dialogue.	"I can actually talk to it and it can give me some explanations and then answer the question. If it's smart enough, I would have liked it to actually entertain me and clarify a few things."
Supporting development	Teaching assesses and adapts to students' experience and abilities	"You might want to be more prescriptive with the prompts, but later on in the course by then, hopefully the student has got a better understanding of how it works and might not need those."
Highlighting connections	Teaching includes showing the links across materials and concepts	"it may be helpful for it to actually link back to maybe an area in the (course materials), but if it can't find the answer then it doesn't know. It won't know where the answer could be either"
Presenting information	Considering how to clearly explain information	"the summary is useful, but it's maybe not presented in the most readable way"

The analysis illustrates that participants saw a need to clarify the roles an i-AIDA would play alongside educators. The prototype system used in these evaluations did not include summative assessment tasks, only formative quizzes. However participants raised several themes related to assessment and feedback and saw educator influence as particularly essential in this. Participants were also concerned about the ability of the assistant to give encouragement, hold rich discussions and support student development, demonstrating concern for affective and academic elements of teaching.

Reflections on designing and embedding AIDA in online courses

As we worked to enable educator influence through the design and trials, several key issues were uncovered.

Creating and harnessing roles

To enable multiple pedagogical approaches, an open-ended mechanism to create and choose roles that the i-AIDA could take on was developed. Roles can be defined by the institution or by educators as a set of instructions for i-AIDA to follow. We drew on Sharples (2023) to create initial roles then defined these in further detail. We identified wider potential to create and adapt roles specific to a subject area or teaching task. Linked to the 'Supporting Development' theme, we also envisage roles that recognise different needs at particular points in the study journey. For example an induction role to help new students. Other roles could assess current understanding and respond appropriately.

Enabling role selection raises questions of student and educator agency. The student could choose which role to engage with, enabling a form of personalisation. However, educators could suggest appropriate roles for a particular situation, or restrict access only to appropriate roles.

Enhancing responses with a course commentary

A key differentiator for an i-AIDA when compared to generic Large Language Models is that its responses can be based on specific approved sources and instructions (Rienties et al., 2025). Course materials are an obvious source, but these alone limit responses to explaining and using the same material in different ways, when further detail, examples and considerations will enrich the dialogue.

This raised the question of how to go beyond course materials while maintaining control, leading us to develop the concept of a 'Course Commentary'. This contains various additional information, including alternative descriptions and explanations of concepts and expected questions and answers. This detail would overburden the course materials but as an additional commentary provides the i-AIDA with relevant further material to draw on. Content for the Course Commentary could include material edited out of course drafts, and can also be created using GenAI tools, guided and reviewed by educators to maintain quality.

Adapting teaching and course production

Introducing an i-AIDA creates new considerations for learning design and additional decisions for educators to make about their teaching. Our work to date has used existing courses. Where these contain elements that the i-AIDA is capable of managing, such as interactive activities or quizzes, decisions arise whether these become part of the dialogue. Time that students are expected to spend engaging with the assistant needs to be accounted for in workload. Students may deviate from expected course journeys in new ways, for example continuing to talk with the assistant rather than progressing through the materials, or asking it for a summary rather than reading materials crafted by the educator.

Additional effort may be required from educators to create course commentary and role descriptions. This is weighed up against the desire for the system to reflect educator expertise and enhance the quality of responses. Looking forward, we envisage 'AIDA-native' courses, with the system integral as the learning design and materials are developed. This could lead to a more integrated experience for students. For educators, reduced time needed for other tasks might be used to instruct the system.

Discussion

Attention to GenAI in education has focused on strategies such as restricting its use by students, and concerns over the misuse of materials and data. A mature vision of how educators can and should influence GenAI tools is needed. Here we identify various methods through which educators can exert influence and consider how these map to areas where this is needed:

1. Instruction: Educators can devise and share prompts which instruct GenAI tools to behave in specific ways. Such prompts provide a basic way to influence behaviour in areas such as 'Providing Encouragement'.

2. Restricted sources: Educators can select course materials or other resources that direct and constrain the assistants responses. This is supported through methods such as Retrieval Augmented Generation (RAG), or Small Language Models (SLMs). Using these approaches, educators may enhance ways of 'Presenting Information' but constraining the assistant may reduce potential for 'Rich Discussions'.

3. Co-authoring: GenAI can create versions of teaching materials, then manually checked, edited and curated by educators (Ullmann et al., 2024). This can enhance 'Presenting Information' but does not support discussion.

4. Role-giving: Educators define the pedagogical roles that an assistant plays and where and how these are deployed. This elevates the potential of 'Instruction' by allowing the educator to suggest or restrict the roles played. It can promote 'Clarifying roles and processes' and their influence over many of the areas identified in table 1, including behaviours around feedback and assessment.

5. Co-assessing: Assistants can provide information about students' behaviour and progress, creating decision-making points for educators. This could enable 'Supporting Assessment Processes' and 'Fairness in Assessment'. Identifying areas that students find difficult could also enhance 'Supporting development'.

6. Course commentary: Educators work with GenAI to create a commentary on how to instruct students to learn the subject matter. By providing more detailed information about the subject, alternative examples, or guidance on how to teach key concepts, this can address themes such as 'Highlighting Connections', 'Presenting Information' and 'Rich Discussions'.

Future work will further explore how these approaches, and others, map to the needs of educators and can enable creative and effective use of GenAI in education.

Competing interests

The authors have no competing interests to declare.

Ethics and consent

This research was approved by the Human Research Ethics Committee of The Open University UK.

Acknowledgements

This research was supported by The Open University UK through the Pro-Vice Chancellor for Research and Innovation. We would like to thank colleagues in the Knowledge Media Institute (KMi) and Institute of Educational Technology (IET) who have contributed to the project, and the participants who gave their time to take part in this and other studies.

References

Chan, C. K. Y., & Tsi, L. H. (2024). Will generative AI replace teachers in higher education? A study of teacher and student perceptions. Studies in Educational Evaluation, 83, 101395.

Deng, R., Jiang, M., Yu, X., Lu, Y., & Liu, S. (2024). Does ChatGPT enhance student learning? A systematic review and meta-analysis of experimental studies. Computers & Education, 227. 105224.

Fan, Y., Tang, L., Le, H., Shen, K., Tan, S., Zhao, Y., ... & Gašević, D. (2024). Beware of metacognitive laziness: Effects of generative artificial intelligence on learning motivation, processes, and performance. British Journal of Educational Technology, 56(2). 489-530.

Furze, L., Perkins, M., Roe, J., & MacVaugh, J. (2024). The AI Assessment Scale (AIAS) in action: A pilot implementation of GenAI-supported assessment. Australasian Journal of Educational Technology, 40(4), 38-55.

Luo, J. (2024). How does GenAI affect trust in teacher-student relationships? Insights from students' assessment experiences. Teaching in Higher Education, 1-16.

Mishra, P., Warr, M., & Islam, R. (2023). TPACK in the age of ChatGPT and Generative AI. Journal of Digital Learning in Teacher Education, 39(4), 235-251.

Molenaar, I. (2022). Towards hybrid human-AI learning technologies. European Journal of Education, 57(4), 632-645.

Mollick, Ethan R. and Mollick, Lilach, Assigning AI: Seven Approaches for Students, with Prompts (2023). The Wharton School Research Paper, Available at SSRN: http://dx.doi.org/10.2139/ssrn.4475995

Rienties, B., Tessarolo, F., Coughlan, E., Coughlan, T., & Domingue, J. (2025). Students' Perceptions of AI Digital Assistants (AIDAs): Should Institutions Invest in Their Own AIDAs?. Applied Sciences, 15(8), 4279.

Rienties, B., Herodotou, C., Tessarolo, F., Domingue, J., Duttaroy, S., & Whitelock, D. (2024). An institutional AI digital assistant: what do distance learners expect and value?. Ubiquity Proceedings, 4(1), 7. https://doi.org/10.5334/uproc.129

Sharples, M. (2023). Towards social generative AI for education: theory, practices and ethics. Learning: Research and Practice, 9(2), 159-167.

Ullmann, T., Edwards, C., Bektik, D., Herodotou, C., & Whitelock, D. (2024). Towards generative AI for course content production: Expert reflections. European Journal of Open, Distance and E-Learning, 26(1).

Yusuf, A., Pervin, N., & Román-González, M. (2024). Generative AI and the future of higher education: a threat to academic integrity or reformation? Evidence from multicultural perspectives. International Journal of Educational Technology in Higher Education, 21(1).

Zhai, X. (2024). Transforming teachers' roles and agencies in the era of generative ai: Perceptions, acceptance, knowledge, and practices. Journal of Science Education and Technology, https://doi.org/10.1007/s10956-024-10174-0.

Co-creating with Generative AI (GenAI) for curriculum design: learning personas

Irina Rets[1], Denise Whitelock[1], Chris Edwards[1], Leigh-Anne Perryman[1], & Beck Pitt[1]

[1] Institute of Educational Technology, The Open University, United Kingdom; irina.rets@open.ac.uk; denise.whitelock@open.ac.uk; chris.edwards@open.ac.uk; leigh-anne.perryman@open.ac.uk; beck.pitt@open.ac.uk

Correspondence: Irina Rets: irina.rets@open.ac.uk

Abstract:

Generative AI (GenAI) presents new opportunities for learner-centred teaching. This study explores its potential in co-creating learning personas—fictional yet research-informed representations of students – for energy digitalisation education, a field that attracts learners from diverse backgrounds. We document the process of generating nine learner personas with GenAI and evaluating their quality through expert review and benchmarking against publicly available LinkedIn profiles of professionals in similar roles. Our findings indicate that GenAI effectively differentiates professional roles, captures key job-related challenges, and reflects learner motivations, making it a valuable tool for curriculum design. However, critical limitations persist, with GenAI creating overly idealised professionals, lacking diversity in the supporting AI-generated images, and overlooking some nuanced real-world complexities. These challenges highlight the need for human oversight to ensure authenticity, inclusivity, and ethical depth. Based on our findings, we provide recommendations for co-creating personas with GenAI for curriculum design.

Keywords: Generative AI, curriculum design, learning personas, co-creation, AI evaluation, learning design

Introduction

Learner-centred teaching approaches emphasize designing content, materials, and assessments that align with the diverse backgrounds and goals of learners. However, understanding a learner base can be challenging, especially in online education, where courses often scale to hundreds or even thousands of learners.

A well-established approach from user experience (UX) design that helps address this challenge is the use of learner personas (Quintana et al., 2017). These fictional yet research-informed representations of typical students provide insight into student demographics, skills, motivations, and potential obstacles. Research suggests that personas encapsulate critical behavioural data in an accessible format, helping instructional designers and educators create targeted, effective learning experiences (Quintana et al., 2017). Additionally, personas offer a shared means of communication between key stakeholders in the course design process (Goodwin, 2009).

Despite their benefits, developing accurate learner personas is resource-intensive. Previous efforts have involved liaising diverse stakeholder groups to ensure realistic and well-informed profiles (Quintana et al., 2017). Some studies have applied predictive modelling using institutional data and student surveys to bridge the gap between data science and learning design, though validation of these personas remains limited (Brooks & Greer, 2014). Both approaches require either extensive expertise or advanced data analysis skills.

Given the challenges of persona development, this study explores the use of Generative AI (GenAI) to create personas for learners in energy digitalisation. As digital energy is increasingly becoming part of everyday life, people from very diverse backgrounds need access to the learning on the topic. To our knowledge, no prior previously published research has explored GenAI-driven co-creation in persona development, making this study an innovative step toward scalable learner-centred teaching.

GenAI in curriculum: friend or foe?

GenAI holds promise in higher education in assisting educators with course material development. From generating course outlines and content to drafting assessment instructions and mapping learning outcomes, GenAI has the potential to streamline curriculum design enhancing student engagement (Fisher et al., 2024; Ullman et al., 2024).

While evaluations of GenAI outputs for course creation and co-creation with GenAI remain limited, emerging studies highlight the critical need for expert review and refinement of AI-generated content. Ullman et al. (2024) examined expert evaluations of AI-generated content for course production and found that while GenAI enabled generation of plausible first drafts of relevant content, human intervention was essential for quality assurance. Meron and Tekmen Araci (2023) having explored two university educators' collaboration with ChatGPT in developing course materials, found that ChatGPT excelled in saving time, structuring textual content, and supporting brainstorming but often produced generic outputs requiring extensive prompting, refinement, and manual editing.

This study examines the process of co-creating learning personas for learners in the energy digitalisation field with GenAI. Co-creation is typically defined as a collaborative process in which participants—whether citizens, end users, or other stakeholders—influence both the production process and the final product, contributing to knowledge generation through collective creativity (Sanders & Stappers, 2008). In this research, we argue that GenAI itself can act as a co-creator and document the steps involved in this co-creation process. We then assess the quality of the GenAI personas by working with energy experts and benchmarking the personas against publicly available LinkedIn profiles of professionals in similar roles. Based on our findings, we offer recommendations for co-creating with GenAI for curriculum design.

Methods

The study was conducted as part of the Every1 project, funded by Horizon Europe/UK Research and Innovation (2022–2026) and managed by an international consortium of researchers and energy experts. The project aims to engage a diverse range of European stakeholders and citizens in energy digitalisation. As part of the project, The Open University UK team is leading the development of a wide range of online learning materials on energy digitalisation for different stakeholders.

Co-creating with GenAI

The GenAI co-creation process began with a consortium-wide brainstorming session to identify key audiences for whom the project's learning materials should be designed. This session followed the methodical collation of a potential list of stakeholder groups from earlier work within the project. At this stage, we focused on specialised stakeholders within the energy ecosystem rather than the general public. This resulted in a list of nine relevant personas, including managers, educators, engineers, and business leaders from energy regulation, investment, electricity retail, digital services, and non-profit sector.

Once the target personas were defined, the next GenAI co-creation step involved preparing a learning persona template. For the purposes of the project, we adapted a template from The Open University's learning design team (https://bit.ly/4kEUdNY) that has been widely tested at the university and used to develop courses for undergraduate and graduate students. This template includes key attributes such as name, age, living situation, motivations, career plans, and qualifications. Since the project's learning materials are not part of a formal programme of study, we expanded the template to include learning outcomes (tailored to the persona's needs), work-related challenges (to refine learning objectives), relevant stakeholders (to explore further engagement opportunities). This adapted template guided the prompts to generate personas. To exemplify, the first prompt used with GenAI was as follows:

Make a profile for [a persona – e.g., a university educator from a technical background looking to teach a course about energy digitalisation]. This topic is new to them. What do the person's qualifications, interests, and motivations tend to be like? What sort of projects/initiatives are they likely to be involved in? What does their life-style tend to be like? Suggest a first name and a last name for them, age, and a location of where they are most likely to be based.

The prompts used aimed to provide a rich contextual background for each persona, acknowledging that learning cannot be separated from its cultural and historical context, and that individuals shape and are shaped by their environments (Kennedy et al., 2025).

Since learning personas are typically presented with images, we used GenCraft (https://gencraft.com/) to generate profile pictures, as it produced more realistic results compared to GenAI chatbots. Each prompt was based on the GenAI-generated persona details, including name, age, location, position, and organisation.

To avoid evaluating a single specific GenAI tool, such as ChatGPT, we used three GenAI chatbots with different architectures and training cut-off points: ChatGPT, DeepSeek, and Claude.

The responses provided by GenAI tools were copied into the adapted learning persona template. An example of the final format is shown in Figures 1 and 2 below.

Andreas Kallioras **Junior Business developer at HEDNO (Greek DSO)**  *(Image generated by gencraft.com)*	
Overall description ***(person and team, product/service, stakeholder needs and gaps)***	Andreas is junior business developer starting at a DSO and has the responsibility to bring innovative solutions to the DSO to increase efficiency in the company. He is based in Athens, Greece. • **Age:** 28 years old • **Marital status:** single but in a committed relationship. He is focused on building his career and gaining experience in the energy sector but values maintaining a meaningful personal life. His partner, who may also work in a professional or creative field, shares his interest in sustainability and technology. They enjoy exploring Greece's natural landscapes and cultural events together, making the most of their free time. • **Living arrangement:** He lives in a modern apartment in the heart of Athens, close to key amenities and public transport. His apartment is a well-designed one-bedroom space with a small home office setup, reflecting his practical and professional mindset. The building is located in a vibrant yet quiet neighborhood, possibly in areas like Pangrati or Koukaki, known for their balance of city life and green spaces.

Figure 1. Excerpt from a GenAI learning persona

Qualifications

- Bachelor's degree in Electrical Engineering or Energy Management.
- Master's degree in Business Administration (MBA) or Renewable Energy Systems.
- Certifications or coursework in innovation management, digital transformation, and smart grid technologies.

Skills

- Analytical thinking and problem-solving.
- Proficiency in data analysis tools and project management software.
- Familiarity with energy markets, regulatory frameworks, and grid modernization.
- Strong communication skills for stakeholder engagement and collaboration.

Figure 2. Excerpt from a GenAI learning persona showcasing generated qualifications and skills

Validating GenAI personas

Each GenAI learning persona was reviewed by energy experts affiliated with the Every1 project. The first persona was used as a test persona and was reviewed by the entire consortium at an in-person consortium meeting. After receiving positive feedback on its quality, seven other personas were reviewed in separate research interviews, and one – in an interactive group workshop. To ensure accurate reviews, we matched reviewing experts with personas based on their field of expertise (e.g., university educators reviewed the university educator persona).

The first author conducted all interviews online via Zoom and Microsoft Teams. To encourage constructive feedback and give time to reviewing experts to reflect on the personas, before the interviews, participants received the persona assigned for review, a link to the chatbot-generated conversation used to create the persona, and the interview questions in advance. The interview focused on evaluating the accuracy and representativeness of the GenAI personas.

As a final validation step, we compared the GenAI personas with real-world professional profiles. Reviewing experts provided LinkedIn links to public profiles of individuals in their networks, who have similar positions to the personas.

Figure 3 below presents the four stages we followed to co-create the learning personas with GenAI: envision, collaborate with GenAI, refine, validate.

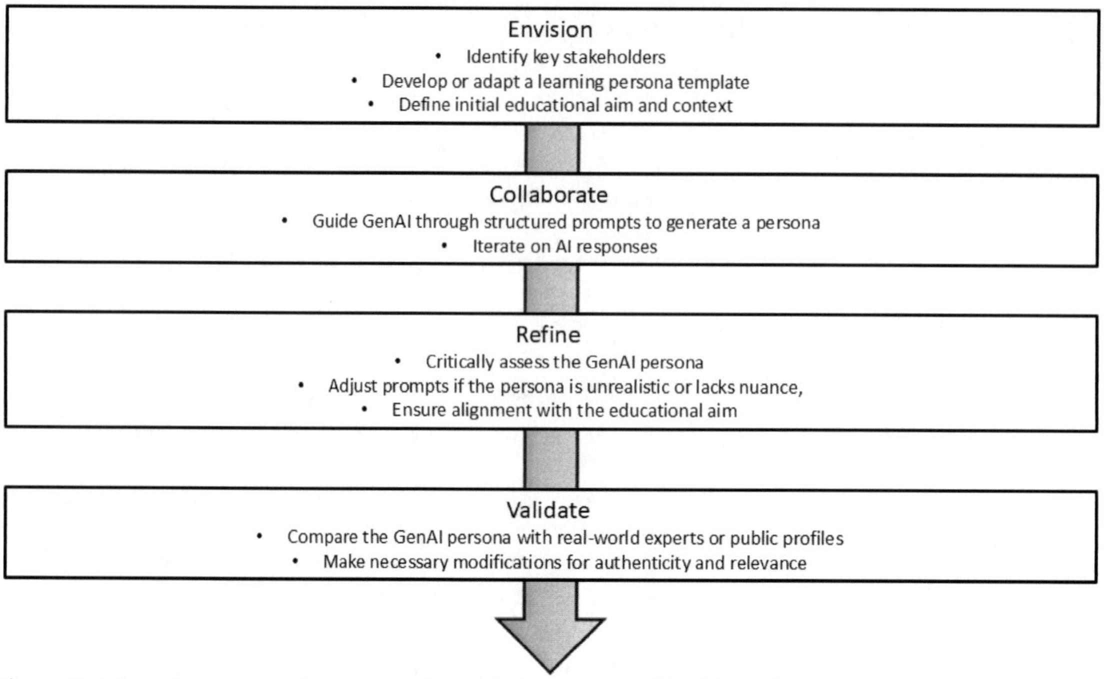

Figure 3. A four-stage approach to co-creating with GenAI adopted in this study

Analysis

The review meeting transcripts were analysed, using thematic analysis (Boyatzis, 1998). Open coding was used to develop the themes and sub-themes, and axial coding was used to identify their repeated occurrences. Following the first round of coding, the interview transcripts were re-read for a critical assessment of assigned codes and adjustments were made. The unit of analysis for coding was one paragraph (i.e., one full answer to an interview question). A particular paragraph could be given multiple codes.

Additionally, the first author reviewed all nine GenAI personas, comparing them for similarities and differences, with particular attention to race and gender representation, living arrangements, and work activities discussed in the personas. LinkedIn profiles suggested by the reviewing experts were explored to complement and triangulate the findings derived from the analysis of the review meetings. The resulting coding scheme is presented in Figure 4 below. The figure illustrates two themes – positive feedback on GenAI personas and identified areas for improvement – along with six sub-themes.

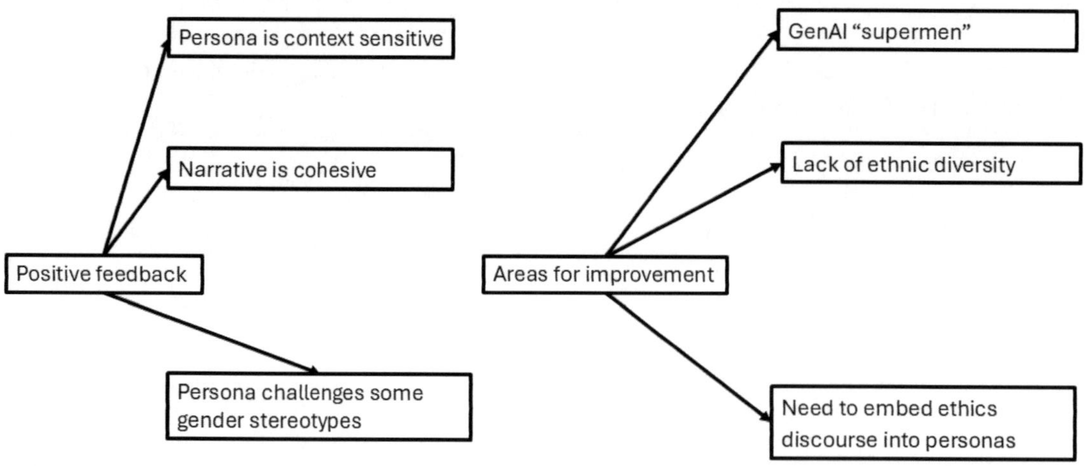

Figure 4. Coding scheme developed in this study

Results

Positive feedback on GenAI personas

Overall, expert reviewers provided positive feedback on the GenAI personas. A key strength noted was the personas' contextual sensitivity to the kind of activities and challenges a persona has to deal with in their daily job. When comparing personas, we noted how GenAI effectively captured differences in professional contexts, such as the contrast between commercial and non-profit roles (e.g., scalability and return of investment – ROI – for commercial roles, systemic change, policy and funding for non-profit roles). The following excerpts from the personas illustrate this point:

- "Marcus must deliver measurable ROI for his solutions while maintaining the company's sustainability goals". (Challenges section, Digital Company Owner persona)
- "Desire to contribute meaningfully to the energy transition by working in a team that drives systemic change across Europe." (Motivations section, project manager persona at a non-profit organisation)

Experts appreciated the authenticity of the challenges described in the personas. One expert in the group workshop reflected:

"The challenges look so realistic, especially the third one, where Clara needs to frequently update her teaching materials. I feel myself represented in this stressful situation". (Project manager / Lecturer in energy and business models, review of Clara – the university educator persona).

Good contextual sensitivity also involved a placement of personas in relevant geographical contexts, GenAI's "spot on" choice of locations. For example, ChatGPT placed a persona working in agri-tech solutions in the Netherlands, which is a leader in digital solutions for farming. Another expert noted how placing a banker in Zurich "makes sense":

"If he comes more the banking side rather than the energy market side, then Zurich for bankers makes sense. I think, probably, Swiss banks invest substantially in European energy markets and energy services". (Chief Operating Officer, COO, at an energy systems think-tank, review of Elliot, Lead portfolio manager at an investment fund).

A few experts highlighted the strong coherence in the personas' life stories: "It all sticks together, the story of the persona follows well" (digital consultant at a digital communication agency, review of Marcus, digital company owner). For example, the investment banker persona, reflective of their financial stability, was the only one among the nine with a secondary/vacation property.

Without explicit gender prompts, GenAI created good female representation in the traditionally male-dominated roles (e.g., Emma, a grid connection engineer persona). Overall, GenAI generated three male and six female personas. Work-life balance was a recurring theme, including for male personas. This challenges gender stereotypes, as previous research indicates that work-family cues are often gendered (e.g., "flexible" work, and "work–family balance" are feminine cues, often used in female-dominated roles vs. "irregular" and "long work hours" are masculine cues, often used to describe male dominated fields, Hu et al., 2024). One expert noted:

"So, it's not the person who is just about, you know, investments and projects, but it's interesting how the tool does keep family in the background. I would say if it would have been a female persona, I would have said that this is something to scrap from the persona, as it's a bit stereotypical. So, it's maybe good that it's in a male persona as well". (COO at an energy systems think-tank, review of Elliot - lead portfolio manager at an investment fund)

Areas for improvement

One major critique was that GenAI tended to create "supermen" – very successful, almost perfect professionals, with extensive skills across different domains. They all got their education from top universities and had a very "structured route directly into energy" (Digital consultant at a digital communication agency, review of Marcus – digital company owner). The reviewing expert further noted:

"In my experience, life is not so linear and balanced. We are all formed by diverse experiences, and our experiences help us make our next steps. I think it would be interesting to know a bit about this person's background that motivated him to get into this line of work. Maybe, he was working some summers as a student in a farm. Maybe he had a different role growing up in another working environment and decided to change that, so that his personality matches his work better? Unless his life was a structural dream". (Digital consultant at a digital communication agency, review of Marcus – digital company owner).

For example, when comparing these personas against LinkedIn profiles, we noted that some professionals had non-traditional educational paths, such as an electrical engineer with a background in teacher education.

Besides being flawless professionals, many personas portrayed an overly idealised environmental consciousness. All generated personas used solar panels at home, energy efficient smart devices, and other eco-friendly "touches", and, overall, looked "instagrammic". One expert in a group workshop reflected:

"She rides a bicycle everywhere she goes, she grows her own stuff, she has solar panels, she is eco-conscious. Working in energy digitalisation doesn't mean that you are eco-conscious, and that you are on the green team. You can work in the oil industry and teach energy digitalisation. You can support big oil and still work in that. So that's interesting how GenAI creates this specific narrative". (Senior research assistant in energy and sustainability, review of Clara, university educator persona).

Another suggestion for improvement was the need to address the lack of ethnic diversity in the GenAI-generated profile photos of the personas. All nine GenAI personas appeared to be white. The personas' appearances also seemed to align with their geographic locations (e.g., slightly tanned for southern Europe, lighter-skinned for northern Europe). One expert commented how the profile photo of the persona they reviewed was very representative of their colleagues:

"She looks exactly like my colleague in my current office in Stuttgart [laughter]. There are, like, ten people in my office that look just like her". (EU project manager working on climate, energy and mobility in a non-profit organisation, review of Emma, a non-profit project manager).

On a different note, some experts noted that it is also important to recognise that some of the portrayals—such as "white males in suits"— "also exist" and may accurately reflect real-world demographics in certain professions. Therefore, this is the responsibility of the person co-creating with GenAI to ensure a balanced representation among the generated personas and prompt the inclusion of individuals from ethnic minority backgrounds as well.

Finally, several experts emphasised the importance of embedding ethical discourse into personas, as learning personas shape the direction of educational materials. Empathy and awareness of ethical issues are essential for guiding both the field and learners toward a more sustainable future, which necessitates the need for an added layer of sensitivity in developing personas. One expert explained:

"Students studying computer science don't always learn about ethics, so it's not surprising that the digital company director persona lacks mention of ethical concerns. This should be included. For example, in the 'Future Trends and Innovations' section, I'd add ethical and social considerations. Farming, isn't just about technology—it's about communities, livelihoods, and societal changes." (Digital consultant at a digital communication agency, review of Marcus – digital company owner)

Recommendations for co-creating with GenAI for curriculum design

Taking into consideration the findings above, and particularly the areas for improvement, we propose the following five key recommendations for co-creating with GenAI for curriculum design:

1. Use narrow, specific prompts (e.g., indicate the size of the company for a digital company owner or the focus of the projects a non-profit persona is likely to work on). These more specific prompts would help avoid "superman" personas.

2. Avoid overly idealised expertise: real-world professionals have areas of strength and areas for growth. Prompt the chatbot to create narratives with career shifts, setbacks, and non-traditional paths and/or discuss life events / events in the wider world that may encourage one to take up a certain line of work.

3. Proactively include diversity: Prompt GenAI for diverse ethnic and gender representation or manually adjust persona demographics.

4. Validate against real-world profiles: Compare personas with LinkedIn profiles of professionals in similar roles. This can provide a reality check and make them appear more human.

5. Incorporate ethical considerations: Prompt GenAI to address ethical and social issues relevant to each persona's role. While the previous recommendation makes the persona more human, this point makes a persona more humane, fostering critical thinking among learners who will engage with the learning materials that the persona motivates.

Conclusion

This study explored the use of Generative AI (GenAI) in co-creating learner personas for energy digitalisation education, evaluating its effectiveness and limitations through expert validation and real-world benchmarking. We adopted a four-stage co-creation approach: envisioning (e.g., defining an educational aim), collaborating (e.g., prompting and iterating GenAI responses), refining (e.g., adjusting prompts), and validating the personas (comparing with expert insights and real-world profiles).

Our findings highlight GenAI's potential to be a valuable co-creator in learning persona development for learner-centred teaching. It effectively differentiates professional roles, captures key job-related challenges, and reflects motivations, supporting its integration into curriculum design. However, critical challenges remain. GenAI tends to generate overly idealised professionals, lacks diversity in GenAI-generated images, and overlooks nuanced real-world complexities such as ethical dilemmas. To enhance GenAI-driven persona creation, we recommend using more specific prompts, intentional inclusion of diversity ethical considerations, and real-world validation.

Our study contributes to the evolving discourse on GenAI in education, reinforcing that while AI can assist in content creation, it requires expert oversight to ensure authenticity, inclusivity, and ethical depth.

Competing interests

The author(s) has/have no competing interests to declare.

Funding Information (optional)

This project has received funding from the European Union under the EU program HORIZON-CL5-2021-D3-02 under grant agreement number: 101075596.

References

Fisher, G. F., Shaw, P., & Fido, D. (2024). Student Judgements of AI-generated and human-generated educational content [Protocol]. The Interdisciplinary Journal of Student Success, (pp. in-press).

Hu, Y., Denier, N., Ding, L., Tarafdar, M., Konnikov, A., Hughes, K. D., ... & Jiang, B. (2024). Language in job advertisements and the reproduction of labor force gender and racial segregation. PNAS nexus, 3(12), pgae526. https://doi.org/10.1093/pnasnexus/pgae526

Kennedy, J., Gabriel, F., Korolkiewicz, M., Rets, I., & Rienties, B. (2025). Editorial: Actionable Learning Analytics in Education: An Opportunity to Close the Learning Loop. Frontiers in Education 10:1571177, https://doi.org/10.3389/feduc.2025.1571177

Goodwin, K. (2009). Designing for the Digital Age. Wiley Publishing Inc., Bloomington, IN.

Meron, Y., & Araci, Y. T. (2023). Artificial intelligence in design education: evaluating ChatGPT as a virtual colleague for post-graduate course development. Design Science, 9, e30. https://doi.org/10.1017/dsj.2023.28

Sanders, E.B.-N., & Stappers, P.J. (2008). Co-creation and the new landscapes of design. CoDesign, 4, 5–18. https://doi.org/10.1080/15710880701875068

Quintana, R. M., Haley, S. R., Levick, A., Holman, C., Hayward, B., & Wojan, M. (2017). The persona party: Using personas to design for learning at scale. Proceedings of the 2017 CHI Conference, pp. 933-941. https://doi.org/10.1145/3027063.3053355

Ullmann, T., Edwards, C., Bektik, D., Herodotou, C., & Whitelock, D. (2024). Towards generative AI for course content production: Expert reflections. European Journal of Open, Distance and E-Learning, 26(S1), 20-34. https://doi.org/10.2478/eurodl-2024-0013

Bridging theory and practice: assessing how pre-service teachers promote self-regulated learning with generative AI through lesson plan analysis

Chen Bitton[1], Guy Cohen[2], Anat Cohen[3], Alla Bronshtein[4]

[1] School of Education, Tel-Aviv University, Israel; chenbitton@mail.tau.ac.il
[2] School of Education, Tel-Aviv University, Israel; guycohen@mail.tau.ac.il
[3] School of Education, Tel-Aviv University, Israel; anatco@tauex.tau.ac.il
[4] Faculty of Medical & Health Sciences, Tel-Aviv University, Israel; allab@tauex.tau.ac.il

Correspondence: Chen Bitton: chenbitton@mail.tau.ac.il

Abstract:

As education shifts toward student-centered learning, evaluating pre-service teachers' ability to foster self-regulated learning (SRL) is essential. This study examines lesson plans as performance-based assessment tools for evaluating pre-service teachers' competence in designing SRL-supportive instruction in online courses. Through qualitative analysis of 37 lesson plans created by 73 pre-service teachers, the research applies a three-dimensional analytical framework focusing on SRL strategy implementation, technology integration, and pedagogical competence. Findings reveal significant variability in how teachers structure SRL, scaffold autonomy development, and incorporate instructional technologies. High-quality lesson plans explicitly embedded metacognitive scaffolds and included structured support for student autonomy, while weaker plans provided inadequate SRL elements and lacked clear instructional rationales. Technology integration varied, with some lesson plans leveraging digital tools to enhance reflection and feedback, while others used technology in a passive, content-delivery manner. These findings reinforce the validity of lesson plans as assessment tools, offering teacher educators a structured alternative to self-reports in evaluating pre-service teachers' instructional reasoning and readiness to promote SRL in diverse learning environments.

Keywords: Self-Regulated Learning (SRL), Online Teacher Education, Pre-Service Teachers, Lesson Planning, Teachers' Professional Competences, Technology Integration

Introduction

Self-Regulated Learning (SRL) is widely recognized as a critical competency for academic success among learners, as it fosters effective learning habits, increases motivation and facilitates positive engagement with learning experiences (Savina, 2021; Xu et al., 2023). SRL is defined as a process in which learners actively plan their learning, use various strategies, monitor, and regulate their cognitive, motivational, and behavioral processes to achieve their goals (Pintrich, 2000; Zimmerman, 2002). These skills extend beyond academic performance, fostering learners' personal development (Moffitt et al., 2011), and lifelong learning capabilities (Alderman & MacDonald, 2015; Taranto & Buchanan, 2020). These capabilities enable learners to continuously evaluate their progress, develop metacognitive awareness, and adapt to an ever-changing world (Zimmerman, 2008). This adaptability has become particularly crucial in today's technology-driven educational settings, making the acquisition of these skills increasingly important for learners (Bogdány et al., 2023; Wong et al., 2018).

Although the benefits of fostering SRL among students are widely acknowledged, achieving this requires mindful instructional design. SRL skills are not innate traits, but rather a set of skills that can be cultivated in any classroom context through guided practice (Pintrich, 1999). Hence, all students have the potential to develop them in different educational settings, with teachers playing a key role in developing students into self-regulated learners (Dignath & Büttner, 2018; Karlen et al., 2020). A balanced integration of these skills as part of the learning process contributes to learners' development and improved achievement (Hong et al., 2021; Zimmerman, 2008), Therefore, effective methods are needed to foster the development of these skills in educational settings so that students can thrive as independent, self-regulated learners.

Online learning environments provide opportunities to foster SRL by promoting independent learning and engagement (Ingkavara et al., 2022; Sutarni et al., 2021). In particular, with the emergence of new opportunities provided by Generative AI (GenAI) tools such as chatbots, teachers can enhance learners' SRL development through adaptive support, personalized feedback, and scaffolded problem-solving processes (Dwivedi et al., 2023). It is important to acknowledge that the effectiveness of these technologies depends heavily on teachers' ability to integrate them meaningfully into their instructional design (Backfisch et al., 2021). This highlights how teacher education programs should equip future educators with the professional competencies—knowledge, skills, and pedagogical beliefs—that enrich instruction through technology-enhanced learning conducive to SRL development (Karlen et al., 2023; Huang & Lajoie, 2021; Sáiz-Manzanares et al., 2022).

Despite this, assessing teachers' SRL-supportive instruction remains a challenge. Current assessment primarily relies on self-report instruments and teachers' subjective perceptions (Zimmerman, 2008), rather than their actual capacity to plan and implement SRL-oriented teaching. The literature highlights a significant gap between self-reported data and actual performance, raising concerns about the reliability of these tools to holistically evaluate SRL-supportive instruction (Bernacki et al. 2012; Jansen et al., 2016; Winne & Jamieson-Noel, 2003). Thus, alternative assessment methods are needed that reflect how teachers conceptualize instruction to foster SRL skills development.

Lesson plans are a core aspect of teacher professional practice, as they guide teachers before implementation in the classroom (Ndihokubwayo et al., 2022). Further to their practical application, they provide insights regarding educational thinking, pedagogical decision-making, and the ability to design SRL-supportive instruction in technology-enhanced settings. Thus, they offer a promising method to evaluate these competencies. This novel assessment approach is particularly valuable since direct observation is often limited and not feasible; for example, pre-service teachers often do not have their own classrooms. Hence, lesson plans serve as structured instruments for evaluating instructional coherence and alignment with learning objectives (Drost & Levine, 2017). Therefore, analyzing lesson plans can serve as an alternative structured means to gauge how effectively teachers integrate SRL and technology into their instructional design.

This study primarily considers the potential of lesson plans as a performance-based assessment tool for evaluating pre-service teachers' competence in integrating SRL strategies into their instructional design, particularly through the integration of GenAI tools. Rather than assessing explicit SRL implementation, it examines how these strategies are embedded in lesson plans while analyzing pedagogical decision-making and technology integration. The present qualitative study identifies SRL strategies, assesses pedagogical competence through the Situational-Specific Skills (PID- Perception, interpretation and decision making) model (Blömeke et al., 2015), and measures the quality of technology integration as discussed in Backfisch et al. (2021), particularly regarding the use of GenAI tools to support SRL development. An evidence-based framework can be useful for assessing SRL-oriented digital pedagogical competencies and can contribute to more authentic evaluation instructional design. In this way, it can capture how future educators conceptualize and plan SRL-supportive instruction, leveraging GenAI tools within technology-enhanced learning environments.

The current research

Research objective and question

This research aims to explore the potential of lesson plans as a performance-based assessment tool for evaluating pre-service teachers' competence in designing SRL-supportive instruction within online learning environments, specifically with the use of GenAI tools. By analyzing how SRL strategies, pedagogical competence, and technology integration – particularly the use of GenAI – are embedded in lesson plans, this study seeks to provide insights into pre-service teachers' instructional thinking before they enter the classroom. Additionally, the study demonstrates whether lesson plans can serve as a viable alternative to self-report measures in evaluating their readiness to foster SRL in technology-driven classrooms.

Consequently, this research is driven by the question: How can lesson plans serve as performance-based assessment tools for evaluating pre-service teachers' competence in designing SRL-supportive instruction, enhanced by GenAI tools?

Research methodology

The present study employs a qualitative research approach which involved pre-service teachers in a digital pedagogical course at a big University as part of their teaching certificate studies. The 73 participants came from diverse backgrounds in regards to age, gender, prior teaching experience, and subject expertise (social sciences and humanities). The study was conducted in an 11-session online (synchronous and asynchronous) intervention course designed to enhance digital and pedagogical competencies that foster SRL in future classrooms. Each session lasted 90 minutes and included foundational SRL concepts and explicit instructions on chatbot integration. Participants engaged with cognitive, metacognitive, and motivational SRL strategies through hands-on activities online (synchronous and asynchronous), supported by innovative tools like Video-based Assisted Self-Regulated Learning Training (VAST) (Cohen et al., 2022) and Gen-AI chatbots, such as ChatGPT.

To complete the course requirements, pre-service teachers were asked to submit lesson plans, individually or in groups (according to their preferences), as a summative assessment task. Lesson plan They followed a three-stage process in developing and submitting their lesson plans: First, pre-service teachers designed a lesson aimed at strengthening students' problem-solving strategies and SRL skills during emergencies. They were instructed to integrate a GenAI chatbot to support independent learning within the context of a specific discipline or as part of a general lesson. Next, pre-service teachers were required to outline clear learning objectives, both related to academic goals as well as the development of SRL skills and describe the four main stages of the lesson. These stages consisted of a) an introduction, b) an instruction which incorporates the chatbot, c) a problem-solving activity that dominates the lesson, and d) a concluding evaluation. Every phase of this lesson would be allowed 15 minutes to complete, with the exception of the problem-solving activity (c), which would require 45 minutes. The pre-service teachers were also asked to develop a rubric to assess students' fulfilment of the lesson objectives and measure how effectively they demonstrated SRL skills. They were also required to propose methods for collecting feedback on the chatbot's role in facilitating learning and engagement of their students during the lesson. Third, pre-service teachers were asked to submit their lesson plans on the LMS system (Moodle) to complete the final course requirement. The guidelines for the lesson plans are presented in figure 1.

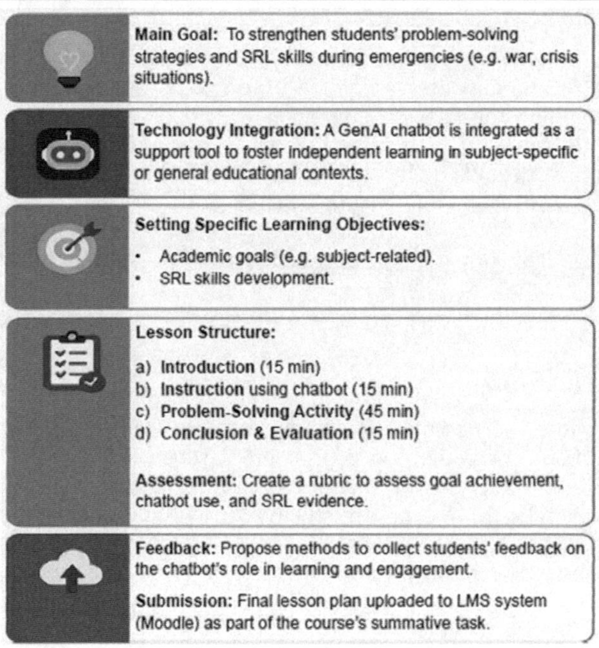

Figure 1: Overview of structured guidelines provided to pre-service teachers for lesson plan development.

A total of 37 lesson plans were retrieved from the university's Moodle system after obtaining informed consent. These lesson plans represented pre-service teachers' instructional thinking (PID), applications of SRL skills, and quality of technology integration.

The analysis was carried out in a structured process. First, lesson plans were individually reviewed to glean initial impressions and identify emerging themes aligned with the research questions and the grounded theoretical frameworks. A second shared reading and discussion confirmed key characteristics. In the third reading, data was coded according to these characteristics. A final shared review ensured consistency and accuracy in coding. Throughout the process, the researchers met to refine labels and reexamine data. They also documented insights related to the research questions.

Lesson plans were analyzed using a structured framework encompassing three key dimensions: SRL strategies, technology integration, and pedagogical competence. Each dimension was assessed based on its role in supporting SRL and instructional effectiveness (see Table 1).

Table 1: Three-Dimensional Framework for Analyzing SRL-Supportive Lesson Plans

Dimension	Guiding Question	Key Components	Evaluation Criteria
SRL Strategies- What to Teach	How does the teacher foster self-regulated learning?	SRL strategies such as goal-setting, self-monitoring, help-seeking, critical thinking, time planning, elaboration, self-evaluation	Explicitness, student autonomy, scaffolding, strategy type (cognitive, metacognitive, motivational)
Technology Integration – Support for Teaching	How does technology support the learning process?	Instructional guidance, technology innovativeness, adaptive methods, multimodality, interactivity	Cognitive challenge, knowledge construction, student engagement, instructional clarity, GenAI integration
Pedagogical Competence (PID) – How to Teach	How does the teacher anticipate and respond to student learning needs?	Perception, interpretation, decision-making	Perception (0-3), interpretation (0-3), decision-making (0-3)

As shown in table 1, all lessons were assessed based on these three areas:

- **SRL strategies implementation:** Lesson plans were examined to identify SRL strategies (e.g. goal-setting, help-seeking, critical thinking, elaboration, and self-monitoring), with emphasis on how they emerged in the lesson, the use of scaffolding, and promotion of student autonomy.
- **The pedagogical competence:** The PID model (Blömeke et al., 2015) was adapted to evaluate how pre-service teachers anticipate student engagement, identify learning challenges, interpret student needs, and make pedagogical decisions. Given that pre-service teachers lack classroom experience, lesson plans were analyzed as indicators of their instructional reasoning. The PID scoring elements evaluating Perception, Interpretation and Decision-Making were assessed on four levels: outstanding (9 points), strong (6-8 points), needs improvement (3-5 points), and insufficient (0-2 points)
- **Technology integration:** The role of technology, particularly GenAI tools, was analyzed for its efficacy in challenging cognitive processes, creating opportunities for knowledge construction, facilitating student participation, and promoting instructional guidance. Technology integration assessment examined five elements as identified by Backfisch et al. (2021): instructional guidance, technology innovativeness, adaptive methods, multimodality, and interactivity. Each factor was measured on a 0-3 scale and evaluated technology integration quality, from no integration (0) to partial integration (1), moderate inclusion (2), and fully high-quality implementation (3).

This approach provided a structured way to assess how pre-service teachers incorporate SRL, pedagogical reasoning, and technology into their lesson plans to foster students' SRL skills.

One limitation of this study was that it was not always clear whether the lesson plans accurately reflected instructional intentions. It could be argued that the participants may have intended to incorporate SRL strategies, but they did not explicitly document them. However, in order to develop effective teaching practices, pre-service teachers must learn to articulate their instructional decisions plainly. Encouraging them to explicitly write their intentions ensures that their pedagogical reasoning is both carefully considered and able to support SRL in their teaching practices. Moreover, this study was limited by a small sample of pre-service teachers from a single university program, though the findings supported the development of a preliminary framework for evaluating lesson plans. Future research will include more participants to further refine and strengthen this assessment framework.

Findings and discussion

This study explored lesson plans as performance-based assessment tools for evaluating pre-service teachers' ability to design SRL-supportive instruction assisted by GenAI tools. Using theoretical frameworks of SRL (Pintrich, 2000), PID (Blömeke et al., 2015), and Technology Integration (Backfisch et al., 2021), the analysis revealed varying levels of SRL integration, pedagogical competence, and technology use across lesson plans.

Lesson plans brought to light considerable variability in how pre-service teachers incorporated SRL strategies. High-quality plans explicitly structured goal-setting, self-monitoring, and autonomy scaffolds with clear instructional rationales, often leveraging GenAI for real-time feedback and metacognitive guidance. In contrast, less effective plans included SRL elements without systematic implementation, aligning with Zimmerman's (2002) finding that explicit SRL instruction produces better outcomes than implicit approaches. From a pedagogical competence perspective, lesson plans with clear SRL rationales demonstrated stronger foresight, effectively differentiating various levels of teaching competence. These variations reveal how lesson plans effectively assess pre-service teachers' understanding and application of SRL principles.

Student autonomy development emerged as another critical factor through the analysis of the lesson plans. More effective lesson plans showed gradual responsibility transitions from teacher-led to student-driven learning, ensuring that students developed independent regulation skills. As such, an emergency preparedness lesson demonstrated this progression, using AI-generated scenarios to develop independent problem-solving skills applicable to real-world contexts. This approach aligns with Hoidn and Reusser (2020), who emphasize that gradual autonomy-building is essential for effective SRL development. In contrast, less structured plans failed to explicitly frame GenAI as a cognitive support tool, leaving students passively interacting with technology rather than engaging in active self-regulation. Results from the pedagogical analysis indicate that many lesson plans scored higher on perception and interpretation components than decision-making elements. This suggests that pre-service teachers often anticipate classroom needs, yet they struggle to address them appropriately, revealing gaps in structuring GenAI to support SRL effectively. These differential patterns in pedagogical reasoning demonstrate how lesson plans can identify specific developmental needs in pre-service teachers' instructional competence.

Technology integration as SRL supportive instruction varied significantly across lesson plans. Some of them effectively utilized GenAI tools for adaptive feedback and metacognitive monitoring, thus supporting SRL development. A drama-based lesson demonstrated this approach by using an AI chatbot to analyze character emotions, facilitating emotional regulation and reflection. This aligns with the SAMR model (Romrell et al., 2014), stating that technology is most effective when it moves beyond substitution to modification and redefinition, thus fostering active engagement rather than passive content delivery. Other plans employed technology in a superficial manner, limiting its effectiveness, and reducing its potential to support deeper self-regulation. Pre-service teachers who aligned GenAI with instructional goals demonstrated stronger pedagogical decision-making, while others integrated technology without clear instructional alignment, lacking justification for GenAI use beyond simple automation. This aligns with Flores and Day's (2006) research, indicating that beginning teachers often identify students' difficulties but require additional support to develop interventions that meet students' needs. These distinctions in technology integration quality demonstrate how lesson plans can effectively assess pre-service teachers' technological-pedagogical knowledge specifically related to using GenAI for fostering SRL.

Implications and Contributions

Building on these insights, the present study suggests a novel assessment framework for evaluating pre-service teachers' SRL-oriented digital-pedagogical competencies, emphasizing the role of GenAI in fostering SRL. The applied integrated analytical framework—examining SRL strategies, pedagogical competence, and technology integration—provides teacher educators with a practical alternative to self-report measures for evaluating instructional design capabilities. The structured analysis of lesson plans offers teacher educators an alternative to traditional self-report measures, providing more objective evaluation of instructional design capabilities. Furthermore, it reveals how teachers conceptualize and justify SRL-supportive instruction enhanced by GenAI tools.

Future research should investigate how lesson plan assessments correlate with classroom teaching effectiveness, and how teacher education programs can enhance pre-service teachers' ability to design SRL-supportive, technology-enhanced learning environments.

Competing interests

The author(s) has/have no competing interests to declare.

Ethics and consent

Research ethics approval was granted by the Institutional Review Board (IRB), approval # 0008223-3, on 25 November 2024. Consent to participate and consent to publish were provided.

Acknowledgements

This research is supported by the Science and Technology Education Center (SATEC) at Tel-Aviv University.

Funding Information

Research was funded by the EU grant 101132603.

References

Alderman, M. K., & MacDonald, S. (2015). A self-regulatory approach to classroom management: Empowering students and teachers. Kappa Delta Pi Record, 51(2), 52-56.

Backfisch, I., Lachner, A., Stürmer, K., & Scheiter, K. (2021). Variability of teachers' technology integration in the classroom: A matter of utility!. Computers & Education, 166, 104159.

Bernacki, M. L., Byrnes, J. P., & Cromley, J. G. (2012). The effects of achievement goals and self-regulated learning behaviors on reading comprehension in technology-enhanced learning environments. Contemporary Educational Psychology, 37(2), 148-161.

Blömeke, S., Hoth, J., Döhrmann, M., Busse, A., Kaiser, G., & König, J. (2015). Teacher change during induction: Development of beginning primary teachers' knowledge, beliefs and performance. International Journal of Science and Mathematics Education, 13, 287-308.

Bogdány, E., Cserhati, G., & Raffay-Danyi, Á. (2023). A proposed methodology for mapping and ranking competencies that HRM graduates need. The International Journal of Management Education, 21(2), 100789.

Cohen, G., Assi, A., Cohen, A., Bronshtein, A., Glick, D., Gabbay, H., & Ezra, O. (2022). Video-Assisted Self-Regulated Learning (SRL) Training: COVID-19 Edition. In Lecture notes in computer science (pp. 59–73). https://doi.org/10.1007/978-3-031-16290-9_5

Drost, B. R., & Levine, A. C. (2015). An analysis of strategies for teaching standards-based lesson plan alignment to preservice teachers. Journal of Education, 195(2), 37-47.

Dwivedi, Y. K., Kshetri, N., Hughes, L., Slade, E. L., Jeyaraj, A., Kar, A. K., ... & Wright, R. (2023). "So what if ChatGPT wrote it?" Multidisciplinary perspectives on opportunities, challenges and implications of generative conversational AI for research, practice and policy. International Journal of Information Management, 71, 1-63. https://doi.org/10.1016/j.ijinfomgt.2023.102642

Dignath, C., and Büttner, G. (2018). Teachers' direct and indirect promotion of self-regulated learning in primary and secondary school mathematics classes - insights from video-based classroom observations and teacher interviews. Metacogn. Learn. 13, 127–157. doi: 10.1007/s11409-018-9181-x

Hong, J. C., Lee, Y. F., & Ye, J. H. (2021). Procrastination predicts online self-regulated learning and online learning ineffectiveness during the coronavirus lockdown. Personality and individual differences, 174, 110673.

Huang, L., & Lajoie, S. P. (2021). Process analysis of teachers' self-regulated learning patterns in technological pedagogical content knowledge development. Computers & Education, 166, 104169.

Hoidn, S., & Reusser, K. (2020). Foundations of Student-Centered Learning and Teaching. In Routledge eBooks (pp. 17–18). https://doi.org/10.4324/9780429259371-3

Ingkavara, T., Panjaburee, P., Srisawasdi, N., & Sajjapanroj, S. (2022). The use of a personalized learning approach to implementing self-regulated online learning. Computers and Education: Artificial Intelligence, 3, 100086.

Jansen, R. S., Van Leeuwen, A., Janssen, J., Kester, L., & Kalz, M. (2017). Validation of the self-regulated online learning questionnaire. Journal of computing in higher education, 29(1), 6-27.

Karlen, Y., Hertel, S., & Hirt, C. N. (2020). Teachers' Professional Competences in Self-Regulated Learning: An approach to integrate teachers' competences as Self-Regulated learners and as agents of Self-Regulated learning in a holistic manner. Frontiers in Education, 5. https://doi.org/10.3389/feduc.2020.00159

Karlen, Y., Hirt, C. N., Jud, J., Rosenthal, A., & Eberli, T. D. (2023). Teachers as learners and agents of self-regulated learning: The importance of different teachers competence aspects for promoting metacognition. Teaching and Teacher Education, 125, 104055.

Moffitt, T. E., Arseneault, L., Belsky, D., Dickson, N., Hancox, R. J., Harrington, H., et al. (2011). A gradient of childhood self-control predicts health, wealth, and public safety. Proceedings of the National Academy of Sciences, 108(7), 2693–2698

Ndihokubwayo, K., Byukusenge, C., Byusa, E., Habiyaremye, H. T., Mbonyiryivuze, A., & Mukagihana, J. (2022). Lesson plan analysis protocol (LPAP): A useful tool for researchers and educational evaluators. Heliyon, 8(1), e08730. https://doi.org/10.1016/j.heliyon.2022.e08730

Pintrich, P. R. (1999). The role of motivation in promoting and sustaining self-regulated learning. International journal of educational research, 31(6), 459-470.

Pintrich, P. R. (2000). The Role of Goal Orientation in Self-Regulated Learning. In Handbook of Self-Regulation (pp. 451–502). Elsevier. https://doi.org/10.1016/B978-012109890-2/50043-3

Romrell, D., Kidder, L., & Wood, E. (2014). The SAMR Model as a Framework for Evaluating mLearning. The Journal Of Asynchronous Learning Networks, 18(2). Retrieved from http://olj.onlinelearningconsortium.org/Index.php/jaln/article/view/435

Sáiz-Manzanares, M. C., Almeida, L. S., Martín-Antón, L. J., Carbonero, M. A., & Valdivieso-Burón, J. A. (2022). Teacher training effectiveness in self-regulation in virtual environments. Frontiers in Psychology, 13, 776806.

Savina, E. (2021). Self-regulation in preschool and early elementary classrooms: Why it is important and how to promote it. Early Childhood Education Journal, 49(3), 493–501.

Sutarni, N., Ramdhany, M. A., Hufad, A., & Kurniawan, E. (2021). Self-regulated learning and digital learning environment: Its' effect on academic achievement during the pandemic. Cakrawala Pendidikan, 40(2), 374-388.

Taranto, D., & Buchanan, M. T. (2020). Sustaining lifelong learning: A self-regulated learning (SRL) approach. Discourse and Communication for Sustainable Education, 11(1), 5-15.

Winne, P. H., & Jamieson-Noel, D. (2003). Self-regulating studying by objectives for learning: Students' reports compared to a model. Contemporary educational psychology, 28(3), 259-276.

Wong, J., Baars, M., Davis, D., Van Der Zee, T., Houben, G., & Paas, F. (2018). Supporting Self-Regulated Learning in Online Learning Environments and MOOCs: A Systematic Review. International Journal of Human-Computer Interaction, 35(4–5), 356–373. https://doi.org/10.1080/10447318.2018.1543084

Xu, Z., Zhao, Y., Liew, J., Zhou, X., & Kogut, A. (2023). Synthesizing research evidence on self-regulated learning and academic achievement in online and blended learning environments: A scoping review. Educational Research Review, 39, 100510.

Zimmerman, B. J. (2002). Becoming a self-regulated learner: An overview. Theory into practice, 41(2), 64-70.

Zimmerman, B. J. (2008). Investigating Self-Regulation and Motivation: Historical Background, Methodological Developments, and Future Prospects. American Educational Research Journal, 45(1), 166–183. https://doi.org/10.3102/0002831207312909

Beyond AI Awareness: How Institutions Are Strategically and Pedagogically Embedding AI Skills Development

Angela Gunder[1], Melissa Vito[2], Marcela Ramirez[3], Cristi Ford[4]

[1] The University of Arizona, United States; agunder@arizona.edu
[2] The University of Texas at San Antonio, United States; melissa.vito@utsa.edu
[3] The University of Texas at San Antonio, United States; marcela.ramirez@utsa.edu
[4] D2L, United States; cristi.ford@D2L.com

Correspondence: Angela Gunder: angela@openedculture.org

Abstract:

As artificial intelligence (AI) reshapes the contours of higher education, institutions are increasingly shifting from isolated experimentation toward strategic, systemic approaches for building AI competencies. This paper examines emergent practices from a range of institutions—including public research universities, Minority-Serving Institutions (MSIs), and professional networks—that are embedding AI literacies into faculty development, curriculum design, institutional planning, and distance learning environments. Drawing from the authors' direct involvement in cross-sector collaborations and professional learning initiatives, this paper surfaces how AI skills development is being scaffolded over time, shaped by mission, and aligned with long-term organizational strategy. Using an ethnographically informed qualitative approach, the authors spotlight patterns in implementation, challenges in sustainability and policy, and the cultural conditions necessary for pedagogically grounded, ethically aware, and contextually responsive AI integration. The findings underscore that institutions treating AI not merely as a technical upgrade but as a catalyst for reimagining teaching, leadership, and academic infrastructure are better positioned to build future-ready, human-centered educational ecosystems.

Keywords: AI literacies, AI competency development, faculty development, institutional strategy, AI-integrated curriculum, workforce alignment

Introduction

The rapid evolution of artificial intelligence (AI) is exerting transformative pressure on higher education institutions worldwide. While AI has long featured in educational systems through analytics, recommendation engines, and automation, recent advances in generative AI and large language models demand a more profound rethinking of teaching, learning, and institutional operations. In this context, higher education institutions face the challenge not merely of understanding new tools, but of developing coherent, sustainable strategies to foster AI literacies across faculty, staff, and leadership (Miao & Cukurova, 2024; Bozkurt, 2023b; Cardona et al., 2023).Many early institutional responses to AI have been reactive: isolated faculty experiments, scattered workshops, and narrowly technical training. These efforts, while often well-intentioned, fall short of equipping educators to navigate AI's pedagogical, ethical, and strategic implications. A more robust approach requires institutions to design AI skills initiatives that are both developmental and systemic—providing differentiated support over time, grounded in pedagogy, aligned with institutional strategy, and attentive to cultural context (Miao & Cukurova, 2024; Castillo-Martínez et al., 2024).

This paper examines a series of case examples that reflect this emerging paradigm. It draws on qualitative data from institutions across the United States, including large public research universities, Minority-Serving Institutions (MSIs), and cross-institutional consortia. MSIs—which include Historically Black Colleges and Universities (HBCUs) and Hispanic-Serving Institutions (HSIs)—offer particularly instructive examples of innovation within resource-constrained environments. These institutions have begun to move beyond AI awareness toward structured capacity-building efforts: faculty learning communities, tiered professional development, AI-integrated curriculum design, and collaborative knowledge-sharing networks. The findings illustrate how AI skills development is being embedded into leadership development, equity-centered pedagogy, and institutional planning.

Across these cases, a common insight emerges: educators and learners require different kinds of support at different stages of readiness. This insight has proven especially important in contexts where infrastructural or staffing limitations are pronounced, yet where innovation and community-led experimentation are actively thriving. Institutions that recognize AI not as a siloed technology but as a vector for institutional and pedagogical transformation are building the strongest foundations for sustainable change (Zawacki-Richter et al., 2019; Bozkurt, 2024).

The authors draw upon their collective experiences supporting AI strategy and professional learning across a wide range of institutional and organizational contexts. Their roles include leading academic innovation units within public research universities, designing digital learning and assessment strategy for organizations globally, conducting empirical research studies on AI competencies and skills, and building custom professional development solutions for postsecondary institutions internationally. These professional vantage points have enabled the authors to collaborate directly with schools, regional consortia, and international networks to support AI-related faculty development and institutional strategy. The insights presented in this paper reflect both formal research engagements and applied consultation, grounded in first-hand experience facilitating AI capacity-building efforts across multiple educational systems and cultural contexts.

Emergent Strategies for AI Competency Development Across Institutions

From Disparate Training to Coordinated Skill-Building

Higher education institutions are beginning to converge on a shared recognition: building AI competency is no longer a matter of one-off workshops or isolated experimentation. Institutions that once relied on stand-alone sessions or informal communities of interest are shifting toward more structured models that offer sustained professional learning and development. These approaches reflect a growing understanding that AI is not a passing trend, but a generational shift in how knowledge is created, evaluated, and applied in academic environments.

At the foundation of these efforts is a pluralistic understanding of AI literacies, recognizing that the competencies needed to navigate, implement, and critique AI vary by context, role, and disciplinary lens (Opened Culture, n.d.; Belshaw, 2023). Drawing from Opened Culture's Dimensions of AI Literacies, which defines AI literacies as "encompass(ing) the skills needed to comprehend, utilize, and critically evaluate AI within complex environments" (Opened Culture, n.d., para. 1), institutions are designing learning ecosystems that honor this complexity. This includes not only building technical skills but also cultivating the critical, civic, communicative, and creative capacities needed to engage AI ethically and imaginatively in education. Tiered development models, structured around this multidimensional view, support early exploration while creating meaningful onramps for deeper, role-specific engagement (Maznev et al., 2024; Almasri, 2024).

Approaches Rooted in Institutional Mission and Context

Among the most compelling strategies are those emerging from MSIs in the US, including both HBCUs and HSIs. These institutions often frame AI not only as a technological skill but as a pedagogical and institutional strategy for expanding access and increasing student opportunity. Rather than isolating AI within technical fields, institutions are embedding AI into broader conversations about how knowledge is shaped and who it serves—ensuring that new tools reflect the cultural and intellectual traditions of their communities (Bali, 2024a; Bali, 2024b; Gupta et al., 2024).

Professional learning communities at these institutions function as critical spaces for reflection, collaborative inquiry, and mutual support. Participants engage with AI tools while simultaneously raising questions about representation in training data, the local relevance of generated content, and the preservation of human judgment in teaching. These initiatives model how institutions can respond to technological change without compromising their commitments to student belonging and academic rigor.

Student Partnerships and Collaborative Ecosystems

Several institutions highlighted the value of inviting students into faculty development processes. Student-led learning communities, ambassador programs, and co-designed course elements are being used to bridge gaps between institutional strategy and student practice. These efforts recognize that many learners are already using AI in creative and productive ways—and that their perspectives can shape more responsive, future-ready teaching.

Beyond individual institutions, partnerships and networks have also played a critical role in scaling efforts. Institutions with limited resources are increasingly joining regional or consortial efforts to share tools, frameworks, and learning design models. These collaborations not only reduce duplication but foster shared accountability and mutual growth, especially across institutions serving historically underrepresented student populations.

Aligning AI Literacies with Institutional Strategy

Finally, some institutions are extending AI competency development beyond the classroom, integrating it into strategic planning and leadership development. This includes scenario-based retreats for senior leaders, strategy mapping sessions that foreground AI-readiness, and multi-stakeholder advisory groups. In these settings, AI is not treated solely as a teaching tool but as a strategic lever—one that intersects with everything from enrollment forecasting to student support infrastructures.

These examples illustrate a broader maturation in how institutions approach AI literacy. Rather than focusing solely on adoption, they are beginning to prioritize coherence, intentionality, and long-term adaptability. The shift reflects a deeper understanding: building AI capacity is not simply about keeping up with technological trends but about preparing institutions—and the communities they serve—for a fundamentally different knowledge environment.

Analysis and Reflections on Implementation

Efforts to embed AI competencies within higher education institutions are revealing both the potential and complexity of organizational learning. While institutions have adopted diverse models to build AI literacies, the success of these efforts often hinges on how they are implemented, aligned, and sustained over time. This section synthesizes findings from across institutional types to examine the design, execution, and ongoing evolution of AI capacity-building initiatives.

Differentiated Support as a Design Imperative

A consistent theme across the case examples collected by the authors is the importance of providing differentiated support to meet the varied needs of faculty and staff. Just as critical, however, is cultivating a culture of experimentation, openness, and play—one that encourages faculty to try new tools without fear of failure, to reimagine familiar practices, and to reflect collectively on outcomes. Successful initiatives framed AI not as a compliance requirement, but as an invitation to creative problem-solving and pedagogical risk-taking. This cultural shift, reinforced through peer communities, iterative design cycles, and leadership modeling, helped reduce resistance and fostered environments where learning and innovation were seen as shared institutional values.

Institutions that grounded their offerings in real-world teaching contexts—rather than generic tool overviews—reported stronger faculty engagement and retention. Particularly effective were project-based approaches in which participants redesigned a course component, built an assessment, or developed new policies informed by AI. This "learn by doing" model was often paired with peer learning structures, enabling participants to exchange strategies and reflect on implementation in real time.

Furthermore, organizations with limited resources and personnel noted that this layered model was essential in environments where staffing and instructional support were limited. By structuring initiatives to unfold over time—rather than relying on one-time workshops—institutions allowed participants to develop confidence gradually while integrating AI into their practices in authentic ways.

Institutional Alignment and Strategic Framing

Another key success factor was the degree to which AI skills development was framed as part of a broader institutional vision. At institutions where these efforts were clearly linked to student success, future-readiness, and digital transformation, buy-in was significantly higher among faculty and leadership alike. In contrast, where AI work remained siloed in individual departments or disconnected from institutional planning, engagement was more sporadic and outcomes were harder to sustain.

Some institutions formalized AI capacity-building within their strategic plans, while others created cross-functional advisory groups that included representation from academic affairs, instructional design, IT, and student services. These structures allowed for coordination across roles and departments, avoiding redundancy and ensuring that AI was integrated into multiple dimensions of institutional life.

Programs that received visible support from senior leadership—through communications, funding, or formal recognition—benefited from increased participation and greater internal legitimacy. In these settings, educators were more likely to perceive their engagement with AI not as extra work, but as part of their contribution to shaping the future of the institution.

Navigating Policy, Ethics, and Infrastructure

While enthusiasm for AI experimentation remains high, implementation efforts also surfaced a range of institutional tensions—particularly around policy gaps, ethical considerations, and technical infrastructure. Educators frequently raised concerns about responsible use of generative AI, data privacy, and the lack of clear guidance on classroom implementation (Smolansky et al., 2023; Gupta et al., 2024). In many cases, these concerns delayed adoption or led to uneven uptake, especially in disciplines where AI was making historical assessment practices in need of reimagination and redesign obsolete.

Some institutions responded by convening internal ethics working groups or AI policy task forces, drawing on faculty expertise to co-develop practical guidelines. These collaborative approaches often led to more nuanced paths forward rather than rote policy creation—paths that accounted for the variability across courses and disciplines while still providing a baseline of institutional consistency.

Infrastructure challenges were also prominent. Institutions with robust digital learning support systems were better positioned to scale AI training across departments. Others reported difficulties in onboarding educators and learners due to limited access to generative AI platforms, inconsistent campus messaging, or administrative uncertainty about licensing and risk. These issues point to the need for clearer governance models—ones that provide flexibility for experimentation but also ensure that institutional values and learner needs remain central.

Sustaining Momentum and Measuring Impact

A final challenge in implementation observed was ensuring sustainability beyond the initial phase of investment and interest. Faculty noted that enthusiasm can wane without continued opportunities for engagement, recognition of effort, and integration into long-term professional pathways. Institutions that addressed this challenge effectively tended to adopt models that included ongoing communities of practice, integration of AI literacies development into recognition structures, or iterative fellowships that encouraged participants to take on mentorship roles in subsequent cohorts.

Several institutions acknowledged that they were still developing appropriate measures for success. While many could point to increased faculty participation or the creation of AI-enhanced courses, few had formal metrics in place to evaluate long-term impact on student learning, curricular coherence, or institutional agility. This lack of evaluation capacity underscores the importance of pairing implementation with a learning strategy—one that uses feedback loops, research partnerships, or annual reviews to assess both progress and persistent gaps.

Despite these challenges, institutions that approached AI skills development as a cultural and structural project—rather than a technical or compliance-oriented one—demonstrated greater staying power. By building adaptable, mission-aligned models rooted in local context, they created the conditions for deeper engagement and more meaningful transformation.

Implications for Distance Education Practice and Policy

The strategies institutions are using to build AI competencies among faculty and staff carry specific relevance for distance education, where digital infrastructures, asynchronous delivery models, and evolving expectations of learner autonomy create unique opportunities and constraints. The case examples examined in this paper offer practical insights for designing reimagined learning experiences that are not only technologically current, but pedagogically sound and strategically responsive to AI's growing influence on higher education.

Designing for Scalability and Responsiveness

Distance education environments are often first to encounter new digital technologies, yet are also at greater risk of superficial adoption due to scale, variability in instructor training, and uneven institutional support. The faculty development models described in this study—particularly those emphasizing layered engagement, interdisciplinary collaboration, and iterative design—demonstrate how AI competency-building can be adapted to distributed learning environments.

Institutions investing in AI literacies development for online educators and learners alike emphasized the importance of self-paced, modular content paired with cohort-based or community-supported engagement. Instructors teaching remotely or across multiple course sections noted the value of having flexible entry points into professional development that still offered structured guidance and collaborative opportunities. Particularly effective were microcredential pathways or fellowship programs that allowed instructors to build AI-related expertise over time, apply it to their course design work, and share outcomes with peers in facilitated learning environments.

Distance learning units can also play a critical strategic role in institutional AI planning, given their experience with instructional technology, course design at scale, and supporting the differentiated needs of learner populations (Xiao, 2024). As institutions consider how to structure AI-enabled learning pathways, design personalized feedback loops, or integrate predictive analytics into student support, these units are well-positioned to shape responsible and contextually relevant practices.

Supporting Learner Belonging and Instructional Flexibility

One of the clearest findings from the authors assessment is that AI integration in distance education requires ongoing attention to student belonging, not just personalization or efficiency. Faculty and instructional designers expressed concern that overuse of generative tools in online spaces might increase transactional distance or diminish the relational aspects of digital learning (Bozkurt, 2023b; van den Berg, 2024). In contrast, institutions that emphasized reflective and intentional use of AI—with attention to tone, cultural specificity, and student voice—were more likely to see instructors design interactions that fostered presence, dialogue, and connection.

Some institutions supported this by offering structured guidance or case examples that guided educators (including faculty, instructional designers, and administrators) through scenarios of ethical AI use in online learning contexts. Others introduced reflective practices into AI training, asking educators to consider when automation enhances learning and when it may obscure the instructor's voice and expertise or the student's agency. These pedagogical tools helped ensure that AI was integrated not simply as a time-saver, but as a means of expanding access, responsiveness, and representation in online courses.

In addition, programs that included students in the development of AI-enhanced distance education offerings saw benefits in both design quality and learner alignment. Student consultants, interns, or peer ambassadors provided real-time feedback on how AI tools were being experienced from the learner side, and often surfaced accessibility or cultural resonance issues that instructors had not anticipated (Chan & Lee, 2023; van Wyk et al., 2023).

Governance for AI in Distributed Learning

Several institutions noted the absence of coherent AI policy frameworks for online learning—particularly in areas such as academic integrity, feedback generation, and grading automation. While some campuses had initiated internal policy discussions, most reported that their AI guidance documents had not been fully adapted to the unique context of distance education.

This gap presents both a challenge and an opportunity. Institutions that are early in this work may benefit from building guidelines directly into the design of AI professional learning initiatives. Faculty learning communities and instructional design teams can play a role in generating values-aligned guidelines that address core questions, including: Are new policies actually needed, or are current policies or guidelines able to be used with regards to broader digital tool usage? What degree of automation is appropriate for formative feedback in asynchronous classes? How should institutions disclose the use of AI-powered interventions to students? What safeguards are necessary to ensure the ethical use of student data in predictive systems?

Some institutions in this study were developing internal review boards, advisory committees, or scenario planning exercises specifically for distance learning units. These groups were charged with developing forward-looking governance practices that could evolve alongside the technology while remaining grounded in pedagogical and learner-centered commitments. By situating these conversations within cross-functional teams, institutions were better able to align policy with practice and reduce the burden on individual instructors to make complex AI decisions in isolation.

Ultimately, the authors observed a notable opportunity: distance education can serve as a strategic proving ground for institution-wide AI integration. With their established infrastructures, expertise in scale, and familiarity with digital experimentation, online learning units are uniquely positioned to lead AI implementation that is pedagogically rigorous, inclusive of varied learning needs, and strategically aligned with long-term planning.

Institutions that recognized and resourced this role—integrating distance education leaders into AI steering groups, elevating online instructors as peer mentors, and aligning AI development with digital learning strategy—were able to move more swiftly and coherently toward institutional readiness.

Conclusion and Future Directions

As AI continues to reshape the possibilities and pressures within higher education, institutions are increasingly being called to respond not only with awareness but with coherence, intentionality, and a long-term view of capacity building. The cases examined in this paper reflect a shift in mindset—from one-time technical interventions to sustained efforts aimed at building institutional fluency in navigating AI's instructional, ethical, and strategic dimensions.

Across these initiatives, several patterns emerged. Institutions that structured AI skills development as part of broader academic transformation efforts—rather than as discrete training events—were better positioned to sustain momentum and scale impact. Faculty learning communities, project-based cohorts, and scaffolded professional development models enabled educators to move from initial curiosity to applied confidence. When designed with flexibility, these models allowed faculty to experiment in ways that were grounded in context, responsive to learner needs, and connected to institutional mission.

This paper also highlights the critical role of institutional context and identity. MSIs in particular demonstrated how AI capacity-building can be closely tied to questions of representation, opportunity, and belonging. These institutions modeled how professional learning can be simultaneously future-oriented and community-rooted, ensuring that the adoption of new technologies does not come at the expense of culturally relevant pedagogy or shared institutional values.

The implications for distance education are equally significant. As digital learning becomes a primary site of innovation—and a central modality of instruction—institutions have an opportunity to position their online learning infrastructures and communities as strategic leaders in AI readiness. Doing so will require thoughtful governance, collaborative design, and continued investment in both people and systems.

Ultimately, numerous institutions taking a holistic approach to AI literacies development show the field pointed toward a promising trajectory. By treating AI as a driver of reflective practice, instructional innovation, and strategic foresight, they are building not just new technical competencies, but new capacities for organizational learning and adaptive leadership within a reimagined future of learning (Castillo-Martínez et al., 2024; World Economic Forum, 2022).

References

Almasri, F. (2024). Exploring the impact of artificial intelligence in teaching and learning of science: A systematic review of empirical research. Research in Science Education, 54(1), 977-997. https://doi.org/10.1007/s11165-024-10176-3

Bali, M. (2024a, February 26). Where are the crescents in AI? LSE Higher Education. https://blogs.lse.ac.uk/highereducation/2024/02/26/where-are-the-crescents-in-ai/

Bali, M. (2024b, October 15). Critical AI literacy is not enough: Introducing care literacy, equity literacy & teaching philosophies. A Slide Deck. Reflecting Allowed. https://blog.mahabali.me/educational-technology-2/critical-ai-literacy-is-not-enough-introducing-care-literacy-equity-literacy-teaching-philosophies-a-slide-deck/

Belshaw, D. (2014). The essential elements of digital literacies. https://dougbelshaw.com/essential-elements-book.pdf

Belshaw, D. (2023, March 18). Applying my digital literacies model to 'AI literacy.' Open Thinkering. https://dougbelshaw.com/blog/2023/03/18/ai-literacy/

Bozkurt, A. (2023b). Unleashing the potential of generative AI, conversational agents and chatbots in educational Praxis: A systematic review and bibliometric analysis of GenAI in education. Open Praxis, 15(4), 261–270. https://doi.org/10.55982/openpraxis.15.4.609

Bozkurt, A. (2024). GenAI et al.: Cocreation, authorship, ownership, academic ethics and integrity in a time of generative AI. Open Praxis, 16(1), 1–10. https://doi.org/10.55982/openpraxis.16.1.654

Cardona, M. A., Rodríguez, R. J., & Ishmael, K. (2023). Artificial intelligence and the future of teaching and learning: Insights and recommendations. United States Department of Education. https://tech.ed.gov/files/2023/05/ai-future-of-teaching-and-learning-report.pdf

Castillo-Martínez, I. M., Flores-Bueno, D., Gómez-Puente, S. M., & Vite-León, V. O. (2024). AI in higher education: a systematic literature review. Frontiers in Education, 9, 1391485. https://doi.org/10.3389/feduc.2024.1391485

Chan, C. K. Y. & Lee, K. K. W. (2023). The AI generation gap: Are Gen Z students more interested in adopting generative AI such as ChatGPT in teaching and learning than their Gen X and millennial generation teachers? Smart Learning Environments, 10(60). https://doi.org/10.1186/s40561-023-00269-3

Gupta, A., Atef, Y., Mills, A., & Bali, M. (2024). Assistant, parrot, or colonizing loudspeaker? ChatGPT metaphors for developing critical AI literacies. Open Praxis, 16(1), 37–53. https://doi.org/10.55982/openpraxis.16.1.631

Maznev, P., Stützer, C. M., & Gaaw, S. (2024). AI in higher education: Booster or stumbling block for developing digital competence? Zeitschrift für Hochschulentwicklung, 19(1), 120-135. https://doi.org/10.21240/zfhe/19-01/06

Miao, F., & Cukurova, M. (2024). AI competency framework for teachers. UNESCO. https://doi.org/10.54675/ZJTE2084

Opened Culture. (n.d.). Dimensions of AI literacies. Opened Culture. https://openedculture.org/projects/dimensions-of-ai-literacies/

Smolansky, A., Cram, A., Raduescu, C., Zeivots, S., Huber, E., & Kizilcec, R. F. (2023). Educator and student perspectives on the impact of generative AI on assessments in higher education. Proceedings of the Tenth ACM Conference on Learning @ Scale (L@S '23) (pp. 378-382). Association for Computing Machinery. https://doi.org/10.1145/3573051.3596191

van den Berg, G. (2024). Generative AI and educators: Partnering in using open digital content for transforming education. Open Praxis, 16(2), 130–141. https://doi.org/10.55982/openpraxis.16.2.640

van Wyk, M. M., Adarkwah, M. A., & Amponsah, S. (2023). Why all the hype about ChatGPT? Academics' views of a chat-based conversational learning strategy at an open distance e-learning institution. Open Praxis, 15(3), 214–225. https://doi.org/10.55982/openpraxis.15.3.563

World Economic Forum. (2022, June 29). A blueprint for equity and inclusion in artificial intelligence. World Economic Forum Publications. https://www.weforum.org/publications/a-blueprint-for-equity-and-inclusion-in-artificial-intelligence/

Xiao, J. (2024). Will artificial intelligence enable open universities to regain their past glory in the 21st century? Open Praxis, 16(1), 11–23. https://doi.org/10.55982/openpraxis.16.1.618

Zawacki-Richter, O., Marín, V. I., Bond, M., & Gouverneur, F. (2019). Systematic review of research on artificial intelligence applications in higher education – where are the educators? International Journal of Educational Technology in Higher Education, 16(39). https://doi.org/10.1186/s41239-019-0171-0

A systematic review of literacies and generative artificial intelligence in education: Evolving concepts, key themes, and directions for future research

Eduardo Junqueira[1]

[1]Instituto Universidade Virtual, Universidade Federal do Ceará, Brazil; eduardoj@virtual.ufc.br

Correspondence: Eduardo Junqueira: eduardoj@virtual.ufc.br

Abstract:

The paper presents the results of a systematic review of studies about evolving conceptualizations of literacies in light of the generative artificial intelligence phenomenon. Findings indicate two main groups of studies. There has been a more technicist perspective of AI literacy that highlights the positive transformations of these technologies to literacy practices and users' needed skills to incorporate and to better take advantage of them. The other group has articulated a more complex and nuanced perspective of AI literacy from a critical point of view, based on the prevalence of human agency and the need to reinforce users' critical thinking and ethical use of the technology. Future research may play a key role in informing the creation of effective pedagogical approaches that integrate GenAI ethically and responsibly, as well as in producing long-term data about the assessment of the impacts of GenAI on literacy development and critical thinking skills.

Keywords: Literacy; Generative Artificial Intelligence; Education; Literature Review.

Introduction: Literacy and Generative Artificial Intelligence

This paper presents the results of a systematic review that investigated the interplay between literacies and generative artificial intelligence (GenAI), particularly in the educational context. The fast proliferation and use of GenAI technologies, such as ChatGPT and DeepSeek, may transform how people interact with machines and use technologies to teach, study, and communicate. This transformative impact has already originated many studies from various countries that have investigated how GenAI influences old and new literacies. This review synthesized central findings from the most recent studies, demonstrating how GenAI is interfering with literacies in theory and practice. The presence of GenAI in education presents opportunities and challenges for all involved, requiring a more complex understanding of its impact and transformation on literacy today.

The core objective of this paper is to provide a comprehensive overview of current research, highlighting key themes, identifying gaps in the literature, and suggesting directions for future research in the field. Results will be presented and analyzed based on 55 articles selected from 5 databases. The analysis indicated a fragmented knowledge base in this emerging field of research, lacking a better integration, and identified themes and problems related to new conceptualizations of literacy. The ultimate goal is to contribute to the development of a broader and more complex conceptual framework about literacy currently. It is essential to unite efforts in the field towards a better conceptualization of the phenomena and to establish a knowledge base to prepare users for a ubiquitous AI era.

The field of literacy theories and practices is not new, but it has undergone significant changes in the last few decades, particularly in light of the new digital technologies and their impacts on how people communicate and learn, as well as due to the social developments in society. Broadly, literacy can be defined as one's ability to use languages and engage in communication with others in various contexts. As people's literacy practices and their understanding of it evolve, many scholars and teacher educators have formulated concepts aiming to detail more specific literacies, such as media literacy (Potter, 2013), digital literacy (Redd et al, 2020), computational literacy (Desessa, 2001), data literacy (Gebre, 2022) and, most recently, AI literacy.

Study design and methodology

The study's guiding questions were: How are literacies defined in the context of GenAI? What are the most relevant conceptual elements for literacies about GenAI? What are the main changes concerning literacy practices in the context of GenAI in the educational context?

The research conducted a mapping of academic articles published on the subject through a literature review (Vosgerau & Romanowski, 2014). The search for English-language articles published in the last five years was carried out in selected databases, using search strings composed of keywords aligned with the objectives and research questions. The articles identified in the searches were selected using inclusion and exclusion criteria developed by the researchers. Articles were searched for in five databases. The search string was refined, resulting in its final version with four variations in order to cover the largest number of relevant studies on the topic: multiliteracies and generative artificial intelligence; literacies and generative artificial intelligence; literacies and automated text; literacies and machine learning. The criteria of database relevance, peer-reviewed articles, and the limited period of 2020 to 2024 were adopted.

This search has resulted in a satisfactory number of articles, given the recent nature of the subject. Two independent coders conducted a title and abstract screening of all 771 collected articles (see Table 1). Discrepancies in the coding were resolved to achieve consensus between the coders. The exclusion criteria were based on the previously detailed guiding questions. The full content of the selected 55 articles was analyzed through thematic categories (Bardin, 2011) based on the research questions.

Table 1: Total of articles collected and selected

Databases	**Search string**	**Collected articles**	**Selected articles**
ERIC; Web of Science; Science Direct; Scopus; Sage	multiliteracies and generative artificial intelligence	38	8
ERIC; Web of Science; Science Direct; Scopus; Sage	literacies and generative artificial intelligence	250	31
ERIC; Web of Science; Science Direct; Scopus; Sage	literacies and automated text	233	9
ERIC; Web of Science; Science Direct; Scopus; Sage	literacies and machine learning	250	7
Total		771	55

Results: Multifaceted dimensions of literacy in the AI paradigm

Researchers have grappled with defining AI literacy, particularly in relation to specific educational goals and contexts, leading to a variety of conceptual frameworks. In the case of the selected articles related to the literacies and generative artificial intelligence string, theories and concepts of literacy varied. They have been used in the narrow sense of learning to use the functionalities of GenAI technologies (Stolpe & Hallstrom, 2024; Pinski & Benlian 2024; Mabuan, 2024; Pretorius, 2023; Long & Mangerko, 2020). In another group of articles, they have developed a critical perspective about the technology, covering, in these cases, questions about the problem of authorship agency and the ethical implications of its use in the school context (Mukhopadhyay, 2024; Chu-Ke & Dong, 2024; Belshaw et al, 2023; Velander et al, 2023; Leander & Burriss, 2020). These differences reflect the fact that there are diverse, evolving definitions and conceptualizations of literacy in the new literature, as well as the term AI literacy, which lacks a universally accepted definition. There are distinct theoretical perspectives about literacies, as well as about the evolving nature of AI technologies and their applications for education.

Long and Magerko (2020) define AI literacy as "a set of skills that enables individuals to critically evaluate AI technologies, communicate and collaborate effectively with AI, and use AI as a tool online, at home, and in the workplace". According to the authors, AI literacy encompasses 17 competencies, such as users' capacity to distinguish between technological artifacts that use and do not use AI, their competency to analyze and discuss features that make an entity "intelligent", including discussing differences between humans, animal, and machine intelligence, and also to understand that agents are programmable and what are the implications for using AI.

Based on an extensive literature review of AI users, Pinski and Benlian (2024) articulated that the main components of AI literacy are grouped under the category of proficiency related to AI, which encompasses knowledge, awareness, skills, competencies/abilities, and experiences about AI. The authors considered that "these proficiency dimensions collectively contribute to the enabling and human-focused AI literacy construct" (p. 9). Additionally, they conceptualized five core AI literacy areas: AI Models, Data for AI, AI Interfaces, AI Tools, and Humans, Organizations, and Society, referring to human roles, interactions, and management of AI. Stolpe and Hallstrom (2024) developed a framework for AI literacy specifically for technology education that includes the dimensions of conceptual technological knowledge, including definitions and theoretical knowledge related to defining AI, recognizing AI, understanding AI, and understanding the role of data in AI. The second dimension refers to technical skills and practical work with AI, identified as procedural, including the abilities to design and make programs work and solve problems using AI. The authors also included contextual knowledge, the socio-ethical technical understanding of the use, and the consequences of AI as another dimension of literacy.

From a distinct perspective in the field, Belshaw et al (2023) articulated that AI literacy involves more than just understanding the technical aspects of AI. It encompasses a set of abilities that enable individuals to critically evaluate AI technologies, communicate and collaborate effectively with AI, and use AI ethically and responsibly in various contexts. These contexts are multiple and varied: the home and workplace, but also in social arenas and liminal spaces between the three. "Consequently, definitions of AI literacies must address how AI influences our decisions, shaping our interactions and challenging our notions of privacy and security in our everyday lives" (Belshaw et al, 2023, p.3). Important elements to be considered are: the centrality of users' ability to critically evaluate generated content, as well as to recognize potential biases and mistakes, and the need to understand and avoid an excessive use of these technologies, thereby avoiding over-reliance on them and promoting responsible use and human agency (Mukhopadhyay, 2024; Cardon et al, 2023, Wijaya et al, 2024).

According to Chu-Ke and Dong (2024), AI literacy should include users' understanding and critical evaluation of knowledge and cultures within which AI systems function, and users' interpretation and ethical use of AI-generated content. Yuan et al (2024) proposed a comprehensive framework for AI literacy by developing a holistic AI literacy scale that considers the individual, interactive, and sociocultural dimensions. The scale included cognitive, behavioral, and normative competencies. Their AI literacy scale comprised six users' competencies needed to navigate and critically engage with the technology regarding AI features, AI processing, algorithm influences, user efficacy, ethical considerations, and threat appraisal.

Adarkwah (2024) argues that AI literacy "includes the ability to understand how large language models are trained; to appreciate the differences between AI tools designed for specialized tasks as opposed to all-purpose ones; and to understand what types of problems current GenAI tools are good at solving" (p. 6). A holistic approach to AI literacy integrates these diverse dimensions, recognizing their interconnectedness and mutual reinforcement (Velander et al, 2024).

Discussion: Towards a more complex understanding of literacy currently

This study confirms that a significant part of research and scholars' current work about literacies "leans towards an instrumental perspective, i.e., focusing primarily on user capabilities, competencies, abilities, and skills-based perspective" (Ng et al, 2021, p. 6). Most of these studies lack a humanistic and holistic perspective on the GenAI's quality of knowledge, human agency, the power of questioning and transformation (Floridi, 2023), as well as the commercial bias and lack of transparency and inscrutability of AI companies and services. To address the nature and power of the GenAI phenomenon globally, it seems necessary to incorporate into the frameworks and analysis some key elements associated to the new ethos created by the AI paradigm shift.

First, it seems important to highlight that a person's literacy goes beyond the ability to decode language and to know how to use technological artifacts. Instead, it encompasses "the breadth of one's symbolic repertoire, the sense and use of competent agency, and the social sophistication to shift one's actions to suit local conditions" (Dyson, 2003, p. 3). Therefore, the issues of power relations, identity, multiculturalism, and diversity are key to understanding, engaging and participating in literacy practices in various contexts of life and also for learning at school today. Many of these are lacking in the set of articles analyzed in this study.

While GenAI opens the possibility of accelerating and even improving many human tasks, its role in education and learning deserves to be more thoroughly scrutinized, given its fast-paced development and the few regulations about it. From a broader perspective, it is essential to keep in mind that AI outputs are never neutral, but they carry biases that may interfere with one's understanding of reality (O'Neil, 2016). And, more specifically, AI can interfere with humans' ability to think critically and independently (Cremer & Kasparov, 2021) as users may become overly dependent on AI-generated services and content, failing to further develop their own analytical and creative abilities.

Addressing the element of human agency in the AI literacy perspective, Cardon et al (2023) articulate some central questions that seem worth pursuing. "Does the communicator retain or expand their personal choices through the use of generative AI? Does the communicator enhance their knowledge and human potential while using generative AI? Can the communicator make independent human decisions while using generative AI?" (p, 279). The authors also articulate two other AI literacy dimensions. The element of authenticity involves a focus on genuine communication and prioritizing human power in AI interactions. Accountability involves taking responsibility for the accuracy and appropriateness of AI-generated content and using GenAI fairly and equitably.

A more complex understanding of AI literacy has various implications for educational policy and curriculum. UNESCO has initiated important work in this direction that encompasses a human-centered mindset, a strong focus on ethics, and fostering problem-solving, creativity, and design thinking, emphasizing interdisciplinary learning at school (Fengchun & Kelly, 2024). Concerning the discussion on the pedagogical perspective of literacies and GenAI, Kohnke et al (2023) point out the qualities and advantages of GenAI, such as providing immediate feedback, expanding language skills, maintaining motivation, reducing the perceived transactional distance between students and teachers, and fostering critical analysis. The authors also highlight the need for the development of a critical evaluation mindset. It is essential to understand GenAI's limitations, use it safely and with integrity, and consider ethical responsibilities as digital citizens, particularly regarding authorship and plagiarism at school. They also point to the need to modify teaching and assessment practices and develop guidelines for the use of AI-driven tools.

Conclusion: Synthesizing findings and future research directions

The importance and impact of GenAI for education and literacy today is indisputable. Relevant and new aspects are emerging in the field of human cognition, writing culture, and media culture in the face of the current expansion of AI and the massive use of bots. It is up to the field to generate data and analysis to better understand these changes, their implications for teacher and student learning, and school practice.

This systematic review has synthesized key findings from a diverse range of studies exploring the complex relationship between literacies and GenAI in education. A group of studies and scholars focused on a more applied and technical perspective towards literacy and GenAI to improve its use and results, integrating it into the educational context. Yet, another group developed a more critical and complex perspective aiming to problematize key aspects of GenAI use, such as ethical dilemmas, critical thinking implications, pedagogical challenges, and students' and teachers' increasing dependency on private companies and their products. The findings have also revealed the transformative potential of GenAI to enhance learning and the simultaneous need for developing appropriate literacies to deal with its complexities. The rapid evolution of AI technologies necessitates ongoing research to fully understand their impact on literacy development and educational practices.

In regards to this study's limitations, it was developed based on some selected highly regarded scientific databases, so the inclusion of more sources of data may bring different perspectives to new studies in this area. Also, the use of four strings of keywords for searching articles may not have covered all available studies, and new ones, published from this year onwards, may provide other important knowledge for the field.

Future research should prioritize longitudinal studies to assess the long-term impacts of GenAI on literacy development and critical thinking skills as well as related school practices. Further development and validation of AI literacy assessment tools are crucial for evaluating the effectiveness of educational interventions and informing policy decisions (Pinski & Benlian, 2024). The creation of innovative pedagogical approaches that integrate GenAI ethically and responsibly is paramount. This includes developing strategies to mitigate potential risks, such as over-reliance on AI tools and algorithmic bias that can severely interfere with literacy practices in general and at school, and to ensure users' hegemony along this endeavour.

Funding Information

This research is funded by Fundação Cearense de Apoio ao Desenvolvimento Científico e Tecnológico (FUNCAP). Grant number PRH-0212-00023.01.00/23.

References

Adarkwah, M. A. (2024). Genai-infused adult learning in the digital era: A conceptual framework for higher education. Adult Learning, 10451595241271161. https://doi.org/10.1177/10451595241271161

Bardin, L. (2011). Análise de conteúdo. Editions 70.

Chu-Ke, C., & Dong, Y. (2024). Misinformation and literacies in the era of generative artificial intelligence: A brief overview and a call for future research. Emerging Media, 2(1), 70–85. https://doi.org/10.1177/27523543241240285

De Cremer, D., & Kasparov, G. (2021). AI should augment human intelligence, not replace it. Harvard Business Review. https://hbr.org/2021/03/ai-should-augment-human-intelligence-not-replace-it

DiSessa, A. (2000). Changing minds: Computers, learning, and literacy. The MIT Press. https://doi.org/10.7551/mitpress/1786.001.0001

Dyson, A. H. (2002). The brothers and sisters learn to write: Popular literacies in childhood and school cultures. Teachers College Press.

Farrelly, T., & Baker, N. (2023). Generative artificial intelligence: Implications and considerations for higher education practice. Education Sciences, 13(11), 1109. https://doi.org/10.3390/educsci13111109

Floridi, L. (2023). Ai as agency without intelligence: On chatgpt, large language models, and other generative models (SSRN Scholarly Paper No. 4358789). https://doi.org/10.2139/ssrn.4358789

Gayed, J. M., Carlon, M. K. J., Oriola, A. M., & Cross, J. S. (2022). Exploring an AI-based writing Assistant's impact on English language learners. Computers and Education: Artificial Intelligence, 3, 100055. https://doi.org/10.1016/j.caeai.2022.100055

Gebre, E. (2022). Conceptions and perspectives of data literacy in secondary education. British Journal of Educational Technology, 53(5), 1080–1095. https://doi.org/10.1111/bjet.13246

Kaspersen, M. H., Bilstrup, K.-E. K., Van Mechelen, M., Hjort, A., Bouvin, N. O., & Petersen, M. G. (2022). High school students exploring machine learning and its societal implications: Opportunities and challenges. International Journal of Child-Computer Interaction, 34, 100539. https://doi.org/10.1016/j.ijcci.2022.100539

Kohnke, L., Moorhouse, B. L., & Zou, D. (2023). Chatgpt for language teaching and learning. RELC Journal, 54(2), 537–550. https://doi.org/10.1177/00336882231162868

Laupichler, M. C., Aster, A., Schirch, J., & Raupach, T. (2022). Artificial intelligence literacy in higher and adult education: A scoping literature review. Computers and Education: Artificial Intelligence, 3, 100101. https://doi.org/10.1016/j.caeai.2022.100101

Leander, K. M., & Burriss, S. K. (2020). Critical literacy for a posthuman world: When people read, and become, with machines. British Journal of Educational Technology, 51(4), 1262–1276. https://doi.org/10.1111/bjet.12924

Lee, S. J., & Kwon, K. (2024). A systematic review of AI education in K-12 classrooms from 2018 to 2023: Topics, strategies, and learning outcomes. Computers and Education: Artificial Intelligence, 6, 100211. https://doi.org/10.1016/j.caeai.2024.100211

Long, D., & Magerko, B. (2020). What is ai literacy? Competencies and design considerations. Proceedings of the 2020 CHI Conference on Human Factors in Computing Systems, 1–16. https://doi.org/10.1145/3313831.3376727

Mabuan, R. A. (2024). Chatgpt and elt: Exploring teachers' voices. International Journal of Technology in Education, 7(1), 128–153. https://doi.org/10.46328/ijte.523

Miao, F., & Shiohira, K. (2024). AI competency framework for students. UNESCO. https://doi.org/10.54675/JKJB9835

Mukhopadhyay, S. (2024). Assessing the impact of generative pre-trained transformers on ai literacy and public awareness in india. Asian Journal of Information Science and Technology, 14(2), 50–56. https://doi.org/10.70112/ajist-2024.14.2.4293

Ng, D. T. K., Leung, J. K. L., Chu, S. K. W., & Qiao, M. S. (2021). Conceptualizing AI literacy: An exploratory review. Computers and Education: Artificial Intelligence, 2, 100041. https://doi.org/10.1016/j.caeai.2021.100041

O'Neil, C. (2016). Weapons of math destruction. Crown Books.

Pinski, M., & Benlian, A. (2024). AI literacy for users – A comprehensive review and future research directions of learning methods, components, and effects. Computers in Human Behavior: Artificial Humans, 2(1), 100062. https://doi.org/10.1016/j.chbah.2024.100062

Potter, W. J. (2013). Review of literature on media literacy. Sociology Compass, 7(6), 417–435. https://doi.org/10.1111/soc4.12041

Pretorius, L. (2023). Fostering AI literacy: A teaching practice reflection. Journal of Academic Language and Learning, 17(1), T1–T8. https://journal.aall.org.au/index.php/jall/article/view/891

Reddy, P., Sharma, B., & Chaudhary, K. (2020). Digital literacy: A review of literature. International Journal of Technoethics, 11(2), 65–94. https://doi.org/10.4018/IJT.20200701.oa1

Stolpe, K., & Hallström, J. (2024). Artificial intelligence literacy for technology education. Computers and Education Open, 6, 100159. https://doi.org/10.1016/j.caeo.2024.100159

Velander, J., Taiye, M. A., Otero, N., & Milrad, M. (2024). Artificial Intelligence in K-12 Education: Eliciting and reflecting on Swedish teachers' understanding of AI and its implications for teaching & learning. Education and Information Technologies, 29(4), 4085–4105. https://doi.org/10.1007/s10639-023-11990-4

Vosgerau, D. S. R., & Romanowski, J. P. (2014). Estudos de revisão: Implicações conceituais e metodológicas. Revista Diálogo Educacional, 14(41), 165-189.

Wijaya, T. T., Yu, Q., Cao, Y., He, Y., & Leung, F. K. S. (2024). Latent profile analysis of ai literacy and trust in mathematics teachers and their relations with ai dependency and 21st-century skills. Behavioral Sciences, 14(11), 1008. https://doi.org/10.3390/bs14111008

Yuan, C. W. (Tina), Tsai, H. S., & Chen, Y.-T. (2024). Charting competence: A holistic scale for measuring proficiency in artificial intelligence literacy. Journal of Educational Computing Research, 62(7), 1675–1704. https://doi.org/10.1177/07356331241261206

Balancing Guided Instruction in Collaborative Learning for Synchronous Critical Thinking and Language Skills Development

Lilit Sargsyan[1]

[1]Faculty of European Languages and Communication, Yerevan State University, Republic of Armenia, 4Lilitvs@gmail.com, sargsyan.lilit@ysu.am

Correspondence: Lilit Sargsyan, 4Lilitvs@gmail.com

Abstract:

The study examines how implementing artificial intelligence tools within organized educational systems improves students' critical thinking abilities and language proficiency. By synthesizing contemporary pedagogical frameworks and empirical studies, the research identifies how structured cognitive models mediate AI's role in collaborative learning environments. The study emphasizes the need for guided teaching methods and examines ethical issues like cognitive offloading. A systematic review of existing literature enables this article to demonstrate AI's transformational power in education and the importance of integrating technological advancements with traditional teaching methods. Intentional use of AI-mediated systems fosters collaborative learning and language skill enhancement.

Keywords: Collaborative learning, balanced guided instruction, synchronous critical thinking, language skills development, AI in education

Introduction

AI technologies progress rapidly which proves their undeniable power to revolutionize educational practices. However, the challenge lies in the successful incorporation of these tools which are utilized to improve critical thinking and language abilities while preserving academic integrity and student autonomy. Interdisciplinary studies in Neurology, Psychology and Education (Stoltz et al., 2024) reveal AI scaffolding activates both (prefrontal cortex) critical thinking and (Broca's area) language processing, suggesting neural basis for synchronous skill development. These educational tools present exciting possibilities to enhance learning experiences yet they bring ongoing challenges around their effective use and maintaining academic integrity while supporting critical thinking and language skill development.

Contemporary debates center on whether AI represents a disruptive innovation requiring entirely new pedagogies or an evolutionary tool that amplifies existing best practices (Essel et al., 2024). This research examines AI's educational applications by studying how critical thinking and linguistic skills develop through guided instruction and collaborative learning methods. Integrating AI technology into educational systems represents more than just technological advancement because it marks a fundamental transformation in how knowledge is understood and taught. Traditional learning theories must be re-evaluated as this shift challenges established beliefs.

Pilot data from Sako (2024) demonstrates AI-mediated groups show greater perspective-taking in debates compared to control cohorts. Constructivist learning theories, particularly those proposed by theorists like Piaget and Vygotsky, offer vital conceptual tools for comprehending how AI may facilitate learning experiences. Piaget's concept of equilibration finds new relevance in AI-augmented environments where adaptive systems provide personalized cognitive challenges (Naseer et al., 2024). These theoretical viewpoints highlight learning as an active, context-dependent process of meaning construction, indicating that AI tools can function as advanced cognitive supports that enhance rather than substitute for human intellectual involvement. Modern AI platforms provide unique opportunities for personalized, adaptive learning pathways. Nevertheless, their deployment must be thoroughly scrutinized through established educational principles.

The integration of AI raises critical questions about epistemic agency (Joseph, 2023). The burgeoning of AI landscape, especially in the domain of LLMs such as GPT-4, reasoning models like Claude 3.7, DeepSeek R1, semantic search systems like Undermind, Litmaps, etc. have catalyzed a disruptive change in education the full impact of which we will yet to realize. These technologies align with the Education 4.0 paradigm, emphasizing autonomous learning (cyberpedagogy), peer learning (peeragogy), and self-directed learning (heutagogy). By creating individualized, interactive, and adaptive learning settings, LLMs hold great promise in augmenting critical thinking and linguistic abilities in tertiary education. Recent incidents of algorithmic bias in AI's low-quality feedback to non-native English speakers (Reusens, M. et al., 2024), as well as language learning AIs (e.g., gender stereotyping in conversational prompts) underscore the need for robust ethical auditing processes (Gerlich, 2025). The adoption of such technologies must, however, be done with caution as it portends ethical and legal concerns, including bias, privacy, and the necessity for strong regulatory frameworks to provide assurance of equitable implementation (Koshiyama A. et al. 2024).

Literature Review

The current discourse about how artificial intelligence may be embedded within learning is delineating a complex landscape of technological impact. Researchers are now considering AI systems as more than simply tools, but rather as advanced cognitive facilitators that can redesign and possibly disrupt learning contexts.

The seminal work of Kirschner, Sweller, and Clark (2010) provides insightful perspective on the thin line between technology applications and effective instruction. They emphasize guided instruction to manage cognitive load, a principle critical to AI-mediated learning environments where unstructured tools risk overwhelming learners. The findings of their work reveal pitfalls of implementing the instructional approaches that offer little guidance, especially for novice learners. This is pivotal particularly in AI-supported Problem-based Learning, where self-directed learning appears to be less beneficial than appropriately guided teaching.

The complex dynamics of instructional scaffolding are accurately captured in Aulls' qualitative research (2002) as it elucidates outstanding educators' methods of strategic intervention during their students' learning experience. The analysis of the core insights convey that top teaching professionals spend much time on concurrent content explanation and procedural support, a precept that is greatly relevant to today's AI-enhanced learning environments (p. 533).

Recent studies have evidenced a broad influence of artificial intelligence tools on the development of critical thinking and language learning. Peláez-Sánchez et al. (2024) link LLMs to personalized feedback and collaborative learning. Their longitudinal study across six universities revealed that AI groups maintained higher retention of critical evaluation skills compared to control groups after 12 months. Similarly, Wei (2023) found that AI-facilitated instruction significantly improves grammar, vocabulary, and reading comprehension in language teaching, in addition to improving students' motivation and promoting self-directed learning strategies. The research, however, identifies the importance of guided instruction in AI-supported learning environments.

Recent empirical studies, including Heung and Chiu's (2025) systematic review, introduce nuanced findings regarding the impact of generative AI tools on student engagement and sheds a new light on the popular claim that AI tolls have the potential to support and augment human creativity (Guzik et al. 2023). Heung & Chiu's meta-analysis quantifies the engagement paradox: while the group of AI users demonstrated a 37% increase in task completion, they exhibited a 15% decline in originality scores on creative thinking assessment Torrance Tests. Most studies in this analysis emphasized the importance of guided reflection protocols to counteract diminishing creativity.

Similar results are found in studies centered upon neuroimaging (Lee et al., 2025) show reduced prefrontal cortex activation during AI-assisted tasks, suggesting the need for deliberate "cognitive calibration" activities, such as unassisted brainstorming, to maintain neural plasticity.

Thus, it can be inferred that while these advanced technologies are seen to have a moderate positive impact on cognitive and behavioral engagement, their effect on higher-order thinking skills remains inconsistent and potentially concerning. GenAI tools may be considered efficient in enhancing specific task outcomes and engagement levels, but their impact on deep understanding and critical thinking skills appears to be limited. The most prevalent cognitive load of using AI tools mimics the lowest common denominator of how we learn, acquiring abilities that are not profoundly internalized. Educators are encouraged to adopt self-assessment techniques after AI-assisted brainstorming activities, focusing on recognizing shortcomings in AI-generated outputs.

Ethical and Cognitive Considerations

Gerlich's (2025) longitudinal study found that learners relying extensively on unmonitored AI tools developed significant gaps in verification skills. Structured reflection practices, however, markedly reduced these deficits, highlighting the value of guided metacognitive interventions. AI mediation reduced confirmation bias in debates but also revealed a tendency among novice learners to over-rely on AI suggestions (Zhang, 2025), emphasizing the need for tiered scaffolding.

One major challenge in AI-supported learning environments is cognitive offloading. Reduced analytical engagement is seen more frequently in less knowledgeable and confident learners with fewer years of learning experience, while advanced learners demonstrated resilience towards the adverse effect of cognitive displacement. This emphasizes adapting teaching methods to balance dependency and AI's transformative potential.

The work market perspective (Lee et al. 2025) introduces measurable trade-offs: their 936-case analysis shows that highly experienced professionals using AI verification protocols maintained their critical evaluation capacity in contrast to unguided novice employees. This aligns with Aulls' (2002) observation that top educators spend considerable amount of intervention time on verification processes.

Methodology

The current research utilizes systematic review methods to explore the incorporation of artificial intelligence tools within educational environments. Adopting a qualitative synthesis approach, the study analyzes patterns across peer-reviewed articles, conference proceedings, and institutional reports published mostly between 2010-2025.

The objective of the study is to enhance the comprehension of AI integration in educational contexts by thoroughly analyzing current research. Research studies chosen for inclusion typically showcased a clear examination of AI integration within educational environments, along with a thorough investigation into the development of critical thinking or language skills. Additional emphasis was placed on the clarity of methodology and the recency of publication to ensure relevance to current discussions.

The comparative examination of theoretical frameworks, coupled with integrated empirical insights, is combined with practical observations and contextual applications to analyze patterns in implementation strategies across diverse educational settings, aiming to uncover factors that may affect learning outcomes. This approach seeks to address the complexities of educational environments shaped by ubiquitous and powerful AI chatbots.

Our study acknowledges several critical factors. The rapidly evolving nature of AI technology indicates possible limitations concerning its temporal relevance, and variations in context may affect the generalizability of the results.

The methodology aims to establish a foundation for understanding AI integration in education, acknowledging its complexity as an emerging field. By focusing carefully on both theoretical frameworks and practical application, the study endeavors to contribute meaningfully to the ongoing academic discourse in this domain.

Integration of Linguistic and Critical Thinking Competencies

The modern interpretation of Bloom's taxonomy as suggested by P. Hardman captures essential elements of 21st-century education, allowing teachers to leverage the multifaceted growth of students' language and critical thinking abilities through active learning while utilizing AI tools.

The application of organized thinking frameworks has shown considerable effectiveness in promoting simultaneous progress in various competency areas. Hardman's Post-AI Learning Taxonomy (2024) shows particular efficacy in Content-Based Learning: students using its tiered framework demonstrated greater lexical density and more complex syntax in case analyses compared to control groups (Wei, 2023).

The fusion of cognitive frameworks and language learning processes has been particularly beneficial when executed via systematic methodological strategies. The implementation of the SOAR framework (Kruger, 2016) in language education settings has shown its effectiveness in fostering high-level linguistic abilities through strategic thinking approaches. If adeptly employed, the framework can improve students' learning experience due to which the language acquisition takes place organically. Inspired by the research conducted by Ellikkal and Rajamohan, according to which AI-enhanced groups of management students produced market analyses with more discipline-specific terminology and greater solution viability compared to AI-free groups of students (2024), SOAR was used, with the mediation of AI systems like Undermind and Perplexity for semantic search for published materials, DeepSeek R1 or Claude 3.7 for preparing group presentations, to enable Master's level Management students to develop strategic intervention strategies for supporting Armenian farmers through Fair Trade principles. Students involved in these integrated educational settings exhibited a greater capacity to express complex analytical ideas while also enhancing their advanced language skills.

The structured examination of synchronous language and critical thinking growth uncovers several notable trends regarding the success of integrated approaches. Kim M. K. & Kim N. J.'s (2024) study suggests that programs combining AI tools with explicit cognitive frameworks achieve greater improvements in argumentation skills compared to isolated AI implementations. Educators have noticed that when learners interact with these frameworks within a well-organized setting, their ability to convey intricate ideas improves significantly, especially in academic environments.

Implementation of Cognitive Frameworks in Language Acquisition

The results from our experimental method of incorporating LLMs with critical thinking development frameworks like Edward de Bono's Six Thinking Hats demonstrate a notable enhancement in collaborative problem-solving abilities. Van Zyl and Zimmerman's (2023) implementation in business contexts shows how AI-enhanced critical thinking development approaches promote equitable participation while maintaining strategic focus – a finding directly applicable to academic group work. Six Thinking Hats integration reduced groupthink by 37% in MBA simulations while increasing minority viewpoint contributions by 29%. Research shows that AI-assisted collaborative settings, when paired with this organized cognitive structure, can actively assess team thought patterns and recommend strategic cognitive adjustments in real-time, especially when discussions tend to be unproductive or lopsided.

Key Mechanisms of LLM-Enhanced Collaboration

Efficacy of Assessing Students' Collaboration: The utilizing LLMs allows evaluation of students' collaboration via implemented quantitative and modular AI-based approach, which is a crucial aspect of learning that traditional assessment methods often struggle to quantify effectively (Tomić et al., 2023).

Bias Mitigation: Teams using AI mediation strategies showed fewer confirmation bias and polarization in debating (Govers et al, 2024).

This enhanced strategy has resulted in measurable advancements in both perspective-taking skills and the quality of solutions generated, surpassing standard applications of the Six Thinking Hats method. The primary benefit of this integration is the system's capacity to pinpoint cognitive roadblocks as they emerge and propose targeted interventions, effectively acting as a metacognitive ally instead of just a procedural tool.

Integration of AI-Enhanced Assessment and Development Methodologies

The incorporation of the Watson-Glaser Critical Thinking Assessment can be greatly improved through the utilization of multimodal AI systems. These sophisticated systems surpass conventional assessment techniques by examining not only the content of students' responses but also the cognitive processes underlying them. By monitoring interactions and studying engagement patterns, multimodal AI offers a more detailed view of critical thinking, especially concerning cognitive flexibility and adaptability. This method has been particularly effective in graduate economics programs, where it has led to enhancements in evidence evaluation skills when compared to traditional assessment strategies.

Multimodal AI systems analyze and consolidate various types of data to provide a thorough assessment of cognitive abilities. This synthesis enables a deeper insight into how students formulate logical arguments and utilize evidence (Stryker, 2024).

Through the simultaneous analysis of various data streams, multimodal AI furnishes detailed feedback on strengths and weaknesses across distinct aspects of critical thinking, such as evidence evaluation and adaptability in argumentation. This feedback is far more thorough than what traditional unimodal methods provide, which tend to emphasize isolated data types like text alone (Curtis, Kidd, 2024).

The deployment of multimodal AI systems for the assessment of students' language and critical thinking skills, as well as their domain-specific knowledge presents numerous benefits over standard unimodal techniques:

- Improved Contextual Understanding,
- Heightened Problem-Solving,
- Cross-Domain Learning.

Thus, by adapting the Watson-Glaser Critical Thinking Assessment through AI-driven approaches, sophisticated formative assessment protocols have been established that evaluate both language and cognitive skills. This integration has enabled the creation of detailed assessment frameworks that offer valuable insights into students' developmental paths across various competency areas.

Findings and Discussion

- Collaborative activities supported by AI boost students' independence and enhance their digital literacy abilities,
- The success of AI tools is contingent upon their correct application and the presence of supportive educator guidance
- Developing critical thinking necessitates a careful equilibrium between the use of AI tools and genuine learning experiences,
- Studies consistently indicate that guided instruction leads to better learning results compared to less structured methods, especially for beginners. In the realm of AI integration, this implies:
    - Strong instructional support is essential when employing AI tools,
    - Scaffolding should be implemented to assist students in effectively using AI resources,
    - Educators must scaffold AI tools to balance autonomy and guidance, ensuring technology complements instead of replacing human instruction.
- AI tools show considerable promise for improving collaborative learning experiences by:
    - Closing perceptual divides among team members,
    - Promoting clearer communication of goals,
    - Assisting in a deeper comprehension of assigned tasks,
    - Fostering more effective group discussions.

Ethical Challenges

1. LLMs provide lower-quality responses to non-native English speakers, especially when recognizing the user's "nativeness" (Reusens, M. et al., 2024).

2. Cognitive offloading poses risks, particularly for novices who over-rely on AI-generated content. Structured intervals of unassisted work (e.g., peer debates) mitigate dependency (Ellikkal & Rajamohan, 2024; Gerlich, 2025).

3. The inclusion of AI tools in educational environments has shown considerable promise in improving critical thinking and language abilities when integrated into well-structured teaching strategies.

Pedagogical Implementation Strategies

The research outcomes highlight the need for advanced strategies in curriculum design that intentionally combine cognitive models with language acquisition goals. Effective execution calls for a deliberate sequential advancement of both language skills and analytical abilities. The successful application of AI-supported learning environments requires comprehensive training programs for educators that cover both technological and pedagogical skills with a special focus on identifying algorithmic bias, privacy compliance. These training initiatives should particularly focus on enhancing assessment comprehension that includes both conventional and AI-supported evaluation strategies.

Future Research Directions:

- Longitudinal studies on equity gaps in AI access and outcomes.
- Development of universal ethical frameworks for AI in education, addressing bias, privacy and epistemic agency.

Conclusion

The strategic use of AI tools in educational contexts presents significant opportunities to enhance learning results, especially when critical thinking skills are developed alongside language skills through problem-based learning (PBL). The success of these implementations greatly depends on following recognized teaching principles and carefully integrating AI tools within structured educational environments. In AI-augmented learning settings, the role of educators is vital, particularly in offering expert support and ensuring that technology enhances rather than substitutes traditional teaching approaches. AI-augmented frameworks succeed when aligned with pedagogical principles, ensuring learners internalize skills rather than offload cognition.

Future studies should concentrate on the long-term effects of AI incorporation in education, particularly regarding student learning outcomes, the roles of teachers, and educational equity. By harmonizing AI with teaching principles, educators can cultivate critical thinking and language skills in Education 4.0.

References

Aulls, M. W. (2002). The contributions of co-occurring forms of classroom discourse and academic activities to curriculum events and instruction. Journal of Educational Psychology, 94, 520-538.

Curtis, A., Kidd, C. (2024). What Is Multimodal AI? https://www.splunk.com/en_us/blog/learn/multimodal-ai.html

De Bono, E. (1985). Six Thinking Hats. Penguin Books: London.

Ellikkal, A., Rajamohan, S. (2024). AI-enabled personalized learning. Vilakshan - XIMB Journal of Management. ISSN: 0973-1954.

Essel, H. B. et al. (2024). ChatGPT effects on cognitive skills of undergraduate students. Computers and Education: Artificial Intelligence, 6, 100198.

Gerlich, M. (2025). AI Tools in Society: Impacts on Cognitive Offloading and the Future of Critical Thinking. Societies, 15(1), 6. https://doi.org/10.3390/soc15010006

Govers, J. et al. (2024). AI-Driven Mediation Strategies for Audience Depolarisation in Online Debates. CHI '24: Proceedings of the 2024 CHI Conference on Human Factors in Computing Systems, Article No.: 803, Pages 1–18. https://doi.org/10.1145/3613904.3642322

Guzik, E. et al. (2023). The Originality of Machines: AI Takes the Torrance Test. Journal of Creativity. https://doi.org/10.1016/j.yjoc.2023.100065

Hardman, P. (2024). A Post-AI Learning Taxonomy. Dr Phil's Newsletter, Powered by DOMS™ AI.

Heung, Y.M.E., Chiu, T.K.C. (2025). How ChatGPT impacts student engagement from a systematic review and meta-analysis study. Computers and Education: Artificial Intelligence, 8. https://www.sciencedirect.com/science/article/pii/S2666920X25000013

Joseph, S. (2023). Large language model-based tools in language teaching to develop critical thinking and sustainable cognitive structures. Rupkatha Journal on Interdisciplinary Studies in Humanities, 15(4).

Kim, M. K., Kim, N. J. (2024). AI-Supported Scaffolding for Writing Academic Arguments. Georgia State University, University of Miami. https://repository.isls.org/bitstream/1/8426/1/ICLS2022_1129-1132.pdf

Kirschner, P. A., Sweller, J., Clark, R. E. (2010). Why minimal guidance during instruction does not work. Educational Psychologist, 41, 75–86.

Koshiyama, A. et al. (2024). Towards algorithm auditing. Royal Society Open Science, 11. https://doi.org/10.1098/rsos.230859

Kruger, S. (2016). https://selskills.com/educators/why-soar-sel-strategies-work/

Lee, H.-P. et al. (2025). The Impact of Generative AI on Critical Thinking: Self-Reported Reductions in Cognitive Effort and Confidence Effects from a Survey of Knowledge.

Mayer, R. (2004). Should there be a three-strikes rule against pure discovery learning? The case for guided methods of instruction. American Psychologist, 59, 14–19.

Naseer, F. et al. (2024). Integrating deep learning techniques for personalized learning pathways in higher education. Heliyon. https://doi.org/10.1016/j.heliyon.2024.e32628

Peláez-Sánchez, I. C. et al. (2024). The impact of large language models on higher education: exploring the connection between AI and Education 4.0. Frontiers in Education, 9. https://doi.org/10.3389/feduc.2024.1392091

Reusens, M. et al. (2024). Native Design Bias: Studying the Impact of English Nativeness on Language Model. Performance. ArXiv. https://doi.org/10.48550/arXiv.2406.17385

Sako, T. (2024). Enhancing Critical Thinking through AI-Assisted Collaborative Task-Based Learning: A Case Study of Prospective Teachers in Japan. Journal of English Language Teaching and Linguistics.

Stoltz, T. et al. (2024). Consciousness and education: contributions by Piaget, Vygotsky and Steiner. Frontiers in Psychology, 15. https://doi.org/10.3389/fpsyg.2024.1411415

Stryker, C. (2024). What is multimodal AI? https://www.ibm.com/think/topics/multimodal-ai

Tomić, B. et al. (2023). An AI-based Approach for Grading Students' Collaboration. IEEE Transactions on Learning Technologies, 16, 292-305.

Van Zyl, D., Zimmerman, M. (2023). How ChatGPT and the Six-Hat Method Present a Powerful Framework for Effective Problem-Solving. Entrepreneur. https://www.entrepreneur.com/leadership/how-chatgpt-can-spark-creative-problem-solving/454702

Vygotsky, L. S. (1999). Scientific legacy. The collected works of L.S. Vygotsky (Vol. 6). New York: Kluwer Academic/Plenum Publishers.

Wei, L. (2023). Artificial intelligence in language instruction: impact on English learning achievement, L2 motivation, and self-regulated learning. Frontiers in Psychology. https://doi.org/10.3389/fpsyg.2023.1261955

Zhang, Z. et al. (2025). Breaking Barriers or Building Dependency? Exploring Team-LLM Collaboration in AI-infused Classroom Debate.

Bridging Borders: Global Faculty Learning Communities on AI for Transforming Teaching and Learning

Angela Gunder[1], Melissa Vito[2], Marcela Ramirez[3], Claudia Arcolin[4]

[1] The University of Arizona, United States; agunder@arizona.edu
[2] The University of Texas at San Antonio, United States; melissa.vito@utsa.edu
[3] The University of Texas at San Antonio, United States; marcela.ramirez@utsa.edu
[4] The University of Texas at San Antonio, United States; claudia.arcolin@utsa.edu

Correspondence: Angela Gunder: angela@openedculture.org

Abstract:

Educators worldwide are experimenting with AI in their classrooms, but without structured collaboration, valuable insights remain siloed. Faculty learning communities (FLCs) provide an essential framework for cross-institutional knowledge exchange, enabling educators to share practices, co-develop AI-integrated pedagogies, and collectively address the challenges and opportunities AI presents in teaching and learning. This paper examines how global FLCs serve as incubators for AI-enhanced instructional innovation, accelerating AI adoption in higher education while fostering professional growth and pedagogical experimentation. Through an autoethnographically informed qualitative approach, the study explores how this community enabled participants to build fluency, navigate uncertainty, and influence institutional conversations about AI integration. Findings highlight how these peer-driven learning communities create structured, supportive spaces for iterative experimentation, ultimately shortening the research-to-practice cycle and equipping educators with the skills to integrate AI ethically, effectively, and creatively. This paper presents a scalable model for AI-enabled FLCs, outlining strategies for institutions to establish, sustain, and scale these collaborative ecosystems. By investing in global FLCs, institutions can move beyond isolated AI exploration toward a more connected, adaptive, and forward-thinking approach to teaching and learning.

Keywords: AI, faculty learning communities, AI-integrated pedagogies, instructional innovation, global collaboration, communities of practice

Introduction

The constant evolution of artificial intelligence (AI) in education has sparked widespread experimentation among educators, yet these efforts often unfold in isolation—without opportunities for structured reflection, knowledge exchange, or shared inquiry. As AI tools become increasingly accessible and pedagogically relevant, educators across institutions and disciplines are grappling with how to integrate them ethically, effectively, and meaningfully into their practice. This moment calls not only for technical upskilling, but for professional spaces that enable collaborative learning, contextual adaptation, and critical reflection on the changing role of teaching in an AI-mediated world.

One promising response to this need is the development of faculty learning communities (FLCs), sometimes referred to as professional learning communities (PLCs), focused on AI integration. These communities provide structured, peer-supported environments where educators can explore emerging tools, examine pedagogical implications, and experiment with intentional course redesign. By fostering sustained collaboration across disciplinary, institutional, and even national boundaries, global FLCs offer a model for professional development that is both generative and adaptive (Gunder & Shellgren, 2022; Tharapos & O'Connell, 2022; Wenger, 1999). They help educators make sense of rapidly evolving technologies within the specific contexts of their learners, institutions, and instructional values.

This paper examines a global faculty learning community co-developed by the University of Texas at San Antonio (USA) and Swinburne University of Technology (Australia), which brought together educators across time zones, disciplines, and instructional modalities to explore the opportunities and challenges of generative AI in higher education. With an autoethnographically-informed approach and grounded in firsthand facilitation, the paper documents how this community supported iterative practice, ethical discernment, and the diffusion of innovation across participants' local contexts.

Overview of the Initiative

FLCs serve as strategic infrastructures through which institutions can collaboratively engage educators on emerging topics and rapidly evolving pedagogical practices. By establishing structured environments for collective inquiry, knowledge exchange, and pedagogical experimentation, FLCs help educators navigate complex educational innovations effectively, especially when confronting rapidly emerging phenomena such as AI (Wenger, 2011; Hoyte et al., 2010). At its core, the establishment of FLCs addresses a critical challenge common across higher education institutions—fragmented, isolated, and often reactive responses to rapidly changing educational technologies. Conventional professional development models, typically consisting of isolated workshops or periodic training sessions, frequently fail to foster sustained engagement or deep pedagogical transformation. By contrast, faculty learning communities operate as structured, longitudinal frameworks wherein educators engage in ongoing dialogue, collaboration, and reflective practice. The generative nature of these communities enables members to iteratively build competencies, share successes and challenges, and jointly refine best practices for pedagogical innovation.

Structure and Design of the UTSA–Swinburne Collaboration

The collaboration between UTSA and Swinburne University of Technology in Australia exemplifies the significant benefits derived from establishing a formal global faculty learning community. Known informally as the Generative AI Global Community of Practice, this initiative united educators from diverse disciplines and international contexts, creating a network that facilitated meaningful exchanges on AI integration into higher education curricula. The initiative was intentionally framed as a faculty-led, inquiry-driven community of practice. Rather than focusing on tool-specific training, the FLC emphasized exploration, experimentation, and iterative learning—grounded in participants' own teaching contexts and disciplinary needs. Faculty from across colleges and programs at both institutions were invited to participate, with no requirement for prior AI expertise. The cohort included instructors from humanities, STEM, business, and health-related fields, bringing diverse pedagogical assumptions and content frameworks to the conversations.

Collaborative Inquiry and Pedagogical Transformation

Participants in this initiative emphasized the critical value of cross-cultural and interdisciplinary collaboration, noting that such engagement provided diverse perspectives that enriched their pedagogical approaches and encouraged innovative practices that individual institutions might not have developed independently (Cronin, Cochrane, & Gordon, 2016; Cochrane et al., 2013). Faculty members involved in the Generative AI Global Community of Practice highlighted enhanced confidence and greater fluency in integrating AI into their teaching and learning environments. Through ongoing dialogue, educators could critically evaluate AI tools, collectively navigating ethical complexities and addressing shared challenges such as ensuring fairness in AI-generated assessments, protecting student privacy, and mitigating potential biases in AI-generated content. Moreover, this sustained collaboration allowed for iterative experimentation, significantly reducing the time typically required to transition from initial exposure to informed application of AI tools within instructional contexts.

One of the central commitments of the FLC was to create a space where faculty could "think with" each other—not to arrive at fixed answers, but to surface key questions and design principles that might guide practice. This included discussion around common tensions: how to retain instructor presence in AI-assisted learning environments; how to scaffold students' understanding of generative outputs; how to balance experimentation with institutional messaging around academic integrity. Rather than treating AI as a disruptive force, the community treated it as an evolving context—one that required thoughtful, collaborative sensemaking. While the sessions were informal in tone, they were scaffolded by a shared framework of reflective inquiry. Participants were invited to contribute to shared documents, develop prototypes or course revisions, and reflect on their own shifting beliefs and practices. This allowed for a form of low-stakes accountability and community witnessing: participants could track their learning over time, while drawing connections between individual experimentation and broader institutional narratives.

Strategic Impact and Scalable Innovation

Crucially, the cross-institutional nature of the community created affordances that would not have emerged in a single-campus model. Faculty compared institutional policies, student expectations, and leadership discourses around AI—surfacing both commonalities and divergences in how the technology was being positioned within their respective institutions. In doing so, the group began to map not just how AI was being used, but how it was being framed and interpreted in different academic cultures—mirroring the cross-cultural AI collaboration patterns noted by McIntosh (2024). While the benefits for the educators in the learning community were vast, the impact of the FLC extended beyond the participants themselves. Several faculty members brought their learnings into departmental meetings or curriculum committees, while facilitators at both institutions synthesized community insights into broader strategy sessions. The initiative ultimately functioned as both a microcosm and a testbed: a space to model AI-integrated pedagogy while contributing to institutional approaches to digital learning transformation.

At the institutional level, the structured design of faculty learning communities supported strategic alignment with broader organizational priorities. Institutional leaders who participated in or facilitated these communities reported improvements in their capacity to make informed, data-driven decisions about resource allocation, faculty development investments, and strategic partnerships aimed at furthering institutional goals. This alignment was crucial in securing administrative support and fostering institutional cultures that valued continuous learning and innovation in teaching and learning practices.

A final significant outcome of these collaborative initiatives, as exemplified by the UTSA and Swinburne partnership, was the creation of replicable, scalable models for global engagement around AI competencies. The Generative AI Global Community of Practice served as a prototype demonstrating how international and interdisciplinary collaboration could effectively address the complexities of AI integration in education. Institutions that participated in similar initiatives reported the development of robust and replicable frameworks that other institutions could adapt to their unique contexts, thereby amplifying their impact beyond initial implementation sites.

Ultimately, this initiative highlights the immense potential of faculty learning communities to facilitate meaningful professional growth, enhance instructional innovation, and strategically position institutions to proactively respond to emerging educational phenomena. Building upon these insights, the subsequent section, Analysis and Reflections on Implementation, will critically explore how these global communities operate in practice, examining key success factors and challenges that influence their effectiveness in supporting educational innovation.

Analysis and Reflections on Implementation

Implementing a global faculty learning community across two institutions with different governance structures, academic cultures, and operational timelines required both intentional design and adaptive facilitation. While the collaboration between UTSA and Swinburne was rooted in a shared curiosity about generative AI, the success of the initiative hinged on more than mutual interest. It relied on a willingness to engage uncertainty together, to embrace experimentation without guarantees of success, and to remain responsive to the rhythms and constraints of each institutional context.

Navigating Time Zones, Calendars, and Capacity

One of the most immediate implementation challenges was logistical: coordinating meetings, schedules, and academic calendars across hemispheres. The facilitation team made intentional choices to keep the structure lightweight—balancing synchronous sessions with asynchronous reflection activities, and minimizing prework to reduce cognitive load. Participants appreciated the low-barrier format, noting that the ability to "drop in" without needing to prepare formal materials made the space feel open, supportive, and non-performative. Still, differences in institutional timelines (semester vs. trimester systems, varying holiday schedules) occasionally disrupted momentum, requiring flexibility and re-grounding at multiple points throughout the process.

Facilitators also acknowledged the challenge of sustaining energy across a voluntary cohort without a formal deliverable or outcome requirement. This decision—deliberate and pedagogically grounded—was both a strength and a limitation. While it preserved a sense of openness and exploration, it also meant that participation varied over time, and some members felt uncertain about what "success" looked like within the community. Reflecting on this tension, facilitators described learning to trust emergence: to design for connection rather than completion, and to measure value in terms of dialogue, confidence-building, and iterative practice rather than discrete outputs (Evans, 2015).

Trust, Vulnerability, and Relational Culture

Several participants remarked on the uniquely relational tone of the community. Early dialogue focused not on AI tools, but on shared questions and open-ended prompts. This established a tone of mutual exploration, where faculty felt comfortable sharing in-progress ideas, pedagogical uncertainties, and early-stage attempts to integrate AI into their courses. That comfort was not accidental—it emerged from intentional choices around facilitation, including modeling vulnerability, foregrounding reflection, and avoiding hierarchies of expertise. One of the organizers described it as "keeping the space warm": reducing the pressure to perform and allowing people to bring not just their professional roles, but their hesitations and hopes.

This relational grounding also supported cross-cultural dialogue. Faculty surfaced differences in how AI was being discussed at their institutions—not only in terms of policy, but in terms of institutional tone, student expectations, and leadership posture. These differences became sites for reflection rather than conflict, and participants used them to deepen their own local strategies. For example, hearing how another institution was framing AI as part of its innovation narrative allowed some participants to advocate for a more expansive, less punitive discourse within their departments.

Shifting from Experimentation to Strategy

A key reflection from both facilitators and participants was the catalytic effect of structured community on institutional readiness. While the group did not produce a formal white paper or toolkit, it nonetheless influenced institutional thinking. Participants brought stories and strategies back to their departments, cited insights in policy discussions, and embedded AI reflection into assessment redesign conversations. At UTSA, for instance, faculty involvement in the community informed internal conversations around course design guidance and professional development programming. And at both institutions, community themes helped shape upcoming learning and teaching initiatives tied to curriculum transformation.

Perhaps most importantly, the community helped faculty and facilitators alike shift from isolated experimentation to strategic visioning. Rather than reacting to the pace of change, they began to identify institutional leverage points—places where reflective pedagogy, student partnership, and AI-supported design could converge into longer-term planning. In this way, the FLC functioned not just as a site of exploration, but as an incubator for institutional imagination.

Reflecting on Role Fluidity and Co-Facilitation

One of the most distinctive features of the implementation process was the porous boundary between "facilitator" and "participant." Facilitators positioned themselves as co-learners, often bringing in their own course challenges, departmental tensions, or ethical questions. This iterative, remix-oriented approach to professional dialogue aligned with emerging models of networked design exploration, where the process of combining, reframing, and repurposing pedagogical ideas becomes a method of faculty learning (Han & Nickerson, 2015). Faculty expressed appreciation for this co-facilitation model, with one of the organizers noting that it felt "less like training and more like growing something together."

Still, this fluidity required active navigation. Facilitators occasionally had to recalibrate when sessions drifted into parallel monologues or when momentum waned. Maintaining the right level of structure—enough to sustain engagement, but not so much as to preempt emergent learning—was a balancing act. Over time, the group developed a shared rhythm, where even pauses or moments of ambiguity became part of the reflective process. As one facilitator noted, "we had to stop thinking of ourselves as content providers and start thinking of ourselves as space-makers."

Implications for Distance Education Practice and Policy

The global faculty learning community at the center of this case study offers a compelling model for how institutions might build distributed, responsive frameworks to support AI integration in distance education. While the learning community itself was not exclusive to online instructors, its structure and ethos resonate strongly with the needs and challenges of digital learning environments (Fox et al., 2021). The initiative's emphasis on collaborative inquiry, asynchronous flexibility, and reflective pedagogy points to several strategic implications for distance education practice and institutional policy.

Flexible Structures Enable Deeper Engagement

The hybrid design of the faculty learning community—combining live sessions with asynchronous reflection, shared documents, and minimal prework—proved especially effective in accommodating the realities of overextended educators. This model offers a roadmap for designing distance education faculty development that is both rigorous and humane. Rather than relying on compliance-oriented training modules or high-stakes assessments of AI readiness, institutions might invest in creating "slow" learning spaces: ones that allow for iterative exploration, relational accountability, and the kind of trust-building that underpins genuine instructional transformation.

For distance education units, this means rethinking how professional learning is delivered. Communities of practice may be more effective than content repositories in helping instructors meaningfully integrate AI into course design, assessment, and feedback strategies—particularly when they are grounded in open, inclusive structures that aim to bridge longstanding digital divides (Lane, 2009; Mills, Bali, & Eaton, 2023). The experience of the UTSA–Swinburne learning community suggests that even modestly structured, time-bound communities can yield insights that outlast the cohort itself—particularly when participation is framed around shared inquiry rather than technical training.

Faculty Voice as a Policy Asset

As institutions race to update policies on AI use—particularly around academic integrity, grading, and student data—distance learning leaders are uniquely positioned to ensure those policies reflect the lived experiences of online instructors and learners. The faculty learning community provided a rare space for policy-adjacent dialogue: where participants could surface gaps in institutional messaging, share alternative framings, and begin to imagine more constructive narratives about AI's role in education.

Participants described using insights from the learning community to reframe AI conversations within their departments—from surveillance and detection toward curiosity and co-design. This shift in discourse is particularly critical in online environments, where instructors often feel disconnected from institutional decision-making and where AI-infused learning tools are most likely to be deployed at scale. The inclusion of distance educators in community-based AI exploration can help institutions avoid reactive policy cycles and move toward more nuanced, contextually grounded guidance.

Reimagining Peer Learning in Distributed Settings

One of the core takeaways from the UTSA–Swinburne initiative was the power of lightly facilitated, transdisciplinary peer dialogue. In distance education contexts—where instructors are often geographically dispersed and pedagogically isolated—such structures can serve not just as development vehicles, but as morale boosters and professional lifelines. Faculty participants repeatedly emphasized that the learning community offered more than just ideas or resources: it offered belonging. That sense of being in community with others who were navigating similar uncertainties helped mitigate the sense of isolation that often accompanies both distance teaching and early-stage AI experimentation.

Institutions supporting distance faculty might consider investing in small-scale, cross-departmental learning groups—ideally facilitated but not overly structured—where instructors can surface questions, reflect on AI integration, and share approaches in real time. These spaces need not be resource-intensive; what they require is a posture of listening, trust in professional judgment, and mechanisms for institutional learning that emerge from the ground up (Huffman et al., 2016).

A Strategic Lever for Institutional Learning

Finally, the structure of the global FLC offered an unexpected benefit: it became a reflective surface for institutional strategy (Fox et al., 2021). Distance education leaders are often tasked with bridging innovation and infrastructure, pedagogy and policy. The learning community served as a microcosm of this work, revealing where institutional AI ambitions aligned—or conflicted—with the realities of faculty experience. In this way, the FLC acted as an informal diagnostic tool, surfacing strategic blind spots while also highlighting pockets of possibility.

For distance learning units seeking to align their AI work with institutional transformation efforts, this case suggests the value of investing in communities that are not only instructional, but strategic. Faculty reflections, when aggregated and framed with care, can inform leadership decisions around technology procurement, support models, and curricular planning. Moreover, they can anchor AI policy in the lived wisdom of educators who are already operating at the frontlines of digital change.

Conclusion and Future Directions

The global faculty learning community between the University of Texas at San Antonio and Swinburne University of Technology offers more than a case of successful AI-related professional learning—it provides a blueprint for how institutions might reimagine collaboration, experimentation, and strategy-building in an era of rapid technological change. By fostering cross-institutional, transdisciplinary dialogue grounded in curiosity rather than compliance, the initiative demonstrated that AI integration is not simply a technical challenge, but a cultural and pedagogical one.

Participants reported increased confidence, ethical clarity, and pedagogical fluency in navigating generative AI tools. But beyond these individual gains, the learning community also surfaced institutional insights: about the role of faculty voice in shaping AI discourse, the tensions between policy and practice, and the value of creating reflective space amid acceleration. These insights were not pre-planned outcomes—they emerged through sustained conversation, shared uncertainty, and a willingness to lead without knowing all the answers.

For institutions seeking to foster intentional AI integration, especially within distributed or digitally mediated learning environments, the lessons from this case are clear. Professional learning must be relational, not transactional. Faculty agency must be centered, not assumed. And communities of practice, when designed with care and humility, can serve as both engines of innovation and mirrors for institutional self-understanding.

Ultimately, the work of embedding AI into higher education is not about catching up to the latest tools—it is about cultivating the capacity to learn, adapt, and reflect in public. The generative potential of faculty learning communities lies not just in what they teach, but in how they model the collective work of shaping education's future, together.

Acknowledgements
The authors extend their deepest gratitude to Rowena Ulbrick, whose vision and leadership as the facilitator of the Swinburne University of Technology AI in Education Community of Practice made this work possible. Her dedication to fostering collaboration and innovation within the SUT community was instrumental in shaping our collective efforts. They also thank Brett Copeland from UTSA and Rohan Gerrard from SUT for their exceptional support in communication strategy and visual design, which enhanced the clarity, reach, and impact of our shared initiatives.

References

Cochrane, T., Buchem, I., Camacho, M., Cronin, C., Gordon, A., & Keegan, H. (2013). Building global learning communities. Research in Learning Technology, 21. https://doi.org/10.3402/rlt.v21i0.21955

Cronin, C., Cochrane, T., & Gordon, A. (2016). Nurturing global collaboration and networked learning in higher education. Research in Learning Technology. http://aut.researchgateway.ac.nz/handle/10292/10959

Evans, P. (2015). Open online spaces of professional learning: Context, personalisation and facilitation. TechTrends, 59(1), 31–36. https://doi.org/10.1007/s11528-014-0817-7

Fox, K., Vignare, K., Yuan, L., Tesene, M., Beltran, K., Schweizer, Halle, Brokos, M., & Seaborn, R. (2021). Strategies for Implementing Digital Learning Infrastructure to Support Equitable Outcomes: A Case-based Guidebook for Institutional Leaders. Every Learner Everywhere. https://www.everylearnereverywhere.org/wp-content/uploads/Strategies-for-Implementing-Digital-Learning-Infrastructure-to-Support-Equitable-Outcomes-ACC-FINAL-1-Updated-Links-by-CF-2.pdf

Gunder, A., & Shellgren, M. (2022). Advancing Universal Access to Quality Digital Learning through Global Coalitions and Narrative Practices. An Open Knowledge Product for the 3rd UNESCO World Higher Education Conference (WHEC 2022). Online Learning Consortium. http://files.eric.ed.gov/fulltext/ED622501.pdf

Han, Y., & Nickerson, J. V. (2015). Understanding the Exploration of Design Space in Remix Networks. In Workshop on Information in Networks. https://papers.ssrn.com/abstract=2670658

Hoyte, D., Myers, S., Powell, L., Sansone, R., & Walter, K. (2010). Communities of practice: An international learning experience. International Journal for the Scholarship of Teaching and Learning, 4(1). https://doi.org/10.20429/ijsotl.2010.040103

Huffman, J. B., Olivier, D. F., Wang, T., Chen, P., Hairon, S., & Pang, N. (2016). Global conceptualization of the professional learning community process: transitioning from country perspectives to international commonalities. International Journal of Leadership in Education, 19(3), 327–351. https://doi.org/10.1080/13603124.2015.1020343

Lane, A. (2009). The Impact of Openness on Bridging Educational Digital Divides. The International Review of Research in Open and Distributed Learning, 10(5). https://doi.org/10.19173/irrodl.v10i5.637

McIntosh, N. (2024). Bridging cultures, advancing AI. ASCILITE Publications, 117–118. https://doi.org/10.14742/apubs.2024.1174

Mills, A., Bali, M., & Eaton, L. (2023). How do we respond to generative AI in education? Open educational practices give us a framework for an ongoing process. Journal of Applied Learning & Teaching, 6(1), 16–30. https://journals.sfu.ca/jalt/index.php/jalt/article/view/843

Tharapos, M., & O'Connell, B. T. (2022). Transnational communities of practice: Their development, operation, and contribution. Journal of Studies in International Education, 26(3), 299–317. https://doi.org/10.1177/1028315320964314

Wenger, E. (n.d.). Communities of practice: Learning as a social system. Retrieved from https://participativelearning.org/pluginfile.php/636/mod_resource/content/3/Learningasasocialsystem.pdf

Wenger, E. (1999). Communities of Practice: Learning, Meaning, and Identity. Cambridge University Press.

Wenger, E. (2011). Communities of practice: A brief introduction. http://scholarsbank.uoregon.edu/xmlui/handle/1794/11736

Building an institutional AI Learning Tutor: A case study on supporting flipped classroom in a business school

Irina Otmanine[1], Denys Giordano[2], Frederic Munier[3]

[1] Innovation & Learner Experience Department, SKEMA Business School, France; irina.otmanine@skema.edu
[2] Innovation & Learner Experience Department, SKEMA Business School, France; denys.giordano@skema.edu
[3] Globalisation Academy, SKEMA Business School, France; frederic.munier@skema.edu

Correspondence: Irina Otmanine: irina.otmanine@gmail.com

Abstract:

This experience presents the design, implementation, and evaluation of an institutional AI Learning Tutor to support undergraduate students' learning within a flipped classroom approach in business school settings. The study begins by presenting the theoretical foundations regarding the role of AI learning assistants in higher education and their potential contributions to the flipped classroom model. It then details the design and implementation process of the AI Learning Tutor for the cohort of 353 students followed by an evaluation of its impact and student feedback. The findings highlight the benefits and challenges of integrating AI-driven learning assistants in educational settings, emphasizing the importance of pedagogical goals, responsible use of AI for learning and institutional strategy.

Keywords: Artificial Intelligence (AI), AI assistant, Digital learning assistant, Undergraduate students

Introduction

The rapid proliferation of Generative artificial intelligence (GenAI) tools such as ChatGPT, Copilot, and Gemini is impacting teaching and learning practices, as well as tools and methods in higher education in general. According to the Digital Education Council Global AI Student Survey 2024, 86% of students in 16 countries have already used AI-powered tools in their academic work. However, 58% report a lack of skills in effectively using AI, and 59% expect educational institutions to provide structured AI integration (Digital Education Council, 2024). This raises the question of responsibly introducing AI tools in the educational context, enhancing AI literacy for teachers and students, and developing new institutional approaches to foster ethical and equitable access to AI tools.

With the aim of investigating these challenges, this paper presents an experiential analysis of the design, implementation, and evaluation of an AI Learning Tutor to support undergraduate students' learning in a business school within the context of a flipped classroom approach. We will start by presenting the theoretical foundations of the experiment regarding the role of AI learning assistants in higher education and their possible contribution to the flipped classroom approach. Then, the design and implementation process of the institutional AI Learning Tutor will be described, followed by the results of the evaluation and students' feedback.

AI learning assistants in higher education

The role of AI assistants and chatbots in higher education has started to be explored in recent academic literature, even though there is not much empirical work currently available (McGrath et al., 2024). For example, Schön et al. (2023) highlight how AI assistants' impact various educational domains, including human interaction, learning processes, institutional organization, and innovation. Their study emphasizes both the benefits—such as personalized tutoring and improved administrative efficiency—and the risks associated with academic integrity and ethical AI use. Similarly, McGrath et al. (2024) offer a comprehensive review of AI chatbots in higher education, analyzing empirical studies conducted after the release of ChatGPT. They identify two prevailing discourses: one optimistic, which views AI chatbots as tools for enhancing personalized learning, and another cautionary, which raises concerns about trust, academic integrity, and the displacement of traditional teaching roles.

One of key conclusions from these studies is the need for structured AI integration that aligns with pedagogical goals while addressing ethical considerations (Schön et al., 2023; McGrath et al., 2024). These findings reinforce the importance of carefully implementing AI-driven tools to optimize learning outcomes while maintaining academic integrity.

In addition to these findings, the study by Renties et al. (2024) reveals that students possess complex views on the role of Generative AI in education. They recognize its benefits for personalized and accessible learning while expressing concerns about academic integrity, data privacy, and depersonalization. This experiment with the distance students' population indicates the preference for institutional AI digital assistance rather than freely available tools like ChatGPT or CoPilot. This approach underscores the advantages of in-house Gen AI tools in enhancing learning experiences without compromising academic integrity or privacy (Renties et al., 2024).

The flipped classroom approach

The flipped classroom model has gained significant attention as an innovative pedagogical approach that enhances student learning by shifting traditional lectures outside the classroom and utilizing class time for interactive activities (Alan & Yurt, 2024). According to recent study, the flipped classroom also has a positive impact on most attitudinal dimensions, highlighting its effectiveness in shaping students' attitudes for attending the real classroom (Cladera, 2025). Research has shown that integrating AI-driven tools, such as ChatGPT, into flipped learning environments can improve student engagement, personalized learning, and overall academic performance by facilitating self-directed learning and fostering course retention (Alan & Yurt, 2024).

Another crucial component of effective flipped classrooms is the use of advanced prompting techniques to guide students through structured inquiry-based learning (Wang et al., 2024). Studies highlight that well-designed AI prompts help students engage critically with materials, formulate meaningful questions, and develop problem-solving skills. By incorporating structured AI-assisted prompts, educators can enhance student autonomy while ensuring alignment with learning objectives (Wang et al., 2024).

These insights have guided the design and implementation of the AI Learning Tutor, as outlined in the Method section.

Method

SKEMA Business School developed an AI Assistant to provide tailored support for students in learning, career development, and entrepreneurship. The initiative addresses issues of cost accessibility, digital equity, and pedagogical integration. Below we will focus on the AI Learning Tutor module, as this part of AI Assistant has been presented to students in Spring 2024.
The experience involved the design stage followed by a pilot study during the 2023-2024 academic year, targeting 170 students enrolled in the " Major Challenges of Consilience " undergraduate course at SKEMA Business School. During 2024-2025 academic year, AI Learning Tutor, integrated with the learning management system (LMS) was deployed within a course for 720 undergraduate students' cohort. A mixed-methods approach was then employed to evaluate the AI Learning Tutor's impact on student learning and integration within undergraduate programs.

Design of the AI Learning Tutor

The AI Learning Tutor was specifically designed to enhance student learning experiences through structured AI support. " Major Challenges of Consilience " core course for undergraduate students incorporates a wide range of mandatory and optional learning materials to foster interdisciplinary critical thinking and academic writing skills: academic articles, video and audio interviews, periodicals. The course was designed within the flipped classroom approach: to be prepared for the course and participate in the session, students need to work through these materials. During every session, students also needed to respond to a real-time MQC test which was graded and contained materials of lectures and optional readings.

The pedagogical approach underlying the Learning Tutor was intended to foster student autonomy and encourage proactive learning strategies. As described by the faculty member overseeing the course, "the Learning Tutor serves as an intellectual gym where students continuously train throughout the semester to excel in their final assessments."

The Learning Tutor operates by leveraging course materials directly uploaded to the school LMS platform (Moodle), ensuring that students work with resources pre-approved by faculty members. The tool was developed using a no-code platform (Glide) that integrates components leveraging different AI models (OpenAI, AzureML, and Google Cloud) depending on the specific use case (e.g., text generation, document-to-text conversion, image-to-text processing). The approach of developing a proper application for the learning purpose provides several advantages, including enhanced control over the user experience, consistency in our prompting strategy, increased flexibility and agility in development, and equitable access for all students. Thus, the prompts used for different functions and incorporated into Glide were first tested by the team of teachers and instructional designers. The students had no need to use specific prompts and had direct access to the application and its functions (see Figure 1).

The design of the tool focused on three primary features:

- **Explore a Concept:** AI assists students in deepening their understanding of key course concepts through access to validated sources from the institutional LMS platform, ensuring accuracy and alignment with course materials.
- **Summarize a Document:** AI Learning Tutor enables students to generate concise summaries of diverse academic resources, including articles, lecture notes, and multimedia content. The students have a possibility to generate a short or a detailed summary of a learning resource, including text, audio or video. The interactive chat feature of the Learning Tutor illustrates that the tool is not limited to simple summarization but rather supports students in actively questioning and deepening their comprehension of the text.
- **Quiz generation:** AI Learning Tutor creates quizzes tailored to individual learning needs, allowing students to practice and reinforce their knowledge in a targeted manner using only materials provided by the pedagogical team. The students have the possibility to generate questions on the course topic of their choice and consult the feedback after answering the questions.

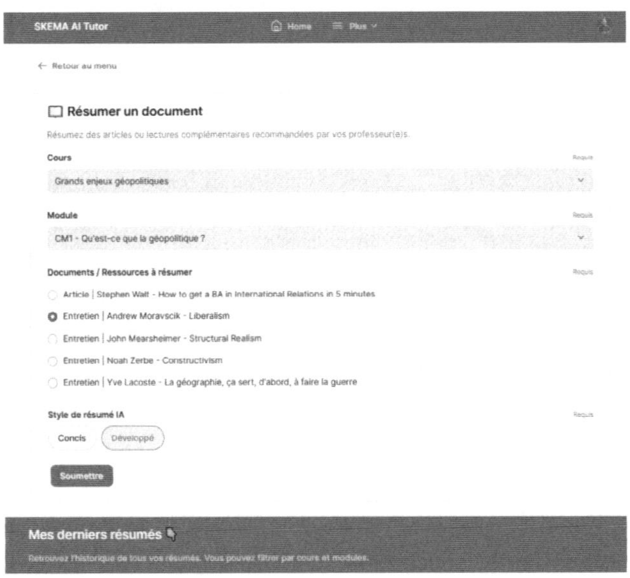

Figure 1: "Summarize a Document" Function of AI Learning Tutor and choice of course resources – student view (in French)

To ensure responsible AI usage, SKEMA Business School has developed an Institutional AI Usage Charter. This document outlines ethical AI practices for teaching, learning, and research while advocating for sustainability and data security. Complementing this effort, a Competency Framework for Responsible AI has been established, defining essential AI literacy skills for all students. These initiatives aim to promote an informed and ethical engagement with AI technologies in educational context, including AI Learning Tutor.

Results

First pilot version

First introduced in January 2024 to a restricted cohort of 170 undergraduate students, the AI Learning Tutor was presented during the first session of the course by the pedagogical team. The use of the tool was optional for students. After this first semester from January to March 2024, a questionnaire and a focus group were organized to gather feedback on students' usage of the tool, its usefulness in supporting learning, and its technical smoothness.

Of the 63 participants, 48 confirmed using the tool at least once during the semester. Among the reasons for non-usage were the preference for other free tools (7 students) and the lack of awareness about the tool's availability (6 students), while 3 other students declared their unwillingness to change their study method during the semester. However, overall feedback from students was positive regarding access (73% rating from good to excellent), ergonomics (70,6% from good to excellent), result relevance (58,3%), and learning usefulness (72,9), as shown on Figure 2. The focus group of voluntary students helped enhance MCQ quality and refine prompts to generate concise and detailed summaries by incorporating reflexive questions.

Figure 2: Results of Questionnaire 1. AI Learning Tutor access, ergonomics, result relevance, and learning usefulness for students. Translated from questionnaire in French.

Second version and its student applications

During the 2024-2025 academic year, the AI Learning Tutor, integrated with the learning management system (LMS), was deployed within a course for a cohort of 720 undergraduate students studying "Major Challenges of Consilience." The use of the tool remained optional for students and was presented at the beginning of the course as an aid for their learning and preparation for the sessions. The students' applications of this second version of the tool were analyzed using connection statistics accessible directly via the Glide application and a questionnaire distributed at the end of the course.

The usage data between October and December 2024 provides further insight into engagement levels.

- **Active participation:** 353 students actively used the tool, representing over 50% of the target cohort.
- **Content creation:** students generated approximately 1,900 summaries and 4,000 questions, with usage spikes observed before lectures and exams.

The distribution of usage based on the total number of queries (2,750) is as follows: Explore a concept: 10%, Summarize a document: 70%, Quiz generation: 20%.

The survey, distributed at the end of the course, was completed by 32 students, representing 9% of users. The limited number of respondents can be attributed to the timing, just before winter break, and the fact that the survey was sent by email instead of being presented in class.However, the survey results demonstrated a positive reception of the AI Learning Tutor, as presented on Figure 3. While 76,9% agreed with the sentence that the tool helps to prepare for tests in class, 57,4 % indicated that the use of AI Learning Tutor enhanced their comprehension of course materials and 73% agreed that the use of this tool reinforced their learning.

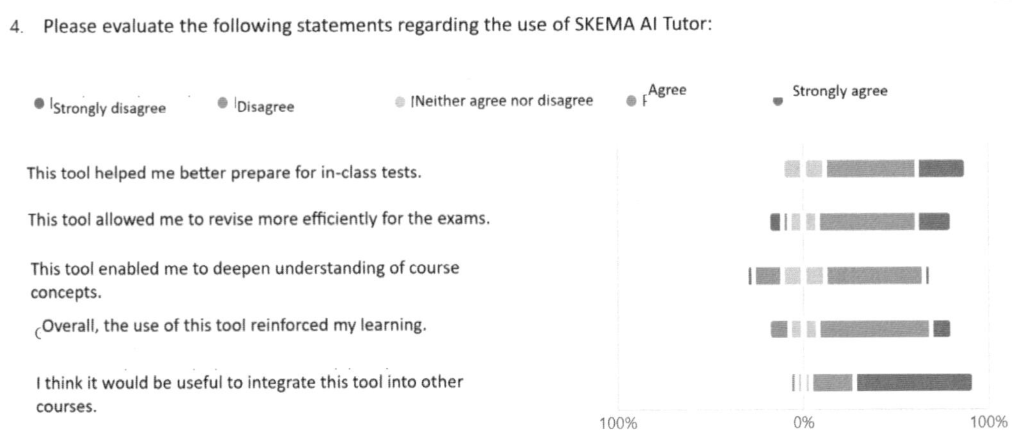

Figure 3: Results of Questionnaire 2. AI Learning Tutor as aid for classroom tests, course concepts comprehension, reinforcement of learning and utility for other courses in the program. Translated from questionnaire in French.

An even higher percentage (88%) of students expressed interest in expanding AI support to other courses, such as law and marketing. As for the improvements suggested by the students, they listed ideas such as generating questions based on the level and progression and having more complex questions similar to those proposed during the final exam. Additionally, some students recommended further enhancements and additional functions:

> "Maybe a feature to help us summarize courses, to help us create revision sheets: key concepts and definitions, important authors..."

> "Offer quizzes that mix all the courses to revise better. And maybe also create a sheet summarizing the course authors with their ideas."

Limits of the experience

Students' feedback

As we can see, the feedback collected from the surveys comes from engaged students who followed the advice of the pedagogical team, utilized the tool, and were likely already motivated by the course content itself. Under these conditions, it is challenging to generalize these feedback results for the entire cohort. A more detailed study is needed to better understand the cases of non-use of the AI Learning Assistant and the reasons behind it.

Pedagogical approach

Since the use of the tool was not mandatory during the course, students had the liberty to explore the content assisted by AI in the way they believed it was useful for them. This opens the question of self-regulated learning strategies and their deployment by students at an individual level. As seen from the experiment, the solicitations of the AI Learning Tutor were elevated at the beginning of the course, just before classes with MCQ graded tests, and before the midterm period in late October. Figure 4 shows the distribution of tool queries from the beginning of the course on September 26, with peaks of usage corresponding to courses with graded tests and midterms (the period from October 22 to October 28 was dedicated to midterm preparation) but very low or no usage during the period without on-campus classes on the subject until November 12, and low usage before and during the last class which had no graded assignment.

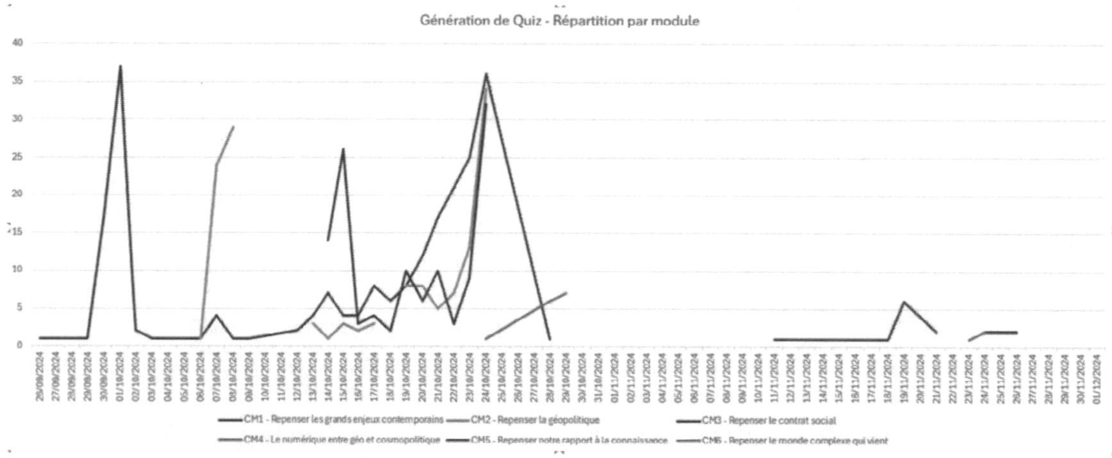

Figure 4: Solicitations of AI Learning Tutor by students through the semester – Quiz generation function by module. Module titles in French (CM) corresponding to different colors.

Conclusion and Perspectives

This experiential paper highlights both the benefits and challenges of AI-powered learning assistants developed within a higher education institution. The design of a proper tool offers an institution the possibility to manage the responsible use of AI, its specific application in accordance with the course scenario (e.g., flipped classroom) and learning objectives, and provides an individual approach to learning and revising materials by ensuring equal access to digital tools.

Students engaged in the experiment with this new tool reported its usefulness in terms of understanding course concepts and reinforcing learning. However, concerns remain regarding increasing engagement and autonomy for all students in the cohort. As highlighted by Darvishi et al. (2024), students tend to rely on rather than learn from AI assistance, and the integration of self-regulation strategies should be supported to develop independent learning skills.

The results also suggest that AI tools can enhance personalized learning, but their use must be carefully structured to maintain critical thinking. For instance, the summary function was one of the most used features among students. While this can be a useful tool for revising learning materials before class, it should not replace the thoughtful reading of articles and other materials essential for acquiring new skills in the domain.

Key lessons learned from the design of the tool itself can be resumed as following:

- Continuous iterations of the application, informed by user feedback, led to enhanced adaptability and effectiveness.
- Students view AI as a catalyst for critical thinking, problem-solving, and deeper learning.
- Increased demand for personalization underscores the need for tailored AI-driven educational support.

In the particular case of this experiment, further developments will focus on improving AI adaptability to different academic disciplines, but also for career development, consolidating the AI learning supports tools in a single-entry point.

Furthermore, the integration of AI assistants at a large scale requires financial and logistical considerations. Budget constraints were initially a challenge for ensuring universal access, which was addressed by optimizing internal resources and offering the tool free of charge to students. This case study suggests that institutions looking to implement similar AI-powered learning assistants should consider scalable and cost-effective strategies.

The AI Learning Tutor project demonstrates the potential of AI-driven educational tools in fostering personalized learning experiences. While student feedback was predominantly positive, institutional policies need to evolve to address ethical and academic integrity concerns, and integration of this type of tools at a large scale to ensure equity in access for all students.

Supplementary files

Supplementary files can be provided at request.

Competing interests

The authors have no competing interests to declare. There is no monetary gain to the authors for the use of the AI Learning Tutor.

Ethics and consent

Written, informed consent was obtained from the survey respondents.

References

Alan, S., & Yurt, E. (2024). Flipped Learning: An Innovative Model for Enhancing Education Through ChatGPT. International Journal of Modern Education Studies, 8(1). https://doi.org/10.51383/ijonmes.2024.328

Cladera, M. (2025). Does the flipped classroom improve undergraduate students' attitudes towards econometrics? Innovations in Education and Teaching International, 62(1), 4–15. https://doi.org/10.1080/14703297.2024.2309319

Darvishi, A., Khosravi, H., Sadiq, S., Gašević, D., & Siemens, G. (2024). Impact of AI assistance on student agency. Computers & Education, 210, 104967. https://doi.org/10.1016/j.compedu.2023.104967

Digital Education Council. (2024). AI or Not AI: What Students Want:Digital Education Council Global AI Student Survey 2024. https://www.digitaleducationcouncil.com/post/what-students-want-key-results-from-dec-global-ai-student-survey-2024

McGrath, C., Farazouli, A., & Cerratto-Pargman, T. (2024). Generative AI chatbots in higher education: a review of an emerging research area. Higher Education. https://doi.org/10.1007/s10734-024-01288-w

Rienties, B., Herodotou, C., Tessarolo, F., Domingue, J., Duttaroy, S., & Whitelock, D. (2024). An institutional AI digital assistant: what do distance learners expect and value? EDEN 2025 Conference Ubiquity Proceedings, 7. https://doi.org/10.5334/uproc.129

Schön, E.-M., Neumann, M., Hofmann-Stölting, C., Baeza-Yates, R., & Rauschenberger, M. (2023). How are AI assistants changing higher education? Frontiers in Computer Science, 5. https://doi.org/10.3389/fcomp.2023.1208550

Wang, M., Wang, M., Xu, X., Yang, L., Cai, D., & Yin, M. (2024). Unleashing ChatGPT's Power: A Case Study on Optimizing Information Retrieval in Flipped Classrooms via Prompt Engineering. IEEE Transactions on Learning Technologies, 17, 629–641. https://doi.org/10.1109/TLT.2023.3324714

How AI changes teaching: digital competences, didactical characteristics, and responsible use

Estela Daukšienė[1], Nemira Mačianskienė[2]

[1] Education Academy, Vytautas Magnus University, Lithuania; estela.dauksiene@vdu.lt
[2] Institute of Foreign Languages, Vytautas Magnus University, Lithuania; nemira.macianskiene@vdu.lt

Correspondence: Estela Daukšienė: estela.dauksiene@vdu.lt

Abstract:

The research aims to discuss how AI transforms teaching and how future teachers see the importance of responsible use of AI tools in education. Digitally competent teachers have to use AI responsibly, foster learners' responsible use of AI, and integrate AI tools focusing on course aims and other didactical characteristics. Focus group discussions were selected as a qualitative research method for data collection. Future teachers were selected as a target group for the research. Research results show that future teachers are sceptical about how teachers use technologies and AI for teaching today. Still, they see the need for teacher digital competence development to use AI responsibly. They suggest teachers start with small steps, testing the tools and learning about them, but neither trust them much nor rely heavily on them to preserve the human touch in teaching.

Keywords: Teacher digital competence, artificial intelligence, responsible AI use, future teachers, AI didactical characteristics, higher education

Introduction

Digital teacher competences and their development are essential in today's schools. Still, this process is associated with various challenges, which are changing with the advancement of technology and the substitution of AI for an increasing number of activities and jobs (Vihar, 2025; Krstic, 2024, Brown et al., 2024). Different researchers (Faloon, 2020), international organisations (European Joint Research Centre, Unesco, UNICEF, etc.) or even countries (National Institute of Educational Technologies and Teacher Training (Spain), 2017, Norwegian Centre for ICT in Education, 2017; Education Wales (Welsh government, UK), 2022, etc.) offer various models for developing teacher digital competencies. Recent technological development and more intense use of generative AI tools have brought revisions, additions or updates of these frameworks by creating additional competences or their subsets to the existing digital competences (Eddico, 2021; Borgne et al., 2023; Miao, & Cukurova, 2024). Some researchers (Borgne et al., 2023; Miao & Cukurova, 2024) also define AI competence for teachers.

This research focuses on teacher digital competence development, where AI competence is defined as part of the existing digital competence. It does not focus on AI technological or responsible development. It supports the idea that in education, we should focus not on AI competence but on the development of human competences and responsible use of AI. Today, AI is not as competent as a teacher; thus, the research analyses teacher digital competence development in the face of changing and increasingly used AI. Therefore, the aim of this research is to discuss AI didactical characteristics, focusing on how AI transforms teaching, and how future teachers see the importance of responsible AI use in education.

Theoretical background

European researchers usually refer to the European Digital Competence Framework (DigCompEdu, Redecker & Punie, 2017) and follow its definition and composition of teacher digital competencies – 3 blocks, 6 domains and 22 competencies. Borgne et al. (2023) explored how this framework could be expanded by introducing AI in the activities while teaching. They suggested what teachers need to know about AI and be able to do with AI in professional development competence, Digital resources competence, Teaching and Learning, Assessment,

Empowering learners and Facilitating learners's digital competence areas. Each digital competence area has its specific subtopics regarding different aspects of AI, such as Data and AI governance, humanity, learning analytics, potential risks, biases, limitations and ethical principles in learning practices. The UNESCO AI framework for teachers (Miao & Cukurova, 2024) outlines a slightly different set of five key competency areas: A human-centred mindset, Ethics of AI and responsible use, AI foundations and applications, AI pedagogy, and AI for professional development. The latter two competencies are, in the context, similar to those in the DigCompEdu model (esp. Area 1 and 3-4). Both frameworks focus on progressing from building awareness and deepening knowledge to applying and creating with AI ethically, from teaching with AI to transforming teaching practices through responsible and socially conscious use of AI.

One of the teacher's digital competencies is to ensure the learner's responsible use of technologies – "To take measures to ensure learners' physical, psychological and social wellbeing while using digital technologies. To empower learners to manage risks and use digital technologies safely and responsibly" (Redecker & Punie, 2017, p.23). This may be ensured when teachers themselves use technologies safely and responsibly. The same may be applied to AI – most teachers are not AI creators but users. Thus, digitally competent teachers have to use AI responsibly and foster learners' responsible use of AI. However, sometimes it may be rather challenging to ensure the responsible use of AI as systems or tool creation, and the data it is using are not something teachers can easily detect and validate themselves. Teachers usually rely on recommendations from educational institutions, colleagues or AI experts. Thus, it becomes very important who and on what criteria provide these recommendations.

The recently updated digital competence frameworks (Borgne et al., 2023; Miao & Cukurova, 2024) also discuss teacher digital competence development for the responsible use of AI. Miao & Cukurova (2024) focus more on political regulation, ensuring trustworthy AI tools, criteria for system validation, national strategies for AI accessibility, local frameworks, assessment tools and national programs for teacher competence development. Borgne et al. (2023) provide more specific suggestions regarding the steps teachers should take to start with AI in teaching (p.p.28-29):

1. Knowledge about AI (what is appropriate according to students' age and subject).
2. Knowledge about underlying pedagogical models of educational applications (why I support AI use for that? How will it help my students reach the intended learning outcomes?).
3. Understanding the technology (when and how to use the tool) and the teaching context.
4. Knowledge about the cognitive processes.

Other researchers (Boscardin et al., 2024) also provide recommendations for teachers on their digital competence to use AI responsibly. This can be done by increasing AI knowledge, understanding the current landscape of AI use in your subject area of education, reviewing strategies for successful AI integration into education, and finally, becoming stewards of the ethical use of AI (Boscardin et al., 2024).

Methodology

The qualitative research approach was selected to reveal future teachers' perspectives towards AI and teacher digital competence development. Focus groups as a research method facilitate and create a possibility to collect diverse perspectives, which are stimulated by interactive dialogue among group participants, enabling researchers to explore complex educational issues in depth. Focus group, as a qualitative research method, elicits "the perspectives and experiences of their participants on a particular topic, especially when the intersubjective dimension is important" (Slovák et al., 2023, p.2).

Four Focus groups with 5-12 participants (students - future teachers in humanities and/or education) were organised at Vytautas Magnus University, Lithuania, in March 2025. A total of 42 participants expressed their views on the research. The focus group participants represented 3-4-year students already working at schools or delivering private lessons, all having previous experience teaching at school. The students in focus groups were also asked to self-assess their digital competencies in using AI tools. Most students indicated 7-8 out of 10 as their digital competence to use AI tools; of course, several students rated their competence as 10/10 and several more critical – 3/10 or 6/10.

There were seven broad questions that focus group participants discussed: Which AI tools are you using now for your teaching-related activities? What teacher activities can AI tools help with or replace? What risks does the use of AI tools by teachers bring? How important is the teacher's digital competence to use AI in teaching? Why? How will AI change the teaching process? How do teachers need to adapt to that? The answers of focus group participants were analysed following the steps of thematic analysis (Braun & Clarke, 2006; Nowell et al, 2017).

Research results

The seven broad questions may be divided into three groups of questions (topics) – AI and teaching now, AI and teaching in the future, and teacher digital competence development to use AI responsibly. The research results are presented according to these three major topics, reflecting on the main ideas and supporting them with the participant responses.

AI and Teaching Now

The first part of the focus group discussion focused on the situation at schools now. The students indicated many AI tools they are using for their studies and teaching activities. They criticised some tools which declare themselves as created for teachers and are more aimed, addressed at helping teachers, that they are not flexible enough for creating lesson plans or activities for non-native language learners (F1S3). The most commonly indicated AI tool mistake in assisting the creation of lesson plans was not properly counted time for the indicated activities or that the suggested activities do not correspond to the age or level indicated. They also mentioned that it is very important to revise the provided activities or tasks because the tools do not know the kids and may prepare or suggest inappropriate content.

They indicated the need for good and precise prompt writing skills to obtain a more proper, better result, more corresponding to your needs. "Being specific about the desired outcomes and activities leads to more targeted and useful responses" (F3S7). The students who rated their competence to use AI tools at the maximum indicated level (10 out of 10) tended to mention that they had been using AI tools for some time and that they were competent in writing proper AI prompts. However, the majority, rating their AI usage at 6-8 out of 10, mentioned that there still were places to improve and understand the processes of working to a better extent (F3S4). The same argument was used by the several participants who rated their competence to use AI as 3 or 5, but the latter also expressed a more critical approach to AI: "Though they are called "generative" tools, they do not generate any new information, but rather recycle that given by other users and available on the Internet. This leads to repetitive patterns in its responses..."(F4S6).

Focus group participants mentioned that during their practice at schools and university studies, they had met some teachers using AI tools for teaching but stressed the word "some". They sceptically addressed some schools where technologies are banned or not used enough (F4S2), as well as criticising students who use AI in "the brain dead usage of AI where you put in the prompt, you ask for the question, and it answers you directly with the same answering style, which you can notice immediately"(F4S3).

Reflecting on the activities that teachers can use AI for, focus group participants mentioned inspiration (F4S2, F3S7) or brainstorming ideas (F1S1, F3S7), lesson plan (F4S2) or project description creation (F1S3); language rule explanations, practice templates for students, especially preparing different sentences (F4S3), making tasks easier or more complicated according to your learner skills and abilities (F1S5). Among the most commonly indicated risks that students saw was teacher overdependence on AI, which may lead to incorrect information (F3S2, F3S7), teacher "laziness"(F3S7) and "loss of creativity"(F4S4), misinforming students (F3S5) and providing improper feedback for students (F3S2).

AI and Teaching in the Future

When trying to think of the future and how teaching may change, focus group participants stress that changes in teaching happen slowly, so they do not envisage drastic changes in the near future. The ideas on how teaching is changing were: more online teaching becoming a reality in schools (F4S3), more schools equipped with technologies and teachers using these technologies when teaching (F4S2). Participants provided some ideas about how AI is changing teaching – through more personalised learning possibilities (F2S3) and by more intense use of immersive technologies (F2S2). However, they also stressed that AI "changes students' learning and creates opportunities for students to "cheat" or rely too heavily on its ideas" (F2S4).

There were many ideas that indicated how teachers could change their approach to AI. The most common idea, reflected in all focus groups, was that teachers should not rely too much on AI, and they need to change their teaching by collaborating across disciplines (F2S2), becoming more flexible and open-minded to make the most of AI tools (F2S3). Teachers need to learn how AI works and how to use it wisely, helping students understand AI's limits and teaching them to think critically about AI-generated content, not taking it for granted (F2S9). However, as AI can provide quick feedback, students stressed that "teachers should still be involved in giving personalised feedback, as AI may not always capture the reality ... teachers know their students better and can offer insights that AI might miss" (F2S1).

Teachers should change their teaching methods to focus on critical thinking, creativity and problem-solving (F2S2), creating more engaging lessons (F2S7), teaching things that only human teachers can do, such as communication and attitudes between people (F2S6), combining AI-driven activities with discussions, group work, and creative tasks that require critical thinking and personal input, this way enhancing learning rather than replacing meaningful interaction (F2S7). Participants stressed the need for teachers to ensure that AI remains a tool for honest and productive learning rather than a replacement of independent thought, and that this may be done by designing specific activities that encourage evaluation and deeper analysis and require honest formulation of thoughts on one or another topic (F2S8). Participants stressed that by guiding students in using AI responsibly, teachers help them prepare for the future (F2S9).

Focus group participants, analysing teacher challenges today, also noted that although there may be more developed AI tools that may recognise AI in the future, they still saw a challenge for a teacher to detect which students are cheating - "to actually catch AI" (F4S3, F4S2). The participants were rather scared of future AI possibilities—what risks technologies may bring to students and how teachers' roles may change (F4S2). Although these potential risks caused concern, the participants remained optimistic. They emphasised the continued importance of the teacher in the classroom (F4S1) and saw more possibilities for teachers to adapt learning to students' individual needs (F4S2). Among the most commonly identified reasons for using AI were improved time management and enhanced inspiration—especially for planning (such as lesson plans) or repetitive tasks (such as creating multiple variations).

The following quotes sum up students' optimistic views of the future: "It will probably be more about evaluating the information, critical thinking than learning the information. Because everything we will be able to find online. So it's good. It will change the teaching itself. I'm just not sure how exactly" (F4S1). Teachers' importance to continuing digital competence development was noted as a necessity: "I believe that we cannot outrun AI, but we can walk with it in like equal intervals. If it and us are "upgrading", so winning over AI is probably impossible (which sounds a bit dystopian), but it is what it is, and I think that could wind up as a positive thing eventually. I'm optimistic about it" (F4S1).

AI and Teacher Competence Development for the Future

Together with the discussions on the changes in teaching processes and changing teaching roles, focus group participants indicated some changes required for teacher knowledge, skills and attitudes. There were many ideas shared, such as teacher "computer skills are a must"(F4S3), teachers should "master the AI skills, of course", but start using AI, teachers should learn step by step (F3S2), they need to have preliminary knowledge of AI (F2S11), they need at least be able to precisely write the prompts (F3S2).

Students emphasised that at least a basic level of digital competence to use AI is essential for teachers. As one student noted, "It is essential to be competent in using AI to at least somehow catch up with students and their interests" (F3S2). Another added, "I believe that a teacher should be at least somewhat proficient with AI to be able to recognize AI generated answers and to create more inventive homework so that students could not use AI to cheat"(F4S5). It was also highlighted that teachers need skills in using learning apps and analysing data (F4S3), along with broader knowledge on various ICT—understanding what these technologies can do and how to apply them in teaching (F1S5). It was even suggested that understanding some programming concepts and having some programming skills can be quite helpful (F4S3).

All of the focus group participants noted that it is important for a teacher to develop digital competence to use AI responsibly—the "presence of AI tools in teachers' lives is beneficial but only if they are working as supplements, not as all-encompassing substitutes for our abilities!" (F2S8), "using AI as a teacher should be done responsibly and should not replace the teacher" (F4S5). The teachers are responsible to teach students how to use technologies responsible—"As teachers of the people who were born into this overwhelming world, it is our task to teach them how to navigate it without becoming completely dependent on it" (F4S6).

Conclusions

Future teachers expressed a sceptical view of the technologies used at school today and recognised the challenges teachers face. While they acknowledged a lack of teacher skills in using AI, they also emphasised the importance of using AI responsibly. The most significant risks identified included teacher overreliance on AI, failure to verify the resources created with AI, and a lack of creativity. On the positive side, AI was seen as a valuable tool for saving time and enabling the personalisation of learning activities and teaching content. Future teachers stressed the urgent need for teachers to develop their digital competencies, though they remained sceptical about teachers' ability to detect students' misuse of AI for tasks in the future. Despite these concerns, they stayed optimistic about the future—particularly regarding the changing teachers' roles and the potential of the upcoming new generation of teachers to integrate technology effectively in the classroom. Their views and suggestions provided aligned with recommendations for teacher digital competence development found in the scientific literature. Focus group participants encouraged teachers to preserve their human qualities and creativity, using AI as a source of inspiration rather than a replacement.

Competing interests

The authors have no competing interests to declare.

Ethics and consent (if applicable)

The research was conducted and published in compliance with the recognised international standards and ethical principles. The identity of the research subject(s) was anonymised whenever possible. Informed consent to participate in the study was obtained from the participants.

Acknowledgements and Funding Information

This research No P-EDU-23-1 is co-funded by the European Union (the project "Breakthrough in Educational Research" No 10-044-P-0001) under the 1st April 2025 Agreement with the Research Council of Lithuania (RCL) and the 17th April 2025 Joint Activity Agreement with Vytautas Magnus University.

References.

Brown, P., Jacquard, A., De Koning, M., Leliaert, I., Leopold, T., Thomas, K., Sharma, S., & Van der Werf, A. (2024). Leveraging Generative AI for Job Augmentation and Workforce Productivity: Scenarios, Case Studies and a Framework for Action. Insight report. World Economic Forum, Switzerland. https://reports.weforum.org/docs/WEF_Leveraging_Generative_AI_for_Job_Augmentation_and_Workforce_Productivity_2024.pdf

Braun, V., & Clarke, V. (2006). Using thematic analysis in psychology. Qualitative research in psychology, 3; 77-101.

Boscardin, C. K., Gin, B., Golde, P. B., & Hauer, K. E. (2024). ChatGPT and Generative Artificial Intelligence for Medical Education: Potential Impact and Opportunity. Academic Medicine, 99(1). https://journals.lww.com/academicmedicine/fulltext/2024/01000/chatgpt_and_generative_artificial_intelligence_for.11.aspx

Borgne, Y.-A. L., Bellas, F., Cassidy, D., Vuorikari, R., Kralj, L., Obae, C., Pasichnyk, O., Beve, P., van Deyzen, B., Ari Laitala, Sharma, M., Wulgaert, R., Niewint-Gori, J., Gröpler, J., Joyce, A., Rondin, E., Gilleran, A., Janakievska, G., & Weber, M. (2023). AI Report by the European Digital Education Hub's Squad on Artificial Intelligence in Education (pp. 1–109). European Union.

Eddico. (2021). Competence Meta-Model for Digital Educators. https://eddico.eu/wp-content/uploads/sites/24/2021/05/2020/content/Competence-meta-model-for-digital-educators.html#/

Education Wales (Welsh government, United Kingdom). (2022). Digital Competence Framework (Part of Cross-Curricular Skills Frameworks. HWB. https://hwb.gov.wales/curriculum-for-wales/cross-curricular-skills-frameworks/digital-competence-framework/

Falloon, G. (2020). From digital literacy to digital competence: The teacher digital competency (TDC) framework. Educational Technology Research and Development, 68(5), 2449–2472. https://doi.org/10.1007/s11423-020-09767-4

Kelentrić, M., Helland, K., & Arstorp, A.-T. (2017). Professional Digital Competence Framework for Teachers (pp. 1–74). The Norwegian Centre for ICT in Education. https://www.udir.no/globalassets/filer/in-english/pfdk_framework_en_low2.pdf

Krstic, Z. (2024). Economic Theory and Artificial Intelligence: A Cross-model Perspective on Labour Market Dynamics. Croatian Regional Development Journal, 5(2), 52–75. https://doi.org/10.2478/crdj-2024-0008

Miao, F., & Cukurova, M. (2024). AI competency framework for teachers. UNESCO; ED/577/1. https://doi.org/10.54675/ZJTE2084

Nowell, L.,S., Norris, J.M., White, D.E., & Moules, N.J. (2017) . Thematic Analysis. Striving to Meet the Trustworthiness Criteria. International Journal of Qualitative Methods. http://journals.sagepub.com/doi/metrics/10.1177/1609406917733847

Redecker, C. & Punie, Y. (2017). European Framework for the Digital Competence of Educators: DigCompEdu. Publications Office of the European Union. https://doi.org/10.2760/178382 (print),10.2760/159770 (online)

Slovák, Ľ., Daněk, J., & Daněk, T. (2023). The use of focus groups in cultural ecosystem services research: A systematic review. Humanities and Social Sciences Communications, 10(1), 1–13. https://doi.org/10.1057/s41599-023-01530-3

The National Institute of Educational Technologies and Teacher Training (INTEF). (2017). Common Digital Competence Framework for Teachers. 1–83.

Vihar, L. (2025). Digital Skills Explored (pp. 1–26). European Digital Education Hub.

Data-Driven Methodologies in a Digital Learning Environment for Mathematics

Elisa Corino[1], Cecilia Fissore[2], Marina Marchisio Conte[2]

[1] Department of Foreign Languages, Literatures and Modern Culture, University of Turin, Turin, Italy; elisa.corino@unito.it
[2] Department of Molecular Biotechnology and Health Sciences, University of Turin, Turin, Italy; {cecilia.fissore, marina.marchisio}@unito.it

Correspondence: Cecilia Fissore: cecilia.fissore@unito.it

Abstract:

Mathematics is undoubtedly one of the school disciplines in which students generally have the most significant difficulties. Numerous studies in Mathematics education have shown that the causes of disciplinary learning difficulties are the acquisition, understanding, and management of language for specific purposes. This paper will illustrate Data-Driven learning activities with automatic formative assessment implemented within a Digital Learning Environment. The research sample comprises 40 students from two upper secondary schools in Turin, Italy. In an L1 context, students were guided to study the language of Mathematics using a concordance to analyse language and specialised texts. Students carried out activities with automatic formative assessment, featuring step-by-step and adaptive questions that guided them in discovering the peculiarities of the language in use and understanding the concepts expressed by the LPS. In this contribution, we will illustrate this close relationship between the use of technologies, the analysis of language, and the subject contents that the LSP conveys.

Keywords: Automatic formative assessment; Data-Driven Learning; Digital Learning Environment; Mathematics; Mathematics Education; Secondary school.

Introduction

Technologies such as mobile devices, learning environments and tools for language analysis, assessment and translation can play a significant role in language learning. Scientific evidence has shown that using digital applications to support different aspects of learning and teaching a second language positively impacts motivation, proactivity, and longer exposure time. All these aspects favour the long-term assimilation of the study object (Read et al., 2018). This is also true for learning LSP and can be particularly important for disciplines often complex and allegedly incomprehensible to students, such as Mathematics. Numerous studies have demonstrated that language acquisition, comprehension, and management are among the factors contributing to disciplinary struggles (Ferrari, 2004). Two methodologies that exploit the potential of technologies and put the student at the centre of learning are Data-Driven Learning (DDL) and formative assessment. In teaching, DDL is an approach that utilises the tools and techniques of corpus linguistics for pedagogical purposes (Gilquin & Granger, 2010). Introducing a corpus-based approach can support reflection on the language of Mathematics to collect meaningful and realistic data on language use (Cobb & Boulton, 2015) and to reflect on the disciplinary content and its applications. Formative assessment is a process in which students have the opportunity to understand what they have learned and how they have taught it (Black & Wiliam, 2009); therefore, it is one of the teaching practices in which technology can provide fundamental support. In a Digital Learning Environment (DLE) integrated with an automatic assessment system (AAS), it is possible to design and implement activities that incorporate automatic formative assessment, providing immediate and interactive feedback (Corino et al., 2022a). Our research aims to design, implement, and test DDL activities with automatic formative assessment in a DLE, enabling students to develop linguistic skills for analysing and describing mathematical objects and operations. Activities have been designed with personalised, immediate and interactive feedback, providing information on how the DDL task was performed and how to answer the question. Our research questions are:

- (RQ1) What were students' main difficulties in carrying out corpus-based activities with automatic formative assessment?
- (RQ2) Do students appreciate data-driven methodologies?

Literature Review

The importance of linguistic skills in Mathematics

Secondary school students are often required to deal with the languages of the disciplines without having an adequate linguistic framework that enables them to make the necessary distinctions between specialised languages and more general linguistic varieties. Numerous studies in mathematics education have shown that the causes of disciplinary learning difficulties lie in the acquisition, understanding and management of its LSP (Ferrari, 2004). Over time, Mathematics has developed its language with almost unique characteristics of universality, precision, conciseness, and effectiveness (Sbaragli et al., 2021). These characteristics can be complex, distant and restrictive regarding learning. According to Halliday (2004), students' difficulties lie more in grammar than in vocabulary, although the two are inextricably linked. The author states: "To understand why scientific writing became difficult in specific ways, we must eliminate our obsession with words. The difficulty lies more with the grammar than with the vocabulary" (Halliday, 2004, p. 161). The Italian school system is characterised by a clear separation between linguistic and scientific education, which is probably why many students do not apply the linguistic skills they demonstrate in other communicative situations in a mathematical context (Viale, 2019). The acquisition of adequate language skills plays a strategic and essential role, which is not the responsibility of the Italian language teacher alone. However, it is a task to be shared among all the teachers in a class. The complexity of language teaching necessitates collaboration among teachers from different disciplines to ensure that all students are adequately integrated into the school environment and learning pathways. Recently, this aspect has become even more important due to the growing need to teach Mathematics in multilingual class communities composed of individuals with heterogeneous linguistic backgrounds and skills (Ferrari, 2004).

Data-Driven Learning and Automatic Formative Assessment in a Digital Learning Environment

DDL is a didactic approach which treats language as data and sees students as researchers engaged in guided discovery activities (Johns, 1991). The basic idea is that learners can discover grammatical patterns, word meanings or other aspects of language by searching linguistic data and examining large amounts of authentic language. A corpus is a collection of texts, or parts of them, in a finite number, in an electronic format that has been processed uniformly to make it computer-manageable and searchable (Barbera, 2013). Tim Johns (Johns, 1991) argues that using the machine as a rather special kind of informant is the heart of the approach. Once the informant has answered the question, students must attempt to make sense of that answer and integrate it with what is already known. DDL is a methodology particularly suitable for teaching and learning LSP, especially regarding typical word choices (sorted by frequency), nuances of meaning, and the appropriate use of collocations. Students' consultation with corpora can make them more active in forming their knowledge, stimulate higher cognitive processes, and encourage autonomy (Sah, 2015). Furthermore, the procedures, query modes, and prompting skills required by DDL tackle the need for cross-functional competencies related to the daily use of web search tools. Many studies (e.g., Boulton, 2019; Crosthwaite, 2020) reach positive conclusions about the impact of using corpora on language learning. However, DDL work in applied linguistics remains relatively unknown in educational circles (Boulton, 2019; Boulton & Vyatkina, 2021), and it often goes unnoticed – if not unknown – in L1 contexts. We define automatic formative assessment as using formative assessment in a digital learning environment (DLE) by automatically processing student responses and providing feedback (Barana et al., 2021a). One of the five key strategies for implementing formative assessment theorised by Black and Wiliam (2009) is to "provide feedback that moves learners forward". According to Hattie and Timperley, feedback is "information provided by an agent about aspects of one's performance or understanding" (Hattie & Timperley, 2007). A DLE integrated with an automated assessment system can enhance automatic formative assessment and provide immediate, interactive feedback (Barana et al., 2020). Our research group has successfully developed and tested an automatic formative assessment model with interactive and immediate feedback in a DLE (Barana et al., 2021b). We conceptualise interactive feedback as a step-by-step process that guides the learner in solving a task after one or more autonomous attempts (Barana et al., 2021a).

Research context and methodology

The research activity involved four classes from two Italian secondary schools, comprising 80 students in grade 11 and their teachers. The two schools are scientific high schools. The didactic experimentation, from

November to December 2021, consisted of four two-hour meetings in the classroom. The activities involved two classes (40 students) and were paired with two other classes, which formed the control group (40 students). The topic chosen for the experiment was the concept of mathematical function, which was agreed upon by the teachers. For the activities, a specific corpus was created by selecting texts related to the concept of function from secondary school textbooks. The research project combined DDL with formative assessment in a DLE. The DLE was implemented on a Moodle platform (available at https://linguaggispecialistici.i-learn.unito.it) integrated with the Möbius Assessment system (https://www.digitaled.com/products/assessment). All activities involved the use of two tools in parallel: AntConc (https://www.laurenceanthony.net/software/antconc/) for linguistic research and the DLE for carrying out tests with automatic formative assessment and other activities. More than 20 corpus-based activities with automatic formative assessment were designed and implemented within the DLE (Corino et al., 2022b). Then, students carried them out independently under the supervision of trainers. At the end of each three-question set, a group discussion was held to reflect on the emerging concepts and consolidate what had been learnt. To study the effectiveness of these methodologies, students took an initial test at the beginning of the experiment and a final test at the end to evaluate students' mathematical and linguistic competences. These results were compared with the results of the initial and final control group tests. In this analysis, we considered the students' performance in 20 corpus-based activities with automatic formative assessment divided into six tests. To answer the first research question, we observed the students in the two experimental classes as they carried out corpus-based activities with automatic formative assessment to understand the possible difficulties (from both linguistic, disciplinary, and technical perspectives) they might have encountered in using the proposed tools. About the second goal of the research, we analysed the responses of 36 students who participated in the research activity to a final questionnaire. In particular, we analysed a Likert scale question related to satisfaction with the proposed activities and methods (DDL and automatic formative assessment). In this question, students were asked to indicate their level of agreement with different statements on a Likert scale, ranging from "1" (strongly disagree) to "4" (strongly agree). Students were asked whether learning new tools was easy, valuable, and engaging and whether they appreciated the immediate and interactive feedback, finding it compelling. An example of a corpus-based activity with automatic formative assessment is illustrated, along with an example of formative and non-formative feedback related to the activity.

Results

When carrying out the first activities (the first two tests), the students encountered some technical difficulties related to using the AntConc software and the AAS, which they were unfamiliar with. The most common difficulties were:

- Setting up the linguistic search and choosing what to search for in the corpus. Some students stared at the screen, unsure how to proceed, or searched extensively without an explicit criterion. In some cases, when they had difficulty understanding the requests from a mathematical perspective and did not know how to answer a question, they searched for the answer in the corpus, even though they were unsure of what to look for, and proceeded by trial. For example, one of the first questions asked students to select from the list of proposed verbs that function as subjects. Sometimes, students entered the verbs proposed in the answer options in the search bar instead of following the instructions. However, they did not conjugate the verb and therefore did not find results.
- Some students confused the AntConc search bar with that of a search engine (e.g., Google), and they entered combinations of multiple words without finding results. They did not understand that the search was for text strings. For example, they did not understand that "funzione" is different from "funzioni" and that entering an entire phrase made it challenging to find a result, that is, an exactly equal string in the corpus.
- Analysing a large number of results. Most linguistic searches produced many results, and the students tended to analyse only the first ones and respond incompletely to the activities.
- Do not consult the corpus to confirm the meanings of terms. To answer the multipart questions, students did not return to the corpus if something was unclear. Continuing the question in the previous example, the second part asked students to insert the identified verbs (which functioned as subjects) into some sentences. Sometimes, students insert the verbs by trial and error rather than consulting the corpus to clarify the verb's meaning.
- Using the available attempts. Many students did not click the "check" button at the end of the first part of a question. In this way, they not only did not receive immediate feedback on the correctness of their answer and lost the opportunity to correct themselves in case of error by making further attempts, but they also did not see the subsequent parts of the question itself.

All these difficulties were gradually overcome during the project. To this end, it was essential to summarise the concepts that had emerged in the collective discussions at the end of each activity and carry out the test together. Regarding the impact of formative assessment on students' performance, the system's ability to provide accurate data on the performance of activities enabled a thorough analysis of the differences between formative and non-formative approaches. Figure 1 illustrates a corpus-based activity with automatic formative assessment. In the first part, students define the "image of an element" in a function, reflecting on terms and relationships between elements and their images. In the second part, students use AntConc software to search for the word "image," analyse the results, and refine the definition accordingly. They must distinguish between the "image" of an element and the "image set" of a function. The third part requires students to apply the same preposition as in the second part to link elements of two sets. After each part, students can click a "verify" button to receive immediate feedback on their answers, allowing them to retry if needed. This feedback helps them improve their understanding of subsequent parts of the activity.

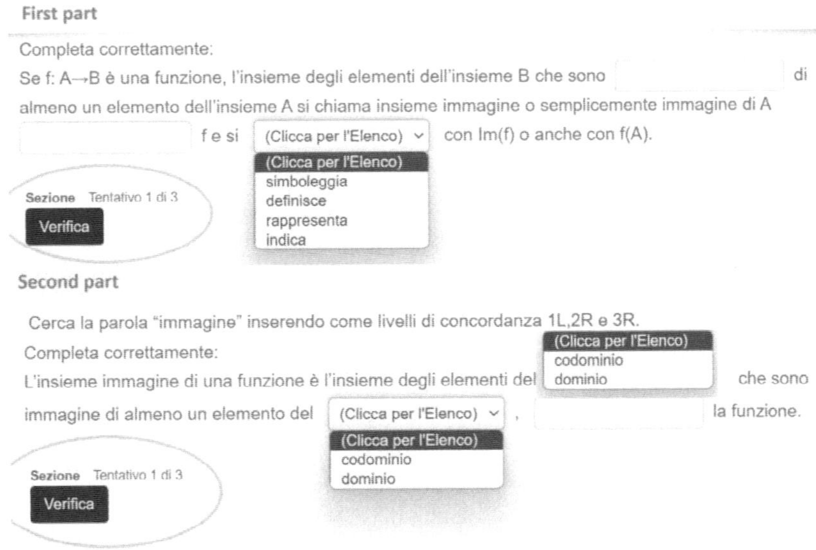

Figure 1: Example of a corpus-based activity with automatic formative assessment.

Figure 2 compares non-formative and formative feedback using two student responses to the question in Figure 1. In the first case (nr1), the student gives incorrect answers for the first two items, using "images" instead of "image" and the wrong preposition "in." Despite three attempts, the student does not change any answers and receives the correct solutions. This feedback is ineffective as the student repeats the same errors. In the second case (nr2), the student initially leaves the second item blank but uses the available attempts and system feedback to revise their answer. The student actively engages with the feedback, utilising the corpus to verify terms and usage, demonstrating a deeper focus on understanding the content rather than just the result. This process provides scaffolding and additional guidance to help the student answer correctly. Table 1 presents students' considerations for using AntConc in linguistic research. They appreciated AntConc for language research because it enabled them to develop new digital and language skills. According to the students, using AntConc (3.09) was easy, understanding how to use it to answer questions (3.14) was also easy, and learning how to use AntConc (3.40) was interesting. They also believe that learning to use text analysis software will be helpful in the future (3.14). The aspects they preferred the most were those concerning automatic formative assessment. Table 2 presents the students' reflections on using the AAS and the potential for receiving immediate and interactive feedback. Students appreciated the possibility of viewing the correct answer immediately after answering a question (immediate feedback) (3.63) and the option to retry the exercise in case of a wrong answer (3.40). They agreed that having the assessment immediately after solving an exercise helped them understand how the question should be answered (3.51). The responses were also optimistic regarding the relationship between language study and mathematical content. According to students, the exercises helped them become more aware of the language to use (3.14), and the exercises on language also made me reflect on meanings and content (2.77). For both the control and experimental groups, the p-value (0.00011368) is below the conventional threshold of 0.05, indicating a statistically significant difference between the pre- and post-test scores. This suggests a significant improvement in test scores from the initial to the final assessment. On average, the control group showed a gain of 1.24 points, while the experimental group exhibited a larger improvement (+ 2.67 points). These findings indicate that the experimental group outperformed the control group.

Conclusions

The complete analysis of the experimental data is still in progress; however, these preliminary results provide sufficient grounds to encourage the increased use of corpora in educational settings. In response to the first research question, the students encountered difficulties using the proposed technologies to carry out corpus-based activities with automatic formative assessment, including setting up the linguistic search, analysing numerous results, and utilising the available attempts.

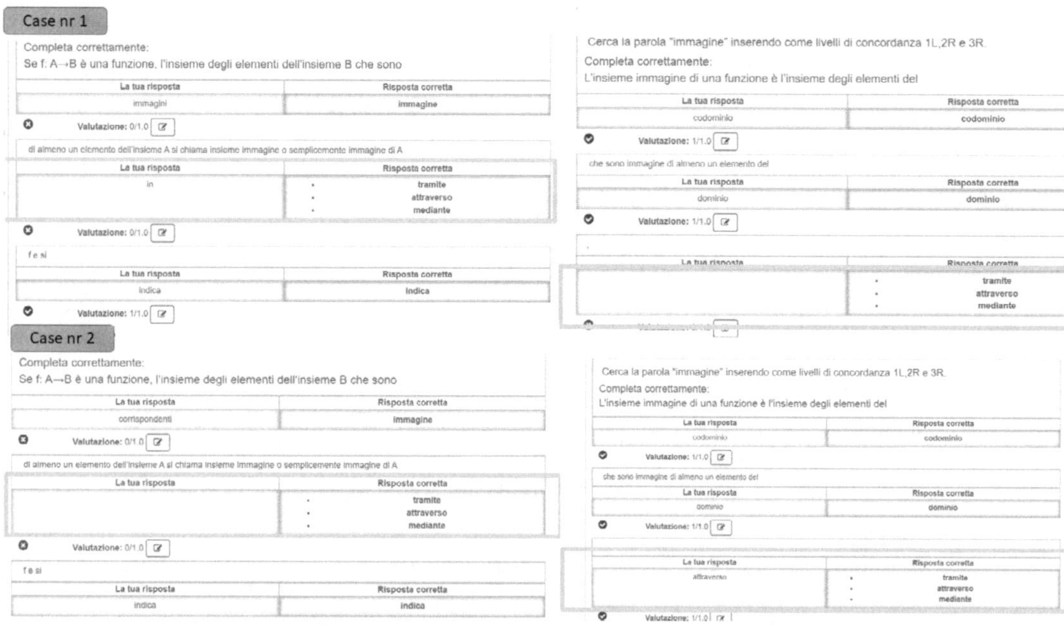

Figure 3: Examples of non-formative and formative feedback.

Table 1: Students' thoughts on the use of AntConc for linguistic research

Item	Mean	Std. dev.
It was easy to use AntConc.	3.09	0.85
It was easy to understand how to use AntConc to answer questions.	3.14	0.85
It was interesting to learn how to use AntConc.	3.40	0.74
Learning to use text analysis software is helpful for the future.	3.14	0.91

Table 2. Students' thoughts on the automatic formative assessment.

Item	**Mean**	**Std. dev.**
It is helpful to view the correct answer immediately after answering a question.	3.63	0.55
When I gave the wrong answer, I would try the exercise again.	3.40	0.69
The assessment immediately after solving an exercise helped me understand how to answer the question.	3.51	0.66

The students quickly overcame all these difficulties, thanks to the trainers' support and the group discussions. In response to the second research question, students appreciated the proposed methodologies and the mathematical activities, which differed significantly from traditional ones. The DDL approach had a very positive and motivating effect on the students. They also appreciated the automatic formative assessment method and the opportunity to receive immediate feedback. This allowed them to correct themselves after several attempts and to see the correct answer at the end of each activity. Technology and a student-centred DDL approach enable students to participate in linguistic tasks, particularly in STEM subjects to which they are not accustomed.

References

Barana, A., Fissore, C., & Marchisio, M. (2020). Automatic Formative Assessment Strategies for the Adaptive Teaching of Mathematics. In International Conference on Computer Supported Education, Springer, Cham, 341-365.

Barana A., Marchisio M. (2021). Analysing Interactions in Automatic Formative Assessment Activities for Mathematics in Digital Learning Environments, International Conference on Computer Supported Education, CSEDU - Proceedings, 1, 497–504.

Barana A., Marchisio M., Sacchet M. (2021a). Effectiveness of Automatic Formative Assessment for learning Mathematics in Higher Education, International Conference on Higher Education Advances, 1-8, 10.4995/HEAd21.2021.13030.

Barana, A., Marchisio, M, Sacchet, M. (2021b). Interactive feedback for learning Mathematics in a digital learning environment", in Education Sciences, vol. 11(6), 2021b, 279.

Barbera, E. F. (2013). Linguistica dei corpora e linguistica dei corpora italiana. Un'introduzione. Milano: Qu. ASAR.

Black, P. & Wiliam, D. (2009). Developing the Theory of Formative Assessment. Educ. Assess. Eval. Account, 21, 5–31.

Boulton, A. (2019). Data-driven learning for younger learners: Obstacles and optimism. In Data-driven learning for the next generation: Corpora and DDL for pre-tertiary learners, Routledge, 14-20.

Boulton, A., & Vyatkina, N. (2021). Thirty years of data-driven learning: Taking stock and charting new directions over time. Language Learning and Technology 25(3), 66–89.

Cobb, T., Boulton, A. (2015). Classroom applications of corpus analysis. In D. Biber, & R. Reppen, Eds., Cambridge Handbook of English Corpus Linguistics, 478–497. doi: 10.1017/CBO9781139764377.027

Corino, E., Fissore, C., & Marchisio, M. (2022a). Adaptive Exercises and Formative Assessment for English Remedial Action. In Orchestration of Learning Environments in the Digital World. Cham: Springer International Publishing, 3-19.

Corino, E., Fissore, C., & Marchisio, M. (2022b). Data Driven Learning activities within a Digital Learning Environment to study the specialised language of Mathematics. In 2022 IEEE 46th Annual Computers, Software, and Applications Conference (COMPSAC), IEEE, 167-176.

Corino, E.; Onesti, C. (2019). Data-Driven Learning: A Scaffolding Methodology for CLIL and LSP Teaching and Learning. Frontiers in Education, 4 (7), 1-12.

Crosthwaite, P. (2020). Data-Driven Learning for the Next Generation, New York: Routledge,.

Ferrari, P. L.. (2004). Matematica e linguaggio: quadro teorico e idee per la didattica. Pitagora.

Gilquin, G., Granger, C. (2010). How can data-driven learning be used in language teaching? In: A. O'Keeffe & M. McCarthy (eds.), Routledge handbook of corpus linguistics, London: Routledge, 359-370.

Halliday, M. A. (2004). The language of science. Londra: Continuum.

Hattie, J., & Timperley, H. (2007). The power of feedback. Review of educational research, 77(1), 81-112.

Johns, T. (1991). Should you be persuaded: two examples of data-driven learning. Classroom Concordancing: ELR Journal, 1-12.

Read, T., Montaner, S., Sedano, B. (2018). Technological Innovation for Specialised Linguistic Domains: Languages for Digital Lives and Cultures. Proceedings of TISLID'18. Mauritius: Éditions universitaires européennes.

Sah, P. K. (2015). Using Data-Driven Learning (DDL) to Enhance Learner Autonomy. IATEFL SIG Independent, 64, 12-15.

Sbaragli S., Demartini S. & Franchini E. (2021). Le difficoltà di comprensione e di gestione dei termini specialistici della geometria all'ingresso della scuola secondaria di primo grado, in La matematica e la sua didattica, 29(1), 7-37.

Viale, M. (2019). I fondamenti linguistici delle discipline scientifiche. L'italiano per la matematica e le scienze a scuola. Padova: Cleup.

Facilitating Flexible Learning by Implementing Blended Learning with Reduced Classroom Time: Research Insights and Implications for Practice

Claude Müller[1]

[1] Zurich University of Applied Sciences, Switzerland; muew@zhaw.ch

Correspondence: Claude Müller; muew@zhaw.ch

Abstract:

The growing demand for flexibility in higher education has led to the development of blended learning models that integrate online and in-person instruction. This study examined the implementation and effectiveness of the FLEX programme, a blended learning initiative designed to enhance flexibility while maintaining learning quality. Using a mixed-methods approach, the research explored three key areas: (1) equivalence testing as a methodological innovation for assessing flexible learning outcomes, (2) a systematic review of the effectiveness of blended learning with reduced classroom time, and (3) the impact of the FLEX format on student learning and stakeholder perceptions. Findings indicate that learning effectiveness in FLEX courses is statistically equivalent to traditional formats, even with a 51 per cent reduction in face-to-face instruction. This aligns with meta-analytic results, which found no significant impact of reduced classroom time on learning effectiveness. However, implementation quality emerged as a crucial factor in student engagement and success, with well-structured courses, interactive learning tasks, teacher presence, and timely feedback proving essential. Stakeholder perceptions varied: Students valued flexibility, while lecturers expressed concerns regarding student engagement in self-learning phases. The study underscores the importance of high-quality instructional design, stakeholder involvement, and institutional support in blended learning implementation. It offers evidence-based recommendations for integrating flexible study formats without compromising learning effectiveness. These findings contribute to ongoing discussions on blended learning in higher education and inform strategies for optimizing flexible learning environments.

Keywords: Blended Learning, Flexible Learning, Higher Education, Equivalence Testing, Learning Effectiveness, Stakeholder Perceptions

Introduction

The demand for flexibility in higher education has been growing for decades (Barnett, 2014; Loon, 2021). As students increasingly balance academic, professional, and personal responsibilities, higher education institutions face the challenge of designing learning experiences that accommodate diverse needs (Wade, 1994). The COVID-19 pandemic further highlighted the importance of flexibility when emergency remote teaching forced both students and educators to adapt to fully online learning. Although few would wish to return to those times, many now value the ability to shape their learning experiences regarding when, where, and how they study (Lockee & Clark-Stallkamp, 2022; Pelletier et al., 2022). This shift has reinforced the necessity of integrating flexible learning elements into higher education without compromising the quality of instruction and learning outcomes.

Flexible learning is more than just incorporating technology—it involves structuring learning experiences in ways that allow students to take ownership of their educational journey (Higher Education Academy, 2015). Previous studies have identified key dimensions of flexibility, including time, place, pace, instructional approaches, assessment methods, and learning goals (Chen, 2003; Li & Wong, 2018). However, understanding how these elements interact in real-world higher education settings remains an important area of enquiry. In particular, universities must ensure that flexibility supports learning outcomes rather than merely offering convenience.

One promising approach to meeting these demands is blended learning, which combines the benefits of in-person instruction with the possibilities of online education. Blended learning allows students to experience social presence and direct engagement while benefiting from the flexibility of multimedia resources, asynchronous learning activities, and self-paced study options (Graham & Halverson, 2023). Beyond individual benefits, this model also allows institutions to provide high-quality education in a scalable and adaptable manner. However, to maximize its effectiveness, this must be implemented thoughtfully, ensuring that flexibility does not come at the expense of pedagogical rigour or student engagement. Despite its potential, blended learning still requires further research to determine how it can best serve students and institutions alike.

This research project addressed these research needs and questions in the context of a systematic flexible learning initiative at a higher education institution. The entire project was extensively evaluated and documented scientifically (Müller et al., 2025; Müller et al., 2023; Müller et al., 2018). Additionally, the project examined and developed the state of the art regarding the methodology of flexible learning research, particularly equivalence testing (Mueller et al., 2020), and a systematic review of blended learning with reduced classroom time (Müller & Mildenberger, 2021). This paper summarizes the research findings and draws conclusions on the effective implementation of flexible learning in the form of blended learning in higher education as part of a synthesis.

The main research topics and research questions (RQ) were:

1 Equivalence testing

Blended learning formats are often compared to traditional methods using statistical tests such as t-tests or ANOVA. However, these methods primarily test for differences rather than the intended goal of a flexible learning context, which is to optimize conditions for students and faculty. Thus, proving similarity is often more relevant than proving difference.

RQ 1: What research methods suit a flexible learning research context?

2 Systematic review

When replacing part of face-to-face classroom instruction with an online learning environment by offering students a blended learning format, the decisive question is whether this creates greater flexibility without compromising educational quality.

RQ 2: Can classroom time be reduced and replaced with an online learning environment to offer more learning flexibility without compromising learning effectiveness?

3 Learning effectiveness and stakeholder perceptions FLEX

The introduction of the flexible learning format (FLEX) in a business administration study programme made it possible to investigate comprehensively the learning effectiveness and perceptions of stakeholders in a pilot study and a study programme over four years with 133 courses across various disciplines.

RQ 3: What are the effects of a flexible study format in a blended learning design in terms of learning effectiveness and stakeholder perceptions?

Research Design

Research context

The Zurich University of Applied Sciences launched a new flexible learning study programme in a blended learning format (FLEX) in 2014 as part of a comprehensive e-learning strategy (Müller et al., 2018). The main goal of the new FLEX blended learning format was to give students the best possible opportunity to combine their work and personal commitments through a flexible study format. Compatibility with remote locations was a guiding principle for the number and distribution of face-to-face sessions over the 14-week term. Specifically, the maximum number of nights away from home acceptable to potential students had to be determined because regular physical classroom sessions were essential to encourage interaction and transfer of online learning. As a result of these considerations, face-to-face teaching for FLEX was reduced by about half (51%) compared to the conventional part-time programme (PT). This means that FLEX students attended the campus for two days every three weeks; the intervening asynchronous self-study phase was intended to allow them to learn flexibly.

The concept for the new blended learning format FLEX was developed in 2014 and tested by running a pilot course in business administration. After evaluating the pilot course, 44 courses were transformed for the Bachelor of Science (BSc) in Business Administration programme (2015-2020). The first cohort of FLEX students graduated in 2019. With the onset of the COVID-19 pandemic in early 2020, the university fully transitioned to distance learning, leading to a significant change and realignment of learning formats. For this reason, scientific evaluation of the FLEX programme focuses on the period before the pandemic.

As shown above, organisational and pedagogical considerations were the guiding principles for the time structure chosen. According to the typology of Allen et al. (2007), the FLEX format can be classified as blended learning. In terms of the dimensions of flexible learning, according to Li and Wong (2018), the FLEX format offered greater flexibility in terms of time, delivery, instructional approach, resources, and support than the conventional study format; however, the format was the same as the traditional face-to-face course in terms of the dimensions of content, entry requirements, orientation or goal, and performance assessment.

Methodology

The project adopted a mixed methods approach using quantitative and qualitative methods. Quantitative methods were mainly used to analyse learning effectiveness, while qualitative methods such as surveys and focus interviews were used to analyse stakeholder perceptions. These methods are described in greater detail in the respective papers.

The research design for the FLEX analyses was tightly controlled for a field study in an educational setting, as the learning objectives and exams were identical, the framework conditions were comparable, the presence of a control group ensured a quasi-experimental design, and selection bias was controlled (see also Fraenkel et al., 2015). Furthermore, this study was not conducted in a model project with special resources, support, and incentives but in a real university setting with the existing lecturers, which ensured high ecological validity. Accordingly, the findings are relevant and valuable for researchers and higher education practitioners.

Results

As a basis for the in-depth FLEX studies, the methodology regarding equivalence testing (Mueller et al., 2020) and the current state of research on flexible learning in a blended learning design (Müller & Mildenberger, 2021) were examined and documented in two articles. Regarding the FLEX projects, the pilot study (Müller et al., 2018), the learning effectiveness (Müller et al., 2023), and stakeholder perceptions (Müller et al., 2025) of the FLEX study programme over five years were thoroughly investigated.

RQ 1: Equivalence testing (Mueller et al., 2020)

The aim of providing flexible learning with blended learning is not primarily to improve learning performance but to maintain it while increasing flexibility, reducing dropout rates, and reaching new student demographics. Traditional statistical methods in educational research face limitations in such a context. A non-significant t-test result is often misinterpreted as evidence of equivalence, despite the well-known principle that "absence of evidence is not evidence of absence." Equivalence testing provides a more appropriate statistical approach, enabling valid judgments about the similarity of study formats. This test follows the logic of a t-test but reverses the null and alternative hypotheses; combining equivalence tests with traditional t-tests enhances accuracy. First, a t-test assesses differences; then, an equivalence test determines similarity. The outcomes can be categorized into four scenarios: (1) statistically equivalent and not different, (2) not equivalent and statistically different, (3) statistically equivalent and statistically different, and (4) not equivalent and not different. Case (4), where no difference or equivalence is shown, usually indicates low power.

In a case study of the FLEX programme, combining these methods allowed statistically confirmed statements for 12 out of 22 courses, whereas a t-test alone would have identified only three. This approach demonstrated that increased flexibility in 55 per cent of courses did not negatively impact learning outcomes, though some results remained inconclusive.

The study demonstrated that incorporating equivalence tests into pedagogical research strengthens methodological rigour, enhances evidence-based decision-making, and supports innovation in higher education.

RQ 2: Systematic review learning effectiveness (Müller & Mildenberger, 2021)

The meta-analysis applied strict inclusion criteria concerning research design, learning outcomes measurement, and blended learning implementation (k=21 effect sizes). In particular, it was a requirement that the attendance time in the blended learning format was reduced by 30–79 per cent compared to the conventional learning environment, drawing on Allen et al. (2007). In this meta-analysis, the estimated effect size (Hedge's g) was 0.0621, although not significantly different from zero. The confidence interval [lower 95th - 0.13, upper 95th 0.25] suggests that overall differences between blended and conventional classroom learning were minor, and, at best, minimal negative or moderate positive effects were plausible. This implies that despite a reduction in classroom time between 30 and 79 per cent, equivalent learning outcomes were found. However—in line with authors of other blended learning reviews—it was pointed out that the number of controlled studies in the field of blended learning is still limited.

RQ 3: Learning effectiveness and stakeholder perceptions FLEX

Pilot study FLEX (Müller et al., 2018)

The study analysed the pilot module FLEX "Introduction to Business Administration" (IBA). The most important aspect of this course is the absence of a self-selection bias because the university's administration assigned the students to the FLEX class. This ensured a semi-experimental setting under highly controlled conditions. The IBA course had 989 students: 140 in the experimental FLEX group and 849 in the control group (CONV).

The final exam results indicate no significant differences in learning effectiveness among the various groups in the IBA course in 2012-2014. A t-test conducted on the 2014 final exam results revealed no significant difference between the FLEX (M=35.9, SD=8.32) and CONV (M=37.20, SD = 8.72) groups, t(987)=-1.56, p=0.10 (ns). The corresponding effect size (Cohen's d=0.15) was low. Furthermore, an equivalence test indicated that the test statistic T(1.64) was lower than the critical value from the noncentral Fisher distribution (3.83), allowing for the rejection of the null hypothesis. Consequently, the exam results for the FLEX and CONV groups can be considered statistically equivalent.

Students in the FLEX group varied in their opinions of the flexible study design. Some would welcome even more classes in the FLEX format, while others pointed out that they had enrolled in a classroom course and were expecting face-to-face classroom instruction. These statements indicate that student needs and choices are highly diverse, reflecting their life context and study skills. For this reason, it may make sense to offer different study formats to cater to the various learning format preferences.

Learning effectiveness FLEX (Müller et al., 2023)

The study assessing the learning effectiveness of the FLEX programme compared the experimental flexible learning group (FLEX, N=278) with a control group of part-time students (PT, N=1,068). No significant differences in personality traits were found between the groups, and all study conditions remained identical. The examination results from FLEX students (N=2,822) and PT students (N=11,638) across 133 courses (2015-2019) were analysed. The summary effect size (d=-0.0562) was not significantly different from zero (CI: [-0.206, 0.094]), indicating minimal differences in learning outcomes between the FLEX and PT formats.

Dropout rates were comparable between the two formats, with FLEX students showing a 34 per cent dropout rate in semesters 1-3 (compared to 35% in PT) and 63 per cent in the final semester (compared to 56% in PT). However, format changes after the assessment level may have influenced these figures.

While the overall effectiveness of the FLEX format was equivalent to the conventional study programme, significant variation in effect sizes across courses was observed. Analysis of relative effect sizes, coupled with detailed surveys, suggests that differences in implementation quality accounted for this heterogeneity. The findings highlight the importance of educational design factors in blended learning programmes. Specifically, a successful implementation should ensure adequate course structure and guidance for students, activating learning tasks, stimulating interaction and social presence of teachers, and timely feedback on the learning process and outcomes. These principles are critical for maintaining the effectiveness of flexible study programmes.

Stakeholder perceptions FLEX (Müller et al., 2025)

The study adopted a multi-stakeholder approach, employing a mixed methods approach to examine the perceptions of students, lecturers, and employers regarding the FLEX format. The findings revealed broad support across stakeholders for reducing classroom teaching time by over 50 per cent. However, perspectives differ: Students valued flexibility as the freedom to tailor their learning process, while lecturers expressed concerns about student commitment and engagement, particularly during self-study phases. These findings highlight the importance of clarifying the study concept and teaching culture, particularly concerning the degree of study flexibility.

Discussion and Implications for Practice

Implementing the FLEX model was examined for over four years in 133 courses across various disciplines, employing a mixed-methods approach. The findings provide robust evidence that increasing educational flexibility through blended learning with reduced classroom time can enhance access to education without compromising learning effectiveness. This aligns with the results of the meta-analysis, which found no significant impact of blended learning environments with reduced classroom time on learning effectiveness.

Moreover, the study highlights that stakeholder satisfaction is generally high, with participants perceiving the flexible learning model as valuable. The analysis of stakeholder perceptions has refined the conceptual understanding of the FLEX format, distinguishing more clearly between the flexible study structure—designed to meet the needs of students and employers—and the blended learning format, which, while beneficial, may pose challenges for instructors.

These findings underscore the potential for higher education institutions to expand flexible study programmes. However, the study also emphasizes the critical role of high-quality implementation in ensuring both the effectiveness of blended learning courses and stakeholder satisfaction. The quality of implementation serves as a key moderating factor, influenced by multiple elements at both the programme and course levels. While specific findings at these levels are outlined below, the success of such initiatives typically depends on dynamic interactions between levels and stakeholders.

Programme Level

Early faculty involvement rewards course development efforts, facilitates structural decisions, and supports blended learning implementation. The FLEX format was systematically developed through stakeholder engagement and strategic change measures to secure lecturer commitment. Initial voluntary participation fostered commitment, with early adopters' positive experiences later easing the transition for less innovation-oriented lecturers.

Concerns about staff reductions due to online learning should be addressed by maintaining equivalent workload allocation between FLEX and traditional formats. While face-to-face instruction is reduced, the freed-up time should be dedicated to online teaching and preparation. Developing digital self-learning modules requires significant initial investment—in FLEX, up to 100 additional hours for a three-ECTS course— and should be remunerated to incentivise lecturer participation.

The transition to flexible learning expands lecturers' roles to include blended course design, online content creation, and asynchronous learning facilitation. To prevent confusion or resistance, training and coaching should be provided. Scripting workshops to design blended courses collaboratively in the FLEX programme proved remarkably effective. These led to the development of the myScripting[1] tool and a supporting manual (Müller, 2025), which aid digital learning design.

Our study also highlights the necessity to clarify the self-conception and teaching culture of a flexible degree programme. In particular, the level of flexibility must be defined through consultation with the relevant stakeholders, most notably the staff and students. As students and faculty may have differing expectations of flexible learning, clear guidelines on student and lecturer roles and responsibilities are essential to fostering a shared understanding while preserving autonomy.

Course Level

Effective design and implementation of blended learning are crucial at the course level. Providing students with a well-structured course, clear guidance, engaging learning tasks, interactive opportunities, strong teacher presence, and timely feedback are also essential. In blended learning with substantial asynchronous self-learning, particular focus should be placed on sustaining student engagement. Additionally, integrating online and face-to-face learning phases is crucial. Our study highlights that student engagement is critical owing to the multiple demands of flexible study programmes, necessitating explicit encouragement and structured tasks. Measures fostering emotional, cognitive, and behavioural engagement—such as varied learning tasks and social interaction tools like collaborative text or video annotation—are particularly effective. While online

[1] The online tool myScripting can be used free of charge at the URL https://myscripting.zhaw.ch.

phases were historically the focus of blended learning design, greater attention should be given to linking online and face-to-face components to enhance student engagement. Assessment is pivotal in guiding student efforts as learners concentrate on evaluated activities and outcomes (Biggs, 1996). For this reason, incentivizing engagement in asynchronous learning may require adjustments to assessment structures at the course, programme, and even institutional levels.

Competing interests

The author has no competing interests to declare.

References

Allen, I. E., Seaman, J., & Garrett, R. (2007). Blending in: The extent and promise of blended education in the United States. Sloan Consortium.

Barnett, R. (2014). Conditions of flexibility: Securing a more responsive higher education system. Higher Education Academy. https://www.heacademy.ac.uk/resource/conditions-flexibility-securing-more-responsive-higher-education-system

Chen, D.-T. (2003). Uncovering the provisos behind flexible learning. Journal of Educational Technology & Society, 6(2), 25-30. http://www.jstor.org/stable/jeductechsoci.6.2.25

Fraenkel, J. R., Wallen, N. E., & Hyun, H. H. (2015). How to design and evaluate research in education (Ninth edition ed.). McGraw-Hill.

Graham, C. R., & Halverson, L. R. (2023). Blended learning research and practice. In O. Zawacki-Richter & I. Jung (Eds.), Handbook of open, distance and digital education (pp. 1159-1178). Springer Nature Singapore. https://doi.org/10.1007/978-981-19-2080-6_68

Higher Education Academy. (2015). Framework for flexible learning in higher education. https://www.heacademy.ac.uk/system/files/downloads/flexible-learning-in-HE.pdf

Li, K. C., & Wong, B. Y. Y. (2018). Revisiting the definitions and implementation of flexible learning. In K. C. Li, K. S. Yuen, & B. T. M. Wong (Eds.), Innovations in open and flexible education (pp. 3-13). Springer Singapore. https://doi.org/10.1007/978-981-10-7995-5_1

Lockee, B. B., & Clark-Stallkamp, R. (2022). Pressure on the system: increasing flexible learning through distance education. Distance education, 43(2), 342-348. https://doi.org/10.1080/01587919.2022.2064829

Loon, M. (2021). Flexible learning: a literature review 2016–2021. https://ctl.uic.edu.cn/2-Loon%202022%20AdvHE_Flexible%20Learning_Lit%20Review%202016-2021.pdf

Mueller, C., Mildenberger, T., & Lübcke, M. (2020). Do we always need a difference? Testing equivalence in a blended learning setting. International Journal of Research & Method in Education, 43(3), 283-295. https://doi.org/10.1080/1743727X.2019.1680621

Müller, C. (2025). Digital learning design: Designing effective online and blended learning. Springer.

Müller, C., Küttel, T., Müller, M., & Reichmuth, A. (2025). Implementation of a flexible learning study program in a blended learning design: Perceptions of students, lecturers, and employers. European Journal of Open, Distance and E-learning.

Müller, C., & Mildenberger, T. (2021). Facilitating flexible learning by replacing classroom time with an online learning environment: A systematic review of blended learning in higher education neu. Educational Research Review, 34, 100394. https://doi.org/10.1016/j.edurev.2021.100394

Müller, C., Mildenberger, T., & Steingruber, D. (2023). Learning effectiveness of a flexible learning study programme in a blended learning design: Why are some courses more effective than others? International Journal of Educational Technology in Higher Education, 20(1), 10. https://doi.org/10.1186/s41239-022-00379-x

Müller, C., Stahl, M., Alder, M., & Müller, M. (2018). Learning effectiveness and students' perceptions in a flexible learning course. European Journal of Open, Distance and E-learning, 21(2), 44-53. https://doi.org/10.21256/zhaw-3189

Pelletier, K., McCormack, M., Reeves, J., Robert, J., Arbino, N., Al-Freih, M., Dickson-Deane, C., Guevara, C., Koster, L., Sanchez-Mendiola, M., Skallerup Bessette, L., & Stine, J. (2022). 2022 EDUCAUSE Horizon report teaching and learning edition. www.learntechlib.org/p/221033/

Wade, W. (1994). Introduction. In W. Wade, K. Hodgkinson, A. Smith, & J. Arfield (Eds.), Flexible learning in higher education (pp. 12-17). Routledge.

How to improve learning cooperation and future skills in cooperative study programs: Insights of a qualitative study among students at a cooperative university

Elena Glüber[1], Prof. Dr. Helge Fischer[2]

[1] IU International University of Applied Sciences, Germany, elena.glueber@iu.org
[2] IU International University of Applied Sciences, Germany, helge.fischer@iu.org

Abstract:

The project ZuKo4Saxony focuses on creating a digital learning environment to enhance collaboration between different institutions (e.g. university and company) and learning locations in cooperative study programs. The presented study is part of the specification process and investigates how the structural characteristics of small and medium-sized enterprises (SMEs) influence the competence development of students in cooperative universities. Through focus group discussions with students from IU International University of Applied Sciences (IU) in Dresden, the research identifies key factors affecting professional and personal growth within cooperative studies. The findings underline the importance of professional supervision, successful theory-practice transfer and the processing of tasks that are thematically relevant to the course. Based on these results, recommendations for the improvement of cooperative study programs in SMEs and suggestions for future research are given.

Keywords: Cooperative study program, theory-practice transfer, practical phases, SMEs, Saxony

Introduction

Cooperative study programs integrate an academic education with practical training within companies, offering a comprehensive educational approach that combines academic learning with practical work experience (Wissenschaftsrat, 2013, p. 5). In Germany, an increasing number of students are opting for cooperative studies. In the Free State of Saxony, a medium-sized German federal state, approximately 6,000 students are inrolled in a cooperative study program. These students are employed regionally in various industries, often in small or very small enterprises located outside urban centers. For many companies, hiring cooperative students represents a forward-looking personnel and innovation strategy in a labor market often described as problematic.

However, cooperative studies come with significant challenges for both students and companies, particularly concerning the integration of different learning locations (company and university). Small or very small enterprises become training companies, even though they often lack the necessary structures, competencies, and capacities. As a result, the integration of the two learning locations and the systematic promotion of cooperative students outside the university often fall short. This leads to decreasing study motivation and performance, as well as increasing dropout rates or changes of practice partners by students. Consequently, many companies struggle to integrate cooperative students optimally into their operations or retain them in the long term.

Strengthening the cooperation between learning locations in cooperative studies and the resulting development of skilled workers are therefore core concerns of the ZuKo4Saxony project (www.zuko4saxony.de). To achieve this, future working skills are to be emphasized, which form the basis of the educational concept at the university and are also significant for the future workplaces (company learning location). Future working skills refer to abilities and competencies that are expected to be in high demand in the coming years as society and the workplace evolve and adapt to technological advancements and the changing economic landscape. Both academia and practice agree that these skills enable graduates to best meet the challenges of the future. The project is jointly implemented by researchers from the Dresden University of Technology, IU International University of Applied Sciences, University of Applied Sciences Mittweida, and TUD FaCE TU Dresden Institute for Further and Continuing Education GmbH, and is funded by the European Social Fund and Saxon State Ministry for Science, Culture and Tourism under the "Future of Vocational Education" funding program.

About the ZuKo4Saxony project

The ZuKo4Saxony project aims to develop a digital learning environment for the development of urgently needed competencies for the future working world, which are required by practice companies for onboarding and supervising cooperative students. The project addresses the following objectives:

- Strengthening the cooperation between learning locations (company and university) to effectively train cooperative students and promote their future working skills through various exchange formats.

- Raising awareness and qualifying employees in SMEs (especially small or very small enterprises) regarding the challenges of modern personnel development in the context of digitalization, particularly the supervision of cooperative students.

- Creating training and further education capacities and prerequisites in companies, especially in small and very small enterprises, to promote company development.

- Improving the quality of cooperative studies and increasing the knowledge transfer between practical work and academic education.

- Assessing the need for future working skills that are expected to be highly needed by society and the labor market in the coming years.

- Designing and implementing certified modules for training and personnel managers as well as cooperative students in the area of developing specific future working skills.

- Implementing communication strategies to promote the development of future working skills and the knowledge transfer between practical work and academic education.

The digital learning environment developed in the project combines various measures/tools of formal and informal education and allows practice companies to flexibly respond to the challenges of supervising cooperative students and build relevant future working skills for company development. It incorporates current educational technology and media didactic developments to provide flexible (mobile), situational, and low-threshold access to high-quality educational content for shaping the future working world. The learning architecture focuses on various facets of future working skills for the new working world, personnel development, and talent management 4.0, as well as corporate transformation in the digital age. Future working skills represent an essential pillar of academic education at the university learning location and are reflected in the curricula of various study programs and modules. They also form the basis for innovation-oriented organizational and personnel development in SMEs, providing significant added value for the company development of practice companies.

The training programme is developed together with SMEs in the region and regional network partners such as business associations and chambers of commerce as part of workshops. This is intended to ensure that the needs of the target group are at the centre of the development and research work.

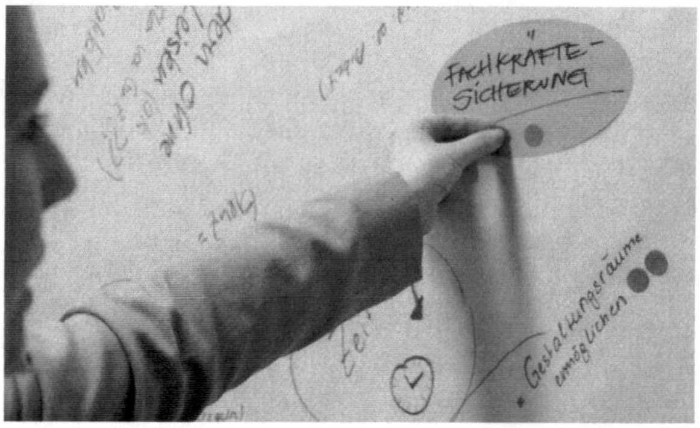

Figure. 1: kick off workhop with SME and business associations

Empirical survey on cooperative study programs in Saxon SMEs

Following the 2024 resolution by the Conference of Ministers of Education and Cultural Affairs, cooperative study programs must ensure the integration of learning locations in terms of content, organization and contractual agreements to qualify for designation and advertising as cooperative studies (Kultusministerkonferenz, 2024, p. 11). However, existing research indicates that cooperative efforts between learning locations present significant challenges for SMEs with fewer than 250 employees (Nickel et al., 2022, p. 315). As already mentioned, the ZuKo4Saxony project aims to improve the conditions for cooperative study programmes by providing digital offerings for learning location cooperation and the development of future working skills. However, this requires a fundamental understanding of the status quo and the problems faced by students. For this reason, the following question was analysed empirically in a first step of the project implementation. "How do cooperative students in Saxony experience the influence of company size and the associated structural framework conditions of small and medium-sized enterprises on their competence development in cooperative studies?"

In this context, this study aims to investigate the extent to which the structures of SMEs influence the skills development of cooperative students and what measures SMEs can implement to enhance learning and development opportunities for cooperative students.

Literature review and method

To approach the research question, a systematic literature review was first carried out. This showed that cooperative students in SMEs tend to work more independently, while in larger companies they tend to receive more supervision and are more intensively integrated into the team structure (Brodsky, 2022, p. 60). The lack of adequate supervision in SMEs can hinder the theory-practice transfer (Langfeld, 2018, p. 12–13). Additionally, ensuring the quality of practical training phases is challenging, as the responsible bodies at the academic learning location have limited ability to oversee company-based training directly (Nickel et al., 2022, p. 103). The alignment of theoretical knowledge with practical tasks is crucial for student satisfaction and retention, with students showing higher commitment when there is a clear connection between their studies and practical work (Rahn, Hettler, & Meyer, 2023, p. 13). Despite these insights, there remains a gap in understanding how cooperative students perceive their competence development within SMEs.

To address the research question, two focus group discussions were conducted with fifteen students (N=15) enrolled in the cooperative Bachelor's program in marketing at IU campus in Dresden. The questionnaire was developed based on the KoMo-Cooperative competence model (Arens-Fischer, Dinkelborg, & Grunwald, 2016), which assesses the contribution of teaching and learning activities at both the academic and company levels to competence acquisition and development. In the KoMo-Cooperative model, overall competence is defined as a combination of the two core competence fields of professional competence and personal competence as well as the three cross-sectional competences of instrumental competence, social competence and competence in scientific thinking and acting (Arens-Fischer, Dinkelborg, & Grunwald, 2016, p. 71). To analyze the focus group data, qualitative content analysis was conducted following Mayring's (2022) procedural model, using a deductive category application based on the predefined categories from the KoMo-Cooperative model.

- **Professional competence: tasks and feedback:** Professional competence involves the ability to independently and appropriately manage tasks from a professional perspective (BMBF, n.d.). The coordination of the tasks in the company with the theoretical content of the course is essential for the development of professional competence. Tasks that lack professional relevance can limit students' ability to deepen their academic knowledge and may cause uncertainty regarding their career preparedness in marketing. Additionally, systematic feedback is crucial for allowing students to learn from their experiences and improve their performance.

- **Personal competence: supervision and role understanding:** Personal competence encompasses the ability and motivation for personal development and the autonomous and responsible management of one's life. High-quality supervision by experienced colleagues is pivotal for developing personal competence. Inadequate supervision can lead to uncertainties and require cooperative students to independently navigate expectations. Clear role definitions prevent frustration and foster a stronger identification with the company, thereby enhancing personal competence and promoting long-term retention.

- **Instrumental competence: use of industry-specific tools:** Instrumental competence refers to the practical application of theoretical knowledge and the effective use of technologies and methodologies. A detailed, technical introduction to industry-specific tools facilitates the rapid development of instrumental competence. SMEs tend to have less standardized processes for implementing these tools, which can hinder the application of industry-specific methods and limit cooperative students' ability to fully leverage their theoretical training.

- **Social Competence: environment and regional connection:** Social competence includes the ability to function responsibly within social contexts, encompassing teamwork, communication skills, and an understanding of societal dynamics (Arens-Fischer, Dinkelborg, & Grunwald, 2016 p. 71). Integration into the company's social environment enhances students' identification with the company and their overall motivation. Especially in SMEs, cooperative students describe a family-like atmosphere. However, this environment can also raise expectations of the work of cooperative students that are too high or lead to them being deployed as low-cost workers in companies with insufficient personnel resources. A decisive factor for students choosing a cooperative study program at the IU in Dresden is the regional connection, for example through family roots or personal relationships. The choice of an SME was not planned for most of them, but resulted from the circumstances, for example due to a lack of alternatives.

- **Competence for scientific thinking and action: application of theoretical knowledge:** The ability to think and act scientifically includes the ability to apply methods, question knowledge and transfer findings into practice (Arens-Fischer, Dinkelborg, & Grunwald, 2016, p. 71). Cooperative students generally benefit from the integration of theoretical knowledge with practical tasks, especially in companies whose core activities align with their studies. However, there are also students who cannot establish a link between theory and practice. If theoretical knowledge is not integrated into working life, cooperative students find it difficult to recognize the value of their academic training. This can lead to them feeling inadequately prepared for starting a career in marketing.

Discussion and recommendations for Effective Cooperative Study Programs in SMEs

The focus group findings align with existing research, particularly regarding task distribution, the integration of theory and practice and supervision quality. A central finding is that the correspondence between the company's core business and the theoretical content of the study program is more influential on competence development than company size. Students engaged in marketing-oriented companies reported more positive experiences due to better alignment with theoretical concepts, whereas those in non-marketing firms more often performed supportive tasks that did not enhance their marketing competencies. Some SMEs tend not to be able to provide adequate professional supervision, which can lead to students being used primarily as full-time workers or as support staff to assist existing employees. This underlines the need for SMEs to balance the cooperative study program in different skill areas to ensure the comprehensive development of cooperative students.

To optimize the implementation of cooperative study programs in SMEs, several key measures should be adopted, e.g.:

- cooperative students should be entrusted with professionally relevant tasks that challenge their capabilities and contribute to their development. Regular, systematic feedback is essential to ensure continuous professional growth.

- structured supervision and clearly defined roles are crucial in fostering cooperative students' personal competence and strengthening their identification with the organization. Clearly outlining responsibilities enhances their ability to navigate professional environments effectively.

- SMEs should ensure access to industry-specific tools and structured training in relevant technologies and methodologies. Providing hands-on experience with essential industry resources supports practical skill acquisition and professional preparedness.

- a supportive and family-like work atmosphere should be cultivated to enhance cooperative student well-being and motivation. However, it is vital to strike a balance, preventing excessive expectations or potential exploitation.

- a strong integration of theoretical knowledge into professional practice must be prioritized. Aligning academic content with workplace tasks enhances competence development and increases student satisfaction with the cooperative study experience.

By implementing these recommendations, SMEs can create an effective and sustainable framework for cooperative study programs, benefiting both students and organizations.

Future Research and Conclusion

Future investigations should focus on establishing criteria for recognizing companies as qualified practical partners in marketing study programs. Additionally, identifying and showcasing SMEs that provide exemplary conditions for competence development could serve as valuable best-practice models. Such research would contribute to enhancing the quality of cooperative studies and optimizing collaboration between universities and companies. The successful development of cooperative study programs in SMEs hinges on the effective integration of theoretical and practical training, the provision of adequate supervision, and the alignment of tasks with academic content. By addressing these factors, SMEs can enhance the competence development of cooperative students, thereby fostering their professional and personal growth and contributing to the sustainability of cooperative study initiatives.

The potential for improvement identified in the study mark the cornerstones for successful project implementation. In further steps, the future competences relevant for SMEs in the Free State of Saxony will be identified on the basis of empirical studies in order to develop digital learning and service offerings. The results of the focus group interviews among the students will be incorporated here, as will the findings from the survey of company representatives. In this way, an environment is being developed that meets the needs of regional companies and leads to a sustainable improvement in cooperative study programmes in the Free State of Saxony.

As part of the presentation of the project, all available empirical findings from the various analyses will be presented.

References

Arens-Fischer, W., Dinkelborg, K., & Grunwald, G. (2016). Theorie-Praxis-Vernetzung und Kompetenzentwicklung in cooperativeen Studiengängen. Hochschule und Weiterbildung, 2, 67–75. :10.25656/01:15203

Brodsky, A. (2022). Lernen am Arbeitsplatz im cooperativeen Studium. Springer Fachmedien.

Kultusministerkonferenz. (2024). Musterrechtsverordnung gemäß Artikel 4 Absätze 1–4 Studienakkreditierungsstaatsvertrag: Beschluss der Kultusministerkonferenz vom 21.11.2024. Retrieved from https://www.kmk.org/fileadmin/Dateien/veroeffentlichungen_beschluesse/2024/2024_11_21-Musterrechtsverordnung.pdf

Langfeldt, B. (2018). Lernortkooperation im cooperativeen Studium – zu viel oder zu wenig Einfluss der Hochschulen auf die betrieblichen Praxisphasen? bwp@ Berufs- und Wirtschaftspädagogik, 34, 1–10.

Mayring, P. (2022). Qualitative Inhaltsanalyse: Grundlagen und Techniken (13th ed.). Julius Beltz GmbH & Co. KG.

Nickel, S., Pfeiffer, I., Fischer, A., Hüsch, M., Kiepenheuer-Drechsler, B., Lauterbach, N., Reum, N., Thiele, A.-L., & Ulrich, S. (2022). Cooperativees Studium: Umsetzungsmodelle und Entwicklungsbedarfe: Wissenschaftliche Studie. CHE Impulse, 8, wbv Verlag.:10.3278/9783763971718

Rahn, S., Hettler, I. S., & Meyer, T. (2023). Die Qualität der Praxisphasen im cooperativeen Studium der Sozialen Arbeit: Zur Relevanz von Aufgabenqualität und Theorie-Praxis-Verzahnung für die Zufriedenheit der Studierenden mit ihren Praxisphasen. Soziale Arbeit (SozA), 72(1), 13–21. :10.5771/0490-1606-2023-1-13

Wissenschaftsrat. (2013). Empfehlungen zur Entwicklung des cooperativeen Studiums: Positionspapier. Retrieved from https://www.wissenschaftsrat.de/download/archiv/3479-13.pdf?__blob=publicationFile&v=4

ZuKo4Saxony. (2024). Zukunftskompetenzen für cooperative Studierende und Unternehmen in Sachsen – praxisnah, digital und vernetzt. Retrieved from https://www.zuko4saxony.de/

E-Mentoring Skills Development in the Online Teaching/Learning Process

Ilona Tandzegolskienė-Bielaglovė[1], Rasa Didžiulienė[2], Nijolė Čiučiulkienė[3]

[1] Education academy, Vytautas Magnus University, Lithuania; Ilona.tandzegolskiene-bielaglove@vdu.lt

[2] Education academy, Vytautas Magnus University, Lithuania; rasa.didziuliene@vdu.lt

[3] Education academy, Vytautas Magnus University, Lithuania; nijole.ciuciulkiene@vdu.lt

Correspondence: Nijolė Čiučiulkienė (nijole.ciuclkiene@vdu.lt) and Rasa Didžiulienė (rasa.didziuliene@vdu.lt)

Abstract:

Manifolded spheres of online education context and e-mentoring as a factor scaffolding it require from e-mentors a wider range of competencies than the traditional mentor would possess. E-mentors must develop a method of gathering, gaining the mentees' trust, providing them with direction toward their goals, maintaining their anonymity via digital means, maintaining balance amongst mentees from diverse cultural backgrounds, and providing them with digital support as well. It means that e-mentor must be ready to answer not only professional questions the mentee may ask but also explain how to deal with any technology-related challenges. This research paper examines the basic theory and characteristics of online learning and e-mentoring. It also investigates how the expansion of IT has affected the development of e-mentoring skills and teaching methods, illuminating the ever-changing nature of modern education.

Keywords: E-Mentoring Skills, Online Teaching/Learning; distance learning.

Introduction

Online mentoring, virtual mentoring, and distance mentoring are synonyms for e-mentoring. However, the term "e-mentoring" is more in line with everyday language. We define e-mentoring as a mutually beneficial relationship organized remotely between a mentor and a mentee that supports a form of distance learning, as well as financial and emotional support, usually provided via e-mail and other electronic means, such as instant messaging, chat rooms, and social networks. Researchers emphasize problems related to the use of technology and information literacy, which can also inspire social problems. These may include a weakening sense of community, decreasing goal orientation, insufficient security, and control. In the context of education there newly arise such problems as careful selection of e-mentors and computer literacy seminars that meet the expectations of e-mentors. Moreover, various spheres of distance education context and e-mentoring require e-mentors to have a wider range of competencies than we should demonstrate while implementing classical mentoring. E-mentors need to create a mentoring system that allows them to gain the trust of their mentees remotely, guide them to achieve their goals, maintain anonymity, and provide digital support to their mentees, helping them cope with any technology-related challenges. Such manifolded online mentoring context inspires the following research questions: what is the priority e-mentor competencies that e-mentors should develop to create a successful system of e-mentoring and how can they be developed in the online mentoring process?

The object of the research: the development of e-mentoring skills.

Aim of research: To investigate how teachers can develop their e-mentoring competencies when mentoring online, highlighting the priority relevant e-mentoring competence list.

Theoretical framework

Online education/e-Learning has been defined as the use of web-based technologies to close the gap between the teacher and the learner, to strengthen the interaction between teacher and student and to help mentees acquire essential competences (Singh &; Thurman, 2019). The e-mentoring can be also characterized as the process of the professional development when more experienced professional via internet provides consultations, and other developmental activities to a less experienced specialist/student. E-mentoring might be one of such forms which is more and more suggested as a means of optimization of the novice mentoring (Perlman et al. 2014). As a result of the integration of new technologies, e-mentoring is a flexible alternative (sometimes as complementary) besides the traditional face-to-face mentoring (Murphy, 2012). E-mentoring provides an opportunity to share knowledge and experience regardless of time and place, it provides different methods of interaction without social prejudices. E-mentoring not only eliminates the status difference but also provides flexibility regarding response time and allows you to reach more people compared to direct mentoring (Hunt et al., 2013). The positive effects of e-mentoring are supported by scientists who have argued that it has some unique advantages over traditional face-to-face mentoring. For example, the online mentoring format allowed trainees to have mentors who were geographically distant from them, giving them access to professional experience and assistance (Aderibigbe at al., 2018). E-mentoring facilitated both synchronous and asynchronous or delayed communication. The asynchronous aspects of online mentoring facilitate more task-oriented interaction than face-to-face discussions, giving more time for reflection (Schechter, 2014).

The potential of e-mentoring becomes even more evident when we compare it to traditional mentoring, especially in a distance learning environment. E-mentoring has filled in geographic gaps, providing learners separated by physical distances with a special and powerful form of assistance. It is remarkable how well e-mentoring and distance learning work together to give students access to insightful advice and encouragement from mentors no matter where they live. E-mentoring has been a game-changer in the field of remote learning, transforming the way students interact with their learning opportunities. In the digital age, traditional mentoring has its limitations because it necessitates physical presence and can be logistically difficult for both mentors and mentees. However, by utilizing digital platforms and communication capabilities, e-mentoring gets beyond these limitations and becomes available to a wider range of students. E-mentoring improves distance learning results and gives students access to a more individualized, effective, and encouraging educational experience (Briscoe, 2019). It should be noted that students sometimes practice their teachers and can share their experiences with them. One of the means may be reverse mentoring, which is practiced when a student becomes a mentor to an old teacher. Both the mentor and the mentee exchange their skills and knowledge. Reverse mentoring is frequently associated with bridging an assumed gap between generations in the workplace and differences in knowledge, expertise, and social values between generations (Murphy, 2012; Eaves, 2018; Browne, 2021).

The authors of this research strived to investigate the prevailing competences that are currently expressed by the e-mentors who have a preliminary practice of distant learning and mentoring. A research group of mentors and paper authors was formed to conduct the research. Mentors considered and addressed potential technical or critical mentoring questions, shared thoughts, and experiences, discussed difficult or particularly interesting mentoring cases, and sought advice from other mentors and facilitators. As a result, an e-mentoring research culture was established. Dialogue, interaction and collaboration between mentors was born which allowed a quite successful procedures of the research.

Methodology

Qualitative research methodology was applied. Research methods: data collection methods: observations of e-mentoring activities, semi structured interviews with the experienced e-mentors and future e-mentors. The received data were analysed while conducting inductive qualitative content analysis (Mayring, 2014). Semi-structured interviews were organized to collect basic data, which were chosen because of the flexibility of this method and the possibility of collecting data from 16 informants. For the implementation of the semi-structured interviews, 20 main questions were prepared relying on an inductive approach. One interview lasted an average of one hour. The interview was conducted by two researchers. The interviews were conducted until the researchers obtained "rich and thick" (Dibley, 2011) data. "Thick data" means a lot of data; "rich data" are many-layered, intricate, detailed, nuanced, and more. For research validity, it is important to have both richness and thickness (Fusch & Ness, 2015). This means that the interview texts (from 6 to 8 pages) were extensive and allowed to proceed with the inductive content analysis (Ciuciulkiene at al., 2023). The responses were recorded and later transcribed. The transcriptions were coded from R1 to R16 to demonstrate the total amount of the produced interviews. The transcriptions were analysed by two independent researchers with the purpose of generating the main ideas and regularities, relying on the meaning of the clearly expressed messages, which were later combined into themes, categories and subcategories.

Participants of the research

The research was conducted with teachers from different fields of studies in Lithuania. The population of the research is teachers who have experience in online teaching and mentoring. Attention is paid to the selection of participants from different education institutions. The purposeful sampling method was used. This is finding and choosing teachers, who are informed about a topic of interest (Cresswell & Plano Clark, 2011). In addition to expertise and experience, other factors include participation readiness, accessibility, and the capacity to share ideas and experiences in an honest, expressive, and thoughtful way. As it was already stated, the research sample consisted of 16 teachers.

Ethics

Each participant agreed to participate in the interview while maintaining their privacy and identity by signing a consent form. Informed permission and privacy safeguards were used to solve ethical issues.

Results

Data analysis was driven by Maying's (2014) qualitative content analysis. There were revealed four major themes: "Providing ongoing support and encouragement to assist learners in the online training phase, meeting new learner needs"; "The online teaching/learning for the development of e-mentees' mentoring skills"; "Help for e-mentee to become comfortable in online environments"; "Forms of e-mentoring".

The first theme "Providing ongoing support and encouragement to assist learners in the online training phase, meeting new learner needs" has been created based on the following 2 main categories, explaining the context: "Learning how to adapt to changes" and "Learning how to work with technology". Each category also includes sub-categories, and they are represented in the 1 table below.

Table 1: Manifestation of the categories and subcategories of the theme "Providing ongoing support and encouragement to assist learners in the online training phase".

Providing ongoing support and encouragement to assist learners in the online training phase			
Learning how to adapt to changes		***Learning how to work with technology***	
Challenges for implementing distant learning	Challenges of technology literacy lack	Problems with managing online	Problems with students' attendance
"It appeared that not all schools were well provided with the consultation basis how to organize the TEAMS meetings" (R1)	"There we were such challenges which seem funny now, for e.g. To share the screen with audience for providing the slides" (R6)	"We could hardly squeeze into 45 min. zoom session period" (R2)	"The mentees were complaining that they failed to connect to the session, but I have some doubts about that... They were simply missing the meeting" (R4)

The main objective of the interview question block was to identify the difficulties that arose when switching to an online learning environment, whether they are related to adjusting to a new setting, strengthening knowledge of technology, efficiently running online courses, or solving issues with attendance <..."It appeared that not all schools were well provided with the consultation basis how to organize the TEAMS meetings"...(R1)>. It appeared that the major challenges were based on technology lack, different time management < "There we were such challenges which seem funny now, for e.g. To share the screen with audience for providing the slides" (R6)> and learning discipline abuse. Through continuous assistance and motivation, instructors can assist learners in overcoming these obstacles and achieving success during the virtual training stage.

The second theme "The online teaching/learning for the development of e-mentees' mentoring skills" has been created based on the following 2 main categories as well: "Implementation of blended learning aspects" and "Development of multitasking skills". Each category also includes sub-categories, and they are represented in the 2 table below.

Table 2: Manifestation of the categories and subcategories of the theme "The online teaching/learning for the development of e-mentees' mentoring skills".

The online teaching/learning for the development of e-mentees' mentoring skills			
Implementation of blended learning		***Development of multitasking skills***	
Group learning skills	Skill development of controlling different numbers of students at once	Skill development of working with other instructors at the same time	Skill development of creating new technology-based methods of teaching
"We gained the experience of group work in "Zoom" and "Teams" (R3)	"I learned how to distribute them into the Zoom rooms and control them. That helped me to work in Blended learning classrooms" (R5)	"Demonstrating video-based tutorials was very popular" (R7)	"I enjoyed video reporting and producing AI designed mentoring task-based clips" (R14)

The focus of the theme is on mentors developing their e-mentoring and blended learning abilities. < "I learned how to distribute them into the Zoom rooms. This experience helped me to work in Blended learning classrooms". (R5) A variety of subcategories include managing different student numbers, working with other teachers (I learned how to distribute them into the Zoom rooms...(R5), developing creative technology-based teaching techniques "I enjoyed video reporting and producing AI designed mentoring task-based clips" (R14)", and mastering group learning techniques. The subject emphasizes how crucial it is for mentors to develop and improve their leading skills to adjust to the dynamic nature of online teaching and learning.

The third theme is "Help for e-mentee to become comfortable in online environments", which is divided into 2 categories: "Qualified in Technological literacy" and "The ability of mentors in an online community to present themselves socially and emotionally, as real people" with substituting sub-categories (See 3 table)

Table 3: Manifestation of the categories and subcategories of the theme "Help for e-mentee to become comfortable in online environments".

Help for e-mentee to become comfortable in online environments			
Qualified in Technological literacy		***The ability of mentors in an online community to present themselves socially and emotionally, as real people***	
Introducing activities helping teachers to progress in online teaching and learning	Demonstrating effective online instruction	Providing guidance when difficulties arise	Being available for the mentee
"We appointed several times in a week for technology management practice" (R11)	"We became effective in 45 min. time" (R9)	"I learned some of the IT discipline, to answer the e-mails and respond to messages in a short time" (R10)	"... we settled the timetable for our meetings" (R14)

Helping mentees feel comfortable in online settings is the main objective of this theme. While the second category emphasizes the interpersonal component and the mentors' capacity to present themselves socially and emotionally <" I learned some of the IT discipline, I mean to answer the e-mails and respond to messages in a short time" > (R10), the first category guarantees technology literacy <"We appointed several times in a week for technology management practice"> (R11). The subcategories focus on certain tactics and actions that are necessary to establish a welcoming and encouraging online learning environment for mentees. These tactics include initiating tasks, modelling successful instruction, offering help during difficulties, and being accessible.

The fourth theme "Forms of e-mentoring" has been created based on the following 3 main categories: Peer mentoring; Team mentoring and Reverse mentoring. Each category also includes sub-categories, and they are represented in the 4 table below.

Table 4: Manifestation of the categories and subcategories of the theme "Forms of mentoring".

Forms of mentoring					
Peer mentoring		***Team mentoring***		***Reverse mentoring***	
From teacher to teacher	Learning community of mentees	Team mentoring questioning sessions	Establishment of mentoring culture	Mentee-mentor dyad relations	Behavioural awareness of a mentee
"Our relation grew to the sharing the experience of e-mentoring with the colleagues who had e-mentoring practice" (R10)	"... we established the network of e-mentees" (R4)	"It was a comfort to work in a group of online mentors" (R7)	"We created our e-mentoring classroom rules" (R9)	"I realized that in some cases my mentee can be my mentor" (R11)	"...I understood that I can trust my mentee..." (R2)

The theme dives into several types of e-mentoring, emphasizing team and peer mentorship < "It was a real comfort to work in a group of online mentors, giving the recommendations to the mentees"> (R7). While team mentoring involves collaborating cooperatively with several mentors and mentees, peer mentoring focuses on relationships between teachers. Aspects of these mentoring forms are highlighted by subcategories including questioning sessions, learning communities, and creating a mentoring culture < "We created our e-mentoring classroom rules"> (R9). These subcategories demonstrate the variety of ways that mentoring can be organized and carried out in an educational setting.

Conclusions

1. The research results highlighted the unique advantages of online mentoring over traditional face-to-face mentoring. The results demonstrated that an online mentoring format allowed trainees to have mentors geographically remote from them, giving them access to professional expertise and assistance that might not otherwise have been available in their given practice environment.
2. E-mentoring facilitated both synchronous and asynchronous or delayed communication. The asynchronous aspects of online mentoring could subsequently facilitate a more reflective, task-oriented interaction than face-to-face discussion by allowing more time to reflect rather than to respond immediately.
3. The e-mentoring relationship appeared to be helpful for enhancing the personal empowerment of mentees and mentors by developing their communication skills while using IT for creating relationships, providing them with the opportunity to assist each other. It appeared that it was more challenging for the protégés than to mentors to relate to social presence in the computer-mediated environment.
4. E-mentoring also provided a foundation for gaining experience of the development of the e-mentoring skills of educators and the growth of cooperative traits in mentors. The content of the categories and subcategories also proved the e-mentors' growing capacities to create adequate tasks for the e-mentees, to optimize the meeting organization time, to apply-mentoring tools (messages, e-mails, and other means of e-mentoring) to improve knowledge gaining process.

References

Aderibigbe, S. A., Gray, D. S., & Gray, L. C. (2018). Understanding the nature of mentoring experiences between teachers and student teachers. International Journal of Mentoring and Coaching in Education, 7(4), 54-71.

Briscoe, P. (2019). Virtual mentor partnerships between practicing and preservice teachers. International Journal of Mentoring and Coaching, 8(4), 235–254. https://doi.org/10.1108/IJMCE-02-2019-0023

Browne, I. (2021). Exploring reverse mentoring; "Win-win" relationships in the multi-generational workplace. International Journal of Evidence Based Coaching and Mentoring, Spec Iss 15, 246–259.

Ciuciulkiene, N., Tandzegolskiene-Bielaglove, I., & Culadiene, M. (2023). Phenomenon-based learning in teaching a foreign language: Experiences of Lithuanian teachers. Social Sciences, 12(12), 670.

Dibley, L. (2011). Analysing narrative data using McCormack's Lenses. Nurse Res., 18(3):13-9. doi: 10.7748/nr2011.04.18.3.13.c8458. PMID: 21560921.

Hunt, J. H., Powell, S., Little, M. E., & Mike, A. (2013). The Effects of E-Mentoring on Beginning Teacher Competencies and Perceptions. Teacher Education and Special Education, 36(4), 286-297. https://www.learntechlib.org/p/156602/

Mayring, P. (2014). Qualitative content analysis: theoretical foundation, basic procedures and software solution. Approaches to Qualitative Research in Mathematics Education, 365-380. Doi: 10.1007/978-94-017-9181-6_13.

Murphy, W. (2012). Reverse mentoring at work: Fostering cross-generational learning and developing millennial leaders. Human Resource Management, 51(4), 549–573. doi: 10.1002/hrm.21489

Singh, V., & Thurman, A. (2019). How Many Ways Can We Define Online Learning? A Systematic Literature Review of Definitions of Online Learning (1988-2018). American Journal of Distance Education, 33(4), 289–306. doi: 10.1080/08923647.2019.1663082

Schechter, C. (2014). Mentoring prospective principals: Determinants of productive mentor–mentee relationship. International Journal of Educational Reform, 23(1), 52–65. https://doi.org/10.1177/105678791402300103

Inclusive Practices in Multisensory Environments: survey of Preschool Teachers experiences

Nijolė Čiučiulkienė[1], Rasa Didžiulienė[2], Birutė Ščiukienė[3]

[1] Education academy, Vytautas Magnus University, Lithuania; nijole.ciuciulkiene@vdu.lt
[2] Education academy, Vytautas Magnus University, Lithuania; rasa.didziuliene@vdu.lt
[3] Education academy, Vytautas Magnus University, Lithuania; birute.sciukiene@vdu.lt

Correspondence: Nijolė Čiučiulkienė (nijole.ciuciulkiene@vdu.lt) and Rasa Didžiulienė (rasa.didziuliene@vdu.lt)

Abstract:

The discussion about inclusion is very relevant for the school community, as it implies the need to analyse the issues of inclusive education and find out what inclusive education methods would be the most effective so that every child, regardless of their physical or psychological condition, has equal opportunities to learn and develop. Although amendments to the Law on Education of the Republic of Lithuania have been adopted, stating that from 2024 all schools and kindergartens should accept children with special educational needs, not all educators are ready to develop their competencies so that they enabled the application of innovative, child-friendly methods that allow the educational process to be adapted to the needs of each child. A multisensory environment stimulates various senses; therefore, it is an effective tool that positively affects children's learning and overall development (Walling, 2014). This paper aims to examine the practices of preschool educators related to the creation and application of multisensory environments, aiming to reach positive inclusion results. The results of the study highlighted that teacher digital and communicative competences are very important for smooth and effective education in multisensory environments.

Keywords: Multisensory Environments; Inclusive education; Preschool Education.

Introduction

The modern era of education is characterized by the fact that not only traditional teaching methods but also innovative environments that can maximize children's learning potential are attracting increasing attention of the scientists (Smith, 2018). Multisensory environments that stimulate various senses are evaluated as an effective tool that positively affects children's learning and overall development. Research studies (Enguito, 2019) highlight the effectiveness of multisensory environments in promoting children's inclusion, but it is necessary to examine in more detail how educators design and adapt these environments to understand their real impact on the development of the competencies that enable to provide positive inclusion. Despite the benefits of multisensory environments, the problem is that not all preschools are able to create effective and fully inclusive multisensory environments due to various challenges, including a lack of knowledge and digital literacy skills among educators, limited resources, and infrastructure constraints.

The problem question: How could the educators develop their competencies by effectively implementing multisensory environments in preschool education?

Aim of research - to investigate the practices of preschool educators while applying multisensory environments.

Theoretical framework

Multisensory education is understood as a teaching method that uses visual, auditory, kinesthetic, and tactile modalities to educate students (Joshi et al., 2002). Research in the field of education (Shams & Seitz, 2008; Scolari et al., 2018; Kress et al., 2021) emphasizes the significant role of representational diversity in the effectiveness of learning. This conceptual shift raises a discussion about the assessment of students' "informal learning strategies" (Scolari et al., 2018) and their inclusion in learning by creating learning environments that embrace the multisensory learning paradigm. Multisensory learning is understood as a learning practice that includes various information channels belonging to different senses: vision, hearing, olfaction, etc. (Kokkinaki et al., 2024).

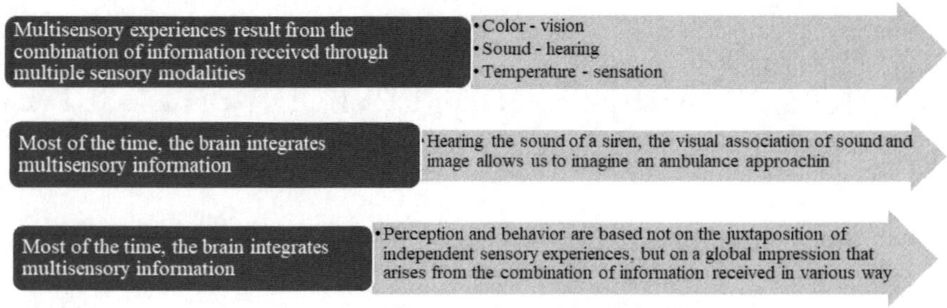

Figure 1: Multisensory integration according to Kokkinaki et al., 2024.

Human perception and behavior are not based on the juxtaposition of independent sensory experiences, but on a global impression that arises from the combination of information received in different ways. This phenomenon is called multisensory integration. In many cases, the survival of the organism depends on appropriate responses to multisensory stimuli. Therefore, the ability to integrate sensory information becomes an essential element of human daily behavior, allowing us to identify events and adapt optimal responses to these events. Educational research (Kress et al., 2021) has shown the benefits of representational learning methods, helping students to be more engaged in the learning process (Shams & Seitz, 2018). An important benefit of multisensory learning is the "double coding", which "reduces cognitive load", because information from different methods can be more easily sorted into short-term memory and used to create long-term representations" Shamso and Seitz (2008). As a result, variations of information repetition with different systems or media (e.g., oral, written, audiovisual, etc.) is prevailing technique for knowledge acquisition and retaining (Kokkinaki et al., 2024).

While summing up, it can be stated that multisensory environments, multisensory rooms are intended not only for learning, but also for self-knowledge, learning to manage emotions (e.g., calming down). Such spaces work for everyone, especially for the children with special needs. It is worth noting that those students who learn in multisensory environments achieve much better results, because their perception and problem-solving approach is broader.

Methodology

Studies such as Joy Ann Enguito (2019) highlight the effectiveness of multisensory environments in promoting children's inclusion, but it is necessary to examine in more detail how educators create and apply these environments in order to understand their real impact on the formation of inclusion competencies. This work aims to investigate the practices of preschool educators related to the creation and application of multisensory environments, and their impact on the formation and development of inclusion competencies. In order to analyse preschool teachers' experiences while applying the multisensory learning the qualitative research methodology was applied.

Data collection methods: semi structured interviews with the preschool educators who are experienced in multisensory teaching and learning was conducted. The received data were analysed while performing inductive qualitative content analysis (Mayring, 2014). Semi-structured interviews were organized to collect basic data, which were chosen because of the flexibility of this method and the possibility of collecting data from 18 informants. For the implementation of the semi-structured interviews, 25 main questions were prepared relying on an inductive approach. One interview lasted an average of one hour. The interview was conducted by two researchers. The interview texts (from 6 to 8 pages) were extensive and allowed to proceed with the inductive content analysis (Ciuciulkiene at al., 2023). The responses were recorded and later transcribed. The transcriptions were coded from E1 to E18 (E stands for "educator") to demonstrate the total amount of the produced interviews. The transcriptions were analysed by two independent researchers with the purpose of generating the main ideas and regularities, relying on the meaning of the clearly expressed messages, which were later combined into subcategories, categories, and themes.

Participants of the research

The research was conducted with teachers from different preschool institutions. The population of the research is teachers who have experience in multisensory teaching/learning. The purposeful sampling method was used. This is finding and choosing teachers, who are informed about a topic of interest (Cresswell, 2013). In addition to expertise and experience, other factors include participation readiness, accessibility, and the capacity to share ideas and experiences in an honest, expressive, and thoughtful way. As it was already stated, the research sample consisted of 18 teachers.

Ethics

Each participant agreed to participate in the interview while maintaining their privacy and identity by signing a consent form. Informed permission and privacy safeguards were used to solve ethical issues.

Results

Data analysis was conducted according by Maying's (2014) qualitative content analysis. There were revealed four major themes: "Teachers' created concept of multisensory environments"; "Teacher's role in multisensory environments"; "Competencies of the teacher working in a multisensory environment"; ""Pros and cons of multisensory education"".

The first theme „Teachers' created concept of multisensory environments" has been created based on the following 2 main categories, explaining the context: "Knowledge about multisensory environments" and "Multisensory usage cases ". Each category also includes sub-categories, and they are represented in the 1 table below.

Table 1: Manifestation of the subcategories and categories of the theme "Teachers' created concept of multisensory environments".

Teachers' created concept of multisensory environments			
Knowledge about multisensory environments		***Multisensory usage cases***	
Multisensory is a therapy	Specific teaching/learning environment	For the development of pupils' competencies	For the development of senses and perceptions
Multisensory is colour therapy, music therapy, aromatherapy (E1)	"Environment used during the adaptation period and when adapting to the educational plan" (E4), "This is the establishment of STEAM environments" (E3) "Environment of holistic education" (E5)	As a stimulating, creative tool for personality development, for the formation of mathematical and communication skills." (E15)	Involves children in tasks where they have to describe different tastes (sweet, sour, bitter), helps develop their senses" E12

Regarding multisensory environments, the informants' answers showed that everyone understands what multisensory environments are and what educational methods/methods are used in multisensory environments: "Multisensory is colour therapy, music therapy, aromatherapy." E1, "Environment that is used during the adaptation period and when adapting according to the educational plan" E4, "This is the establishment of steam environments" E3 "Environment of general education" E5 "Adaptation according to the weekly theme, a way for spending free time" E6. Almost all informants emphasized that they often use multisensory environments. All informants revealed their knowledge about multisensory environments, emphasizing how they apply multisensory environments to children's education, "As a stimulating, creative tool for developing counting and communication skills." E1, "<...> Involving children in tasks in which they have to describe different tastes (sweet, sour, together) helps develop their senses" E2.

The second theme ""Teacher's role in multisensory environments"" has been created based on the following 2 main categories as well: "Teacher for empowerment" and "Teacher for motivation". Each category also includes sub-categories, and they are represented in the 2 table below.

Table 2: Manifestation of the subcategories and categories and of the theme "Teacher's role in multisensory environments".

Teacher's role in multisensory environments				
Teacher for empowerment			***Teacher for motivation***	
A promoter of student engagement	Stimulator of students' interest	Teacher for inclusion	Provider of a positive environment	Positive reflector
"A teacher can empower students <...>" (E1)	Teacher plans the multisensory activities so that they could inspire creativity (E2)	Makes individual activity plan so that all pupils were indulged in activities (E7)	"I try to help my pupils feel comfortable" (E13)	I always highlight the positive day achievements so that they could see their progress (E16)

After analysing the answers of the interview participants about the role and competences of the teacher when transferring education to multisensory environments, it became clear that the role of the teacher in multisensory environments is no less important than during traditional education: <...>"The teacher can empower students <...>" E1 "He/she helps children get involved, creates and organizes activities, encourages and motivates" E2 "<....>the teacher becomes not only a transmitter of knowledge, but also a leader of activities, an observer and a promoter of student involvement.<....>" E3. The teacher observes the children and during the observation, imperceptibly guides them in the right direction, towards the right tools The answers show that the role of the teacher in multisensory environments is very important, the teacher becomes an observer, a promoter, a motivator, scaffolder of the inclusion.

The third theme is ""Competencies of the teacher working in a multisensory environment".", which is divided into 2 categories: "Priority competencies" and "Competencies of inclusive education" (See 3 table)

Table 3: Manifestation of the categories and subcategories of the theme "Competencies of the teacher working in a multisensory environment".

Competencies of the teacher working in a multisensory environment				
Priority competencies			***Competencies of inclusive education***	
Digital competence	Artistic competence	Communicative Competence	Knowledge about special educational needs	Abilities and skills for applying multisensory environments
The teacher working in a multisensory environment should be well trained to use its tools (E14)	He/she/ should have a sense of everyday life aesthetics (E11)	Good command of dealing with kids and parents is a must (E9)	One must be very qualified and have good knowledge about psychological, physiological needs of the pupils, like a doctor (E10)	"Good command of group activities while using specific technologies" (E3), "...one must be technologically friendly" (E14)

After the analysis of the prevailing competencies the researchers have picked the mostly repeating competencies which were accompanied by such evaluating phrases as "the most Important competencies" (E1, E5, E7, E11, E12, E16). They are digital competence, artistic competence, and communicative competence. The messages that teachers had sent had the modalities showing the inevitability of the existence of the mentioned competences if the goal is the success of the learning process < The teacher working in a multisensory environment ***should be*** well trained to use its tools (E14)>, " He/she/ ***should have*** a sense of everyday life aesthetics"(E11), < Good command of dealing with kids and parents ***is a must"*** > (E9). As the basis of a successful inclusion teachers pointed out the understanding of SEN "One must be very qualified and have good knowledge about psychological, physiological needs of the pupils, like a doctor (E10)" which should be interrelated with good command of the competencies for professional usage of multisensory education (See table3).

The fourth theme "Pros and cons of multisensory education" has been created based on the following 2 juxtaposed main categories:" Positive students' achievements in multisensory environment and "Challengers of multisensory teaching/learning". Each category also includes sub-categories, and they are represented in the 4 table below.

Table 4: Manifestation of the categories and subcategories of the theme "Forms of mentoring".

Positive students' achievements in multisensory environment		Challengers of multisensory teaching/learning.	
Maintaining the attention of children with special needs	Higher level of perception	Overstimulation	Not sufficient teacher training
Students stay focused longer, are interested." E1,	"Better concentration, relaxation, improved perception of sensations, management of emotions, motor coordination, cognitive skills <..>" E3	"There may be overstimulation <...>" E2	Insufficient preparation of educators, lack of training on how to work with equipment (E 2)

Teachers noticed that during education in multisensory environments, children are more easily involved in the educational process, greater motivation appears, children understand the world around them more smoothly, and children's curiosity and creativity are stimulated: "Involvement, motivation, encouragement, stimulation and calming." E1All informants emphasized that the biggest problems and shortcomings are the lack of information and help: "Information, help, support, funds" E1 "Information, help from management, seminars and materials, funds." E2 "<.> seminars, funds, tools." P3 "Everything is missing, it is probably easier to say what is not missing, <.> E4. All teachers who participated in the survey, who have experience working with children with special educational needs, emphasized that the biggest challenge is to integrate children with SEN into the general work of the group, to interest and maintain their attention. After reviewing the answers to questions in this category, the main problems become clear: lack of information, materials, seminars, courses, funds and help in integrating multisensory environments into the educational process. Teachers noticed that during education in multisensory environments, children are more easily involved in the educational process, greater motivation appears, children understand the world around them more smoothly, and children's curiosity and creativity are stimulated: "Involvement, motivation, encouragement, stimulation and calming." E1

Finalizing

Teachers understand how to work in multisensory environments, which educational methods to use, which ones are most suitable, how to apply them to educational activities, which methods are most suitable for children and for improving the educational process, but problems still emerge hindering the possibilities of effectively applying multisensory environments in the educational process. While summing up teachers' experiences, it can be stated children with SEN are more easily involved in general educational activities when they take place in multisensory environments, education proceeds more smoothly, and the development of children's competencies proceeds more smoothly. Children whose education is transferred to multisensory environments absorb the received material faster, willingly engage in the educational process, all five most important senses of the child (smell, vision, hearing, touch, and speech) are developed simultaneously, children focus more easily, calm down, understand the world around them more easily, willingly explore, their desire to learn increases, and they become more independent.

References

Ciuciulkiene, N., Tandzegolskiene-Bielaglove, I., & Culadiene, M. (2023). Phenomenon-based learning in teaching a foreign language: Experiences of Lithuanian teachers. Social Sciences, 12(12), 670.

Cresswell, J. (2013). Qualitative inquiry & research design: Choosing among five approaches.

Enguito, J. A. (2019). The multisensory method for six-year-old children at a daycare centre.

Kokkinaki, K., & Georgiadou, Z. (2024). Multisensory Perception and Multimodal Communication In Primary Education. Exploring Aesthetic Experience and Ways of Communication the 'Box Of Senses'. European Journal of Alternative Education Studies, 9(1).

Kress, S., Neudorf, J., Ekstrand, C., & Borowsky, R. (2021). Unmasking the effects of orthography, semantics, and phonology on 2AFC visual word perceptual identification. Visual Cognition, 29(10), 657-678.

Mayring, P. (2014). Qualitative content analysis: theoretical foundation, basic procedures, and software solution. Approaches to Qualitative Research in Mathematics Education, 365-380. Doi: 10.1007/978-94-017-9181-6_13.

Scolari, C. A., Masanet, M. J., Guerrero-Pico, M., & Establés, M. J. (2018). Transmedia literacy in the new media ecology: Teens transmedia skills and informal learning strategies. Profesional de la Información, 27(4), 801-812.

Shams, L., & Seitz, A. R. (2008). Benefits of multisensory learning. Trends in cognitive sciences, 12(11), 411-417. Smith, 2018

Walling, D. R. (2014). Designing learning for tablet classrooms: Innovations in instruction. Springer Science & Business Media.

The "Flipped Classroom" In Primary Education for the Development of Digital Competence: Pros and Cons

Nijolė Čiučiulkienė[1], Ilona Tandzegolskienė-Bielaglovė[2], Rasa Didžiulienė[3]

[1] Education academy, Vytautas Magnus University, Lithuania; nijole.ciuciulkiene@vdu.lt
[2] Education academy, Vytautas Magnus University, Lithuania; Ilona.tandzegolskiene-bielaglove@vdu.lt
[3] Education academy, Vytautas Magnus University, Lithuania; rasa.didziuliene@vdu.lt

Correspondence: Nijolė Čiučiulkienė (nijole.ciuclkiene@vdu.lt) and Rasa Didžiulienė (rasa.didziuliene@vdu.lt)

Abstract:

The Flipped Classroom model is a didactic method that has gained popularity in recent years due to its potential to improve students' learning experiences. This study investigates the impact of flipped classroom pedagogy on digital competence in primary education. The study analysed how the flipped classroom model improves students' digital literacy. The results of the study highlighted the positive impact of the flipped classroom model on the formation of digital competence in primary education, as well as the related pros and cons. The results of the study highlighted that flipped classrooms promote active learning, collaboration, and engagement, improve digital competences; by implementing flipped classrooms in primary education, students with essential digital literacy are prepared.

Keywords: "Flipped Classroom"; Digital Competence; Primary Education.

Introduction

The increasing mobility of society implies the need to connect the learning process with digital technologies and transfer it to environments accessible to students. The modern digital generation spends a lot of time in the virtual world, seeking to reach not only friends, but also learning content everywhere: not only in the classroom, but also outside it. Today, in the digital age, every learner can find many free learning resources, such as video lessons, which they can watch anywhere, at their convenience (Richter & McPherson, 2012). Therefore, it is important to organize the educational process in a digital learning environment, combining it with the traditional classroom model. The flipped classroom is a new learning model that allows video lessons and practical problem-solving to be done at home, and active group activities to develop problem-solving skills in the classroom (Bishop & Verleger, 2013). The flipped classroom model can be applied at all levels of education, including primary, secondary and tertiary education (Ozdamli & Asiksoy, 2016). Furthermore, the flipped classroom strategy offers a unique opportunity to improve digital competence while promoting deeper learning. Although there is more support for the flipped classroom strategy in the evaluation, more research is needed to determine its effectiveness in developing digital literacy and to identify didactic practices that will make the flipped classroom successful (Ozdamli & Asiksoy, 2016).

The problematic question arises how do flipped classroom participants use digital tools to ensure a successful learning process in the flipped classroom?

The object of the study is the development of digital competence in the flipped classroom.

Aim of research: to investigate the development of digital competence in the flipped classroom.

Theoretical framework

The flipped classroom is an educational model that changes traditional educational activities. In flipped classrooms, teachers record lectures and upload them to a learning management system (LMS) where students can review them before class. During the lesson, students engage in activities, discussions, and problem-solving that reinforce what they have learned by analysing the material presented in the videos. Flipped learning has been studied by Bergmann & Sams (2012); Geyer-Hayden (2016) among others. The learning culture in the flipped classroom has been analysed by Osman, Jamaludin and Mokhtar (2014) among others. Caliskan & Bicen (2016) investigated teachers' attitudes towards the use of the flipped classroom. It is worth noting that the flipped classroom education model not only develops digital competence but also encourages students to take responsibility for their own learning, scaffolds collaboration, and develops critical thinking skills.

Table 1: Comparative analysis of Traditional education and flipped classroom didactic practices (according to Bhavsar et al., 2022)

Didactic aspects	**Traditional Education**	**Flipped Classroom Methodology**
Classroom Setup	Teacher-centered	Student-centered
Lecture Delivery	In-class lectures	Pre-recorded lectures
Homework	After-class assignments	Pre-class assignments
In-class Time	Lectures, discussions	Collaborative learning
Teacher's Role	Primary source of info	Facilitator and guide
Student's Role	Passive listener	Active participant
Pace of Learning	Same for everyone	Individual pace
Feedback	Limited and delayed	Immediate during activities
Flexibility	Limited	More flexibility
Collaboration	Limited opportunities	Emphasizes collaboration
Technology	Minimal use	Depends on technology

The use of technology in the Flipped Classroom model facilitated the development of IT skills, including digital literacy, information management and communication using a variety of technology tools. The authors believe that the Flipped Classroom model should be considered an educational innovation for capacity building in higher education institutions. It can be said that the Flipped Classroom model changes the educational paradigm. The teacher is no longer the main centre of knowledge, he/she becomes the organizer of the learning process. Compared to the traditional classroom model, the flipped classroom model flips the expected levels of cognition upside down, thus swapping classroom and home activities. In the classroom, learners are enabled to develop higher (applying, analysing, evaluating, creating) skills through active activities, and they acquire basic knowledge using technology before class. The insights of the theoretical analysis clearly revealed the positive attitude of scientists towards the application of the Flipped Classroom. The main pros: Flipped Classroom enables active formation of digital literacy and formation and improvement of digital competence, information management and communication using various digital tools. The main cons (against): limited digital literacy of teachers, negative attitude of parents towards Flipped Classroom-type homework; teachers' fear of applying innovative digital technologies in lessons.

While summing up, it can be stated that the Flipped Classroom model changes the educational paradigm. The teacher is no longer the main centre of knowledge, he becomes the organizer of the learning process. Compared to the traditional classroom model, the Flipped Classroom model turns the expected levels of cognition upside down, thus replacing classes in the classroom and at home. In the classroom, through active activities, learners are given the opportunity to develop higher (application, analysis, evaluation, creation) skills, and using digital technologies, they acquire the necessary knowledge before the lesson.

Methodology

Qualitative research methodology was applied. Data were collected during the observations of Flipped classroom activities, semi structured interviews with the experienced teachers who implemented the Flipped classroom practices. The semi-structured interview had 5 blocks of questions: block for demographic data; block of questions on didactic knowledge about flipping; question block on the positive experience of flipping (pros for flipping); question block on negative flipping experience (cons); question block for the teachers' experience analysis of the usage of flipped classroom for the development the digital competence. The received data were analysed while conducting deductive qualitative content analysis (Mayring, 2014; Ciuciulkiene et al., 2023). The minutes of observations of flipped classroom activities and semi-structured interviews were organized to collect basic data, which were chosen because of the flexibility of this method and the possibility of collecting data from 22 informants. 30 main questions were prepared relying on a deductive approach. One interview lasted an average of one hour. The interview was organized by one researcher. The interviews were conducted until the researchers obtained "rich and thick" (Dibley, 2011) data. This means that the interview texts (from 6 to 8 pages) were extensive and allowed to proceed with the inductive content analysis (Ciuciulkiene at al., 2023). The responses were recorded and later transcribed. The transcriptions were coded from P1 (Participant1) to P22) to demonstrate the total amount of the produced interviews. The transcriptions were analysed by three independent researchers with the purpose of generating the main ideas and regularities, relying on the meaning of the clearly expressed messages, which were later combined into themes, categories, and subcategories.

Participants of the research

The research was conducted with teachers from different fields of studies in Lithuania. The population of the research is teachers who have experience in online teaching and in conducting the Flipped Classroom. Attention is paid to the selection of participants from primary education institutions, considering the proportion of participants from private and state sectors. For this reason, the purposeful sampling method was used. This is finding and choosing teachers, who are informed about a topic of interest. In addition to expertise and experience, other factors include participation readiness, accessibility, and the capacity to share ideas and experiences in an honest, expressive, and thoughtful way. As it was already stated, the research sample consisted of 22 primary school teachers.

Ethics

Each participant agreed to participate in the interview while maintaining their privacy and identity by signing a consent form. Informed permission and privacy safeguards were used to solve ethical issues.

Results

Data analysis was organized by Maying's (2014) qualitative content analysis. There were revealed three major themes: "Teacher's vision of flipping"; "Flipped classroom experience that made me feel positive"; "Cons for flipping".

The first theme "Teacher's vision of flipping" has been created based on the following 2 main categories, explaining the context: "Flipping as an educational innovation" and "Didactics of flipping". Each category also includes sub-categories, and they are represented in the 1 table below.

Table 1: Manifestation of the categories and subcategories of the theme "Teacher's vision of flipping".

"Teacher's vision of flipping".			
Flipping as an educational innovation		*Didactics of flipping*	
Motivation to be innovative	Good command of digital tools	Good command of curriculum planning skills	The implementation of the universal design in blended learning
"I wanted something different for my multicultural class" (P1)	"I as a teacher was competent while using digital tools, so I could start thinking about flipping (P3)	"Students always wanted to demonstrate their homework findings, so I had to find the optimal ways of lesson planning" (P2)	"The teacher has to be aware how to match online tutorials and face to face classes" (P4)

The main objective of the interview question block was to identify how the teachers define the concept of Flipped classroom, whether they qualify it as an inevitable and scary innovation or accept it as a positive change. The research data demonstrated that the concept of flipping in major cases was regarded as a motivating, inspiring innovation, motivating both: students and teachers for further development not only the subject knowledge, but also digital skills <..."I wanted something different for my multicultural class"...(P1)>, which enhance the understanding of authentic didactics that is working in a flipped class <"The teacher has to be aware how to match online tutorials and face to face classes" (P4). The positive attitude towards the innovation inspired not only digital, but also professional growth < "Students always wanted to demonstrate their homework findings, so I had to find the optimal ways of lesson planning" (P2)>.

The second theme "Flipped classroom experience that made me feel positive" has been created based on the following 2 main categories as well: "Encouragement of active learning" and "Development of multitasking skills". Each category also includes sub-categories, and they are represented in the 2 table below.

Table 2: Manifestation of the categories and subcategories of the theme "Flipped classroom experience that made me feel positive".

Flipped classroom experience that made me feel positive			
"Encouragement of active learning"		*Development of multitasking skills*	
Group learning skills	Tutorials "From a student to a student: diminishing the	Skill development of teaching and controlling	Skill development of creating new technology-

	misunderstandings of "what-to-do"	different numbers of students at the same time	based methods of teaching
"We gained the experience of group work in "Zoom" and "Teams when we tried to plan our class materials" (P3)	"I noticed that students started to organize kind of their own consultations and teach each other. The number of declarations that I "do not know what to do significantly decreased." (P5)	"I learned how to separate the attention to the students in classroom and in the distance" P22)	"I enjoyed video reporting and producing AI designed problem - based learning clips" (P14)

The focus of the theme is on the factors that make teachers feel positive about the flipped classroom. The first and the most relevant factor that almost all participants mentioned was dynamic group learning, resulting in peer tutorials < "I noticed that students started to organize kind of their own consultations and teach each other. The number of declarations that I "do not know what to do significantly decreased." (P5)". A variety of subcategories include the development of creative technology-based teaching techniques "I learned how to separate the attention to the students in classroom and in the distance" P22; "I enjoyed video reporting and producing AI designed mentoring task-based clips" (P14)", and mastering group learning techniques "We gained the experience of group work in "Zoom" and "Teams when we tried to plan our class materials" (P3). The subject emphasizes how important it is for teachers to develop and improve their digital skills to adjust to the dynamic nature of flipped classroom.

The third theme is "Cons for flipping", which is divided into 2 categories: "Hidden fear for the digital innovation" and "Students' attitudes towards the "independent homework" with corresponding sub-categories (See 3 table)

Table 3: Manifestation of the categories and subcategories of the theme "Cons for flipping".

Cons for flipping			
"Hidden fear for the digital innovation"		***"Students' attitudes towards the "independent homework"***	
Poor primary experience of using digital innovations	Increased responsibility for the students' achievements	Traditional homework missing problems	Refusing to participate in the innovative class
"I do not trust technologies" (P11)	"I have some doubts about the time management in the class if I have to reexplain everything they have done (P12)"	Students are traditional in finding the excuses for not doing homework: "I could not read the task in electronic register, there was no internet" (P10)	"I do not like when everything is vice versa" - such was the explanation of the cheating student (P14")

The preliminary range of possible negative attitudes towards flipping testify the traditional content of teacher – student apprehensions connected with the innovative approach towards the development of digital literacy. It is poor experience of the usage of digital means "I do not trust technologies" (P11), constant fear that the students will not demonstrate the required competences and skills "I have some doubts about the time management in the class if I have to reexplain everything they have done (P12)". Still, while comparing the content of categories and subcategories expressing negative attitudes towards flipping with those that express positive experience aspects it is possible to note that flipping serves as a stimulating setting for the professional development opportunities of the educators. The flipped classroom involves group work and collaborative activities during lessons. However, educators note that not all students were motivated to prepare for effective group work. The reason for demotivation is the fear of applying innovations in the lesson. Students had difficulty engaging in meaningful discussions, taking responsibility for their group's learning. The main advantage of flipped classrooms is the formation of student responsibility for their own learning. According to teachers, some students found it difficult to take responsibility for their education and use their time and resources wisely. In order to help students develop a sense of autonomy and independence, educators emphasized the importance of teaching self-regulation techniques and providing ongoing support.

The results of this study confirm previous studies that have shown the advantages of flipped classrooms in various educational contexts (Bergmann & Sams, 2012; Betihav et al., 2016; Blair et al., 2016). The flipped classroom model allows students to learn and apply information technology skills in a more engaging and personalized way, using digital resources and technological tools. Flipped classrooms allow students to explore subjects at their own pace, strengthening knowledge and skills.

Finalizing

The results of the study confirm that the implementation of the flipped classroom strategy in primary education can greatly help students improve their information technology skills. The flipped classroom strategy develops critical thinking and student collaboration. Interactive flipped classroom lessons encourage student collaboration, problem solving, and critical thinking. The flipped classroom applied in primary education does not significantly change the role of the teacher - he remains important in planning the teaching process, planning didactic activities. Teachers also act as facilitators, helping students develop digital literacy skills and creating an attractive environment.

References

Bergmann, J., & Sams, A. (2012). Flip your classroom: Reach every student in every class every day. International society for technology in education.

Betihav, J., Bridgman, H., Kornhaber, M. L., & Cross, C. (2016). Flipping the classroom and studio: Strategies for developing intellectual skills. Innovations in Education and Teaching International, 53(3), 298-308.

Bhavsar, M. H., Javia, H. N., Mehta, S. J., Bhavsar, M., & Mehta, S. (2022). Flipped classroom versus traditional didactic classroom in medical teaching: a comparative study. Cureus, 14(3).

Blair, E., Maharaj, C., & Primus, S. (2016). Flipped classroom: An approach to improve student learning and engagement. Journal of Education and Training Studies, 4(7), 35-44.

Caliskan, T., & Bicen, H. (2016). A case study on pre-service teachers' perception of the flipped classroom. Journal of Education and Learning, 5(3), 80-89.

Ciuciulkiene, N., Tandzegolskiene-Bielaglove, I., & Culadiene, M. (2023). Phenomenon-based learning in teaching a foreign language: Experiences of Lithuanian teachers. Social Sciences, 12(12), 670.

Dibley, L. (2011). Analysing narrative data using McCormack's Lenses. Nurse Res., 18(3):13-9. doi: 10.7748/nr2011.04.18.3.13.c8458. PMID: 21560921.

Geyer-Hayden, L. E. (2016). The flipped classroom model for college algebra: Effects on student achievement, skills preparedness, and perceptions. PhD dissertation, The University of Akron.

Mayring, P. (2014). Qualitative content analysis: theoretical foundation, basic procedures and software solution. Approaches to Qualitative Research in Mathematics Education, 365-380. Doi: 10.1007/978-94-017-9181-6_13.

Osman, A. M., Jamaludin, R., & Mokhtar, M. (2014). Flipping the classroom: A new learning culture to enhance higher cognitive learning among engineering students. Procedia - Social and Behavioural Sciences, 116, 646-654.

Ozdamli, F., & Asiksoy, G. (2016). Flipped classroom approach. World Journal on Educational Technology: Current Issues, 8(2), 98-105.

Richter, S., & McPherson, M. (2012). Open educational resources: Education for the world? Distance Education, 33(2), 201-219.

Singh, V., & Thurman, A. (2019). How Many Ways Can We Define Online Learning? A Systematic Literature Review of Definitions of Online Learning (1988-2018). American Journal of Distance Education, 33(4), 289–306. doi: 10.1080/08923647.2019.1663082

The Links Between Teacher's Digital Competence and Professional Motivation

Rasa Didziuliene[1], Nijole Ciuciulkiene[2], Salomeja Karaseviciute[3]

[1] Education academy, Vytautas Magnus University, Lithuania; rasa.didžiuliene@vdu.lt
[2] Education academy, Vytautas Magnus University, Lithuania; nijole.ciuciulkiene@vdu.lt
[3] Kauno kolegija Higher Education Institution, Lithuania; salomeja.karaseviciute@kaunokolegija.lt

Correspondence: Rasa Didžiulienė: rasa.didziuliene@vdu.lt and Nijolė Čiučiulkienė: nijole.ciuciulkiene@vdu.lt

Abstract:
Strengthening digital competence in teacher work creates opportunities to create a digital learning experience that promotes engagement and motivation not only to draw students' attention to the content of education, but also to ensure that students are able to purposefully apply digital information flows and learn meaningful things. In qualifying training, teachers practice using various digital tools and discovering their benefits for the effective education of students, assessing the mutual respect, reliable social ties, safety and professional meaningfulness of teachers and learners. This article analyzes the research question: How does strengthening a teacher's digital competence affect teachers' professional motivation? The aim of the study is to establish a link between teachers' digital competence and professional motivation.

Keywords: Digital Competence; Professional Motivation; Digital Skills.

Introduction

The school community is constantly improving its digital competence (information and data literacy; communication and cooperation using digital technologies; creation of digital content; security and problem solving), applies innovations in the learning / educational process (Falloon, 2020; Chang at al., 2022). Digital literacy includes aspects such as cybersecurity and the management of personal data and online presence, digital citizenship, ethics and decision-making, knowledge acquisition and collaboration in a virtual environment (Falloon, 2020). Currently, non-formal education tools such as puzzles, games, comics, etc., are attractive, but creating a digital learning experience that promotes engagement remains a difficult task (D'Mello, 2021). While the digital technology experience is immersive, it often demotivates teachers by diverting students' attention from the content and not always ensuring that students learn meaningful things. In qualifying training, teachers practice using digital technologies for the effective education of students, i.e. to be able to assess not how many and what digital tools need to be used, but when and why we intend to apply them (Girdzijauskienė at al., 2022). In the educational process, it should be remembered that mutual respect, reliable social ties, security and professional meaningfulness are equally important (Sokal et al., 2020; Du Plooy, Tommasi at al., 2024). The research question of this study is: How does strengthening a teacher's digital competence affect teachers' professional motivation? The aim of the study is to identify the link between teachers' digital competence and professional motivation.

Theoretical framework

The development of digital technologies is changing the way the school community social life, cooperates, communicates and creates new lives. An increasing number of students in general education schools are learning, in whole or in part, in an environment dominated by digital technologies - laptops, educational digital technologies and an advanced learning environment have become a reality, not an aspiration (Schleicher, 2021). The European Commission has recognised digital competence (technology-related skills) as one of the eight key competences for lifelong learning and it combines reliable and critical use of digital tools for work, leisure and communication. Digital competence is a combination of knowledge, skills and approaches to using technology to perform tasks, solve problems, communicate, manage information, collaborate, as well as create and share content efficiently, properly, safely, critically, creatively, independently and ethically (Anders Skov, 2016). The above-mentioned competence is associated with logical and innovative thinking, advanced information management skills and well-developed communication skills (Radhamani & Kalaivani, 2023) and an integral tool of the teacher's work in creating the content of the lessons. The areas of digital competence acquisition are presented in Figure.

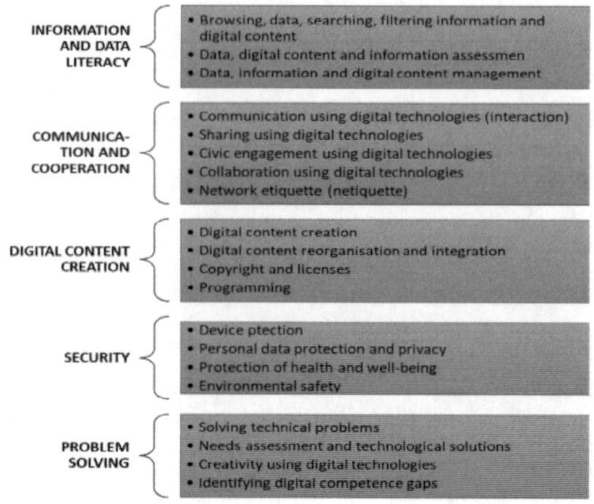

Figure: The areas of digital competence acquisition (compiled by the authors according to Anders Skov, 2016).

A few years ago, the pandemic time caused a lot of stress to the school community, when it was necessary to organize and implement distance learning in a short time (Besser et al., 2022). Due to the specifics of remote work, the work environment was limited (Kim & Asbury, 2020). Some studies (Tommasi et al., 2022; Huge, 2023; Didziuliene, 2023) showed an increased risk of professional burnout of teachers, when the consequences of remote work became more tense not only in terms of digital competence, knowledge and mastery of new teaching platforms, but also in terms of digitization of teaching tools, etiquette of cooperation with students in the virtual space, subtleties of communication, evaluation of training results in the virtual space. When solving the above-mentioned challenges, most teachers are looking for opportunities to improve digital competence - professional obligations encourage them to grow and learn throughout their careers. Professional development is the practice of creating a meaningful professional change for a teacher, which promotes professional satisfaction in the context of the predominance of digital technologies (Yoon ir Kim, 2022). The modern teacher feels the current affairs of specific activities related to technology, work organization and other aspects, so he seeks to constantly update and improve his digital competence (Didziuliene, 2023). This confirms that the needs for the improvement of the teacher's qualifications are constantly changing, depending on various external and internal factors of change in the educational system. Teachers' professional development is a lifelong process, because knowledge ages, new methods appear, and the content of education changes (Gedviliene & Tutlys, 2017; Smidt et al., 2017). Motivation is the effect of energetic forces that activate human behaviour in the work environment in a certain way, time and strength (Westerman, 2020). Professional motivation determines the direction and changes in behaviour at work, encourages concentration and purposeful action, achieving compliance with personal needs and organizational interests, and gives value and meaning to activities. Motivated teachers work more creatively, are more enthusiastic, tend to cooperate, and seek opportunities for professional growth (Mazgon et al., 2021). Technology-Enhanced Learning (TEL) environments can facilitate learning by providing opportunities for timely feedback, monitoring learning progress, offering innovative approaches, and increasing transparency. However, teachers may face challenges due to a lack of digital assessment competencies (Greenspon &; Volungeviciene, 2023), which can promote motivation to strengthen digital competence or, conversely, may increase professional demotivation (Didziuliene, 2023).

Methodology

For the theoretical explanation of the research problem, an analysis of the scientific literature was chosen, and for empirical research, a quantitative research methodology was applied. The indicators on the questionnaire scales provided an opportunity to determine the links between digital competences of the teacher and teaching and learning of students.

Study participants

Educators of educational institutions (N-424) participated in the questionnaire survey. This corresponds to the real relative distribution of men and women in the Lithuanian teacher community (the representative sample of the survey - 381 respondents). The average age of the teachers who participated in the survey was 50.1 ± 9.2. Their professional teaching experience ranged from 1 to 30 years.

Organization of the study

The survey was conducted in 2024 in March in Lithuanian general education institutions. The teachers who participated in the survey had the opportunity to fill in the questionnaire online: the questionnaire was uploaded to the freely available online survey portal www.apklausa.lt. Teachers had the opportunity to rate the intensity of their attitudes according to the Likert (1932) linear scale (from 1 - "not at all important" to 5 - "very important"). Statistical analysis was performed using SPSS 24. Research participants had the opportunity to fill out the questionnaire online at the freely available online survey portal www.apklausa.lt.

Ethics and consent

During the study, the main ethical principles characteristic of social research was observed: the right not to be violated, the right not to be exploited, the usefulness of the investigation, justice, respect for the privacy of individuals, anonymity and confidentiality (Zyzdiunaite & Sabaliauskas, 2017). The questionnaire was accompanied by an introductory letter indicating the subject of the study, the purpose, and a brief description and contacting the investigator (name, institution, e-mail address) in case of questions.

Results

To improve digital competence, teachers participate in trainings and seminars, the goals and tasks of which are focused on analysis, systematization, selection and evaluation. Teachers share the acquired knowledge and experience with students, integrating innovations into the teaching process. The results obtained allow us to determine the level of skills of the teacher in working with digital tools. The teachers who participated in the study assessed the areas of digital competence acquisition, such as: information and data literacy, communication and collaboration, digital content creation, security and problem solving.

When analysing the digital competence of the study participants, it was coded whether the teacher improves/does not improve digital competence. Most (87%) teachers indicated that they constantly improve digital competence, but there are still teachers (13%) who are confident in their level of digital literacy. It was meaningful to check how qualification improvement/lack of improvement affects the level of individual areas of digital competence. A psychometric scale consisting of 5 primary statements (indicators) was developed to measure the dependent variable – digital competence. The results of the verification, using the t-test for independent samples, are presented in Table 1.

Table 1: The impact of teacher qualification development/non-development on the level of digital competence, N = 424

	Levine test		t-test				Difference of means in the group
					Group averages		
					Comparisons of groups		
	F	p value	t	p value	Improved digital competence (N = 367)	Did not improve digital competenc e (N = 57)	
Information and data literacy	2,92	0,088	2,757	0,006	3,92	4,11	0,20
Communication and collaboration	14,88	0,000	3,210	0,001	3,79	4,05	0,26
Creating digital content	0,051	0,022	3,536	0,000	2,87	3,21	0,33
Security	16,15	0,000	3,244	0,001	3,60	3,89	0,29
Problem solving	5,92	0,015	1,997	0,047	3,57	3,75	0,18

(Compiled by authors)

As can be seen from the t-test data in Table 1, a statistical model has been established that in all cases, teachers who tend to develop their qualifications are relatively more likely to assimilate areas of digital competence than their colleagues who do not participate in in-service training and seminars. In all studied cases, the statistical pattern found satisfies the conditions of statistical reliability ($p \leq 0.05$). It can be assumed that the continuous improvement of digital competences allows teachers to strengthen the level of all areas of digital literacy (such as information and data literacy, communication and collaboration, creation of digital content, security and problem solving).

Next, it was tested how the fact of qualification improvement/non-improvement affects the links between teachers' professional motivation and the strengthening of digital competence. The dependent variable – the links between a teacher's professional motivation and the strengthening of digital competence – was measured by assessing three summative factors: the strength of digital competence based on intrinsic motivation, demotivation and the strength of digital competence based on extrinsic motivation. Test results using independent samples t-test, are presented in Table 2.

Table 2: The impact of teacher qualification development/non-development on the indicators of the relationship between teachers' professional motivation and digital competence strengthening, N = 424

	Levine test		**t-test**				**Difference of means in the group**
					Group averages		
					Comparisons of groups		
	F	**p value**	**t**	**p value**	**Improved digital competence (N = 367)**	**Did not improve digital competence (N = 57)**	
Strengthening digital competence based on intrinsic motivation	1,44	0,230	–3,146	0,002	0,03	–0,22	–0,25
Demotivation	0,11	0,745	2,118	0,035	–0,02	0,14	0,16
Strengthening digital competence based on extrinsic motivation	0,06	0,806	–1,270	0,205	0,01	–0,08	–0,09

(Compiled by authors)

As can be seen from the data in Table 2, teachers who improve their professional qualifications are more likely than their colleagues who do not participate in digital literacy training and seminars to experience the enhancement of digital competences based on both internal and external professional motivation. The identified statistical models meet the conditions for statistical reliability ($p < 0{,}05$). The data of the study suggests that teachers who ignore the possibilities of professional development are more likely to demotivate the application of digital technologies in the educational process.

Conclusions:

1. Strengthening the digital capacity of teachers provides an opportunity to make better use of interactive and inclusive learning environments that support flexible and adaptable learning through the development of technology-based teaching and learning methods.
2. The professional motivation (internal and external) of teachers affects the strengthening of digital literacy. Teachers who are constantly improving their professional qualifications are more motivated to use digital technologies for the effective education of students, assessing mutual respect, safety and professional meaningfulness.

References

Anders Skov (2016). What is digital competence? Center for Digital Dannelse. Retrieved from: https://digital-competence.eu/front/what-is-digital-competence

Besser, A., Lotem, S., & Zeigler-Hill, V. (2022). Psychological stress and vocal symptoms among university professors in Israel: implications of the shift to Online synchronous teaching during the COVID-19 pandemic. Journal of Voice: official journal of the Voice Foundation, 36(2), 291.e9–291.e16. Doi: 10.1016/j.jvoice.2020.05.028.

Chang, C. Y., Panjaburee, P., Lin, H. C., Lai, C. L., & Hwang, G. H. (2022). Effects of online strategies on students' learning performance, self-efficacy, self-regulation and critical thinking in university online courses. Educ. Technol. Res. Dev., 70, 185–204.

Du Plooy, H., Tommasi, F., Furlan, A., Nenna, F., Gamberini, L., Ceschi, A., & Sartori, R. (2024). A Human-Centered Perspective on Individual Risks for Digital Innovation Management: An Integrative Conceptual Review. European Journal of Innovation Management. Doi: 10.1108/EJIM-092023-0821.

Didziuliene, R. (2023). Subjective perception of professional happiness in the teaching community: gender comparison. Doctoral Dissertation. Social Sciences, Education (S 007): 76-79.

Falloon, G. (2020). From digital literacy to digital competence: the teacher digital competency (TDC) framework. Education Tech Research Dev. Doi: 10.1007/s11423-020-09767-4.

Gedviliene, G., & Tūtlys, V. (2017). The role of key competences in adult education: the case of Lithuania. New educational review, 49(3), 40–53. Doi: 10.15804/tner.2017.49.3.03

Girdzijauskiene, R., Norviliene, A., Smitiene, G., & Rupsiene, L. (2022). Strengthening Student Engagement in Learning Through Use of Digital Tools. Acta Paedagogica Vilnensia, 49. 115-130. Doi: 10.15388/ActPaed.2022.49.8.

Greenspon, R., & Volungeviciene, A. (2023). How Can a Technology Enhanced Learning Environment Support Learning-Oriented Assessment in Higher Education? Pedagogika 150(2): 58-74. Doi: 10.15823/p.2023.150.4.

Yoon, I., & Kim, M. (2022). Dynamic patterns of teachers' professional development participation and their relations with socio-demographiccharacteristics, teacher self-efficacy, and job satisfaction. Teaching and Teacher Education, 109, 103565. Doi: 10.1016/j.tate.2021.103565.

Mažgon, J., Kalin, J., Kaminskiene, L., Gedviliene, G., Tutlys, V., & Skubic Ermenc, K. (2021). Coping with challenges of the COVID-19 lockdown in public education of Lithuania and Slovenia: views of school heads. Pedagogika, 143(3), 5–22. DOI: 10.15823/p.2021.143.1

D'Mello, S. (2021). Improving student engagement in and with digital learning technologies. In A. Schleicher (Ed.), Pushing the Frontiers with Artificial Intelligence, Blockchain and Robots, 79–104. Paris: OECD Publishing.

Kim, L. E., & Asbury, K. (2020). Like a rug had been pulled from under you: The impact of COVID-19 on teachers in England during the first six weeks of the UK lockdown. Br. J. Educ. Psychol, 90, 1062–1083. Doi: 10.1111/bjep.12381.

Schleicher, A. (2021). Editorial. In A. Schleicher (Ed.), Pushing the Frontiers with Artificial Intelligence, Blockchain and Robots (pp. 3–5). Paris: OECD Publishing.

Sokal, L. J., Trudel, L. G. E., & Babb, J. C. (2020). Supporting teachers in times of change: The job demands-resources model and teacher burnout during the COVID-19 pandemic. International Journal of Contemporary Education, 3(2), 67–74. Doi: 10.11114/ijce.v3i2.4931.

Zydziunaite, V., & Sabaliauskas, S. (2017). Kokybiniai tyrimai: principai ir metodai. Vilnius: Vaga, 375 p. ISBN:9785415024575.

Enhancing Skills, Transforming Worlds: Personalized Learning and Global Learning with the TalkTech Project

Mark Frydenberg[1], Diana Andone[2]

[1] Computer Information Systems Department, Bentley University, USA; mfrydenberg@bentley.edu
[2] eLearning Center, Politehnica University of Timisoara, Romania; diana.andone@upt.ro

Correspondence: Mark Frydenberg: mfrydenberg@bentley.edu

Abstract:

The TalkTech 2024 project, a collaborative partnership between US and Romanian universities, leverages virtual reality (VR) to foster global collaboration and enhance students' digital skills. This study examines how the project, where students create VR tours of their local communities for international partners, facilitates personalized learning and global engagement. Utilizing Puentedura's SAMR (Substitution, Augmentation, Modification, Redefinition) model, the research investigates how technological integration through VR transforms the learning experience. By creating immersive VR environments, students engage in collaborative research, communication, and digital media production, effectively building "digital bridges" between their communities. The analysis explores how progressing through SAMR stages, from simple substitution to redefining global collaboration through innovative VR experiences, empowers students to develop original digital content. The study concludes that SAMR provides a valuable framework for instructors to integrate immersive learning, demonstrating how incorporating technology can enhance skills, transform learning environments, and foster a deeper understanding of global communities. TalkTech 2024 serves as a model for creating impactful, technology-driven educational experiences.

Keywords: Virtual Reality, SAMR, Co-creation, Global Learning, Personalized Learning

Introduction

Global collaboration and developing personal digital literacy skills are necessary for student succcess in a world that is increasingly reliant on technology. The TalkTech project, a collaboration between universities in the United States and Romania, has, since 2008, provides a forum for students to develop these skills by pairing students from these institutions to work as members of international teams. In the TalkTech 2024 project, together the students explore innovative places and spaces in their home communities and prepare virtual reality tours for their international partners. Students form a community of global learners working as members of international teams to create a tangible work product in a short amount of time, selecting and using a variety of information and communication technologies (ICTs) and digital media applications to research, communicate, and work together. The website www.talktechproject.net provides additional information about this and prior iterations of the TalkTech project.

This paper extends previous research (Frydenberg & Andone, 2018b) by analyzing the TalkTech 2024 project through the lens of Puentedura's SAMR (Substitution, Augmentation, Modification, Redefinition) model (R. R. Puentedura, 2014). SAMR is often used to identify ways to introduce technology to enhance and transform learning. This paper will discuss how the model can apply to creating immersive experiences using VR as members of collaborative international teams and foster personalized learning.

The following research questions are the focus of this study:

- How does creating VR artefacts in the TalkTech 2024 project facilitate the development of both global collaboration and personalized learning experiences for students?
- How can progressing through the SAMR stages (Substitution, Augmentation, Modification, Redefinition) enhance students' digital skills and transform their understanding of global communities?

The SAMR Model and Immersive Learning

SAMR (Substitution, Augmentation, Modification, Redefinition) is a model used to evaluate the integration of technology an educational context and provides guidelines for creating projects to assess students' learning through their evolving use of technology (Campos Retana, 2021; R. Puentedura, 2018; R. R. Puentedura, 2014).

The SAMR framework presents four levels by which to examine the use of new technology in an educational context, as shown in Figure 1.

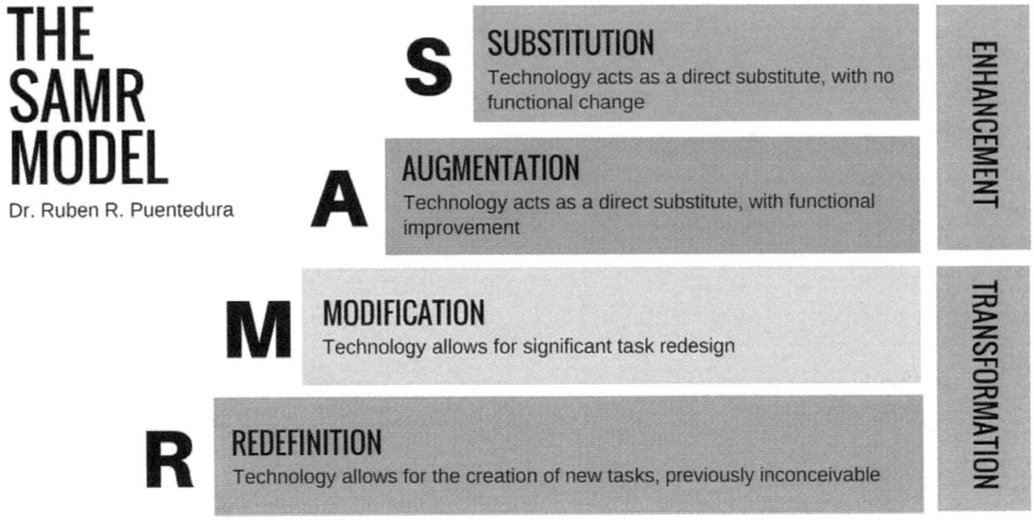

Figure 1. The SAMR Model. (This file is licensed under the Creative Commons Attribution-Share Alike 4.0 International license. Attribution: https://commons.wikimedia.org/wiki/File:The_SAMR_Model.jpg)

SAMR is a popular model for evaluating scenarios that involve immersive learning with VR across multiple disciplines. Wang, et al. (2024) use SAMR to address challenges of assessing learning in immersive medical environments. Their research shows that VR experiences enhance student engagement and provide feedback to learners. Another recent study investigated the use of immersive technology and real-time applications in industry-based training using the SAMR model. The research, conducted at TAFE Queensland, evaluated student experiences in learning about VR/AR technology and its associated real-time applications. The authors concluded that VR/AR technology can transform learning experiences by offering students the opportunity to explore and be immersed in imaginative environments intuitively (Stevens & Moussa, 2023).

The SAMR framework encourages educators to reevaluate teaching methods and consider new ways to use technology to advance student learning. "Embracing the SAMR model empowers educators to harness the true potential of technology in education. By progressing through each level, educators can elevate their teaching practices and create engaging, innovative, and impactful learning experiences for their students." (Afzal, 2023)

Learning in Community with Virtual Reality

According to the World Economic Forum, VR will reshape the future of education (Aldhaheri & Hamade, 2022). Colleges and universities are evaluating how VR can be integrated arcoss the curriculum, not only for technology courses. Educators are incorporating immersive technologies to enhance learning about the metaverse (Frydenberg et al., 2024; Phakamach et al., 2022), group collaborative work, data visualization, public speaking, and career readiness (Mentzer et al., 2024). The affordability of VR headsets along with the availability of multiple device management (MDM) software has enabled the use of VR across classrooms and institutions.

Recent developments incorporating artificial intelligence technologies with VR create new environments for students to praticipate in immersive simulations to develop essential skills. Tools such as Talespin, Bodyswaps, and VirtualSpeech provide virtual environments for students to develop soft skills in interviewing, communication and presentation skills, and navigating difficult conversations (Alsaffar, 2021; Evangelou et al., 2025; Shilling et al., 2025) .

TalkTech 2024: Exploring Innovative Places and Spaces

The authors offered the TalkTech 2024 project during the Fall 2024 semester at their respective universities. A total of 39 students participated (18 honors students in a first-year introductory Information Technology course at Bentley University in the United States, and 21 students enrolled in a Technologies of Multimedia course in their fourth year at Politehnica University of Timisoara).

Students used UniCampus, an online collaboration tool managed by the university in Romania, to share their group's progress with each other and with their instructors. Each team's working space included a blog for tracking their work and sharing short summaries; an upload area for sharing files (though most students shared files through their own OneDrive, Google Drive, or other cloud storage accounts), and a home page with project information (descriptions, clocks showing the current time in each country), and announcements from their instructors.

Students from each university worked in pairs to visit local landmarks or establishments based on the theme of innovation, and used CoSpaces, a web and mobile app for creating, sharing, and viewing immersive digital media, to create a digital story that conveys the significance of their locations. They combined their scenes with those of their international partners, so students from each country could experience similar locations in their partner's country and easily teleport between them.

The instructors identified, and teams chose one of these themes for their projects:

- Innovation Co-Working Spaces
- Campus Entrepreneurship (E-hub/ Innohub)
- Innovation from Tech History (local technology-based museums)
- University Innovative Spaces (maker spaces, interdisciplinary creativity spaces)
- Digital innovation in education (VR classrooms, digital education classrooms)
- Innovation in Research (research labs)
- Innovation in Business (stock trading room, electric car facility)

All students had prior experience using the web, collaboration tools, and mobile devices, and working collaboratively. Participants formed self-selected groups of four (two students from each country) Students were mostly between 21-23 years old (49%), and between 18-20 years old (44%). The Romanian students were, on average, about 3 years older than their American counterparts. The authors understood that students differed in age, programs, technical abilities, and class sizes across universities. However, they saw these differences as an opportunity to create a collaborative learning experience that would benefit all participants. The project's common language is English.

Matching students enrolled in similar courses at universities across the globe has become more common with the proliferation of free web-based messaging and conferencing tools such as Instagram, Facebook Messenger, WhatsApp, Zoom, and Discord, all of which support real-time communication in some combination of text messaging, voice calling, or video conferencing over the Internet. "The ability to communicate and collaborate across the globe has transformed education,"(Frydenberg & Andone, 2017, p. 2) as it has transformed the workplace (Lipnack & Stamps, 1999; Townsend, DeMarie, & Hendrickson, 1998) in order to meet evolving business needs. By choosing from a range of communication and collaboratoin tools, designing multimedia, and researching and navigating online content, students build their digital skills. They collaborative capabilities by selecting and using tools and platforms to communicate (synchronous and asynchronous), share files, create multimedia, and manage projects. By working together on a collaborative international project, students also learn about the communities and culture where their partners live. Deliverables include links to the VR scenes created in CoSpaces, video tours, and weekly blog posts summarizing their teams' progress.

Creating Immersive Content with CoSpaces

The authors chose CoSpaces for this project, because of its ease of use to design 3D spaces and add interactions using a block-based coding environment. "Working with CoSpaces Edu develops digital literacy and 21st Century learning skills such as collaboration and coding, which prepare [students] for their future while empowering them to become creators." (CoSpaces EDU: Make AR & VR In the Classroom, 2021) Students can also view their VR creations in a browser as well as on a Meta Quest headset with no additional support other than its integrated web browser. It provides an instructor's dashboard that simplifies the classroom management process.

To design a VR scene with CoSpaces, students create a 3D model or upload an original image created using a 360-degree camera. They enhance their scenes with avatars, dialog, animations, video, and user interactions (such as quiz question popups or clickable signposts to navigate between scenes) to tell a digital story. As an example, one group of students created a VR experience based on visits to technology museums in their home cities, and then built a 3D model of their own virtual innovation museum based on their in-person experiences. The dialog between avatars conveys the research that students did learning about the museum's exhibits.

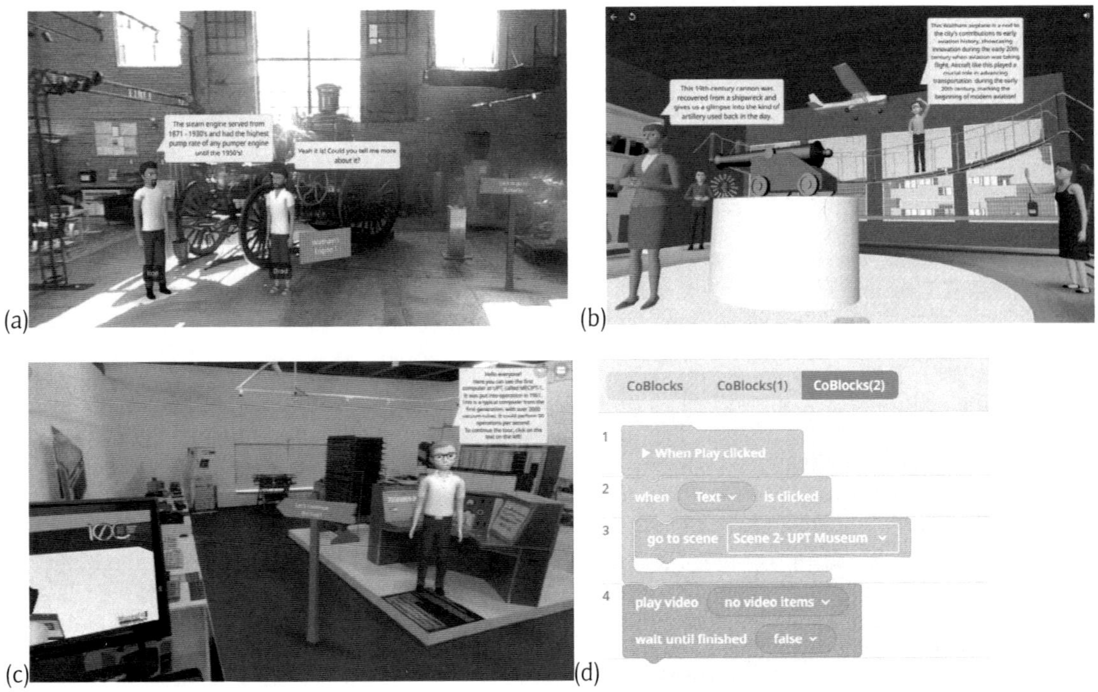

Figure 2. Visiting Technology Museums in the United States (a) and Romania (c), CoBlocks code to animate a scene(d), and designing a 3D model of a museum scene (b).

Students met witih their teams synchronously to present their virtual tours and critique each other's work. They also visited the school's VR lab to view their scenes on Meta Quest VR headsets. Students can also view their VR scenes with the CoSpaces app on a mobile device or laptop in a browser. By providing a link or QR code, sharing their scenes with others is accomplished easily.

A student on this team commented, "By developing a virtual reality scene based on this location, I learned how to use coding and design tools in unison to illustrate a greater story and present information about the different exhibits in the museum. CoSpaces provided me with an opportunity to experiment with 3D renderings of characters, shapes, and objects, helping bring various pieces of information to life. I also found it fascinating to work with a 3D camera to capture the museum site. Adding the 3D elements via CoSpaces truly brought the environment to life. ... I became familiar with incorporating a jumpstart button and coding the movements of characters within the 3D visualizations."

Another student said:

> "I have never done anything like this before, including working with international partners. Working with CoSpaces taught me more about using design tools to illustrate a story. It was difficult at first using the co-blocks to animate the people and objects, but once we figured it out it became a useful tool for our project. Creating the image also helped me learn more about the museum itself, as we had to do more research to incorporate facts into space. The task wasn't nearly as daunting as I thought it was going to be, the program was pretty simple to work with. In terms of learning about our partner's culture, it was a bit difficult to connect at that level, but overall, I got the sense that we aren't so different after all, despite the different countries, languages, and time zones. I think our scenes were similar in terms of the fact that they displayed different inventions and devices in rooms, however, they differed in that ours was a museum and theirs seemed to be just a room. We took different approaches to creating our scenes as well. While we had

people talking about our different inventions, they seemed to have people who described different aspects of their room. Virtual reality was a cool aspect of this project, creating these interactive worlds to see different locations. I think the project really showed me that the applications of Virtual Reality are widely applicable."

Applying the SAMR Model to TalkTech 2024 with Virtual Reality

In a prior iteration of the TalkTech project, students explored augmented reality (AR) technologies and created collaborative AR models to share with their international partners. Previous research (Frydenberg & Andone, 2018b, 2018a) analyzed this iteration of the TalkTech project using the SAMR model. The following analysis applies SAMR to the current project utilizing virtual reality.

Substitution

At the SAMR Substitution level, technology serves as a direct replacement for traditional tools, providing a fist step toward integrating digital experiences as part of the TalkTech project. Students incorporate the use of technology to complete the same tasks that they might have performed without it, with no functional change. In the TalkTech2024 project, students could have presented their findings through a written report or poster. In TalkTech 2024, CoSpaces and their virtual reality scenes substitute for these more traditional methods. They take 360-degree images to create a virtual visit that will substitute for a physical visit (which would be unlikely, if not impossible) for their international partners.

The focus of the Substitution level is largely on the functional replacement of tools with technology. Students get to choose the locations and themes for their project, and the communication tools they will use with their international partners, creating a persnoalized learning experience.

Augmentation

Augmentation occurs when using technology provides an improvement or more effective tool for competing the same task without using technology. By enhancing their scenes with interactive quizzes, 3D models and avatars engaging in dialogue and animations, students add functionality to their immersive scenes that they could not accomplish with a written presentation. Using the CoBlocks development environment in CoSpaces allows them to add engaging elements to their digital scenes.

In the augmentation stage, students often choose synchonous video conferencing or text chats over asynchronous email to begin their work This improves team efficiency, helps to create personal connections among the team members each team. When creating their scenes, sutdents often add clickable items that visitors can discover in any order they choose, to find out more information. These augmentations are an improvement over looking at a static photograph, and create a more persnalized learning experence for the

Modification

Modification occurs when the use of technology changes the way learning previously might have taken place. Students must collaborate internationally to build a shared digital artefact in VR. This level of global collaboration and sharing digital content is new to most students, especially the first-year American students, and requires them to learn new ways to interact with their team members and learn together.

TalkTech 2024 provides an opportunity for cultural exchange by working with students from other countries, and virtually visiting locations through shared VR experiences. Using Unicampus as a centralized hub for tracking group progress, sharing digital files, and communicating with their instructors modifies prior experiences of teamwork patterns and introduces students to using tools for project management.

Redefinition

Afzal (2023) notes that "Redefinition is the pinnacle where technology leads to entirely new learning experiences. Virtual field trips using AR/VR is a prime example." The TalkTech 2024 project redefines the concept of exploring new cultures by enabling students to visit similar places in their partners' countries using virtual reality. Students can view the scenes on their laptops or use Meta Quest headsets for a more immersive experience.

The process of creating digital experiences provides a forum for students to share what they learned about the locations they visited, redefining their roles from passive learners to active "creative creators" (Friedman & Mandelbaum, 2012) of digital experiences. By advancing through the different stages of SAMR, the TalkTech

2024 project enhances students' digital skills and transforms their understanding of both physical and virtual worlds through global collaboration and creating personal virtual spaces.

Discussion

Creating VR scenes in the TalkTech 2024 project required students to work in global communites enabled by technology. From researching their locations to creating 360-degree images and incoroporating them into an immersive CoSpaces scene, and determining how and when to communicate with their international partners, students worked collaboratively to create, share, and critique digital media using virtual reality.

The VR artefacts that they created became digital bridges that linked students home communities and enabled virtual visits that would otherwise not be possible. The project developed problem solving skills and empowered them to contribute to creating innovative digital spaces. They built global partnerships as they crafted worlds that depicted locations in thier home communities, and experienced those of their partners.

Conclusion

The authors contend that SAMR can provide a valuable model for instructors looking to incorporate immersive learning in their courses across disciplines. In previous research, Frydenberg and Andone (2018b) described how the SAMR framework can be extend from VR to projects incorporating technology across disciplines, by using this model shown in Table 1.

Table 1. SAMR Model Applied to Projects Incorporating Technology across Disciplines

Enhancement of Learning	Substitution	Allow students to choose and decide by themselves which tools and technologies they can use when working on their projects. Give students control over their learning environment in project-based learning.
	Augmentation	Students recognize the benefit that using an enhanced technology solution provides to improve a process or make it more efficient or cost effective.
Transformation of Learning	Modification	Students develop solutions that make use of their technology skills. Allow students to use their creativity to adopt new solutions to improve or change their project results.
	Redefinition	Students innovate and develop original digital content and solutions to problems across many disciplines.

TalkTech 2024 shows how instructors can leverage SAMR to develop learning scenarios that incorporate immersive experiences in global communities. This can be accomplished by substituting traditional methods, augmenting them with interactivefeatures, modifying them to convey realism, and ultimatley, redefining global collaboration to create opportunities thet would otherwise not be possible. TalkTech 2024 demonstrates how carefully incorporating technology within the learning processcan enhance skills and transform worlds by empowering students to create original digital content and develop new, innovative VR experiences.

References

Afzal, M. (2023, July 17). Enhancing Education with SAMR Model – Tech in Teach. https://techinteach.com/enhancing-education-with-samr-model-a-guide-for-educators/

Aldhaheri, A. B. H., & Hamade, M. A. (2022, May 23). Experiential learning and VR will reshape the future of education. World Economic Forum. https://www.weforum.org/stories/2022/05/the-future-of-education-is-in-experiential-learning-and-vr/

Alsaffar, M. J. (2021). Virtual Reality Software as Preparation Tools for Oral Presentations: Perceptions From the Classroom. Theory and Practice in Language Studies, 11(10), 1146–1160. https://doi.org/10.17507/tpls.1110.02

Campos Retana, R. (2021). Technology Integration Models into adult education: TPACK and SAMR. Actualidades Investigativas En Educación, 21(1), 429–456. https://doi.org/10.15517/aie.v21i1.42411

CoSpaces EDU: Make AR & VR In the Classroom. (2021). Delightex GmbH. https://cospaces.io/edu

Evangelou, D., Mulders, M., & Sekerci, B. (2025). The VR Landscape in Education: A Non-Technical Guide for Researchers and Practitioners. https://doi.org/10.20944/preprints202502.2187.v1

Friedman, T. L., & Mandelbaum, M. (2012). That Used to Be Us: How America Fell Behind in the World It Invented and How We Can Come Back. Macmillan.

Frydenberg, M., & Andone, D. (2018a). Creating Virtual Reality Artefacts to Enhance and Transform Digital Learning. 1543–1552. https://www.learntechlib.org/primary/p/184376/

Frydenberg, M., & Andone, D. (2018b). Enhancing and Transforming Global Learning Communities with Augmented Reality. Journal of Information Systems Education, 29(1), 37.

Frydenberg, M., Yates, D., & Noonan, A. (2024). Teaching the Metaverse: Applying TPACK to a Multidisciplinary First Year Seminar Course Design. ISEDJ, 22(5), 18.

Mentzer, K., Frydenberg, M., & Li, S. (2024). Exploring VR-Enhanced Learning in Business Education: A Multi-Site Study.

Phakamach, P., Senarith, P., & Wachirawongpaisarn, S. (2022). The Metaverse in Education: The Future of Immersive Teaching & Learning. RICE Journal of Creative Entrepreneurship and Management, 3(2), Article 2. https://doi.org/10.14456/rjcm.2022.12

Puentedura, R. (2018). Transformation, technology, and educaton. Hippasus. http://hippasus.com/resources/tte/puentedura_tte.pdf

Puentedura, R. R. (2014). SAMR: A contextualized introduction. http://hippasus.com/rrpweblog/archives/2014/01/15/SAMRABriefContextualizedIntroduction.pdf

Shilling, V., Starkings, R., & Fallowfield, L. (2025). Feasibility and acceptability of a virtual learning module for navigating angry conversations in clinical encounters. BMC Medical Education, 25(1), 167. https://doi.org/10.1186/s12909-025-06726-6

Stevens, A., & Moussa, A. (2023). Investigating the Use of Immersive Technology and Real-Time Applications in an Industry-Based Training Using the SAMR Model. 1187–1192. https://www.learntechlib.org/primary/p/222634/

Wang, Y., Li, Y., Chen, C., Zhang, W., Wang, Y., Sha, K., & Wang, S. (2024). Research on virtual reality-based assessment framework and application path in medical education. PLOS ONE, 19(11), e0310782. https://doi.org/10.1371/journal.pone.0310782

Digital OBL, AI and Robotics for inclusive heritage education experiences

Antonella Poce[1], Carlo De Medio[2],Mara Valente[3], Luca Contardi[4], Eliana Maria Torre[5], Sabina Pirchi[6], Maria Tolaini[7]

[1]History, Cultural Heritage, Education and Society, University of Rome Tor Vergata, Italy; antonella.poce@uniroma2.it
[2]History, Cultural Heritage, Education and Society, University of Rome Tor Vergata, Italy; carlo.demedio.572666@uniroma2.eu
[3]History, Cultural Heritage, Education and Society, University of Rome Tor Vergata, Italy; mara.valente.582975@uniroma2.eu
[4]Department of Classics, University of Rome La Sapienza, Italy; luca.contardi@uniroma1.it
[5]Department of Classics, University of Rome La Sapienza, Italy; elianamaria.torre@uniroma1.it
[6]History, Cultural Heritage, Education and Society, University of Rome Tor Vergata, Italy; sabina.pirchi@gmail.com
[7]Languages and Cultures Department, University of Genoa, Italy; maria.tolaini@edu.unige.it

Correspondence: Antonella Poce, antonella.poce@uniroma2.it

Abstract:

Object-Based Learning (OBL) is a pedagogical methodology that fosters interactive and immersive engagement with cultural heritage, while promoting key transversal skills: Creativity, Communication, Collaboration, and Critical Thinking (4Cs). Digital OBL has been employed within the ARTISTIC (AI and Robotics for Inclusive Heritage Education Experiences) project which foresees the integration of advanced digital technologies—such as artificial intelligence (AI), robotics, and virtual reality (VR)—in museum education. The project's primary goal is to enhance the accessibility and inclusivity of Ligurian cultural heritage through innovative approaches, particularly supporting individuals with cognitive or physical disabilities, children, and the elderly. The present contribution describes a pilot study carried out at Giardini Luzzati in Genoa where the employment of these methodologies was tested. A humanoid robot, Pepper, was involved as a teaching facilitator, guiding participants through structured activities such as the "I See, I Think, I Wonder" thinking routine. This multimodal learning experience combined physical and digital heritage objects, including 3D-printed artefacts and virtual museum content, enhancing observational and analytical skills. The study also evaluated participants' acceptance of robotics in educational settings, with promising preliminary results, particularly for children with protected characteristics. While initial findings suggest that AI-driven and robotics-enhanced learning can foster engagement and accessibility in museum education, further research is needed to assess the long-term pedagogical impact. Ongoing and future pilot activities will refine methodologies and explore their applicability across different audiences and learning contexts, contributing to the broader discourse on digital innovation in cultural heritage education.

Keywords: Artificial Intelligence; educational robotics; digital OBL; cultural heritage

Introduction

The ARTISTIC (Ai and RoboTics for IncluSive heriTage educatIon experienceS) project aims to develop and validate an innovative technological solution designed to enhance the Ligurian museum heritage through heritage digitization systems, educational robotics, humanoid robots, artificial intelligence, and virtual reality. The project's focus is on heritage valorization, communication, and education, particularly to promote social inclusion and well-being for specific groups, including individuals with cognitive or physical disabilities, children, and the elderly.

The ARTISTIC technological solution employs the educational methodology of Object-Based Learning (OBL) to foster an in-depth and active understanding of selected artistic and cultural heritage. This approach encourages direct interaction with the heritage and promotes the development of transversal skills, specifically the 4Cs: Creativity, Communication, Collaboration, and Critical Thinking. The project is designed to facilitate community engagement and participatory efforts in constructing meanings and interpretations of both material and intangible heritage.

The research group has developed and executed OBL and educational robotics workshops, acting as a bridge between local associations, municipal bodies in Genoa, participating schools, and families involved in the experiences. Additionally, the group is responsible for monitoring and evaluating the project's activities. This paper outlines the current state of the art regarding the selected methodologies and describes the procedures implemented. The evaluation results and ongoing implementation of workshops will be addressed in future publications.

State of the Art

Museums have increasingly been recognised as significant educational spaces, with visitor experience at the core of contemporary research in the field (Parry, 2010; Nardi, 2014; Poce, 2018; 2019). Integrating technology within museum education offers new opportunities to enhance visitor engagement and accessibility while promoting critical digital literacy and transversal skills (Carretero, Vuorikari, & Punie, 2017). Moreover, educational activities in the museum setting can promote well-being and social inclusion (Kanda et al., 2004; Chatterjee & Noble, 2017). However, the pedagogical design of technological interventions remains crucial to ensuring their effectiveness (Poce, 2018). The application of digital tools in museum learning environments has been extensively studied, demonstrating their potential to foster interactive and personalised experiences. Digital resources, including mobile applications, interactive displays, and AI-based guides, can provide tailored content and promote inclusive education, particularly benefiting audiences with cognitive or sensory disabilities, children, and older adults (Rosales et al., 2018; Gustke et al., 2023). Implementing robotics, artificial intelligence (AI), and virtual reality (VR) in museum education has further expanded these possibilities, making heritage experiences more immersive and accessible.

Digital Object-Based Learning

Object-Based Learning (OBL) is a well-established pedagogical approach that emphasises direct engagement with physical objects to enhance learning (Durbin, Morris, & Wilkinson, 1990; Lane & Wallace, 2007). This methodology fosters critical thinking, creativity, and collaboration, supporting the development of 21st-century skills (Chatterjee & Hannan, 2015). The advent of digital technologies has led to the emergence of Digital Object-Based Learning, which extends traditional OBL principles through virtual environments, 3D modeling, and interactive interfaces. The digitisation of cultural objects allows for more flexible and inclusive educational experiences, overcoming limitations related to physical accessibility (Karreman, Ludden, & Evers, 2015). Digital OBL is particularly valuable when direct object manipulation is impractical due to conservation concerns, geographic constraints, or user needs (Klahr, Triona, & Williams, 2007). Integrating robotics, AI, and VR can enhance object-based interactions since it enables users to examine artifacts in detail, manipulate digital replicas, and participate in immersive storytelling experiences. Furthermore, studies indicate that AI-driven educational robots can facilitate object-based learning by providing contextualised explanations and adapting content to users' cognitive levels (Spezialetti et al., 2020).

Robotics, Artificial Intelligence, and Virtual Reality in Museum Education

The use of robotics in museums has been explored in various contexts, particularly through so-callled 'social robots' that guide visitors, provide information, and facilitate interactions. Studies highlight that robotic guides can enhance visitor experience by offering personalised tours, responding to questions, and collecting feedback (Castellano et al., 2020). Additionally, remote-controlled robotic systems allow users to explore museums virtually, overcoming physical barriers and enabling access during closures (Cigola et al., 2014). Evidence suggests that social robots can positively influence visitors' engagement and emotional response, enhancing the overall quality of the museum experience (Draghici et al., 2022).

Artificial intelligence (AI) is increasingly employed in museum education to improve both communication strategies and content creation. AI-powered chatbots and virtual assistants enable visitors to interact dynamically with museum exhibits, enhancing personalised learning (Gustke et al., 2023). Furthermore, AI-integrated robotics have been utilised to greet visitors, guide them through exhibitions, and provide context-based recommendations (Yang et al., 2024). AI-driven applications also play a role in museum gaming environments, where interactive virtual tutors support learning experiences and encourage active engagement (Liang et al., 2024). From a pedagogical perspective, AI fosters inquiry-based interaction and contributes to deeper learning processes. Studies indicate that AI-enhanced museum experiences promote prolonged visitor engagement, facilitate question-driven learning, and increase self-confidence in information-seeking behaviors

(Fast et al., 2019). Additionally, AI tools can support accessibility and inclusion by offering adaptive content delivery for diverse audiences, addressing language barriers, and providing alternative formats for sensory-impaired users (Gustke et al., 2023).

Recent research underscores the potential of AI and humanoid robots in pedagogical applications, particularly in formal and informal learning settings. Studies suggest that AI-powered educational robots can support personalised learning by adjusting instructional strategies in real-time and providing immediate feedback (Pesovski, 2024). The ability of these robots to simulate natural human interactions has been linked to increased student engagement and motivation (Wang et al., 2023). Moreover, humanoid robots equipped with emotion recognition capabilities have been employed in inclusive education to support students with social and cognitive challenges (Spezialetti et al., 2020).

The role of virtual reality (VR) in museum education has also gained significant attention due to its potential to create immersive and personalised learning experiences (Alvarado et al., 2023). VR applications enable users to interact with digital reconstructions of heritage objects, facilitating engagement and comprehension regardless of physical location or ability (Li et al., 2023). Research demonstrates that VR-based learning enhances emotional and cognitive engagement, improving retention and understanding of museum content (Xin, 2022).

Integrating robotics, AI, and VR within museum settings represents a significant advancement in inclusive and interactive learning methodologies, particularly when combined with structured pedagogical frameworks such as Object-Based Learning (OBL).

Methodology

Procedure

During July 2024, at the Giardini Luzzati in Genoa, a pilot activity of Object-Based Learning (OBL) and educational robotics workshops was carried out with the support of all the institutions involved in the ARTISTIC project. The workshop lasted two hours and involved 20 children attending the summer camp organized by the Il Ce.Sto cooperative at the same venue. After setting up the materials, including the humanoid robot selected for the activity (Pepper) and the necessary materials for the participating children, the workshop began. To prevent the presence of the robot from distracting or confusing the participants, it was decided to introduce the activity outdoors, initially away from the robot. At the Giardini Luzzati square, two members of Rome Tor Vergata research team seated the participants in a circle and explained the planned activities for the day. They then distributed the entry tests, reading each question aloud to facilitate understanding. The test was designed to assess participants' knowledge of the city's history and heritage, as well as their digital skills. It included three multiple-choice questions about the city's history, accompanied by images to aid young children's understanding, and two questions using a Likert scale with emojis to evaluate their digital skills. Once the tests were completed, the participants were guided to the archaeological area, where the Pepper robot and the facilitator from EHT managing its interaction—supported by a remote connection with the BLABS partner—were waiting. Once positioned on the ground and divided into four groups, the participants and Pepper took turns introducing themselves by stating their name and city of origin. The mediators then provided some historical information on the foundation of Genoa and the populations that previously inhabited the area, serving as an introduction to the first digital Object-Based Learning (OBL) activity. Each group received a small architectural element (an arch, a capital, and two column sections) created using a 3D printer. The goal of the activity was to manipulate the object to promote a deeper understanding of cultural heritage and develop transversal skills such as communication, collaboration, and critical thinking. Pepper asked a series of questions following the OBL model "I see, I think, I wonder," aiming to guide object manipulation and encourage interaction. Each group, in turn, manipulated the object and responded to Pepper's questions. Subsequently, the mediators provided a summary of the discussion, integrating additional information. In the second OBL activity, each group received a tablet that allowed them to manipulate virtual museum objects. Once again, Pepper posed questions to guide the manipulation of the objects, with each group responding in turn. After the digital interaction with the objects and Pepper, the mediators provided another summary of the key points that emerged. At the end of the activity, participants received sticky notes: a green one to indicate what they enjoyed about the workshop and a red one for aspects they did not like. Pepper called on each group in turn to stick the green notes on a dedicated board, followed by the red ones. Finally, the exit tests were distributed. The tests followed the same structure as the entry tests, with slightly different questions. As at the beginning, the questions were read aloud collectively to aid comprehension and completion. After finishing the tests, the participants said goodbye to Pepper.

Use and Functions of the Thinking Routine

During the OBL activities, Pepper asked a series of questions following the "I see, I think, I wonder," thinking routine structured into three following phases:

1. I SEE
2. I THINK
3. I WONDER

The first phase, I SEE, aims to capture participants' attention on the physical aspects of the object they are handling through guiding questions such as What do you see? What do you perceive? The second phase, I THINK (What do you think it is?), allows participants to interpret the object based on their visual analysis and connect it to their prior knowledge. In the third phase, I WONDER (What questions does this object raise?), the mediator steps in to answer participants' questions (e.g., What is it? What was it used for? How was it used? Where was it found? What material is it made of?), revealing the function, history, and characteristics of the object. During the different phases of object description, emphasis is placed on:

- Operational aspects (technique, materials, dimensions; prompted by direct questions such as What material is the object made of? How was it created? What are its dimensions?)
- Figurative aspects (What does it depict? Are there colors? If so, which ones?)
- Function and meaning (What is it? How would you use it? What modern object could it be compared to?)

The role of the Robot

The humanoid robot Pepper was used to support the educational activity designed and implemented by researchers from Tor Vergata. It provided participants with instructions for carrying out the various activities, offering specific stimuli and engaging children in the phases of description and discussion. The research team at Tor Vergata predefined the instructions that the robot would deliver to the students, preparing a list of phrases, comments, and guidelines for each stage of the workshop.

Despite these promising developments, the pedagogical impact of AI and robotics in museum education remains underexplored. The potential of AI-enhanced OBL in fostering critical thinking and engagement with heritage objects represents an area for future exploration, particularly in the context of inclusive and accessible museum education. Integrating advanced technologies in museum education—particularly robotics, AI, and VR—offers unprecedented opportunities for interactive, inclusive, and personalised learning experiences. Combining these technologies with Digital OBL methodologies represents a promising direction for enhancing cultural accessibility and engagement. However, further research is needed to assess the long-term pedagogical impact of these innovations, particularly concerning visitor learning outcomes, cognitive development, and social inclusion. The ARTISTIC project aims to contribute to this ongoing discourse by implementing and evaluating a technology-enhanced, object-based educational model tailored to diverse audiences in the museum context.

Conclusion

This project study explores the integration of advanced digital technologies - in particular robotics, artificial intelligence (AI) and virtual reality (VR) - in museum education, focusing on their potential to improve social inclusion and well-being by promoting visitor engagement and accessibility as well as 4C's skills and learning outcomes. Based on the evidence emerging from the reference literature. object-based learning (OBL) was considered an excellent pedagogical approach for the purposes of the project as it is capable of extending traditional museum experiences through interactive and immersive methodologies. The experimental workshop conducted at the Giardini Luzzati in Genoa offered the opportunity to test the impact of these technologies and methodology, in particular through the use of the humanoid robot Pepper as a teaching facilitator.

During the activity, the structured implementation of the "I See, I Think, I Wonder" thinking routine allowed participants to interact more deeply with both physical and digital heritage objects, thanks to the integration of 3D printed artefacts and virtual museum objects that supported a multimodal learning experience, allowing children to develop observational and analytical skills and to engage in historical narratives actively. These first pilot activities also allowed to test the script that will be used autonomously by the humanoid robot in further activities, thanks to the help of Artificial Intelligence, as well as the digital OBL methodology, so as to contribute to the enrichment of the specialist literature in this sector. Another objective achieved was to observe how children reacted to the interaction with the robot, especially children with protected characteristics. The workshop allowed to examine the general degree of acceptance of the technologies and of the humanoid robot specifically.

While this pilot study is promising, further experimentation and analysis are needed to determine the long-term pedagogical impact of AI, robotics, and VR on museum education. To this end, additional pilot activities were conducted in February and will be conducted in April, to refine the methodologies employed and explore their applicability with different age groups and learning contexts.

Preliminary informal observations collected from these tests suggest that the integration of robotics and OBL digital methodologies has significant potential to promote inclusive and engaging learning experiences. By adopting AI-driven learning techniques and virtual reality, museums can provide personalised educational paths suitable for different audiences, such as children, the elderly, and people with cognitive or sensory disabilities. Furthermore, the use of social robots, such as Pepper, has shown to improve interaction, stimulate curiosity and facilitate meaningful discussions on cultural artefacts as suggested by the literature. The ARTISTIC project experiments continue in this direction, contributing to the ongoing discourse on the role of digital technologies in cultural heritage education. However, further research is needed to assess their effectiveness and long-term impact on visitor learning. Possible future developments may concern the further optimisation of processes aimed at promoting the use of the artificial intelligence methodology and the implementation of the user experience evaluation phase to verify the increase in digital skills in the long term in order to contribute to improving practices for accessibility to cultural heritage.

Competing interests

The authors have no competing interests to declare.

Ethics and consent (if applicable)

The research was conducted and published according to recognised international standards, e.g. the Declaration of Helsinki. The research was approved by an appropriate ethics committee and informed consent to participate in the study was obtained from the participants' legal guardians.

Funding Information (optional)

Authors' contributions (optional)

The research is coordinated by Antonella Poce and all the authors equally contributed to the editing of the paper.

References

Alvarado, Y., Guerrero, R., & Serón, F. (2023). Inclusive learning through immersive virtual reality and semantic embodied conversational agent: a case study in children with autism. Journal of Computer Science and Technology, 23(2): https://doi.org/10.24215/16666038.23.e09

Carretero, S., Vuorikari, R., & Punie, Y. (2017). DigComp 2.1: The Digital Competence Framework for Citizens with eight proficiency levels and examples of use. Luxemburg: Publications Office of the European Union:10.2760/38842

Castellano, G., Macchiarulo, N., De Carolis, B., & Vessio, G. (2020). Pepper4Museum: Towards a Human-like Museum Guide. Proceedings of *AVI2CH* 2020: Workshop on Advanced Visual Interfaces and Interactions in Cultural Heritage.

Chatterjee, H., & Noble, G. (2017). Museums, Health and Well-Being. Routledge.

Cigola, M., Gallozzi, A., Ceccarelli, M., Carbone, G., De Stefano, C., & Scotto di Freca, A., (2014). Strategie robotiche ed informatiche per la fruizione museale. SCIentific RESearch and Information Technology, 4(1), 59-68: 10.2423/i22394303v4n1p59.

Chatterjee, H.J., & Hannan, L. (2015). Engaging the Senses: Object-Based Learning in Higher Education (1st ed.). Routledge. https://doi.org/10.4324/9781315579641

Draghici, B.G., Ovidiu, P. S., Dobre, A. E., & Misaros, M., (2022). Development of a human service robot application using Pepper Robot as a museum guide. 2022 IEEE International Conference on Automation, Quality and Testing, Robotics (AQTR), 1-5, doi: 10.1109/AQTR55203.2022.9802037.

Durbin, G., Morris, S., & Wilkinson, S. (1990). Learning from objects: A teacher's guide. London: English Heritage.

Fast, E., Chen, B., Mendelsohn, J., Bassen, J. & Bernstein, M. (2018). Iris: A conversational agent for complex tasks. CHI '18: Proceedings of the 2018 CHI Conference on Human Factors in Computing Systems, 1 - 12: 10.1145/3173574.31740.

Gustke, O., Schaffer, S., & Ruß, A. (2023). CHIM—Chatbot in the Museum. Exploring and Explaining Museum Objects with Speech-Based AI. In: Sonja Thiel/ Johannes C. Bernhardt (Eds.), AI in Museums (257-264). Bielefeld: transcript Verlag. https://doi.org/10.14361/9783839467107-024

Kanda, T., Hirano, T., Eaton, D., & Ishiguro, H. (2004). Interactive Robots as Social Partners and Peer Tutors for Children: A Field Trial. Human–Computer Interaction, 19(1–2), 61–84: 10.1080/07370024.2004.9667340

Karreman, D., Ludden, G. & Evers, V., 2015. Visiting cultural heritage with a tour guide robot: A user evaluation study in-the-wild. Social Robotics: 7th International Conference, ICSR. Proceedings 7, 317-326.

Klahr, D., Triona, L., & Williams, C. (2007). Hands on What? The Relative Effectiveness of Physical Versus Virtual Materials in an Engineering Design Project by Middle School Children. Journal of Research in Science Teaching, 44. 183 - 203. 10.1002/tea.20152.

Lane, J., & Wallace, A. (2007). Hands On: Learning from Objects and Pain- tings. A Teacher's Guide. Glasgow: Scottish Museums Council.

Li, K. C., & Wong, B. T. M. (2023). Features and trends of personalised learning: A review of journal publications from 2001 to 2018. Interactive Learning Environments, 29(2), 182–195: 10.1080/10494820.2020.1811735

Liang, H.-Y., Hwang, G.-J., Hsu, T.-Y., & Yeh, J.-Y. (2024). Effect of an AI-based chatbot on students' learning performance in alternate reality game-based museum learning. British Journal of Educational Technology, 55(10), 2315–2338. https://doi.org/10.1111/bjet.13448

Nardi, E. (2014). Musei e pubblico. Milano: FrancoAngeli.

Parry, R. (2010). Museums in a Digital Age. New York: Routledge.

Pesovski, I., Santos, R., Henriques, R., & Trajkovik, V. (2024) Generative AI for Customizable Learning Experiences. Sustainability, 16, 3034: 10.3390/su16073034

Poce, A. (2018). Il patrimonio culturale per lo sviluppo delle competenze nella scuola primaria. Milano: Franco Angeli.

Poce, A. (2019). Studi Avanzati di Educazione Museale. Lezioni. Napoli: ESI.

Rosales, R., Castanon-Puga, M., Lara-Rosano, F., Flores-Parra, J., Evans, R., Osuna Millan, N. & Gaxiola-Pacheco, C. (2018). Modelling the interaction levels in HCI using an intelligent hybrid system with interactive agents: A case study of an interactive museum exhibition module in Mexico. Applied Sciences, 8(3), 446: 10.3390/app8030446

Spezialetti, M., Placidi, G. & Rossi, S. (2020). Emotion recognition for human-robot interaction: Recent advances and future perspectives. Frontiers in Robotics and AI, 7, p.532279.

Wang, K., Sang, G.-Y., Huang, L.-Z., Li, S.-H., & Guo, J.-W. The Effectiveness of Educational Robots in Improving Learning Outcomes: A Meta-Analysis. Sustainability 2023, 15, 4637. https://doi.org/10.3390/su15054637

Xin, Y. (2022). Influence of learning engagement on learning effect under a virtual reality (VR) environment. International Journal of Emerging Technologies in Learning (iJET), 17(5), 226–237.

Yang, Z., Xia, M., Wan, X., Wang, M. & Tang, W. (2024). Artificial Intelligence Technology Enabling Innovation in Museum Public Cultural Service Models. Applied Mathematics and Nonlinear Sciences, Sciendo, 9(1): 10.2478/amns.2023.2.01661

Flexible personal itineraries for learners' agency in digital environments

Gemma Tur[1], Laia Riera[1], Sofía Vialltoro[1], Antònia Darder[1], Adolfina Pérez[1]

[1] Institute of Educational Research and Innovation. Department of Applied Pedagogy and Educational Psychology. University of the Balearic Islands. Spain. gemma.tur@uib.es
[1] Institute of Educational Research and Innovation. Department of Applied Pedagogy and Educational Psychology. University of the Balearic Islands. Spain. laia.riera@uib.es
[1] Institute of Educational Research and Innovation. Department of Applied Pedagogy and Educational Psychology. University of the Balearic Islands. Spain. antonia.darder@uib.es
[1] Institute of Educational Research and Innovation. Department of Applied Pedagogy and Educational Psychology. University of the Balearic Islands. Spain. fina.perez@uib.es

Correspondence: Gemma Tur, gemma.tur@uib.es

Abstract:

Agency has been generally defined as the ability to take control of one's own decisions and choices, and in the educational context, it has been described from a sociocultural perspective, in which individual, relational and contextual sources of agency are defined. This is an aligned background to support students' autonomy in flexible learning enhanced by designs such as personal itineraries. In this study, a pedagogical design based on flexible learning itineraries in digital environments is presented, and from a Design Based Research methodology, the second iteration is developed and analysed from participants' perceptions on agency activation. Results suggest that students who perceive greater opportunities for choice and autonomy in their learning itinerary are also more likely to perceive their learning environments as supportive and resource-rich, both socially and materially.

Keywords: learners' agency, flexible learning, personalized learning, learning itineraries, digital technologies, teacher education

Introduction

Flexible learning is a pedagogical approach that requires a conceptual shift of educational practices towards student-centered strategies, which at the same time involves the change in the teachers' role. Designing for flexible strategies means not only the change of the participants' role but also the transformation of the whole educational landscape including materials and their organization (Salinas et al., 2022). Furthermore, digital technologies have facilitated such an evolution by challenging not only traditional designs but also supporting autonomous and self-paced learning (de Benito et al., 2020; Castañeda & Tur, 2020), such as flexible itineraries.

Although flexibility has promised democratization of education by allowing access to a wide target audience, the fact is that it has been critized for having privileged those who have skills and other material conditions to navigate through such 'anytime' and 'anyplace ' claims (Houlden & Veletsianos, 2019). In order to address this issue, the pedagogic strategy of flexible learning itineraries offers a balanced design between flexibility and scaffolding by offering options in which the diverse elements are presented accordingly. This means that flexibility requires offering learning strategies such as itineraries or pathways, enhanced by digital technologies, in which there is adaptation of content organization, aims, time and participating requirements, media and other elements in the instructional design (Salinas & de Benito, 2020; Salinas et al., 2022).

Flexible itineraries or pathways were defined as "sets of one or more learning activities leading to a particular learning goal" (Janssen et al., 2011, p. 2018), and from which learners can make their own choices. In order to take these decisions, students require key information such as aims, contents, tasks, workload etc. Both pedagogical lessons and materials offering such information allow students' self-regulation, since they can take decisions before starting learning, deciding in relation to motivation and needs, monitor their performance and finally, self-reflecting on achievements, success, and failure to prepare their next learning steps, according to the model by Zimmermann (2002). The self-regulation cycle has been paramount into designing learning for autonomous aims, in particular regarding the individual element of the person learning. However, it has not offered a wider framework that includes other aspects such as the sociocultural contexts, which are also relevant to offer fair flexibility to all. Aligned with this approach, the agency offers the sociocultural background required.

Agency has been related to the autonomous ability to choose and take control of one's own decisions, and it has been explored from a variety of approaches. In the recent literature review by Marín et al. (2025) it has been seen that the one by Jaäskela et al. (2017) is among the most cited. The sociocultural perspective adopted by Jaäskela et al. (2017) described agency for learning aims, including not only individual aspects, but also the relational and contextual elements of formal educational settings. In particular, Jäaskela et al. (2017) include four resources of agency at an individual level: interest and motivation, self-efficacy, competence beliefs and participation activity; four more factors as relational sources of agency: equal treatment, teacher support, peer support and trust; and, two in the contextual dimension: opportunities to influence and opportunities to make choices. In the work by Zhang and Tur (2024) in which e-portfolios were addressed from a co-design approach, agency was explored and it was concluded that those sources of greater agency were at different stages of the e-portfolio development: competence beliefs (individual domain), peer learning (relational domain), and the opportunities to make choices (contextual domain). Apart from that, Marín et al. (2025) conclude about the limited knowledge of the pedagogical designs that activate agency, and claim for future experiences in which designs and contexts in technology enhanced learning are carefully described. Therefore, this work is aimed at answering the following research question: Which sources of agency are mostly activated by students in flexible learning itineraries?

Based on the sociocultural perspective of learner agency and the pedagogical design of flexible learning itineraries, this study hypothesizes that:

The design proposal based on flexible itineraries favours the perceived activation of different dimensions of student agency (individual, relational, and contextual), in an ecosystemic framework of the agency. Furthermore, within the contextual dimension, the perception of flexibility—understood as opportunities for participation and decision-making—shows positive correlations with sources of individual and relational agency, suggesting a possible cross-facilitative effect of flexibility on the development of agency.

More specifically, it is expected that the perception of the flexible itineraries regarding autonomy in choosing tasks, objectives, content, and digital tools will be positively associated with:

1. Increased motivation and self-regulatory behaviors (individual agency),
2. Stronger perceptions of teacher and peer support (relational agency),
3. Opportunities to participate and make choices (contextual agency).

This hypothesis is grounded in the assumption that the ability to make meaningful choices within the learning process fosters engagement, peer-collaboration and active participation—core components of agency in higher education contexts.

Method

In this section, we present the design of the educational context, and the aligned research design, including instruments, data collection and results.

Educational context

This research reports the learning design implemented over two school years, 2023-24 and 2024-25, in a course on digital technologies for Primary Education in the Teacher Education program of the University of the Balearic Islands, in the off-campus centre in Ibiza. The design is a new iteration developed from the one reported in Pérez Garcias et al. (2022), in which the first pilot of flexible itineraries in digital environments was analysed in order to explore quality design and students' perceptions on learning impact and other individual aspects such as motivation and interests. Although conclusions allowed the confirmation of the successful outcome of the pedagogical experience, the fact is that students and lecturers' perceptions on workload and other organization issues (such as a complex group organization with different members joining for different tasks) led the team to further work on new designs. So, the new pedagogical strategy was organized into two main parts: a minor one with the individual task, common for all students; and a group task, introducing flexibility by presenting diverse learning sequences with adapted aims, contents, organization, technologies, and tasks. In short, all students had to develop one group task, choosing topics, technologies, and pedagogical designs.

Research design and instrument

This study is developed under the framework of the Design Based Research methodology, from which we develop, implement, evaluate and improve the pedagogical designs based on flexible itineraries in a cyclic and iterative workflow (Reeves, 2006; de Benito & Salinas, 2016). This methodological approach collects data from a variety of sources in order to learn in detail about the process and products generated. In this case, the first iteration was aimed at knowing about the quality of the designs and the learning impact, and it was concluded that although the designs were pedagogically sound and participants were satisfied to a great extent, the overwhelming amount of information and itineraries recommend a new iteration with a simpler structure, which is reported here. In order to carry out the aligned study, an existing survey was used to collect data on students' perception. Thus, the instrument created for the research by Zhang and Tur (2024) on e-portfolios was adapted and delivered to students at the end of the term. The online questionnaire follows the agency background by Jäaskela et al. (2017) and with a Likert scale format explores the level of agreement in relation to students' perception of the activation of individual, relational or contextual sources of agency.

Results

This section presents the results from a quantitative analysis aimed at examining the students' perceived development of their agency. Table 1 provides descriptive statistics for all analyzed variables, including the overall flexibility index, items measuring individual, relational and contextual agency. These statistics offer a general overview of how participants responded to each item, helping to understand the central tendencies and variability within the sample.

Table 1: Descriptive statistics for all measured variables.

Dimension	Variable	count	mean	std	min	25%	50%	75%	max
Contextual Agency	Choice of learning objectives	34.00	3.82	0.67	2.00	3.25	4.00	4.00	5.00
	Choice of tasks	34.00	3.79	0.72	2.00	3.0	4.00	4.00	5.00
	Choice of content	34.00	3.74	0.86	1.00	3.0	4.00	4.00	5.00
	Choice of digital tools	34.00	3.97	0.76	2.00	4.0	4.00	4.00	5.00
	Technology-supported participation	34.00	4.53	0.56	3.00	4.00	5.00	5.00	5.00
Individual Agency	Motivation	34.00	4.09	0.67	3.00	4.00	4.00	4.75	5.00
	Self-confidence	34.00	4.26	0.71	3.00	4.00	4.00	5.00	5.00
	Planning	34.00	4.21	0.73	3.00	4.00	4.00	5.00	5.00

	Self-monitoring	34.00	4.00	0.65	3.00	4.00	4.00	4.00	5.00
	Self-assessment	34.00	4.15	0.78	2.00	4.00	4.00	5.00	5.00
Relational Agency	Teacher support	34.00	4.59	0.56	3.00	4.00	5.00	5.00	5.00
	Teacher support for understanding content	34.00	4.44	0.66	3.00	4.00	5.00	5.00	5.00
	Teacher support for digital skills	34.00	4.44	0.75	2.00	4.00	5.00	5.00	5.00
	Peer support	34.00	4.44	0.75	3.00	4.00	5.00	5.00	5.00
	Peer support for understanding content	34.00	4.03	1.03	1.00	3.00	4.00	5.00	5.00
	Peer support for digital skills	34.00	4.03	1.09	1.00	3.00	4.00	5.00	5.00

To examine students' perceived flexibility within the learning design, we focused on four items from the questionnaire that capture their sense of autonomy in key aspects of the course: choice of learning objectives, tasks, content, and digital tools. These items were theoretically grounded in the contextual dimension of agency, as described by Jääskelä et al. (2017), specifically reflecting the opportunities to make decisions and participate in the learning process. Taken as a whole, they form a composite measure that we refer to as flexibility, representing a specific and operationalizable facet of contextual agency. The strong internal consistency among these items supports their use as an integrated indicator of students' perceived freedom to shape their own learning pathway. Although flexibility is understood as a contextual dimension of agency—reflecting students' perceived opportunities to make decisions and participate actively—it may also function as a catalyst or enabler for other types of agency. In particular, students who perceive greater flexibility in choosing content, tools, or tasks may also feel more motivated (individual agency) and better supported by peers and teachers (relational agency). To explore this potential transversal role of flexibility, a correlation analysis was conducted in order to examine the associations between students' perceived flexibility and other agency indicators. This allows us to investigate whether students who feel empowered to make learning decisions also experience higher engagement, confidence, and support throughout the learning process.

To identify potential relationships between students' perceived flexibility and their reported levels of agency, a Spearman correlation matrix was computed. Figure 1 displays the correlation coefficients between all variables. Warmer colours indicate stronger positive correlations, while cooler colours indicate weaker or negative ones. This visual representation helps in detecting clusters of relationships and possible patterns among the variables under study. The matrix reveals several noteworthy associations. As expected, the four items related to flexibility—Choice of learning objectives, Choice of tasks, Choice of content, and Choice of digital tools—were strongly correlated with the Flexibility index, with coefficients ranging from 0.76 to 0.85. These high correlations confirm the internal consistency of the composite flexibility measure and validate its use as an aggregate indicator. Within the relational agency dimension, substantial correlations were observed among variables reflecting teacher and peer support. For example, Teacher support showed a strong positive correlation with both Teacher support for understanding content ($r = 0.75$) and Teacher support for digital skills ($r = 0.72$). Similarly, Peer support correlated strongly with Peer support for digital skills ($r = 0.73$), suggesting consistency in the students' perceptions of social support across different learning domains. Contextual agency variables also exhibited strong internal coherence. Resources helpful for understanding and Useful resources were closely related ($r = 0.70$), and both were moderately associated with perceptions of the subject being interesting ($r = 0.68$) and useful ($r = 0.75$). On the other hand, several variables showed weak or negligible correlations. Notably, Self-confidence exhibited very low correlation values with all flexibility items, such as Choice of learning objectives ($r = 0.07$) and Choice of tasks ($r = 0.13$).

Additionally, Planning showed virtually no association with Peer support for digital skills (r = 0.00), and Self-assessment was weakly and negatively associated with the same variable (r = -0.04). These findings suggest that while perceived flexibility aligns closely with motivation and participation, it may be less strongly related to self-reported indicators of confidence and metacognitive regulation.

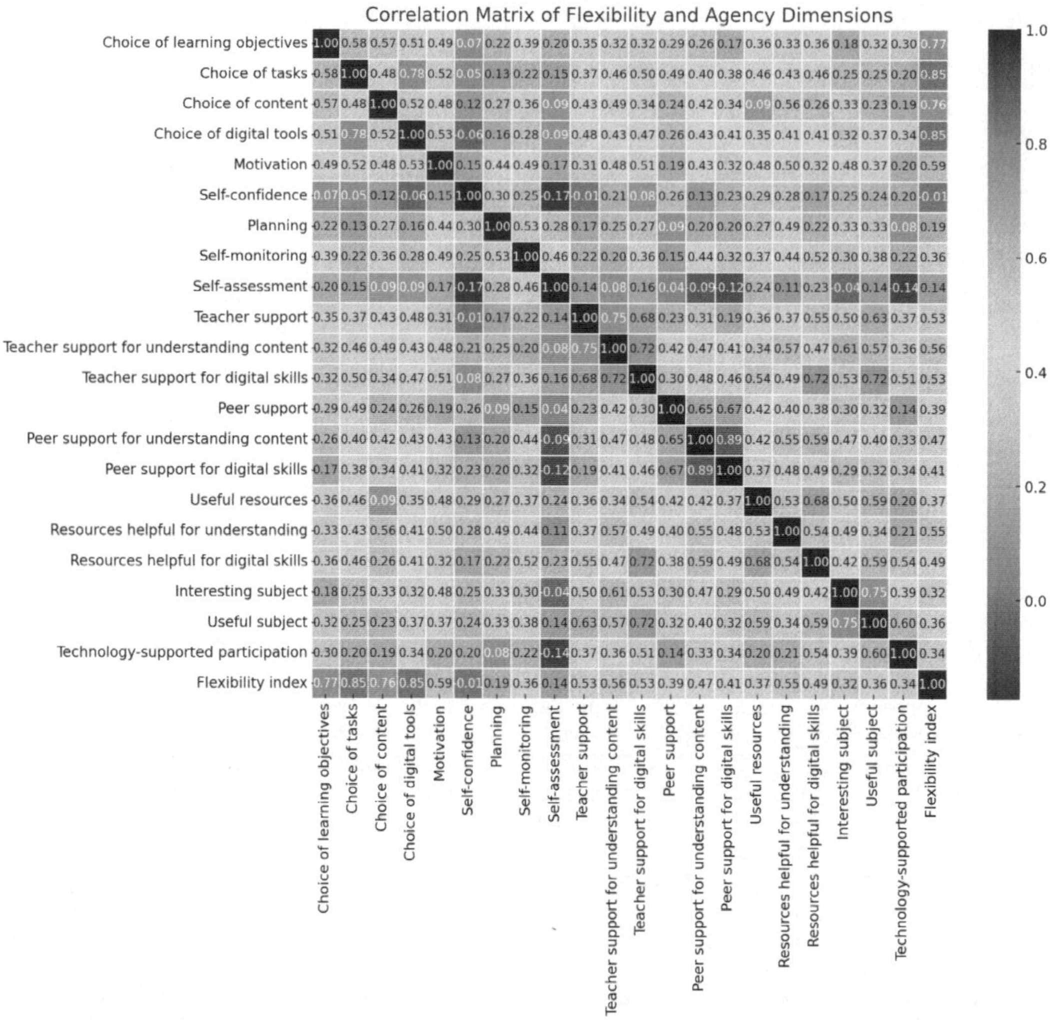

Figure 1: Spearman correlation matrix showing associations between flexibility and other indicators.

To further explore the role of flexibility as an internal component of contextual agency, we conducted independent samples t-tests comparing students with high and low perceived flexibility (as measured by their reported opportunities to make learning choices). Although flexibility is part of the broader construct of contextual agency, this analysis aimed to examine whether students who experience higher levels of flexible decision-making also report significantly different perceptions in other agency dimensions. The only statistically significant difference among the individual agency variables was observed in motivation (t = 3.19, p = 0.003), suggesting that students with higher flexibility tended to feel more motivated. However, significant differences also emerged across several dimensions of relational agency, indicating a broader impact of flexibility perceptions. Specifically, students in the high-flexibility group reported significantly higher levels of teacher support (t = 3.59, p = 0.0014), including both support for understanding content (t = 4.11, p = 0.0003) and for developing digital skills (t = 3.44, p = 0.0022). Similarly, they reported greater peer support, both overall (t = 2.18, p = 0.0372), for understanding content (t = 2.73, p = 0.0109), and for digital skill development (t = 2.16, p = 0.0383).

These results suggest that students who perceive greater opportunities for choice and autonomy in their learning itinerary are also more likely to perceive their learning environments as supportive and resource-rich, both socially and materially. This supports the idea that flexibility can act as a contextual enabler of agency, not only internally (through motivation), but also in how students engage with others and with the tools and materials provided. Overall, the results highlight the value of designing flexible learning environments not only to foster contextual agency directly, but also to strengthen students' perceived motivation and social embeddedness—two key aspects of individual and relational agency.

Discussion and conclusion

The aim of this study was to explore how a pedagogical design based on flexible learning itineraries, enhanced by digital technologies, fosters students' perceived agency across individual, relational, and contextual dimensions, following the framework proposed by Jääskelä et al. (2017) and adopting a sociocultural perspective on agency. Specifically, the study hypothesized that students would report activation of all three dimensions of agency through this design, and that flexibility—understood as opportunities to make decisions and participate—would play a particularly relevant role within contextual agency and might be positively associated with individual and relational components. The results provide substantial support for this hypothesis, while also suggesting a nuanced interaction between flexibility and other forms of agency.

The data analysis shows that students reported generally high levels of perceived agency across all three dimensions. Within the contextual dimension, the flexibility indicators—specifically students' perceived opportunities to choose learning objectives, tasks, content, and digital tools—stood out as particularly strong. These items were also positively correlated with motivation, the only self-regulatory variable showing a statistically significant association. Although other individual agency indicators such as self-confidence, planning, monitoring, and self-assessment presented higher mean scores in students with higher perceived flexibility, these differences were not statistically significant. More importantly, flexibility as part of contextual agency showed consistent and meaningful correlations with relational agency indicators, including teacher and peer support, as well as students' perceptions of the usefulness and accessibility of learning resources. Future research should further investigate the nature of these associations, particularly whether they are strengthened by content-related or digitally mediated interactions that might serve as additional sources of agentic learning.

This study reinforces the notion that student agency is strengthened when genuine opportunities for choice, collaboration, and self-construction of learning are present, as flexible itineraries in digital environments offer (Salinas & de Benito, 2020; Salinas et al., 2022; Pérez Garcias et al., 2022). A pedagogical design based on flexible digital itineraries, grounded in a sociocultural perspective, emerges as an effective strategy to address the current challenges of higher education, while also contributing to the development of pedagogical frameworks that explicitly support agency, as highlighted by Marín et al. (2025). The results offer compelling evidence for the value of incorporating contextual and relational dimensions—particularly flexibility and social support—into the design of higher education experiences. By enabling students to make meaningful decisions about what, how, and with whom they learn, instructors may foster not only academic engagement but also a deeper sense of ownership and participation.

Competing interests

The author(s) has/have no competing interests to declare.

Ethics and consent

Informed consent to participate in the study was obtained from participants, who were informed about the research aims and allowed to dropout whenever they needed.

Funding Information

This study has been supported by the Project PID2020-113101RB-I00 "Codiseño de itinerarios personales de aprendizaje en entornos conectados en educacion superior", funded under the State Programme for R&D&I Oriented to the Challenges of Society, from the State Plan for Scientific and Technical Research and Innovation 2017-2020 of the Spanish Ministry of Science and Innovation. State Research Agency.

References

Bovill, C. (2020). Co-creation in learning and teaching: the case for a whole-class approach in higher education. Higher Education, 79(6), 1023–1037. https://doi.org/10.1007/s10734-019-00453-w

de Benito, B., & Salinas, J. (2016). La investigación basada en diseño en Tecnología Educativa. Revista Interuniversitaria de Investigación en Tecnología Educativa, 0, 44-59. https://doi.org/10.6018/riite2016/260631

de Benito, B., Moreno-García, J., & Villatoro Moral, S. (2020). Entornos tecnológicos en el codiseño de itinerarios personalizados de aprendizaje en la enseñanza superior. Edutec Revista Electrónica de Tecnología Educativa, 74, 72-93. https://doi.org/10.21556/edutec.2020.74.1843

Díaz Barriga, Á. (2013). Secuencias de aprendizaje. ¿Un problema del enfoque de competencias o un reencuentro con perspectivas didácticas? Profesorado. Revista de Currículum y Formación de Profesorado, 17(3), 11-33. https://bit.ly/3iwKxEh

Houlden, S., & Veletsianos, G. (2019). A posthumanist critique of flexible online learning and its "anytime anyplace" claims. British Journal of Educational Technology, 50(3), 1-14. https://doi.org/10.1111/bjet.12779

Jääskelä, P., Poikkeus, A. M., Vasalampi, K., Valleala, U. M., & Rasku-Puttonen, H. (2017). Assessing agency of university students: validation of the AUS Scale. Studies in Higher Education, 42(11). https://doi.org/10.1080/03075079.2015.1130693

Janssen, J., Berlanga, A. J., & Koper, R. (2011). Evaluation of the Learning Path Specification. Educational Technology & Society, 14(3), 218-230. https://bit.ly/3e9UTcs

Marín, V. I., Tur, G., Castañeda, L., Peguera-Carré, M. C., Orellana, M. L., Villagrá, S., & Carrera, X. (2025). Agencia y aprendizaje en la Educación Superior: una revisión sistemática. UTE Teaching & Technology (Universitas Tarraconensis), (1), e4035. https://doi.org/10.17345/ute.2025.4035

Pérez-Garcias, A., Tur Ferrer, G., Villatoro Moral, S., & Darder-Mesquida, A. (2022). Flexible Learning Itineraries in Digital Environments for Personalised Learning in Teacher Training. RIED-Revista Iberoamericana de Educación a Distancia, 25(2), pp. 175-193. https://doi.org/10.5944/ried.25.2.32326

Salinas, J., & de-Benito, B. (2020). Construction of personalized learning pathways through mixed methods. Comunicar: Revista Científica de Comunicación y Educación, 28(65). https://doi.org/10.3916/C65-2020-03

Salinas-Ibáñez, J., de Benito-Crosetti, B., Moreno-García, J., & Lizana Carrió, A. (2022). Nuevos diseños y formas organizativas flexibles en educación superior [New flexible designs and modes of organisation in higher education]. Pixel-Bit.Revista de Medios y Educación, 63, 65-91. https://doi.org/10.12795/pixelbit.91739

Zhang, P., & Tur, G. (2024). An exploration of agency enactment in e-portfolio learning co-design. Digital Education Review, (45), 190-203. https://doi.org/10.1344/der.2024.45.190-203

Zimmerman, B. J. (2002). Becoming a self-regulated learner: an overview. Theory into Practice, 41(2), 64-70. https://doi.org/10.1207/s15430421tip4102_2

Competency Recognition in AI Education: Investigating Higher Education Students' Perceptions of Open Educational Badges Using Technology-Acceptance Model.

Ilona Buchem[1], Franziska Schmid[2], Annika Ermel[3]

[1] Department of Economics and Social Sciences, Berlin University of Applied Sciences, Germany; buchem@bht-berlin.de
[2] mycelia gGmbH, Germany; franzi@mycelia.education
[3] mycelia gGmbH, Germany; annika@mycelia.education

Correspondence: Ilona Buchem: buchem@bht-berlin.de

Abstract:
In the age of Artificial Intelligence (AI), digital credentialing is transforming how competencies are recognized in AI education. Open Educational Badges (OEBs) have emerged as an alternative to traditional paper-based and PDF certificates, offering a more transparent and verifiable way to showcase skills. However, the factors driving the acceptance of OEBs among students participating in AI education remain uncertain. This study investigates first-semester university students' perceptions of OEBs compared to PDF participation certificates, using the Technology Acceptance Model (TAM3) as a theoretical framework. A survey with 65 business students was conducted after they completed an online course related to the Foundations of AI and received both credential formats. The study examined perceived usefulness, ease of use, job relevance, output quality, and result demonstrability as key factors influencing student acceptance. Results indicate that while both formats were perceived as useful, PDF certificates were preferred for formal applications, whereas OEBs were valued for digital professional visibility on platforms like LinkedIn. Ease of use was a barrier to OEB adoption, whereas perceived usefulness and quality were key drivers of acceptance. The findings from our study contribute to ongoing discussions on digital credentials in AI education and provide insights into enhancing OEB adoption for competency recognition in AI education.

Keywords: Artificial Intelligence (AI), Technology Acceptance Model (TAM3), Digital Credentialing, Open Educational Badges (OEBs), Competency Recognition.

Introduction

Background and Context

In the age of Artificial Intelligence (AI) in education, the recognition and validation of competencies related to AI is evolving rapidly, embracing digital solutions that align with the dynamic nature of modern education and professional development. As AI becomes more deeply embedded in both professional and educational landscapes, higher education institutions must rethink their pedagogical strategies both in relation to providing competency-oriented teaching/learning opportunities as well as credentialing practices which align with current technologies (Gimpel et al., 2024) and ensure that students/graduates receive a recognition of their AI skills they can utilise easily in different digital platforms. Traditional methods of assessing and certifying student competencies, such as paper-based or PDF certificates, are becoming challenged by digital alternatives, metadata-based standards like Open Badges (OB) offer opportunities to make learning achievements easily shareable across professional networks like LinkedIn and e-portfolios, facilitating transparent and skill-based recognition (Gimpel et al., 2024).

We define Open Educational Badges (OEBs) as Open Badges which are used for the recognition of skills in educational contexts (Buchem, Orr & Brunn, 2019) as opposed to other uses of Open Badges, such as content consumption and generation (Lu, Xie & Chen, 2022) or as a toolkit for measuring and shaping face-to-face social interactions (Lederman et al., 2017). By recognising and referencing skills to frameworks such as ESCO (European Classification of Skills, Competences, Qualifications and Occupations), OEBs enable the earners (e.g. students) to showcase their skills in digital platforms, such as LinkedIn, and the receivers (e.g. employers) to understand and validate these skills in a wider context, e.g. in the context of skill classifications maintained by the European Commission (Buchem, Orr & Brunn, 2019).

Research Gap

While research has highlighted the role of digital badges in fostering motivation and self-directed learning, promoting lifelong learning and enhancing employability a broader adoption of OEBs seems to be influenced by how students perceive their relevance in academic and professional contexts (Ahn, Pellicone & Butler, 2014). Understanding the factors influencing student acceptance of OEBs is crucial to their broader adoption, particularly in AI education, which in itself aims at enhancing technological literacies. Gimpel et al. (2024) emphasize that AI competencies are essential for future-proof graduates and can be categorized into AI Literacy, AI Reflection, AI Technology, AI Innovation, AI Management, and AI Application areas. With higher education institutions attempting to increasingly integrate AI competencies in education, the need for an effective, skill-focused credentialing approach becomes an important question and task. Ahn, Pellicone & Butler (2014) highlight that while digital badges can serve as both extrinsic and intrinsic motivators, their impact varies depending on contextual factors such as institutional endorsement and employer recognition. The acceptance of Open Badges possibly depends on multiple factors including students' perceptions of their credibility and applicability in real-world scenarios. The Technology Acceptance Model provides a theoretical framework for understanding technology adoption, focusing on key determinants such as perceived usefulness, ease of use, job relevance, output quality, and result demonstrability (Venkatesh & Bala, 2008). Applying TAM3 to the context of OEBs allows for an in-depth examination of how students evaluate and intend to use digital badges as compared to traditional credentials. Understanding adoption factors is crucial for educators and policymakers looking to implement digital credentialing systems for AI competencies that align with student expectations and demands of the digital shifts in education and at work.

Research Questions

This study aims to investigate the acceptance of OEBs compared to PDF participation certificates among first-semester university students enrolled in an AI-focused course. By applying the TAM3 framework, the study seeks to address the following research questions:

1. How do students perceive the usefulness, relevance, ease of use, reputation, demonstrability of their results and the quality of OEB digital credentials focused on recognising competencies compared to traditional PDF certificates focused on certifying attendance in the context of AI education?

2. What are students 'current and planned uses of OEBs compared to PDF certificates?

3. Which factors significantly predict the intention to use OEB credentials compared to PDF certificates?

Structure of the Paper

The paper is structured as follows: Section 2 presents the theoretical background, including an overview of the Technology Acceptance Model (TAM3) and the role of digital credentialing in AI education. Section 3 describes the research methodology, including study design, data collection, and analysis. Section 4 presents the results, comparing students 'perceptions of OEBs and PDF certificates. Section 5 discusses the findings in relation to digital credentialing adoption in AI education. Finally, Section 6 concludes the paper with implications for educators and recommendations for future research.

Theoretical Background

Technology Acceptance

Understanding the factors that influence acceptance of technologies is crucial for their successful implementation in educational contexts. The Technology Acceptance Model (TAM) introduced by Davis (1989), includes two primary determinants of technology use, i.e. perceived usefulness (PU) and perceived ease of use (PEU). Perceived usefulness refers to the degree to which a person believes that using a particular system would enhance their job performance, while perceived ease of use related to the degree to which a person believes that using the system would be low effort (Davis, 1989).

Over time, the TAM model has undergone several extensions. TAM2 expanded the original model by including social influence processes (e.g., subjective norms) and cognitive instrumental processes (e.g., job relevance, output quality) as antecedents of perceived usefulness (Venkatesh & Davis, 2000). Further refinement led to the TAM3 model, which integrated factors such as computer self-efficacy, perceptions of external control, computer anxiety, and perceived enjoyment, providing a more comprehensive understanding of technology acceptance (Venkatesh & Bala, 2008). This study applied TAM3 for a more nuanced investigation of a range of factors.

The application of TAM and its extensions has been widespread across various domains, including education. The meta-analysis by Ma & Liu (2004) synthesized findings from multiple studies, confirming the robustness of TAM in predicting technology acceptance, especially confirming the strong correlation between usefulness and acceptance. Researchers have also used TAM to assess factors influencing both educators' and students' acceptance of digital learning platforms, highlighting the model's relevance in educational technology research (Šumak et al., 2011).

Open Badges

Open Badges (OBs) have emerged as a promising alternative to traditional paper-based and PDF certificates, providing a digital and verifiable means of recognizing competencies (Hickey & Buchem, 2021). Open Badges were initially introduced by the Mozilla Foundation in 2011 and have since gained traction among various institutions, including universities, corporations, and online learning platforms (Fadel, Bialik, & Trilling, 2017). These digital credentials include embedded metadata with information about the earner (e.g. students) issuer (e.g. university), assessment criteria, expiration date and other additional information such as workload and evidence of competency acquisition (Buchem, Orr, & Brunn 2019).

In higher education, Open Badges have been increasingly explored as a means to promote competency-based learning. The report by Buchem, Orr & Brunn (2019) emphasized the role of Open Badges in making competencies more visible for both education and employment. The report highlights how digital credentialing with Open Badges can support flexible learning pathways, improve employability, and address the limitations of traditional certification systems, which are no longer aligned with current digital practices. The report underscores the importance of institutional recognition and interoperability for the adoption of Open Badges, particularly in bridging the gap between education and employment (Buchem, Orr, & Brunn 2019).

Despite their potential, Open Badges still face barriers to adoption, including limited awareness both among educators and employers and concerns regarding their inflationary use and assessment rigour (Buchem Orr & Brunn, 2019). Hickey & Buchem, 2021 also discussed concerns that traditional credentialing practices may hinder the deployment of Open Badges as innovations in education. Efforts to align Open Badges with competency frameworks, such as the European Skills, Competences, Qualifications, and Occupations (ESCO) system, have aimed to enhance their legitimacy and recognition in professional settings. Nevertheless, the acceptance of Open Badges in higher education remains a subject of debate and the integration of OEBs as a new digital credentialing mechanism requires a shift in perception.

Methods

Study Context

The study aimed to evaluate students 'perceptions and factors driving acceptance of both formats (PDF and OEB), using the Technology Acceptance Model 3 as a framework. 65 students participated in the study. The study was conducted as part of the course "Fundamentals of Digital Media" in the first semester of an undergraduate study program in Digital Economy (BSc.). This course introduces students to key digital media concepts and tools, including Foundations of Artificial Intelligence (AI). As part of the course requirements, students completed the "AI for All" online course hosted on the educational platform KI-Campus[1]. The online course provided students with foundational knowledge in AI, including different AI/ML methods, application areas including business, basic programming skills in Python and ethical considerations related to AI. After completing 10 weeks of the online course "AI for All", all participants received a PDF certificate of attendance as well as a digital competency badge in the form of an Open Educational Badge (OEB). The OEBs were issued via the openbadges.education platform and included a detailed list of acquired competencies with references to the ESCO repository[2], while the PDF certificate listed the topics covered (see Figure 1).

[1] https://ki-campus.org
[2] https://esco.ec.europa.eu/en/use-esco/use-esco-services-api

Figure 1: The PDF Certificate of Attendance and the OEB Credential issued via the OEB platform[3].

Data Collection and Analysis

To assess students 'perceptions of both certificate types (PDF and OEB), an online survey was administered at the end of the course. The survey included Likert-scale items rated on a scale from 1 = strongly disagree, 7 = strongly agree. The TAM3 model was used to structure the survey, focusing on selected acceptance factors, i.e. behavioral intention, perceived usefulness, perceived ease of use, job relevance, image, output quality, and result demonstrability. Additionally, two questions were asked about the actual use of both certificate formats, asking whether students uploaded their credentials to LinkedIn or other online platforms, and two open-ended question about whether and how students plan to use both certification formats in the future. The final part of the survey collected demographic and experience-related data, i.e. age (predefined age groups), gender (female, male, non-binary, other), and knowledge about Open Badges (0 = none; 6 = high). The collected data were analyzed using IBM SPSS Statistics, employing both descriptive and inferential methods.

Participants

A total of 65 students participated in the study. The majority were between 18 and 23 years old. The largest age group was 18–20 years old (44.6%, 29 students), followed by 21–23 years old (24.6%, 16 students). The remaining participants were: 24–26 years old: 15.4% (10 students), 27–29 years old: 6.2% (4 students), 30–32 years old: 1.5% (1 student), 33 years and older: 3.1% (2 students). The gender distribution was as follows: male students: 38 (58.5%), and female students: 27 (41.5%). Participants self-rated their knowledge of Open Educational Badges (OEB) on a scale from 0 (no knowledge) to 6 (high knowledge). The average rating was $M = 3.15$ ($SD = 1.29$). A wide range of responses was observed, with most participants rating their knowledge between 3 and 4 (22 students rated 4, and 19 rated 3). A gender-based comparison found no significant differences in OEB knowledge ($x^2 = 7.843$, $df = 6$, $p = .250$). However, a linear correlation analysis indicated a significant positive association ($p = .021$), suggesting a slight variation in OEB knowledge based on gender with Spearman's $p = .265$, $p = .033$. About halt of the students reported having a LinkedIn profile, i.e. 32 students (49.2%). This nearly even distribution suggests that while about half of the students in their first semester already use LinkedIn, the other half may not yet see the need or are unaware of its use and/or benefits.

Results

Comparing PDF Certificates and OEB Credentials

The following results are related to the comparison of descriptive statistics (mean rating scores and standard deviations) for PDF certificates and OEB credentials. Additionally, paired samples t-tests or Wilcoxon Signed Ranks Tests were conducted to test whether the differences (PDF – OEB) were statistically significant:

[3] https://openbadges.education/public/start

- **Perceived Usefulness:** The PDF certificate was rated as useful, with a mean score of M = 4.97 (SD = 1.854). The OEB received a slightly lower score of M = 4.72 (SD = 1.883). The t-test was not statistically significant (p = 0.099). These results indicate that both formats were perceived as useful.
- **Academic relevance:** The PDF certificate was rated as academically more relevant, with a mean score of M = 4.78 (SD = 1.763) compared to OEB with M = 4.57 (SD = 1.820). The t-test was statistically significant with an average difference of 0.215 points in favour of the PDF, a t-value of 2.225 (df = 64) and a moderate effect size (Cohen's d = 0.780). These results suggest that participants perceive the PDF certificate as academically more relevant than the OEB.
- **Career Relevance:** The PDF certificate and the OEB were both rated as professionally relevant, with a mean scores of M = 4.80 (SD = 1.822) and M = 4.83 (SD = 1.876) respectively. The t-test showed an average difference of -0.031 points, with a t-value of -0.322 (df = 64), but was not statistically significant (p = 0.748). This suggest that both formats are relevant for students 'career.
- **Output Quality:** The PDF and the OEB were perceived as high-quality certificates, with a mean scores of M = 5.06 (SD = 1.580) and M = 4.88 (SD = 1.682). The paired t-test was not statistically significant (p = 0.083), which suggests that both formats were seen to be of high quality.
- **Perceived Ease of Use:** The PDF certificate was perceived as easier to use, with a mean score of M = 5.17 (SD = 1.654) compared to the OEB with a score of M = 4.63 (SD = 1.850). The paired t-test was statistically significant (p = 0.003) with an average difference of 0.538 points, a t-value of 3.142 (df = 64) and a large effect size (d = 1.382). These results indicate that participants found the PDF certificate significantly easier to use than the OEB.
- **Image/Reputation**: The PDF participation certificate was rated slightly lower with a mean score of M = 4.48 (SD = 1.760), compared to the OEB with the score of M = 4.68 (SD = 1.760). The t-test was was not statistically significant. This shows that both formats enjoy a high reputation among students.
- **Result demonstrability** (being able to articulate its benefits to others): The PDF certificate was rated slightly lower with a mean score of M = 4.48 (SD = 1.760) compared to the OEB with the score of M = 4.68 (SD = 1.760). The t-test was not statistically significant, which suggest that students found both credential formats equally easy to explain to others.
- **Behavioral intention:** The PDF participation certificate was rated slightly lower with a mean score of M = 4.71 (SD = 1.869) compared to the OEB with M = 4.88 (SD = 1.772). The t-test was not statistically significant, which shows that participants have similarly positive intentions to use both formats.
- **Actual use:** To compare the actual use of both formats, students could choose one of these options: Not yet, As a LinkedIn certificate, and In a LinkedIn post. The majority of participants did not share either format (89.2% PDF certificate, 86.2% OEB). 9.2% (n = 6) uploaded their PDF and 12.3% (n = 8) their OEB as a LinkedIn certificate. Only 1 student had shared the PDF and the OEB in a LinkedIn post. The Wilcoxon Test was no statistically significant, indicating that LinkedIn sharing was similar for PDF and OEB. A possible explanation for rare sharing may be the short time between credential issuance and the survey (one week), which may not have been sufficient for students to share their credentials.
- **Planned Use:** A comparison of the responses to the question about planned used revealed the following similarities and differences: Both PDF and OEB are planned to be used primarily for job applications, job searches, or résumés (PDF: 48 mentions; OEB 42 mentions) and hardly in academic settings (both under 5 mentions). OEBs intended for online visibility on platforms such as LinkedIn (14 mentions) more often than PDF certificates (6 mentions). No specific planned use was reported for both PDF certificates (10 mentions) and OEBs (7 mentions). Additionally, 4 participants stated that they do not plan to use either credential format, as they already have a job.

These findings indicate that both credential formats are primarily planned to be used for professional purposes. However, a clear shift in preference emerges as the PDF certificate is more strongly associated with traditional, formal applications such as résumés and job applications. The OEB format is particularly valued for its digital advantages, especially for enhancing online presence on networking platforms like LinkedIn.

Predictors of Acceptance

The first regression model examined the factors influencing the Behavioral Intention to use PDF certificates. The model included Perceived Usefulness (PU) and Perceived Ease of Use (PEU) as predictors. Results showed that PU had a significant positive effect on Behavioral Intention (B = 0.632, $p < .001$), while PEU was not statistically significant (B = 0.161, p = 0.249). Together, these factors explained 54% of the variance in Behavioral Intention ($R^2 = 0.540$). To analyze PU, six determinants were tested: Result Demonstrability (RD), Image (IM), Job Relevance (Studies) (JR1), Job Relevance (Career) (JR2), Output Quality (OQ), and PEU. The model explained 79.2% of the variance in PU ($R^2 = 0.792$, $p < .001$). The strongest predictors were JR2 (B = 0.461, p = .008) and RD (B = 0.245, p = .034), while other factors were not significant. These findings show that the professional relevance of PDF certificates and the result demonstrability are key predictors of usefulness. In turn, PU strongly predicts the intention to use the PDF certificate, while ease of use plays a minor role. These findings suggest that the career-related relevance and the demonstrability of the certificate have a significant positive effect on the future use of PDF certificates of attendance.

The second regression model examined the factors influencing the Behavioral Intention to use OEB credentials. Perceived Usefulness (PU) significantly predicted Behavioral Intention (B = 0.520, $p < .001$), while Perceived Ease of Use (PEU) had no significant effect (B = 0.186, p = 0.097). The model explained 47.1% of the variance in Behavioral Intention ($R^2 = 0.471$, $p < .001$). For PU, six determinants were tested: Result Demonstrability (RD), Image (IM), Job Relevance (Studies) (JR1), Job Relevance (Career) (JR2), Output Quality (OQ), and PEU. The model explained 73.9% of the variance in PU ($R^2 = 0.739$, $p < .001$). Only OQ had a significant positive effect on PU (B = 0.458, p = .004), while other factors were not significant. These findings indicate that Output Quality was the key predictors of PU, which in turn predicts Behavioral Intention to use OEBs. These results indicate that improving the perceived quality of OEB credentials could enhance their acceptance and future use.

Discussion

This study examined the acceptance and perception of two formats: traditional PDF certificates of attendance and digital competency recognition with Open Educational Badges (OEBs). Participants were 65 first-semester students in the undergraduate Digital Economy program, who participated in the online course "AI for All". Upon completion, they received both credential formats and assessed their perceptions of usefulness, relevance, quality, ease of use, image, result demonstrability, behavioral intention, as well as actual and planned use in an online survey at the end of semester. The results indicate that both formats (PDF and OEB) were perceived as useful and relevant. The PDF certificate was primarily valued for traditional professional contexts, such as job applications or résumés, while OEBs were valued for online professional presence in digital platforms such as LinkedIn. This suggests that OEBs are particularly perceived as a tool for enhancing online professional visibility and networking. Both formats received similar ratings in terms of perceived usefulness and image (reputation), but he PDF format was rated significantly higher in terms of ease of use. A regression analysis of the selected TAM3 constructs showed that perceived usefulness was a key determinant of intention to use both PDF certificates and OEBs, which aligned with the results from prior research (Ma & Liu, 2004). For PDF certificates, perceived usefulness was primarily predicted by job relevance and result demonstrability. For OEBs, perceived usefulness was significantly predicted by the quality of the credential. These findings suggest that improving the quality, relevance, and explainability of Open Educational Badges (OEBs) could positively impact their acceptance and future use.

Recommendations

Our recommendations for future use of OEBs in AI education are based on the three scenarios proposed by Buchem, Orr, & Brunn (2019), each reflecting different levels of institutional, pedagogical, and labor market engagement. Our recommendation is to progress from the supplemental recognition (minimal scenario), in which OEBs are used informally to acknowledge micro-achievements and skills to partial integration (medium scenario), in which OEBs are embedded to formal education as tools of competency-based credentialing, and possibly going further to full integration (maximum scenario), in which OEBs are fully integrated into credentialing systems allowing for personalised learning pathways and competency tracing in relation to AI skills. The progression from medium to maximum scenario would be from using OEBs to provide granular recognition of specific AI competencies, e.g. in Machine Learning (ML), to using OEBs as stackable micro-credentials which recognise AP specialisations, e.g. Natural Language Processing (NLP), which can be stacked to full degrees and hold the same credibility as traditional certifications.

As integration of OEBs into AI education depends on individual and institutional acceptance, more research is needed on factors driving the acceptance of different stakeholders. Moreover, as the digital credentialing ecosystem evolves too, with recent advancements such as Open Badges 3.0 and Verifiable Credentials (VCs), the next generation of secure and trusted credentials, which are cryptographically verifiable opens new possibilities for the recognition of skills in AI education.

Competing interests

The author(s) has/have no competing interests to declare.

Ethics and consent (if applicable)

The research was conducted and published according to recognised international standards including the Declaration of Helsinki. The informed consent to participate in the study was obtained from the participants.

References

Ahn, J., Pellicone, A., & Butler, B. S. (2014). Open badges for education: What are the implications at the intersection of open systems and badging? Research in Learning Technology, 22.

Buchem, I., Orr, D., & Brunn, C. (2019). Making competences visible with Open Badges – Final report of the HFD Community Working Group Competence Badges. Working Paper Nr. 48. Hochschulforum Digitalisierung.

Davis, F. D. (1989). Perceived usefulness, perceived ease of use, and user acceptance of information technology. MIS Quarterly, 13(3), 319–340.

Gimpel, H. et al. (2024). Generative AI competencies for future-proof graduates: Inspiration for higher education institutions. University of Hohenheim.

Hickey, D., & Buchem, I. (2021). Advancing sustainable educational ecosystems with open digital credentials and badges. In S. Jagannathan (Ed.), Reimagining digital learning for sustainable development (pp. 293-307). Routledge.

Lederman, O., Calacci, D., MacMullen, A., Fehder, D. C., Murray, F. E., & Pentland, A. (2017). Open badges: A low-cost toolkit for measuring team communication and dynamics. ArXiv, abs/1710.01842.

Lu, S., Xie, Y., & Chen, X. (2022). Immediate and enduring effects of digital badges on online content consumption and generation. International Journal of Research in Marketing, 40 (1), 146-163.

Ma, Q., & Liu, L. (2004). The technology acceptance model: A meta-analysis of empirical findings. Journal of Organizational and End User Computing, 16(1), 59–72.

Šumak, B., Heričko, M., & Pušnik, M. (2011). A meta-analysis of e-learning technology acceptance: The role of user types and e-learning technology types. Computers in Human Behavior, 27(6), 2067–2077.

Venkatesh, V., & Bala, H. (2008). Technology acceptance model 3 and a research agenda on interventions. Decision Sciences, 39(2), 273–315.

Venkatesh, V., & Davis, F. D. (2000). A theoretical extension of the technology acceptance model: Four longitudinal field studies. Management Science, 46(2), 186–204.

Assessment and micro-credentials in distance learning for VET educators

Evangelia (Gelly) Manousou[1], Maria-Eleftheria Galani[2]

[1]Hellenic Open University, Greece; manousoug@eap.gr
[2] University of the Peloponnese, Greece; megalani@go.uop.gr

Correspondence: Maria-Eleftheria Galani: megalani@go.uop.gr, Evangelia Manousou, manousoug@eap.gr

Abstract:

The Erasmus+ KA2 project "Improving VET distance learning through a Gamified Asynchronous eLearning Methodology" (d-ICT) addresses the evolving needs of Vocational Education and Training (VET) educators in the digital era by integrating assessment tools and micro-credentialing mechanisms into distance learning. With the shift towards online education, particularly during the COVID-19 pandemic, VET educators faced significant challenges in engaging learners, evaluating competencies, and ensuring the credibility of remote training programs. This project developed an innovative, gamified, and asynchronous e-learning approach, equipping educators with structured methodologies for assessment and digital credentialing. Through research conducted across seven European countries, the project identified key gaps in digital competencies and designed a comprehensive e-Toolkit featuring assessment strategies, interactive learning techniques, and a micro-credentialing framework based on ECVET points. The findings highlight the effectiveness of game-based learning, peer review assessments, and digital tools in fostering engagement and validating competencies. By enhancing the professional recognition and mobility of VET educators, the d-ICT project contributes to a more structured, inclusive, and competency-based approach to distance learning and digital education.

Keywords: assessment, micro-credentials, digital learning, gamification, VET education, ECVET points

Introduction

The digital transformation of Vocational Education and Training (VET) has accelerated in response to technological advancements and the increased demand for flexible learning pathways. The Erasmus+ KA2 project "Improving VET distance learning through a Gamified Asynchronous eLearning Methodology" (d-ICT) aimed to enhance VET educators' digital skills and competencies by creating an interactive and gamified e-learning experience. As the COVID-19 pandemic necessitated distance learning due to the closure of educational institutions, VET centers in several European countries, including Greece, Cyprus, Belgium, France, Italy, Spain and Portugal, faced challenges in ensuring effective online learning. This project provided a structured approach to address these challenges by integrating innovative assessment tools and micro-credentialing mechanisms to enhance the digital learning landscape.

This paper explores the role of assessment and micro-credentials in VET distance learning, focusing on the d-ICT initiative. It outlines how structured assessment strategies and micro-credentials can validate educators' competencies, ensuring that their skills are recognized and transferable across various educational and professional contexts.

1. The Erasmus+ KA2 project "Improving VET distance learning through a Gamified Asynchronous eLearning Methodology" (d-ICT)

The project d-ICT aimed to improve Vocational and Educational Training (VET) educators' digital skills and competencies in distance learning training by creating an innovative gamified eLearning experience. That resulted in building a more interesting and interactive environment that boosted the curiosity of VET learners and lessened any potential dropouts.

The Covid-19 pandemic brought to the forefront the need for distance learning due to the closure of VET centers. Distance learning was a unique opportunity for the consortium countries – Greece, Cyprus, Italy, Spain, Portugal,

Belgium and France– to make VET education more interactive as they struggled to communicate effectively with the learners through the lockdowns. Therefore, the target groups were VET educators and learners that benefited from this project's outcome.

The project offered the following resources:

- Lessons Learned: Explore the resolutions that were used during the Covid-19 era.
- D-ICT e-Toolkit: Introduce distance learning practices and digital tools to facilitate the e-Learning experience end prevent dropouts.
- Development of a Gamified asynchronous eLearning experience (Serious Game).

The Erasmus+ KA2 d-ICT project was coordinated by the University of the Peloponnese (GR) and involved a strategic partnership among several European institutions, including Centro Servizi Formazione (IT), IASIS (GR), C.I.P Citizens in Power (CY), ISQ e-learning (PT), F.C.B Forum Citoyens – Burgers (BE), Association de Gestion des Fonds Européens (FR), and INFODEF Instituto para el fomento del desarrollo y la formación (ES). The project ran for a two-year period, from 28 February 2022 to 27 February 2024, aiming to enhance digital competencies in vocational education and training (VET) through innovative approaches and collaborative efforts among partner organizations across Europe.

2. Methodology

The field research was carried out as part of the final report with the aim of identifying digital skills, competencies, gaps, and needs related to distance learning in Vocational Education and Training (VET). A mixed-method approach was employed, combining three methodologies—questionnaires, focus groups, and digital interviews—to gather both qualitative and quantitative educational data through a bottom-up process.

The primary target group of this project was VET educators, who worked in VET centers. To ensure the collection of high-quality quantitative data, each partner organization from seven European countries (Greece, Cyprus, Italy, Spain, Portugal, France, and Belgium) approached 20 VET educators and invited them to complete a questionnaire focused on distance learning. For the qualitative component, 8 VET educators per partner participated in a focus group, while an additional 5 educators per partner provided insights through digital interviews.

The selection of VET educators was based on the following criteria: ▪ Their experience in vocational education and training, ▪ a demonstrated interest in the project's subject matter, ▪ a willingness to share best practices, ideas, experiences, and personal skills, along with being flexible, enthusiastic, and dependable, ▪ their fluency in English.

Questionnaire

The questionnaire included 20 VET educators (per partner)through emails, calls, and social media. It was open online from 10-2022 to 11-2022. It contained 15 questions with multiple choices. Using a questionnaire, 20 trainers self-assessed their competencies (e.g. supporting their self-regulated learning) before and after the COVID pandemic.

Focus Group

Qualitative data was gathered through focus groups and interviews. Each partner selected 8 VET educators from various fields within VET education to participate in the focus group. The session lasted around two hours and facilitated a productive exchange of ideas. Follow-up questions and a structured discussion were also included.

The objective of the d-ICT focus group was to explore the working conditions during the lockdown period, the challenges trainers faced in delivering engaging and effective distance learning to students at home, the digital solutions and tools they employed, and to identify areas for improvement along with potential solutions or suggestions. This approach encouraged collaborative brainstorming around participants' needs, gaps, strengths, preferences, and capabilities. Participants shared personal accounts of their working environments, challenges, needs, and expectations within the VET system as shaped by the impact of COVID-19. The group also discussed a range of flexible learning strategies using digital technologies, with a focus on addressing the varied needs of trainees and supporting the learning of new material in innovative ways.

Digital interviews

Five Digital Storytelling interviews were video-recorded per partner, featuring 5 VET educators who shared their personal experiences and offered recommendations on how to enhance distance learning, making it more engaging and enjoyable while also helping to reduce school dropout rates.

Overall, although they encountered numerous challenges related to online training during the lockdowns, they recognized the potential benefits of distance learning for both students and trainers. The VET educators expressed genuine interest in the project's intellectual outputs, particularly the asynchronous gamified experience, as they believed it could significantly support and enrich the distance learning process.

The findings of the questionnaires and the focus groups provide us the survey results and helped the consortium of the project to develop the D-ICT e-Toolkit divided into 7 modules which were the following:

Module 1: Introduction to VET distance learning

Module 2: Digital skills in VET distance learning

Module 3: Methodologies and tools to enhance learners' interaction and teamwork in VET distance learning

Module 4: Methodologies and tools to enhance learners' motivation in VET distance learning

Module 5: Gamification in distance learning I

Module 6: Gamification in distance learning II

Module 7: Assessment Tools for Distance Learning

3. Definition and characteristics of VET Distance Learning

Vocational Education and Training (VET) plays a crucial role in equipping individuals with the essential skills and expertise required for employment and career advancement. In recent years, VET has experienced a profound evolution, driven by the emergence of digital technologies and the expansion of online learning platforms, reshaping traditional training methodologies and enhancing accessibility. VET Distance Learning refers to a remote education and training approach that enables learners to engage with study materials and resources through digital technologies, eliminating the need for in-person interactions with instructors or trainers. This learning method is widely recognized for its flexibility, accessibility, and convenience, allowing individuals to access educational content from any location at any time. Moreover, VET Distance Learning often integrates multimedia tools, online platforms, and communication technologies to enhance learning experiences and foster collaboration.

4.1 Overview of digital resources for VET distance learning

Distance learning in VET depends extensively on a variety of digital resources that support the learning process and boost student engagement. These resources come in multiple formats, such as text, images, audio, video, and interactive content. They allow learners to access educational materials remotely, collaborate with both peers and instructors, and participate in interactive learning experiences. When used effectively, digital resources enrich the learning environment, increase student involvement, and contribute to the development of essential vocational skills.

4.2 Multimedia tools and resources for VET distance learning

Multimedia tools and resources are essential in VET Distance Learning, as they offer dynamic, interactive experiences that enrich the educational process. These tools include a wide range of applications, platforms, and software that support the creation, modification, and distribution of multimedia content. A key example is video production and editing software. Programs such as Adobe Premiere Pro and Camtasia enable educators to develop engaging video lectures, tutorials, and demonstrations, which can be easily shared with learners. These tools provide features like video editing, screen recording, and the addition of special effects, helping educators deliver visually rich and informative content.

Graphic design software also plays an important role in VET Distance Learning. Tools like Canva and Adobe Photoshop allow educators to craft visually appealing infographics, presentations, and other instructional materials. With user-friendly interfaces and ready-made templates, these platforms help create professional visuals that support better understanding and retention of vocational topics.

Virtual reality (VR) has also become increasingly popular in VET Distance Learning due to its immersive capabilities. Platforms such as Engage and Mozilla Hubs allow educators to build virtual environments where learners can engage in realistic simulations and scenarios. VR technology offers hands-on learning opportunities, enabling students to practice tasks—like operating equipment or following safety procedures—in a safe, virtual space. This form of experiential learning greatly enhances engagement and knowledge retention in vocational contexts.

In addition, simulation software is a valuable asset in distance learning for VET. Tools like SimScale and Labster allow educators to replicate real-world scenarios and experiments that might be difficult to perform in traditional settings. Learners interact with these simulations, make decisions, and observe outcomes, thereby building critical thinking and problem-solving abilities. Simulation-based learning is particularly effective in fields such as engineering, healthcare, and various technical trades.

4.3 Online platforms and Learning Management Systems (LMS) for VET distance learning

Online platforms and Learning Management Systems (LMS) function as centralized environments for organizing and delivering VET Distance Learning programs. These platforms offer a wide array of features that support both the management and dissemination of educational materials. Moodle, for example, is a widely used open-source LMS that provides a robust set of tools for educators. It supports content development, assessment administration, progress monitoring, and collaborative learning activities, fostering a structured and engaging educational experience. Additionally, Moodle allows for extensive customization through plugins and extensions, enabling educators to tailor the platform to meet the specific needs of vocational training.

Canva is another popular platform known for its intuitive interface and user-friendly course design capabilities. Educators can efficiently create and manage course materials, assignments, and discussions within a visually organized layout. Canva also offers real-time collaboration tools, multimedia integration, and flexible assessment options, allowing instructors to deliver interactive and engaging VET Distance Learning experiences.

Blackboard is a comprehensive LMS offering a broad range of tools for content delivery, communication, assessments, and learner analytics. With Blackboard, educators can organize and present course materials, facilitate interactive discussions, evaluate learners, and monitor progress through a streamlined interface. The platform also supports integration with external applications, allowing for smooth incorporation of multimedia elements and other digital tools into the virtual classroom.

Google Classroom, another widely used solution, utilizes Google's suite of tools to support VET Distance Learning. Educators can easily distribute assignments, share resources, and offer timely feedback through the platform. Its seamless integration with Google Drive enables collaborative document creation and storage. Furthermore, Google Classroom includes communication tools, such as announcements, comments, and private messaging, to facilitate ongoing interaction between educators and learners.

4.4 Communication technologies for VET distance learning

Effective communication is essential in VET Distance Learning, as it promotes interaction and collaboration between educators and learners. Communication technologies offer both synchronous and asynchronous channels, allowing participants to connect and engage in meaningful exchanges. Common tools used in VET Distance Learning include video conferencing platforms such as Zoom and Microsoft Teams, online discussion forums, instant messaging services, and collaborative document editing tools. These technologies support real-time conversations, group discussions, peer-to-peer feedback, and joint project work, fostering a dynamic and socially engaging learning environment within vocational education and training.

5. Assessment and evaluation methods for VET distance learning

Assessment and evaluation play a fundamental role in VET distance learning, ensuring that learners successfully attain the intended learning objectives. A range of assessment techniques, including quizzes, examinations, assignments, and project-based evaluations, can be utilized to measure learners' knowledge and competencies. Additionally, evaluation tools such as surveys and feedback forms provide valuable insights into learners' experiences, helping to identify strengths and areas for improvement within the learning process.

As part of the d-ICT project and based on the findings of research conducted across seven European countries, the project consortium developed an e-Toolkit, which includes the e-Curriculum with carefully structured guidelines, outlining a systematic process from the definition of e-Units to the allocation of ECVET points, ensuring a well-defined and robust educational framework. The e-Book which serves as a valuable resource for VET educators, enhancing their digital teaching competencies by integrating practical methodologies, gamification strategies, and theoretical foundations. Moreover, the e-Tool which represents an advanced innovation aimed at significantly enhancing the distance learning experience, providing educators with dynamic, interactive, and technology-driven instructional solutions.

In this paper, we focus on Module 7 of the e-Toolkit, which is dedicated to assessment tools in VET distance learning and presents specific examples of their application.

e-Curriculum:

Module 7: Assessment Tools for Distance Learning

Objectives	After the completion of this Module the learner will be able to: To provide educators with a range of assessment tools and strategies that can be used to evaluate learners in a distance learning environment. To explore the advantages and disadvantages of different assessment tools, such as formative assessments, summative assessments, self-assessments, and peer assessments. To help educators design and implement effective assessment plans that align with their learning objectives, construction methods and student needs. To promote the use of technology-enabled assessment tools, such as online quizzes, surveys, and other digital tools that can enhance the assessment process and provide timely feedback to students. To support educators in monitoring and assessing student progress and adjusting their teaching strategies as needed.
Total Hours	25 hours
ECVET Points	1
KNOWLEDG E	Identify the key assessment tools for synchronous and asynchronous learning. Outline the best practices of how to develop an effective assessment in distance learning. Emphasize the needs of students creating a student- centre assessment in distance learning.

	Choose the relevant assessment tools. Design an effective assessment strategy directed at the needs of learners.
RESPONSIBILITY AND AUTONOMY	Summarize the findings of the implementation of the assessment strategy. Compare face-to-face and distance learning assessments based on students' performance.
HOURS DISTRIBUTION	Contact hours: 5 Hands-on practice hours: 13 Self-study hours: 5 Assessment hours: 2

e-Tool I: Assessment Tools in Distance Learning

Tool Activity Title	Asynchronous Video Interviewing as a New Technology
Duration	1-3 minutes Video recording The recommended length for a video-answer in an assessment can vary depending on the purpose and nature of the assessment. Generally, a video-answer should be long enough to adequately address the question or prompt, but not so long that it becomes cumbersome for the instructor to review and grade. In some cases, instructors may provide specific guidelines regarding the length of the video-answer. For example, they may require a video-answer to be between 1-3 minutes or limit it to a specific number of words or slides. In other cases, the length of the video-answer may be more flexible. As a general rule, a video-answer should be long enough to provide a comprehensive response to the question or prompt, while also being concise enough to hold the attention of the instructor and other viewers. It's important to note that the purpose of a video-answer is to demonstrate understanding of the material and to communicate ideas clearly and effectively. As such, the quality of the response is more important than the length of the video-answer.

Process	Video-based assessment tools can offer a valuable alternative to traditional written assignments in distance learning, enabling students to showcase their knowledge and skills in a new format. Asynchronous or recorded video is a newly emerging technology that can be utilized in the initial screening phase of an assessment. Students can record their responses to assessment questions posed by educators on camera, and then submit them online. Following this, the educator can evaluate the answers based on pre-defined criteria drawn from the module's curriculum. Online oral assessments can prove to be even more effective than traditional in-person assessments due to reduced anxiety for students and the ability to revisit their recorded speaking multiple times. Additionally, encouraging students to use multimedia components can enhance the engagement level of their presentations. For instance, the 'record' function available in Microsoft PowerPoint allows students to combine their voice with a slide presentation while some may experiment with editing software to produce more sophisticated multimedia presentations. Podcasts may serve as a viable substitute for conventional oral presentations, and group presentations can be more stimulating and foster dynamic discussions. To prepare students for online verbal communication, educators may coach them on the basics of speaking clearly and into a microphone. It may also be helpful to have students submit test recordings to troubleshoot any uploading issues. If

	feasible, live presentations on platforms such as Zoom, Teams or Skype can be a valuable addition to the assessment process. However, it is important to remember that the content of the presentation should be prioritized, and engaging multimedia should be used to support information and expression, rather than replace it. The general steps for a video-assessment process are the following: 1. Define the learning outcomes and assessment criteria: Determine the specific knowledge, skills, and competencies that learners are expected to demonstrate in the video assessment, and identify the criteria that will be used to evaluate their performance. 2. Provide clear instructions and guidelines: Clearly communicate the requirements and expectations for the video assessment, including the duration, format, and technical specifications. 3. Support learners with resources and feedback: Provide learners with relevant resources and support to help them create high-quality videos, such as templates, examples, and feedback on drafts. 4. Use a rubric to evaluate videos: Develop a rubric that aligns with the learning outcomes and assessment criteria and use it to evaluate the videos submitted by learners. 5. Provide feedback and follow-up: Provide feedback to learners on their video assessments, highlighting strengths and areas for improvement, and follow up with additional instruction and support as needed.

Here is an example of a video-assessment process in Vocational Education and Training (VET):

1. Learning outcomes and assessment criteria: In a VET course on cooking, the learning outcome might be for learners to demonstrate the ability to prepare a specific dish, such as spaghetti carbonara. The assessment criteria might include factors such as ingredient selection, preparation techniques, presentation, and taste.
2. Instructions and guidelines: Learners are provided with clear instructions on how to record and submit their video, including guidance on camera angles, lighting, and sound quality. They are also given a detailed recipe and instructions for preparing the dish.
3. Resources and feedback: Learners are provided with access to relevant resources, such as cooking videos, recipes, and tips for presentation. They can also receive feedback on their video drafts from their instructor or peers.
4. Rubric: The rubric for evaluating the videos might include criteria such as ingredient selection, preparation techniques, presentation, and taste. Each criterion might be rated on a scale of 1-5, with specific indicators of performance at each level.
5. Feedback and follow-up: After reviewing the videos, instructors provide learners with feedback on their performance, highlighting areas of strength and areas for improvement. Learners may also be given the opportunity to revise their videos and resubmit them for additional feedback.

Further Resources or References	Miller, M., Lu, Y., & Montplaisir, L. (2017). The effects of asynchronous video interviews on interviewing processes and perceptions. Online Learning Journal, 21(1), 75-94. https://doi.org/10.24059/olj.v21i1.3398 Video Length: How Long Should Instructional Videos Be? (New Data): https://www.techsmith.com/blog/video- length/ Barbour, M.K. & Harrison, K.U. (2016). Teachers' Perceptions of K-12 Online: Impacting the Design of a Graduate Course Curriculum. Journal of Educational Technology Systems, 45(1), 74-92. Retrieved March 22, 2023 from https://www.learntechlib.org/p/175706/.

e-Tool II: Assessment Tools in Distance Learning

Tool Activity Title	Game-based Scenario Assessment Tool (GSAT)
Duration	40 minutes
Materials	Laptops and Internet Connection
Process	GSAT is a web-based assessment tool that utilizes game-type scenarios to evaluate vocational skills and competencies. The tool presents learners with a simulated work environment where they must complete tasks and make decisions that reflect real-world work situations. The tool is designed to provide learners with an engaging and interactive learning experience while also allowing trainers to assess learners' progress and competencies in real-time. GSAT consists of a series of scenarios that simulate different work environments and tasks. Each scenario is designed to evaluate specific vocational skills and competencies, such as problem-solving, teamwork, communication, and technical skills. As learners navigate through the scenarios, they are required to make decisions, solve problems, and perform tasks that are directly related to their vocational training discipline provided by their educator. Trainers can use GSAT to evaluate learners' performance in real-time, through a dashboard that provides detailed analytics

	on learner progress and competencies. The tool also provides learners with immediate feedback on their performance, allowing them to identify areas for improvement and adjust their learning accordingly. Overall, GSAT is an effective assessment tool for VET that combines game-type activities with scenario-based learning to evaluate vocational skills and competencies in a fun and engaging way. In an asynchronous setting, GSAT could be designed as a standalone activity that learners complete on their own time, rather than as a live activity that requires learners to be present at the same time. For example, learners could be given access to the GSAT tool through an online platform, and could complete the assessment at their own pace. One advantage of using game-based assessments in asynchronous settings is that learners can complete the assessment on their own schedule, without having to coordinate with other learners or trainers. This can be particularly useful for VET programs that have learners with different schedules and time zones. However, it's important to note that asynchronous game-based assessments may not be able to provide the same level of social interaction and collaboration as synchronous assessments, which can be an important aspect of VET

programs. Therefore, it's important to carefully consider the goals of the assessment and the needs of the learners when deciding whether to use a synchronous or asynchronous approach to game-based assessment in VET.

Example – GSAT for Gardening and Landscaping:

The GSAT for gardening and landscaping could present learners with a simulated garden or outdoor space that requires maintenance and design. The tool would simulate real-world gardening and landscaping tasks, such as plant identification, soil preparation, pruning, planting, and design.

The tool could present learners with a series of scenarios, each of which would require the learner to complete specific gardening or landscaping tasks. For example, a scenario could present learners with a garden plot that requires soil preparation and planting. The learner would be required to select and use the appropriate gardening tools, such as a hoe or a spade, to prepare the soil and plant the seeds. The learner's performance would be evaluated based on their ability to complete the task correctly and efficiently.

Another scenario could focus on plant identification and pest management. The learner would be presented with a variety of plants and pests and would be required to correctly identify them and select the appropriate pest management strategies.
The learner's performance would be evaluated based on their

	ability to accurately identify the plants and pests and select the appropriate management strategies. The GSAT for gardening and landscaping could also include a design component, where learners would be required to design and implement a landscape plan for a simulated outdoor space. The tool would provide learners with a variety of design elements, such as plants, hardscaping materials, and decorative elements, and would require learners to create a cohesive and aesthetically pleasing landscape design.
Further Resources or References	• Pauschenwein, J., Goldgruber, E. & Sfiri, A. (2013). The Identification of the Potential of Game-based Learning in Vocational Education within the Context of the Project "Play the Learning Game". International Journal of Emerging Technologies in Learning (iJET). 8. 10.3991/ijet.v8i1 • 12 Best Virtual Games for Classroom Fun & Learning: https://www.splashlearn.com/blog/best-virtual-games-for-classroom-fun-learning/

e-Tool III: Assessment in Distance learning

Tool Activity Title	Microsoft Form as an assessment Tool
Duration	1 hour
Materials	Laptops or smartphones, internet connection
Process	During the Covid-19 pandemic, the utilization of Microsoft Forms was extensively adopted as an assessment tool due to its ease of use and minimal digital competency requirements. This form of assessment allows educators to implement a hybrid approach by utilizing both multiple-choice and essay-type questions, along with the capacity to incorporate images that can aid in descriptive responses from students. In vocational education and training (VET), Microsoft Forms can be an incredibly useful tool for conducting assessments and evaluating students' knowledge and skills. One way to use Microsoft Forms in VET education is by creating quizzes and assessments to test students' knowledge of specific topics or concepts. With Microsoft Forms, teachers can easily create multiple-choice questions, open-ended questions, and rating scales to assess different aspects of student learning. Additionally, Microsoft Forms can be used for self-reflection and self-assessment activities. For example, teachers can create forms that students can use to reflect on their learning

	progress, identify areas where they need improvement, and set goals for future learning. This can be an effective way to promote self-directed learning and empower students to take ownership of their learning journey. Another way Microsoft Forms can be used in VET education is for peer assessment. Teachers can create forms for students to evaluate each other's work, such as presentations, projects, or practical skills assessments. This can help to foster collaboration and teamwork skills while also providing valuable feedback for students to improve their work. Overall, Microsoft Forms is a versatile tool that can be used in many different ways in VET education. Whether for assessment, self-reflection, or peer assessment, it offers a user- friendly interface that can help teachers and students streamline the learning process and improve learning outcomes.
Further Resources or References	• How to Use Microsoft Forms: https://www.youtube.com/watch?v=ouFKWHQMxtQ/ • What it is? https://teachinghub.bath.ac.uk/microsoft-forms/ • 6 InterActive Ways to Use Microsoft Forms https://www.themerrillsedu.com/blog-1/2020/6/27/5-interactive-ways-to-use-microsoft-forms/

Conclusions

The d-ICT project has demonstrated the critical role of structured assessment and micro-credentials in distance learning for VET educators. Through the development of the e-Toolkit, the project provided innovative solutions to address the challenges faced by VET educators in digital learning environments (Carretero et al., 2017). The research conducted across seven European countries highlighted the gaps in digital skills and the need for targeted training. By integrating gamification strategies, interactive methodologies, and asynchronous e-learning approaches, the project successfully enhanced educators' ability to design and deliver engaging online learning experiences (Deterding et al., 2011; Hamari et al., 2014).

The development of standardized assessment tools has ensured that digital learning within VET is competency-based, measurable, and aligned with European frameworks such as ECVET and DigCompEdu (Redecker & Punie, 2017). The inclusion of formative and summative assessments, peer reviews, and gamified evaluation techniques provided a diverse and effective way of measuring learners' progress and engagement. The integration of micro-credentials in VET distance learning addresses the need for formal recognition of digital skills, ensuring portability and transferability across educational and professional institutions (Oliver, 2019). By embedding ECVET points, the project created a scalable system for lifelong learning and career development.

The findings indicated that gamification and asynchronous methodologies significantly increase learner motivation, reduce dropout rates, and improve engagement in digital learning environments (Hamari et al., 2014; Kapp, 2012). The Serious Game methodology and the Game-Based Scenario Assessment Tool (GSAT) proved to be effective in simulating real-world vocational skills training (Sailer & Homner, 2020). The pilot testing and feedback mechanisms confirmed that the tools and methodologies developed under the d-ICT project are applicable and beneficial for VET educators. The sustainability of the project is ensured through long-term hosting of resources by partner institutions, supporting continuous professional development in the VET sector (Facer & Shelwyn, 2021).

The d-ICT project provides a replicable model for enhancing digital learning in vocational education, with a strong emphasis on assessment innovation, competency-based education, and micro-credentialing (OECD, 2019). The insights gained can be leveraged for future policy-making, integration of AI-driven assessment tools, and expansion of cross-border recognition of digital qualifications in VET education.

References

Carretero, S., Vuorikari, R., & Punie, Y. (2017). DigComp 2.1: The Digital Competence Framework for Citizens with eight proficiency levels and examples of use. Publications Office of the European Union. https://doi.org/10.2760/38842

Deterding, S., Dixon, D., Khaled, R., & Nacke, L. (2011). From game design elements to gamefulness: Defining "gamification". Proceedings of the 15th International Academic MindTrek Conference: Envisioning Future Media Environments, 9-15. https://doi.org/10.1145/2181037.2181040

Hamari, J., Koivisto, J., & Sarsa, H. (2014). Does gamification work? A literature review of empirical studies on gamification. Proceedings of the 47th Hawaii International Conference on System Sciences (HICSS), 3025-3034. https://doi.org/10.1109/HICSS.2014.377

Kapp, K. M. (2012). The gamification of learning and instruction: Game-based methods and strategies for training and education. Wiley.

OECD. (2019). Trends shaping education 2019. OECD Publishing. https://doi.org/10.1787/trends_edu-2019-en

Oliver, B. (2019). Making micro-credentials work for learners, employers and providers. Deakin University. https://doi.org/10.13140/RG.2.2.26887.50088

Redecker, C. & Punie, Y. (2017). European Framework for the Digital Competence of Educators: DigCompEdu. Publications Office of the European Union. https://doi.org/10.2760/159770

Sailer, M., & Homner, L. (2020). The gamification of learning: A meta-analysis. Educational Psychology Review, 32(1), 77-112. https://doi.org/10.1007/s10648-019-09498-w

Facer, K. & Shelwyn, N. (2021). Digital learning and the future of education. https://unesdoc.unesco.org/ark:/48223/pf0000377071

Creativity and AI in Teacher Education: A Structured Framework for Future Educators

Rena Alasgarova[1], Jeyhun Rzayev[2]

[1] Baku-Oxford School, Azerbaijan; rena.alasgarova@bakuoxfordschool.net

[2] School of Education, ADA University, Azerbaijan; jrzayev@ada.edu.az

Correspondence: Rena Alasgarova: rena.alasgarova@bakuoxfordschool.net

Abstract:

Creativity is an essential competency for teachers in the 21st century, yet it remains underrepresented in many teacher education programs. This study explores how teaching creativity can be systematically integrated into BA-level teacher training applying AI-driven tools to enhance learning outcomes. Drawing on the Hierarchical Pyramid, AI TPACK, and UNESCO AI Competency Frameworks, the study investigates teacher-students' and faculty perceptions of creativity and AI integration in three Azerbaijani pedagogical universities. A qualitative methodology, including semi-structured interviews with 15 teacher-students and 6 faculty members, revealed significant gaps in structured creativity training and AI literacy. Findings highlight the complementary potential of the three frameworks in fostering creativity and professional development. To address these gaps, this study proposes a structured process for integrating creativity teaching and AI tools into teacher education, providing practical strategies aligned with global competency standards. Implications for curriculum design, professional development, and further research are discussed.

Keywords: creativity in education, teacher education, artificial intelligence in education, UNESCO AI Competency Frameworks, TPACK, professional development

Introduction

Fostering creativity in teaching practices is increasingly recognized as essential in teacher education, as it equips future educators to address complex challenges and support innovation in diverse classrooms. However, despite its importance, creativity often remains underrepresented in many teacher education curricula, leaving teacher-students without the necessary competencies to implement creative approaches effectively in their future classrooms.

The integration of artificial intelligence (AI) tools into teacher training programs provides an opportunity to bridge this gap. AI can support creativity by offering tools for personalized learning, collaborative teaching strategies, and innovative content delivery. Frameworks such as the Hierarchical Pyramid (Alasgarova & Rzayev, 2024a), AI TPACK Model (Mishra & Koehler, 2006; Alasgarova & Rzayev, 2024b), and the UNESCO AI Competency Framework ("AI Competency Framework for Teachers," 2024) highlight the potential of AI in enhancing creativity while emphasizing the importance of ethical and pedagogical alignment.

This study aims to address this critical area through three objectives: (1) to explore why and how teacher-students should be explicitly taught creativity during their training to prepare them for creative teaching practices; (2) to analyze how AI tools can enhance the teaching and learning of creativity, aligning with established frameworks; and (3) to design and propose a structured process for integrating creativity teaching and AI tools into BA-level teacher education programs. By examining these objectives, the study seeks to offer actionable insights and strategies for fostering creativity and AI integration in teacher education.

Literature Review

The Importance of Creativity in Teacher Education

Creativity is a core competency for teachers in the 21st century, essential for engaging students and addressing diverse classroom challenges. Recent studies continue to underscore the significance of creativity in education. For instance, Moirano et al. (2020) provide a systematic review of creative interdisciplinary collaboration, highlighting strategies that enhance creativity across organizational, educational, and research contexts. Additionally, a systematic review by Bullard and Bahar (2023) identifies common barriers in teaching for creativity in K-12 classrooms, emphasizing the challenges educators face in nurturing creativity among students.

Simpson et al. (2022) found that pre-service teachers who underwent explicit training in creative teaching approaches significantly improved their understanding and application of creativity. They argue that creativity should not be seen as an innate trait but as a skill that can be taught and developed through structured interventions. As such, it is essential that pre-service teacher education programs prioritize the development of creativity as a core competency.

AI as a Tool for Enhancing Creativity

AI tools offer unprecedented opportunities to enhance creativity in teacher education. Generative AI applications, such as ChatGPT and Canva, provide teacher-students with innovative ways to design lessons, solve problems, and engage learners. In their research, Bae et al. (2024) highlighted pre-service teachers' dual perspectives on AI: recognizing its potential to foster creativity while expressing concerns about its trustworthiness and ethical implications.

Liu et al. (2023) demonstrated that integrating design thinking models with AI tools significantly enhances pre-service teachers' creative self-efficacy and problem-solving skills. These findings align with the TPACK framework, which emphasizes the intersection of technological, pedagogical, and content knowledge (Mishra & Koehler, 2006). The adaptation of this framework for AI integration provides a roadmap for effectively embedding AI tools into teacher education programs to enhance creativity.

Competency Frameworks Guiding AI and Creativity Integration

The Hierarchical Pyramid

The Hierarchical Pyramid model (Alasgarova & Rzayev, 2024a) outlines a progressive framework for developing teacher competencies, from foundational knowledge and skills to advanced professional skills and lifelong learning (Figure 1). This conceptualization aligns with the literature's portrayal of educators as collaborative leaders engaged in lifelong professional development, emphasizing a shift from static knowledge acquisition to dynamic skill-building for adaptability and resilience in modern education (Darling-Hammond, 2006; Trinter & Hughes, 2021). This framework informs the current research by providing a developmental basis for integrating creativity and AI into teacher education programs.

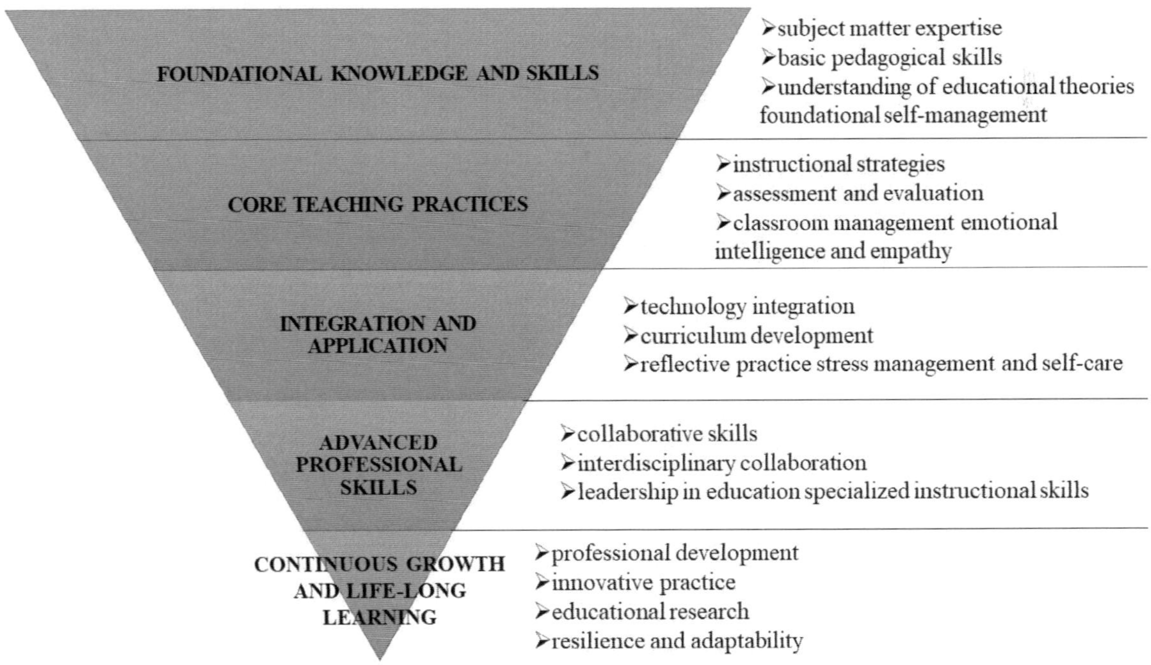

Figure 1: Hierarchical Pyramid. From The Paris Conference on Education 2024: Official Conference Proceedings, by R. Alasgarova & J. Rzayev, 2024b.

TPACK Framework for AI Integration

The TPACK framework provides a robust model for integrating AI into pedagogy. The integration should begin with relevant changes in educational policies, and its success of AI in education depends on how well teachers are prepared to use and critique these technologies. (Aljemely, 2024; Almasri, 2024; Selwyn, 2019; Wang et al., 2018).

The AI TPACK Model, as presented by Alasgarova and Rzayev (2024b), builds on the established TPACK framework by incorporating AI-specific competencies. The model explores how the integration of AI tools can intersect with pedagogical and content knowledge to enhance teaching practices (Figure 2).

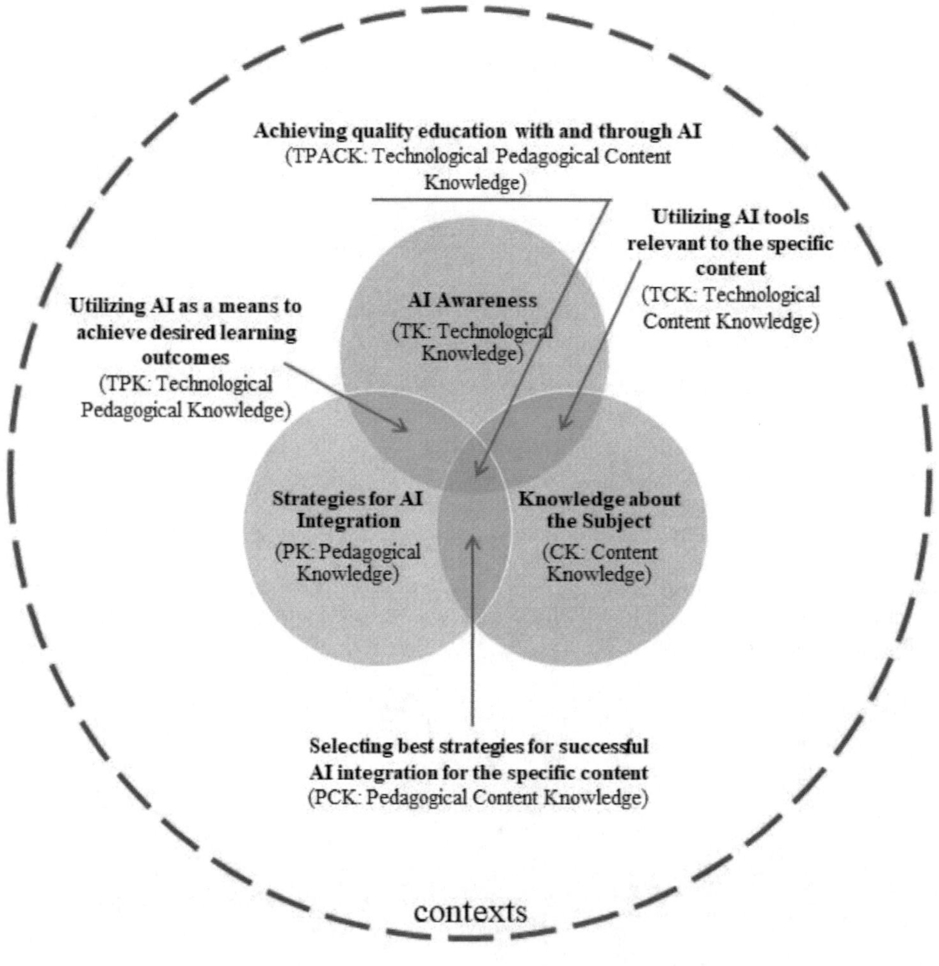

Figure 2: AI TPACK model. by R. Alasgarova & J. Rzayev, 2024b, Ubiquity Proceedings.

The emphasizes the need to align AI tools with pedagogical objectives and subject-specific content, providing a foundation for addressing the challenges and opportunities associated with AI adoption in teacher education. Wang et al. (2018) similarly argue that preservice teacher education programs should embed frameworks like TPACK to systematically develop technological and pedagogical competencies as they relate to emerging technologies such as AI.

UNESCO AI Competency Framework

The UNESCO AI Competency Framework for Teachers (2024) outlines three progression levels to guide educators in integrating AI effectively into educational settings. These levels scaffold teachers' competencies from foundational AI literacy to advanced innovation in AI-driven teaching practices. At the Acquire stage, educators develop basic knowledge of AI concepts, ethical considerations, and the use of AI tools in classrooms. The Deepen stage emphasizes integrating AI into pedagogical strategies to enhance creativity, personalize learning, and foster collaboration. Finally, the Create stage focuses on advanced competencies, enabling educators to innovate with AI tools, lead institutional AI integration, and address complex ethical issues.

This framework also emphasizes the importance of ethical considerations at every stage, ensuring that educators not only use AI tools effectively but also responsibly. The focus on collaboration and creativity highlights the transformative potential of AI in fostering dynamic and inclusive educational environments. As educators reach the advanced stages, the framework prepares them to take on leadership roles, advocating for and driving meaningful AI integration across their institutions ("AI Competency Framework for Teachers," 2024). However, research on the framework remains limited, as it was only introduced in 2024, leaving significant opportunities for further exploration and adaptation to diverse educational contexts.

Challenges and Barriers

Despite the potential of AI to enhance creativity, several challenges remain. Bae et al. (2024) identify barriers such as limited familiarity with AI tools among teacher-students and faculty, ethical concerns, and skepticism about reliability of AI systems. Addressing these challenges requires targeted training, access to resources, and ongoing professional development for faculty and students alike.

This study aims to address these challenges and contribute to the literature by exploring the following research questions:

Primary Research Question:

- How can teacher education programs teach creativity effectively to prepare teacher-students to become creative teachers, and how can AI tools support this process?

Secondary Research Questions:

1. Why is teaching creativity to teacher-students essential for their future roles as creative teachers?
2. How can AI tools, aligned with the AI TPACK Model and UNESCO AI Competency Framework, enhance creativity teaching in teacher education?
3. What are the key stages and components of a structured process for integrating creativity teaching and AI into teacher education programs, based on the Hierarchical Framework?

By drawing on relevant frameworks, such as the Hierarchical Pyramid, AI TPACK, and UNESCO AI Competency Framework, teacher education programs can equip future educators with the skills and tools needed to foster creativity in their classrooms. This study introduces a structured process to address barriers and provide practical strategies for integrating creativity and AI into teacher training, ensuring they become integral components of teacher education.

Methodology

This exploratory qualitative study investigated the perceptions and experiences of teacher-students and faculty regarding creativity and AI integration in three Azerbaijani pedagogical universities. These institutions were selected for their relevance to teacher education programs, where creativity and AI integration remain underexplored. The selection of a qualitative method is validated by its ability to explore in-depth perceptions and experiences (Creswell & Creswell, 2022).

Participants were selected through purposive sampling, comprising 15 BA teacher-students across various disciplines and academic years and six faculty members with over four years of teaching experience in pedagogy and methodology courses. Inclusion criteria required participants to be either enrolled in BA teacher education programs or actively teaching creativity-related or AI-focused courses. Ethical considerations included informed consent procedures, ensuring participants' anonymity, and maintaining confidentiality in line with APA 7 guidelines (American Psychological Association 7th Edition, 2019).

Data were collected through semi-structured interviews conducted online, lasting approximately 45 minutes. Semi-structured interviews were chosen for their flexibility and ability to capture detailed, context-rich data on participants' experiences and perceptions, aligning with qualitative research best practices (Cohen et al., 2017). The interviews were guided by a structured instrument adapted from the TPACK Assessment Instrument for Preservice Teachers (Schmidt et al., 2009), tailored for qualitative inquiry. Additional questions were developed to align with frameworks such as the Hierarchical Pyramid (Alasgarova & Rzayev, 2024a) and the UNESCO AI Competency Framework ("AI Competency Framework for Teachers," 2024). Expert feedback was sought to validate the adapted instrument. All interviews were recorded for transcription and analysis.

The data were analyzed using thematic analysis to identify patterns and framework analysis to align findings with theoretical models (Cohen et al., 2017). Qualitative analysis software Taguette was used to assist in coding and organizing the data (Rampin et al., n.d.).

Potential limitations include the reliance on self-reported data, a limited sample size, and time constraints. These were mitigated by diverse participant selection and triangulating data with multiple frameworks to enhance credibility.

Findings

Thematic analysis revealed three major themes aligned with the study objectives: (1) creativity training in teacher education, (2) the role of AI tools in fostering creativity, and (3) alignment with theoretical frameworks, including the Hierarchical Pyramid, AI TPACK, and the UNESCO AI Competency Framework. These themes were derived through an iterative coding process, where data segments were assigned codes reflecting key ideas. For clarity, teacher-students are coded as S (e.g., S1, S2) and teachers as T (e.g., T1, T2).

Creativity Training in Teacher Education

Teacher-Students

Teacher-students frequently described creativity as vital for teaching but noted a lack of formal training. The code "creativity as self-driven" emerged as students highlighted the absence of structured approaches in their coursework. One participant remarked, "Creativity is something I need to figure out on my own; there's no dedicated training" (S3). Another expressed a desire for more practical workshops, stating, "We need guidance on how to apply creative techniques in real classrooms" (S5).

Teachers

For teachers, the theme "personal initiative in creativity" was dominant. They reported embedding creativity into their teaching practices without formal support. One teacher explained, "I integrate open-ended tasks and encourage collaboration to foster creativity" (T2). However, the sub-code "institutional gaps in creativity training" highlighted the lack of professional development opportunities. As one teacher noted, "We're expected to teach creativity, but there's little guidance on how to do it effectively" (T4).

The Role of AI Tools in Fostering Creativity

Teacher-Students

The code "AI as a creativity enhancer" was prominent in teacher-students' responses, with many citing tools like ChatGPT and Canva as helpful for generating lesson ideas. One participant shared, "AI tools save time and give me fresh ideas for engaging content" (S7). However, ethical concerns emerged under the code "AI ethical uncertainty," with one student stating, "I'm not sure about the ethical implications of relying on AI for teaching" (S9).

Teachers

Teachers similarly recognized the utility of AI, with the code "AI as an efficiency tool" describing its role in streamlining routine tasks. One teacher explained, "AI allows me to focus on creative aspects by handling repetitive work" (T1). Yet, the theme "balancing AI and critical thinking" emerged as a concern. As one teacher observed, "We need to ensure students use AI responsibly without becoming dependent on it" (T5).

Alignment with Theoretical Frameworks

The thematic analysis reveals a shared recognition of creativity and AI tools as critical for modern education but highlights gaps in training and institutional support. Teacher-students reported foundational challenges in developing creativity and integrating AI into pedagogical practices, while teachers emphasized the need for ongoing professional development and institutional support to advance these competencies (Table 1).

Table 1: Framework-based analysis of teacher and teacher-student responses

Framework Component	Teacher-Students (S)	Teachers (T)
Hierarchical Pyramid	The code "stuck at foundational stage" reflected students' struggle to advance beyond basic knowledge (S8).	Teachers emphasized the need for ongoing professional development, captured under "progress through stages" (T3).
AI TPACK	Teacher-students noted difficulties integrating AI into content knowledge, highlighted under "disconnect between AI and pedagogy" (S4).	Teachers described the potential of AI TPACK but stressed the need for professional development to strengthen "technological-pedagogical alignment" (T2).
UNESCO AI Competency Framework	The theme "limited AI literacy" was prevalent, with students feeling unprepared to move beyond initial stages (S6).	Teachers identified a lack of institutional support for advancing from AI literacy to leadership ("institutional barriers") (T6).

Discussion

The findings of this study provide insights into how creativity and AI can be integrated into teacher education, revealing gaps in structured training and opportunities for innovation. These findings are examined through the interconnected lenses of the Hierarchical Pyramid, AI TPACK, and UNESCO AI Competency Framework, demonstrating how these frameworks collectively address the challenges and opportunities of fostering creativity and AI literacy in education.

Consistent with prior research, teacher-students emphasized the importance of creativity in teaching but reported a lack of formal training in their programs. This reflects broader trends identified by Simpson et al. (2022), who argue that structured interventions are necessary for developing creative teaching skills. Teachers, in contrast, described using personal strategies to foster creativity but acknowledged institutional gaps in professional development opportunities, aligning with Darling-Hammond (2006) and Trinter and Hughes (2021). The emphasis of the Hierarchical model on scaffolding creativity aligns with these findings, as both groups highlighted the need for systematic progression from foundational knowledge to advanced creative practices (Alasgarova & Rzayev, 2024a).

AI tools, such as Canva and ChatGPT, were recognized as valuable for enhancing creativity in teaching. Teacher-students reported using these tools to generate ideas and streamline lesson planning, which reflects the findings described by Liu et al. (2023) on the potential of AI-driven tools to foster creative self-efficacy. However, ethical concerns and over-reliance on AI emerged as significant barriers, echoing Bae et al. (2024). Teachers similarly noted the efficiency of AI tools but stressed the importance of balancing AI use with fostering students' critical thinking. The AI TPACK framework provides practical guidance here, which emphasizes the need to align technological tools with pedagogical and content knowledge to ensure meaningful and ethical integration.

The findings reveal how the Hierarchical Pyramid, UNESCO AI Competency Framework, and AI TPACK Model can work together to address gaps in creativity training and AI integration. For example, teacher-students' struggles with foundational creativity and AI skills reflect the Acquire stage of the UNESCO framework, the foundational level of the Hierarchical Pyramid, and the technological domain of AI TPACK (Alasgarova & Rzayev, 2024b). Teachers' emphasis on the need for professional development aligns with the focus of the Pyramid on lifelong learning and the Deepen and Create stages of UNESCO framework ("AI Competency Framework for Teachers," 2024). AI TPACK bridges these frameworks by operationalizing their principles, offering a roadmap for integrating AI tools into pedagogical practices while addressing ethical considerations.

Implications for Teacher Education

This study highlights the critical need for teacher education programs to adopt a unified and systematic approach to integrating creativity and AI tools. To address the gaps identified in the findings, this study proposes a Structured Process for Integrating Creativity Teaching and AI Tools (Figure 3). The structured process consists of five stages: assessing the current curriculum, introducing AI literacy, developing core creative pedagogies, fostering advanced professional skills, and evaluating implementation.

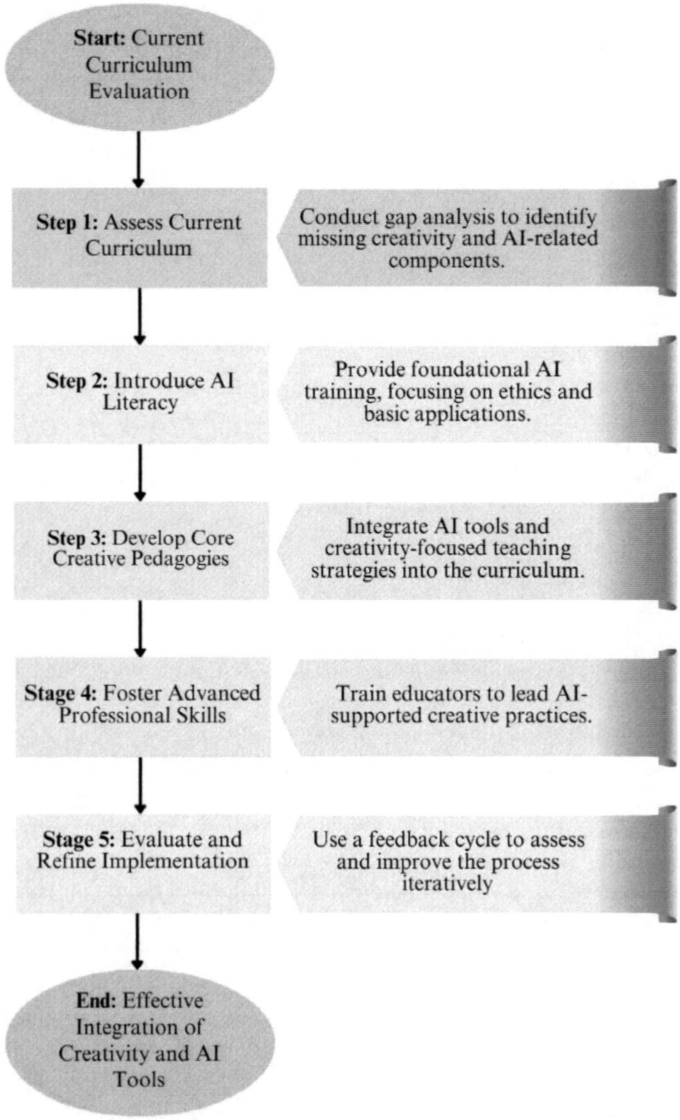

Figure 3: Structured Process for Integrating Creativity Teaching and AI Tools

This structured process aims to guide teacher education programs in fostering creativity and equipping future educators with the skills to integrate AI effectively into their teaching practices. It aligns theoretical frameworks with actionable strategies, ensuring that programs address both foundational and advanced competencies.

Conclusion

This study underscores the critical role of creativity in teacher education and the potential of AI tools to enhance both teaching and learning. The findings reveal significant gaps in current teacher education programs, i.e. the lack of structured training in creativity and AI literacy. While teacher-students rely on self-directed approaches to foster creativity, teachers take personal initiatives to incorporate creative strategies despite limited institutional support. Both groups recognize the utility of AI tools, yet concerns regarding ethical considerations and over-reliance highlight the need for careful integration into pedagogical practices.

Addressing these gaps requires a systematic and comprehensive approach. The proposed structured process offers a practical roadmap for integrating creativity teaching and AI tools into BA-level teacher education programs. By aligning with the Hierarchical Pyramid, AI TPACK, and UNESCO AI Competency Frameworks, this process ensures that teacher-students can progress from foundational competencies to advanced, innovative practices. Implementation of this process demands institutional commitment to curriculum redesign, professional development opportunities, and ongoing evaluation to ensure its effectiveness.

Despite these contributions, this study has limitations. The sample size was relatively small and limited to three Azerbaijani pedagogical universities, which may affect the generalizability of the findings. Additionally, reliance on self-reported data introduces potential biases (Creswell & Creswell, 2022). Future research could address these limitations by expanding the study to include a broader range of institutions and employing mixed-method approaches to validate findings.

Further research is also needed to explore the long-term impact of integrating creativity and AI tools into teacher education. Investigating the effectiveness of the proposed structured process in diverse educational contexts would provide valuable insights for refining its implementation. Exploring the intersection of creativity and emerging AI technologies, such as adaptive learning systems and AI-driven collaboration tools, could open new avenues for innovation in teacher education.

Ethics Statement

This study was conducted in accordance with the ethical principles outlined by the American Psychological Association's (APA) 7th Edition ethical guidelines. Prior to participation, all participants provided informed consent through signed consent forms. Their identities were anonymized, and all data were stored securely to ensure confidentiality.

References

AI competency framework for teachers. (2024). In UNESCO eBooks. https://doi.org/10.54675/zjte2084

Alasgarova R., & Rzayev J. (2024a) Evaluating Pedagogical University Preparation for Educators of Tomorrow ISSN: 2758-0962 The Paris Conference on Education 2024: Official Conference Proceedings (pp. 35-49) https://doi.org/10.22492/issn.2758-0962.2024.4

Alasgarova, R., & Rzayev, J. (2024b). The changing role of educators in the age of artificial intelligence: Molding minds at the digital dawn. Ubiquity Proceedings, 6. https://doi.org/10.5334/uproc.128

Aljemely, Y. (2024). Challenges and best practices in training teachers to utilize artificial intelligence: a systematic review. Frontiers in Education, 9. https://doi.org/10.3389/feduc.2024.1470853

Almasri, F. (2024). Exploring the Impact of Artificial intelligence in teaching and learning of Science: A Systematic Review of Empirical research. Research in Science Education, 54(5), 977–997. https://doi.org/10.1007/s11165-024-10176-3

American Psychological Association 7th Edition. (2019). Ethical principles of psychologists and code of conduct. American Psychological Association. https://www.apa.org/ethics/code

Bae, H., Hur, J., Park, J., Choi, G. W., & Moon, J. (2024). Pre-service Teachers' Dual Perspectives on Generative AI: Benefits, Challenges, and Integrating into Teaching and Learning. Online Learning, 28(3). https://doi.org/10.24059/olj.v28i3.4543

Bullard, A. J., & Bahar, A. K. (2023). Common barriers in teaching for creativity in K-12 classrooms: A literature review. Journal of Creativity, 33(1), 100045. https://doi.org/10.1016/j.yjoc.2023.100045

Cohen, L., Manion, L., & Morrison, K. (2017). Research methods in education (8th ed.). In Routledge eBooks. https://doi.org/10.4324/9781315456539

Creswell, J. W., & Creswell, J. D. (2022). Research design: Qualitative, quantitative and mixed methods approaches (6th ed.). SAGE.

Darling-Hammond, L. (2006). Constructing 21st-century teacher education. Journal of Teacher Education, 57(3), 300–314. https://doi.org/10.1177/0022487105285962

Liu, X., Gu, J., & Xu, J. (2023). The impact of the design thinking model on pre-service teachers' creativity self-efficacy, inventive problem-solving skills, and technology-related motivation. International Journal of Technology and Design Education, 34(1), 167–190. https://doi.org/10.1007/s10798-023-09809-x

Mishra, P., & Koehler, M. J. (2006). Technological Pedagogical Content Knowledge: A Framework for Teacher Knowledge. Teachers College Record, 108(6), 1017-1054. https://doi.org/10.1111/j.1467-9620.2006.00684.x

Moirano, R., Sánchez, M. A., & Štěpánek, L. (2019). Creative interdisciplinary collaboration: A systematic literature review. Thinking Skills and Creativity, 35, 100626. https://doi.org/10.1016/j.tsc.2019.100626

Rampin, R., Rampin, V., & DeMott, S. (n.d.). Taguette [Software]. https://www.taguette.org/

Schmidt, D. A., Baran, E., Thompson, A. D., Mishra, P., Koehler, M. J., & Shin, T. S. (2009). Technological Pedagogical Content Knowledge (TPACK). Journal of Research on Technology in Education, 42(2), 123–149. https://doi.org/10.1080/15391523.2009.10782544

Selwyn, N. (2019). Should robots replace teachers?: Ai and the Future of Education. Polity Press.

Simpson, R., Newton, D. P., & Newton, L. (2022). Developing creative teaching skills in Pre-Service teachers. International Journal for Talent Development and Creativity, 10(1–2), 163–178. https://doi.org/10.7202/1099950ar

Trinter, C. P., & Hughes, H. E. (2021). Teachers as curriculum designers: Inviting teachers into the productive struggle. RMLE Online, 44(3), 1–16. https://doi.org/10.1080/19404476.2021.1878417

Wang, W., Schmidt-Crawford, D., & Jin, Y. (2018). Preservice Teachers' TPACK Development: A Review of literature. Journal of Digital Learning in Teacher Education, 34(4), 234–258. https://doi.org/10.1080/21532974.2018.1498039

Artificial Intelligence and Large Language Models in Higher Education: Results of a Systematic Review

Thomas Leitgeb[1], Michael Leitgeb[2]

[1] Centre for Digital Education and STEAM, University College of Teacher Education, Austria; thomas.leitgeb@ph-burgenland.at
[2] Centre for Digital Education and STEAM, University College of Teacher Education, Austria; michael.leitgeb@ph-burgenland.at

Correspondence: Thomas Leitgeb: thomas.leitgeb@ph-burgenland.at

Abstract:

Artificial Intelligence (AI)—especially Large Language Models (LLMs)—has become increasingly important in higher education, offering applications ranging from personalized learning paths to administrative process automation. Despite these advancements, there is a clear need for integrative frameworks that address both technical efficiency and ethical standards, particularly in data-sensitive academic contexts. This paper presents findings from a systematic literature review of 111 relevant studies (2014–2024) identified in Web of Science, Scopus, and Google Scholar. Guided by PRISMA methodology, we synthesized the potential benefits (e.g., adaptive feedback, administrative automation) and significant challenges (e.g., privacy issues, algorithmic bias, lack of model explainability). We propose three essential pillars for responsible and effective AI integration in higher education:

1. Institution-owned AI systems to ensure robust data governance,
2. Continually updated policy guidelines emphasizing transparency and academic integrity, and
3. High-quality professional development for faculty to build both technical and ethical capacities.

Our findings underscore the need for holistic approaches that unite technical innovation with ethical accountability, thus facilitating sustainable, equitable, and data-protective AI adoption in universities. The conclusions and recommendations presented here provide a practical roadmap for institutions seeking to optimize learning processes while maintaining the highest standards of fairness and privacy.

Keywords: Artificial Intelligence in Higher Education, Systematic Literature Review, Large Langauge Models

1. Introduction

Artificial Intelligence (AI) has undergone a significant surge in importance within higher education, transforming teaching, learning, and institutional operations (Kasneci et al., 2023). Large Language Models (LLMs), including chatbots capable of generating human-like text, offer new possibilities for creating adaptive learning environments and automating assessments. However, empirical evidence suggests that many institutions still struggle to balance these tools' technical potential with stringent ethical and legal requirements (Vincent-Lancrin & Vlies, 2020).

The question of how to implement AI in higher education in a manner that prioritizes fairness, privacy, and transparency remains underexplored (Holmes et al., 2019). While existing literature points to broad trends—such as AI-based predictive systems for academic performance and the personalization of learning materials (Zawacki-Richter et al., 2019)—few studies provide an integrative perspective encompassing both the technical and ethical dimensions. Thus, this paper seeks to contribute to "Empowering Inclusion, Innovation and Ethical Growth" by presenting results of a comprehensive review that addresses the following research question:

How can AI systems—particularly LLMs—be designed and implemented in higher education to improve learning processes while ensuring technical efficiency and compliance with ethical standards, such as data protection and fairness?

2. Theoretical Background and Research Gaps

Early work on AI in education often centered on discrete technical gains—e.g., improved predictive models or more automated grading—without considering the broader context of data privacy, fairness, or user acceptance (Selwyn, 2019). Meanwhile, ethical concerns about bias, transparency, and accountability have garnered increased attention (Floridi & Cowls, 2019).

Despite a variety of systematic reviews (Zawacki-Richter et al., 2019; Crompton & Burke, 2023; Chu et al., 2022) and domain-specific investigations (e.g., chatbots in language learning; Fryer et al., 2019), several gaps persist:

1. **Holistic Approaches**

   Existing studies rarely integrate technical efficiency (e.g., accuracy, reliability) with stringent ethical concerns (e.g., privacy, equity).

2. **Concrete Mitigation of AI Challenges**

   Issues such as "hallucinations" in LLMs (Valentin et al., 2024) and the "black box" nature of advanced AI models (Lipton, 2018) require targeted solutions.

3. **Privacy Solutions in Institutional Contexts**

   Few sources provide actionable strategies for implementing data protection measures that comply with, for instance, the General Data Protection Regulation (GDPR).

4. **Bias Avoidance**

   Systematic distortions in datasets and models risk reinforcing social inequities (Baker & Hawn, 2022; Omughelli et al., 2024). Few studies offer institution-level frameworks to detect and mitigate algorithmic biases.

These gaps underline the urgent need for integrative research that combines technical and ethical dimensions to build trust in AI systems (Drachsler & Greller, 2016).

3. Methodology

3.1 PRISMA-Based Systematic Review

We conducted a systematic literature search following the PRISMA guidelines (PRISMA, 2020). Searches were carried out in September 2024 in three databases: Web of Science, Scopus, and Google Scholar. We focused on the period 2014–2024 to capture recent trends and included only English- and German-language publications pertinent to higher education and AI/LLM applications.

Search Strings and Selection

- Combined Boolean operators (e.g., "AI" AND "Higher Education" AND "Data Privacy")
- Yielded 1,946 initial results (845 from Web of Science, 367 from Scopus, 734 from Google Scholar)
- After removing duplicates, 467 records remained

Studies were retained only if they explicitly addressed AI or LLM applications in higher education and provided empirical or theoretical insights relevant to data protection, bias, explainability, or technical integration.

3.2 Qualitative Content Analysis

We adopted an inductive–deductive scheme (Mayring, 2015) to categorize the final pool of 111 articles. Core categories included:

1. **Potentials of AI and LLMs** (personalized learning, automated assessment)
2. **Challenges** (data quality, resource requirements)
3. **Ethical Implications** (data protection, bias)
4. **Recommended Measures** (guidelines, professional development, institutional AI systems)

Intercoder reliability was established through iterative review of coding procedures, ensuring consistent interpretation.

4. Findings

4.1 Potential of AI and LLMs in Higher Education

4.1.1 Personalized Learning

Adaptive learning models guided by LLMs enable real-time student profiling and customized feedback (Wen et al., 2024; Ng & Fung, 2024). For instance, GPT-4–driven course management systems can dynamically suggest tasks aligned with individual performance data (Zawacki-Richter et al., 2019). Empirical studies point to increased student motivation, especially when LLM-based platforms adapt content difficulty in real time (Suresh & Misra, 2024).

4.1.2 Efficiency Gains

AI-based automation can expedite administrative tasks (Abimbola et al., 2024) and reduce manual grading workloads (Larondo et al., 2024). LLMs employed in intelligent tutoring systems also generate personalized feedback—improving student outcomes while freeing academic staff for more in-depth pedagogical engagement (Stamper et al., 2024).

4.1.3 Innovative Teaching Methods

Chatbots—such as Jill Watson at Georgia Tech—showcase how AI can offer immediate guidance and address common queries at scale (Taneja et al., 2024). In language-learning contexts, chatbots can serve as conversational partners, fueling interest and skill development (Fryer et al., 2019). Studies also confirm a positive correlation between adaptive chatbot usage and learners' self-reported critical thinking (Ali et al., 2024).

4.2 Challenges

4.2.1 Data Quality and Infrastructure

Machine learning outcomes heavily depend on comprehensive, high-quality datasets (Budach et al., 2022). Institutions lacking sufficient resources or infrastructure may face suboptimal model performance, hampering broad access to AI's pedagogical benefits (Li, 2023). Additionally, advanced AI systems consume substantial energy, raising sustainability concerns (Strubell et al., 2019).

4.2.2 Algorithmic Bias

Systemic biases in training data risk perpetuating social inequities (Baker & Hawn, 2022). In educational contexts, biased models can influence admission decisions or academic performance predictions, undercutting equal opportunities for students (Omughelli et al., 2024). Tools for bias detection and mitigation are critical but often underutilized (Pagano et al., 2023).

4.2.3 Privacy and Security

Compliance with GDPR and other data-protection laws is a key institutional barrier (Drachsler & Greller, 2016). The large-scale processing of sensitive student data raises serious confidentiality questions. A single breach can deeply undermine trust in AI, thereby stalling further integration (Slade & Prinsloo, 2013).

4.3 Ethical Implications

Data Protection: The broad adoption of LLMs in universities magnifies data privacy risks. Systems must incorporate encryption and anonymization to safeguard student information (Singhal, 2024).
Transparency: The "black box" nature of deep learning raises accountability challenges, prompting calls for explainable AI (XAI) frameworks (Chaudhary, 2024).
Fairness and Inclusion: Ongoing audits are required to detect and correct algorithmic discrimination (Chinta et al., 2024).

4.4 Recommended Measures

Institution-Owned AI Systems: Developing and hosting AI solutions on institutional servers allows universities to maintain end-to-end control over data flows (Drachsler & Greller, 2016). This approach mitigates privacy concerns, ensures alignment with university-specific requirements, and lessens reliance on external vendors (Bai et al., 2024).
Continually Updated Guidelines: Rapid advancements in LLM and generative AI necessitate dynamic policy environments. Institutions should define clear usage policies—covering data collection, permissible scope of AI-based assessments, and intellectual property—reviewing and revising them regularly (Leitgeb et al., 2024).
Comprehensive Professional Development: Teachers require both technical (ML concepts, platform usage) and ethical–pedagogical training (fairness, bias detection, data responsibility) to integrate AI effectively

(Brandão et al., 2024). Long-term professionalization fosters sustainable AI adoption and helps navigate moral dilemmas posed by advanced automation.

5. Discussion

By synthesizing 111 studies, this review provides evidence that AI—particularly LLMs—can advance higher education through greater personalization, enhanced efficiency, and novel teaching approaches. However, to avoid the pitfalls of algorithmic bias, data breaches, and unsustainable resource usage, institutions must embed AI solutions within robust ethical and regulatory frameworks.

Our analysis supports the notion that universities should take deliberate steps—owning AI infrastructures, establishing dynamic guidelines, and emphasizing human-centered professional development—if they hope to harness AI responsibly (Holmes et al., 2019).

Limitations

1. **Study Heterogeneity**: Our sources vary widely in methodology and focus, limiting strict comparability of results.
2. **Underrepresentation of Long-Term Outcomes**: Empirical data on the sustained impacts of AI tools remain scarce.
3. **Insufficient Cost–Benefit Analysis**: Financial constraints faced by smaller institutions or developing regions are underexplored.

6. Conclusion

This systematic review demonstrates that AI and LLMs can revolutionize learning experiences, streamline administrative tasks, and foster dynamic pedagogical innovations in higher education. Nonetheless, harnessing these advantages requires carefully balancing technical robustness with ethical oversight. We propose three foundational pillars for institutions:

1. **Adopt Institution-Specific AI Systems**: Enhance privacy protection and adapt solutions to local needs.
2. **Implement Evolving Guidelines**: Ensure academic integrity, legal compliance, and transparent governance structures.
3. **Invest in Professional Development**: Equip educators with the technical and ethical competencies necessary to implement AI responsibly.

Future research should include longitudinal studies to investigate the sustained efficacy of AI in higher education, deeper cost–benefit analyses, and more detailed strategies for mitigating bias. By employing these strategies, universities can cultivate an environment where AI technologies enrich teaching and learning while upholding fairness, transparency, and accountability—key elements in realizing a future guided by "Empowering Inclusion, Innovation and Ethical Growth."

References

Baker, R. S., & Hawn, A. (2022). Algorithmic bias in education. International Journal of Artificial Intelligence in Education, 31(4), 595–626.

Crompton, H., & Burke, D. (2023). Artificial intelligence in higher education: The state of the field. International Journal of Educational Technology in Higher Education, 20, 22.

Drachsler, H., & Greller, W. (2016). Privacy and analytics: It's a DELICATE issue. In Proceedings of the Sixth International Conference on Learning Analytics & Knowledge (pp. 89–98).

Holmes, W., Bialik, M., & Fadel, C. (2019). Artificial intelligence in education: Promises and implications for teaching and learning. Center for Curriculum Redesign.

Kasneci, E., Sessler, K., Kasneci, G., & Seidel, T. (2023). ChatGPT for good? On opportunities and challenges of large language models for education. Learning and Individual Differences, 103, 102274.

Leitgeb, T., Maitz, K., Sitter, G., Matischek-Jauk, M., Mößlacher, C., et al. (2024). KI-Leitlinien für den PH-Verbund Süd-Ost – Leitlinien für die Nutzung von Künstlicher Intelligenz in der Hochschule. University College of Teacher Education Burgenland, Eisenstadt. https://doi.org/10.5281/zenodo.13638314

Mayring, P. (2015). Qualitative Inhaltsanalyse: Grundlagen und Techniken (12. Aufl.). Beltz.

Ng, C., & Fung, Y. (2024). Educational Personalized Learning Path Planning with Large Language Models. Retrieved from https://arxiv.org/abs/2407.11773

Omughelli, D., Gordon, N., & Al Jaber, T. (2024). Fairness, bias, and ethics in AI: Exploring the factors affecting student performance. Journal of Intelligent Communication, 4(1), 100–110.

PRISMA. (2020). Preferred Reporting Items for Systematic Reviews and Meta-Analyses. http://www.prisma-statement.org/

Suresh, S., & Misra, S. M. (2024). Large Language Models in Pediatric Education: Current Uses and Future Potential. Pediatrics, 154(3), e2023064683.

Vincent-Lancrin, S., & van der Vlies, R. (2020). Trustworthy artificial intelligence (AI) in education: Promises and challenges. OECD Education Working Papers, No. 218.

Wen, Q., Liang, J., Sierra, C., Luckin, R., Tong, R., Liu, Z., Cui, P., & Tang, J. (2024). AI for education (AI4EDU): Advancing personalized education with LLM and adaptive learning. https://doi.org/10.1145/3637528.3671498

Zawacki-Richter, O., Marín, V. I., Bond, M., & Gouverneur, F. (2019). Systematic review of research on artificial intelligence applications in higher education—Where are the educators? International Journal of Educational Technology in Higher Education, 16(1), 39.

Between Technical Assistance and Authorship: Researchers' Ethical considerations of Using Generative AI for Scientific Writing

Hagit Meishar-Tal[1]

[1]Faculty of Instructional technologies, Holon Institute of Technology, Israel; hagitmt@hit.ac.il

Correspondence: Hagit Meishar-Tal: hagitmt@hit.ac.il

Abstract:

Scientific writing is essential for sharing research findings, yet it poses significant challenges due to the need for precision, clarity, and adherence to strict standards. Generative AI (GenAI) tools, such as ChatGPT, have emerged as potential aid in this process, offering capabilities in linguistic editing, translation, and summarization. However, the integration of GenAI in academic writing raises ethical concerns regarding plagiarism, data fabrication, authorship and the preservation of the researcher's original voice. This study empirically investigates researchers' ethical considerations regarding the use of generative AI in scientific writing. Through a survey of 102 researchers and research students in Israeli academia, the study explores the perceived ethical boundaries and conditions for appropriate GenAI use. Findings indicate that while GenAI can be beneficial for technical tasks, its role in content creation remains contentious. Transparency, critical evaluation of GenAI outputs, and maintaining originality are highlighted as essential conditions for ethical AI integration.

Keywords: ethics, ChatGPT, generative AI, academic writing, scientific writing

Introduction

Scientific writing is crucial for researchers to share their knowledge but poses challenges due to the need for precision, clarity, and adherence to strict standards. Generative AI (GenAI) tools, which became accessible to the public in 2022, can assist with various writing tasks, potentially saving time. However, these tools are not always reliable and require careful review by researchers. Additionally, scientific writing must follow strict ethical guidelines, which GenAI usage can complicate. Most of the literature on ethical considerations of Using GenAI for Scientific Writing is theoretical or based on researchers own experience. This study empirically explores researchers' ethical considerations regarding the appropriate use of these tools.

Literature review

Scientific writing

Scientific writing is essential in academia and research as it facilitates communication, sharing of findings, and advancement of collective knowledge (Sengupta et al., 2014; Somashekhar,2020). It demands precision, systematicity, and objectivity, adhering to strict structural and design rules (Alley, 1996; Gopen & Swan, 1990). Typically, scientific articles are structured to include an abstract, introduction, literature review, methodology, results, discussion, and conclusions, allowing readers to follow the research logically (Grimm & Harvey, 2022; Sengupta et al., 2014).

Writing a literature review is a fundamental aspect of scientific writing, requiring a review of large volumes of sources and integration of key ideas to present the state of research and address gaps relative to previous studies (Webster & Watson, 2002; Steward, 2004). This task should reflect the author's voice through language, connections, evaluations of previous sources, and presentation of insights (Mhilli, 2023).

Detailed documentation of information sources is crucial, as every claim must be backed by reliable references, enhancing the review's credibility and allowing readers to verify the information (Grimm & Harvey, 2022;

Sengupta et al., 2014). Scientific writing also includes critical analysis and interpretation of findings, relating them to the literature review, considering alternative explanations, and discussing implications for theory and the field (Hasemi et al., 2019).

The challenge of academic writing is particularly complex for advanced research students who often lack sufficient guidance and support in acquiring academic writing skills (Gupta et al., 2022). Non-native English writers face additional difficulties in expressing deep ideas and avoiding grammatical errors, which can affect their confidence and professional identity (Gupta et al., 2022; Hadan et al., 2024).

Integrating GenAI in Academic Writing

GenAI applications like ChatGPT and Claude have been adopted by many researchers to improve and streamline academic writing tasks (Khalifa & Albadawy, 2024). GenAI has proven effective for tasks such as phrasing, proofreading, and linguistic editing (Altmäe rt al., 2023; Semrl et al, 2023), particularly for non-native English speakers looking to publish in English journals (Golan et al., 2023; Hutson, 2022; Giglio & Costa, 2023; Hwang et al., 2023; Ingley & Pack, 2024). However, maximizing AI-generated writing outputs requires precise instructions and effective integration, which can be challenging for those not fluent in English (Warschauer et al., 2023).

GenAI tools are also helpful in planning literature reviews, creating titles, organizing, and suggesting outlines, as well as writing abstracts, introductions, and summaries (Aydın et al., 2022; Hutson, 2022). However, for actual literature review content, these tools often produce superficial and inaccurate information, with instances of AI-generated "hallucinations" presenting fabricated information and references (Athaluri et al., 2023; Zheng & Zhan, 2023). Thus, these tools are considered unreliable for this purpose.

ChatGPT and similar tools improve users' performance by enabling them to produce high-quality outputs without needing extensive skills or knowledge (Meishar-Tal, 2024). Users must have enough expertise to critically evaluate the AI-generated content and not rely on it blindly (Bozkurt, 2024). Researchers also express their concern that using ChatGPT for academic writing by students will harm their critical thinking and will encourage "shortcuts" (Meishar-Tal, 2024; Weimann-Sandig, 2023).

Ingley and Pack (2024) advocate using GenAI tools interactively to enhance writing by providing feedback on self-written text. They suggest using these tools as advisors throughout the writing process, from selecting a research topic to proofreading. This approach is effective and responsible, empowering authors and improving their writing quality.

Ethical Issues in Integrating GenAI in Scientific Writing

Adhering to ethical standards is crucial in scientific writing (Vargas, 2019). Researchers must avoid data fabrication, falsification, and plagiarism (Carver et al., 2011). The use of GenAI increases the risk of plagiarism, as researchers lack information about the sources the GenAI tool relies on and are also exposed to AI hallucinations (Hwang et al., 2023; Salimi & Saheb, 2023; Zheng & Zhan, 2023).

Moreover, GenAI models are typically trained on public web pages, databases like Wikipedia and news sites, not on peer-reviewed academic articles. These sources contain biases and inaccuracies, making them unsuitable for academic writing. Researchers must critically evaluate AI-generated information, ensuring its reliability and tracing its sources to avoid scientific integrity violations (Hacker, 2024).

Additionally, GenAI poses ethical challenges of authorship and ownership, in relation to copyright laws and AI-generated content (Bozkurt, 2024). Referencing to GenAI tools as information sources is not accepted in the academic community (Guleria et al., 2023). They cannot be cited or included as authors, although some attempts have been made to publish articles written by ChatGPT (Stokel-Walker, 2023).

Detecting GenAI use in academic articles is nearly impossible (Hadan et al., 2024; Homolak, 2023). Nonetheless, addressing ethical issues, and transparency about the use of GenAI tools is required. Authors should declare the tools used and how they were utilized (Guleria et al., 2023). The number of journals requiring such declarations is growing, shifting full responsibility for the content to the authors (Salimi & Saheb, 2023; Tang, 2023; Draxler et al., 2024).

Methodology

This study is part of a larger research project examining the attitudes of academic researchers toward the use of GenAI for research and scientific writing. The study is based on a questionnaire distributed among researchers and research students in academia in Israel, examining the characteristics of use, dependency perception, and ethical perceptions of researchers using GenAI tools in their research work, with an emphasis on academic writing.

The study includes researchers and research students in the Israeli academia who have experience using generative GenAI for academic writing and research purposes. A total of 111 respondents completed the questionnaire. However, 9 respondents were excluded because their questionnaires indicated no use of GenAI for academic writing and research, resulting in 102 valid questionnaires for the study.The average age of the participants was 50.6 years (SD = 11.7), with 59 women and 43 men.

In the questionnaire, participants were asked an open-ended question: "What is your ethical stance on using GenAI tools for scientific writing?". Eighty-five participants answered this question. The respondents' answers were analyzed using inductive thematic analysis based on a content analysis approach (Braun & Clarke, 2006).

The analysis process involved several steps: initially, all responses were thoroughly reviewed to familiarize with the content and identify initial themes. The data were then divided into meaningful segments, each labeled with a descriptive code. These codes were grouped into central thematic themes, reflecting the main topics. The themes were repeatedly reviewed to ensure accurate representation of the data.

Findings

The findings regarding ethical attitudes of researchers towards using GenAI for academic writing can be divided into two aspects:

1. Types of appropriate and inappropriate Actions
2. Conditions for Proper Use of GenAI

Types of ethical and unethical Actions

The actions perceived by respondents as appropriate are those considered "technical actions." First and foremost are actions related to linguistic editing and translation. Regarding these actions, there was broad agreement that they are acceptable, as reflected in the following quotes: "If the tool helps in phrasing, it's fine. It's like a professional performing proofreading."

Additional uses perceived as "technical" include bibliographic listing, information source search, summarization, and translation. Examples of this can be found in the following quotes:

> "For bibliographic listing, it's a technical matter, and there's no objection."
>
> "I support using these tools in technical ways for locating sources, summarizing, and translating."
>
> "As a tool for processing information, summarizing, and translating, especially for those who are not native English speakers, there is no issue."
>
> "It is legitimate to use it as a research assistant, particularly for the technical work of searching for citations, summarizing, and translating."

Another research activity perceived as legitimate and appropriate is consulting with AI: "As long as it is at the consultation and brainstorming stage with the system and not actual writing at the copy-paste level, it is fine, in my opinion."

Conversely, actions mentioned as inappropriate and unacceptable mainly relate to content writing. One respondent stated: "I think it is permissible regarding finding materials but less so for actual writing." Another respondent noted that they are "against the model adding substantial content to the work, including the writing stage itself." The following quote clarifies the fine line between usage for phrasing improvement and content writing: "Helping with phrasing is possible, writing in place of it is bad." It should be noted that not all respondents see content writing itself as an illegitimate action but set conditions for relying on content generated by GenAI, as presented in the following section.

Given the awareness of AI's ability to fabricate information, data fabrication was mentioned as an action perceived as ethically unacceptable in academic writing: "[As long as] the user did not ask AI to invent results or data [the use is legitimate]."

Conditions for Ethical Use of GenAI

In addition to actions perceived by respondents as appropriate or inappropriate for GenAI, the respondents presented the conditions necessary to rely on GenAI for academic writing and research.

The first and most common condition raised by respondents is transparency. Respondents argued that for their use of GenAI tools to be legitimate, they must disclose the use: "It is necessary to declare the use of it". Transparency is not just a matter of academic integrity but also a requirement of journals. Therefore, one respondent stated: "It is essential to check the position of the journal to which the article is intended to be submitted and to disclose where necessary."

Another condition raised by respondents is the overall responsibility of the researcher for appropriate use of GenAI. According to this view, AI is merely an assistive tool, and the researcher must take responsibility for the process and the outputs. Responsibility is seen as "leading" the process, as expressed in the following quote: "I will not let AI tools lead the writing. I will use it only as an aid to writing." AI is seen as a "personal assistant": "AI is like my personal assistant. I must lead, know what I want, and review".

This responsibility is expressed in critically examining the texts generated by GenAI. Criticism can be based on self-checking, as claimed by the researchers: "It requires the researcher to review and verify the reliability of the AI tool's insights. You cannot rely on the tool without supervision." Another way to checking AI is by cross-referencing sources: "Everything written with AI assistance is checked through at least one additional external source until a genuinely reliable version is achieved."

Another condition emerging from the findings is maintaining originality and expressing the researcher's voice throughout the research process. Respondents argued that proper use must ensure that researcher's personal contribution remains original, and this should be evident already at the idea stage: "It is not appropriate for generating ideas that are supposed to be original."

The responsibility for originality does not end at the idea stage; it must be maintained throughout the research, including analysis, discussion, and conclusions. Therefore, "using them to write full scientific outputs such as research proposals or articles is not ethical since the conceptual and analytical contribution must be personal."

Discussion

The findings of this study reveal a nuanced perspective among researchers regarding the use of GenAI tools in academic writing. Many researchers consider the use of GenAI for technical tasks, such as linguistic editing, translation, bibliographic listing, information source search, summarization, and statistical analysis, to be ethically acceptable. These tasks are viewed as supportive, not replacing the core intellectual contributions of the researcher.

The findings support previous studies that claim GenAI tools offer significant benefits for non-native English speakers (Golan et al., 2023; Hutson, 2022; Giglio & Costa, 2023; Hwang et al., 2023; Ingley & Pack, 2024). Israeli researchers whose native language is Hebrew can benefit from GenAI, which helps improving their written expression and thus reduces linguistic barriers in academic publishing. However, these researchers must still ensure that AI-generated text is critically reviewed and appropriately integrated into their work.

Transparency in the use of GenAI is also deemed crucial, with researchers agreeing that disclosing the use of these tools in the research and writing process is essential to maintain academic integrity. This aligns with the growing trend of journals requiring such declarations, highlighting the increasing importance of transparency (Salimi & Saheb, 2023; Tang, 2023; Draxler et al., 2024).

However, there is a consensus among researchers that relying on GenAI for actual content creation, such as writing the main text, generating ideas, or drawing conclusions, may be ethically problematic. Over-reliance on

GenAI for idea generation and content creation might undermine the unique insights and critical analysis that define scholarly work (Weimann-Sandig, 2023). Nonetheless, researchers do not entirely dismiss the use of GenAI for content creation but propose conditions that limit and scrutinize its use. According to the researchers, such actions are permissible as long as there is critical review of AI-generated content, verification of its accuracy, and assurance of its alignment with ethical standards.

Researchers agree that the responsibility for maintaining the quality and reliability of the research lies with the human researcher. Preserving the originality of the researcher's contributions and the expression of their personal voice is crucial. However, it seems that the balance between ethical and unethical use of GenAI is very delicate, and keeping the fine line between the two is challenging

Conclusion

The use of GenAI in scientific writing is contentious. While some see it as a valuable tool for enhancing writing performance, others worry about its potential to impair value of mastering scientific writing and critical thinking skills. These findings underscore the need to balance the potential benefits of GenAI for technical support with the imperative to maintain the intellectual integrity and ethical standards of scholarly work, and highlights the need for ongoing dialogue and the development of comprehensive ethical frameworks to navigate the evolving landscape of AI-assisted scientific writing.

Competing interests

The author has no competing interests to declare.

Ethics and consent

The research was approved by the Instructional Technologies faculty's ethical committee at Holon Institute of Technology.

References

Alley, M. (1996). The craft of scientific writing. New York: Springer.

Athaluri, S. A., Manthena, S. V., Kesapragada, V. S. R. K. M., Yarlagadda, V., Dave, T., & Duddumpudi, R. T. S. (2023). Exploring the boundaries of reality: Investigating the phenomenon of artificial intelligence hallucination in scientific writing through ChatGPT references. Cureus, 15(4), e37432. https://doi.org/10.7759/cureus.37432.

Altmäe, S., Sola-Leyva, A., & Salumets, A. (2023). Artificial intelligence in scientific writing: A friend or a foe?. Reproductive BioMedicine Online, 47(1), 3-9. https://doi.org/10.1016/j.rbmo.2023.04.009

Aydın, Ö., & Karaarslan, E. (2022). OpenAI ChatGPT Generated Literature Review: Digital Twin in Healthcare. In Ö. Aydın (Ed.), Emerging Computer Technologies (Vol. 2, pp. 22-31). İzmir Akademi Derneği. Available at SSRN: https://ssrn.com/abstract=4308687 or http://dx.doi.org/10.2139/ssrn.4308687

Bozkurt, A. (2024). GenAI et al. Co-creation, authorship, ownership, academic ethics, and integrity in a time of generative AI. Open Praxis, 16(1), 1-10. https://doi.org/10.55982/openpraxis.16.1.654

Braun, V., & Clarke, V. (2006). Using thematic analysis in psychology. Qualitative Research in Psychology, 3(2), 77-101. https://doi.org/10.1191/1478088706qp063oa

Carver, J. D., Dellva, B., Emmanuel, P. J., & Parchure, R. (2011). Ethical considerations in scientific writing. Indian Journal of Sexually Transmitted Diseases and AIDS, 32(2), 124-128. https://doi.org/10.4103/0253-7184.85425.

Draxler, F., Werner, A., Lehmann, F., Hoppe, M., Schmidt, A., Buschek, D., & Welsch, R. (2023). The AI ghostwriter effect: When users do not perceive ownership of AI-generated text but self-declare as authors. ACM Transactions on Computer-Human Interaction, 3637875. https://doi.org/10.1145/3637875.

Giglio, A. D., & Costa, M. U. P. D. (2023). The use of artificial intelligence to improve the scientific writing of non-native English speakers. Revista da Associação Médica Brasileira, 69(9), e20230560.

Golan, R., Reddy, R., Muthigi, A., et al. (2023). Artificial intelligence in academic writing: A paradigm-shifting technological advance. Nature Review Urology, 20, 327–328. https://doi.org/10.1038/s41585-023-00746-x.

Gopen, G. D., & Swan, J. A. (1990). The science of scientific writing. American Scientist, 78(6), 550-558. https://www.americanscientist.org/blog/the-long-view/the-science-of-scientific-writing

Grimm, L. J., & Harvey, J. A. (2022). Practical steps to writing a scientific manuscript. Journal of Breast Imaging, 4(6), 640-648. https://doi.org/10.1093/jbi/wbac059.

Gupta, S., Jaiswal, A., Paramasivam, A., & Kotecha, J. (2022). Academic writing challenges and supports: Perspectives of international doctoral students and their supervisors. Frontiers in Education, 7, 891534. https://doi.org/10.3389/feduc.2022.891534.

Guleria, A., Krishan, K., Sharma, V., & Kanchan, T. (2023). ChatGPT: ethical concerns and challenges in academics and research. The Journal of Infection in Developing Countries, 17(09), 1292-1299. https://doi.org/10.3855/jidc.18738

Hadan, H., Wang, D., Mogavi, R. H., Tu, J., Zhang-Kennedy, L., & Nacke, L. E. (2024). The great AI witch hunt: Reviewers' perception and (mis)conception of generative AI in research writing. arXiv preprint arXiv:2407.12015.

Hacker, P., Mittelstadt, B., Borgesius, F. Z., & Wachter, S. (2024). Generative Discrimination: What Happens When Generative AI Exhibits Bias, and What Can Be Done About It. arXiv preprint arXiv:2407.10329.

Hasemi, A., Bahadoran, Z., Mirmiran, P., Hosseinpanah, F., & Shiva, N. (2019). The principles of biomedical scientific writing: Discussion. International Journal of Endocrinology and Metabolism, 17(3), e95415. https://doi.org/10.5812/ijem.95415.

Homolak, J. (2023). Exploring the adoption of ChatGPT in academic publishing: Insights and lessons for scientific writing. Croatian Medical Journal, 64(3), 205-207. https://doi.org/10.3325/cmj.2023.64.205.

Hutson, M. (2022). Could AI help you to write your next paper? Nature, 611(7934), 192-193.

Hwang, S. I., Lim, J. S., Lee, R. W., Matsui, Y., Iguchi, T., Hiraki, T., & Ahn, H. (2023). Is ChatGPT a "fire of Prometheus" for non-native English-speaking researchers in academic writing? Korean Journal of Radiology, 24(10), 952-959. https://doi.org/10.3348/kjr.2023.0773.

Ingley, S. J., & Pack, A. (2023). Leveraging AI tools to develop the writer rather than the writing. Trends in Ecology & Evolution, 38(9), 785-787. https://doi.org/10.1016/j.tree.2023.05.007

Meishar-Tal, H. (2024). ChatGPT: The challenges it presents for writing assignments. TechTrends, 68, 705–710. https://doi.org/10.1007/s11528-024-00972-z.

Mhilli, O. (2023). Authorial voice in writing: A literature review. Social Sciences & Humanities Open, 8(1), 100550. https://doi.org/10.1016/j.ssaho.2023.100550

Salimi, A., & Saheb, H. (2023). Large language models in ophthalmology scientific writing: Ethical considerations blurred lines or not at all? American Journal of Ophthalmology, 254, 177-181.

Sengupta, S., Shukla, D., Ramulu, P., Natarajan, S., & Biswas, J. (2014). Publish or perish: The art of scientific writing. Indian Journal of Ophthalmology, 62(11), 1089-1093. https://doi.org/10.4103/0301-4738.146760.

Somashekhar, S. P. (2020). Art of scientific writing. Indian Journal of Gynecologic Oncology, 18, 1-3. https://doi.org/10.1007/s40944-020-00382-y.

Steward, B. (2004). Writing a literature review. British Journal of Occupational Therapy, 67(11), 495-500. https://doi.org/10.1177/030802260406701105.

Stokel-Walker, C. (2023). ChatGPT listed as author on research papers: Many scientists disapprove. Nature, 613(7945), 620-621.

Tang, A., Li, K. K., Kwok, K. O., Cao, L., Luong, S., & Tam, W. (2024). The importance of transparency: Declaring the use of generative artificial intelligence (AI) in academic writing. Journal of Nursing Scholarship, 56(2), 314-318.

Vargas, M. A. P. (2016). Ethical guidelines for conducting experiments and writing scientific reports in psychology. International Journal of Psychological Studies, 8(3), 1. https://doi.org/10.5539/ijps.v8n3p1.

Warschauer, M., Tseng, W., Yim, S., Webster, T., Jacob, S., Du, Q., & Tate, T. (2023). The affordances and contradictions of AI-generated text for writers of English as a second or foreign language. Journal of Second Language Writing, 62. https://doi.org/10.2139/ssrn.4404380.

Webster, J., & Watson, R. T. (2002). Analyzing the past to prepare for the future: Writing a literature review. MIS Quarterly, xiii-xxiii. https://www.jstor.org/stable/4132319.

Weimann-Sandig, N. (2023). Digital literacy and artificial intelligence–does chat gpt introduce the end of critical thinking in higher education?. In EDULEARN23 Proceedings (pp. 16-21). IATED.

Zheng, H., & Zhan, H. (2023). ChatGPT in scientific writing: A cautionary tale. The American Journal of Medicine, 136(8), 725-726. https://doi.org/10.1016/j.amjmed.2023.02.011

Unmasking Online Harassment: A Longitudinal Analysis of Cyberbullying by Gender

Davoud Masoumi[1], Maryam Bourbour[2], Silvia Edling[3]

[1] Department of Educational Sciences, University of Gävle, Sweden: davoud.masoumi@hig.se
[2] Department of Educational Sciences, University of Gävle, Sweden: Maryam.Bourbour@hig.se
[3] Department of Educational Sciences, University of Gävle, Sweden: Silvia.Edling@hig.se

Abstract:

This paper presents a comprehensive longitudinal analysis of cyberbullying incidents, focusing on gender disparities, conducted from 2019 to 2024 in a Swedish municipality. Our study, which is part of a broader research project examining students' learning environments and expectations for educational development, engaged approximately 6,000 students across grades 4 to 9 and generated over 63,500 data points. The survey was implemented biannually, enabling a detailed exploration of the prevalence and evolution of cyberbullying. Descriptive and inferential statistical analyses, including t-tests, ANOVA, and time-series analysis, reveal key findings: girls consistently report higher rates of cyberbullying compared to boys, with a notable upward trend in reports from 2019 to 2023, followed by a slight decline in 2024. Preliminary findings indicate that girls consistently reported higher rates of cyberbullying than boys, especially in the later years of the study. Notably, non-traditional gender categories such as 'Other', 'Uncertain', and 'Prefer not to answer' demonstrated a significant increase in reported incidents in 2023 and 2024, suggesting a shift in reporting behavior or increased vulnerability. The time-series analysis revealed a general increase in cyberbullying reports up until 2023, followed by a slight decrease in 2024. This trend suggests a potential rise in cyberbullying incidents or an improvement in reporting mechanisms, with the recent decline possibly indicating the impact of targeted interventions. This study underscores the critical role of digital literacy and proactive educational policies in combating cyberbullying and fostering a safer online environment for children and adolescents.

Keywords: Digitalization, cyberbullying, social media, students, school

Introduction

The digital age has redefined human interaction and identity construction, embedding Information and Communication Technologies (ICT) into the fabric of daily life, especially for the younger generation. These technologies are central to molding young people's meanings, subjectivities, and relationships, giving rise to unprecedented practices and sensibilities (Echeveste, Francia, and Venegas, 2024).

The integration of digital environments, devices, and platforms, however, has not been entirely benign. The ubiquity of the 24/7 connectivity and mobile technology has revolutionized social interactions, often extending the reach of negative behaviors such as bullying beyond physical schoolyards into digital spaces (Evangelio et al., 2022; Azumah et al., 2023; Stoilova et al., 2024). This digital transformation has raised significant concerns regarding mental health and wellbeing, posing risks of long-lasting adverse effects on children's academic achievements and mental health (WHO, 2023 OECD 2023; Edling et al., 2024; Moore & Woodcock, 2017; Schoeler et al., 2018).

Compounding these issues is the alarming rate of problematic digital usage among youth. Current statistics reveal that approximately 7% of Swedish adolescents aged 11 to 15 faces with problematic social media use (Folkhälsomyndigheten, 2024). Similar findings by Edling et al. (2022) in a population study within a Municipality show that, in terms of type and frequency, bullying varies between schools and between classrooms within schools, where the variations between school classes can be greater than those between schools. Internationally, the prevalence of cyberbullying tends to increase with age, with a peak involvement occurring around the age of 15 (Wright, 2018; Camerini et al., 2020; Li et al., 2022; Esposito et al., 2023).

Cyberbullying, as a complex of psycho-social phenomenon, entails a wide range of actions, such as excluding individuals from online forums and/or groups, spreading rumours, threatening, sending offensive comments, including commenting about gender/sexuality, on social media and posting offensive and degrading digital content on online platforms (Masoumi et al.; Evangelio et al., 2022; Erikson et al., 2023). Addressing these critical concerns, this paper introduces a large-scale research project that aims to build upon prior individual-based findings by employing a longitudinal design. This strategic approach will enable us to meticulously trace the dynamics and developmental patterns of cyberbullying behavior among children from 2019 to 2024 within a specific Swedish municipality.

Methodology

Research Context and Objectives

This study is an integral component of a broader research initiative aimed at understanding students' perspectives on their learning environments, their evolving needs, and expectations for educational development. This specific segment of the research focuses on identifying the locations where bullying occurs, how these incidents evolve over time, and exploring the potential relationships between gender and the locations of bullying incidents.

Survey Design and Data Collection

The study utilizes data from a large-scale, longitudinal survey conducted over six years (2019–2024), encompassing approximately 6,000 students and generating over 63,500 data points. The survey was administered biannually to students in grades 4 through 9, providing a comprehensive overview of students' experiences at various educational stages. Thanks to a high participation rate, the dataset offers robust insights into the prevalence of bullying, its temporal trends, and the contextual factors that influence its occurrence.

The survey was administered between March and October each year from 2019 to 2024. It is a digital survey that was conducted anonymously and voluntarily within classroom settings. Parents were notified in advance and given the opportunity to opt their children out of the study. The administration of the survey across schools adhered to a standardized protocol to ensure consistency.

Data Analysis Procedures

Data analysis was conducted using SPSS, incorporating both descriptive and inferential statistical techniques to address the study's objectives. Descriptive statistics were utilized to identify general trends, frequencies, and distributions of bullying incidents across different cohorts and time points. To explore deeper patterns, inferential statistical methods were applied. t-tests were conducted to examine gender-based differences in bullying experiences, while ANOVA (Analysis of Variance) was employed to assess variations across different grades and time periods, providing insights into how bullying incidents may differ by age and over time. Additionally, a time-series analysis was performed to track changes in bullying trends throughout the study, offering a dynamic perspective on the evolution of bullying behaviors. These analytical methods collectively enabled a comprehensive understanding of cyberbullying trends and variations across different demographic and temporal dimensions.

Preliminary Findings

A general upward trend in cyberbullying reports is observed from 2019 to 2023, followed by a slight decline in 2024. The study's findings highlight clear trends in cyberbullying reports when examined by year and gender. Flicka (Girls) consistently report higher rates of cyberbullying compared to Pojke (Boys), with this disparity becoming especially pronounced in 2022 and 2023. This trend suggests that girls may be more frequently targeted or are more likely to report cyberbullying incidents than boys.

Additionally, in 2023 and 2024, there is a notable rise in cyberbullying reports among individuals identifying under alternative gender categories, including Annat alternativ (Other), Osäker (Uncertain), and Vill ej svara (Prefer not to answer). This increase may indicate that these individuals experience cyberbullying differently or at higher rates, potentially due to greater vulnerability, increased awareness, or changing social dynamics in online spaces. These findings underscore the need for further research into gender-related disparities in cyberbullying, ensuring that preventive measures and interventions address diverse identities and experiences effectively.

To gain deeper insights into these trends, a time series analysis is conducted to visualize the evolution of cyberbullying reports over different years (see Figure 1). This analysis aims to identify long-term patterns, seasonal variations, and external factors that may contribute to fluctuations in reported incidents. By mapping these changes, the study provides a clearer understanding of how the cyberbullying reporting landscape has been shaped over time and what underlying dynamics influence its progression.

Figure 1: Yearly Trends in Cyberbullying Reports

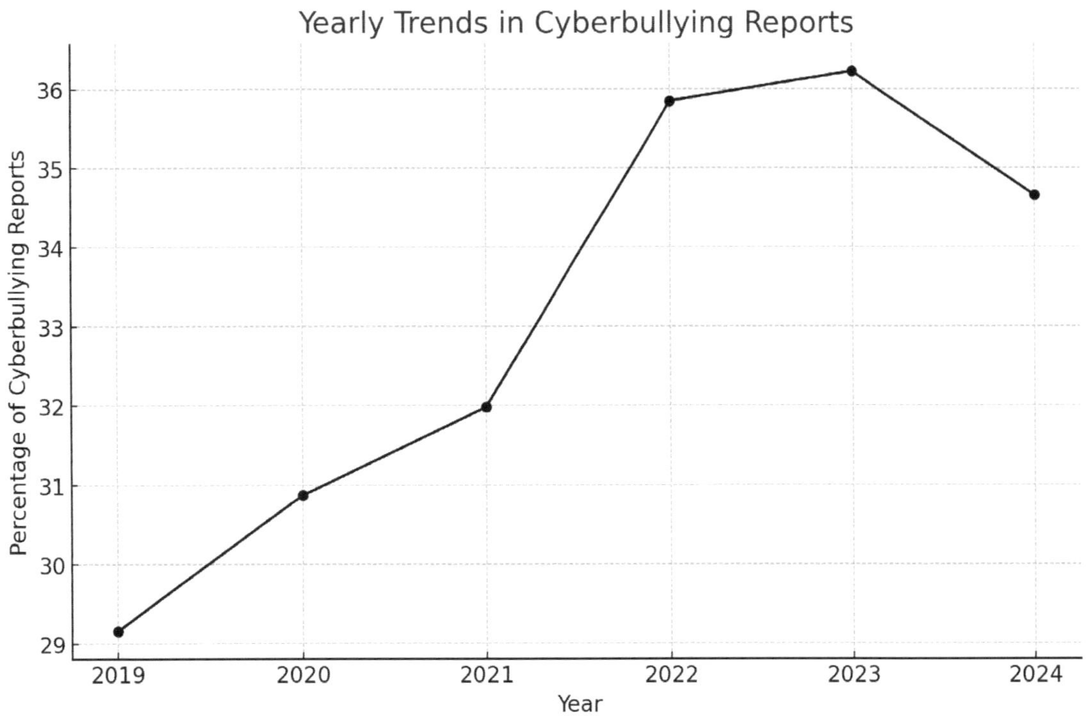

As indicated in Figure 1, the percentage of reported cyberbullying incidents shows a clear upward trajectory from 2019 to 2023. This increasing trend is likely influenced by multiple interrelated factors that require in-depth investigation to understand the underlying causes. Further analysis is crucial to determine whether this trend reflects an actual rise in cyberbullying incidents or improvements in detection and reporting practices over time.

One significant factor contributing to this trend is greater digital engagement, which has expanded the scope of online interactions and, consequently, increased exposure to cyberbullying risks. The widespread adoption of social media, instant messaging apps, and online gaming platforms has created more opportunities for cyberbullying and online harassment, as digital spaces become integral to social communication. Additionally, the COVID-19 pandemic (2020–2022) played a key role in accelerating digital interactions, shifting many aspects of socialization, education, and professional communication online. This shift likely contributed to the rise in cyberbullying cases, as individuals, particularly students, spent more time in virtual spaces where online conflicts, peer pressure, and digital aggression became more prevalent. At the same time, the proliferation of anonymity-driven platforms and encrypted messaging services has made cyberbullying more difficult to detect and regulate.

In 2024, a slight decline in cyberbullying reports suggests a potential shift in the cyberbullying landscape. While this may indicate genuine progress in combating online harassment, the trend could have been influenced by a series of initiatives that emerged following the publication of alarming findings about the increasing number of cyberbullying reports at the beginning of 2024 (Edling et al., 2024). These findings, along with subsequent actions at the municipal, school, and classroom levels, may have contributed to heightened awareness, shifts in reporting behaviors, and policy interventions, all of which could have played a role in the observed decline. However, further investigation is needed to determine whether this decrease reflects a sustained reduction in cyberbullying incidents or merely temporary fluctuations in reporting patterns.

References

Azumah, S. W., Elsayed, N., ElSayed, Z., & Ozer, M. (2023). Cyberbullying in text content detection: an analytical review. International Journal of Computers and Applications, 1-8. https://doi.org/10.1080/1206212X.2023.2256048

Camerini, A.-L., Marciano, L., Carrara, A., & Schulz, P. J. (2020). Cyberbullying perpetration and victimization among children and adolescents: A systematic review of longitudinal studies. Telematics and Informatics, 49, 101362. https://doi.org/https://doi.org/10.1016/j.tele.2020.101362

Edling, S., Francia, G., Bourbour, M., Masoumi, D., & Gill, P. (2024). I skuggan av mobbning och kränkande behandling på mellanstadiet från ett genusperspektiv: Resultat från en fallstudie https://hig.diva-portal.org/smash/get/diva2:1851040/FULLTEXT01.pdf

Edling, S., Gill, P. E., Francia, G., Matton, P., & Simonsson, B.-E. (2022). Motverka mobbning: och annan kränkande behandling - en handbok för lärare. Studentlitteratur AB.

Erikson, J., Håkansson, S., & Josefsson, C. (2023). Three Dimensions of Gendered Online Abuse: Analyzing Swedish MPs' Experiences of Social Media. Perspectives on Politics, 21(3), 896-912. https://doi.org/10.1017/S1537592721002048

Esposito, C., De Masi, F., Dragone, M., & Bacchini, D. (2023). Technology-Based Interventions for Preventing Youth Violence: A Systematic Review of Programs, Tools, and Evidence. Adolescent Research Review. https://doi.org/10.1007/s40894-023-00222-y

Evangelio, C., Rodríguez-González, P., Fernández-Río, J., & Gonzalez-Villora, S. (2022). Cyberbullying in elementary and middle school students: A systematic review. Computers & Education, 176, 104356. https://doi.org/https://doi.org/10.1016/j.compedu.2021.104356

Folkhälsomyndigheten. (2024). Digitala medier och barns och ungas hälsa: En kunskapssammanställning. https://www.folkhalsomyndigheten.se/contentassets/20a0ad3202d54bc9be156ff3e407b55c/digitala-medier-barns-ungas-halsa-kunskapssammanstallning.pdf

Li, C., Wang, P., Martin-Moratinos, M., Bella-Fernández, M., & Blasco-Fontecilla, H. (2022). Traditional bullying and cyberbullying in the digital age and its associated mental health problems in children and adolescents: a meta-analysis. European Child & Adolescent Psychiatry. https://doi.org/10.1007/s00787-022-02128-x

Masoumi, D., Bourbour, M., Edling, S., Gill, P., & Francia, G. School Staff Strategies for Identifying, Dealing with and Preventing Cyberbullying Among Swedish Primary School Pupils. Computers in the Schools, 1-22. https://doi.org/10.1080/07380569.2024.2416426

Stoilova, M., Livingstone, S., & Khazbak, R. (2024). Investigating children's health and wellbeing in a digital world: A rapid review of the evidence on children's internet use and outcomes. In J. Kuriansky & P. Kakkattil (Eds.), Resilient Health (pp. 809-818). Academic Press. https://doi.org/https://doi.org/10.1016/B978-0-443-18529-8.00067-6

Wright, M. F. (2018). Youths and Cyberbullying: Description, Theories, and Recommendations. In V. C. Bryan, A. T. Musgrove, & J. R. Powers (Eds.), Handbook of Research on Human Development in the Digital Age (pp. 364-384). IGI Global. https://doi.org/10.4018/978-1-5225-2838-8.ch016

AI Literacies and the TPACK Framework: Insights from a Global Study on AI in Education

Angela Gunder[1], Cristi Ford[2]

[1] The University of Arizona, United States; agunder@arizona.edu
[2] D2L, United States; cristi.ford@D2L.com

Correspondence: Angela Gunder: angela@openedculture.org

Abstract:

How can educators develop the technical, pedagogical, and content knowledge needed to integrate AI ethically, impactfully, and responsibly? As artificial intelligence (AI) becomes increasingly embedded in education, aligning AI literacies with the TPACK framework provides a structured approach to developing the essential competencies educators need to navigate AI-enhanced teaching and learning. This paper presents findings from a UNESCO IITE-commissioned global study that collected perspectives from over 50 educators across 25 countries, representing diverse teaching and leadership roles. The study highlights how AI literacies development is filling critical gaps in technical AI proficiency, pedagogical strategies, and subject-matter applications, enabling educators to align AI usage with ethical principles, effective teaching methodologies, and meaningful content engagement. Findings illustrate how AI literacies support: (1) Technical Knowledge: Understanding AI capabilities, limitations, and responsible use; (2) Pedagogical Knowledge: Designing AI-infused learning experiences that foster engagement, creativity, and student agency; (3) Content Knowledge: Applying AI tools to discipline-specific instructional challenges and research. Through a qualitative portraiture method, this research surfaces how AI literacies are being integrated into professional development programs, instructional design frameworks, and institutional strategies worldwide. The study also reveals ongoing challenges in scaling AI literacies equitably, ensuring ethical AI use, and adapting AI for diverse learning contexts. By positioning AI literacies as a core competency within the TPACK framework, this paper offers a global perspective on the evolving role of AI in education and presents a replicable model for embedding AI literacies into faculty development, curriculum design, and institutional capacity-building efforts.

Keywords: artificial intelligence, AI literacies, TPACK framework, faculty development, instructional design, ethical AI integration

Introduction

As artificial intelligence (AI) becomes increasingly embedded in teaching and learning, educators and learners are being asked to make high-stakes decisions about technologies and approaches they may not fully understand. While AI can enhance educational access, personalize learning, and optimize instruction, it also introduces challenges related to ethics, transparency, and pedagogical coherence. These tensions are especially pronounced in distance education, where digital infrastructures are central to instructional delivery and human mediation may be limited. AI-driven tools are reshaping how educators design, assess, and facilitate learning—but successful integration requires more than technical fluency. It demands an interplay of technological, pedagogical, and content knowledge to ensure ethical and pedagogically aligned use.

The Technological Pedagogical Content Knowledge (TPACK) framework offers a valuable lens for understanding how AI literacies can be cultivated among educators. Traditionally applied to technology integration in classroom instruction, TPACK's emphasis on the dynamic relationship between technology, pedagogy, and content is increasingly relevant as AI reshapes the instructional landscape. Educators must develop not only fluency with AI tools, but also the capacity to assess their pedagogical implications and align AI-generated content with disciplinary standards. Without an integrated approach, there is a risk of misalignment between technological affordances and best practices, leading to automation-driven inequities and diminished learner agency.

This paper examines the intersection of AI literacies and TPACK through findings from a global research initiative commissioned by UNESCO IITE. Drawing on the perspectives of over 50 educators from 25 countries, the study uses an ethnographically informed portraiture methodology to explore how AI is being integrated across technical, pedagogical, and content domains. While AI tools are increasingly accessible, many educators lack structured opportunities to evaluate outputs, align tools with their teaching values, and adapt AI-generated content for meaningful disciplinary engagement.

By analyzing this intersection, the paper contributes to ongoing conversations about AI literacies in professional development, curriculum design, and institutional strategy. It considers how AI reshapes technological knowledge through automation, pedagogical knowledge through adaptive design, and content knowledge through AI-generated materials. The paper concludes by identifying practical strategies and ethical imperatives for ensuring that AI supports inclusive and intentional teaching in digital learning environments.

TPACK and AI: Critical Knowledge Development

The rapid expansion of artificial intelligence (AI) technologies in education has necessitated a comprehensive approach to educator preparedness, encompassing technological, pedagogical, and content knowledge. Several frameworks have emerged to support educators and learners in navigating the complexities of AI, including UNESCO's competency frameworks for both teachers and students (Miao & Cukurova, 2024; Miao & Shiohira, 2024), and Opened Culture's (n.d.) Dimensions of AI Literacies taxonomy. Emerging instructional design models are beginning to integrate scaffolded AI literacies development for learners across educational levels (MacCallum et al., 2024). Within this burgeoning ecosystem of guidance for AI usage in education, the Technological, Pedagogical, and Content Knowledge (TPACK) framework emerges as a particularly insightful structure to examine the competencies educators require to implement AI ethically and effectively.

Technological knowledge within AI integration involves educators' proficiency with AI-driven tools, such as intelligent tutoring systems, learning analytics platforms, and generative AI applications. Educators require familiarity with the capabilities, limitations, and operational nuances of these tools. Recent studies emphasize the necessity for educators to possess AI literacies—skills enabling them to critically assess AI outputs for bias, accuracy, and privacy concerns (Castillo-Martínez et al., 2024; Ng et al., 2023; Opened Culture, n.d.). A lack of AI-specific technological knowledge can lead to unethical applications, such as reinforcing biases or compromising student data privacy. Research highlights that professional development aimed at enhancing educators' AI technical skills correlates positively with ethical decision-making in AI use.

Pedagogical knowledge refers to an educator's ability to design and deliver instruction effectively. When AI is involved, pedagogical knowledge must extend to strategies for integrating AI tools in ways that complement human instruction, fostering meaningful learning experiences. Scholars emphasize that effective AI integration requires educators to adapt their teaching methodologies, emphasizing learner-centered practices that AI can support. AI tools offer potential advantages in formative assessment, personalized learning pathways, and immediate feedback, yet their ethical deployment hinges on informed pedagogical practices that maintain transparency, equity, and inclusivity. Without strong pedagogical knowledge, educators risk over-reliance on automation, potentially diminishing critical thinking and student agency in learning processes.

Content knowledge is vital for educators to effectively evaluate and contextualize AI-generated content. Within higher education, where content is specialized, robust subject-matter expertise allows educators to critically examine AI outputs, identify inaccuracies, and align generated materials with curricular objectives. Moreover, educators increasingly require foundational knowledge of AI itself, particularly those incorporating AI literacies or data literacies into curricula across disciplines. Recent investigations underscore the importance of content knowledge, asserting that educators must understand the principles underlying AI, including algorithmic thinking, data ethics, and machine learning basics, to responsibly incorporate AI into their courses.

Integrating AI effectively and ethically is contingent upon the interplay of technological, pedagogical, and content knowledge as represented by the TPACK framework. Professional development initiatives in higher education increasingly emphasize the holistic cultivation of competencies and skills to prepare educators for AI integration, underscoring ethical use, data-informed decision-making, and responsible pedagogical alignment. Thus, a comprehensive approach to professional learning that fosters integrated TPACK competencies can better equip educators to address the complex challenges and opportunities AI presents. The TPACK framework provides educators and researchers a structured approach to navigate the integration of AI in education ethically and effectively. Enhancing educators' combined technological, pedagogical, and content knowledge is essential to responsibly harness AI's potential in education, promoting learning experiences that are not only innovative but also equitable and inclusive.

Methodology

This study employs a qualitative research design, drawing on portraiture methodology (Lawrence-Lightfoot & Davis, 1997) to investigate how educators worldwide are developing AI literacies within the framework of Technological, Pedagogical, and Content Knowledge (TPACK). Given the rapid expansion of artificial intelligence in education, this study seeks to capture the lived experiences of educators, illuminating how they navigate AI integration and competency development across diverse educational contexts (Lawrence-Lightfoot, 2005).

Research Design and Rationale

The study follows an ethnographically informed portraiture approach, a qualitative research method designed to document participants' experiences in a structured yet narrative-driven manner. Portraiture methodology is particularly suited for this study because it foregrounds educators' voices, allowing for a nuanced exploration of how AI literacies intersect with technological, pedagogical, and content knowledge in practice. By combining rich, descriptive accounts with systematic analysis, portraiture provides insight into the challenges, strategies, and transformations educators undergo when engaging with AI tools in their teaching.

Participants and Sampling Strategy

This study engaged over 50 educators across 25 countries, ensuring a broad representation of teaching and leadership roles in higher education. The participant pool included faculty members, instructional designers, academic leaders, and administrators from diverse institutional contexts. The selection of participants was purposeful, aiming to capture a range of experiences with AI integration (Suri, 2011).

Key criteria for participant selection included:

- Direct experience with AI tools in teaching and learning
- Engagement in faculty development, curriculum design, or leadership related to AI integration
- Representation from different disciplinary backgrounds and institutional types

Participants were recruited through professional networks, educational conferences, and AI-focused faculty development programs. Invitations to participate were extended via email and professional community groups, with an emphasis on ensuring geographic and institutional diversity.

Data Collection and Analysis

Data were collected through a combination of survey data and semi-structured interviews. These methods were chosen to provide both depth and breadth in capturing educators' perspectives on AI literacies and their application within the TPACK framework. All participants provided informed consent, and the study adhered to ethical guidelines for research involving human subjects.

A grounded theory approach (Strauss & Corbin, 1997; Glaser & Strauss, 2017) was taken in coding the qualitative data using the open coding software, Taguette. Data were analyzed through open, axial, and selective coding, as well as using a priori codes created by the researchers from their work creating the Dimensions of AI Literacies taxonomy (Opened Culture, n.d.).

The TPACK framework (Mishra & Koehler, 2006) served as a guiding analytical lens, allowing the research team to categorize findings within the interplay of technological, pedagogical, and content knowledge. This structured approach ensured that the study not only captured individual experiences but also provided generalizable insights for institutional strategy and policy development.

Findings and Discussion

Unlike static platforms or linear content delivery systems, AI tools require educators to make real-time judgments about appropriateness, reliability, and ethical use—often without the benefit of established norms or institutional guidelines (Mishra et al., 2023; Zawacki-Richter et al., 2019; Kamalov et al., 2023). The integration of AI into educational contexts is prompting a rearticulation of the TPACK framework, challenging educators to synthesize technological, pedagogical, and content knowledge in new ways. AI tools, with their generative and predictive capacities, introduce dynamic affordances that do not align neatly with earlier forms of educational technology.

Technological Competencies within Context

Participants in this study identified a persistent gap in AI-specific technological knowledge. Even among educators with significant digital competencies and skills, there was a widespread sense that AI tools demand a qualitatively different kind of understanding—one that includes awareness of how outputs are shaped by training data, algorithmic bias, and opaque design. While some participants felt confident navigating digital learning management systems or assessment software, they acknowledged that AI presented unfamiliar epistemological terrain (Almasri, 2024; Lee et al., 2024; Maznev et al., 2024). This lack of structured guidance often led to inconsistent adoption, with some educators experimenting enthusiastically and others hesitating out of concern for unintended consequences.

The findings also emphasize that AI literacies cannot be understood purely in functional terms. Technological knowledge, in this context, must be conceptual as well as operational (Ng et al., 2023; Miao & Cukurova, 2024; Miao & Shiohira, 2024). Educators indicated the need for professional development that situates AI within a broader conversation about values, teaching philosophies, and institutional responsibilities. They expressed particular interest in understanding not just how AI works, but how it might reinforce or disrupt their pedagogical commitments—especially with regard to learner agency, inclusivity, and the evolving nature of academic labor.

Pedagogical Fluency and Adaptive Instructional Design

A second theme that emerged was the tension between efficiency and intentionality in AI-enhanced pedagogy. Educators described both the promise and the risk of automation: on one hand, AI offers tools to support personalized learning, generate feedback at scale, and streamline administrative tasks (Gupta, 2023; Druga et al., 2022; Cardona et al., 2023); on the other hand, it can erode the relational and dialogic dimensions of teaching if deployed uncritically. Participants shared concerns that students might disengage from critical thinking, rely too heavily on generative tools, or lose opportunities for formative interaction if AI is used primarily as a time-saving measure.

Those who reported more confident integration of AI tools often framed their practice as grounded in clear pedagogical intent. Rather than beginning with a tool and finding a use for it, they began with a teaching challenge—scaffolding metacognition, diversifying assessment, creating space for student voice—and explored how AI might support that goal. This pattern aligns with existing models of reflective instructional design and underscores the importance of pedagogical clarity in navigating emerging technologies (Davis, 2023). Participants noted that faculty learning environments which allow for experimentation, collaborative critique, and iterative redesign were far more helpful than compliance-oriented workshops.

Content Knowledge and Disciplinary Judgment

Content knowledge—especially in its critical and disciplinary forms—emerged as essential to responsible AI integration (Castillo-Martínez et al., 2024). Educators emphasized that the ability to evaluate AI outputs is highly contextual. In fields like engineering or data science, it might mean verifying technical accuracy or examining how predictive models function. In the humanities and social sciences, it often involved analyzing the assumptions embedded in AI-generated narratives or questioning whose voices and histories are represented. The data suggest that disciplinary expertise plays a crucial role in mitigating AI's limitations. Participants were particularly attuned to the risk of uncritically accepting AI-generated material, especially in domains where nuance, interpretation, and positionality are central. They described developing strategies for triangulating AI responses, embedding critique into assignments, and using AI as a comparative lens rather than a definitive authority. These practices require both content fluency and a broader set of critical literacies that allow educators to model ethical discernment and contextual judgment.

Evolving Understandings of AI Literacies

Together, the findings affirm a vision of AI literacies that transcends functional proficiency. The TPACK framework offers a useful lens not because it provides a checklist, but because it illuminates the interdependence of technological awareness, pedagogical reasoning, and content expertise. Educators' reflections point to a growing recognition that AI competence involves layered knowledge: the ability to evaluate tools technically, align them pedagogically, and interpret them through a disciplinary lens (MacCallum et al., 2024; Opened Culture, n.d.).

Importantly, the study also highlights the need for AI literacies to be situated within broader institutional and social contexts. Educators described how structural factors—such as policy ambiguity, time constraints, and uneven access to resources—shaped their ability to meaningfully engage with AI. They called for professional development models that are not only informative, but dialogic and developmental—spaces where faculty can explore, iterate, and reflect in ways that build confidence and maturity over time.

By mapping educator insights onto the TPACK framework, this study contributes to a more holistic understanding of what AI literacies require and how they might be cultivated. It underscores the importance of moving beyond isolated competencies toward a more integrated, critical, and context-aware approach—one that equips educators to navigate AI not as a passive tool, but as a co-shaping force in the future of teaching and learning.

Implications for Distance Education

Rethinking Professional Development as Pedagogical Formation

Traditional models of faculty development—centered on tools, compliance, or technical fluency—are insufficient in the age of AI. The findings suggest that AI literacies must be cultivated not just through exposure to emerging tools, but through iterative processes of inquiry, reflection, and contextual application. Rather than positioning AI as a specialized skill set for select faculty, institutions should embed AI literacies into broader professional formation. This includes supporting instructors in developing critical dispositions—such as ethical discernment, evaluative skepticism, and pedagogical imagination—alongside technical competencies. Faculty learning communities, design studios, and use-case-driven fellowships may be more effective than standalone workshops in building sustainable, reflective engagement with AI.

AI as Infrastructure: The Role of Policy and Governance

Distance education leaders are often at the forefront of decisions about platforms, data use, and instructional automation. As AI tools become more embedded in LMS environments and institutional workflows, the distinction between pedagogy and infrastructure becomes increasingly porous. Rather than reacting to AI as a threat, distance learning offices are positioned to convene cross-role conversations that surface values, anticipate tensions, and generate proactive guidance. These policies should not be static. As AI capabilities and practices evolve, institutions will need to revisit and revise frameworks that shape how faculty and students interact with AI—ideally through mechanisms that invite diverse perspectives and ongoing dialogue.

Supporting Learner Agency and Disciplinary Belonging

Perhaps most critically, the study's findings highlight the importance of aligning AI integration with the needs and identities of learners—particularly in digital contexts where students may encounter AI with limited instructor mediation. Faculty in the study expressed concern that uncritical use of AI tools could compromise student agency, encourage surface learning, or reinforce disciplinary hierarchies.

Distance learning leaders should treat AI integration as an opportunity to deepen, rather than dilute, the intellectual character of online learning. This includes designing prompts and activities that position students as critical readers of AI, co-creators of knowledge, and evaluators of disciplinary relevance. The TPACK lens can support this work by helping faculty scaffold student engagement with AI at the intersection of disciplinary practice, pedagogical intention, and tool functionality.

At a policy level, this also means ensuring that AI adoption does not exacerbate access gaps, overwhelm already-burdened faculty, or displace the relational dimensions of teaching. Institutions committed to inclusive digital learning must ask not only what AI can do, but what learners need to thrive in AI-mediated environments—and how instructors can be equipped to guide that process with care and intentionality.

Conclusion

As artificial intelligence becomes increasingly enmeshed in the tools, platforms, and pedagogical rhythms of higher education, educators must be equipped with more than just operational fluency—they need frameworks that support ethical discernment, disciplinary alignment, and pedagogical intentionality. This study demonstrates that the TPACK framework, when applied to AI contexts, offers a valuable structure for cultivating AI literacies that are adaptive, reflective, and grounded in the realities of diverse teaching and learning environments. The findings reveal that educators are not merely seeking technical training—they are asking deeper questions about what AI means for their students, their disciplines, and their professional identities. By mapping AI literacies onto the interdependent domains of technological, pedagogical, and content knowledge, the study provides a pathway for more holistic and sustainable approaches to faculty development and instructional design. This work is especially urgent in distance education, where AI systems are often deployed at scale and with limited human mediation. In these contexts, the risks of bias, misalignment, and learner disempowerment are amplified—but so too are the possibilities for innovation, access, and transformation. Institutions that approach AI integration as a pedagogical and ethical endeavor, rather than a technical upgrade, will be better positioned to support faculty and students in navigating this evolving landscape. As AI continues to evolve, the role of educators will be not only to adapt to new tools, but to shape how those tools are used—to ask better questions, design more just systems, and keep learning human at the center of innovation.

References

Almasri, F. (2024). Exploring the impact of artificial intelligence in teaching and learning of science: A systematic review of empirical research. Research in Science Education, 54(1), 977-997. https://doi.org/10.1007/s11165-024-10176-3

Cardona, M. A., Rodríguez, R. J., & Ishmael, K. (2023). Artificial intelligence and the future of teaching and learning: Insights and recommendations. United States Department of Education. https://tech.ed.gov/files/2023/05/ai-future-of-teaching-and-learning-report.pdf

Castillo-Martínez, I. M., Flores-Bueno, D., Gómez-Puente, S. M., & Vite-León, V. O. (2024). AI in higher education: a systematic literature review. Frontiers in Education, 9, 1391485. https://doi.org/10.3389/feduc.2024.1391485

Davis, V. (2023, January 5). Is AI the new homework machine? Understanding AI and its impact on higher education. WCET. https://wcet.wiche.edu/frontiers/2023/01/05/is-ai-the-new-homework-machine/

Druga, S., Otero, N., & Ko, A. J. (2022, July 7). The landscape of teaching resources for AI education. Proceedings of the 27th ACM Conference on on Innovation and Technology in Computer Science Education Vol. 1. ITiCSE 2022: Innovation and Technology in Computer Science Education, Dublin Ireland. https://doi.org/10.1145/3502718.3524782

Glaser, B. G., & Strauss, A. L. (2017). Discovery of grounded theory: Strategies for qualitative research. Routledge.

Gupta, G. (2023, September 18). The AI advantage: Boosting student engagement in self-paced learning through AI. Faculty Focus | Higher Ed Teaching & Learning; Magna Publications. https://www.facultyfocus.com/articles/teaching-with-technology-articles/the-ai-advantage-boosting-student-engagement-in-self-paced-learning-through-ai/

Kamalov F, Santandreu Calonge D, & Gurrib I. (2023). New era of artificial intelligence in education: Towards a sustainable multifaceted revolution. Sustainability, 15(16):12451. https://doi.org/10.3390/su151612451

Lawrence-Lightfoot, S. (2005). Reflections on portraiture: A dialogue between art and science. Qualitative Inquiry, 11(1), 3–15. https://doi.org/10.1177/1077800404270955

Lawrence-Lightfoot, S. & Davis, J. H. (1997). The art and science of portraiture. Jossey-Bass.

Lee, D., Arnold, M., Srivastava, A., Plastow, K., Strelan, P., Ploeckl, F., Lekkas, D., & Palmer, E. (2024). The impact of generative AI on higher education learning and teaching: A study of educators' perspectives. Computers and Education: Artificial Intelligence, 6(100221). https://doi.org/10.1016/j.caeai.2024.100221

MacCallum, K., Parsons, D., & Mohaghegh, M. (2024). The Scaffolded AI literacy (SAIL) framework for education: Preparing learners at all levels to engage constructively with artificial intelligence. He Rourou, 1(1), 23. https://doi.org/10.54474/herourou.v1i1.10835

Maznev, P., Stützer, C. M., & Gaaw, S. (2024). AI in higher education: Booster or stumbling block for developing digital competence? Zeitschrift für Hochschulentwicklung, 19(1), 120-135. https://doi.org/10.21240/zfhe/19-01/06

Miao, F., & Cukurova, M. (2024). AI competency framework for teachers. UNESCO. https://doi.org/10.54675/ZJTE2084

Miao, F., & Shiohira, K. (2024). AI competency framework for students. UNESCO. https://doi.org/10.54675/JKJB9835

Mishra, P. (2019). Considering contextual knowledge: The TPACK diagram gets an upgrade. Journal of Digital Learning in Teacher Education, 35(2), 76–78. https://doi.org/10.1080/21532974.2019.1588611

Mishra, P., & Koehler, M. J. (2006). Technological pedagogical content knowledge: A new framework for teacher knowledge. Teachers College Record, 108(6), 1017–1054. https://doi.org/10.1111/j.1467-9620.2006.00684.x

Mishra, P., Warr, M., & Islam, R. (2023). TPACK in the age of ChatGPT and generative AI. Journal of Digital Learning in Teacher Education, 39(4), 235–251. https://www.tandfonline.com/doi/abs/10.1080/21532974.2023.2247480

Ng, D. T. K., Leung, J. K. L., Su, J., Ng, R. C. W., & Chu, S. K. W. (2023). Teachers' AI digital competencies and twenty-first century skills in the post-pandemic world. Educational Technology Research and Development, 71(1), 137–161. https://doi.org/10.1007/s11423-023-10203-6

Opened Culture. (n.d.). Dimensions of AI literacies. Opened Culture. https://openedculture.com/projects/dimensions-of-ai-literacies/

Strauss, A., & Corbin, J. M. (1997). Grounded theory in practice. Sage.

Suri, H. (2011). Purposeful sampling in qualitative research synthesis. Qualitative Research Journal, 11(2), 63–75. https://doi.org/10.3316/QRJ1102063

Zawacki-Richter, O., Marín, V. I., Bond, M., & Gouverneur, F. (2019). Systematic review of research on artificial intelligence applications in higher education – where are the educators? International Journal of Educational Technology in Higher Education, 16(39). https://doi.org/10.1186/s41239-019-0171-0

How to select the right AI tool for the job? An Autonomy-values framework for educational AI with a focus on academic advising

Jan Petrus Bosman[1], Wim Van Petegem[2], Tinne De Laet[3], Nompilo Tshuma[4]

[1] Centre for Learning Technologies, Stellenbosch University, South Africa; jpbosman@sun.ac.za
[2] Faculty of Engineering Technology, KU Leuven, Belgium; wim.vanpetegem@kuleuven.be
[3] Faculty of Engineering Science, KU Leuven, Belgium; tinne.delaet@kuleuven.be
[4] Faculty of Education, Stellenbosch University, South Africa; ntshuma@sun.ac.za

Correspondence: Jan Petrus Bosman: jpbosman@sun.ac.za

Abstract:

This study presents an Autonomy-values framework for analysing, designing, and selecting AI academic advising systems. Through focus groups with advisors using Nominal Group Technique, we identified contextually specific values that were then generalised using Legitimation Code Theory's Autonomy lens. The resulting framework maps advising values across four positions: Student-Centred, Advisor-Centred, Institution-Centred, and Social-Centred. By combining values-sensitive design with LCT Autonomy, this work advances knowledge on human-centred approaches to AI implementation in academic advising and broader educational contexts.

Keywords: Autonomy-values, academic advising, values-sensitive design, Legitimation Code Theory (LCT), AI in Education, Nominal Group Technique (NGT), Autonomy translation device

Introduction: Values-sensitive design and AIEd

Values-sensitive design (VSD), a sub-discipline of Human-Computer Interaction (HCI), has been making inroads in the design of education technologies, especially AI-infused systems (Zahran et al., 2025). VSD is a "human-centered and theory-grounded approach to technology design that explicitly elicits and accounts for human values" (Prieto et al., 2025, p.950). The growing interest in the values perspective around AI tools comes as there are calls for the social sciences to assist with designing AI tools and systems that are based upon and support human-driven needs and values (Miller et al., 2017). In this development, two challenges arise. The first is around the concept of values. "What values?" and "whose values?" become essential questions[1]. The second concerns how these values are "sourced" or identified in a specific user group. This paper will unpack these challenges in the form of a case study of how a values-sensitive design process was followed and how the concept of values can be transformed from a very localised expression to a more generalised one.

Values-sensitive design in education

In the field of academic advising, there is a growing realisation that AI technologies, especially large language models (LLM), could be of great benefit to support students in their academic success journeys and also academic advisors in their advising practice (Assayed et al., 2024). A growing body of research into the potential of generative AI (GAI) advisor chatbots indicates the direction of technology development (Albinali et al., 2024). It has become essential to build systems and tools that support students and advisors in a consistent and human-centred way. To understand and identify what human-centred means in the context of academic advising AI-infused systems, one can follow a values-sensitive design (VSD) process, generalise the academic advising values through connecting them to Legitimation Code Theory's Autonomy dimension and then

[1] See, e.g., Kasirzadeh and Gabriel (2023) for an in depth analysis of how to align language models with human values.

develop a translation device and a practical-theoretical framework for informing academic advising with AI practices[2].

Values-sensitive design case study: European Academic Advisors on Machine Values

For this study the Nominal Group Technique (NGT) was used to facilitate Values-sensitive design sessions. In NGT, the participating expert practitioners represent or identify human-centred values relating to the envisioned technological system through a consensus-building process (Harvey & Holmes, 2012). The NGT "facilitates equal participation and allows all opinions to be respectfully considered" (McMillan et al., 2014, p.2). For our case study, two NGT sessions (n=10) were conducted with academic advising practitioners in a European university. In the consensus-building process, several values or human-centred characteristics of an envisioned AI-infused academic advising system were identified. These prioritised values or system characteristics include holistically developmental, relationships-supporting, connections-fostering, inclusive, non-biased, trustworthy, "knowing its limits", respectful of privacy, and an evidence-based approach[3].

These values are valuable to a specific institution in a localised context (like this specific European institution), but they lack generalisability by default. Although qualitative research is beneficial in showing the depth of a particular educational reality and should not necessarily aim for generalisability, the question was asked how the localised VSD process outcomes (like the values and characteristics) could inform the development of a framework with which other practitioner groups, institutions or companies could interrogate or express their values-needs when it comes to designing or selecting future AI-based academic advising systems. To build such a framework, one needs to go deeper into the recorded and transcribed qualitative data by analysing the ideas and concepts expressed by the NGT focus group participants. The data was subsequently coded according to the Autonomy dimension of Legitimation Code Theory (LCT) to develop an Autonomy-values translation device and framework for analysing, designing or selecting academic advising AI systems.

An Autonomy-values framework for academic advising AI systems

We will now discuss LCT Autonomy, explain how we envision developing the concept of Autonomy Values, and build an Autonomy-values translation device and an accompanying framework.

LCT and Autonomy

Legitimation Code Theory[4] (LCT) is a "sociological framework for revealing the organizing principles underlying achievement in education and other social fields of practice" (Maton et al., 2024). Autonomy (a set of concepts with which to uncover these principles) is one of three LCT dimensions. Autonomy codes explore how knowledge practices are constructed by actors (e.g. academic advising practitioners) in the context being studied (e.g. an academic advising AI system in a university context) (Maton & Howard, 2018). In Autonomy analysis, the focus is on finding the positions and principles of a set of practices and "their ways of working, their aims, their purposes, and so on" (Adendorff & Blackie, 2021, p.237). Autonomy codes can be analytically distinguished as:

- Positional autonomy (PA) between constituents positioned within a context or category and those positioned in other contexts or categories. Here we identify the what? or the "content" (knowledge base) of the legitimised practice. The PA can be stronger (PA+) or weaker (PA-) on a continuum of strengths. Stronger PA (PA+) is, e.g., when academic advising practice knowledge is drawn upon, while weaker PS (PA-) is, e.g., when knowledge and practices outside of the academic advising domain are referenced.

---

[2] **A note on methodology:** Due to space constraints the paper follows several methodological steps without in-depth description. One could summarise the steps followed: a) A case study was developed using NGT; b) An LCT-based academic advising values Autonomy translation device was conceptualised; c) The transcribed data from the focus groups were then analysed according to the translation device; d) An Autonomy-Values theoretical framework was validated for the specific.

[3] These priorities are a mix of what can be called "functional" values that can be translated into functional requirements for a system (e.g. privacy, evidence-based) and "non-functional" values that are "more social, epistemic or contextual in nature" and do not directly translate to specific features (like holistically developmental, trustworthy) (Sadek et al., 2024, p.3).

[4] For research and practice enacting LCT, see www.legitimationcodetheory.com.

- Relational autonomy (RA) is the relations among constituents of a context or category and relations among constituents of other contexts. Here, we identify the purpose or the why? (the goal or effect) of the legitimised practice. The RA can also be stronger (RA+) or weaker (RA-). In stronger RA (RA+), the purpose is, e.g., towards supporting academically successful students, whereas weaker RA (RA-) is constructed for furthering other goals or purposes than solely student academic success.

The innovation in this inquiry is to relate the insights of LCT Autonomy into the specialised field of academic advising with what is valued (legitimised) and, therefore, could function as a more generalisable Autonomy-values framework. The other interesting "tack" in this paper is the fact that the values (Autonomy codes) we identify are meant to be "instilled" (through design) into an envisioned machine-learning machine – almost like giving it a values "compass" or an advisor's "heart"[5].

Connecting academic advising values and the LCT Autonomy Dimension

Values discussions around AI often fall into simplistic dichotomies—progressive versus oppressive, embracing versus rejecting AI advising systems. Instead, understanding values through their affinity to a knowledge community's specific Autonomy knowledge values offers more nuance. Analysing academic advising practices through an Autonomy lens reveals underlying values that legitimise approaches while highlighting the diverse richness and tensions within practitioner communities. This maps dimensions of academic advising values on an Autonomy-values plane, freeing practices from locally specific values toward a more generalisable, non-dichotomous framework. Such a theoretical framework becomes a practical tool for understanding institutional or company values in academic advising, guiding the analysis, design, or selection of values-based, human-centred AI advising systems.

An academic advising Autonomy-values translation device

Translation devices are theoretically solid and practically powerful in research as they invite broader and more transparent participation in the interpretation of data and how it relates to practice (Maton & Chen, 2016). In a previous study, (Bosman et al., 2024) a dialogic-relational translation device for identifying advising personas was developed. In this study, we introduce the concept of an Autonomy-values translation device. The basic two codes, in terms of our data and with a focus on the Autonomy domain of academic advising, are:

- Stronger or weaker Positional autonomy (PA+/-), which is indicated by the nearness to the practice of academic advising with the ultimate goal of student academic success. From the data, we see PA+ in developmental approaches that lead to reflection and useful interpreted statistics for students to gain insights into their student success journey. PA- is uncovered when the focus is on more indirect things related to academic advising (like chatting just for chatting sake), when it takes on a related role (like a psychologist or expert career advisor), or when it gives predictions for student performance without actionable insights (or when it is just plain wrong).

- Stronger or weaker Relational autonomy (RA+/-) is seen in the data when the goal or focus of the activity becomes clear. RA+ is when the focus is on holistic student success, and even when it is about strengthening academic advisors to help students better. RA- is when the focus/ outcome is on things other than student success, like putting the institution in a positive light, creating effectiveness for advisors, students and teachers, and things like surveillance and privacy intrusion.

To look for these aspects in the data separately is already meaningful, but when one combines PA and RA as a lens, then we get really interesting insights that can form a framework for ethical or values-sensitive AI advising systems.

Towards an Autonomy-values framework for academic advising AI systems

When we combine the principal Autonomy codes on a plane, we get four broad codes: Sovereign (PA+RA+), Introjected (PA-RA+), Projected (PA+RA-), and Exotic (PA-RA-). The qualitative transcribed focus group (NGT) data were coded according to not only stronger or weaker PA and RA, but also according to the co-occurring combination of PA (+/-) and PR (+/-) in the semantic data. Through iterative coding, it was possible to express

[5] Here we are in the realm of technography, or social science fiction – where the machine's dreams, needs, and (values) orientation are inferred and reconstructed through human advisors' dreams, needs and orientations (Berg, 2022).

participants' values-perspectives in four Autonomy-values positions and subsequently map them on an Autonomy-values plane.

In Table 1, we unpack the four AI System Autonomy-values types as a translation device that enables the movement from theory (the type and code) to practice (the system type description with an example from the data). A translation device provides a potential mechanism to lift a localised understanding to a more generalisable approach and framework. It also functions as a window into the researcher's process of interpretation of the qualitative data, as it is made transparent and can be confirmed or refuted by other researchers.

Table 1: Translation Device for Values-sensitive Autonomy Academic Advising AI System Types

AI System AVS Type	Code	Description of the type of system	Example from the data
Student-Centred (Sovereign)	PA+RA+	The system gives trusted and evidence- and practice-based academic advising. This includes giving correct information, using reflective processes, and following a dialogic approach. The outcome of the advising supports holistic student success in terms of the student's academic, psycho-social and career journeys. It can also support academic advisors' to help students better.	So, if it's like we as a human advisor should be trustworthy or reliable. As well an AI system, if we would use it, should also be trustworthy, reliable, transparent and so on ... guide students around study choice, maybe also ask a few reflective questions and integrate those answers and direct them to - This is a list of things you can study that align with what your interests are ... guiding the choice basically. (NGTFG1)
Advisor-Centred (Introjected)	PA-RA+	The system uses related and indirect academic advising knowledge and practices and sometimes even non-academic advising practice knowledge from other fields (like psychology) and sometimes even hallucinates or just plainly makes students feel welcome. The aim is more prone towards academic advisor support (like making the admin lighter for advisors or even teachers) but also is zoned in on holistic student support and success.	I have to give feedback to the teachers about teaching styles, exam questions linked to the feeling of the student. You know whether that's clear ... Just also give feedback to the teachers. I think that's important not only to the students, but also to teachers. (NGTFG1)
Institution-Centred (Projected)	PA+RA-	The system uses academic advising knowledge and practice approaches (like predictive learning analytics) but are used for purposes other than holistic student success, like forcing students out of the system and automating the role of academic advisors, ombuds, and other roles. The focus is more on the institution's needs.	It will show that we as a university do care about the individual students. (NGTFG2)
Social-Centred (Exotic)	PA-RA-	The system does not use academic advising knowledge and practices, and the purpose is towards something else than student success (like social life connections). It could be using technology for technology's sake, keeping students busy with "chatting" or sometimes even for surveillance.	I have another approach is what the system should not be. It should not be too intrusive. If it's impeding learning or making students feel more powerless or disconnected or lonely. We don't, we don't want this. So, if this would be a side effect of new systems or if it's not transparent. (NGTFG2)

Table 2: Results of coded qualitative NGT Focus group data according to Values-sensitive Autonomy (n=10)

AVS AI System type	**Student-Centred Sovereign) PA+RA+**	**Advisor-Centred (Introjected) PA-RA+**	**Institution-Centred (Projected) PA+RA-**	**Social-Centred (Exotic) PA-RA-**
All voices (n=10)	**50%** (72/145 Codes)	39% (57/145 codes)	3% (5/145 codes)	8% (11/145 codes)

Visually mapping the same data in Table 2 on a Cartesian plane shows the overall distribution of the Values-sensitive Autonomy codes (Fig. 1).

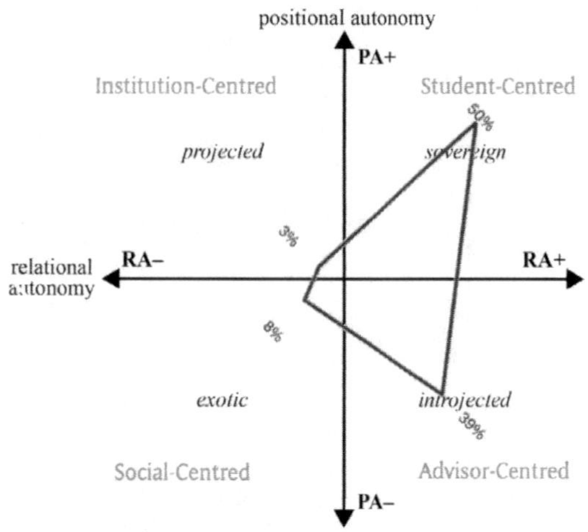

Figure 1: Academic advising Autonomy-value AI system types mapped on the LCT Autonomy plane

Mapping the data this way shows where this group of academic advisors' localised Autonomy-values lie. A very strong Relational Autonomy (RA+ - 89% of the codes) indicates a strong preference for an AI system to almost exclusively support students' and advisors'/ teachers' needs. About half (53%) of the codes show a stronger Positional Autonomy (PA+) and half show a weaker PA (PA- 47%). This indicates a preference for an AI system design that is more flexible regarding using very exclusive academic advising knowledge practices (Student-Centred) but also utilising knowledge and practices from other domains that are potentially helpful and supportive of student and advisor success (Advisor-Centred). The fact that there are very limited Institution-Centred (3%) and Social-Centred (8%) positions mapped from the data is perhaps expected as the idea of doing a Values-sensitive Design process is to identify what the insider values needs of a group are and then build the AI Advisor machine system to match and perform those values.

Conclusions and implications

The Autonomy-values framework was developed through an NGT-enabled Values-sensitive design process by academic advising practitioners mapping their expressed needs and expectations of a future AI-infused academic advising system using the Autonomy lens of LCT. The localised values of a specific academic advising practitioner group could be expressed in terms of a more generalisable Autonomy-values framework.

The implications of this technique and framework are practical and theoretical. Practically, other academic advising contexts could utilise the NGT method coupled with an Autonomy-values analysis and visual mapping in terms of the Student-, Advisor-, Organisation-, or Social-Centredness range of practices. It could also be used to facilitate discussions between, e.g. university management and advisors, IT engineers and practitioners, or institutions and EdTech companies. As an analytical tool, it has the potential to serve as an institutional tool for introspection (identifying the Autonomy-values of all stakeholders in an academic advising project). As a design tool, it could guide values-based alignment and guardrail development when building academic advising AI-infused systems. As a selection tool, it could fortify more robust and values-sensitive selection criteria for academic advising AI systems.

Theoretically, analysing academic advising values in terms of the LCT Autonomy lens and developing a translation device contributes to the emerging body of knowledge around how to use social-science approaches and insights to understand, design and develop more human-centric AI systems. Showing how a localised inquiry into contextually expressed prioritised values can be generalisable through a framework such as academic advising Autonomy-values potentially opens very interesting and enticing future opportunities to develop similar Autonomy-values frameworks for other practitioners, like teachers, tutors, and even students.

The study and subsequent translation device and practical-theoretical Autonomy-values framework were based on the data from one case study in a European university context. Future research invites the application and validation of the translation device and framework as case studies in other academic advising sites of practice.

Competing interests

The authors have no competing interests to declare.

Ethics and consent

Ethical clearance for the study was granted (KU Leuven—SMEC—G-2023-6280-R5(MAR); Stellenbosch University – REC SB: 27224). Informed consent was obtained from research participants, and their identities were anonymised in the data.

References

Adendorff, H., & Blackie, M. A. L. (2021). Decolonizing the science curriculum: When good intensions are not enough. In C. Winberg, S. McKenna, & K. Wilmot (Eds.), Building knowledge in Higher Education: Enhancing teaching and learning with Legitimation Code Theory (pp. 237–254). Routledge.

Albinali, K., Iahad, N. A., & Fadhil, A. (2024). A Systematic Literature Review of the Artificial Intelligence Role in Transformative Academic Advising : A Study of AI Applications in Higher Education. 14(12), 1429–1443. https://doi.org/10.6007/IJARBSS/v14-i12/24100

Assayed, S. K., Alkhatib, M., & Shaalan, K. (2024). A Systematic Review of Conversational AI Chatbots in Academic Advising. In A. M. Khalid, A. M. Farzana, A. D. Solomon, & A.-E. Mostafa (Eds.), BUiD Doctoral Research Conference 2023, LNCE 473 (pp. 346–359). Springer. https://doi.org/https://doi.org/10.1007/978-3-031-56121-4_33

Berg, M. (2022). Digital Technography: A Methodology for Interrogating Emerging Digital Technologies and Their Futures. Qualitative Inquiry, 28(7), 827–836. https://doi.org/10.1177/10778004221096851

Bosman, J. P., Petegem, W. Van, Laet, T. De, & Tshuma, N. (2024). Cracking the AIEd code : Dialogic-relational academic advising. 4 (June), 16–18. https://doi.org/https://doi.org/10.5334/uproc.131

Harvey, N., & Holmes, C. A. (2012). Nominal group technique: An effective method for obtaining group consensus. International Journal of Nursing Pratice, 18, 188–194. https://doi.org/10.1111/j.1440-172X.2012.02017.x

Kasirzadeh, A., & Gabriel, I. (2023). In Conversation with Artificial Intelligence: Aligning language Models with Human Values. Philosophy and Technology, 36(2), 1–30. https://doi.org/10.1007/s13347-023-00606-x

Maton, K., & Chen, R. T.-H. (2016). LCT in qualitative research: Creating a translation device for studying constructivist pedagogy. In K. Maton, S. Hood, & S. Shay (Eds.), Knowledge-building: Educational studies in Legitimation Code Theory. Routledge.

Maton, K., Doran, Y. J., Howard, S. K., Nothman, J., & Quilpatay, M. (2024). Making bigger waves: Automating theoretical coding to generate educationally meaningful learning analytics. In K. Bartimote, S. K. Howard, & D. Gašević (Eds.), Theory informing and arising from learning analytics. Springer. https://doi.org/10.1007/978-3-031-60571-0

Maton, K., & Howard, S. K. (2018). Taking autonomy tours A key to integrative knowledge-building. LCT Centre Occasional Paper, 1, 1–35.

McMillan, S. S., Kelly, F., Sav, A., Kendall, E., King, M. A., Whitty, J. A., & Wheeler, A. J. (2014). Using the nominal group technique : how to analyse across multiple groups. Health Services and Outcomes Research Methodology, 14 (3), 92–108. https://doi.org/10.1007/s10742-014-0121-1

Miller, T., Howe, P., & Sonenberg, L. (2017). Explainable AI: Beware of Inmates Running the Asylum Or: How I Learnt to Stop Worrying and Love the Social and Behavioural Sciences. Proc. IJCAI Workshop Explainable AI (XAI), 36–42. http://arxiv.org/abs/1712.00547

Prieto, L. P., Alfredo, R., Benjamín, H., Martinez-Maldonado, R., & Echeverría, V. (2025). VALA / AID : A Method for Rapid , Participatory Value-sensitive Learning Analytics and Artificial Intelligence Design. LAK25: The 15th International Learning Analytics and Knowledge Conference (LAK 2025), March 03–07, 2025., 950–956. https://doi.org/https://doi.org/10.1145/3706468.3706553

Sadek, M., Calvo, R. A., & Mougenot, C. (2024). The Value-Sensitive Conversational Agent Co-Design Framework. International Journal of Human-Computer Interaction. https://doi.org/10.1080/10447318.2024.2426737

Zahran, R., Xu, J., Liang, H., & Forshaw, M. (2025). Data Science Students Perspectives on Learning Analytics: An Application of Human-Led and LLM Content Analysis. January, 1–17. http://arxiv.org/abs/2502.10409

Download Complete: Mapping AI adoption in academic spaces

Martina Plantak[1], Matevž Mandl[2],Vesna Lešnik Štefotič[3]

[1] Project Office, DOBA Business School, Slovenia: martina.plantak@doba.si
[2] Project Office, DOBA Business School, Slovenia: matevz.mandl@doba.si
[3] Project Office, DOBA Business School, Slovenia: vesna.lesnik-stefotic@net.doba.si

Correspondence: Martina Plantak: martina.plantak@doba.si

Abstract:

The integration of artificial intelligence (AI) tools in education has significantly influenced the experiences of both students and university faculty. This study examines usage patterns of AI tools among students and professors, comparing current data with last year's student survey. It explores which tools are most commonly used, why they are preferred, and their perceived usefulness in online learning. The research highlights benefits such as improved efficiency, learning outcomes, and personalized support, as well as concerns like over-reliance and ethical issues. It also assesses student proficiency with AI tools and identifies areas for improvement. In parallel, faculty perspectives are analyzed, including concerns about academic integrity, teaching limitations, and the need to adapt instructional practices. By comparing both groups' experiences, the study offers insights into AI's evolving role in higher education and informs strategies for its ethical and effective integration.

Keywords: artificial intelligence, higher education, online learning, teaching adaptation, comparative analysis.

Introduction

Artificial intelligence (AI) is no longer a concept of fiction but a fundamental part of our reality. With AI tools like ChatGPT becoming increasingly common, technological advancements in robotics and AI have accelerated over the past decades. The rapid development of AI is driven by three key factors: (1) decreasing costs in IT, along with increased computing power and memory capacity; (2) the expansion of the internet and digital communication, enabling big data analysis; and (3) reduced capital costs, which have facilitated market entry for startups experimenting with AI technologies (Ernst et al., 2019, 3). The future of AI is expected to bring even more transformative changes, significantly impacting economic systems and societies worldwide.

For example, in the context of online education, e-learning platforms leverage AI to offer adaptive learning, automate grading, and provide real-time feedback, improving student engagement and knowledge retention. In recent years, e-learning has emerged as a dynamic educational method, providing adaptable, scalable, and tailored learning opportunities. (Gligorea et al., 2023)

From an economic standpoint, AI in e-learning can improve efficiency and lowers costs, making education more accessible on a global scale. However, significant challenges persist, including the digital divide and the necessity of upskilling educators to effectively integrate AI tools into teaching practices. Furthermore, despite the rapid adoption of AI in education, there remains a noticeable lack of research, clear guidelines, and policy frameworks to address the unique ethical concerns it raises. Around the world, efforts to regulate or provide structured approaches for the responsible use of AI in learning environments are still in their infancy, leaving educators and institutions without clear direction. (Holmes et al., 2018) While technological advancements have historically reshaped the workforce, AI's capability to automate complex tasks raises critical questions about the future of human-led instruction. In recent years, the rapid development of AI tools has introduced a transformative dimension to e-learning, not only enhancing the learning process but also revolutionizing assessment and grading methods.

Following Arslan et al. (2020), using AI can offer several key advantages that enhance human expert performance. AI can match human graders in diagnostic accuracy, sensitivity, and specificity, while operating much faster and more cost-effectively. Nevertheless, alongside its advantages, AI introduces several challenges that need to be carefully managed to guarantee its ethical, equitable, and effective use. Educators and professionals must be prepared to apply AI tools thoughtfully, adapting them to suit the unique needs of different learning environments. Furthermore, it is essential to investigate how core skills like critical thinking, teamwork, and creativity can be preserved and fostered within AI-enhanced educational settings. (Gligorea et al., 2023)

As a leading fully online business school in Southeastern Europe, DOBA Faculty is committed to delivering high-quality, innovative education. With its strong focus on digitalization and modern pedagogical approaches, the integration of AI naturally aligns with the school's mission. Building on a 2023 study (see Plantak and Štefotič, 2024) that revealed both growing interest in AI tools and significant gaps in experience and understanding among students, this research was designed to track how those patterns have evolved over time. To support this goal, DOBA Faculty regularly conducts surveys among students and professors to monitor AI usage, perceptions, and emerging trends. By comparing last year's and this year's survey data, we aim to better understand how both groups are engaging with AI and to provide insights that support its responsible and effective integration in online education. To gain a deeper understanding of how students and faculty are using artificial intelligence in higher education, and how their perceptions are evolving over time, the following research questions were formulated:

1. How have student usage and perceptions of AI tools changed since last year?
2. What benefits and challenges do AI tools present in learning and assessment?
3. How do faculty view AI's impact on teaching, academic integrity, and learning?
4. What strategies support ethical, effective AI use in higher education?

Methodology

An electronic survey was administered in February of 2025 to gather data from higher education students and faculty members at Doba Faculty. A total of 104 students participated, responding to questions about their demographics, experience with AI tools, and attitudes toward AI in their studies. The student sample spanned a range of ages (roughly 15% were 18–25 years old, 32% were 26–35, 33% were 36–45, with smaller proportions above 45). About 27% of the student respondents identified as male and 73% as female. In terms of study level, the majority (74%) were undergraduate students, with 22% in Master's programs and a small number of doctoral students.

The teacher survey collected responses from 44 faculty members in higher education. The teacher cohort was also diverse in age, though skewed slightly older (over half were between 46–55 years old). Similar to the student sample, about one-third (34%) of the faculty members were male and two-thirds (66%) female. Response rate was around 40 %.

Both surveys included multiple-choice and rating-scale questions about AI tool usage frequency, self-assessed proficiency, specific tools and use cases, perceived usefulness and benefits, as well as concerns regarding AI in the educational context. Students came from various bachelor's and master's programmes, while faculty represented different fields, including management, marketing, and informatics. Most students had some experience using AI tools such as ChatGPT, Grammarly, or AI-supported search engines. Faculty members had varying levels of AI usage in their teaching practices.

Where applicable, results from a comparable survey conducted in 2023 are referenced to identify trends over time. All participants responded voluntarily, and the questions were presented in their respective native languages (Slovene, Croatian or English). The data were analyzed by calculating response frequencies, percentages, and mean agreement scores for scaled items.

Surveys for both faculty and students were conducted using comparable questions that were slightly updated each year to reflect the rapid changes in AI and its uses. The participation rate was similar through all the previous years.

Results

The 2025 survey data indicate a marked increase in the adoption of AI tools among both students and faculty, with faculty exhibiting a marginally higher rate of integration. Approximately one-third (33%) of students reported never using AI for academic purposes, whereas 51% use such tools occasionally and 16% regularly. Faculty responses reflect broader engagement: only 19% indicated no AI use in teaching, while 44% use AI occasionally and 36% regularly. These figures suggest that a greater proportion of faculty have embedded AI tools into their academic routines. Compared to 2023, when 47% of students had never used AI, the decline to 33% in 2025 marks a significant shift toward experimentation and occasional use. Faculty adoption levels are now broadly aligned with those of students, suggesting that instructors are adapting in parallel with the evolving digital landscape.

This increased exposure to AI has been accompanied by notable gains in self-reported proficiency (Figure 1). In 2025, only 11% of students identified as having "entry-level" knowledge (a substantial decline from 43% in 2023). A plurality (44%) rated themselves at a basic level, while 35% reported advanced competence, and 11% identified as experts. Faculty self-assessments reflect even greater confidence: none rated themselves at entry level, 55% reported basic knowledge, 31% advanced, and 14% expert-level proficiency. These findings suggest that faculty, bolstered by professional development opportunities such as DOBA Business School's AI-focused seminars, are generally more assured in their use of AI tools.

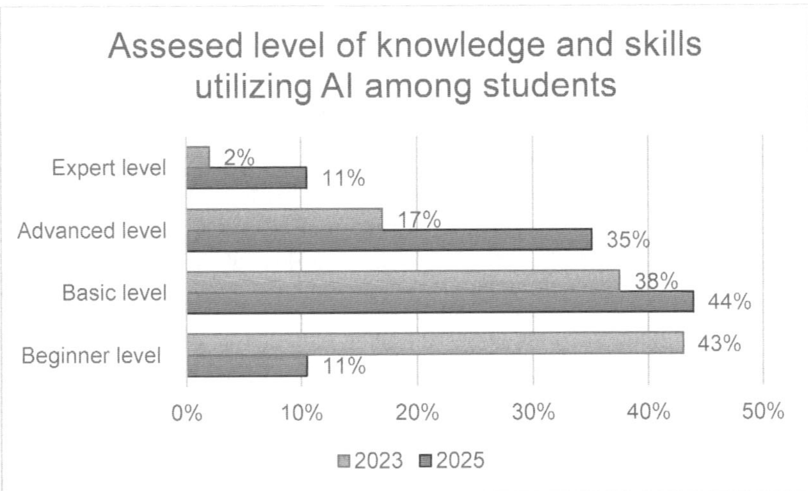

Figure 1: Assessed level of knowledge and skills utilizing AI among students in 2023 and 2025 survey

Regarding specific tools, ChatGPT emerged as the most widely used AI application among both cohorts. While some students and faculty mentioned using alternatives such as GitHub Copilot, Google's Gemini, and AI features in platforms like Canva, these tools were cited far less frequently. The dominance of ChatGPT underscores the role of generative AI, particularly large language models, as primary entry points into AI use in educational contexts.

Despite differences in experience, students (Figure 2) and faculty members report similar patterns of use, primarily leveraging AI for idea generation, summarization, translation, and information retrieval.

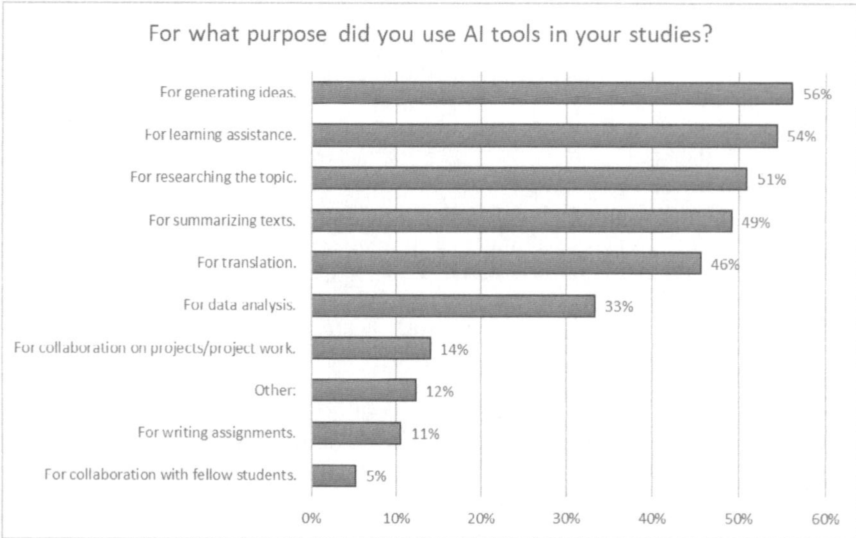

Figure 2: Purpose of AI Use in Studies – Student Survey 2025

Students rated the perceived benefits of AI tools (on a 4-point scale (1 = Strongly Disagree, 2 = Disagree, 3 = Agree, 4 = Strongly Agree)), showing the highest agreement for time-saving in information searches and improved understanding of study material (3.3). They also agreed that AI supports skill development and study efficiency (3.1 -3.2). Moderate benefits were seen in areas like exam prep and personalized learning (2,7 – 2.9), while the lowest benefit was noted in enhancing collaboration with peers and teachers (2.1). Faculty members reported the highest benefits of AI tools in enhancing teaching materials (3.4) and improving the clarity and structure of content (3.3). They also agreed (3.1–3.2) that AI supports efficiency in preparing lectures, provides inspiration for new teaching approaches, and aids in student assessment. Moderate benefits (2.7–2.9) were seen in supporting student engagement and simplifying administrative tasks. The lowest benefit (2.3) was reported for AI's role in fostering collaboration with students.

Nonetheless, the surveys also highlight persistent concerns. Both groups expressed scepticism regarding the reliability of AI-generated content (86% of students and 93% of lecturers) and raised ethical questions related to academic integrity, including plagiarism and fairness. Over two-thirds of faculty members reported facing ethical dilemmas concerning AI use. Students similarly recognized the potential for misuse (44 %), underscoring the need for institutions to provide clear, actionable guidelines.

Discussion

Overall, the findings reflect a dynamic and rapidly evolving integration of AI into higher education. Student adoption has grown significantly over the past two years, and faculty engagement has expanded in tandem. The data suggests that instructors are not only keeping pace but, in many cases, leading in the regular use of AI tools, potentially driven by the imperative to understand emerging technologies and guide their appropriate application in the classroom. As familiarity with AI increases, both groups are progressing along the learning curve, resulting in higher overall proficiency and confidence.

AI is viewed as a supportive tool that enhances productivity and creativity, rather than as a replacement for human input. The most frequently cited benefits, respectively, efficiency and improved understanding, align with broader trends in educational technology, wherein AI augments routine academic tasks and supports higher-order learning.

The ethical concerns raised by faculty members and students are already addressed by DOBA Business School. It has taken proactive steps in this direction by issuing formal AI usage policies for both students and faculty members.

Assessment integrity in the context of AI presents additional challenges. While a slight majority of students (51%) believe their instructors can detect AI-generated work, many faculty members expressed uncertainty about their ability to distinguish between human- and AI-produced content. This gap highlights the need for improved detection tools and pedagogical strategies that foster authentic student engagement, such as in-class assessments or oral examinations. Rather than prohibit AI outright, educational efforts might focus on teaching students how to use these tools ethically and transparently.

Another area of concern is AI's limited perceived capacity to facilitate collaboration and communication. Both groups rated these as the least developed aspects of current AI applications (14 % students and 12% of teachers), indicating that AI is predominantly seen as an individual aid. As new tools emerge, this may evolve; however, the centrality of human interaction in education remains evident. Educators could leverage the time saved by AI-supported automation to invest more in personalized instruction and peer-based learning activities.

In sum, comparisons across the 2023–2025 survey data reveal a clear trajectory: AI is becoming increasingly embedded in academic practice. Students are gaining experience and becoming more discerning in their use, while faculty are expanding their engagement and application of AI across a range of teaching tasks. Although the core benefits and concerns have remained stable, efficiency, improved learning, ethical risks, and accuracy, the growing prevalence of AI underscores the urgent need for comprehensive institutional support. This includes integrating AI literacy into curricula, providing faculty development opportunities, and updating academic policies to ensure ethical and effective use of AI in education.

Conclusion

In summary, the survey of students and faculty on AI usage in higher education reveals a dynamic yet cautious embrace of AI tools. AI adoption is widespread and increasing, with most students and an even larger proportion of faculty members now integrating tools like ChatGPT into their academic work. Both groups report that these tools serve valuable purposes – from brainstorming and research to translating materials and providing learning support – and they largely agree that AI can make studying and teaching more efficient and effective. The comparison to the previous year's data shows a clear uptick in engagement with AI and a growing confidence in using it, particularly among students who have quickly moved from novice to intermediate skill levels.

While enthusiasm for AI in education is growing, it is tempered by a clear awareness of associated challenges and responsibilities. Concerns about content accuracy, academic integrity (particularly plagiarism), and data privacy are widely shared by both students and faculty. As AI tools become more integrated into learning environments, the need for clear guidelines and open discussion becomes urgent. Institutions should not only establish policies on AI use but also promote AI literacy alongside core academic skills like critical thinking and problem-solving to prevent over-reliance.

Faculty perspectives range from skepticism to proactive engagement. Some remain cautious, requiring reassurance around AI's ethical application, while others are already experimenting with innovative uses in teaching. The findings suggest several practical implications: faculty training on AI integration, curriculum enhancements that engage students critically with AI, and updated academic integrity and data protection policies.

Overall, the results reflect cautious optimism. AI offers substantial potential to support personalized and effective learning, but its benefits will be fully realized only through thoughtful, balanced integration that maintains academic rigor and emphasizes human-centered learning.[1]

References

Arslan, J., Samarasinghe, G., Benke, K. K., Sowmya, A., Wu, Z., Guymer, R. H., & Baird, P. N. (2020). Artificial intelligence algorithms for analysis of geographic atrophy: a review and evaluation. Translational vision science & technology, 9(2), 57-57.

Ernst, E., Merola, R. i Samaan, D. (2019). Economics of Artificial Intelligence: Implications for the Future of Work. IZA Journal of Labor Policy, 9(4).

[1] Language and grammar in this article were reviewed and refined with the assistance of ChatGPT, an AI-based language model developed by OpenAI. All content and interpretations remain the responsibility of the authors.

Gligorea, I., Cioca, M., Oancea, R., Gorski, A. T., Gorski, H., & Tudorache, P. (2023). Adaptive learning using artificial intelligence in e-learning: A literature review. Education Sciences, 13(12), 1216.

Holmes, W., Bektik, D., Whitelock, D., & Woolf, B. P. (2018). Ethics in AIED: Who Cares?. In Artificial Intelligence in Education: 19th International Conference, AIED 2018, London, UK, June 27–30, 2018, Proceedings, Part II, Rosé, C. P., Martínez-Maldonado, R., Hoppe, H. U., Luckin, R., Matriki, M., Porayska-Pomsta, K., McLaren, B. and Du Boulay, B (ed) Vol. 10948. Lecture Notes in Computer Science. Cham: Springer International Publishing. https://doi.org/10. 1007/ 978-3-319-93846-2.

Plantak, M., & Štefotič, V. L. (2024). Artificial Intelligence and the Future of Online Learning: Opportunities and Challenges. Ubiquity Proceedings, 4(1).

Is Learning with an AI-Powered Chatbot for Everyone? A First Look at How Learning Preferences May Influence Learning Outcomes

Katharina Frosch[1], Friederike Lindauer[2], Carmen Winkel[3]

[1] Department of Business & Management, Brandenburg University of Applied Sciences, Germany; frosch@th-brandenburg.de
[2] Department of Business & Management, Brandenburg University of Applied Sciences, Germany; lindauer@th-brandenburg.de
[3] Project ELI Incubator, Brandenburg University of Applied Sciences, Germany; winkel@th-brandenburg.de

Correspondence: Katharina Frosch: frosch@th-brandenburg.de

Abstract:

In an era where AI-powered chatbots are increasingly being integrated into education and corporate learning, it is critical to determine whether these approaches benefit all learners or primarily cater to those with specific preferences. This study explores the interplay between learning preferences and learning outcomes in communication training using an AI-powered chatbot. In a field experiment with 17 participants, systematic thinkers and intrinsically motivated learners reported higher satisfaction and greater skill improvement, while those who preferred model learning and direct feedback benefited less. These findings suggest that AI-powered chatbots should be carefully designed to accommodate diverse learners and mitigate potential negative effects.

Keywords: AI-powered chatbots, learning preferences, cognitive style, learning outcomes

Introduction

Recently, AI chatbots - AI-powered software that converses with users in natural language (Holmes, 2019, pp. 142-143) - have become an integral part of modern education. Recent reviews have highlighted their potential to enhance the learning experience in higher education (Ma et al., 2024; Schei et al., 2024; Zhang et al., 2024): AI chatbots can provide adaptive learning paths, simplify complex concepts, assist with idea generation and task solving, and provide personalized feedback. A meta-analysis by Wu & Yu (2024) shows that AI chatbots improve various learning outcomes, including performance, motivation, interest, self-efficacy, and perceived value of learning, especially in higher education.

Increasingly, AI chatbots are being used not only to provide predefined interactions, such as answering questions and providing feedback, but also to create interactive, realistic learning experiences by simulating specific contexts and roles, such as acting as a virtual patient in medical education (e.g., Li et al., 2024). In their recent review, Yusuf et al. (2025) found that over 15% of 92 educational applications of conversational agents served this "simulate & experience" purpose. According to Nikolopoulou (2024, p. 106), such AI chatbot applications are particularly useful for simulating realistic, interactive learning experiences that are difficult to replicate in traditional settings due to resource constraints, such as the availability of instructors to act as role-players or conversation partners.

However, the promise of AI to improve education should not lead us to ignore potential limitations. As we experiment and innovate with AI technologies to improve average learning outcomes and satisfaction, we may overlook whether all learners can effectively use and benefit from these advances. This concern was raised in a recent study by Wu et al. (2024), which calls for further research into this issue.

This paper aims to provide initial insights into whether learning with an AI-powered chatbot is suitable for all learners, or whether certain types of learners are at risk of being left behind. We begin with a brief literature review, followed by research hypotheses about how learning preferences might influence outcomes when engaging with AI chatbots for learning. We then present a field experimental study with 17 participants using an AI chatbot to improve their communication skills. A pre-post survey design allows us to assess the impact of learning preferences on satisfaction and learning outcomes. We then discuss findings, limitations, and implications for research and practice, and conclude with ideas for future work.

State-of-the Art and Hypotheses

The question of whether and how individual learning styles and preferences affect learning effectiveness is an ongoing discussion in educational research. Technology-enhanced learning formats, including those powered by artificial intelligence, add an additional dimension to this discussion by enabling the design of adaptive learning experiences that take into account learners' styles and preferences to optimize learning outcomes (for reviews, see Ezzaim et al., 2024; Halkiopoulos & Gkintoni, 2024; Khamparia & Pandey, 2020; Truong, 2016). The Felder-Silverman learning style model (Felder & Silverman, 1988) is by far the most dominant one, followed by the VARK model (Fleming & Mills, 1992). While the Felder-Silverman model distinguishes between active/reflective, sensing/intuitive, visual/verbal, and sequential/global learners, the VARK model accommodates between visual (V), aural (A), read/write (R), and kinaesthetic (K) learning modes (Fallace, 2023; Prithishkumar & Michael, 2014). Another model that is used, albeit less frequently, when discussing learning styles in the area of technology-enhanced learning is Kolb's. In this model, Individuals may prefer and cope well with certain stages of a four-stage learning cycle—concrete experience, abstract conceptualization, active experimentation, and reflective observation—highlighting learning as a continuous and interactive process (Kolb 1976, 1984).

However, substantial meta-analytic evidence has discredited the matching hypothesis, which posits that individuals learn optimally when instruction matches such learning styles, which are thought to be relatively stable constructs (Hattie & O'Leary, 2025). However, it could be argued that novel learning and training formats, such as chatbot-assisted learning, have not yet been included in the evidence base of reviews and meta-analytic studies. In fact, the most recent meta-analysis discussed by Hattie & O'Leary (2025), Erdem & Kaf (2023) only includes studies up to 2017, long before the significant increase in AI-based learning and training methods.

In this paper, instead of using learning style models that describe rather stable indicators ("styles") of how learners learn best, we propose to use the related but somewhat more concise concept of learner preferences as a starting point for exploring the extent to which chatbot-assisted learning is a viable approach for all learners or only for some. Cassidy (2004, p. 421) defines learning preferences as "the preference for one method of instruction over another (e.g., group work over independent study)". This approach emphasizes that learners may prefer certain learning formats or situations over others (Deale, 2019; Loo, 2004; Rohani et al., 2024), such as group work vs. independent study, writing seminar papers vs. doing practical exercises. However, this does not necessarily mean that these preferred formats are closely linked to a concise learning style that is most effective (or: the only effective one) for their learning (ibid.). Nevertheless, as Deale (2019) points out, such preferences may be highly relevant for capturing learners' interest, engaging them, and increasing their overall satisfaction. Increased satisfaction, in turn, can lead to improved participation and enhanced learning opportunities in more indirect ways.

In what follows, we will briefly summarize existing research on learners' preferences regarding chatbot-assisted learning. This summary helps us to derive hypotheses about how preferences for specific instructional features within chatbot-based learning may vary across learners.

Recent reviews of chatbot-assisted learning (Zhang et al., 2024) indicate that chatbots are currently used primarily for exercises and instructions, and, although much less frequently and primarily in specific educational domains such as language learning (Dai et al., 2025) and patient simulation in health care (Li et al., 2024), for role-playing. In this context, chatbot technology is used to present learning materials, provide exercises, assess students' performance by providing immediate feedback, answer students' questions, and ask guiding questions to enhance the learning process (Zhang et al., 2024, p. 4535). The above-described ability of chatbots to provide dynamic, real-time responses (e.g., error correction, concept clarification, and adaptive guidance) to learner input may be particularly appealing to learners who prefer immediate, direct feedback on their learning performance:

H1: Chatbot-based learning provides a better learning experience for learners with a high preference for direct feedback.

While, as described above, the conversational nature of chatbot-based learning opens up opportunities to implement forms of learning in which learners actively engage in exploration, ask questions, and reflect on their understanding, one instructional feature that chatbot-based learning does not inherently include is observational learning. Rooted in Bandura's Social Learning Theory and being a building block of informal learning processes at the workplace (Eraut, 2007), observational learning describes the "acquisition of attitudes, values, and styles of thinking and behaving through observation of the examples provided by others" (Bandura, 2008) and is sometimes also referred to as "modelling". With respect to observational learning, we hypothesize:

H2: Chatbot-based learning provides a better learning experience for learners with a low preference for observational learning.

Another key instructional design feature often mentioned in the context of chatbot-based learning is self-regulated learning, in which learners construct their own understanding through interactions with the chatbot. This process involves setting learning goals, selecting, monitoring, and modifying their learning strategies to successfully complete specific tasks (for a recent review, see Guan et al., 2025). It is well established that successful self-regulation processes are highly dependent on learners' motivation and interest (Pintrich, 2004; Puustinen & Pulkkinen, 2001; Vollmeyer & Rheinberg, 2006; Yin et al., 2021), as "the stronger the learner's internal motivation, the more active they are in learning, the more cognitively engaged they are, and the more self-regulated they are" (Lee et al., 2025, p. 3). Therefore, we suggest that

H3: Chatbot-based learning provides a better learning experience for learners with high intrinsic motivation.

In our fourth hypothesis, we examine learners' cognitive styles, which, while not directly related to preferences for specific instructional features of chatbot-based learning, refer to the habitual patterns or strategies individuals use in educational situations (Armstrong, 2000). This concept, in turn, is thus again closer to the stable learning styles discussed above. We include it because the study by Iku-Silan et al. (2023) is one of the few that uses a control-group experimental design to examine whether learners' engagement and performance with chatbots varies based on individual characteristics. Their findings suggest that while chatbot-based learning resulted in higher performance compared to other formats, it also increased cognitive load. Specifically, analytical learners experienced less cognitive load and achieved better results than intuitive learners, suggesting that they may be better equipped to handle the demands of chatbot interactions. Therefore, we formulate the following hypothesis:

H4: Chatbot-based learning provides a better learning experience for learners with an analytical approach as compared to learners with an intuitive approach.

Research Methods and Materials

Sample and procedure

Our field experiment explored the interplay between learner preferences and learning outcomes with AI-powered chatbots, involving 32 students from a German university. Over the course of six weeks, participants engaged in multiple conversations with the chatbot and participated in a face-to-face role play to practice their leadership communication skills. The inclusion of face-to-face role-playing in the experimental design is important because it allows us to explore, at least to some extent[1], whether differences in how learners perceive chatbot-based learning and IT outcomes related to individual preferences are specifically related to the chatbot-based learning format, or whether the observed effects are more general (e.g., intrinsically motivated learners may generally tend to have better experiences; those who prefer observational learning may generally find fewer adequate learning experiences in traditional educational settings such as higher education). To assess learning preferences and approaches, participants completed online questionnaires before the training (pre-test) and reported on their experiences with the chatbot afterwards (post-test). The final sample (N=17) includes students with matched pre-test and post-test data who consented to the use of their data for research purposes.

Design of the AI-Powered Chatbot

The chatbot plays the role of the team member, while the participants play the role of the team leader. When the chatbot starts, participants are given a context for the conversation (e.g., discussing a new feedback system

[1] Parshler (2008) recommends randomly assigning learners to two groups, with each group undergoing a different learning or training intervention, followed by measuring identical outcome variables for both groups. In contrast, our study adopts a different approach to achieve the same objective: all participants engage in the same two learning activities (chatbot-based learning and face-to-face role play for practicing communication skills) and subsequently report their experiences with each format, respectively.

with a sceptical team member) and a brief description of their conversation partner (name, age, role, tenure, hobbies). Each conversation varies in the chatbot's characteristics and typical behaviours, such as being talkative or quiet, seeking feedback but defensive, or overflowing with ideas versus sticking to routines. Participants do not have access to this additional information. During the conversation, the chatbot maintains its character by offering realistic responses and incorporating basic nonverbal cues in parentheses (e.g., "[crosses arms and looks down]"). After the conversation, participants reflect by answering questions about the difficulty, goal attainment, and challenges of the conversation. This reflection helps them understand their performance and identify areas for improvement. The chatbot then highlights best practices and areas for improvement to enhance the user's communication skills. For the in-person role play that was also part of the training program, human actors took on the role of the team member.

Measures

Independent Variables: Preferred Learning Strategies

In the pre-test, we assessed learning preferences using items from the Informal Workplace Learning Scale (IWL, Decius et al., 2023), which closely reflect the previously discussed learner preferences that may be particularly important in chatbot-assisted learning. Thus, we measure

- observational learning, called “model learning in the IWL Scale, (“I look at how others work in the company/in my studies to improve my work"),
- direct feedback (“I ask my colleagues/my peer students when I am not sure how well I worked"), and
- intrinsic intent to learn (“I want to learn something new for myself because then I can solve problems at work/in my studies faster.")

with a 6-point Likert scale. In addition, a binary variable was operationalized to indicate whether the respective aspect is high (equal to or greater than the 25% percentile of the respective variable) or low.

We also measured cognitive thinking style using a 4-item version of the Cognitive Reflection Test (Thomson & Oppenheimer, 2016). Scores range from -4 to +4, with positive scores indicating a systematic thinking style (i.e., more correct than incorrect answers).

Dependent Variables: Learning Outcomes

Learning outcomes and experiences were measured using adapted items from Kron et al. (2017), which were used in a training context comparable to ours, specifically to evaluate communication skills training in the healthcare setting. We assessed participants' perceptions of training engagement, quality, and willingness to participate in future sessions with a similar instructional design. Participants also self-reported improvements in communication, handling emotionally charged situations, and leadership skills. Similar questions were asked about enjoyment, satisfaction, and self-perceived learning outcomes for the face-to-face role-play training session.

Results

Our sample reflects a typical business science student population: 59% female, mostly in their twenties. Most participants prefer model learning, see themselves as intrinsically motivated and like direct feedback (see Figure 1). CRT test results show that about one third of the participants use a systematic thinking style, with more correct answers than intuitive or incorrect ones (see also Figure 1).

An analysis of how different groups of learners rated the AI-powered chatbot training based on mean comparisons revealed the following differences: Participants with a strong preference for model learning found the chatbot-based communication training less engaging (Δ=-0.5, $p<0.05$) and showed less interest in participating in future sessions based on this learning format (Δ=-0.6, $p<0.05$). Similarly, those with a strong preference for direct feedback found the training less engaging (Δ=-0.4, $p<0.1$). Conversely, participants with high intrinsic motivation rated the training more positively (Δ=0.5, $p<0.1$) and were more willing to participate in similar activities in the future (Δ=0.6, $p<0.05$). In addition, learners classified as “systematic" thinkers reported higher overall satisfaction with the training (Δ=0.8, $p<0.05$).

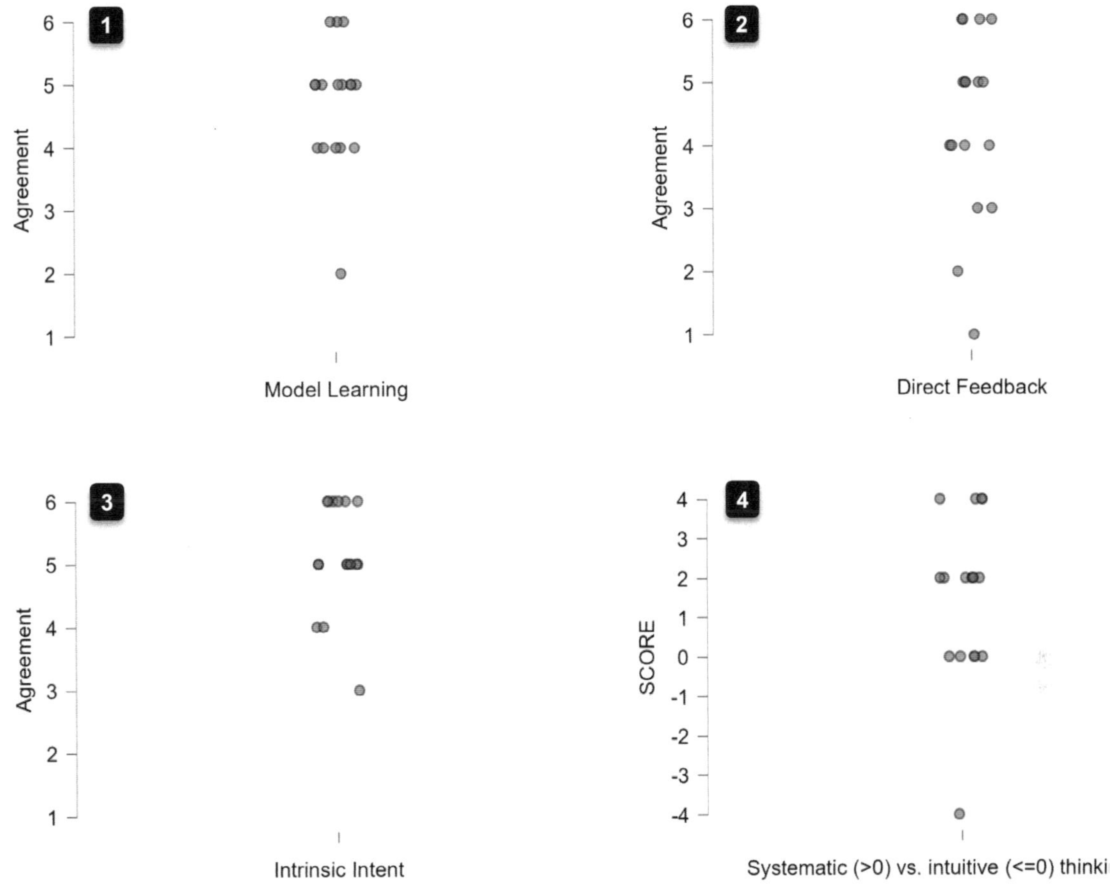

Figure 1: Jitter plots for selected learning preferences. Own illustration.

Notes: N=17, no missings. Graphs (1) - (3): 6-point Likert scale with options agree 1=strongly disagree, 2=mostly disagree, 3=somewhat disagree, 4=somewhat agree, 5=mostly agree, 6=strongly agree. Graph (4): Total score for the 4-item CRT ranges from -4 to +4, with positive values indicating a systematic thinking style.

In summary, learners with high intrinsic motivation and systematic thinking rated the training more positively, while those who preferred model learning and direct feedback found it less engaging. These differences are statistically significant despite the small sample size. In contrast, when analysing the face-to-face role-play, none of the mean differences were statistically significant and, in fact, even pointed in the opposite direction for some preferences and approaches, suggesting that the differences in the learning experience using a chatbot for learning may, to some extent, actually be specific to this format.

Table 1: Mean scores for different aspects related to training evaluation, by different learning strategies

	Model learning		**Direct feedback**		**Intrinsic intent**		**Syst. think. style**	
	low	high	low	high	low	high	no	yes
Engaging	4.5	4.0 **	4.4	4.0 *	4.3	4.0	4.2	4.2
Overall	4.2	3.9	3.9	4.1	3.8	4.3 *	3.5	4.3 **
Further	4.5	3.9 **	4.1	4.1	3.9	4.5 **	4.2	4.1
Enjoyment (f2f)	3.8	4.1	3.6	4.3	3.9	4.2	4.1	3.9
Satisfaction (f2f)	4.0	4.4	4.1	4.3	4.1	4.5	4.3	4.2

*Notes: N=17, no missings. The asterisks denote the results of a one-sided T-Test for independent samples (Mann-Whitney U test), indicating the statistical significance of differences between group means: */ **/*** indicates a p-value <0.01/<0.05/<0.1.
Survey questions: **Engaging** = "This training was engaging"; **Overall** = "Overall, this was an excellent training experience; **Further** = "I would like to take part in other trainings like this again in the future." **Enjoyment (f2f)** = "I enjoyed the face-to-face conversation with my role-play partner."; **Satisfaction (f2f)** = "Overall, I was satisfied with the face-to-face conversation as a learning format".

Table 2 shows the perceived skill development in communication, handling emotionally charged situations, and leadership after the AI-powered chatbot training. With the exception of preference for direct feedback, all learning preferences are associated with perceived skill development. Participants who prefer model learning reported lower skill development in handling emotionally charged situations (Δ=-0.7, p<0.1) and leadership (Δ=-0.4, p<0.1). Conversely, students with high intrinsic motivation reported greater improvements in managing emotionally charged situations (Δ=1.0, p<0.05). The most pronounced differences were observed between systematic and intuitive thinkers, with systematic thinkers showing higher improvements in all skill dimensions (Δ=0.7/0.8/0.6, p<0.05/0.1/0.05). Again, we do not observe statistically significant differences with respect to any of the learning preferences and approaches when analysing self-reported learning in the face-to-face role-playing format.

Table 2: Mean scores for different aspects related to perceived skill building, by different learning strategies

	Model learning			**Direct feedback**			**Intrinsic intent**			**Syst. think. style**		
	low	**high**		**low**	**high**		**low**	**high**		**no**	**yes**	
Communication	3.7	4.1		3.8	4.1		3.9	4.0		3.5	4.2	**
Handling emotions	4.0	3.3	*	3.5	3.6		3.2	4.2	**	3.0	3.8	*
Leadership	4.3	3.9	*	4.0	4.1		4.1	4.0		3.7	4.3	**
Learning (f2f)	4.0	3.8		3.9	3.9		3.7	4.2		4.0	3.8	

*Notes: N=17, no missings. The asterisks denote the results of a one-sided T-Test for independent samples (Mann-Whitney U test), indicating the statistical significance of differences between group means: */ **/*** indicates a p-value <0.01/<0.05/<0.1.
Survey questions: **Communication** = "Based on this training, my communication skills improved"; **Handling emotions** = "This training was effective for learning how to handle emotionally charged situations; **Leadership** = "This training will help me improve my leadership skills." **Learning (f2f)**: "I learned a lot from the face-to-face conversation."

Discussion

In this study, we analysed how different learner preferences and approaches affect the evaluation and outcomes of communication training delivered through an AI-powered chatbot. Our results suggest that learners with systematic thinking strategies and high intrinsic motivation benefited more, as they found the training more engaging and reported greater self-perceived improvement in communication skills. Conversely, those who preferred model learning and direct feedback were less satisfied. A preference for model learning was also associated with lower reported skill development when practicing communication skills with such a chatbot-based learning format. This supports our previous hypotheses. In contrast, no significant differences in learner preferences were observed in face-to-face role-playing, suggesting that it may have been the specific instructional features of chatbot-based learning that shape the different learning experiences.

However, our study has limitations. Our small sample size restricted us to considering a narrow range of learning strategies and prevented us from exploring interaction effects or potential confounding factors. The small sample size also limits the generalizability of our findings. Furthermore, small samples can lead to estimation biases. We have addressed this concern by employing the non-parametric Mann-Whitney U test, which is particularly well-suited for small samples. Nevertheless, our results should be considered very preliminary given the small sample size.

We hope this exploration of how learner differences affect experiences and outcomes in chatbot-based learning will inspire further large-scale studies. If individual preferences and approaches indeed influence how learners experience chatbot-based learning, instructional design should account for this. For instance, the chatbot-based communication training in this study appears less suitable for model learners. Incorporating sample dialogues that illustrate effective conversation practices could enhance the learning experience for those who prefer learning through observation and practical demonstrations of communication behaviours.

Conclusions

Future research could aim for larger samples to increase the generalizability of findings, and consider a broader range of learner characteristics that may lead to differences in how chatbot-based learning is experienced. In addition, a mixed-methods design that includes qualitative research methods would provide deeper insights into the learner experience and the potential impact of preferences when engaging with AI-based chatbots. The most important aspect of future research, however, is not only exploring whether individual preferences and approaches affect learning experiences, but also understanding why certain groups benefit from or struggle with chatbot-based training. Gaining insight into the underlying mechanisms of the learning process will be crucial for developing inclusive training solutions that cater to different learning preferences and approaches, and ultimately make AI-powered chatbots a truly effective and inclusive learning technology.

References

Armstrong, S. J. (2000). The influence of individual cognitive style on performance in management education. Educational Psychology, 20(3), 323–339. https://doi.org/10.1080/014434100750018020

Bandura, A. (2008). Observational learning. In W. Donsbach (Ed.), The International Encyclopedia of Communication (1st ed.). Wiley. https://doi.org/10.1002/9781405186407.wbieco004

Cassidy, S. (2004). Learning Styles: An overview of theories, models, and measures. Educational Psychology, 24(4), 419–444. https://doi.org/10.1080/0144341042000228834

Dai, D. W., Suzuki, S., & Chen, G. (2025). Generative AI for professional communication training in intercultural contexts: Where are we now and where are we heading? Applied Linguistics Review, 16(2), 763–774. https://doi.org/10.1515/applirev-2024-0184

Deale, C. (2019). Learning preferences instead of learning Styles: A case study of hospitality management students' perceptions of how they learn best and implications for teaching and learning. International Journal for the Scholarship of Teaching and Learning, 13(2). https://doi.org/10.20429/ijsotl.2019.130211

Eraut, M. (2007). Learning from other people in the workplace. Oxford Review of Education, 33(4), 403–422. https://doi.org/10.1080/03054980701425706

Erdem, E., & Kaf, Ö. (2023). Effect of learning styles on academic achievement: A meta-analysis. TAY Journal, 7(1), 26–43. https://doi.org/10.29329/tayjournal.2023.537.02

Ezzaim, A., Dahbi, A., Aqqal, A., & Haidine, A. (2024). AI-based learning style detection in adaptive learning systems: A systematic literature review. Journal of Computers in Education. https://doi.org/10.1007/s40692-024-00328-9

Fallace, T. (2023). The long origins of the visual, auditory, and kinesthetic learning style typology, 1921–2001. History of Psychology, 26(4), 334–354. https://doi.org/10.1037/hop0000240

Felder, R. M., & Silverman, L. K. (1988). Learning and teaching styles in engineering education. Engineering Education, 78(7), 674–681.

Fleming, N. D., & Mills, C. (1992). Not another inventory, rather a catalyst for reflection. To Improve the Academy, 11(1), 137–155. https://doi.org/10.1002/j.2334-4822.1992.tb00213.x

Guan, R., Raković, M., Chen, G., & Gašević, D. (2025). How educational chatbots support self-regulated learning? A systematic review of the literature. Education and Information Technologies, 30(4), 4493–4518. https://doi.org/10.1007/s10639-024-12881-y

Halkiopoulos, C., & Gkintoni, E. (2024). Leveraging AI in e-learning: Personalized learning and adaptive assessment through cognitive neuropsychology—A systematic analysis. Electronics, 13(18), Article 18. https://doi.org/10.3390/electronics13183762

Hattie, J., & O'Leary, T. (2025). Learning styles, preferences, or strategies? An explanation for the resurgence of styles across many meta-analyses. Educational Psychology Review, 37(2), 31. https://doi.org/10.1007/s10648-025-10002-w

Holmes, W. (2019). Artificial intelligence in education: Promises and implications for teaching and learning. Center for Curriculum Redesign.

Iku-Silan, A., Hwang, G.-J., & Chen, C.-H. (2023). Decision-guided chatbots and cognitive styles in interdisciplinary learning. Computers & Education, 201, 104812. https://doi.org/10.1016/j.compedu.2023.104812

Khamparia, A., & Pandey, B. (2020). Association of learning styles with different e-learning problems: A systematic review and classification. Education and Information Technologies, 25(2), 1303–1331. https://doi.org/10.1007/s10639-019-10028-y

Kolb, D. A. (1976). The Learning Styles Inventory: Technical manual. Boston: McBer & Company.

Kolb, D. A. (1984). Experiential learning. Englewood Cliffs, NJ: Prentice Hall Inc..

Kron, F. W., Fetters, M. D., Scerbo, M. W., White, C. B., Lypson, M. L., Padilla, M. A., Gliva-McConvey, G. A., Belfore II, L. A., West, T., & Wallace, A. M. (2017). Using a computer simulation for teaching communication skills: A blinded multisite mixed methods randomized controlled trial. Patient Education and Counseling, 100(4), 748–759.

Lee, Y.-F., Hwang, G.-J., & Chen, P.-Y. (2025). Technology-based interactive guidance to promote learning performance and self-regulation: A chatbot-assisted self-regulated learning approach. Educational Technology Research and Development. https://doi.org/10.1007/s11423-025-10478-x

Li, Y., Zeng, C., Zhong, J., Zhang, R., Zhang, M., & Zou, L. (2024). Leveraging large language model as simulated patients for clinical education (No. arXiv:2404.13066). arXiv. https://doi.org/10.48550/arXiv.2404.13066

Loo, R. (2004). Kolb's learning styles and learning preferences: Is there a linkage? Educational Psychology, 24(1), 99–108. https://doi.org/10.1080/0144341032000146476

Ma, W., Ma, W., Hu, Y., & Bi, X. (2024). The who, why, and how of ai-based chatbots for learning and teaching in higher education: A systematic review. Education and Information Technologies. https://doi.org/10.1007/s10639-024-13128-6

Nikolopoulou, K. (2024). Generative artificial intelligence in higher education: Exploring ways of harnessing pedagogical practices with the assistance of ChatGPT. International Journal of Changes in Education, 1(2), Article 2. https://doi.org/10.47852/bonviewIJCE42022489

Pashler, H., McDaniel, M., Rohrer, D., & Bjork, R. (2008). Learning styles: Concepts and evidence. Psychological Science in the Public Interest, 9(3), 105–119. https://doi.org/10.1111/j.1539-6053.2009.01038.x

Pintrich, P. R. (2004). A Conceptual framework for assessing motivation and self-regulated learning in college students. Educational Psychology Review, 16(4), 385–407. https://doi.org/10.1007/s10648-004-0006-x

Prithishkumar, I. J., & Michael, S. A. (2014). Understanding your student: Using the VARK model. Journal of Postgraduate Medicine, 60(2), 183–186. https://doi.org/10.4103/0022-3859.132337

Puustinen, M., & Pulkkinen, L. (2001). Models of self-regulated learning: A review. Scandinavian Journal of Educational Research, 45(3), 269–286. https://doi.org/10.1080/00313830120074206

Rohani, N., Sowa, S., & Manataki, A. (2024). Identifying learning preferences and strategies in health data science courses: Systematic Review. JMIR Medical Education, 10(1), e50667. https://doi.org/10.2196/50667

Schei, O. M., Møgelvang, A., & Ludvigsen, K. (2024). Perceptions and use of AI chatbots among students in higher education: A scoping review of empirical studies. Education Sciences, 14(8), Article 8. https://doi.org/10.3390/educsci14080922

Thomson, K. S., & Oppenheimer, D. M. (2016). Investigating an alternate form of the cognitive reflection test. Judgment and Decision Making, 11(1), 99-113.

Truong, H. M. (2016). Integrating learning styles and adaptive e-learning system: Current developments, problems and opportunities. Computers in Human Behavior, 55, 1185–1193. https://doi.org/10.1016/j.chb.2015.02.014

Vollmeyer, R., & Rheinberg, F. (2006). Motivational effects on self-regulated learning with different tasks. Educational Psychology Review, 18(3), 239–253. https://doi.org/10.1007/s10648-006-9017-0

Wu, R., & Yu, Z. (2024). Do AI chatbots improve students learning outcomes? Evidence from a meta-analysis. British Journal of Educational Technology, 55(1), 10–33. https://doi.org/10.1111/bjet.13334

Yin, J., Goh, T.-T., Yang, B., & Xiaobin, Y. (2021). Conversation technology with micro-learning: The impact of chatbot-based learning on students' learning motivation and performance. Journal of Educational Computing Research, 59(1), 154–177. https://doi.org/10.1177/0735633120952067

Yusuf, H., Money, A., & Daylamani-Zad, D. (2025). Pedagogical AI conversational agents in higher education: A conceptual framework and survey of the state of the art. Educational Technology Research and Development. https://doi.org/10.1007/s11423-025-10447-4

Zhang, R., Zou, D., & Cheng, G. (2024). A review of chatbot-assisted learning: Pedagogical approaches, implementations, factors leading to effectiveness, theories, and future directions. Interactive Learning Environments, 32(8), 4529–4557. https://doi.org/10.1080/10494820.2023.2202704

Supporting Students in Distance Education: A Case Study of the PENER-16 Programme at the Hellenic Open University

Thomas Vangelis[1], Evangelia Manousou[2], Eleni Niarchou[3], Kyriaki Rassia[4]

[1] School of Humanities, Hellenic Open University, Greece, thomasvanggelis@gmail.com
[2] School of Humanities, Hellenic Open University, Greece, manousoug@eap.gr
[3] School of Humanities, Hellenic Open University, Greece, elniarchou@gmail.com
[4] School of Humanities, Hellenic Open University; Greece, kyriaki.rassia@ac.eap.gr

Correspondence: Thomas Vangelis: thomasvanggelis@gmail.com

Abstract:

This research focuses on student support in distance education by gathering data for the development of a comprehensive support framework. More specifically, the research, through the method of literature review, explores students' needs and examines the potential of utilizing support mechanisms to address these needs. As a case study, the PENER-16 research project of the Hellenic Open University is chosen, which aims at the smooth familiarization of students with distance education by preventing dropout. The research findings demonstrate that students need support, instructional design, self-regulation, and communication. Moreover PENER-16 guidelines are aligned with the needs of students, promoting equal inclusion and reducing inequalities in both access to and success in education.

Keywords: student support, students' needs, distance education, PENER-16 research project, Hellenic Open University

Introduction

Students' smooth integration and adaptation to distance education play an important role in their academic success and in preventing dropout. Several transition and adaptation difficulties occur in the early stages of studies, highlighting the challenges that institutions and students may face in adapting to the distance education environment (Rahmani et al., 2024). In this context, support mechanisms play a crucial role in ensuring equitable access and participation in the educational process. Utilizing all available support services at an early stage of studies helps create a safe environment for students to continue their education journey (Raju & Kohli, 2015). Another relevant study, that of Kara et al. (2019), argues that creating flexible learning environments, adapted to individual differences and challenges, is essential to prevent attrition from e-learning programs. In this context, institutions should provide support to students, who from the outset are aware that they must organize their own learning due to the physical distance from their tutor. Within this framework, the PENER-16 programme is chosen as a case study. PENER-16 is a research project developed by the Hellenic Open University (HOU), which aims to improve student support by providing tools and guidance to facilitate the adaptation to e-learning.

This study explores the needs of students at the beginning of their study in distance education and examines the extent to which the support mechanisms provided by PENER-16 address these needs. Through a literature review, this research maps the challenges faced by students during the early phases of their studies, while a content analysis of PENER-16 identifies the main thematic axes related to student support.

Research scope and research questions

The present research aims to investigate the needs of students in higher distance education and examine how HOU's PENER-16 support mechanism facilitates their smooth adjustment for a successful academic career.
The research questions, derived from the research's main objectives, are as follows:

1. What are the needs of students at the beginning of their studies in distance education?
2. How do the support mechanisms provided by PENER-16 research project address students' needs for early adaptation to distance education?

Theoretical framework

Student support framework in Distance Education

Tait (2015) argues that student support in distance education should not be viewed merely as an integral part of an institution's organizational system, but as a comprehensive framework that encompasses the whole student learning experience. The aim of institutions should be to make this integrated system available to all stages of study from the enrollment to the graduation. In this context, preventing dropout should be a main goal of student support mechanisms to remove the barriers and challenges faced by students and enhance their academic success (Ologbura, 2023).

Tait (2015) distinguishes seven key elements essential for effective student support

- Information and guidance prior to the commencement of studies
- Curriculum design that promotes student success
- Crisis intervention to address students' needs
- Assessment strategies that support learning and evaluate performance
- Personalized and tailored student support systems
- Information and logistical systems that facilitate communication among all stakeholders
- Effective management focused on ensuring student achievement

Lionarakis et al. (2018a) imply that an institution should provide support in administrative matters, promoting collaboration and communication skills, and enhancing digital literacy.

Factors Influencing Student Retention

The educational process, especially after enrollment, is very significant to students' decision to drop out (Bağrıacık Yılmaz and Karataş, 2022). Regarding the difficulty in adapting to the new environment of distance education at the beginning of their studies (Schweighart et al., 2024). The issue of exploring all the characteristics of students just entering their first year of study can contribute to a successful academic career by utilizing all available support mechanisms at an early stage, in order to create a safe environment for students to prevent them from dropping out of their studies (Raju & Kohli, 2015). Willging and Johnson's (2009) study focuses on the preparatory phase before the start of studies, examining the factors that influence students' decisions to drop out of online courses. Specifically, the authors reported that students are more likely to drop out courses if they have difficulty adjusting at the beginning of the course, suggesting that the initial stages of preparation and adjustment are critical to student retention. Another related study, conducted by Kara et al. (2019), argues that creating flexible learning environments that adapt to individual differences and challenges is essential to prevent dropout in e-learning programs. In a similar context, Muljiana and Luo's (2019) research highlighted factors that influence retention rates in distance education, including institutional support, program difficulty, enhancement of sense of belonging, facilitation of learning, course design, student behavioral characteristics, and demographic and personal issues. The ease of adjustment at the beginning of the course (Willging & Johnson, 2009), flexibility in a learning environment tailored to students' needs (Kara et al., 2019), support, sense of belonging to a group, course design, focus on student behavioral characteristics, and student demographics and personal issues (Muljiana & Luo, 2019) are key factors that contribute to student retention in distance universities and academic success.

Addressing Student Needs in Distance Education

The needs of students are many. First, they need technical support, guidance, a sense of connection, and feedback from tutors, as well as communication and interaction with their peers (Mypigna et al., 2006; Koper, 2015). Additionally, students seek flexibility and convenience, with a focus on self-motivation and efficiency in course design (Fedynich et al., 2015). It is crucial for all distance education institutions to identify the factors that hinder students from continuing their studies, and, indeed, it is vital to identify early on those who are at risk of dropping out in the early stages (Heilporn & Lakhal, 2021). Investigating the needs of students in open and distance higher education is crucial. This approach forms an appropriate theoretical framework. In practice, it helps formulate a comprehensive student support system that addresses some inherent weaknesses of distance education and balances the inequalities associated with openness and access.

PENER-16

PENER-16 is a key mechanism for providing students with assistance and support. It serves as a vital tool that ensures equal access to the educational process, helping to bridge gaps, reduce inequalities, and promote inclusion. According to Lionarakis et al. (2018b) PENER-16 research project actively addresses several challenges, including student isolation, lack of personal contact and support, absence of intermediary infrastructure, and the admission of students who have been out of formal education for years and may lack academic skills or a collaborative learning culture. According to the researchers, PENER-16 consists of a tele-support platform (Moodle) based mainly on asynchronous communication with the possibility of activating synchronous communication services. The model includes a variety of narrative modes and multimodal support materials for all thematic categories, using animated videos and presentations with a combination of audio and visual material, with the aim of providing information and answering possible questions. At the same time, according to the researchers, PENER-16 promotes self-directed learning, digital literacy and the provision of support mechanisms.

Methodology

Data Collection and analysis

This research uses a mixed research methodology with a qualitative approach. The first research question, "What are the needs of students at the beginning of their studies in distance education?" is answered through a literature review. Data were collected through a search of electronic databases. It contains papers that are published in the field of distance education. The search was conducted in the following databases: Google Scholar, Scopus, ScienceDirect, SpringerLink, Wiley Online Library, Taylor & Francis Online Journals, SAGE Journals Online, Educational Resources Information Center (ERIC). The included keywords in the search are distance education, needs, perceptions, factors, dropout, support, challenges, services, frameworks, mechanisms. The second research question, 'How do the support mechanisms provided by PENER-16 address students' needs for early adaptation to distance education?' is answered through an institutional analysis approach by browsing to the official PENER-16 website (https://eeyem.eap.gr/pener-eap-16). All support services were identified that address the needs and challenges of students. The research questions will be explored and answered through thematic analysis. Appropriate thematic areas were identified based on the aims of the study, guided by the first research question, shaping the analytical process (Tsiolis, 2018). The analysis of qualitative data provides meaningful insights that help address the main research questions (Tsiolis, 2018). The NVivo 20 software (https://lumivero.com/products/nvivo/) was used to extract the following thematic areas: a) needs for support, b) needs for well-organized instructional design, c) needs for self-regulation and skills development, and d) needs related to communication and collaboration. For the second research question, the data were again analyzed utilizing NVivo 20 software. The analysis emerged the following thematic fields: a) Support, b) Instructional design c) Self-regulation and skills development, d) Communication and collaboration. This classification enables the connection of PENER-16 services with students' needs, emphasizing how PENER-16's supportive practices contribute to the smooth adaptation of students to distance education.

Findings

Students' needs

Need for support

Students need psychological and instructional support to feel independent and confident in continuing their studies. An essential aspect of this support is the feedback provided by tutors through assignments, as well as guidance on using technical equipment (Kauffman, 2015). On an emotional level, satisfaction and goal achievement play a key role, alongside the development of study organization skills (Rahmmani et al., 2024). Additionally, self-esteem and self-efficacy play significant role, because students with higher emotional intelligence demonstrate greater self-awareness of their needs, effective self-regulation, organizational abilities, and self-evaluation skills (Kauffman, 2015). Furthermore, technological support is necessary, as inadequate technical preparation for a program can negatively impact students' progress (Willging & Johnson, 2009).

Need for instructional design

This category includes instructional design with an emphasis on course structure, learning materials, and the degree of flexibility in studies. Enhancements in teaching methods are sought to increase students' interest in interactive courses (Mohammad et al., 2021). Students need a variety of educational materials, direct access to courses, and flexibility in examinations (Turan et al., 2022). They, also, prefer to have well-organized courses, which may connect the theoretical knowledge with real-world, and activities that encourage them to maintain their learning progress and deepen their understanding of the material (Kauffman, 2015). Pre-arranging lessons with supportive activities is a strong request from students, allowing access to the material from the beginning, enhancing time management (Fayer, 2014).

Need for self-regulation and skills development

This category relates to a sense of autonomy and self-regulation, as well as the development of skills for achieving personal and professional goals to ensure a successful pathway of study. Students often feel isolated and experience emotional instability due to a lack of self-regulated learning and various challenges that, combined with technical issues, affect their communication with peers and professors (Uzir et al., 2024; Rahmani et al., 2024). Additionally, students struggle with study time management (Aydin et al., 2019). Finally, there is a need for academic and social integration, as well as access to university facilities (Bağrıacık Yılmaz & Karataş, 2022).

Need for communication and collaboration

The fourth category refers to the notions of communication and collaboration. The need for collaboration fosters engagement in online learning environment and enhances the overall learning experience (Bolliger & Martin, 2018). This practice promotes two-way communication and helps create an engaging learning environment (Kauffman, 2015; Mohammad et al., 2021), while also facilitating interaction with professors, peers, and course materials (Baturay & Yukselturk, 2015). Moreover, the provision of continuous feedback, resulting from communication among stakeholders, strengthens the sense of belonging to a community, enabling smoother integration into the learning environment (Diep et al., 2019).

Addressing needs through the mechanisms provided by PENER-16

The analysis of data demonstrates the influence of the practices of PENER-16 and how they can address students' needs.

Support

A major function of PENER-16 is the provision of information on psychological support. It highlights how important is the mental well-being and identifies critical points where students may require support during their studies. Additionally, it offers information on the counseling and psychological support structures available at HOU and other institutions.

Instructional Design

PENER-16 includes an introductory and supportive thematic unit named "Introduction to University Studies." This section provides essential information on the structure, functions, and procedures governing open university studies, helping students familiarize themselves with the philosophy of distance education

Self-Regulation and Skills Development

To address the need for self-regulation, PENER-16 includes the thematic category "Organization of Study," which explains the demands of university-level learning and provides guidance on time and study management. Another significant category is "Academic Writing," which explores the principles of academic writing and methodologies for composing scientific texts. Additionally, the "Preparing a Dissertation" section offers structured support for organizing and developing a dissertation. In addition, the "Digital Tools" section provides to the students the necessary skills to complete assignments and tasks using various digital platforms.

Communication and Collaboration

The thematic category "Community and Collaborative Learning" defines the dimensions of communication and collaboration. Moreover, it provides guidelines how to use collaborative learning tools and videoconferencing platforms to enhance interaction and engagement, because communication and collaboration are very important for students to have a sense of being part of an academic community

Discussion and Conclusions

The research highlights students' needs to ensure their support and a successful academic career. The use of support mechanisms such as PENER-16 is a key factor in student retention and dropout prevention. Specifically, regarding the first research question, the findings indicate that students need support and guidance to succeed and stay well-organized (Fedynich et al., 2015; Kauffman, 2015; Koper, 2015; Mupinga et al., 2006; Rahmani et al., 2024). They also require a well-structured educational design with flexibility and easy access to the learning process (Fayer, 2014; Koper, 2015; Mohammad et al., 2021; Turan et al., 2022). Additionally, the research demonstrated that students need self-regulation and skill development to enhance their academic success (Aydin et al., 2019; Fedynich et al., 2015; Rahmani et al., 2024; Uzir et al., 2024). Finally, students seek an engaging learning environment (Bolliger & Martin, 2018; Kauffman, 2015; Mohammad et al., 2021) and emphasize the importance of communication and collaboration (Fedynich et al., 2015; Koper, 2015; Mupinga et al., 2006), with direct interaction with all participants in the educational process (Baturay & Yukselturk, 2015).
The second research question, which examines the supportive practices of PENER-16, suggests that these mechanisms effectively address and fulfill students' needs. The thematic categories of psychological support and informing students about the philosophy of distance education and instructional design (Tait, 2015) can contribute to their psychological empowerment and help prevent dropout (Heilporn & Lakhal, 2021), while aligning with Tait's (2015) support framework. Furthermore, the thematic categories 'Organization of Study,' 'Academic Writing,' and 'Preparing a Dissertation' support the development of self-regulation, study organization, and self-directed learning (Lionarakis et al., 2018b). The need for communication and collaboration is addressed through the thematic category 'Community and Collaborative Learning,' which enhances students' sense of engagement and improves their learning experience (Bolliger & Martin, 2018).

In conclusion, the research data shows how importance is the establishment of a support framework for students. Understanding students' needs, outlining their profile, and examining the conditions that influence their learning journey are crucial not only for their academic success but also for institutions seeking to implement effective support mechanisms and policies. The early activation of support systems can play an important role in preventing students from dropping out. This should be done from the very beginning of a student's academic journey and should also help them to feel part of an academic community.

Competing interests

The author(s) has/have no competing interests to declare.

References

Aydin, S., Öztürk, A., Büyükköse, G. T., Er, F., & Sönmez, H. (2019). An Investigation of Drop-out in Open and Distance Education. Educational Sciences: Theory and Practice, 19(2), 40-57. http://dx.doi.org/10.12738/estp.2019.2.003

Bağrıacık Yılmaz, A., & Karataş, S. (2022). Why do open and distance education students drop out? Views from various stakeholders. International Journal of Educational Technology in Higher Education, 19(1), 28. https://doi.org/10.1186/s41239-022-00333-x

Baturay, M., & Yukselturk, E. (2015). The role of online education preferences on student's achievement. Turkish Online Journal of Distance Education, 16(3), 3-12. http://dx.doi.org/10.17718/tojde.47810

Bolliger, D. U., & Martin, F. (2018). Instructor and student perceptions of online student engagement strategies. Distance Education, 39(4), 568–583. https://doi.org/10.1080/01587919.2018.1520041

Diep, A. N., Zhu, C., Cocquyt, C., De Greef, M., Vo, M. H., & Vanwing, T. (2019). Adult learners' needs in online and blended learning. Australian Journal of Adult Learning, 59(2), 223-253. https://files.eric.ed.gov/fulltext/EJ1235812.pdf

Fayer, L. (2014). A multi-case study of student perceptions of online course design elements and success. International Journal for the Scholarship of Teaching & Learning, 8(1), 1–27. https://doi.org/10.20429/ijsotl.2014.080113

Fedynich, L., Bradley, K. S., & Bradley, J. (2015). Graduate students' perceptions of online learning. Research in Higher Education Journal, 27(1), 1–13. https://files.eric.ed.gov/fulltext/EJ1056187.pdf

Heilporn, G., & Lakhal, S. (2021). Environmental Facilitators and Barriers to Student Persistence in Online Courses: Reliability and Validity of New Scales. The Journal of Continuing Higher Education, 1–19. https://doi.org/10.1080/07377363.2020.1847972

Kara, M., Erdogdu, F., Kokoç, M., & Cagiltay, K. (2019). Challenges faced by adult learners in online distance education: A literature review. Open Praxis, 11(1), 5-22. http://dx.doi.org/10.5944/openpraxis.11.1.929

Kauffman H. (2015). A review of predictive factors of student success in and satisfaction with online learning. Research in Learning Technology, 23. Article 26507. https://doi.org/10.3402/rlt.v23.26507

Koper, R. (2015). How Do Students Want to Learn in Online Distance Education? Profiling Student Preferences. International Review of Research in Open and Distributed Learning, 16(1), 307–329. https://doi.org/10.19173/irrodl.v16i1.2000

Lionarakis, A., Niaris, M., Apostolidou, A., & Hartofylaka, A.-M. (2018a). Development of an integrated support system for distance education students. 4th International Conference on the Promotion of Educational Innovation,Larissa, October 12–14, 2018. https://elearn.eap.gr/pluginfile.php/249/mod_resource/content/6/eepek2018.pdf

Lionarakis, A., Apostolidou, A., Hartofylaka, A.-M., Niari, M., & Sfakiotaki, K. (2018). Individual and institutional support in ODL: How the macro may benefit from the micro. In A. Volungeviciene & A. Szűcs (Eds.), Proceedings of the European Distance and E-Learning Network 2018 Annual Conference (pp. 38-46). EDEN. https://www.researchgate.net/publication/326228908_INDIVIDUAL_AND_INSTITUTIONAL_SUPPORT_IN_ODL_HOW_THE_MACRO_MAY_BENEFIT_FROM_THE_MICRO

Mohammad, W. A. W., Wahab, N. A., Mydin, A. M., Omar, M., Abd Samat, A. A., & Gumilar, L. (2024). Identifying Students' Preference in Learning Through ODL (Open Distance Learning) for Multimedia Course. Journal of Advanced Research in Applied Sciences and Engineering Technology, 132-141. https://doi.org/10.37934/araset.62.1.132141

Mupinga, D. M., Nora, R. T., & Yaw, D. C. (2006). The learning styles, expectations, and needs of online students. College Teaching, 54(1), 185–189. https://doi.org/10.3200/ctch.54.1.185-189

Muljana, P.S., & Luo, T. (2019). Factors contributing to student retention in online learning and recommended strategies for improvement: A systematic literature review. Journal of Information Technology Education Research, 18, 19–57. https://doi.org/10.28945/4182

Olugbara, C. T., Letseka, M., & Akintolu, M. (2023). Student Support as a Panacea For Enhancing Student Success in an Open Distance Learning Environment. Journal of Educators Online, 20(3). https://doi.org/10.9743/JEO.2023.20.3.9

Rahmani, A. M., Groot, W., & Rahmani, H. (2024). Dropout in online higher education: a systematic literature review. International Journal of Educational Technology in Higher Education, 21(1), 19. https://doi.org/10.1186/s41239-024-00450-9

Raju, D., & Kohli, D. (2015). Exploring Student Characteristics of Retention that Lead to Graduation in Higher Education Using Data Mining Models. Journal of College Student Retention: Research, Theory & Practice, 16(4), 509-528. https://doi.org/10.2190/CS.16.4.e

Schweighart, R., Hast, M., & Trautwein, C. (2024). Transition into distance education: A scoping review protocol. PloS One, 19(2), e0298882. https://doi.org/10.1371%2Fjournal.pone.0298882

Tait, A. (2015). Student success in open, distance and e-learning. The ICDE reports series, 1–10. International Council for Open and Distance Education. https://www.icde.org/wp-content/uploads/2023/01/studentsuccessreport.pdf

Tsiolis, G. (2018). Thematic analysis of qualitative data. In G. Zamakis (Ed.), Research trajectories in the social sciences: Theoretical-methodological contributions and case studies (pp. 97–125). University of Crete, Lab of Social Analysis and Applied Social Research. https://eclass.uowm.gr/modules/document/file.php/NURED412

Turan, Z., Kucuk, S., & Cilligol Karabey, S. (2022). The university students' self-regulated effort, flexibility and satisfaction in distance education. International Journal of Educational Technology in Higher Education, 19(1), 35. https://doi.org/10.1186/s41239-022-00342-w

Uzir, N. A., Khairuddin, I. E., Zaini, M. K., & Izzuddin Izham, M. A. A. N. (2024). Towards a conceptual framework to mitigate dropout risk in open and distance learning (ODL) in higher education institutions. In: Lecture notes in networks and systems (Vol. 488, pp. 907–914). https://doi.org/10.21834/e-bpj.v9iSI18.5465

Willging, P. A., & Johnson, S. D. (2009). Factors that influence students' decision to dropout of online courses. Journal of Asynchronous Learning Networks, 13(3), 115-127. https://files.eric.ed.gov/fulltext/EJ862360.pdf

Revitalise an Endangered Language and Writing Via Mooc: What and How

Jue Wang Szilas[1, 2]

[1]Centre for Continuing and Distance Education and Faculty of Humanities, University of Geneva, Switzerland; jue.wangszilas@unige.ch
[2]PLIDAM, Institut National des Langues et Civilisations Orientales, France

Correspondence: Jue Wang Szilas: jue.wangszilas@unige.ch

Abstract:

The Dongba script, recognized as a UNESCO Memory of the World in 2003, is considered the world's last living pictographic writing system but remains critically endangered. In response, the Institut National des Langues et Civilisations Orientales (Inalco), the University of Geneva (Unige), and Beijing Language and Culture University (BLCU) collaboratively developed a MOOC to revitalize the script. Offered in four languages, the course teaches 300 high-frequency Dongba characters and incorporates "graphoculture" to highlight cultural contexts. During its first launch in 2023, the MOOC attracted over 2,000 participants from 80 countries, with 234 earning completion badges. This article examines the course's design, learner engagement, and its impact on endangered language preservation. It explores whether MOOCs can contribute to revitalizing endangered writing systems and identifies key design factors influencing learner experience. The paper argues that MOOCs can function not only as educational tools but also as research platforms for digital heritage preservation.

Keywords: MOOC, endangered language, Dongba script, Naxi culture, cultural heritage preservation, language teaching, pedagogical design.

1. Introduction

The Dongba script, used by the Naxi people in northwestern China, is often described as the world's "only living pictographic script," still used mostly in religious rituals. Despite its 2003 UNESCO Memory of the World designation, the script faces extinction. Traditionally confined to priests, the script doesn't consistently represent the spoken language (Naxi language) and incorporates mnemonic devices, rebuses, and phonetic pictograms, making interpretation challenging without expert guidance. With fewer than 350 active users, the script is critically endangered.

Conventional preservation efforts have largely confined the Dongba script to museums and folkloric displays rather than encouraging active use. As Poupard (2019) notes, these approaches risk creating a "cultural living death" where the script is preserved but disconnected from actual use. To ensure its survival, younger generations must be engaged in revitalization.

To address this challenge, the Institut National des Langues et Civilisations Orientales (Inalco), the University of Geneva, and Beijing Language and Culture University (BLCU), with UNESCO's support, developed the "Initiation to the Dongba Script" MOOC (hereafter the Dongba MOOC). This initiative combines script acquisition with cultural context, offering interactive learning beyond passive preservation.

Beyond serving as an educational tool, this project explores the broader role of digital platforms in language preservation. Specifically, it examines two questions:

- Can a MOOC contribute to the revitalization of an endangered writing system?
- What key design factors shape the effectiveness of such a course from the learner's perspective?

As MOOC designers, we address the first question through purposeful course design supporting active script transmission, while gathering learner feedback to inform refinements for the second question.

2. Why a MOOC ?

The rise of MOOCs has influenced education by offering accessibility, scalability and interactive learning. More than a decade after their inception, MOOCs have expanded into language learning (Martín-Monje, E., & Bárcena, E., 2015; Jitpaisarnwattana, N., Reinders, H., & Darasawang, P., 2019). Unlike traditional preservation methods, MOOCs allow for global participation and hands-on engagement. Their massive dimension, reflected in their large reach, diverse participant profiles, and active learner engagement, enhances knowledge dissemination and fosters a dynamic learning community. This dimension is crucial for the revitalization of endangered scripts.

Initiatives such as the Yup'ik Language and Culture course (edX, University of Alaska Fairbanks), Exploring Afrikaans Language and Culture (edX, Stellenbosch University) and Les hiéroglyphes égyptiens (FUN, Université de Liège) demonstrate both the potential and the challenges of using MOOCs to preserve cultural heritage. Based on these examples and our previous experience with language-related MOOCs, we believe that MOOCs can effectively contribute to the preservation of the Dongba script. However, challenges in their pedagogical design need to be addressed in order to maximize their impact.

3. Insights from the Chinese Introductory MOOC

The Dongba MOOC draws on insights from our experience with the Chinese Introductory MOOC (FUN, Inalco), particularly in teaching non-alphabetic scripts. Despite their distinct historical contexts, Dongba pictographs and the Chinese writing system share structural similarities (Milnor, 2005), allowing us to apply key principles from Chinese as a Second Language (CSL) didactics (Bellassen, J., 2010; Gong, Y., Lyu, B., & Gao, X., 2018).

The design of the Dongba MOOC is inspired by the Dualism-Based Teaching Method (Bellassen, J.,1989; Wang-Szilas & Bellassen, 2017), which was successfully implemented in the Chinese Introductory MOOC. This approach views characters as independent carriers of meaning rather than mere phonetic transcriptions. It emphasizes high-frequency characters as foundational elements, systematic visual recognition, and cultural contextualization. Additionally, by focusing on the visual identification of graphical elements, this method enhances character memorization, making it particularly suited to the pictographic nature of the Dongba script.

Research on Dongba scripts provides a foundation for developing a pedagogical corpus for the MOOC. Naxi scholar Fang Guoyu (1995), author of Naxi Xiangxing Wenzipu (A dictionary of Naxi pictographic characters), classified Dongba characters into ten categories, including basic pictographs, ideograms, and phono-semantic compounds. Recent advancements, such as Unicode encoding (Hohhot meeting, 2017) and the Pangloss Project's Naxi language audio database of the LACITO (Langues et Civilisations à Tradition Orale), further support digital representation and pronunciation resources. Collaboration with Dongba priests, teachers, and researchers ensures a solid foundation for building an introductory-level corpus.

4. Design of the Dongba MOOC

The Dongba MOOC consists of seven modules (Figure 1). Module 1 serves as an introduction, while Modules 2–7 follow a structured format with five sequences each. Sequences 1–4 focus on character learning, guiding learners through a pictographic writing logic, as shown in the horizontal menu. Sequence 4 serves as a summary exercise to reinforce learning. Sequence 5 explores cultural aspects and includes forum discussions to foster community engagement. Each module concludes with a quiz, and learners who successfully complete all modules earn a badge.

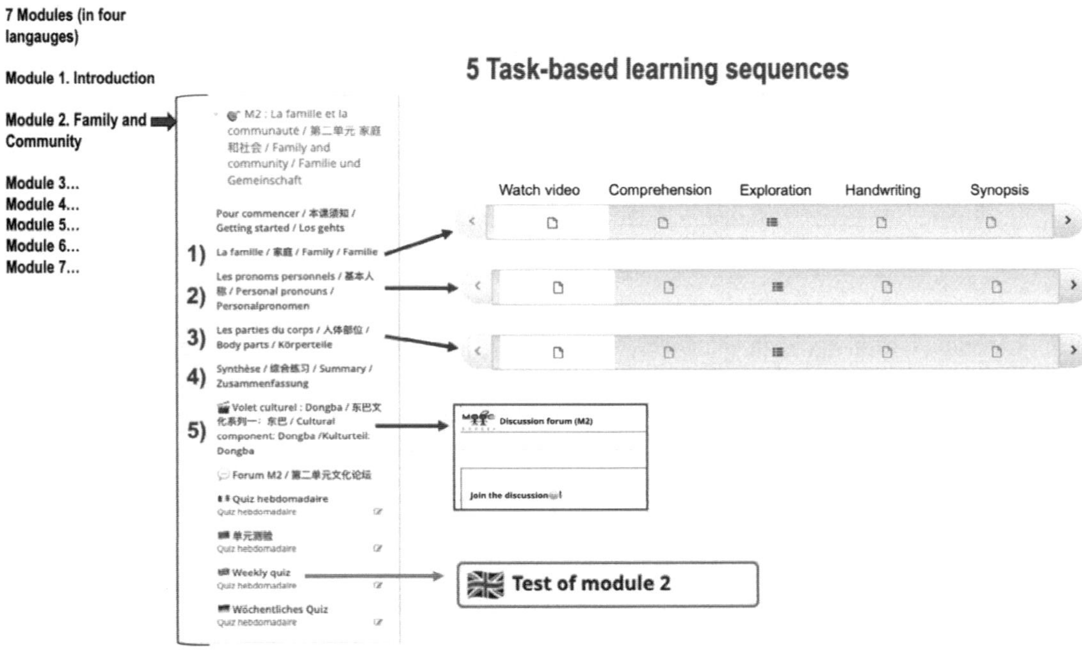

Figure 1. The Dongba MOOC's course plan.

Key design principles are presented as follows:

Separation of Oral and Written Language

The MOOC focuses on literacy in Dongba writing rather than spoken Naxi, reducing cognitive load and ensuring accessibility.

Economy and "Threshold Level" Approach

Inspired by the Threshold Level framework (Van Ek, 1975; Council of Europe, 2001) and the principle of economy ("less is more") (Ellis, 1997), the course optimizes learning by focusing on a core set of 300 essential characters. This selection ensures learners gain a functional grasp of the script, fostering confidence without overwhelming them.

Character Selection

- **Simplicity and Combinability**: Focuses on basic characters that serve as building blocks for compound characters. This approach introduces learners to the logic of Dongba character formation, promoting both understanding and creativity. For example, the character  (man, husband, son) serves to learn characters such as  (woman, wife, daughter),  (father),  (mother), etc.
- **Meaning-Linked Forms**: Emphasizes pictograms and ideograms with clear visual representations, making them easier to understand and remember. This selection fosters a more intuitive learning experience. For example, the pictograms as  (sky),  (sun),  (moon),  (cloud), etc., are used to form the ideograms as  (sunny day),  (cloudy day),  (light).

- **High Frequency**: Selects commonly used characters to ensure practical relevance.
- **Graphic Families**: Groups visually similar characters to reinforce pattern recognition. For instance, a single base character might serve as the root for multiple compound forms, as shown in the table below.

man	I, me	sitting	jumping	dancing

- **Cultural Significance**: Integrates characters central to Naxi traditions, beliefs, and daily life. For example, the symbol  shows a seated priest (Dongba) wearing the sacred 5-lobed headdress (only 3 lobes are represented in the Dongba symbol) and reciting the Dongba classics.

Learning Activities

The course takes inspiration from Diana Laurillard's six learning activities (2018) for structured, autonomous learning, with certain adaptations:

- Watch & Read: Introduces basic characters through videos and readings.
- Comprehension Exercises: Reinforces recognition through matching activities.
- Watch& Explore: Presents compound characters, prompting learners to deduce meanings.
- Practice Handwriting: Allows learners to replicate characters, emphasizing memorization over strict orthography.
- Collaboration: Promotes interaction between learners and the tutors.
- Assessment & Badging: Learners complete quizzes and receive badges for progress.

Embedding Cultural Knowledge

- Graphoculture: Examines the cultural significance of individual characters, such as the symbol for milk churns  , a key element of Naxi cuisine. It represents a churn used for yak butter tea, an essential part of daily life for the Naxi people.
- Naxi heritage: Highlights important traditions, such as sacred places (e.g.,  Jade Dragon Mountain, the sacred mountain of the Naxi people) and marriage rituals (e.g.,  the statue of a Dongba anointing butter on the foreheads of newlyweds).

Learning Community

To enhance engagement, the MOOC includes multilingual tutoring, with a team of doctoral researchers and experts providing support in French, Chinese, English, and German.

5. First Launch and Results

The Dongba MOOC, launched from April 24 to June 26, 2023, attracted over 2,000 learners from 80 countries, with France having the highest enrollment (65.36%). Other participants came from China (5.91%), Switzerland (2.36%), Belgium (2.17%), Germany (1.47%), and several other countries, including the U.S., Spain, Italy, Canada, Morocco, and Japan. Of the 2,039 enrolled learners, 503 completed the first quiz and were considered active students (Celik & Cagiltay, 2024). By the end of the session, 234 completion badges were awarded, representing a 47% success rate, which is quite high compared to the average for standard MOOCs.

6. Data Collection and Analysis

The high success rate of the MOOC suggests strong learner engagement. However, do participants believe that a MOOC can contribute to the revitalization of the Dongba script? What are their views on the course design, particularly regarding the separation of spoken and written language, the participatory activity, and the multilingual interface? And do they continue using the Dongba script after completing the MOOC?

To address these questions, we analyzed data collected from:

- Two questionnaires: a Pre-MOOC and a Post-MOOC questionnaire, both including a standard set of questions from the French MOOC Platform France Université Numérique (FUN), along with 5 additional questions proposed by the designers.
- Forum discussions
- Email exchanges, LinkedIn posts, and other participant interactions.

Analysis of the Pre-MOOC and the Post-MOOC Questionnaires

The Pre-MOOC questionnaire received 396 responses (19.4% response rate) from 2,039 registrants. Participants were mostly female (74%), highly educated (48% with master's degrees, 15% with doctorates), and professionally active (52% working), aged 17 to 88. Most were native French speakers (80%) with prior MOOC experience (72%). The Post-MOOC questionnaire received 196 responses, with 188 participants earning certificates, representing 80% of the 234 certificate recipients. The analysis focuses on the additional questions included in both the Pre-MOOC and Post-MOOC questionnaires.

The five additional questions in the Pre-MOOC questionnaire assess participants' prior knowledge, attitudes, and motivations regarding language and writing systems. The five Post-MOOC questions evaluate how the course has impacted their views on language learning and revitalization. The table below illustrates the connection between these Pre-MOOC and Post-MOOC questions, providing a framework for addressing the research questions in this paper.

Table 1: Connection Between Pre- and Post-MOOC Questions

Category	Pre-MOOC Question	Post-MOOC Question	Connection
Knowledge and Prior Experience →Continued Interest/ Motivation	Q1: Do you know any writing systems other than your own?	Q1: If a MOOC on the Dongba script is offered in the future, would you consider enrolling?	Examines whether prior exposure to multiple writing systems and multilingualism influences continued interest in both the Dongba script and the Naxi language.
	Q2: Apart from your mother tongue, do you speak any other languages?	Q2: Would you like to learn the Naxi language?	Investigates whether learning the Dongba script encourages learners to study the Naxi spoken language, considering if the unique features of the script stimulate interest in oral language acquisition.
Motivation → Future	Q3: What motivated you to	Q1: If a MOOC on Dongba script is offered in the future,	Learners' initial motivations provide insight into their likelihood of continued

Engagement	take this MOOC?	would you consider enrolling?	engagement, helping assess the MOOC's impact on sustaining interest in Dongba script.
Conceptual Understanding – Perception Change	Q4: Can a language be approached solely through one of its two forms, oral or written?	Q4: After following this MOOC, has your perception of what constitutes a language changed?	The Pre-MOOC question assesses participants' views on spoken and written language, while the Post-MOOC response evaluates the MOOC's impact on their perspective.
Utility Perception → Value for Preservation	Q5: Do you think learning a rare language is useful?	Q3: Do you think universities need to offer the teaching of rare languages? Q5: Can a MOOC be useful for the maintenance and preservation of an endangered language and culture?	The Pre-MOOC question identifies learners' initial views on rare languages. The Post-MOOC responses reveal whether the course reinforced their belief in the value of endangered language preservation and the role of universities in supporting such efforts.

Knowledge and Prior Experience —Continued Interest/ Motivation

In Pre-MOOC Q1 (Do you know any writing systems other than your own?), all 396 respondents answered "yes." The most cited were Chinese/Kanji (88 respondents), followed by Russian/Cyrillic (44) and Japanese (42). Other frequently mentioned scripts included Arabic, Hebrew, Greek, Korean, and, less commonly, Sanskrit and ancient scripts such as Egyptian hieroglyphics, Yi, Manchu, Mayan, and runes.

For Pre-MOOC Q2 (Do you speak any languages other than your native language?), all 396 respondents again answered "yes." English was the most widely spoken second language (86.11% of respondents), followed by Spanish, Chinese, German, and French, each spoken by roughly a quarter of participants. Additionally, 28.03% reported proficiency in other languages, including Russian, Korean, Dutch, and Arabic, among others.

These responses indicate that participants possess diverse linguistic knowledge and are highly multilingual, forming a group well-versed in linguistic and textual diversity.

For Post-MOOC Q1 (If a MOOC on Dongba script is offered in the future, would you consider enrolling?), 92% of respondents said "yes." In Post-MOOC Q2 (Would you like to learn the Naxi language?), 75% expressed motivation to do so.

Given that the Naxi language is also endangered, this raises an important question: Can the Dongba MOOC contribute to a broader revitalization of Naxi beyond preserving the script? One possible approach is to use the MOOC as a gateway to spark interest in learning Naxi. If more people—especially those outside the Naxi-speaking community—engage with the language, this external interest could, in turn, encourage greater enthusiasm among Naxi speakers, ultimately supporting its preservation and continued use.

Motivation —Future Engagement

The analysis of Pre-MOOC Q3 (What motivated you to take this MOOC?) supports this conclusion. Most participants enrolled in the MOOC for the joy of learning (84.09%), with a specific interest in the topic motivating over half of the respondents (53.79%). When asked about their particular interest in Dongba, the originality of the writing system was the main attraction for 87.37% of participants, followed by curiosity about ethnic customs (55.81%) and a desire to compare Dongba with other writing systems (36.36%).

Conceptual Understanding —Perception Change

The responses to Pre-MOOC Q4 (Can a language be approached solely through one of its two forms, oral or written?) were divided. Half of the respondents (50%) believed that oral and written language are interconnected and essential for a complete understanding of grammar, vocabulary, and cultural context. The remaining 25% of respondents thought that it was possible to learn a language through only one form, citing examples like Latin, where the written form is dominant, or languages like Farsi, where the writing system does not always directly reflect spoken language. Several participants also pointed out that, in the digital age, written language often enables communication without speech, such as through Edongba (a software program developed to facilitate the digital input of Dongba scripts, Yang, 2001), making written-only learning more relevant for some languages.

For Post-MOOC Q4 (After following this MOOC, has your perception of what constitutes a language changed?), responses were nearly split, with 47% reporting a shift in perspective and 53% stating that their understanding had not changed. Those who did not experience a change typically had prior experience with diverse writing systems. However, those who did note a change in perception highlighted several key insights, such as:

- recognizing Dongba as a memory aid rather than a direct representation of speech,
- appreciating pictographic communication as a distinct form of language,
- understanding the deeper connections between language, culture, and religion.

Utility Perception —Value for Preservation

Regarding Pre-MOOC Q5 (Do you think learning a rare language is useful?), 77% of participants affirmed the value of rare languages, citing cultural preservation, cognitive benefits, and exposure to alternative perspectives. Some also challenged conventional definitions of "utility," comparing linguistic diversity to biodiversity and emphasizing the responsibility to preserve cultural heritage.

For Post-MOOC Q3 (Do you think universities need to offer the teaching of rare languages?), 96% of participants supported university involvement, recognizing the role of higher education in cultural preservation, intellectual enrichment, and fostering diverse worldviews. While most saw universities as essential for this mission, some suggested that specialized institutions might be better suited.

For Post-MOOC Q5 (Can a MOOC be useful for the maintenance and preservation of an endangered language and culture?), 96% of participants believed MOOCs could contribute to language preservation. They highlighted benefits such as:

- Raising global awareness about endangered languages
- Providing accessible education to diverse audiences
- Motivating native speakers to value their linguistic heritage
- Creating comprehensive digital documentation
- Inspiring deeper study of endangered languages

One participant encapsulated this idea: "On ne protège que ce qu'on aime, et on n'aime que ce qu'on connaît" (We only protect what we love, and we only love what we know).

Overall, the Post-MOOC responses reinforced the participants' belief in the importance of endangered language preservation and the potential role of both universities and online education in this effort.

Key Insights and Participant Engagement Beyond the MOOC

In addition to the questionnaire results, we observed participant engagement beyond the MOOC.

Participatory Task Engagement

In the forum, learners were encouraged to take part in a hands-on activity. The aim was to link online learning with real-world engagement (see Figure 2).

Mission: A la recherche de manuscrits Dongba / Mission: Searching for Dongba scriptures / 学习任务：寻找东巴经 / Mission: Auf der Suche nach Dongba-Manuskripten

Poster une réponse

Hello Everyone,

After several weeks of study, you learned that the Dongba scriptures are the classics of Dongba religion, a primitive religion unique to the Naxi people. It records philosophy, history, religion, astronomy, folklore, literature, medicine, and other disciplines. These scriptures are the encyclopedia of Naxi people. Nowadays, there are over 40,000 volumes of the existing Dongba Classic, including more than 1,000 different categories. In addition to the scriptures collected in Chinese domestic museums and by private collectors, a large number of Dongba scriptures are scattered all over the world.

The MOOC team would like to invite everyone to join in the mission of finding the Dongba scriptures. Let's try to find collections or presentations about the Dongba scriptures in museums, libraries, or websites in your country, your city, or even in a flea market, and then, you can share your discoveries in this discussion.

We hope that with your participation, more people will have the opportunity to see different Dongba scriptures or receive information about the collection of Dongba scriptures.

We look forward to your sharing!

MOOC team

Figure 2. Screenshot of the mission description from the MOOC interface on the FUN platform.

Participants actively contributed to Dongba script preservation by documenting manuscripts and artifacts. One participant in Paris discovered a Dongba manuscript at the Musée Guimet, while another identified Dongba artifacts in a private collection and provided photographs. Several others reached out to regional museums to inquire about potential holdings. Although engagement was primarily from French-speaking participants, some contacted the authors via email to share personal collections and request script interpretations.

Academic Research and Further Studies

Two students at the University of Geneva wrote their Master's theses on the Dongba script. Some participants expressed interest in studying in Lijiang, where the script is used by the Dongba priests.

Creative Artistic Applications

Some graphic designers have incorporated the Dongba script into their work. As shown in Figure 3, one participant shared her design using the Dongba script she learned in the MOOC.

Figure 3. Screenshot of a participant's design work from the Dongba MOOC.

These cases suggest that the MOOC not only promoted learning but also inspired real-world applications as well as deeper and sustained engagement with the Dongba script.

7. Reflections and Prospects

This Dongba MOOC highlights the potential of MOOCs as an effective tool for revitalizing endangered writing systems. Our analysis reveals several key aspects and prospects.

The Combination of XMOOC and CMOOC

The Dongba MOOC integrates both XMOOC (eXtended MOOCs) and CMOOC (Connectivist MOOCs) approaches. XMOOCs focus on traditional knowledge delivery through structured content, such as course videos, quizzes, and assignments, while CMOOCs emphasize learner-driven connections and collaboration (Downes, S., & Siemens, 2013). This hybrid design offers:

- XMOOC elements: Structured modules, clear learning objectives, and formal assessments.
- CMOOC elements: Collaborative forums, peer learning, and participant-driven research tasks.

This combined approach provides learners with essential knowledge about the Dongba script while also promoting community building and knowledge co-creation. The success of this integrated model depends on factors such as cultural relevance and resource availability to support collaboration.

The Participatory Task: Sustaining Engagement Beyond the MOOC

The participatory task in the Dongba MOOC redefines traditional pedagogical "tasks" by applying an action-based approach to online language learning. Participants were encouraged to identify and describe Dongba manuscripts in their countries, transforming the task into a real-world activity connected to the preservation of Dongba manuscripts. This task serves as a form of crowdsourcing or citizen science, where learners actively participate in knowledge production. By engaging a global community, it helps promote the documentation and preservation of endangered languages and cultural heritage.

However, sustaining learner engagement beyond the course is a critical consideration for the success of the MOOC. The platform successfully attracted a linguistically and intellectually sophisticated audience, with many participants holding advanced degrees. Despite this, maintaining engagement across a diverse learner base—especially those with less formal training—remains a challenge. To ensure long-term participation, future iterations of the course should:

- Develop advanced modules for continued learning.
- Implement collaborative translation projects.
- Create regional learning communities.
- Establish connections with Naxi communities.

In addressing engagement, one of the key challenges lies in balancing interactivity with scalability. While interactive elements such as peer-reviewed tasks, discussion forums, and collaborative projects are essential, they require careful facilitation and clear community guidelines to maintain effective participation. Additionally, dropout rates—common in MOOCs—can be mitigated by improving onboarding processes, incorporating structured progress tracking, and offering timely feedback.

Some participants requested features such as live Q&A sessions, group projects, and pronunciation support, which are proven to enhance learner retention in other language MOOCs. These suggestions align with the need for an interactive and personalized learning environment, which can make the course more engaging for a broader audience.

By comparing the Dongba MOOC with other digital language revitalization efforts—such as those for Hawaiian, Māori, or Scottish Gaelic—we can contextualize its success and identify areas for improvement. These programs also focus on community-based learning and digital platforms but differ in terms of the role of native speakers, instructional design, and engagement strategies. Incorporating best practices from these initiatives could strengthen the Dongba MOOC's effectiveness and its ability to engage a wide range of learners.

Establishing a Specialized Research Community Through the MOOC

Of the 396 responses from the pre-course questionnaire, approximately 60 participants hold doctoral degrees, and the depth and professionalism of their answers demonstrate the platform's potential for research engagement. The MOOC platform could serve not only as a learning environment but also as a potential research hub, facilitating communication and collaboration among researchers.

Moving forward, we can enhance these exchanges by:

- Creating specialized research discussion forums
- Facilitating collaborative research projects
- Hosting virtual conferences on endangered language preservation
- Developing AI-powered chatbots to provide real-time expert support for all learners

8. Conclusion

Our findings strongly affirm that MOOCs can contribute to endangered writing system revitalization. The high completion rate (47%), sustained engagement, and overwhelming participant belief (96%) in MOOCs' potential for language preservation validate this approach. Several critical factors are identified and recognized:

- Focus on high-frequency characters (pedagogical economy)
- Integration of cultural context (graphoculture)
- Separation of written and oral language to reduce cognitive load
- Real-world application through citizen science
- Multilingual interface accessibility

Participants - a linguistically sophisticated group with knowledge of multiple writing systems - showed remarkable engagement, with 92% expressing interest in future Dongba courses and 75% motivated to learn the Naxi language itself. This suggests the MOOC could serve as a gateway to broader language revitalization, potentially generating enthusiasm among native Naxi speakers.

Participant feedback for improvement included clearer instructions and community guidelines, progress tracking, audio recordings for pronunciation, sentence-building exercises, handwritten character submission capabilities, and advanced courses with interactive elements like live Q&A sessions and group projects.

Future research should focus on the effectiveness of interactive learning and integrating online with offline community engagement. Challenges remain in balancing interactivity with scalability and adapting to different linguistic contexts. Expanding this approach to other endangered languages could provide further insights while contributing to broader digital heritage preservation efforts.

References

Bellassen, J. (1989). Méthode d'initiation à la langue et à l'écriture chinoises. La Compagnie, Paris.

Bellassen, J. (1989). Méthode d'initiation à la langue et à l'écriture chinoises. La Compagnie, Paris.

Bellassen, J. (2010). La didactique du chinois et la malédiction de Babel. Émergence, dynamique et structuration d'une discipline. Études chinoises. *漢學研究* hors-série pp. 27-44. https://hal.science/hal-03935858v1

Celik, B., & Cagiltay, K. (2024). Uncovering MOOC completion: A comparative study of completion rates from different perspectives. Open Praxis, 16(3), 445-456. DOI: 10.55982/openpraxis.16.3.606

Fang Guoyu 方国瑜, & He Zhiwu 和志武. (1995). Nàxī Xiàngxíng Wénzì Pǔ (A dictionary of Naxi pictographic characters) (纳西象形文字谱). Yunnan Renmin Press.

Gong, Y., Lyu, B., & Gao, X. (2018). Research on teaching Chinese as a second or foreign language in and outside mainland China: A bibliometric analysis. The Asia-Pacific Education Researcher, 27(4), 277-289. https://doi.org/10.1007/s40299-018-0385-2

Jitpaisarnwattana, N., Reinders, H., & Darasawang, P. (2019). Language MOOCs: An expanding field. Technology in Language Teaching & Learning, 1(1), 21-32. https://doi.org/10.29140/tltl.v1n1.142

Laurillard, D., Kennedy, E., Charlton, P., Wild, J., & Dimakopoulos, D. (2018). Using technology to develop teachers as designers of TEL: Evaluating the learning designer. British Journal of Educational Technology, 49(6), 1044-1058. https://doi.org/10.1111/bjet.12697

Martín-Monje, E., & Bárcena, E. (Eds.). (2015). Language MOOCs: Providing learning, transcending boundaries. Walter de Gruyter GmbH & Co KG. https://doi.org/10.2478/9783110420067

Milnor, S. J. (2005). A comparison between the development of the Chinese writing system and Dongba pictographs. University of Washington Working Papers in Linguistics, eds. Daniel J. Jinguji and Steven Moran, pp 30-45, Seattle, WA chrome-extension://efaidnbmnnnibpcajpcglclefindmkaj/https://depts.washington.edu/uwwpl/vol24/pub_submission_Milnor.pdf.

Oppitz, M., & Hsu, E. (1998). Naxi and Moso ethnography: Kin, rites, pictographs. Zurich: Volkerkundemuseum Zurich, 1998. 396 pages.

Poupard, D. (2019). Revitalising Naxi Dongba as a 'pictographic' vernacular script. Journal of Chinese Writing Systems, 3(1), 53-67. https://doi.org/10.1177/2513850218814405

Results of the ad-hoc meeting on Naxi Dongba in Hohhot, 2017-09-21. Working Group Document, Universal Multiple-Octet Coded Character Set International Organisation for Standardisation. https://www.unicode.org/L2/L2017/17337-n4895-naxi-dongba-adhoc.pdf.

Siemens, G., & Downes, S. (2013). What is a MOOC. Recuperado en: http://cemca.org.in/ckfinder/userfiles/files/EdTech%20Notes%202_Littlejohn_final_1June2013.pdf.

Wang-Szilas, J., & Bellassen, J. (2017). Dualism-based design of the introductory Chinese MOOC "Kit de contact en langue chinoise". Research-publishing.net. https://doi.org/10.14705/rpnet.2017.mooc2016.670

Yang Xiaohui. (2001). Edongba (Version 7.01.) [Computer software] http://www.zmnsoft.com/edongba/en/Edongba.html

Sparking institutional change: The experience of implementing a Learning Analytics project in an online university

José Israel Reyes[1], Anna Calvo[2], Efrem Melián[2], Julio Meneses[1,2]

[1] Faculty of Psychology and Education Sciences, Universitat Oberta de Catalunya, Spain; jreyesrey@uoc.edu, jmenesesn@uoc.edu
[2] eLearning Innovation Center, Universitat Oberta de Catalunya, Spain; anna.calvo@uoc.edu, emelian@uoc.edu

Correspondence: José Israel Reyes: jreyesrey@uoc.edu

Abstract

Learning analytics have gained relevance in online higher education over the last decade, focusing on supporting teaching and learning processes while enhancing students' academic performance. These methods leverage students' academic data to inform decision-making and interventions aimed at improving educational outcomes. However, recent research suggests that large-scale learning analytics applications in online courses have primarily focused on describing and predicting student behaviours, with a notable lack of prescriptive approaches to guide specific actions. In this paper, we present the experience of implementing a dashboard project across the entire academic body of an online university. The project seeks to inform institutional change by providing the university's key decision-makers responsible for teaching with visual representations of classroom activity, promoting improvements in students' academic performance. It regularly gathers users' needs and expectations using an iterative development approach to facilitate continuous improvements based on user feedback. Additionally, the project develops a comprehensive scaffolding strategy to support end users in effectively engaging with the dashboards, translating these insights into enhanced teaching practices. By carefully considering the needs and expectations of learning analytics users and providing structured support to transform data into pedagogical improvements, institutions can move beyond descriptive analytics towards a more prescriptive, data-informed educational approach.

Keywords: Learning analytics, visualisation dashboards, online higher education, data-informed decisions, student success.

Over the last decade, online higher education (OHE) institutions have increasingly adopted learning analytics (LA) to enhance educational outcomes. These institutions leverage LA tools to promote better students' academic performance based on data-informed insights and interventions (Dennehy et al., 2023; Foster et al., 2020; Tabuenca et al., 2015), reinforce the internal support aiming to improve the teaching and learning processes (Herodotou et al., 2021), and guide the curricular design (Claassen et al., 2025). When effectively implemented, LA dashboards can serve as powerful triggers for academic success (Ifenthaler & Yau, 2020), with some research indicating that students who utilised LA dashboards demonstrated better academic performance than those who did not (Kim et al., 2016), though additional variables influencing this performance remain unexplored. Using students' educational data to create new knowledge and develop strategies to meet their needs represents an opportunity for universities offering hybrid or online education to guarantee a better learning experience for all learners.

Apart from supporting students, LA dashboards can provide significant opportunities within OHE contexts by addressing multiple institutional challenges. Most LA dashboards are designed to predict learners' behaviours aiming to reduce dropout and underachievement (Larrabee et al., 2019), with successful results in decreasing student attrition (Cambruzzi et al., 2015) and increasing student engagement (Huberth et al., 2015). Furthermore, these tools could also be used as promoters of professors' self-regulation (Chen et al., 2021; Huang et al., 2024), encouraging educators to move beyond simply interpreting what they see to reflecting on its meaning and determining appropriate actions, essentially transitioning from understanding "what" the data shows to knowing "how" to respond effectively (Kaliisa & Dolonen, 2023).

While expectations for learning analytics contributions to online universities are high, research indicates that its implementation in large-scale courses still faces some limitations (Kaila et al., 2024). Until now, most LA applications in OHE have focused on description and prediction (Kaliisa et al., 2023), emphasising students' current behaviours and attempting to alert professors or institutions about future risks, particularly failure and dropout (Tsai & Gasevic, 2017). However, to leverage all the potential that LA can provide, OHE institutions should move forward, transforming these insights into actionable practices that professors can employ to improve students' academic performance. Few studies have focused on informing both academic administrators and faculty about such practices and their critical role in improving academic outcomes (Kaila et al., 2024; Kaliisa et al., 2023). This prescriptive dimension is essential for moving beyond pattern identification, enabling proactive, evidence-based interventions that directly enhance the learning experience.

The adoption of LA in OHE still presents relevant challenges, particularly in the area of pedagogical infrastructure, which is crucial to implementing the interventions effectively. Online higher education institutions do not seem to have a well-designed strategy guiding the implementation of LA within their systems (Herodotou et al., 2021; Márquez et al., 2024). Although previous studies have identified the absence of a technological infrastructure that allows the integration of LA within their systems and inconsistencies between LA technologies and the users' needs, the most significant concerns remain regarding training for LA implementation under a transformative philosophy.

Beyond promoting students, faculty, and staff (as LA users) literacy to understand and analyse LA academic data, institutions should also offer comprehensive training and support with practical guidelines on incorporating tangible actions to enhance students' academic performance (Kaliisa et al., 2023). One of the most pressing challenges to address is helping professors transform their pedagogical practices to suit students' needs, while enabling academic administrators to make data-informed decisions that catalyse significant institutional change. According to Herodotou (2021), professors' resistance to change and the reluctance of academic administrators to adopt new policies represent important barriers to effectively applying LA in OHE. To overcome these challenges, it is essential to consider the needs and expectations of beneficiary stakeholders by involving them in the design processes (Klein et al., 2019; Márquez et al., 2024). Most importantly, the accompaniment provided during the implementation should demonstrate the tangible impact of interventions on teaching and learning outcomes.

In this paper, we share our experience in implementing a strategic institutional project focused on educational innovation, developed by the eLearning Innovation Center of the Open University of Catalonia (UOC). The primary objective of the project is to enhance students' academic performance by boosting data-informed decision-making among professors and educational administrators. We aim to illustrate how suitable institutional support can transform dashboards into catalysts for evidence-based educational change in online universities. Specifically, this work exemplifies the transition from a descriptive and predictive application of LA in OHE to a more prescriptive approach, where all stakeholders can utilise new knowledge, insights, and understandings to strengthen their educational practices.

Context

The UOC is a fully online university founded in Barcelona, Spain, in 1994. UOC's educational model is based on a student-centred philosophy. The student's academic journey is supported by practice-based learning activities and complemented by asynchronous interaction with instructors and peers through the learning management system (LMS). To guarantee an effective learning experience, the university is organised through a distributed and standardised structure. Learning activities take place within the LMS, where courses are separated according to the language of instruction (primarily Spanish and Catalan, with some in English). At the most granular level are the classrooms, where instructors teach and interact with students. These classrooms are grouped into courses, each managed by a full professor. These professors design learning resources, activities, and assessments, and coordinate the team of instructors to ensure consistency across all classrooms. Courses have as many classrooms as needed based on student enrolment, with a maximum ratio of 70 students per classroom. Courses belong to programmes, where the Programme Directors set up learning guidelines for the team of full professors (who coordinate instructors who teach in the classrooms). Programmes are hosted by 7 Faculties, coordinated by deans who direct each Faculty's teaching policies through the Programme Directors, supported by the teaching deputies. At the highest level, the Vice-Rectorate of Teaching and Learning establishes the guidelines for all educational processes, ensuring a cohesive learning experience across the university.

The SAA dashboards

The Classroom Activity Monitoring dashboards (SAA, its acronym in Catalan for Seguiment de l'Activitat a les Aules) have been created to enhance learners' academic performance by providing evidence on how learning and teaching practices take place in classrooms, enabling data-informed decision-making at various levels. The project was initiated in 2022 and continues to evolve with ongoing enhancements and expansion across academic years. Figure 1 illustrates the university's teaching organisation, where the SAA dashboard is implemented, and its scope for the 2024-2025 academic term. Aligned with this structure, various academic roles are in charge of designing and guaranteeing an effective learning experience for students under the leadership of the Vice Rector of Teaching and Learning, as well as the deans and teaching deputies in the seven Faculties. Coordinating decisions across different levels of responsibility for improving teaching quality is complex and requires organising, sorting, and aggregating information to guide a consistent strategy. To this end, we have developed four visualisation dashboards as a foundation to promote institutional change.

Figure 1. UOC's teaching structure and scope of the SAA dashboards for the 2024-2025 academic year.

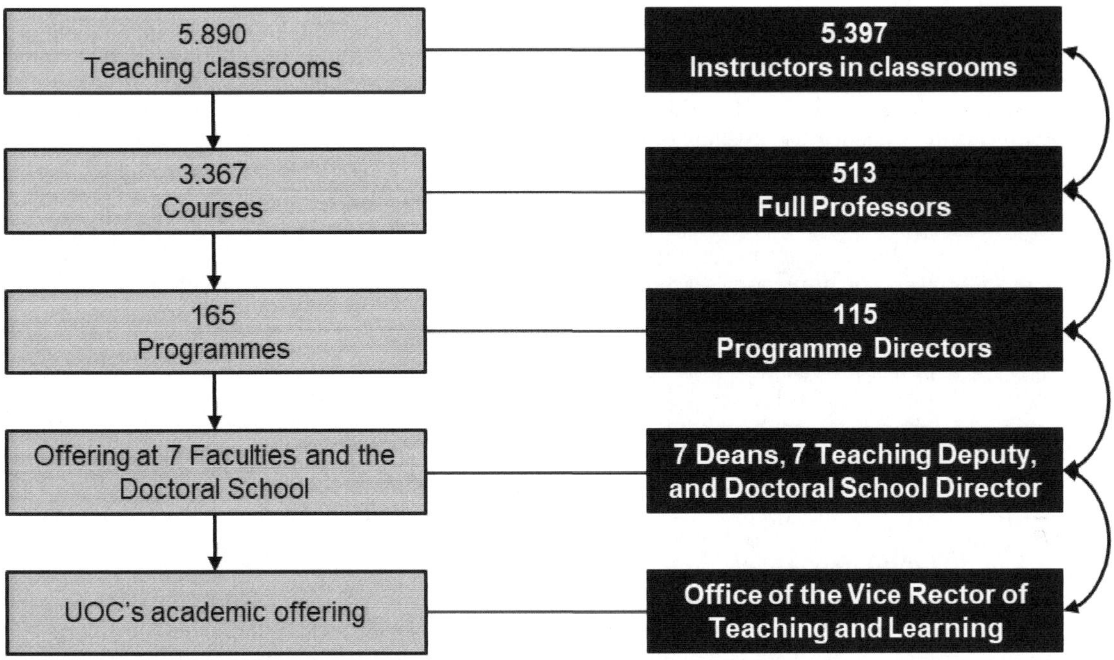

The SAA dashboard project integrates multiple data sources from across the university's ecosystem. Mainly, the dashboards capture detailed information about the activity in the classrooms within the LMS, while being enriched with supplementary data on enrolment and academic characteristics of students, courses, and programmes from the educational management system. As Figure 2 illustrates, all the necessary information provided by the various data sources is consolidated into Snowflake, where we generate a normalised dimensional schema to develop a cohesive data model. This unified model connects to Power BI to support the design of the visualisations, displaying nearly real-time data to enable stakeholders to access up-to-date insights for informed decision-making.

Figure 2. The technical infrastructure of the SAA dashboards.

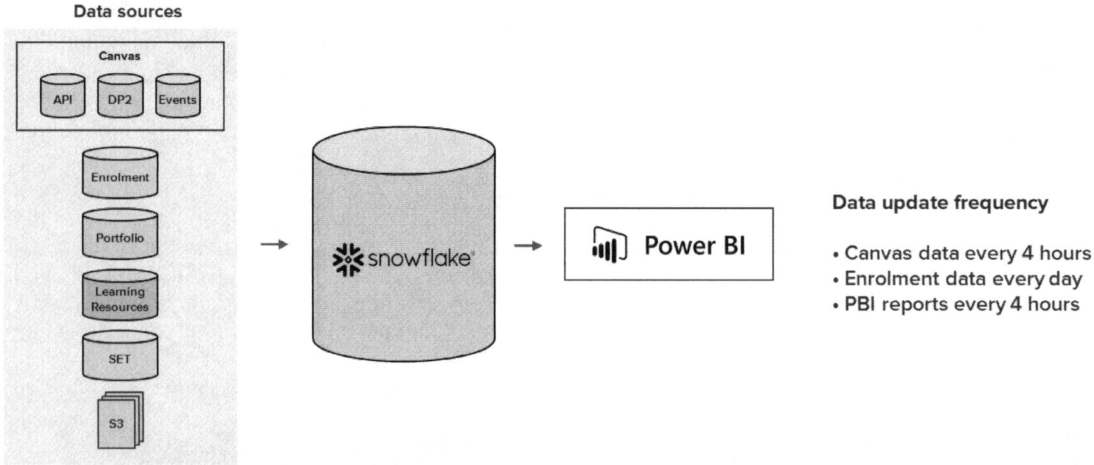

In line with the SAA dashboard's strategy of influencing educational change, the visualisations work as triggers for conversations aimed at improving teaching and learning practices. To facilitate this process, the project provides information about students' involvement within the classroom's main spaces, along with key sociodemographic and academic characteristics. Regarding students' academic activity, each dashboard encompasses five domains of information: access to the classroom and its spaces, interaction with peers and instructors in the discussion spaces (forums and workspaces), interaction with instructors, use of learning resources, and completion of assessment activities (including a report of plagiarism evidence). The dashboards also provide insights about instructors' teaching activity in the classroom, such as their performance in the assessment and feedback processes and interaction with students.

The ultimate goal of these visualisations is to promote institutional change based on evidence, enabling each stakeholder to reflect on identified issues and, accordingly, deploy policies and interventions according to their responsibilities to improve the entire educational model. Therefore, each dashboard displays the information relevant to the specific role and level of responsibility exclusively. This means that each decision-maker (full professors, programme directors, deans, teaching deputies, and the Office of the Vice Rector of Teaching and Learning) has access only to the activity of the courses, programme, or faculty for which they are responsible.

Implementation of the SAA dashboards

SAA dashboards have been developed following a continuous improvement strategy, designed to suit users' needs and expectations as these are incorporated into decision-making. The development of the dashboards begins with a minimum viable product, which is tested with a small sample of end users through individual interviews and group feedback sessions. These insights inform the development of a beta version, which is then piloted with all relevant users. Based on their feedback, it evolves into the production phase, undergoing continuous improvements informed by these diverse experiences. The iterative nature of the project facilitates the incorporation of improvements semester by semester in line with users' requirements, enabling an ongoing development strategy to refine and expand the dashboards.

As reflected in the literature, the mere availability of dashboards does not lead to transformations in the learning processes. Beyond its development, the real challenge of this project lies in encouraging the involved stakeholders to use these tools as catalysers for sparking institutional change. To address this issue, we have implemented a structured scaffolding strategy to support and accompany the stakeholders involved in educational decision-making processes in the university through multiple approaches. For instance, we conduct introductory sessions for all these stakeholders and provide training for the management team responsible for supporting them each time a new visualisation dashboard is released. We also organise training sessions every time the dashboards experiment modifications as a product of improvements or the addition of new information domains, offering new insights for the decision-making process. At the beginning of each semester, we also share an official update outlining the latest features of the visualisations and the future directions of the project. Furthermore, we regularly provide users with workshops, support materials, infographics, and video tutorials for each dashboard. Table 1 summarises the approaches of support on which the SAA dashboards' focus to guide the continuous improvement strategy.

Table 1. Scaffolding strategies for the implementation of SAA dashboards

Approaches of support	Actions	Materials and resources
Documentation and initial training	• Guidance through the support portal. • Introductory training for dashboard use. • Integration of the SAA dashboards into onboarding for new faculty. • Informative sessions to present new dashboards or new features on the existing ones.	Tutorials, infographics, and guidelines. Group feedback sessions. Training sessions. Dictionaries of indicators for each dashboard.
Resolution of doubts and collection of requests	• Training for the SAA dashboards support team. • Assistance for users on how to access and navigate the dashboards. • Monthly collection of suggestions to improve the dashboards.	Dedicated support channel for the SAA dashboards. In-person support sessions.
Incorporation of SAA dashboards in the decision-making process	• Targeted training sessions to promote the adoption of SAA dashboards. • Ongoing training for professors and programme directors based on practical cases.	Workshops. User-centred working sessions. Video tutorials. Practice-based examples.

Conclusions

The future of LA in OHE lies in transforming data into targeted interventions that effectively address learners' difficulties and needs. In terms of teaching, online universities should align their policies to support faculty in adapting their pedagogical practices based on evidence, thus increasing the chances of students' success. As a result, the impact of LA insights will reach students, who ultimately are the beneficiaries of the analysis and interpretation of teaching and learning data generated in the classrooms. However, a gap exists between merely consuming dashboard visualisation data and effectively translating the evidence provided into enhanced student learning experiences and academic outcomes. To address this issue, online universities must promote commitment and engagement among all stakeholders involved in teaching, fostering institutional change guided by data-informed decisions.

We derived several key considerations based on our experience implementing SAA dashboards in large-scale online courses. Developing an institutional strategy to support all stakeholders in applying learning analytics insights to their teaching and learning practices is crucial for effectively leveraging these methods. The implementation of institutional projects such as SAA dashboards requires a combination of technological and pedagogical infrastructure. Given the tendency of online universities to invest primarily in technology, the next essential step is to focus on supporting stakeholders within their role of responsibility, not only in using the dashboards but in translating LA insights into real-world interventions that produce a positive impact on students' learning. By involving end users in the design and development of visualisation dashboards, they will take ownership of the project and feel motivated to apply changes in their practices.

So far in the project's implementation, we have focused on the academic roles in charge of decision-making, coordinating courses, programmes, and faculties, and leading the entire structure at the university. The next steps will concentrate on moving on to the lower levels in the structure, specifically to support learners' self-regulation processes and assist instructors in identifying specific needs and risks within their classrooms. We are aware that fostering the institutional change we aim for comes with challenges. It requires engaging all stakeholders, encouraging their active participation, and overcoming potential resistance. In this regard, it is crucial for online universities to assess the impact of applying prescriptive LA on students' academic performance by contrasting their satisfaction and perspectives post-implementation. This final step is essential not only to ensure the achievement of the project's objectives but also to maintain a continuous improvement approach, which ultimately contributes to aligning the SAA dashboards with the evolution of the users' needs as these are being incorporated into policy and practice.

Competing interests

The authors have no competing interests to declare.

References

Cambruzzi, W., Rigo, S., & Barbosa, J. L. V. (2015). Dropout prediction and reduction in distance education courses with the learning analytics multitrail approach. JUCS - Journal of Universal Computer Science, 21(1), Article 1. https://doi.org/10.3217/jucs-021-01-0023

Chen, Y., Hmelo-Silver, C. E., Lajoie, S. P., Zheng, J., Huang, L., & Bodnar, S. (2021). Using teacher dashboards to assess group collaboration in problem-based learning. Interdisciplinary Journal of Problem-Based Learning, 15(2), Article 2. https://doi.org/10.14434/ijpbl.v15i2.28792

Claassen, A., Mirriahi, N., Kovanović, V., & Dawson, S. (2025). From data to design: Integrating learning analytics into educational design for effective decision-making: From Data to Design. Proceedings of the 15th International Learning Analytics and Knowledge Conference, 558-567. https://doi.org/10.1145/3706468.3706541

Dennehy, D., Conboy, K., & Babu, J. (2023). Adopting learning analytics to inform postgraduate curriculum design: Recommendations and research agenda. Information Systems Frontiers, 25(4), 1315-1331. https://doi.org/10.1007/s10796-021-10183-z

Foster, E., Siddle, R., Crowson, P., & Bonne, P. (2020). It's all about the intervention: Reflections on building staff capacity for using learning analytics to support student success. En Adoption of Data Analytics in Higher Education Learning and Teaching (p. 241-256). Springer, Cham. https://doi.org/10.1007/978-3-030-47392-1_13

Herodotou, C., Maguire, C., McDowell, N., Hlosta, M., & Boroowa, A. (2021). The engagement of university teachers with predictive learning analytics. Computers & Education, 173, 104285. https://doi.org/10.1016/j.compedu.2021.104285

Huang, L., Zheng, J., Lajoie, S. P., Chen, Y., Hmelo-Silver, C. E., & Wang, M. (2024). Examining university teachers' self-regulation in using a learning analytics dashboard for online collaboration. Education and Information Technologies, 29(7), 8523-8547. https://doi.org/10.1007/s10639-023-12131-7

Huberth, M., Chen, P., Tritz, J., & McKay, T. A. (2015). Computer-tailored student support in introductory physics. PLOS ONE, 10(9), e0137001. https://doi.org/10.1371/journal.pone.0137001

Ifenthaler, D., & Yau, J. Y.-K. (2020). Utilising learning analytics to support study success in higher education: A systematic review. Educational Technology Research and Development, 68(4), 1961-1990. https://doi.org/10.1007/s11423-020-09788-z

Kaila, E., Lokkila, E., & Rytilahti, J. (2024, juny 15). Utilizing learning analytics in large online courses. Education and New Developments 2024 – Volume 2. Education and New Developments 2024. https://doi.org/10.36315/2024v2end035

Kaliisa, R., & Dolonen, J. A. (2023). CADA: A teacher-facing learning analytics dashboard to foster teachers' awareness of students' participation and discourse patterns in online discussions. Technology, Knowledge and Learning, 28(3), 937-958. https://doi.org/10.1007/s10758-022-09598-7

Kaliisa, R., Jivet, I., & Prinsloo, P. (2023). A checklist to guide the planning, designing, implementation, and evaluation of learning analytics dashboards. International Journal of Educational Technology in Higher Education, 20(1), 28. https://doi.org/10.1186/s41239-023-00394-6

Kim, J., Jo, I.-H., & Park, Y. (2016). Effects of learning analytics dashboard: Analyzing the relations among dashboard utilization, satisfaction, and learning achievement. Asia Pacific Education Review, 17(1), 13-24. https://doi.org/10.1007/s12564-015-9403-8

Klein, C., Lester, J., Rangwala, H., & Johri, A. (2019). Technological barriers and incentives to learning analytics adoption in higher education: Insights from users. Journal of Computing in Higher Education, 31(3), 604-625. https://doi.org/10.1007/s12528-019-09210-5

Larrabee, A. S., Hughes, E., & Smith, J. (2019). The efficacy of learning analytics interventions in higher education: A systematic review. British Journal of Educational Technology, 50(5), 2594-2618. https://doi.org/10.1111/bjet.12720

Márquez, L., Henríquez, V., Chevreux, H., Scheihing, E., & Guerra, J. (2024). Adoption of learning analytics in higher education institutions: A systematic literature review. British Journal of Educational Technology, 55(2), 439-459. https://doi.org/10.1111/bjet.13385

Tabuenca, B., Kalz, M., Drachsler, H., & Specht, M. (2015). Time will tell: The role of mobile learning analytics in self-regulated learning. Computers & Education, 89, 53-74. https://doi.org/10.1016/j.compedu.2015.08.004

Tsai, Y.-S., & Gasevic, D. (2017). Learning analytics in higher education --- challenges and policies: A review of eight learning analytics policies. Proceedings of the Seventh International Learning Analytics & Knowledge Conference, 233-242. https://doi.org/10.1145/3027385.3027400

Streaming attendance of on-campus lectures and student outcomes: a correlational study

Mara Soncin[1], Adalberto Polenghi[2], Margherita Pero[3], Francesca Fumero[4]

[1] Politecnico di Milano, School of Management, Italy; mara.soncin@polimi.it
[2] Politecnico di Milano, School of Management, Italy; adalberto.polenghi@polimi.it
[3] Politecnico di Milano, School of Management, Italy; margherita.pero@polimi.it
[4] Politecnico di Milano, School of Management, Italy; francesca.fumero@polimi.it

Correspondence: Mara Soncin: mara.soncin@polimi.it

Abstract

This study explores the relationship between streaming attendance and student academic performance in higher education. Drawing on data from two Management Engineering courses at a large Italian university, it combines administrative records, Webex usage logs, and student surveys to examine motivations, attendance behaviors, and outcomes. Findings indicate that while live streaming is widely used and offers flexibility, it does not negatively impact grades or exam pass rates. Instead, prior academic performance and engagement – regardless of modality – are the strongest predictors of success. These results suggest that hybrid models incorporating streaming could be adopted without detriment on the cognitive sphere.

Keywords: Hybrid learning; live streaming; student achievement

Introduction and Research Questions

The COVID-19 pandemic prompted a rapid and large-scale adoption of hybrid learning models in higher education. These models, combining in-person and online teaching simultaneously, provided continuity during emergency conditions. In the post-pandemic landscape, however, the pedagogical viability and effectiveness of hybrid learning remain underexplored, particularly in non-emergency settings. While some studies report benefits such as increased flexibility and perceived student satisfaction (Kohnke & Moorhouse, 2021), concerns persist regarding its implementation and educational outcomes (Li et al., 2022; Raes et al., 2020).

Hybrid learning has often been conflated with blended learning, yet its distinct nature—allowing synchronous online participation during in-person lectures—introduces new dynamics. Saichaie (2020) highlights this shift, emphasizing the evolving pedagogical frameworks. Despite a growing body of literature on hybrid and blended learning, there is limited direct empirical evidence on the impact of live streaming specifically in higher education. Streaming allows for real-time access to lectures without physical presence, yet its effects on learning remain ambiguous. While some studies suggest that it offers convenience and comparable learning experiences, others raise concerns about reduced engagement, multitasking, and lack of interaction (Li et al., 2022; Raes et al., 2020). Importantly, most existing studies focus on student perceptions or self-reported satisfaction rather than academic outcomes such as grades or pass rates (Kohnke & Moorhouse, 2021). Furthermore, the literature tends to overlook heterogeneity across student populations—such as prior academic ability or international status—which may moderate the effectiveness of streaming. The lack of fine-grained data on actual usage of streaming tools, as opposed to declared availability, further limits our understanding. Among the few robust empirical investigations, Cacault et al. (2021) conducted a randomized controlled trial in Geneva, finding no average performance effect but increased disparities by student ability. Ragni et al. (2024) employed a quasi-experimental approach at Politecnico di Milano and observed a minor increase in ECTS credits but reduced GPA. This latter study is particularly relevant for the present research, as it uses data from an Italian institution. However, that previous research has not access to the information about the actual use of streaming by students, and thus the observed impact is based on availability of streaming but not on the actual use. The current aims instead to fill this gap.

In detail, this study contributes to the literature by examining detailed streaming attendance data alongside academic performance, controlling for relevant student characteristics. The research aims to address the following questions:

- What are the main motivations for students to attend lectures via live streaming?
- How do different attendance modalities (in-person, live streaming, or no attendance) impact student performance, measured by grades and exam pass rates?

To address these questions, the paper presents a correlational study based on two pilot courses in a Management Engineering program at a large Italian university. The study integrates administrative records, detailed streaming data, and student survey responses to explore the relationship between attendance modality and academic outcomes. The next section describes the data sources and methodological approach, including the strategies adopted to handle missing or incomplete data. This is followed by a presentation of the main results, including descriptive statistics, regression analyses, and heterogeneity checks. The paper concludes with a discussion of the implications for hybrid learning design, acknowledges limitations, and suggests directions for future research.

Data and Methodology

The study was conducted within the Management Engineering program at a major Italian technical university, during the second semester of the 2022/23 academic year. Two pilot courses were selected to represent different levels of education: "Leadership and Innovation" (Master's level, N=241) and "Operations Research Optimization Methods" (Bachelor's level, N=127). Attendance for both courses was non-mandatory, and students could choose among three attendance modalities: in-person, live streaming via Webex, or no attendance. Three main sources of data were used: (i) Administrative data: this included students' demographic characteristics, historical academic performance (e.g., GPA, ECTS), and enrollment status (e.g., international student). (ii) Webex platform data: used to compute the actual duration of live streaming attendance per student throughout the semester. (iii) Student surveys: administered monthly during the semester to gather students' self-reported attendance modality and their motivations for choosing one format over another.

The use of student surveys was crucial for distinguishing between in-person attendance and complete non-attendance. While Webex data provided detailed information about the duration and frequency of live streaming, this platform could not capture what students were doing during the rest of the course hours. Specifically, the Webex logs allowed us to observe only the streaming portion of attendance. Without further input, we would be unable to determine whether the remaining portion of attendance was spent attending in person or if the student was entirely absent. To fill this gap, students were asked to indicate their predominant attendance modality (in-person, streaming, or no attendance) in a short survey.

These surveys were administered monthly by the course instructor, typically at the end of class sessions in which data collection was scheduled. To ensure full coverage, the surveys were subsequently uploaded to the course's Learning Management System (LMS), allowing students who were not physically present to participate as well. This approach ensured a broader and more inclusive data collection, helping to triangulate Webex data with students' own reported behaviors.

To estimate the relationship between attendance modality and academic performance, a correlational approach was adopted. The dependent variables were final exam grade and pass/fail outcome. The key explanatory variable was the proportion of lectures attended via live streaming, with control variables including prior GPA, international status, and other personal characteristics. For each course j, we estimate the following model considering the i-th student:

$$y_i = \beta_0 + \beta_1 X_i + \varepsilon_i$$

Where y is the final outcome (score or exam passed); X are the controlling covariates+attendance modality

X can be further defined as = $[X_c, X_p, X_a]$, where: X_c covariates related to the student career; X_p student personal characteristics; X_a attendance modality synthetized by three variables: (i) proportion of the course attended via live streaming (coming from Webex log data); (ii) proportion of the course attended in presence; (iii) proportion of the course not attended.

A particular methodological challenge arose due to incomplete responses to the survey instrument: 79 students failed to complete all three monthly surveys. For these students, we observed a notable inconsistency between the streaming data and the self-reported attendance patterns. Specifically, the amount of streaming activity recorded via Webex exceeded the total declared attendance reported in the partial survey responses. This discrepancy arose precisely because the surveys were not fully completed: missing entries led to an underestimation of the declared attendance, creating an apparent mismatch between observed streaming intensity and self-reported behaviors. To address this issue and account for uncertainty in the missing data, we adopted a dual-assumption modeling approach:

- Case 1 (Worst-case scenario): Missing attendance data were treated as non-attendance.
- Case 2 (Best-case scenario): Missing attendance data were assumed to be in-person attendance.

This dual-scenario approach ensured robustness of results against possible survey-related bias.

Descriptive statistics were computed for all variables, and multiple regression models were employed to assess correlations between attendance modality and academic performance. Additional heterogeneity analyses explored whether the effects varied by students' prior academic ability, streaming intensity, or international status.

Results

The first set of results explores the motivations driving students' choice of attendance modality. Data from the monthly surveys indicate that while a majority of students initially planned to attend in person, many eventually shifted to streaming. Figure 1 illustrates the main motivations students reported for selecting either in-person or streaming attendance. For students who predominantly attended in person, the key drivers were the ability to follow the lecture more effectively, the value of group work and classroom interaction, and the opportunity for social engagement. Conversely, those who primarily attended via streaming cited organizational constraints related to their weekly schedule, the perception that streaming was equally effective for learning, and practical considerations such as time and cost savings. These findings underscore the multifaceted nature of attendance decisions and suggest that live streaming is not simply a substitute for physical presence, but a flexible alternative shaped by diverse academic and logistical factors.

Figure 1. Attendance modality declared by students

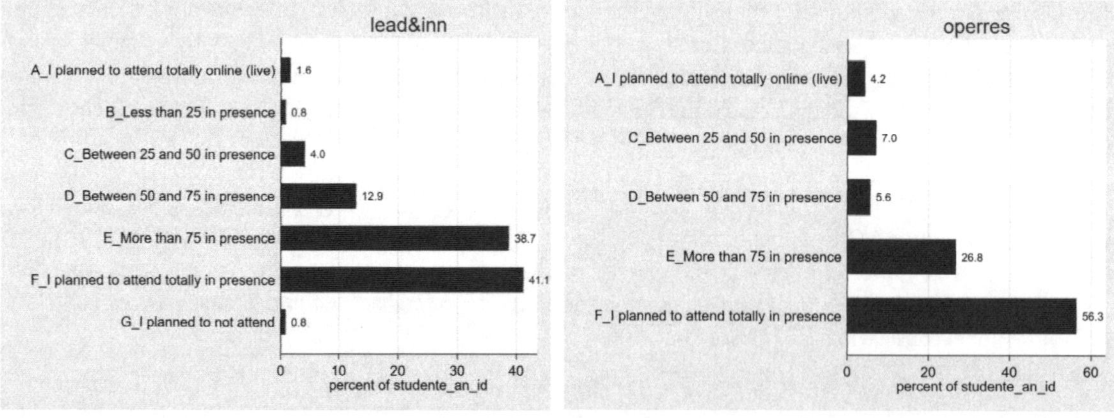

Table 1 presents descriptive statistics on the distribution of attendance modalities across both courses, under the two assumptions used to address missing survey data. These figures reveal how students combined in-person attendance, live streaming, and non-attendance during the semester. The table highlights a notable shift in attendance habits when comparing the best-case and worst-case scenarios. In Case 1 (where missing data are treated as non-attendance), the proportion of students categorized as non-attending is higher, and in-person attendance appears more limited. In contrast, Case 2 (where missing data are interpreted as in-person attendance) shows a more balanced distribution between modalities. Across both cases, however, live streaming plays a significant role in students' learning experience, often substituting but not completely replacing in-person participation. These insights support the idea that students adopted hybrid patterns in a flexible and personalized manner, making use of the live streaming option when convenient, but not abandoning the in-person experience entirely.

The following table provide descriptive statistics and analytical insights into students' academic performance. Table 2 presents the main descriptive statistics for both pilot courses. It shows the average final exam grades and the proportion of students who passed the exam in the two courses. Notably, pass rates and exam scores are higher for the Leadership and Innovation course compared to Operations Research Optimization Methods, as it reasonable to expect given the first is a course at master level.

Table 3 presents the correlation coefficients between streaming attendance and the main academic outcomes. The results are displayed separately for Case 1 and Case 2. Across both cases, the correlation between the proportion of live streaming attendance and final grade is weak or non-significant, reinforcing the earlier descriptive finding that streaming per se is not associated with poorer outcomes. Instead, stronger correlations are observed between previous academic performance and probability to pass the exam, suggesting that attending increases the probability of passing, with a higher magnitude of correlation for the in-person modality than the streaming one. Together, these descriptive and correlation analyses provide a foundation for the multivariate regression models discussed in the following section, where confounding factors and heterogeneity are explicitly accounted for.

Table 1. Descriptive statistics of the attendance modalities.

Case 1

course	var	prop_streaming	prop_person	prop_unattend
lead&inn	mean	0.239	0.164	0.597
	sd	0.262	0.229	0.322
operres	mean	0.214	0.211	0.575
	sd	0.264	0.276	0.36
Total	mean	0.231	0.18	0.59
	sd	0.263	0.247	0.336

Case 2

course	var	prop_streaming	prop_person2	prop_unattend2
lead&inn	mean	0.239	0.396	0.365
	sd	0.262	0.394	0.505
operres	mean	0.214	0.384	0.402
	sd	0.264	0.383	0.43
Total	mean	0.231	0.392	0.378
	sd	0.263	0.39	0.48

Table 2. Descriptive statistics of the output variables.

course	var	grade	passed
lead&inn	mean	25.268	0.822
	sd	2.467	0.384
	count	198	241
operres	Mean	22.329	0.598
	Sd	3.344	0.492
	count	76	127
Total	mean	24.453	0.745
	sd	3.033	0.437

Table 3. Correlation analysis between outcomes and attendance modality.

Case 1

	grade	passed	prop_streaming	prop_person	prop_unattend
grade	1.000				
passed	.	1.000			
prop_streaming	-0.083	**0.1519***	1.000		
prop_person	0.033	**0.2605***	-0.006	1.000	
prop_unattend	0.019	**-0.3017***	**-0.5583***	**-0.826***	1.000

Case 2

	grade	passed	prop_streaming	prop_person2	prop_unattend2
grade	1.000				
passed	.	1.000			
prop_streaming	-0.083	**0.1519***	1.000		
prop_person2	0.070	**0.2251***	-0.091	1.000	
prop_unattend2	-0.024	**-0.2803***	**-0.3938***	**-0.8796***	1.000

Note: * means that the correlation is significant at 5%.

Building on these preliminary findings, we estimated multivariate regression models to isolate the association between attendance modality and student performance, while controlling for relevant individual-level characteristics. The baseline regression results are consistent across both Case 1 and Case 2 as shown in Table 4. Specifically, the proportion of lectures attended via live streaming is not significantly associated with the final course grade. Instead, prior academic performance (e.g., previous GPA) and international student status emerge as the most robust predictors of success. These findings suggest that, when student background is accounted for, the specific mode of attendance (streaming vs. in-person) does not play a determining role in explaining variations in academic achievement. Regarding exam pass rates, the analysis reveals that attending lectures—regardless of the modality—is positively correlated with the probability of passing the exam. However, the specific choice between in-person and streaming attendance does not significantly alter this relationship. This confirms the idea that engagement in course activities matters more than how students access the content.

We also conducted heterogeneity analyses to test whether the effects of streaming varied across different subgroups of students. These include: (i) Students with high vs. low prior academic performance; (ii) Students with high vs. low intensity of streaming attendance; (iii) Domestic vs. international students. Across all subgroups, the results remain consistent: no significant differential impact of streaming on academic outcomes is observed. These robustness checks reinforce the general conclusion that streaming, as a modality, does not compromise student performance, and can be considered an effective complement to in-person learning in a hybrid educational model.

Table 4. Results from the regression analysis

	Course: lead&inn		Course: operres	
Dep var: exame grade	**Case 1**	**Case 2**	**Case 1**	**Case 2**
prop_streaming	-0.334	-0.641	0.301	0.007
prop_unattend	0.112	-0.296	0.042	-0.607
ects_semester	-0.001	-0.010	-0.010	-0.009
ects_tot	-0.001	-0.007	-0.009	-0.010
avg_grade	0.376***	0.376***	1.202***	1.189***
international	-1.360***	-1.324***	-	-
italian	-	-	0.076	0.032
N	198	198	76	76
R2	0.34	0.34	0.48	0.48
Dep var: exam passed	**Case 1**	**Case 2**	**Case 1**	**Case 2**
prop_streaming	0.549	1.004	-0.010	1.154
prop_unattend	-1.135**	-0.762**	-1.618**	-0.869**
ects_semester	-0.026	-0.027	-0.012	-0.007
ects_tot	0.009*	0.009*	0.019***	0.020***
avg_grade	0.078***	0.085***	0.247**	0.289***
international	0.467**	0.518**	-	-
italian	-	-	0.148	0.702
N	241	241	127	127
R2	0.23	0.23	0.44	0.42

Discussion and Implications

The findings of this study offer meaningful insights into the role of live streaming in higher education. First and foremost, the preliminary evidence suggests that live streaming can be effectively integrated into hybrid course designs without detriment to student performance. The lack of a statistically significant association between streaming attendance and either final grades or exam pass rates supports the view that synchronous remote participation is not academically inferior to in-person attendance, provided students remain engaged. These results align with the broader shift in post-pandemic pedagogy toward flexibility and personalization in learning. Students' motivations for selecting different modalities reveal that practical considerations – such as scheduling and commuting constraints – often drive the decision to stream lectures. At the same time, a substantial proportion still values the pedagogical and social benefits of face-to-face instruction. This points to the continued relevance of in-person teaching, but within a system that can accommodate diverse student needs and preferences. For educators and academic institutions, the findings underscore the importance of maintaining high-quality interactions and learning support across modalities. Since engagement, rather than the mode of attendance, seems to be the key factor influencing performance, instructional design should focus on strategies that promote active learning and participation, regardless of whether students are physically present or attending remotely.

Several limitations should be considered when interpreting the results. First, the analysis relies in part on self-reported survey data, which may be affected by recall bias or selective response. While efforts were made to administer surveys consistently and to reach all students via the LMS, response completeness varied, requiring the formulation of two contrasting scenarios (Case 1 and Case 2) to account for missing data. Second, the study is based on only two courses within a single academic program, which may limit the generalizability of the results to other contexts or disciplines. Future research should expand the scope to include a wider range of courses, institutions, and student populations. Third, the study focuses solely on academic performance as measured by grades and exam pass rates. It does not explore other important educational outcomes such as student satisfaction, engagement, long-term retention of knowledge, or skill acquisition. Finally, while live streaming attendance was tracked accurately via Webex, data on in-person attendance relied on student reporting, which introduces potential inaccuracies. Future studies could benefit from integrating additional digital tools or institutional tracking systems to enhance data reliability.

Despite these limitations, this study provides a valuable contribution to the understanding of hybrid learning by highlighting how streaming can serve as a flexible and effective component of modern university teaching. The results support a nuanced view of attendance, one that recognizes quality of engagement over physical presence, and opens the door for more inclusive and adaptable educational models. These results of this correlational study suggest that hybrid learning can be a viable alternative to traditional in-person education without negatively affecting academic performance. However, limitations regarding the response rate to student surveys as well as the impact on other outcomes that are not exam scores should be considered.

References

Cacault, M. P., Hildebrand, C., Laurent-Lucchetti, J., & Pellizzari, M. (2021). Distance learning in higher education: evidence from a randomized experiment. Journal of the European Economic Association, 19(4), 2322-2372.

Li, K. C., Wong, B. T., Kwan, R., Wu, M. M., & Cheung, S. K. (2022, June). Evaluation of hybrid teaching effectiveness: The perspective of academics. In International Conference on Blended Learning (pp. 265-274). Cham: Springer International Publishing.

Kohnke, L., & Moorhouse, B. L. (2021). Adopting HyFlex in higher education in response to COVID-19: Students' perspectives. Open Learning: The Journal of Open, Distance and e-Learning, 36(3), 231-244.

Raes, A., Detienne, L., Windey, I., & Depaepe, F. (2020). A systematic literature review on synchronous hybrid learning: gaps identified. Learning environments research, 23, 269-290.

Ragni, A., Ippolito, D., & Masci, C. (2024). Assessing the impact of hybrid teaching on students' academic performance via multilevel propensity score-based techniques. Socio-Economic Planning Sciences, 92, 101824.

Saichaie, K. (2020). Blended, flipped, and hybrid learning: Definitions, developments, and directions. New Directions for Teaching and Learning, 2020(164), 95-104.

Let's Save Our Environment! Empowering Students to Create VR Games in Disadvantaged Primary Schools

Rosa Bellacicco[1], Barbara Bruschi[2], Fabiola Camandona[3], Manuela Repetto[4], Melania Talarico[5]

[1] Department of Philosophy and Educational Sciences, University of Turin, Italy; rosa.bellacicco@unito.it
[2] Department of Philosophy and Educational Sciences, University of Turin, Italy; barbara.bruschi@unito.it
[3] Department of Philosophy and Educational Sciences, University of Turin, Italy; fabiola.camandona@unito.it
[4] Department of Philosophy and Educational Sciences, University of Turin, Italy; manuela.repetto@unito.it
[5] Department of Philosophy and Educational Sciences, University of Turin, Italy; melania.talarico@unito.it

Correspondence: Manuela Repetto: manuela.repetto@unito.it

Abstract:

This research addresses environmental issues through innovative educational approaches, aimed at fostering soft skills in children from disadvantaged neighborhoods and at enhancing local community engagement. The study, which employs a Design-Based Research method, involved the creation of immersive educational escape rooms designed by students and focused on environmental themes. The outcomes reported increased environmental awareness, improved collaboration and digital skills, and enhanced community involvement. Civic, educational, and playful dimensions were successfully integrated to benefit underserved children.

Keywords: game-based learning, extended learning, children inclusion, digital escape room, active citizenship

Introduction

In 2024, a network of researchers and local community associations implemented an integrated and innovative educational intervention for 4th-grade children in a vulnerable neighborhood of a northern Italian city. The initiative aimed to enhance their socio-cognitive and digital skills while fostering awareness of environmental issues. Although these topics were addressed at a local level, they align with European frameworks such as DigComp 2.2 and GreenComp, as well as the 2030 Agenda, which served as key reference points for the intervention's approach and activities. Furthermore,

The integration of environmental education with digital skill development was a fundamental aspect of this research-driven initiative. The intervention focused on the creation of virtual reality (VR) games and immersive teaching, both of which are emerging themes in K-12 education. VR experiences enhance immersion and engagement, supporting attention processes and emotional involvement (Tilhou et al., 2020). Moreover, when combined with appropriate teaching strategies, VR positively influence learning processes and motivation. The immersive and interactive nature of certain VR games place students in authentic contexts, fostering experiential learning through hands-on activities (Angel-Urdinola et al., 2021; Di Natale et al., 2020). Presenting environmental preservation through VR-based gaming transform it into a challenge to be tackled or a problem to be solved, allowing students to engage in practical experiences within a safe play space where simulated consequences encourage reflection.

The pedagogical approach of this intervention is rooted in a constructionist framework for game design (Harel & Papert, 1991; Kafai, 2006; Li et al., 2013), emphasizing active student participation in creating VR games rather than merely consuming them. Usinga an environment for game development programming, students designed videogames that explore environmental issues, thereby deepening their understanding and engagement.

Our research hypothesis posited that involving nine- and ten-year-old children from disadvantaged urban contexts in game design lead to more effective learning and foster behavioral change, particularly by enhancing environmental awareness. Furthermore, by adopting eco-friendly behaviors and actively engaging in the educational intervention, children influence their families and inspired broader community change.

This study employed a Design-Based Research (DBR) methodology (Anderson & Shattuck, 2012), which integrated theory-driven approaches with empirical evaluation across two iterative cycles. The first cycle, conducted in the previous year, involved a quasi-experimental study investigating how students improved socio-cognitive skills and developed pro-environmental attitudes. Findings indicated that students from at-risk neighborhoods showed significant improvement compared to their peers in more affluent areas. Consequently, the second iteration of the intervention targeted a broader population of disadvantaged students. This study aims to present the research design approach adopted in this initiative and its outcomes, with the expectation that this can be adopted also in other similar urban schooling contexts in Europe.

This work aims to present the prototype design approach developed through this research. By sharing these insights, we invited European researchers participating in the panel discussion to consider adopting and applying this model within their own urban schooling contexts.

Theoretical framework

Stories can be a good way to enhance territories and help people view places from different perspectives. Regarding this, let us take the example of the Neighborhood of Detroit project, which, through the stories of its inhabitants, sought to restore value to the city of Detroit to promote civic engagement actions after falling victim to the economic crisis and thus experiencing social, economic, and cultural degradation for several years. When we combine storytelling with play, especially for younger children, it can convey significant themes such as environmental education, which should be more effectively approached in an inclusive manner. However, to work on current and delicate issues, it is necessary to consider the operation Europe has long adopted to help citizens develop key competencies for citizenship (2018). These competencies are cited in the 2018 Recommendations document:

- digital competence;
- personal, social, and learning to learn competence;
- social and civic competence in citizenship.

These objectives are transversally included within those listed in the 2030 Agenda (2015), in which it is essential for our discussion to work on goal number 4, referring to quality education, with a focus on point 4.7. This point aims to ensure that all learners acquire the knowledge and skills needed to promote sustainable development, including education for sustainable development and sustainable lifestyles, human rights, gender equality, the promotion of a culture of peace and non-violence, global citizenship, and the appreciation of cultural diversity and culture's contribution to sustainable development.

Furthermore, a recent UNESCO report (2023) emphasizes the role of innovative pedagogical approaches and digital technologies in fostering inclusive and equitable education, highlighting that the focus should be on education and its three challenges: quality, as well as equity, inclusion, and efficiency. In light of these three challenges, immersive games created by students on environmental issues can support active citizenship and engagement in disadvantaged communities, bridging educational gaps and empowering marginalized learners, who become agents of change.

As reported by ISTAT data, Barriera di Milano is one of the neighborhoods in Turin experiencing particular social hardship, with a high youth unemployment rate of about 13.1%, creating cultural impoverishment and economic and social impoverishment. According to ISTAT, the Social Vulnerability Indicator of Barriera di Milano is equal to the weighted average of 101.2 (2017). Although much has been done, the degradation that the neighborhood often experiences, both socially and environmentally, is relatively high. Hence, it is necessary to rebuild social awareness from the ground up to work on the sense of citizenship and consequently focus on the related competencies. The care of spaces and places can become an action that gains meaning and value for both individual citizens and the community. People, including children, become accustomed to living in these places, and as a result, degradation starts to feel normal. For this reason, we aimed to work in this area, starting from primary school, so that children can develop critical thinking skills about the issues in their environment—specifically, environmental concerns—and, together with the community, rebuild a vision of beauty to restore social value to the territory through virtual game projects and game-based learning.

Methodology and research design

A Design-Based Research (DBR) has been conducted in this research, encompassing two cycles (pilot phase and scaling up phase), in which the latter is still undergoing in order to progressively enhance the design approach obtained in the former. The specific DBR approach adopted envisages the four iterative phases recommended by Reeves (2006). The design approach that emerged was aimed at guiding innovative educational interventions targeted at fourth graders of the vulnerable neighborhoods.

During the first cycle of DBR, the pilot phase, the development of collaborative and cognitive skills within experimental groups of students tasked with designing Virtual Reality (VR) games structured as escape rooms (Repetto et al., 2023) were compared with control groups engaged in the creation of physical escape rooms. A pretest-posttest design was deliberately selected, using two calibrated teachers' and students' scales as an instrumental metric for assessing the enhancement of collaborative skills. The results of this first cycle suggest that experimental groups of students engaging with immersive VR environments enhanced situated, experiential, and transformative learning processes. In contrast, the control group involved in constructing physical escape rooms showed minimal improvements in on teachers' and students' assessment scales. Moreover, the notable improvements observed in two classrooms comprising foreign students, many of whom experience learning difficulties, underscore the necessity of expanding the sample size of these students in the ongoing second cycle of Design-Based Research (DBR).

During this scaling up phase, it was imperative to establish a network of associations to provide support for this demographic and to provide training for primary school teachers in immersive teaching and learning. This involved adopting the same educational approach utilized during the first cycle - with a more active participation of teachers trained on this approach - and applying it to a larger sample of students in disadvantaged situations.

The three "Is" of DBR, as outlined by Hall (2020), were utilized in our research, that can be considered an interventional, innovative, and iterative one. Firstly, the research involved intervention to alter and enhance the learning experience and the relationship that students facing disadvantaged situations have with environmental issues. Secondly, the research, due to its advancement of environmental education through immersive and novel technology and methods, can be regarded as pioneering in the realm of learning and teaching. Thirdly, the two interconnected cycles, which encompass conceptualization, design, implementation, and evaluation, represent one of the most contemporary and adaptable approaches to learning design.

The sample

The study led during the scaling-up phase involved 13 fourth-grade classes from four primary schools, engaging approximately 350 students. A team of three or more teachers per class, including special education teachers, participated due to the high presence of foreign students and Newly Arrived in Italy (NAI) students.

The study phases

The study was organised into the following phases:

- Teacher Training on the Design of Escape Rooms: Between February and April 2024, five meetings of two hours each were held to train teachers on game-based learning and digital educational escape rooms to learn the fundamental theoretical and design principles.
- Creation of Stories and Puzzles by the Children: Between May and June, after the training, teachers began working with their classes to create the story and puzzles to be included in the games. Teachers could choose between actual escape rooms or fantasy escape rooms. In the first case, the story is based on the local context using issues related to their neighborhood. In the second case, teachers and their classes chose to create escape rooms that address real problems within a fantasy narrative. Each class created its own story, resulting in 13 stories and future games.
- Game Development: This phase involves creating escape rooms using the CoSpaces Edu software. Children can use their resources, such as 2D or 360-degree images, and take advantage of the 3D environments available in the software to create animated objects, dialogues, and scene transitions. Additionally, the software allows for coding and stimulates logical thinking. Figure 1 provide an example of the development of a game scene.

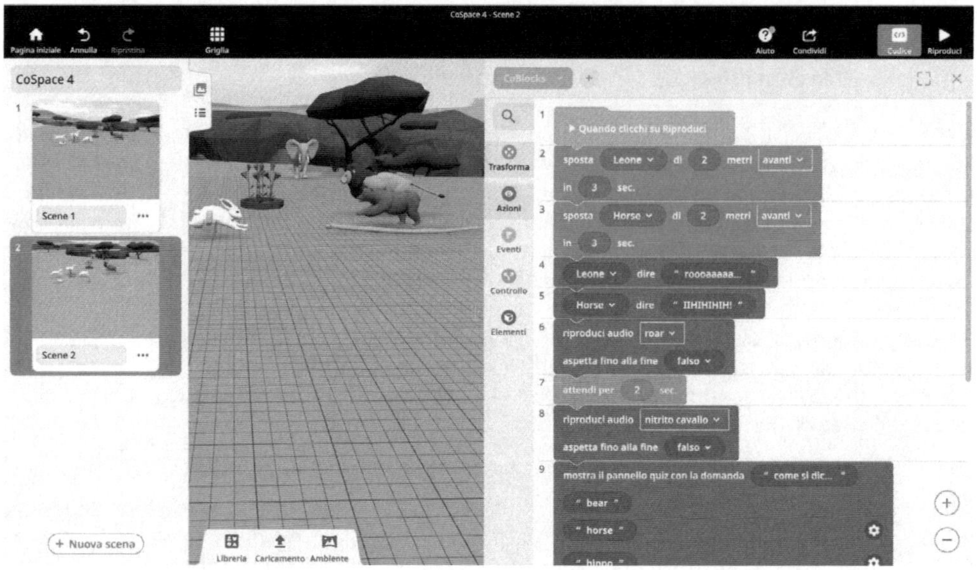

Figure 1: Example of a 3D Scene with scene transition on the left and 3D object programming code on the right

- Sharing at the Sotto18 Film Festival: To add value to the games, children had the opportunity to showcase their work through a video at a conference organized by an association operating on cinema-related topics.

Research tools

Throughout the scaling-up phase, teachers and researchers collected qualitative data through reflective journals, student interviews, and classroom observations, allowing for continuous refinement and scaling of the intervention. Adjustments were made to enhance student engagement, address technological challenges and foster better collaboration. The DBR approach ensured that the project remained adaptable, effectively improving digital skills, environmental awareness, and collaborative learning while addressing the specific needs of disadvantaged students.

Results

From a thematic analysis of reflective journals and interviews, several interesting data points emerged related to the qualitative observation of the activities, which have merged into a set of thematic cores.

Firstly, there was a cultural gap between students, influenced by their home backgrounds, and a general low-to-medium level of knowledge about environmental education. The development of digital escape rooms has proven to be an effective and engaging way to teach environmental concepts. Many students were able to solve puzzles and retain the information about the environment, even recalling it at later times.

Students digital competences were distributed in a specific manner: while most students were familiar with using mobile phones, tablets, and gaming consoles, fewer were skilled in using computers or digital tools. However, game-based learning (GBL) proved to be effective, leading to growth not only in collaboration skills but also in creativity and the basic functions of using computers. These activities allowed for significant development in students' digital literacy, including improvement of children computational thinking. As students became more familiar with the tools and platform used, they showed greater independence and speed in both creating and using the escape room scenes, as well as in collaborative work.

There were noticeable differences in group dynamics across different classes. Some groups struggled to collaborate effectively, while others demonstrated excellent teamwork, particularly in resolving conflicts through democratic voting or open dialogue. The cultural diversity of the students also posed challenges in communication, especially in mixed-language groups.

Students with certified disabilities or special needs actively participated in the coding and virtual reality activities. The adoption of cooperative attitudes were evident, with students supporting each other, especially those with less experience with computers or virtual reality headsets. The use of virtual reality has been particularly beneficial for students with disabilities, for increasing inclusion and motivation.

The level of motivation and involvement of the teachers greatly influenced the success of the project. When teachers were well-prepared and engaged, they created a more productive and smooth learning environment. However, some teachers showed lower engagement and needed more guidance, which sometimes resulted in less organized class dynamics.

Conclusion

The results garnered from the pilot phase of this research, in conjunction with the outcomes of the ongoing scaling-up phase, underscore the imperative nature of initiatives tailored for children experiencing disadvantaged situations, wherein access to diverse and innovative educational opportunities leveraging emerging technologies is limited.

One primary outcome involves the establishment and maintenance of a comprehensive network encompassing university entities, schools and local cultural and environmental associations. This network aims to provide integrated socio-educational support to the most vulnerable neighborhood within a city in northwest Italy. Collaboration with existing entities operating within the designated territory is integral to this endeavor, fostering synergy with ongoing local initiatives.

Another outcome involves the enhancement of teaching methodologies among primary school teachers in the targeted neighborhood. Through innovative training programs, teachers were equipped to revamp their approaches to teaching and learning. This initiative cascades to sensitize students and, subsequently, the broader community on topics related to prevention and environmental conservation. Leveraging novel immersive learning technology, this effort not only promotes active citizenship but also fosters an inclination towards advocacy and ecological transition.

Furthermore, dissemination and adoption of the design approach developed within this research is worthy of consideration: this integrated perspective not only encompasses environmental considerations but also permeates social, cultural, and educational dimensions. It is envisioned that this approach will serve as a model inspiring similar initiatives and studies in other urban areas facing similar socio-cultural challenges across Europe.

References

Angel-Urdinola, D. F., Castillo-Castro, C., Hoyos, A.: Meta-analysis assessing the effects of virtual reality training on student learning and skills development. World Bank, Washington, DC (2021).

Di Natale, A. F., Repetto, C., Riva, G.; Villani, D. (2020). Immersive virtual reality in K-12 and higher education: A 10-year systematic review of empirical research. British Journal of Educational Technology, 51(6), 2006-2033.

Hall, T. (2020). Bridging practice and theory: The emerging potential of design-based research (DBR) for digital innovation in education. Education Research and Perspectives, 47, 157-173.

Harel, I. & Papert, S. (1991). Constructionism. Norwood, NY: Ablex Publishing Corporation.

Kafai, Y. (2006). Playing and making games for learning: instructionist and constructionist perspectives for game studies. Games and Culture, 1, 1, 36–40.

Li, Z. Z., Cheng, Y. B., & Liu, C. C. (2013). A constructionism framework for designing game-like learning systems: Its effect on different learners. British Journal of Educational Technology, 44(2), 208-224.

Reeves, T. (2006). Design research from a technology perspective. In Educational design research (pp. 64-78). Routledge.

Repetto, M., Bruschi, B., & Talarico, M. (2023). Key issues and pedagogical implications in the design of Digital Educational Escape rooms. Journal of e-Learning and Knowledge Society, 19(1), 67-74.

Tilhou, R., Taylor, V., Crompton, H. 3D Virtual Reality in K-12 Education: A Thematic Systematic Review. In: Yu, S., Ally, M., Tsinakos, A. (eds): Emerging Technologies and Pedagogies in the Curriculum. Bridging Human and Machine: Future Education with Intelligence. Springer, Singapore (2020).

Use of plagiarism detection software in higher education: A case study of Croatia

Anja Đurđević[1], Dan Stipić[2], Sandra Kučina Softić[3]

[1] University of Zagreb University Computing Centre, Croatia; anja.djurdjevic@srce.hr
[2] University of Zagreb University Computing Centre, Croatia; dan.stipic@srce.hr
[3] University of Zagreb University Computing Centre, Croatia, sskucina@srce.hr

Correspondence: Sandra Kucina Softic, sskucina@srce.hr

Abstract:

The increasing incidence of academic misconduct among students in written assignments and final papers has prompted academic institutions to implement various measures, including using plagiarism detection software. In this paper, we present the experiences of the University of Zagreb University Computing Centre (SRCE) in conceptualising and establishing the technical prerequisites for a strategic approach to plagiarism prevention within the student population in Croatia's higher education system. Plagiarism detection software undoubtedly holds a prominent role in identifying and preventing academic misconduct today; however, its effectiveness largely depends on how well it is integrated into institutional policies and everyday practices. In Croatia, such software has been available to public higher education institutions for nearly six years and has become essential in promoting academic integrity. More recently, the widespread use of generative AI tools for academic writing has further emphasised the importance of plagiarism detection software. Accordingly, this paper discusses the use of plagiarism detection tools, focusing on the support provided to Higher Education Institutions (HEIs) in their adoption and examining the challenges and successes observed during implementation and use.

Keywords: plagiarism detection software, higher education, academic integrity

Introduction

Plagiarism, defined as using someone else's work without proper credit, and more broadly, ethics in education and academic integrity, has long been a key topic on the agenda of higher education policymakers. With the recent ubiquity of generative AI technologies, the topic has gained renewed urgency. A decade ago, the Council of Europe established the Pan-European Platform for Ethics, Transparency and Integrity in Education (ETINED, 2015), aiming to promote and safeguard academic integrity, with a particular emphasis on tackling plagiarism. The importance of academic integrity among higher education institutions was particularly emphasised due to the increasing number of students at the time and the growing competition between universities. The European Commission also acknowledged the significance of this issue. Between 2010 and 2013, the Impact of Policies for Plagiarism in Higher Education Across Europe (IPPHEAE) project investigated national policies and institutional practices designed to uphold academic integrity and address plagiarism across the European Higher Education Area (Glendinning, 2015).

Many European universities have established strict definitions and policies to address this issue. Plagiarism detection software is crucial in a systematic approach to detecting plagiarism and maintaining academic integrity in higher education. These tools support the assessment of textual originality by comparing submitted content against a wide range of sources, including online materials, scientific and professional articles from selected commercial databases and journals, open-access publications, and previously submitted papers stored within the software. Additionally, users can include their own documents as sources for comparison. Following the analysis of the similarity report generated by the software, the user determines whether any portion of the document constitutes plagiarism. However, it is important to note that software tools alone cannot establish a clear boundary between original and plagiarised papers. Interpreting results requires careful consideration and a thorough understanding of their context. Additionally, the software analysis results in terms of similarity percentage cannot be uniformly interpreted across all scientific fields. For example, many common technical terms or mathematical formulas cannot be considered plagiarism, as they are repeatedly used across various papers. The same applies to other types of generic content. For this reason, users (i.e. academic staff) are expected to review the analysis report in detail and draw a definite conclusion on whether plagiarism has occurred.

In 2016 and 2017, SRCE conducted a comprehensive review of plagiarism detection software available on the market, using a predefined set of criteria tailored to the specific needs of higher education institutions (Birkić et al., 2016, 2017). The aim of this report was to encourage dialogue on the topic of plagiarism in higher education in Croatia with a particular focus on the role of detection software and to present and share up-to-date knowledge with both experts and the broader public. Representing the academic community and drawing on the findings of these reports, SRCE initiated discussions with the Ministry of Science, Education, and Youth to negotiate the possibility of acquiring plagiarism detection software for public higher education institutions in Croatia. Following a positive response from the Ministry, the first license was purchased in the academic year 2019/2020. Since then, plagiarism detection software has been available to public higher education institutions in Croatia. SRCE leads its distribution and serves as a focal point of support for academic staff and students using the software.

The role of SRCE in coordinating the software usage for HEIs

The University of Zagreb University Computing Centre (SRCE) (https://www.srce.unizg.hr/en) is a central infrastructure institution responsible for planning, developing, and enhancing e-infrastructure and digital services for Croatia's academic and scientific community, while also providing support for their use. In addition, SRCE also acts as a competence centre for information and communication technologies (ICT) and serves as a hub for education and support in ICT applications.

Within SRCE's E-learning Centre, a plagiarism detection software team (https://www.srce.unizg.hr/spa) coordinates the distribution of software to public higher education institutions in Croatia, provides user support, conducts training for academic and non-academic staff, and plays an active role in promoting awareness of ethical principles and academic integrity in higher education.

Public higher education institutions can access Turnitin software to check various types of student papers, ranging from seminar papers to final theses and doctoral dissertations, in accordance with institutional procedures and needs. Students, academic, and non-academic staff can do this according to the institution's procedures and needs, using their AAI@EduHr electronic identities.

Setting up the scene

Based on criteria defined by SRCE experts during the 2016 and 2017 analysis, software selection focused on several key factors: applicability at the national or institutional level (universities or faculties), its ability to reference relevant sources in Croatian language, primarily HRČAK - portal of Croatian scientific and professional journals (https://hrcak.srce.hr/en) and DABAR - Digital Academic Archives and Repositories (https://dabar.srce.hr/en) platform, as well as its compatibility with essential information systems, such as Merlin (https://moodle.srce.hr/), the national e-learning platform developed and maintained by SRCE and based on Moodle LMS.

The defined criteria for evaluating plagiarism detection software included the following (Birkić et al., 2016, 2017):

- available application programming interface (API) and plug-in to integrate the software into DABAR and Merlin systems
- service location (locally on institutions' or SRCE servers or online on software manufacturers' servers)
- database scope and the possibility to include personal content

- support
- distribution (usage of software in the world, Europe and neighbouring countries)
- costs of using the system and the license

Based on the reports conducted and the state of the use of plagiarism detection software at higher education institutions in Croatia at that time, it was concluded that such specialised tools are essential for verifying the originality of student papers, master's and doctoral theses, seminar papers, and scientific publications.

While SRCE generally favours open-source solutions, none of the available options could adequately support the needs of a large student population, high paper volume, or the required workflow. Therefore, commercial solutions were selected. SRCE proposed the procurement of licenses for two software solutions, enabling the checking of an unlimited number of student submissions.

The aim was to raise awareness of plagiarism and emphasise the importance of academic integrity within the student population. Plagiarism detection software plays a crucial role in preventing plagiarism. Its use is intended to empower students to review their own work and take responsibility for the originality of their seminar papers, graduate theses, doctoral dissertations, and similar academic work before submission for assessment. Furthermore, the implementation of plagiarism detection tools contributes to increasing students' awareness of the ethical dimensions of academic integrity. The main idea behind that is that when students become more familiar with these tools and their purpose, they are more likely to pay closer attention to correct referencing practices. This, in turn, promotes a culture of academic honesty and responsibility on a practical level.

Prior to SRCE acquiring licenses, several higher education institutions in Croatia already used plagiarism detection software, with Turnitin being the most commonly adopted. Consequently, the proposal was to procure licenses for two software solutions: PlagScan, a German-developed tool that received the highest evaluation based on the analysis and predefined criteria, and Turnitin, an American software already in use at some of Croatia's public higher education institutions.

SRCE undertook the procurement, distribution, and usage coordination tasks. At the same time, the Ministry of Science, Education, and Youth ensured that financial resources were allocated for purchasing the software from the academic year 2019/2020 onwards. The procurement model was based on the number of students enrolled at the public higher education institutions, enabling unlimited checks of students' papers per enrolled student. Paper checks can be conducted by teachers, non-teaching staff, and students using these tools, following the procedures and needs of each higher education institution.

Each public higher education institution could choose which plagiarism detection software to use for each academic year. However, the majority of institutions retained their original selection. During the first four years, three institutions switched to a different software. In the academic year 2019/2020, 68 public higher education institutions utilised plagiarism detection software, with 52.94% using Turnitin. In academic years 2020/2021, 2021/2022, and 2022/2023, 70 public higher education institutions used software, and 54.2% of them used Turnitin.

In 2021, Turnitin acquired Ouriginal, a company that included PlagScan as one of its software products. Beginning with the 2023/2024 academic year, Turnitin became the primary plagiarism detection software used in public higher education institutions in Croatia, as PlagScan was discontinued and is no longer available.

It is also crucial to ensure that users receive high-quality guidance and support. While Turnitin provides documentation in English, the SRCE team has prepared documentation in Croatian (https://www.srce.unizg.hr/spa) for academic staff, students, and institutional administrators. These resources include detailed explanations of each feature within the software interface and practical instructions tailored to the SRCE license.

Furthermore, since users may not always be inclined to read detailed instructions, "quick start" guides have been created for teachers and students. These guides concisely summarise the originality review process, highlighting the most important steps. In addition, video tutorials have been developed to explain key aspects of the software, such as logging in, interpreting similarity reports, and managing stored papers, including how to delete them.

Purchasing software licenses alone is insufficient; clear instructions and guidelines are also necessary, along with education on topics such as academic integrity and proper referencing. As part of its education and training programs, which SRCE has been providing for over 50 years, dedicated online courses on this topic are available: self-paced online courses "Authorship, Plagiarism, and Citation: What, How, and Why" for students and "The Use of Creative Commons Licenses in Educational Content" for academic staff. Moreover, institutions are encouraged to approach this topic independently and through collaborative efforts at the institutional level, involving academic staff, librarians, and other staff members to organise training activities on using plagiarism detection software, as well as other educational activities related to academic writing and ethics.

Methodology

To monitor the application and use of plagiarism detection software, the SRCE team conducts annual surveys to assess the extent and types of usage and gauge users' satisfaction with the software and the support provided. The survey consists of 12 questions and is completed by designated representatives at the institutional level. At the end of the survey, institutions also have the opportunity to leave comments and share additional feedback on their experiences with the software and SRCE support. Based on their responses, it can be concluded that users are generally satisfied with the software provided.

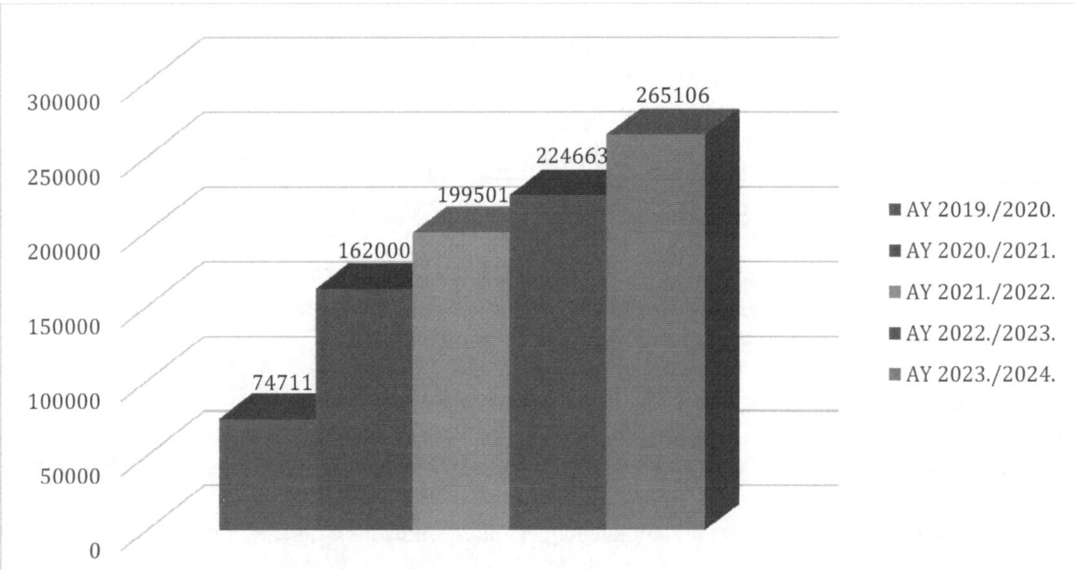

Graph 1: Total number of papers checked by the plagiarism detection software for each academic year

In Graph 1, the number of papers checked using plagiarism detection software increases annually. While some institutions and academic staff were initially sceptical about using the software or did not recognise its benefits, the number of checked papers at public higher education institutions has since increased significantly. As shown in Graph 1, in the academic year 2023/2024, the number of checked papers was 265.106. Taking the first academic year as the pilot, a comparison of data between the academic years 2020/2021 and 2023/2024 shows an increase of 64.65%. Recently, an increasing number of higher education institutions have made it mandatory to check master's and doctoral theses, and this trend is expected to persist in the foreseeable future.

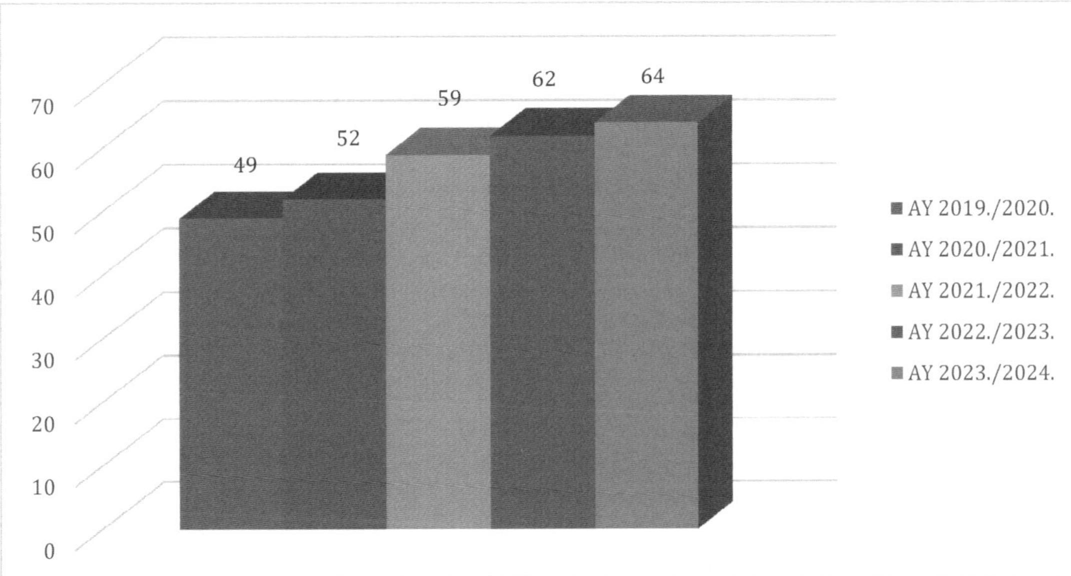

Graph 2: Number of institutions that have enabled students to check their papers independently

Through SRCE's advocacy, the number of institutions that have recognised the importance of allowing students to check their papers independently (assignments, seminars, final theses, etc.) has increased significantly over the years. Today, 62 of 70 public higher education institutions in Croatia have enabled students to check their papers independently before submitting them for evaluation.

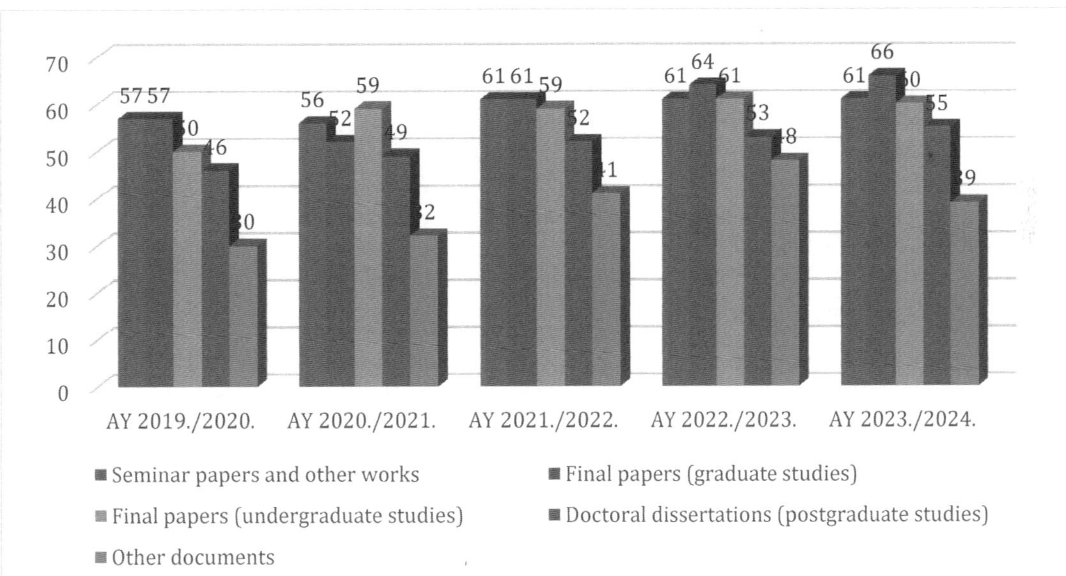

Graph 3: Overview of document types checked using the selected software

Graph 3 shows a steady increase in the number of checked papers across all types, particularly final papers for undergraduate and graduate studies. These figures are important for monitoring higher education institutions' overall usage and needs.

All public higher education institutions in Croatia consistently report satisfaction with the support provided by SRCE in distributing and using plagiarism detection software. Additionally, SRCE teams respond to approximately 300 inquiries of varying complexity each year.

Following the increased interest expressed by institutions in both surveys and ongoing communication with users regarding the challenges posed by AI-generated content, starting from the academic year 2024/2025, Turnitin's AI-generated text detection tool is also available to academic and non-academic staff as a part of the SRCE license, integrated directly as a feature within the software interface. As of the writing of this paper, the tool is only available for papers written in English and Spanish (Turnitin, n.d.), allowing institutions and academic and non-academic staff to prepare, test, and familiarise themselves with the tool and the concept, ultimately helping them to make informed decisions regarding the use of AI tools for detecting AI-generated content in academic papers. Although this functionality is not currently available in Croatian, it has sparked significant interest among academic staff and higher education institutions in Croatia.

Current developments and future plans for plagiarism detection in Croatia

According to the survey results, the licences for the use of Turnitin software for public higher education institutions in Croatia are consistently rated as satisfactory. However, with the growing capabilities of AI tools, it will become increasingly important for plagiarism detection software to support checks in all languages, not just the most widely used ones. At the same time, clear rules and guidelines should be established at the institutional level to ensure students understand how to use AI tools responsibly. Likewise, academic staff must be equipped to comprehend and effectively integrate AI tools into teaching and learning.

As plagiarism detection tools have expanded to include identifying AI-generated text, they now incorporate features to detect content likely produced by generative AI. These tools analyse characteristics such as writing style, sentence structure, word choice, and other elements that may distinguish AI-generated text from the more unpredictable nature of human-written. Given that this concept is undoubtedly more complex and challenging to substantiate than the traditional comparison of the submitted text with external sources, it is essential to understand the capabilities and limitations of these tools in terms of their accuracy. AI detection tools cannot definitively assess whether a paper or a portion of it was written using AI; instead, they primarily indicate the possibility of AI involvement. Therefore, as with traditional text comparison methods, AI detection tools require a more comprehensive analysis, including incorporating educational context into their usage. The increasing number of academic articles and research studies on the impact of generative AI tools, such as ChatGPT, on academic writing further underscores the urgency and relevance of this topic.

Guided by a continuous commitment to upholding academic integrity and staying abreast of emerging trends, SRCE will continue to monitor the software plagiarism market, providing the best possible solutions for the Croatian academic community and collaborating with them to maintain high ethical standards.

Final thoughts and conclusions

Over the years, the significant growth in plagiarism detection software usage underscores its value and highlights its critical role, as evidenced by positive feedback from institutions gathered through annual surveys. Specifically, the results regarding satisfaction with the service and support provided by SRCE may suggest that, although these software solutions are neither flawless nor perfectly tailored to every user's preferences, institutions nonetheless appreciate the efforts invested in creating a strategic and comprehensive approach to plagiarism prevention and the continuous support offered to both institutions and all user categories.

Institutional participation is also a key factor in the success of this initiative. Since the start of implementation, SRCE has actively encouraged the development of internal usage guidelines, emphasising the importance of allowing students to independently check their work and thereby fostering practical awareness of proper source citation. Equally important is the emphasis on transparency and the open accessibility of theses and dissertations through institutional repositories, in line with the principles of openness. Furthermore, higher education institutions are responsible for ensuring the appropriate use of plagiarism detection software and establishing clear internal procedures. At the same time, the individual author bears personal responsibility for the authenticity of their work.

As we navigate the ongoing challenges of generative AI tools, these established practices can also serve as a foundation for integrating artificial intelligence into academic contexts. Effective plagiarism prevention among students should be rooted primarily in education and open dialogue rather than relying on punitive measures. Although regulating the use of emerging technologies presents significant challenges, prioritising ethical awareness and personal accountability helps reinforce the established foundations.

References

Birkić, T., Celjak, D., Cundeković, M., & Rako, S. (2016). Analiza softvera za otkrivanje plagiranja u sustavu znanosti I visokog obrazovanja. Sveučilišni računski centar Sveučilišta u Zagrebu.

Birkić, T., Celjak, D., Cundeković, M., & Rako, S. (2017). Analiza softvera za otkrivanje plagiranja u sustavu znanosti I visokog obrazovanja 1.1. Sveučilišni računski centar Sveučilišta u Zagrebu.

Glendinning, I. (2015). Promoting Maturity in Policies for Plagiarism across Europe and beyond. Presented at: 7th Prague Forum: Towards a Pan-European Platform on Ethics, Transparency and Integrity in Education, Prague.

Pan-European Platform for Ethics, Transparency and Integrity in Education (ETINED) (2015). http://www.coe.int/en/web/ethics-transparency-integrity-in-education.

SRCE, Turnitin upute i animacije. https://wiki.srce.hr/spaces/CEU/pages/121963891/Turnitin+upute+i+animacije.

Turnitin. (n.d.). Turnitin AI. https://www.turnitin.com/products/features/ai/.

Rematerialising and revitalising synchronous distance learning with moving hands

Nicolas Szilas[1], Sophie Bénard-Linh Quang[2]

[1] University of Geneva, Switzerland; nicolas.szilas@unige.ch
[2] University of Geneva, Switzerland; sophie.linhquang@unige.ch

Correspondence: Nicolas Szilas: nicolas.szilas@unige.ch

Abstract:

To move beyond traditional online lectures, we propose an innovative approach in which slides are replaced by real-time hand movements filmed by a camera. The moving hands manipulate objects to convey learning content. The iterative design of the course is described, and three challenges are highlighted: technical optimisation, the teacher's cognitive load and note-taking. Student evaluations conducted over three years shows a majority of satisfied learners, while also highlights the difficulties of dealing with a course without prior slides. Solutions to this problem are currently being worked on.

Keywords: Synchronous Distance Learning, Videoconferencing, Moving Hands, Innovation

Distance synchronous learning: potential and limits

Distance learning is classically divided into synchronous and asynchronous modes, depending on whether the participants can communicate in real time during an online course or whether they undertake learning activities at their own pace (Hrastinski, 2008). In the field of distance education, asynchronous distance learning is preferred, because it allows for more flexibility (Asaduddin & Maulani, 2021; Ghilay, 2022).

However, during the 2020 pandemic, synchronous distance learning suddenly became widespread, replacing traditional courses. It was easy to convert an in-person course into a videoconference course. Nevertheless, ease does not equal quality, and it received a lot of justified criticism, since distance course is not the mere transposition of a presence course but needs a specific pedagogical design (Peraya & Peltier, 2020).

While the pandemic has demonstrated the technical feasibility of synchronous learning and has largely influenced today practices (not necessary positively), it also has shown to which extent it could be poorly designed. Should distance synchronous learning be simply discarded, because it put learners in uncomfortable and inefficient learning situations?

One advantage of synchronous courses must be pointed out: it allows a more lively communication within the virtual class, between learners and between the learners and the teachers. Potentially, it can help to reduce one of the main burdens of distance learning, namely learner isolation (Hrastinski, 2008). While hybrid learning, combining presence and distance is often recognised as reducing such isolation, the inclusion of synchronous sessions within a whole distance course also has the same potential benefits, without requiring the logistic of presence courses.

In this article, we will explore one modality of synchronous distance learning that was conceived as a response to the poor quality online courses that were prevalent during the pandemic (Szilas et al., 2023). The next section will criticise the dominant model of online synchronous courses in order to introduce an innovative alternative.

Criticism of slides & talking head

The dominant model today is to present slides while being filmed by a frontal camera, with the teacher's face inserted on the screen, as a "talking head". It uses the technical functionalities of videoconferencing systems, camera streaming and screen sharing.

Split attention

Although this format may enhance learners' satisfaction, it can also impair learning (Sondermann & Merkt, 2023). Research has shown that it requires learners to split their attention between the teacher's face and the instructional content, increasing extraneous cognitive load and thereby reducing learning effectiveness (Ayres & Sweller, 2005; Mayer & Fiorella, 2014).

The excesses of immateriality

What is striking about this approach is that it stages a learning situation that is totally dissociated from any materiality. First the slides, which take up most of the space and represent the major focus of visual attention.

Then the teacher, reduced to his face. Most of the body gestures are discarded, as are any stage effect used in classroom. If the face can express emotion, the associated gaze is fixed, towards the camera. In addition, any notion of space is removed: no desk, no chairs, even no background. Particularly symptomatic of this deletion of space was the massive use of virtual backgrounds during the pandemics. Practically and officially, these virtual backgrounds enable users to keep their privacy – their home should not be exposed to the public. But we believe they express the implicit acceptance that, if a course is not in class, it must be "nowhere", in the virtual immaterial world of networks.

As we will demonstrate later, moving away from the assumption that distance learning is immaterial opens up several new horizons for synchronous distance learning.

The oddity of not projecting slides

It is enlightening to recall where the idea of sharing slides through videoconferencing software came from. First there was the blackboard (and the whiteboard), followed by overhead transparencies, whose main advantage was to facilitate the teacher's work, as most material was written in advance. Note however that it was common to write directly on the transparencies. The main characteristic of transparencies is their small format, compared to the screen on which they are projected. Then the transparencies were computerized, which not only eased their management but also largely improved the possibilities for animation: the presenter did not have to move objects or transparencies in real-time because the animation was automated, triggered only by the presenter. Finally, such a slide-based presentation is transmitted directly to the learner's digital device, as a streaming video, without being projected at all.

Therefore, a key property of digital slides and their physical ancestors (overhead transparencies) is their ability to transform a small document handled by the teacher into a large one visible to a large audience. This is no longer the case with videoconferencing. Streaming possibilities are therefore used in an old-fashioned way, by legacy, without taking into account the specificity of the distance learning situation, technically characterised by video streaming communication.

Proposed new modality: filmed moving hands

Questioning the relevance of streaming slides and wishing to re-introduce the materiality of the teacher's space, we propose the idea of supporting the teacher's discourse not with animated slides but with physical objects on a desk, manipulated in real time during the lesson.

The filmed physical objects can be of any kind: images, text labels, action figures, strings, construction kits (e.g. LEGO® elements), plants, rocks, etc., depending on the course subject. These objects are manipulated or pointed at by the teachers as s/he speaks, while the camera films the desk from a top view (see Fig. 1).

This top view alternates with two more traditional views: the camera pointing at the teacher (but not necessarily limited to his/her face) and the screen sharing, to show a website or a software.

The minimum technical requirement consists of a computer equipped with a camera capable to film from above, and another camera facing the teacher. The keyboard and mouse are only used during screen sharing.

Following an analogy with the theatre, it is interesting to structure the lesson into scenes, corresponding to one set of physical elements handled by the teacher, some of which are added/removed as the scene progresses. A scene would match with the digital equivalent of a slide with animations. Within a scene, continuing with the theatre analogy, the hands could be seen as the main (and only) character with three different functions:

- Animation: the hands can add, move, deform, and remove objects to support the teacher's explanations.
- Pointing: with the index finger (in our culture), the hands have a deictic function that accompanies speech (in expressions such as « this », « here », etc.)
- Expressivity: as in any speech interaction, the hands move to emphasise some words, producing what are called beat gestures or batons (Wagner et al., 2014).

A last important concept is the backstage, that is, all the physical that is not visible when the hands are filmed (the stage being the part of the desk in the camera field). The backstage includes the off-camera part of the desk where the unseen elements are located (the storage space): elements that will be seen and elements that have been seen. The backstage also includes all the space in front of the teacher; it is used as a prompter. In this space, it is convenient to have a computer screen displaying what the camera is filming.

Figure 1: Workspace viewed from behind the teacher, illustrating the stage and the backstage (cameras, storage space, prompters, and feedback screens).

Challenges

Before entering into the detail of the lesson design, we would like to underline three distinct challenges that characterise the moving hand approach.

Technical optimisation: the technical apparatus is not simple. It should not suffer from technical issues that would disturb the teacher's discourse. A difficult issue is the switching between the three views (hands, face, screen sharing).

Teacher's cognitive load: even if the technical device is perfectly smooth, handling physical elements is more difficult than navigating through slides. First, the teacher needs to carry out the animation that was automatised with digital slides. This task can be compared to playing a musical instrument. Second, the comfortable linear nature of the slides, in particular in the digital format where the user can see what comes next, gives way to a more improvised discourse in which the teacher must perfectly know his/her subject.

Note taking: after the lesson, the students do not have any printout, making it difficult for them to recall the content of the lesson. They must rely entirely on their note-taking, a skill that is already challenged by the omnipresence of digital handouts (Stacy & Cain, 2015).

Iterative design of the course

The filmed hand modality has been implemented three consecutive years for a 60-minute lesson within an annual university course on educational technology. This lesson introduces the use of Learning Management Systems (LMS) for distance and hybrid learning, including concepts such as tutoring, mediatisation, and co-modality. Prior to this, the course was taught with digital slides. The following section is a description of the iterations of the course to illustrate the design space of this innovative modality.

4.1 The iterations

The first iterations consisted of transforming digital slides into the filmed hands modality, that is, translating a content from a media to another media. More precisely it consists in materialising a digital media, the opposite of the mediatisation process in digital learning (Peraya, 2008). This materialisation depends on the learning content. Specifically, the first part of the lesson describes pedagogical platforms. Interestingly, the term "platform" is a metaphor referring to a physical object. The materialisation was then straightforward: we used a large LEGO base plate on which we added bricks representing learning modules. Actors around the platform (learners, teachers, etc.) were represented as LEGO characters, while the relation between them was represented with strings. This made the first scene. The second scene represented the mediatisation of in-class activities to distance activities via a base plate with two parts. The third scene represented the time organisation of distance or presence sessions with LEGO elements sliding on a glitter (see Fig. 1). The technical device consisted of one camera on a tripod in front of the large computer screen. The teacher would rotate this camera to switch from the top view to the facing view (Fig. 2a). Two teaching assistants helped with the preparation and running of the course unfolding, in particular with backstage management.

The session went well, but the change of view was not quite smooth and the general cognitive load for the teacher was high, despite the support of the assistants. The students also complained not to have slides. So we edited the video recording to provide them with a digest summary of the course.

The second iteration used a different device. We found that a computer released in the mid-2010, the Sprout computer from HP, dedicated to multimedia was quite relevant: it is an all-in-one large screen computer with a top camera, a top projection facility, a tactile pad, and a front camera (see Fig. 2b). The existence of these two cameras were perfectly suited to our need to switch between the two views. The projection and tactile interaction features, although not used for this iteration, was also a promise of innovations for future teaching lessons. The teaching content was the same. After the course we build a-posteriori slides, based on screenshots taken from the video recording of the session.

a) b) c)

Figure 2: Teaching device for the first three successive iterations of the course.

This second session went well, but we encountered two technical problems. First, the quality of the top camera was not as good as previously, even forcing us to rewrite some text labels with larger fonts. Second, the switching from one camera to the other was tedious, because there were more than two cameras in the camera list of the videoconferencing system (Zoom).

The third iteration will be described in the next session. It comes back to the initial design (same top camera used), but with a distinct additional camera for the facing view, placed on the side, and other slight improvements.

4.2 Final design

We will describe the design following the structure of the three challenges described above.

The **technical device** consists of a laptop computer put at the right of the desk, with its built-in camera pointed towards the teacher. In this view, the teacher is seen more globally than the usual face camera, allowing gestural communication. A mouse and a wireless keyboard are also available, used in the screensharing view. A second screen, facing the teacher, provides visual feedback from the top-camera. This latter camera is placed between the screen and the teacher, on a tripod, filming a space of approximately 50 cm wide. The backstage include 1) the left-hand part of the desk, used as storage space for physical elements (mainly pre-assembled LEGO pieces) and 2) the second screen, supplemented by various text supports sticked to the side of the screen (see Fig. 1 and 2c). The switching camera was parametrised with a keyboard shortcut on the videoconferencing software that worked fine. In addition, we used a foot pedal connected to the computer to activate this shortcut with the foot (visible on Fig. 2c). This way, the switching between the two cameras was perfectly smooth, since the hands could remain the focus of the top view.

In order reduce the **teacher's cognitive load**, we sequenced the animation steps for each scene in a very structured way. In the rehearsal phase, without the filming device, the teacher listed the precise sequence of physical elements that needed to be successively added to the. Then, in the preparation phase, the storage space was set up according to this ordered list. Visually, the teacher can see the different steps of the animation, providing a support similar to printing the slides or seeing in advance the next slide. The other supporting device is the stickers placed around the facing screen. The assistant managed the interaction with the students and helped with the management of the storage space.

In order to supplement **students' note-taking**, we decided to provide students with a-posteriori handouts, based on the recording of the session. It is expected that such handouts would be more engaging for student as they relate to the happenings during the on-line session. To this end, we implemented an innovative solution that involves the assistant as a note-taker. He or she uses the chatting tool offered by the videoconferencing system to take notes, using the screenshot functionality to capture relevant images for the slides. The note-taker prefixes the text with an underscore ("_") to specify that it is intended for the handouts. When such a text occurs just after the screenshot, it means that the text is the title of the slide with the screenshot as image, otherwise, it appears under the image (See Fig. 3). It should be pointed out that the assistant's note taking activity is also useful for the students during the course, because it highlights important notions. From the transcript outputted by the videoconferencing software, we applied a script to convert the text file into an html file using the Reveal.js library dedicated to slideshows (Reveal, s. d.). With this approach, the slides are automatically created! In practice, because it was our first attempt, we had to manually modify the initial text, to correct minor errors (e.g. shortening a title). The script was developed in Python, with the help of ChatGPT (free version).

Figure 3. Seven slides generated from the assistant's notes (slightly modified after generation).

5 Reception

Each lesson in the one-year course is provided with a short evaluation questionnaire consisting of a ternary evaluation ("cool", "ok", "not so good") and an open question asking for comments. We collected these data for the three above-mentioned iterations. The evaluation results are shown in Table 1.

Table 1: Student evaluation (multiple choice question)

	Year 1	Year 2	Year 3
Not so good	1	3	5
Ok	13	7	8
Cool	16	13	11

We are going to comment these results, without carrying out any statistical analysis, given the limited amount of data. First, we observe that more than the half of students gave the best evaluation (52% of respondents), but that unsatisfied students represent 12% of the respondents. Unfortunately, we cannot see any improvements over the years, and we even observe a growing number of students finding it "not so good".

If we look at qualitative answers, we have 24 comments over the three years. Nine of them (either "ok", or "not so good"), that is 37.5% of commenters, find it difficult to follow, usually because of the lack of slides. Twelve comments were quite positive, matching the above quantitative data. Most enthusiastic comments praised the originality of the presentation (e.g.: "The idea of Lego bricks was original and enriching from a pedagogical viewpoint", 2024; Legos were a good way for representing links. I loved it!", 2025). Three out of these 12 positive comments recognized that they were sceptical at the beginning but that after a while, they really appreciated the course.

Globally the students' feedback is rather positive, but there are still a few students who express their reservations, preferring some more classical formats. If we refer to the three challenges mentioned above, it must be pointed out that the two first challenges are not mentioned by students: no technical issue reported, nor teacher's difficulties with handling the equipment. The main focus lies in the absence of slides. Our efforts with a-posteriori slides do not solve the issue that many students appreciate slides both as guidance during the lesson and as support for notetaking. Regarding the guidance, the filmed hands modality seems to require more focus of attention from the students. This is, we believe, related to the three comments mentioning that at the beginning they were not convinced but then, when they understand that they must focus on the teacher's speech in relation to his/her hands, it gets manageable and rewarding. One of the three students who were sceptical at the beginning stated: "in the end, I really liked the concept, especially in terms of maintaining attention". This summarizes well the challenge of such a lesson: getting students to leave their long-term habits with slides for adopting an attitude requiring more attention on what is happening "there and now".

The other issue, the note-taking issue, is also related to previous students' habits. It must be mentioned that for other lesson in the same course, when slides are available, they are given after the synchronous lesson, not before, which is the subject of recurrent complaints. This is consistent with other research that confirmed that students do prefer having slides beforehand. Research also shows that the learning benefits of having slides beforehand is controversial, some results showing a learning benefit (Chen & Lin, 2008; Marsh & Sink, 2010), some showing no difference (Atarés et al., 2009; Marsh & Sink, 2010), and some showing a drop in learning performance (Worthington & Levasseur, 2015). In any case, it is a pedagogical choice made for the whole course, and the filmed-hand based lesson is aligned with the other sessions on that respect. The filmed hand modality just stresses the teacher's choice to bring students to higher their attention level during synchronous distance sessions, should it come at the price of not satisfying the student's desire to use handouts for taking notes.

Conclusion

Escaping from the excessive disembodiment of synchronous distance learning, we have designed and iteratively implemented an innovative modality of distance teaching, called the "moving hands". Three challenges have been identified, and we are progressively addressing them. Regarding the most delicate one, the lack of slides to guide students, we plan to provide them with a course plan beforehand that, combined with slides immediately created after the session, should facilitate the learning process during the course.

As demagogical and commercial discourses tend to make us believe that digital tools make learning easy, the moving hands modality reminds us that both teaching and learning require effort, to achieve quality learning.

References

Asaduddin, A., & Maulani, U. (2021). Beyond Synchronous and Asynchronous Systems towards Blended Learning : Perspective on Medical Education through COVID-19 Pandemic. Journal of Academia Perspectives, 1. https://doi.org/10.30998/jap.v1i2.733

Atarés, L., Bonet, P., & Serra, B. (2009). THE CLASS HANDOUT... SHOULD IT BE GIVEN BEFORE OR AFTER CLASS? EDULEARN09 Proceedings, 4900-4908. 1st International Conference on Education and New Learning Technologies.

Ayres, P., & Sweller, J. (2005). The Split-Attention Principle in Multimedia Learning. In R. Mayer (Éd.), The Cambridge Handbook of Multimedia Learning (p. 135-146). Cambridge University Press.

Chen, J., & Lin, T.-F. (2008). Does Downloading PowerPoint Slides Before the Lecture Lead to Better Student Achievement? International Review of Economics Education, 7(2), 9-18. https://doi.org/10.1016/S1477-3880(15)30092-X

Ghilay, Y. (2022). Quantitative Courses in Higher Education : A Comparison Between Asynchronous and Synchronous Distance Learning. Journal of Education and Learning, 11(5), 93. https://doi.org/10.5539/jel.v11n5p93

Hrastinski, S. (2008). Asynchronous and Synchronous E-Learning. EDUCAUSE QUATERLY, 4, 51-55.

Marsh, E. J., & Sink, H. E. (2010). Access to handouts of presentation slides during lecture : Consequences for learning. Applied Cognitive Psychology, 24(5), 691-706. https://doi.org/10.1002/acp.1579

Mayer, R. E., & Fiorella, L. (2014). Principles for Reducing Extraneous Processing in Multimedia Learning : Coherence, Signaling, Redundancy, Spatial Contiguity, and Temporal Contiguity Principles. In R. E. Mayer (Éd.), The Cambridge Handbook of Multimedia Learning (p. 279-315). Cambridge University Press.

Peraya, D. (2008). Un regard critique sur les concepts de médiatisation et médiation : Nouvelles pratiques, nouvelle modélisation. Les Enjeux de l'information et de la communication, 9(2). https://lesenjeux.univ-grenoble-alpes.fr/2008/supplement-a/12-un-regard-critique-sur-les-concepts-de-mediatisation-et-mediation-nouvelles-pratiques-nouvelle-modelisation

Peraya, D., & Peltier, C. (2020). Ce que la pandémie fait à l'ingénierie pédagogique et ce que la rubrique peut en conter. Distances et médiations des savoirs. Distance and Mediation of Knowledge, 30, Article 30. https://doi.org/10.4000/dms.5198

Reveal. (s. d.). reveal.js. Consulté 17 mars 2025, à l'adresse https://revealjs.com/

Sondermann, C., & Merkt, M. (2023). Like it or learn from it : Effects of talking heads in educational videos. Computers & Education, 193, 104675. https://doi.org/10.1016/j.compedu.2022.104675

Stacy, E. M., & Cain, J. (2015). Note-taking and Handouts in The Digital Age. American Journal of Pharmaceutical Education, 79(7), 107. https://doi.org/10.5688/ajpe797107

Szilas, N., Nguyen, T.-V. T., Yong Xin, L., & Le, T. K. O. H. (2023). Synchronous Online Teaching : Exploring New Horizons. 108-109.

Wagner, P., Malisz, Z., & Kopp, S. (2014). Gesture and speech in interaction : An overview. Speech Communication, 57, 209-232. https://doi.org/10.1016/j.specom.2013.09.008

Worthington, D. L., & Levasseur, D. G. (2015). To provide or not to provide course PowerPoint slides? The impact of instructor-provided slides upon student attendance and performance. Computers & Education, 85, 14-22. https://doi.org/10.1016/j.compedu.2015.02.002

New ways of employing TLC in education: Immersive Object-Based Learning and AI Integration for Cultural Heritage Education. The case of the Restart Project

Antonella Poce[1], Mara Valente[2], Carlo De Medio[3]

[1] Department of History, Humanities and Society, University of Rome Tor Vergata, Italy; antonella.poce@uniroma2.it

[2] Department of History, Humanities and Society, University of Rome Tor Vergata, Italy; mara.valente.582975@uniroma2.eu

[3] Department of History, Humanities and Society, University of Rome Tor Vergata, Italy; carlo.demedio.572666@uniroma2.eu

Correspondence: Antonella Poce: antonella.poce@uniroma2.it

Abstract:

RESTART - Innovative telecommunication solutions for the enhancement and heritage experience: the totems and the Virtual Museum of the University of Tor Vergata" represents an advanced research initiative that is located at the intersection of technology, culture and education within the recovery funding project RESTART RESearch and innovation on future Telecommunications systems and networks, to make Italy more smART foundation. The main objective is to develop and implement innovative solutions in the field of telecommunications to improve accessibility, enjoyment and enhancement of cultural heritage, with a specific focus on the campus of the University of Tor Vergata.

The research activity herewith described represents a use case within Spoke 8 of the RESTART project as it embodies the mission to develop innovative solutions for the experience and enhancement of cultural heritage through the integration of cutting-edge technologies and advanced educational methodologies, realized through two demonstrators, two totem installed in the engineering macro-area. Thanks to the use of augmented reality, virtual reality, and 3D digitization, the project not only promotes inclusive and immersive access to local heritage but also tests and validates replicable models of connection between culture, technology, and society. Through the installation of interactive totems, a dedicated 5G network, and devices such as VR headsets and haptic gloves, the Virtual Museum acts as an innovation laboratory for testing educational approaches like digital Object-Based Learning, which enhance users' soft skills.

Additionally, the totems play a crucial role in disseminating the results of the RESTART project and its scientific products, serving as strategic access points for communication and interaction with digital content, thereby strengthening the social and cultural impact of the initiative.

The RESTART project at the University of Rome Tor Vergata herewith presented is an innovative endeavor that employs Object-Based Learning (OBL) and advanced digital solutions to redefine contemporary education. Its primary objective is to nurture essential competences for the 21st century—Creativity, Collaboration, Communication, and Critical Thinking—while emphasizing participant well-being. Central to RESTART is the Tor Vergata Virtual Museum, a fully immersive virtual reality (VR) domain featuring twenty meticulously chosen objects, which guide users through the historical and cultural richness of the local area. The experience is further enhanced by a haptic glove simulating tactile feedback, offering a multisensory approach that fosters deeper engagement and retention.

Inclusivity stands at the core of RESTART's mission. Dedicated workshops ensure that all learners, regardless of physical or cognitive abilities, have equitable access to these cutting-edge educational methods. By harnessing AI-driven personalization, the initiative tailors' experiences to individual needs, reinforcing an inclusive and adaptable environment. Of particular note is RESTART's dual commitment to both scholarly success and holistic well-being. By tracking academic metrics alongside indicators of emotional health, the project aims to demonstrate how technologically enriched OBL can heighten engagement, comprehension, and personal satisfaction. In doing so, RESTART paves the way for future models that integrate advanced educational technologies with progressive pedagogies.

Ultimately, RESTART represents a significant milestone in the fusion of digital innovations and instructional strategies. By embracing avant-garde solutions and prioritizing inclusivity, this project helps shape the future of teaching and learning, inspiring new generations to value cultural heritage while enhancing their academic and emotional development.

Keywords: Cultural Heritage; Inclusive Education; AI Personalization; Object-Based Learning; Well-being; Gamification.

State of the art

Research on educational innovation increasingly highlights the value of Artificial Intelligence (AI) in promoting deeper engagement with content and boosting inclusive access to cultural resources. Within museum contexts, AI has been employed to enhance accessibility through automated captioning, interactive exhibits, and personalized curation (Tussyadiah & Zach, 2013). Likewise, immersive technologies—virtual reality (VR) and augmented reality (AR)—have seen a surge in application, enabling learners to interact with otherwise distant or fragile artifacts, thus transforming passive observation into a hands-on, exploratory activity (Antonioli et al., 2014).

Object-Based Learning (OBL), initially adopted in Anglo-Saxon educational frameworks (Durbin et al., 1990; Paris, 2002; Lane & Wallace, 2007), expands this dynamic further by using real or digitized objects to support knowledge construction. When enhanced by AI, OBL can deliver personalized pathways—shaping difficulty levels, offering tailored prompts, or autonomously highlighting connections between objects to spark curiosity. Gamification principles, integrating game mechanics into learning, have likewise proven effective in sustaining motivation, establishing trust, and encouraging progressive mastery (Ryan & Deci, 2000; Kapp, 2012). Storytelling, an element often woven into gamified designs, plays a vital role in activating emotional engagement, creativity, and critical thinking (Giakalaras, 2016).

Coupled with AI mechanisms, immersive storytelling experiences have broadened cultural heritage education's reach, especially in urban or remote settings. Virtual replicas of archaeological sites, historically themed reconstructions, and interactive narratives enable a participatory approach, wherein users not only "visit" but actively discover contextual links between objects and their historical relevance. This approach aids in developing transversal competencies—collaboration, communication, creativity, and critical thinking—essential for modern professions (Poce, 2018).

Further, researchers acknowledge that meaningful, participatory learning can positively influence well-being and encourage social inclusion. By reducing barriers to entry (such as mobility constraints or geographic distance) and offering engaging, multisensory experiences, immersive OBL endeavours can foster emotional connections, lower stress, and augment user satisfaction. Nonetheless, implementing such advanced setups can require sizable financial and technical resources, underlining the need for robust evaluation frameworks. Projects like RESTART exemplify how AI-driven personalization and immersive tech can converge.

Methodology

Research questions and objectives

The research explores two primary questions that define the development of the RESTART project:

- How can digital Object-Based Learning activities, enhanced by VR and haptic technologies, nurture transversal skills—particularly critical thinking?

This line of investigation seeks to determine how merging digitized objects with immersive solutions—such as virtual reality and haptic gloves—creates engaging learning contexts. Through these setups, learners practice creativity, reflection, and communication. RESTART aims to foster dynamic, innovative learning opportunities where interactions with cultural heritage deepen comprehension and spark critical thinking.

- Can interaction with the AI-enabled totem improve the local community's well-being?

This second focus addresses whether AI-assisted totems, specifically through the empathetic chatbot Romolo, can offer emotional support by reducing anxiety and heightening inclusivity. By delivering personalized responses, the system seeks to craft a supportive and inclusive digital environment—particularly relevant in a busy urban setting like Tor Vergata.

The strategic objectives of adopting the Virtual Museum and deploying 5G-connected totems on campus are:

- Encouraging transversal skills by investigating cultural heritage via VR and haptic technology
- Providing captivating, hands-on educational experiences that inspire both creativity and critical reflection
- Enhancing collective psychological well-being by fostering belonging and inclusion through empathetic interactions with the AI-infused totem.

The Tor Vergata virtual museum: a digital platform for heritage valorization and social inclusion

The Tor Vergata Virtual Museum is structured as a unifying platform to enhance tangible and intangible heritage, promoting inclusive learning experiences that reinforce social cohesion. Rooted in pedagogical theories specific to heritage studies, it addresses the needs of a broad user base—students, university professionals, community residents, and especially individuals with cognitive or physical impairments. By spotlighting Tor Vergata's cultural and historical milestones, the Virtual Museum underscores the University's pivotal contributions to local development.

The museum's guiding principle posits that awareness of one's surroundings strengthens critical understanding of cultural and social capital, thereby reinforcing inclusion and emotional well-being. To this end, the collection is organized along decisive historical phases:

Early Settlement

- The Roman Era and Its Aftermath
- The Post-Empire Transformation and Agrarian Shift
- The Advent of Towers and Castles
- The University's Emergence and Key Scientific Milestones (e.g., Marconi's radio experiments)
- Neighboring Communities and Their Activities

In keeping with Digital Object-Based Learning strategies, a carefully curated set of artifacts underpins the museum's narrative. Inspired by MacGregor's (2012) approach to "A History of the World in 100 Objects," the museum constructs "The History of Tor Vergata in 20 Objects," enriched by interactive 3D models and storytelling-based content.

Users engage with the digitized material through VR, while haptic gloves (WEART technology) provide simulated tactile sensations spanning temperatures between 15 and 42 degrees Celsius, coupled with an array of surface textures. This immersive dimension allows participants to virtually handle archaeological pieces, historical documents, or artistic works—thereby deepening the investigative aspect of OBL. Additionally, Leap Motion is employed to map precise finger movements, enabling fluid manipulation such as turning pages in an ancient manuscript, lifting relics from storage crates, or striking chords on a digital musical instrument.

A preceding pilot, the E-Trouria application (Poce et al., 2020), showcased VR's potential within a museum context. Twenty graduate learners specializing in museum education tested a prototype featuring Etruscan artifacts from Villa Giulia. Preliminary results indicated a heightened emotional response, with participants expressing "wonder" and "pleasure" linked to personalized learning pathways. These findings confirmed the capacity of immersive technologies to galvanize engagement, provoke introspection, and advance skills that transcend disciplinary boundaries.

Romolo chatbot

The Romolo chatbot, a key component of the RESTART ecosystem, exemplifies how empathetic AI systems can elevate well-being for individuals interacting with smart kiosks across the University of Rome Tor Vergata. Grounded in advanced machine learning and natural language processing, Romolo skilfully detects emotional nuances, tailoring responses to user sentiment.

Recent investigations into Large Language Models (LLMs) and empathy indicate that contemporary GPT-based architectures can surpass human performance in recognizing emotional states, crafting supportive statements, and adapting messages to diverse profiles. Within Tor Vergata's socially varied landscape, Romolo caters to both student inquiries (administrative, academic, or mental health support) and the broader local population seeking practical information or general reassurance. Its empathetic dialogues reduce stress and foster a sense of belonging—critical in an urbanized environment where quick, personable interactions can significantly enhance user satisfaction.

Moreover, Romolo's integration into campus Totem aligns with broader efforts to cultivate psychological well-being. Studies comparing AI-generated guidance to professional advice reveal that empathetic responses, even if system-generated, can alleviate anxiety (Maida et al., 2024). Although AI lacks human intuition, empathetic modeling constructs a comforting environment for individuals requiring emotional support. By delivering immediate, user-specific feedback, Romolo transforms the totem experience into a nexus for accessible mental health resources.

Generation of interactive adventures: the RESTART project's crime story in comic form

An additional layer of immersion is provided by a series of interactive adventures, presented as a "crime story" graphic novel, that chronicle a group of reporters unearthing mysteries tied to RESTART's discoveries and outputs. Users become active detectives, solving riddles and uncovering hidden details by gathering clues within the virtual environment and conversing with AI-driven characters. By weaving science and culture into a gripping narrative, this format boosts intrigue, challenges critical thinking, and democratizes access to complex content. The narrative was designed to captivate the audience through a storyline that combined elements of fantasy and reality. The main characters' profiles depicted in the comic were inspired by Tor Vergata University's most significant research achievements, presented not only as scientists but also as protagonists in a story brimming with adventures and discoveries. The "Restart to the Future" comic opened by introducing an interdisciplinary group of young researchers involved in the RESTART project—a visionary initiative that aimed to unite science, technology, and cultural heritage. Each character brought a personal story and a distinct goal, making the group a prime example of academic collaboration. Three chapters had been produced, and the plan is to release six in total.

In the project's final phase, these instalments would serve as prequels for an interactive, serious gaming–style virtual experience. Users would be able to follow one of the researchers' adventures within the virtual museum by engaging with the comic's protagonists and aiding them in solving a case for their section.

The comic book was intended for distribution through a multichannel strategy, leveraging both interactive totems and the campus's LED wall. Dissemination was set to follow a regular release schedule, keeping the audience interested and building anticipation around upcoming chapters. The LED wall would also promote the comic book, employing teasers and promotional materials to instil a sense of excitement and curiosity.

The crime story in comic form thus offers a unique fusion of creativity, inquiry-based learning, and gamified exploration—turning the cultural heritage experience into an engaging intellectual quest.

The involvement of schools

Schools from the surrounding area and across Rome Province, including high schools, comprehensive institutes, and art academies, were invited to assume a central role in the project, contributing not only to the museum's usability but also to content creation for the Tor Vergata Virtual Museum. Through a specially organized contest, students explored the local cultural heritage and portrayed their territory's history via artistic and digital outputs, moving beyond individual expression into a collaborative environment where multiple institutions could share and intertwine narratives. These efforts were supported by the establishment of collaborative spaces—both physical and virtual—where students, working closely with teachers, artists, and researchers, collectively shaped the historical narrative of the Tor Vergata area by experimenting with digitized objects, multimedia storytelling, and interactive tools. This co-creation process enriched the Virtual Museum with distinct perspectives, enabled the formation of a shared social memory embracing the breadth and complexity of local histories, and fostered a deeper awareness and sense of responsibility toward the community. In alignment with the leadership and faculty of upper secondary schools, the educational program was structured as "Percorsi per le Competenze Trasversali e per l'Orientamento - Pathways for Transversal Skills and Orientation" (PCTO). The Department of Electronic Engineering at the University of Rome Tor Vergata hosted these activities, through which students gained insight into the enhancement of tangible and intangible heritage by using cutting-edge technologies such as generative AI, virtual reality, and augmented reality, while also engaging with didactic methodologies including digital Object-Based Learning, Digital Storytelling, and Gamification. Through these experiences, participants strengthened their digital competencies, developed critical and creative thinking, and refined their communication skills. By the conclusion of the program, they had become proficient in the use of VR and AR headsets, 3D digitization software, haptic gloves for virtual manipulation, AI platforms for interactive content creation, and mixed reality interfaces capable of integrating virtual components into real settings. They also employed digital storytelling and educational gaming to foster engagement and operated 5G-enabled interactive totems to disseminate cultural and scientific information. In so doing, the students not only acquired technical expertise and artistic aptitudes but also evolved from passive recipients of content into principal agents dedicated to the preservation and promotion of their local cultural heritage, leaving a concrete legacy for future generations through their contributions to the Tor Vergata Virtual Museum.

Discussion

Drawing on several research and testing, the RESTART project activities, represents a pioneering synthesis of advanced educational methods and interactive technology. Equipped with a 5G-enabled totem network, the project marks a defining milestone in leveraging digital solutions to teach cultural heritage—chiefly through OBL. The museum's flexible structure appeals to students, university personnel, and community residents alike, providing an accessible platform to explore artifacts and narratives that bring local history to life.

Past studies have identified a relationship between personality traits (e.g., introversion/extroversion) and user preferences for immersive exhibits. In response, this initiative seeks to create a robust customization system that adapts each museum visit according to individual user profiles. Introverted users may be guided to calmer, more contemplative settings, whereas extroverted users are offered dynamic, interactive group activities. Combined with personalization of haptic or Leap Motion interactions, this user-centered approach strives to heighten engagement, enjoyment, and knowledge retention.

A notable innovation is the synergy with an AI-powered companion, Romolo, delivering tailored feedback and in-depth cultural insights. By adopting GPT-4 as a foundation, the project aspires to forge a truly interactive learning space. Every user session with the totems generates valuable data—critical for evaluating how effectively OBL fosters transversal skills (including creativity, collaborative reasoning, and critical thinking). Tracking participants' learning outcomes is also vital in gauging the project's contribution to emotional health, as immersive educational environments can mitigate stress and sharpen cognitive engagement.

Collecting and analyzing these user interactions will validate whether the Tor Vergata Virtual Museum achieves its core aims: augmenting key skill sets, improving local community well-being, and enhancing appreciation for the University's cultural significance. As part of the broader RESTART agenda, the museum ties into urban innovation projects, supporting a holistic vision where technological advances serve both academic outcomes and social needs.

Conclusion

The RESTART project stands as a visionary convergence of cultural heritage preservation, technology-enhanced pedagogy, and social inclusion. By harnessing the power of Object-Based Learning, immersive 3D experiences, haptic and Leap Motion technologies, and empathetic AI chatbots, the initiative proposes a novel educational paradigm that engages users on multiple levels—cognitive, emotional, and communal.

Ongoing data collection and detailed evaluations will ascertain how effectively this approach encourages transversal competencies such as critical thinking, creativity, and collaboration, while simultaneously promoting emotional well-being. The insights gained will guide refinements to the museum's design and generate evidence-based strategies for scaling its methods. Already, the integration of 5G networks, AI-driven customization, and interactive storytelling demonstrates a forward-looking vision of how academic institutions can leverage emerging technologies to preserve local heritage, expand access, and enrich the learning experience.

By nurturing a deeper bond between learners and their environment, the RESTART project exemplifies how inclusive, immersive education can empower individuals, strengthen communities, and cultivate a shared sense of identity. Its dual emphasis on skill development and personal fulfilment offers a sustainable model for future initiatives, underscoring the potential of education to address both intellectual pursuits and broader societal well-being.

References

Durbin, G., Morris, S., & Wilkinson, S. (1990). Learning from objects: A teacher's guide. English Heritage.

Paris S.G. (2002). Perspectives on Object –Centred Learning in Museums. Routledge.

Lane, J., & Wallace, A. (2007). Hands on: Learning from objects and paintings. A teacher's guide. Scottish Museums Council.

Ryan, R. M., & Deci, E. L. (2000). Self-determination theory and the facilitation of intrinsic motivation, social development, and well-being. American Psychologist, 55(1), 68–78. https://doi.org/10.1037/0003-066X.55.1.68

Kapp, K. (2012). The gamification of learning and instruction: Game-based methods and strategies for training and education. Pfeiffer.

Giakalaras, M. (2016). Gamification and storytelling. University of the Aegean.

Poce, A. (2018). Il patrimonio culturale per lo sviluppo delle competenze nella scuola primaria. FrancoAngeli.

Johnson, D., Deterding, S., Kuhn, K. A., Staneva, A., Stoyanov, S., & Hides, L. (2016). Gamification for health and wellbeing: A systematic review of the literature. Internet Interventions, 6, 89–106.

Antonioli, M., Blake, C., & Sparks, K. (2014). Augmented reality applications in education. The Journal of Technology Studies, 40(2), 96–107.

Maida, E., Moccia, M., Palladino, R., Borriello, G., Affinito, G., Clerico, M., Repice, A. M., Di Sapio, A., Iodice, R., Spiezia, A. L., & Sparaco, M. (2024). ChatGPT vs. neurologists: A cross-sectional study investigating preference, satisfaction ratings and perceived empathy in responses among people living with multiple sclerosis. Journal of Neurology, 1–10. https://doi.org/10.1007/s00415-024-12053-7

MacGregor, N. (2012). A history of the world in 100 objects. Penguin Books.

Poce, A., Caccamo, A., Amenduni, F., Re, M. R., De Medio, C., & Valente, M. (2020). A virtual reality Etruscan Museum exhibition – Preliminary results of the participants' experience. In Enhancing the human experience of learning with technology: New challenges for research into digital, open, distance & networked education (pp. 40–49). https://doi.org/10.38069/edenconf-2020-rw-0005

Development of Micro-credentials ecosystem at the University of Maribor

Boštjan Vlaovič[1]

[1] Faculty of Electrical Engineering and Computer Science, University of Maribor, 2000 Maribor, Slovenia; bostjan.vlaovic@um.si

Correspondence: Boštjan Vlaovič: bostjan.vlaovic@um.si

Abstract:

Traditional occupation-based education is increasingly complemented by lifelong learning, with competencies taking precedence over specific job roles. Micro-credentials are emerging as a flexible response to these evolving demands. This paper presents the University of Maribor's approach, including the guidelines for the development of micro-credentials. A key focus is the integration of competency frameworks and classifications, enabling structured lifelong learning pathways. Additionally, we introduce the Curriculum Management System (CMS), an AI-supported platform designed to facilitate the mapping of learning outcomes to multiple competency frameworks and classifications, ensuring transparency, quality assurance, and cross-border recognition. The system aims to bridge the gap between higher education offerings and labour market needs, fostering a more agile and competency-driven education ecosystem.

Keywords: lifelong learning, micro-credentials, competence frameworks, competence classifications, curriculum management system, quality assurance

1. Introduction

Technological development, the green transition, and economic and demographic changes are reshaping the global labour market, necessitating lifelong learning and the acquisition of competencies required for the (future) job market. Higher education is also undergoing significant transformations, as traditional focus on occupations does not provide the necessary resilience to the ever-accelerating changes. Competencies are coming to the forefront, and higher education is increasingly complemented by lifelong learning. Leading these changes are micro-credentials – shorter educational courses that enable the acquisition of specific competencies tailored to societal, personal, and cultural needs or labour market demands.

According to the Organisation for Economic Co-operation and Development (OECD, 2023), only 40% of adults in Europe currently participate in lifelong learning. According to the World Economic Forum, 44% of the global workforce will require additional training or reskilling in the next five years, as two-fifths of their existing competencies will be reshaped or become obsolete between 2025 and 2030 (WEF, 2025). To address these challenges, the European Union (EU) adopted the Council of European Union (2022) Recommendation on a European Approach to Micro-Credentials for Lifelong Learning and Employability, which provides a foundation for developing flexible learning pathways in member states, including their integration into national qualification systems.

In Slovenian higher education, activities to promote lifelong learning and establish a unified micro-credential system began at the national level in the second half of 2022. At the University of Maribor (UM), we started 23 pilot projects within the European Union – NextGenerationEU, under the Recovery and Resilience Plan, co-financed by the Republic of Slovenia, the Ministry of Higher Education, Science and Innovation. In June 2023, the University of Maribor approved the first version of the Guidelines for the Development of Micro-Credentials, thereby taking a leading role and making a significant contribution to shaping the professional foundations for the national framework for micro-credential development in Slovenian higher education. Guidelines are regularly updated (UM, 2024). We have contributed to the development of the Guide for the Development of a Micro-Credentials System in Slovenian Higher Education (Ines Gergorić, 2025), published by the Ministry of Higher Education, Science, and Innovation in collaboration with the National Agency for Quality Assurance in Higher Education.

The University of Maribor recognizes micro-credentials as a part of its lifelong learning offerings. We see an opportunity to establish an innovative mechanism for long-term collaboration with both the business and non-business sectors to accelerate the transfer of research results and create new high-value-added jobs. In this context, we strive to involve representatives from the professional environment already at the conceptual planning stage of short courses for micro-credentials and establish a unified system of collaboration with external partners. Additionally, we aim to enhance existing mechanisms for involving external experts in the university's educational activities.

A crucial element in this process is establishing digital support, i.e., a platform that connects information about competencies acquired through study programs and short courses with identified labour market and societal needs. Within the Agile Development of Education and Micro-Credentials pilot project, we are developing university-wide support for all forms of education, backed by competency frameworks and classifications. The accreditation process, monitoring of development, and quality assurance of study programs and short courses will also be digitally supported. Quality assurance mechanisms for micro-credentials are paramount for long-term recognition by employers. We have followed well-established best practices in higher education while aiming for agile development that could be completed from concept to implementation within three months. The platform will also include a catalogue of educational programs to promote and support applications for short courses. Additionally, within the pilot project Development of flexible learning approaches with micro-credentials for the digital and green transition of education to Society 5.0 we are developing support for micro-credential management in the form of verifiable credentials.

The success of micro-credentials will depend on effective collaboration with external stakeholders and establishing a system that ensures quality, transparency, cross-border comparability, recognition, and transferability. The approach should be based on explicitly defined credentials linked to assessed learning outcomes. Micro-credentials can reach their full potential only with a common approach and tools that will empower developers to provide the required information.

In the second section, we present short courses for lifelong learning at UM, focusing on micro-credentials. In the third section, we present our approach to managing the diverse landscape of competencies to provide a systematic approach to developing European Skills, Competences, Qualifications and Occupations (ESCO) (European Commission, 2017). In the fourth section, we present a developed Curriculum Management System that supports various competency frameworks and classifications of competencies. We conclude with an overview of the lessons learned and proposed approaches for addressing identified challenges.

2. Short Courses

At the University of Maribor, short courses are categorized as follows:

1. Non-accredited short courses without assessment and evaluation of learning outcomes, resulting in a certificate of attendance.
2. Non-accredited short courses with assessment and evaluation of learning outcomes, resulting in a certificate of attendance.
3. Accredited short courses with assessment and evaluation of learning outcomes, resulting in a micro-credential.

Non-accredited short courses without assessment and evaluation of learning outcomes are part of regular staff training and various offerings based on individual agreements with employers. These programs already have an established support environment, which will be upgraded to accommodate lifelong learning and the inclusion of external participants.

Non-accredited short courses with assessment and evaluation of learning outcomes, leading to a certificate of attendance, are implemented at UM member institutions. Certificates are issued by UM member institutions in accordance with the standardized certificate template.

UM, micro-credentials will be issued exclusively for accredited short courses with assessment and evaluation of learning outcomes during the accreditation. All accredited short courses leading to the micro-credentials will be published in the UM lifelong learning catalogue. All participants will be enrolled in the Academic Information Subsystem (AIPS), where information will be managed by the same standards as are valid for the rest of the UM students. With the unique identifier, they will have access to the university infrastructure.

Quality assurance and reporting will be carried out per legislation, sectoral regulations, and guidelines for developing micro-credentials at UM.

At the University of Maribor, the recommended minimum scope of a short training program for awarding a micro-credential is 1 ECTS. The number of work hours required by participants is determined by the program developer in accordance with the European Credit Transfer and Accumulation System (ECTS) (European Commission, 2015), Criteria for Credit Evaluation of Study Programs under ECTS (NAKVIS, 2019), and the Processes of Internal Management and Quality Monitoring of Study Programs at the University of Maribor (UM 2017).

The minimum level of short training programs for awarding a UM micro-credential is level 6 within the European Qualifications Framework (EQF). It is recommended that learning outcomes be defined between 1 and 8, depending on the scope of the short training program. The learning outcome description must include an appropriate verb based on the selected taxonomy (e.g., Bloom's taxonomy). It must be measurable, achievable, and assessed through evaluation and assessment processes.

Mandatory elements to describe micro-credential were extended with the member of the UM that provides the short course, participating institutions, acronym, course coordinator (habilitated teacher), short description (maximum 1000 characters), link to the list of competencies based on the selected competency framework (e.g., DigComp, IEEE, ACM) or competency classification (e.g., ESCO), the language of instruction, level of qualification framework (SOK – Slovenian Qualifications Framework, EQF – European Qualifications Framework, EHEA – European Higher Education Area Framework), KLASIUS P-16 classification (defined at the third classification level, 4-digit code), ISCED-F classification (defined at the first classification level, 2-digit code), grade achieved, grading system, grading scale and unique identifier of the issued micro-credential.

The accreditation of a short course for awarding a micro-credential must reasonably follow the well-established procedures at member institutions of the University of Maribor. The accreditation process is initiated by the Application for Accreditation of a Short Course, along with the curriculum, a statement by the short course coordinator, financial assessment, and confirmation from the Senate of the member institution.

The definition of the relevance of the short course and assessment should be conducted in close cooperation with social partners, employers, the expressed interests of the target group, research and innovation organizations, professional associations or civil society organizations, employment and social inclusion services, as well as local, regional, and national authorities and strategies.

The appropriateness of the short course should be examined in terms of supporting the professional development of workers and meeting mandatory upskilling and reskilling requirements. The impact of the short course on identified target groups should be explicitly stated, including opportunities related to employment or career advancement. Applications are managed by the Center for Lifelong Learning at UM. The accreditation process concludes with a recommendation of approval by the Commission for Education and Study (vice-deans of education from all member institutions and student representatives) and a decision by the Senate of the University of Maribor.

The internal monitoring and quality assurance process of short courses for awarding micro-credentials will be part of UM's broader quality assurance system. This system will operate in accordance with national quality assurance guidelines and will contribute to the comprehensive and continuous improvement of education and the effectiveness of short courses for awarding micro-credentials at the UM. Changes to short courses for awarding a micro-credential follow the standard procedure for modifying study programs at UM. However, there is no fixed timeline for accrediting modifications, meaning that short courses can be adjusted throughout the year. The process for modifying an accredited short course is also finalised by a decision of the Senate of the UM.

3. Competences

The Council of the European Union has identified that within Europe, a growing number of people need to update and improve their knowledge, skills and competencies to fill the gap between their formal education and training and the needs of a fast-changing society and labour market. One of the major challenges facing European businesses and employers is an insufficient supply of relevant skills in the EU labour market. Simultaneously, workers are facing unprecedented changes in how work is organised. It is essential that people can access quality and relevant education and training, upskilling and reskilling throughout their lives.

Procedures for the recognition of prior learning, the validation of non-formal and informal learning, and the recognition of awarded micro-credentials by employers must be based on competencies. This is not an easy task, since competencies are presented in very diverse forms. We envision a shift from occupation-based to competencies-based learning, but this requires a coordinated and EU-wide or worldwide approach.

At UM we have identified two major collections of competencies – competencies frameworks (CF) and classifications of competencies (CC). In ideal circumstances, the worldwide classification of competencies would include all existing competencies and would be updated on a regular basis based on the well-defined editorial procedures that would include all stakeholders in the education area. Next, for each of the identified professional fields, we would have worldwide competencies frameworks that would identify required competencies and level of expertise. Competencies frameworks could be closely linked to current occupations. All competencies from frameworks would be present in the world-wide classification of competencies. One classification of competencies, multiple competencies frameworks that are linked to the occupations (collection of competencies from various frameworks).

3.1. Competence frameworks

We have identified several hundred CF that address the various education fields at UM. Some of the frameworks are provided by prominent professional organizations, e.g., the Institute of Electrical and Electronics Engineers (IEEE, 2025) and the Association for Computing Machinery (ACM, 2012), but most of the frameworks are part of national or international projects of focus groups. Some frameworks are based on the systematic categorisation of the professional field; some are focused on education and training; others describe the needs of specific fields, e.g., Tourism. Some use descriptions of broader concepts, while others include only narrower competencies. Some complement competencies with levels of proficiency, e.g., DigComp. Most of the CF are not available in machine-readable format. Compared to the structured and formally defined occupations, diversity, and lack of international standards for the description of competencies present a great challenge. There were some propositions that Artificial Intelligence could be used to solve identified challenges, but we believe that, while AI is a very useful tool, quality CF cannot be built without human experts from the field.

3.2 Competence classifications

ESCO is a European Commission project run by the Directorate General Employment, Social Affairs and Inclusion (DG EMPL). Its first full version (ESCO v1) was published on the 28th of July 2017. The latest version of the classification can be downloaded or retrieved through the ESCO API. ESCO is the European multilingual classification of Skills, Competencies and Occupations. ESCO provides descriptions of 3,039 occupations and 13,939 skills linked to these occupations, translated into 28 languages (European Commission, 2017). The aim of ESCO is to support job mobility across Europe and, therefore, a more integrated and efficient labour market by offering a "common language" on occupations and skills that can be used by different stakeholders on employment and education and training topics. It is available in an online portal and can be consulted free of charge. It is predominately used in the EU. Our first attempt to use ESCO was with partner universities at the ATHENA European University project in 2022. We have asked a selected group of professors to map the learning outcomes to the classification. The objective was to find courses related to these subjects at nine partner universities. It has been found that the classification is incomplete and unsuitable for higher education, as it is dominated by competencies that are more relevant to lower levels of education. We have identified areas not included in the classification or the set of competencies was insufficient. For the intended purpose we would also need proficiency levels for each of the selected competencies.

Lightcast is a labour market analytics company that provides data-driven insights on workforce trends, skills demand, and economic development. The Lightcast Open Skills Library delivers comprehensive, current, crowd-sourced common skills language. It provides more than 32,000 skills from real-world use cases. They have a dedicated team of taxonomists and engineers that provide an accurate and up-to-date picture of the labour market. It is predominately used in the USA.

4. Curriculum Management System

Based on our experiences during the European University Athena project, we decided to develop a Curriculum Management System (CMS) to support multiple competence frameworks and classifications. Our goal is to establish digital support for the agile development of education offerings at UM. This paper will focus only on the functionalities related to the learning outcomes and competencies.

Figure 1 demonstrates an overview of learning outcomes and competencies in CMS as selected by the professor using the web interface of the ESCO and manually selecting competencies. This can be overwhelming and results in incomplete records. Therefore, we have developed artificial intelligence assistance for the user with support for multiple competence frameworks and classifications. Where applicable, we support proficiency levels. The description of the learning outcome and selected competencies are used to provide a list of additional candidate competencies that can be selected by the user (Figure 2). Coloured stars mark suggestions based on already selected competencies at any CF or CC. White stars mark suggestions are based on the learning outcome's description. Where possible, we use the Slovenian language, e.g. ESCO. However, English descriptions are used for AI assistance since they provide better results. Figure 3 demonstrates suggestions from IEEE CF and Figure 4 suggestions from Lightcast CC. Each added competence improves the quality of the suggested recommendations and builds connections between different CFS and CC that can be used to provide the basis for proposals for the development of the ESCO competency classification based on well-established competency frameworks.

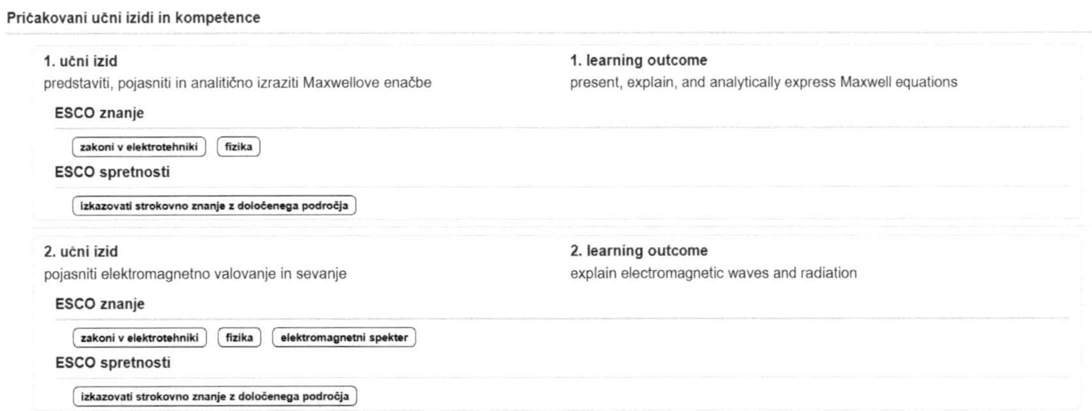

Figure 1: Two of the expected learning outcomes and competencies in Slovenian and English for the course Electromagnetic Waves that were linked to the ESCO by the professor during the ATHENA European University project in 2022.

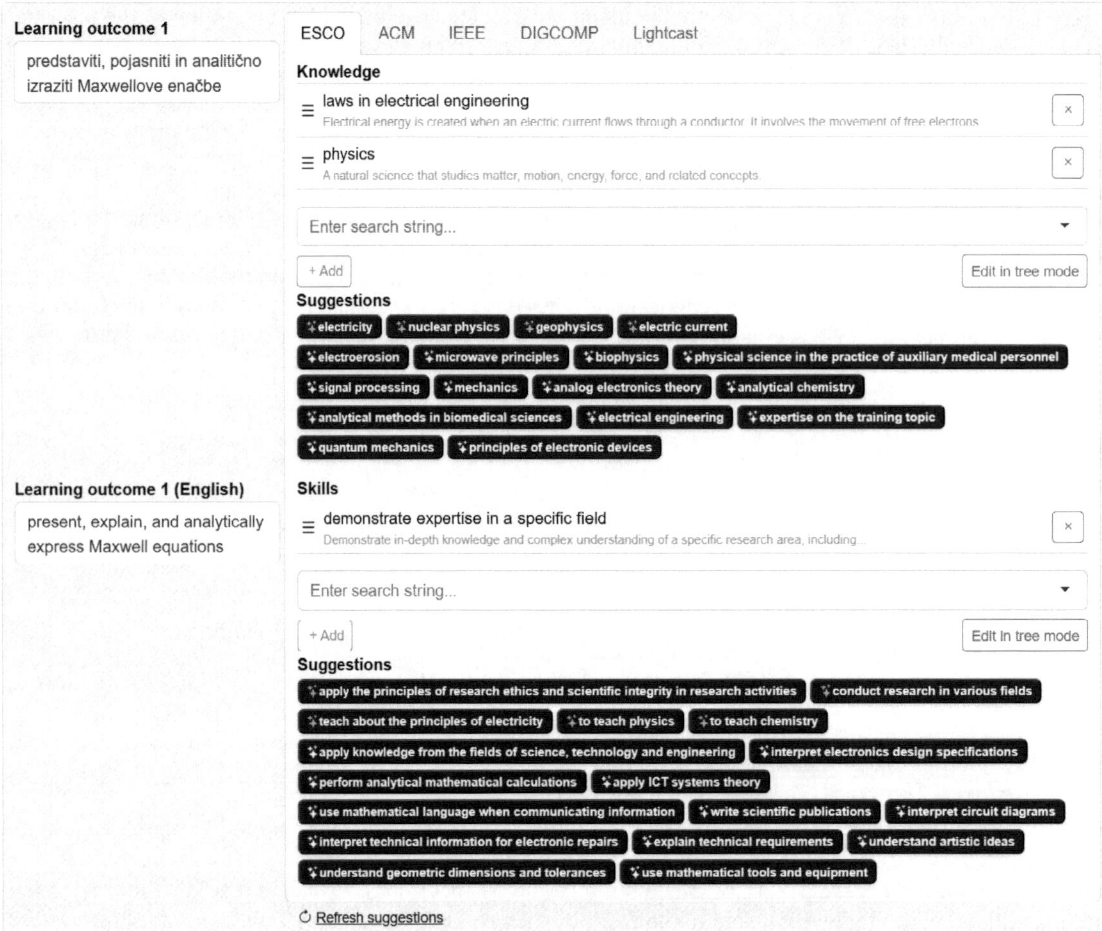

Figure 2: Additional suggestions from the selected competence classification ESCO.

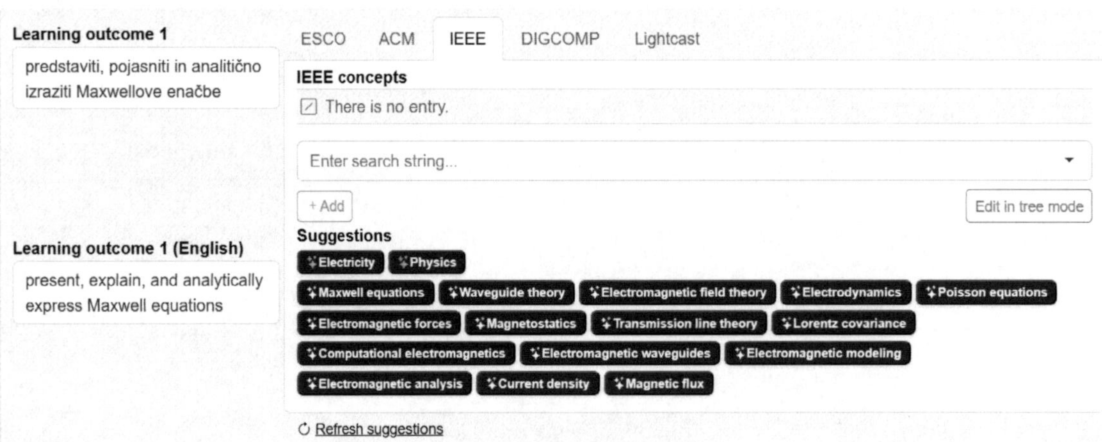

Figure 3: Suggestions from the selected competence framework IEEE.

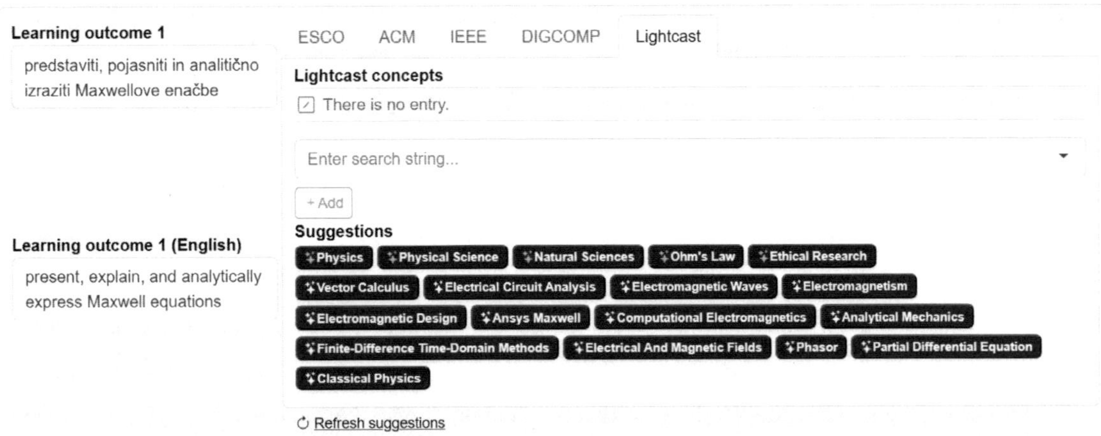

Figure 4: Suggestions from the selected competence classification Lightcast.

5. Conclusion

Higher education is undergoing a paradigm shift, driven by rapid technological, economic, and societal changes that demand a more flexible and competency-based approach to learning. Traditional, occupation-focused education models are no longer sufficient to ensure long-term employability and resilience in an evolving labour market. In response, micro-credentials have emerged as a vital mechanism for lifelong learning, offering targeted, skills-oriented education that aligns with labour market needs and individual learning goals.

At the University of Maribor, we have taken significant steps to integrate micro-credentials into our educational offerings, contributing to the development of a national framework. Our approach includes defining clear accreditation procedures, establishing quality assurance mechanisms, and fostering collaboration with external stakeholders to ensure the relevance and recognition of micro-credentials. The Guidelines for the development of Micro-Credentials at UM provide a structured foundation for designing, assessing, and implementing short courses that meet academic and professional standards.

A critical challenge in micro-credential development is competency classifications and frameworks' diverse and fragmented nature. To address this, we have developed a Curriculum Management System (CMS) with AI support, enabling the systematic mapping of learning outcomes to multiple competence frameworks and classifications. By leveraging artificial intelligence, our system enhances the efficiency and accuracy of competency alignment, ensuring better transparency, comparability, and recognition of acquired skills.

Micro-credentials' success depends on continued collaboration among universities, employers, policymakers, and professional organisations. Future efforts should focus on improving digital tools for education developers and refining ESCO. By embracing these innovations, higher education institutions can enhance their role as key drivers of lifelong learning, supporting workforce adaptability and societal progress in an era of constant transformation.

Competing interests

The author has no competing interests to declare.

Acknowledgements

The author would like to express gratitude to all professional colleagues from the Center for Lifelong Learning, with special thanks to its head, Anita Ješovnik. Appreciation is also extended to the head of Department of Education and Study at the University of Maribor, Sebastijan Frumen. A special acknowledgement goes to the invaluable contributions of Faculty of Electrical Engineering and Computer Science (FERI) colleagues, particularly Miha Strah and Uroš Brglez, for their dedicated work on the Curriculum Management System (CMS).

Funding Information

The project is co-financed by the Republic of Slovenia, the Ministry of Higher Education, Science and Innovation, and the European Union – NextGenerationEU under the Recovery and Resilience Plan, reference number C3330-22-953012 - NOO.

References

Association for Computing Machinery (2012), ACM Computing Classification System, https://dl.acm.org/ccs.

Council of European Union (2022), Council Recommendation on a European approach to micro-credentials for lifelong learning and employability 2022/C 243/02, Official Journal of the European Union, https://eur-lex.europa.eu/legal-content/EN/TXT/?uri=CELEX:32022H0627(02)

European Commission (2015), European Credit Transfer and Accumulation System (ECTS), https://education.ec.europa.eu/education-levels/higher-education/inclusive-and-connected-higher-education/european-credit-transfer-and-accumulation-system

European Commission (2017), European Skills, Competences, Qualifications and Occupations (ESCO), https://esco.ec.europa.eu/

Ines Gergorić (2025)., Guide for the Development of a Micro-Credentials System in Slovenian Higher Education. Ministry of Higher Education, Science, and Innovation in collaboration with the National Agency of the Republic of Slovenia for Quality in Higher Education, https://moja.um.si/vsezivljenjsko-ucenje/Documents/2024.12-Vodnik_za_razvoj_sistema_mikrodokazil_v_Slovenskem_visokem_solstvu.pdf

Institute of Electrical and Electronics Engineers (IEEE) (2025), January 2025 IEEE Thesaurus, https://www.ieee.org/content/dam/ieee-org/ieee/web/org/pubs/ieee-thesaurus.pdf

National Agency for Quality Assurance in Higher Education (NAKVIS) (2019), Criteria for Credit Evaluation of Study Programs under ECTS, https://www.nakvis.si/wp-content/uploads/2019/11/Merila-za-kreditno-vrednotenje-%C5%A1tudijskih-programov-po-ECTS.docx

Office of the Republic of Slovenia for Recovery and Resilience Plan, Ministry of Finance (2021), https://www.gov.si/en/registries/projects/the-recovery-and-resilience-plan/about-the-recovery-and-resilience-plan/

Organisation for Economic Co-operation and Development (2023), OECD Skills Outlook 2023: Skills for a Resilient Green and Digital Transition, OECD Publishing, Paris, https://doi.org/10.1787/27452f29-en

University of Maribor (UM) (2017), Processes of Internal Management and Quality Monitoring of Study Programs at the University of Maribor, https://www.um.si/wp-content/uploads/2022/03/Procesi-notranjega-upravljanja-in-spremljanja-kakovosti-studijskih-programov-na-Univerzi-v-Mariboru.pdf

University of Maribor (UM) (2024), Guidelines for the Development of Micro-Credentials, https://moja.um.si/vsezivljenjsko-ucenje/Documents/2024.01.18-Smernice_za_razvoj_mikrodokazil_na_UM_2.0.pdf

World Economic Forum (2025). Future of Jobs Report 2025, Word Economic Forum Publishing, Switzerland, https://reports.weforum.org/docs/WEF_Future_of_Jobs_Report_2025.pdf

From AI Anxiety to AI Empowerment: Transforming Teacher Education with Generative AI

Aysegul Liman Kaban[1], Meltem Ozmutlu[2], Sefika Feza Orhan[3], Lara Ozer[4], Taha Aydogmus[5], Fatma Nazire Kolat[6]

[1] STEM Education Department, Mary Immaculate College, University of Limerick, Ireland; aysegul.limankaban@mic.ul.ie
[2] Computer Education and Instructional Technologies Department, Bahcesehir University, Turkiye
[3] Computer Education and Instructional Technologies Department, Bahcesehir University, Turkiye
[4] Computer Education and Instructional Technologies Department, Bahcesehir University, Turkiye
[5] Computer Education and Instructional Technologies Department, Bahcesehir University, Turkiye
[6] Computer Education and Instructional Technologies Department, Bahcesehir University, Turkiye

Correspondence: Aysegul Liman Kaban: aysegul.limankaban@mic.ul.ie

Abstract:

The accelerated integration of generative artificial intelligence (GenAI) into educational settings has underscored a significant preparedness gap among teachers, particularly in terms of digital competence, ethical literacy, and emotional readiness. This study examines the impact of a structured, two-day professional development (PD) program on public school teachers in Türkiye, aimed at mitigating AI-related anxiety and enhancing instructional integration of GenAI tools. Grounded in Roblyer's Technology Integration Planning Model (TIPM), the program introduced participants to educational AI applications such as Lessonplans.ai, MagicSchool.ai, CanvaAI, and Gradescope through interactive workshops and reflective sessions. Quantitative analyses using the Artificial Intelligence Anxiety Scale and Wilcoxon Signed-Rank Test revealed statistically significant reductions in learning anxiety and job replacement anxiety following the intervention. However, no significant changes were observed in sociotechnical blindness or AI configuration anxiety. While participants reported high satisfaction with the training, these findings suggest that short-term PD initiatives, though effective in addressing operational concerns, are insufficient for fostering critical, ethical, and sustainable AI integration. The study concludes that meaningful teacher empowerment in the AI era requires longitudinal, ethically grounded, and psychologically supportive professional development models that go beyond technical proficiency to cultivate reflective and resilient educational practice.

Keywords: Generative AI in Education, Teacher Professional Development, AI Anxiety and Literacy, AI-Enhanced Instructional Design, Technology Integration in Teaching, Ethical AI in Education.

Introduction

The integration of Generative Artificial Intelligence (GenAI) in education is revolutionizing pedagogical practices, offering teachers new avenues to enhance lesson planning, instructional design, assessment, and student engagement. However, the rapid advancement of AI tools has introduced a dual challenge: while AI presents unparalleled opportunities for improving teaching efficiency and personalization, it also generates uncertainty, skepticism, and ethical concerns among educators. Many teachers experience AI anxiety, stemming from a lack of structured professional development programs that foster AI literacy, ethical awareness, and pedagogical integration strategies.

This study seeks to bridge this gap by investigating how structured teacher professional development (TPD) programs can facilitate the meaningful adoption of AI in education. Grounded in Roblyer's Technology Integration Planning Model (TIPM) and teacher education frameworks, the research explores the implementation of AI-driven tools such as Lessonplans.ai, MagicSchool.ai, CanvaAI, and Gradescope in real-world classroom settings.

Through a two-day AI-enhanced professional development program, teachers engaged in hands-on activities that introduced them to AI-assisted lesson planning, instructional material creation, personalized learning design, and formative assessment methods. The training followed a pedagogically sound, ethics-driven approach, ensuring that AI was framed as a teacher-supporting tool rather than a replacement for educator agency. This study examines the pre- and post-training impact on teachers' AI confidence, and instructional practices, providing empirical insights into how AI literacy can be sustainably developed among educators.

In this context, answers to the following questions were sought in the study.

1. Is there a statistically significant difference in teachers' anxiety regarding the use of generative AI (GAI) tools in the classroom before and after the teacher training?
2. What is the level of teachers' satisfaction with the training they attended, and does it vary according to different demographic or contextual variables?

Methodology

This study employs a quantitative research design, integrating quantitative approaches to examine the impact of structured professional development on teachers' adoption of Generative AI (GenAI) in instructional design, assessment, and pedagogical practices. The research was conducted as part of a two full day AI-enhanced teacher training program, designed to systematically introduce AI tools while addressing teacher perceptions, confidence, and ethical considerations in AI integration.

Participants and Sampling

The study targeted primary and secondary school teachers working in public schools in Istanbul, Türkiye. A purposive sampling strategy was employed to select participants who met specific inclusion criteria: (1) being a state school teacher, (2) having an intermediate level of digital literacy, (3) having no prior structured training in AI-assisted teaching, and (4) demonstrating willingness to participate in AI-focused professional development. A total of 40 teachers participated in the training, divided into two cohorts. A total of 40 participants completed the post-test survey. The sample consisted of 32 female participants (80%), with 8 male participants representing a smaller proportion (20%). The most common age group was 38–43 years, accounting for 12 participants. In terms of professional background, the largest group comprised classroom teachers (n = 15), followed by English teachers (n = 11). Mathematics and science teachers (including physics, chemistry, and biology) each represented five participants, while smaller groups included social studies/history (n = 2), Turkish/literature (n = 1), and fine arts/physical education teachers (n = 1). The participants were generally experienced educators, with the most frequent range of professional experience being 12–15 years (n = 9). This demographic profile reflects a relatively homogeneous group of mid-career teachers, primarily from primary education and English language instruction backgrounds.

Study Design and Intervention

Participants engaged in interactive workshops, hands-on exercises, and collaborative lesson design tasks, applying AI tools to their specific subject areas. The training also incorporated peer discussions and expert-led reflections to facilitate critical thinking about AI's limitations, ethical use, and long-term sustainability in education. The training program was a two-day structured professional development (PD) intervention designed for public school teachers in Türkiye, aiming to reduce AI-related anxiety and build competence in using generative AI tools for teaching. The design followed Roblyer's Technology Integration Planning Model (TIPM) to ensure pedagogical coherence. During the AI-enhanced professional development program, our goals were to influence teachers' lack of AI knowledge and artificial intelligence (AI) anxiety.

For this purpose, the flow of the two-day training, which lasted 6 hours a day, was as follows.

Day 1: Foundational Concepts & Lesson Planning

- **Morning Session:**
  Introduction to Artificial Intelligence in Education.
  Ethical considerations: bias, data privacy, and the role of human oversight.
  Exploring AI's role in personalized learning environments.
- **Afternoon Session:**
  Hands-on training with **Lessonplans.ai** and **MagicSchool.ai**.
  Teachers created AI-supported lesson plans aligned with their subject areas.
  Focus on AI-human collaboration in curriculum design.

Day 2: Instructional Materials, Assessment, and Feedback

- **Morning Session:**
  Interactive use of **CanvaAI** for visual instructional materials.
  Automated and formative assessment strategies using **Gradescope**.
- **Afternoon Session:**
  Use of **Quizgecko** and AI-powered rubrics for grading and feedback.
  Designing AI-enhanced assessment scenarios.
  Group work and reflection on pedagogical integration of AI tools.

Data Collection Instruments

The scale used in this study is the Artificial Intelligence Anxiety Scale, originally developed by; Wang & Wang (2019) ,and adapted into Turkish by Terzi (2020). The adaptation study confirmed the scale's reliability and validity in measuring AI-related anxiety levels. The high Cronbach's Alpha values in this study align with Terzi's findings, supporting the scale's robustness across different participant groups. The Cronbach's Alpha coefficients for the pre-test and post-test are 0.939 and 0.968, respectively. These values indicate a high level of internal consistency, demonstrating that the scale is highly reliable for measuring the intended construct of AI-related anxiety. The strong reliability of the scale supports the validity of the findings and confirms that the measurement instrument consistently captures the participants' responses.

Findings

Descriptive analyses were conducted to summarize satisfaction and anxiety scores across participants ($N = 19$). Participants reported high levels of satisfaction ($M = 4.18$, $SD = 0.22$) and low to moderate levels of anxiety ($M = 2.03$, $SD = 0.55$) on a 5-point Likert scale. Mean satisfaction and anxiety scores across different school types are shown in Table 2.

Table 2 : Mean Satisfaction and Anxiety Scores by School Type

School Type	Satisfaction Mean (±SD)	Anxiety Mean (±SD)
Primary	4.22 (±0.17)	2.23 (±0.42)
Middle	4.12 (±0.25)	1.67 (±0.28)
High	4.21 (±0.27)	2.14 (±0.44)

Participants from primary schools exhibited slightly higher anxiety scores compared to those from middle schools; however, satisfaction scores remained consistently high across all groups.Given the small sample size and potential violations of normality assumptions, non-parametric tests were utilized. A Kruskal-Wallis H test indicated that there were no statistically significant differences in satisfaction scores between school types, $H(2) = 0.76$, $p = .68$. Similarly, no significant differences were found in anxiety scores across school types, $H(2) = 4.10$, $p = .13$. Although the p-value for anxiety approached significance, it remained above the conventional threshold of .05. Spearman's rank-order correlations were used to examine the relationships between teaching experience and satisfaction/anxiety scores.

Table 3: Spearman Correlation Results (Experience and Scores)

Variables Compared	Spearman`s p	P value
Experience vs Satisfaction	+0.06	0.82
Experience vs Anxiety	−0.38	0.11

There was no significant correlation between experience and satisfaction (ρ = .06, p = .82). A moderate negative correlation was observed between experience and anxiety (ρ = −.38, p = .11), suggesting that more experienced teachers tended to report lower anxiety levels. However, this association did not reach statistical significance. Overall, findings indicate that teachers were highly satisfied with the training, and reported relatively low levels of anxiety regarding AI integration.Neither school type nor teaching experience showed statistically significant effects on satisfaction or anxiety levels. While there was a non-significant trend suggesting that more experienced teachers might feel less anxious, further research with larger samples is required to validate these findings.

In order to analyse the main question of the study, 'Is there a significant difference between teachers' anxiety about the use of GAI tools in the classroom before and after AI-enhanced professional development program?', Wilcoxon Signed-Rank Test (because the data were not normally distributed) was performed for statistically significant difference analysis between the pre-test given 10 days before the training program and the post-test given after the training and presented in Table 2.

Table 4: Wilcoxon Signed-Rank Test (non-parametric) analyses:

Dimension	**Participants**	**Wilcoxon Statistic**	**p-value**	**Pre-test Mean**	**Post-test Mean**
Learning Anxiety	27	33.0	0.000047	2.87	1.57
Job Replacement Anxiety	27	20.5	0.000082	2.91	1.48
Sociotechnical Blindness	27	127.0	0.217	3.02	2.71
AI Configuration Anxiety	27	131.5	0.843	2.41	2.36

Table 4 presents the Wilcoxon Signed-Rank Test results comparing pre- and post-training anxiety scores across the four dimensions. Learning Anxiety and Job Replacement Anxiety show statistically significant decreases after the training program ($p < 0.001$), meaning participants felt less anxious about learning AI and less worried about AI replacing their jobs. Sociotechnical Blindness and AI Configuration Anxiety show no significant change ($p > 0.05$), indicating the training did not affect participants' deeper understanding of AI's societal impacts or their confidence in configuring or using AI properly.

Discussion

The findings of this study reveal that structured AI training significantly reduced teachers' learning anxiety and job replacement anxiety, while failing to make meaningful improvements in sociotechnical blindness and AI configuration anxiety. These results align with prior research indicating that while hands-on training interventions are effective for operational skills development, they often fall short when addressing deeper socio-ethical dimensions of AI adoption.

Terzi (2020) emphasized that AI anxiety is multidimensional, rooted not just in fears about learning or job security, but also in sociotechnical blindness—the inability to grasp AI's broader societal impacts. The present study's insignificant change in sociotechnical blindness anxiety reflects exactly this complexity. Similar to Terzi's findings, the intervention appeared more successful in alleviating immediate personal concerns, but inadequate in promoting critical socio-technical awareness among teachers. Liu and Liu (2025) developed a five-dimensional AI anxiety scale for Chinese EFL teachers, emphasizing that job displacement fears and technological proficiency concerns are the most dominant sources of anxiety. In parallel, our study demonstrated a clear reduction in job replacement anxiety. However, just like Liu and Liu pointed out, dealing with teachers' AI anxiety requires a broader approach beyond technical training. Emotional aspects, such as fear of losing professional identity or the role of the teacher, remain unaddressed without ongoing psychological support and systematic institutional backing. Supporting this, Hopcan et al. (2024) also argue that while teachers are less concerned about learning AI itself, their anxiety spikes around employment insecurity and social displacement. Our study mirrors these patterns, confirming that short-term interventions can effectively teach AI tools but do little to dissolve deeper existential concerns. Furthermore, gender differences highlighted by Hopcan et al. and Zhang et al. (2023) suggest that female teachers may experience higher anxiety levels, particularly related to perceived ease of use and AI configuration. While our study did not explicitly analyze gender differences, the heavily female sample (80%) and the insignificant change in AI configuration anxiety suggest that this factor might have subtly influenced the outcomes. Moreover, Zhang et al. (2023) applied the Technology Acceptance Model (TAM) and found that AI anxiety negatively impacts perceived ease of use and perceived usefulness, thereby blocking technology adoption. Our findings similarly indicate that without addressing AI configuration anxiety, teachers' actual adoption rates may remain limited despite reductions in learning or job fears. In other words, getting teachers comfortable enough to experiment with AI is not the same as getting them critical and strategic about it. Satici et al. (2025) further argue that AI attitudes are deeply intertwined with mental health variables such as stress and well-being. Teachers with higher baseline anxiety tend to maintain more resistant or skeptical attitudes toward AI. The lack of change in sociotechnical blindness in our results suggests that interventions need to consider participants' broader emotional and psychological profiles, not just their technical skills. Simply put, AI literacy must be taught together with emotional literacy if long-term change is expected. The need for critical engagement is particularly crucial when considering the societal risks outlined by Satici et al. (2025)—such as algorithmic bias, privacy violations, and discrimination—that teachers will inevitably encounter in AI-integrated classrooms. Training programs that avoid discussing these issues create a false sense of competence, leaving teachers ill-prepared for real-world ethical challenges.

The findings of the present study are strongly supported by recent international frameworks and scholarly critiques emphasizing the urgent need for a more holistic approach to AI training in education. UNESCO's AI Competency Framework for Teachers (2024) explicitly outlines that technical skills acquisition, while important, is only one dimension of AI preparedness. The framework advocates for a balanced development across five key domains: human-centered mindset, ethics of AI, AI foundations and applications, AI pedagogy, and AI for professional learning. Without sustained attention to ethics and socio-technical implications, training risks producing teachers who can operate AI tools but lack the critical understanding necessary to engage responsibly with their broader societal impacts. This concern is echoed by Cukurova (2025), who critiques the dominant view of AI as mere technological tools and calls for a paradigm shift towards hybrid intelligence—a model that extends rather than diminishes human agency and critical thinking. The insignificant reduction in sociotechnical blindness found in this study reflects precisely the gap that Cukurova warns against: training interventions that address only immediate, operational anxieties while neglecting the deeper cognitive and ethical dimensions of AI integration.Furthermore, Bulathwela et al. (2024) argue that the prevailing techno-solutionist narrative in AI and education risks exacerbating educational inequalities rather than resolving them. They stress that inclusive and sustainable AI education must be participatory, critically reflective, and attuned to ethical concerns—principles largely absent from short-term technical training programs.

Finally, Giannakos et al. (2024) similarly caution against the hasty and uncritical adoption of generative AI in education. They emphasize the necessity for human-centric, ethically sound, and pedagogically robust frameworks to guide AI integration, highlighting that efficacy alone is insufficient if broader ethical and societal impacts are ignored. Taken together, the findings of this study reinforce a growing consensus: professional development that focuses narrowly on technical proficiency without embedding critical socio-technical literacy and emotional resilience will ultimately fail to prepare teachers for the complexities of AI-mediated education. As UNESCO (2024) and leading scholars argue, fostering critical, ethical, and emotionally intelligent engagement with AI is not optional—it is fundamental to safeguarding the future of education. To sum up, the results confirm the concern raised by Satici et al. (2025) and Liu and Liu (2025) that short workshops, no matter how well-designed, are not enough. Effective interventions must be longitudinal, interdisciplinary, and critically reflective, combining technical skills, ethical awareness, and emotional resilience training. The literature converges on one critical point that our findings now reinforce: AI training that treats teachers as mere "users" rather than as critical co-designers of technology is fundamentally inadequate. Without sustained, reflective, and ethically grounded training models, educational AI risks becoming yet another top-down innovation that teachers superficially adopt but internally resist. In conclusion, the significant reduction in learning and job replacement anxieties is a hollow victory if teachers remain ethically blind and insecure about AI's configuration and societal role. What our findings show—starkly—is that if AI professional development continues to prioritize tool operation over critical literacy, it will fail both teachers and the students they serve.

Conclusion

The findings across these studies deliver a clear message: while artificial intelligence holds transformative potential for education, the teaching profession is critically underprepared to navigate its challenges. Despite UNESCO's global push for AI competency frameworks, the actual systemic support for teachers remains alarmingly sparse, leaving individuals to manage complex transitions largely on their own. Targeted professional development interventions have demonstrated real potential to reduce AI anxiety and build confidence. However, these interventions are short-term solutions to what is fundamentally a long-term, structural challenge. If AI is to be meaningfully and ethically integrated into education, policymakers, teacher educators, and institutional leaders must move beyond aspirational frameworks and invest in sustained, psychologically-informed, and equity-focused support structures. Otherwise, the risks will not only undermine AI adoption efforts but also deepen existing fractures in the teaching profession.

Competing interests

The authors have no competing interests to declare.

Funding Information (optional)

This research (Project No: 123B828) is funded by the TUBITAK 4005 Innovative Educational Practices Support Programme under the project titled "Innovative Technology Education for Branch Teachers Based on the Technology Integration Planning Model."

References

Bulathwela, S., Pérez-Ortiz, M., Holloway, C., Cukurova, M., & Shawe-Taylor, J. (2024). Artificial intelligence alone will not democratise education: On educational inequality, techno-solutionism and inclusive tools. Sustainability, 16(2), 781. https://doi.org/10.3390/su16020781

Cukurova, M. (2025). The interplay of learning, analytics and artificial intelligence in education: A vision for hybrid intelligence. British Journal of Educational Technology, 56(2), 469–488. https://doi.org/10.1111/bjet.13514

Çakıroğlu, Ü. (2021). Teachers' AI literacy: Overcoming anxiety and embracing digital pedagogies. Journal of Educational Technology & Society, 24(3), 77-92.

Darling-Hammond, L., Hyler, M. E., & Gardner, M. (2017). Effective teacher professional development. Learning Policy Institute.

Desimone, L. M. (2009). Improving impact studies of teachers' professional development: Toward better conceptualizations and measures. Educational Researcher, 38(3), 181-199.

Giannakos, M., Azevedo, R., Brusilovsky, P., Cukurova, M., Dimitriadis, Y., Hernandez-Leo, D., Järvelä, S., Mavrikis, M., & Rienties, B. (2024). The promise and challenges of generative AI in education. Behaviour & Information Technology. https://doi.org/10.1080/0144929X.2024.2394886

Holmes, W., Bialik, M., & Fadel, C. (2022). AI and education: A critical review. OECD AI & Society.

Hopcan, S., Türkmen, G., & Polat, E. (2024). Exploring the artificial intelligence anxiety and machine learning attitudes of teacher candidates. Education and Information Technologies, 29, 7281–7301. https://doi.org/10.1007/s10639-023-12086-9

Kaplan-Rakowski, R., Yang, M., & Chien, S. Y. (2023). Teachers' attitudes toward AI-driven educational technologies: Opportunities and challenges. Educational Technology Research and Development, 71(1), 35-57.

Liu, X., & Liu, Y. (2025). Developing and validating a scale of artificial intelligence anxiety among Chinese EFL teachers. European Journal of Education, 60(e12902). https://doi.org/10.1111/ejed.12902

Luckin, R. (2017). Towards AI-powered education: Intelligence unleashed. Pearson Research Report.

Luckin, R., Holmes, W., Griffiths, M., & Forcier, L. B. (2016). Intelligence unleashed: An argument for AI in education. Pearson Research Report.

Roblyer, M. D., & Doering, A. H. (2013). Integrating educational technology into teaching (6th ed.). Pearson Education.

Satici, S. A., Okur, S., Yilmaz, F. B., & Grassini, S. (2025). Psychometric properties and Turkish adaptation of the artificial intelligence attitude scale (AIAS-4): Evidence for construct validity. BMC Psychology, 13(297). https://doi.org/10.1186/s40359-025-02505-6

Selwyn, N. (2022). Should robots replace teachers? AI and the future of education. Polity Press.

Teo, T. (2011). Factors influencing teachers' intention to use technology: A model of AI adoption. Journal of Educational Computing Research, 45(4), 439-464.

Terzi, R. (2020). An adaptation of artificial intelligence anxiety scale into Turkish: Reliability and validity study. International Online Journal of Education and Teaching (IOJET), 7(4). 1501-1515. http://iojet.org/index.php/IOJET/article/view/1031

UNESCO. (2024). AI competency framework for teachers. United Nations Educational, Scientific and Cultural Organization. https://doi.org/10.54675/ZJTE2084

Wang, Y. Y., & Wang, Y. S. (2019). Development and validation of an artificial intelligence anxiety scale: An initial application in predicting motivated learning behavior. Interactive Learning Environments, 1-16.

Zhang, C., Schießl, J., Plößl, L., Hofmann, F., & Gläser-Zikuda, M. (2023). Acceptance of artificial intelligence among pre-service teachers: A multigroup analysis. International Journal of Educational Technology in Higher Education, 20(49).

Exploring AI Skills Training For Lifelong Learning Staff: A Reflection From The University Of Geneva

Patrizia Birchler Emery[1] & Jue Wang Szilas[2]

[1] Centre for Continuing and Distance Education, University of Geneva, Switzerland Patrizia.Birchler@unige.ch
[2] Centre for Continuing and Distance Education and Faculty of Humanities, University of Geneva, Switzerland; Jue.WangSzilas@unige.ch

Correspondence: Jue Wang Szilas

Abstract:

The advent of artificial intelligence (AI) has posed significant challenges to higher education, particularly in staff training for digital competencies. The Centre for Continuing Education and Distance Learning (CCDE) at the University of Geneva has implemented a "three-level" support model in its efforts to digitise continuing education courses and train staff. This model includes the Threshold level, the Standard level, and the Advanced level, which have been continuously refined and tested. As AI technologies become more widely used, there is a need to redefine the objectives of each training level and explore more feasible implementation strategies. This paper outlines our exploratory process, shares the results of preliminary projects, and offers constructive recommendations on how AI competency training can be integrated into the broader digital skills development for continuing education teaching staff.

Keywords: Artificial Intelligence, Digital Transformation, Digital Competence, Teacher Training, Design-Based Research, Lifelong Learning, University Continuing Education.

1. Introduction

Generative Artificial Intelligence (GenAI) have caused a new disruption in teaching practice: barely recovered from the one induced by the COVID pandemic, which brought distance learning to the forefront, teachers must go back to school to learn how to teach with AI and how to teach AI. The gap that existed before the pandemic between those who favoured teaching augmented by techno-pedagogical tools and those who preferred to continue with traditional face-to-face teaching has widened still further with the arrival of ChatGPT and others. This obviously raises the question of agency of teachers and their adaptability to new technologies: the exercise of rethinking oneself and having to call into question what has taken a long time to learn is never easy, and in the coming years we will certainly have to deal with a wide variety of teacher and teaching profiles.

The arrival of GenAI is said to be revolutionising education: it will obviously bring about many transformations, since it affects all levels of our education systems. Software producers are promising teachers time savings, but this will depend on the level of confidence and ease of use of the users.

The digital transformation in higher education, accelerated by the rise of AI technologies, has created new challenges for lifelong learning institutions, particularly in terms of staff training and digital competency development. The University of Geneva (UNIGE) is addressing these challenges by focusing on integrating AI skills into its existing digital skills training for continuing education staff. This paper explores how AI can be incorporated into training programs to ensure ongoing quality in the institution's continuing education offerings.

1.1. *The UNESCO and UNIGE frameworks*

To guide such initiatives, global frameworks like UNESCO's AI Competence Framework for Teachers provide valuable principles and structured approaches to integrating AI in education (Cukorova & Miao 2024). The UNESCO AI Competence Framework for Teachers (AI CFT) is built on a human-centred approach, prioritizing inclusivity, human agency, and respect for diversity (Miao & Holmes 2021). It is structured around five key areas—teachers' mindset, AI ethics, AI foundations, AI pedagogy, and AI for professional development—offering a progression pathway for teachers to develop their AI competencies, from basic awareness to advanced application. The framework underscores that AI should complement, not replace, teachers, reinforcing their critical role in education. Its primary goal is to equip educators with the knowledge and skills to use AI responsibly and effectively, ensuring that AI enhances learning while minimizing risks to students and society.

At a more local level, the University of Geneva (UNIGE) issued recommendations on the use of generative artificial intelligence in October 2023, then updated in June 2024 to emphasise individual responsibility, academic integrity and data protection (University of Geneva position paper on artificial intelligence). In its guidelines, the UNIGE recognises the potential of generative artificial intelligence and supports its responsible use. The UNIGE sees AI as an opportunity in research, teaching and administration. It encourages a critical and informed approach, with a focus on key principles such as individual responsibility, legality, academic integrity and transparency, economy and ecology. In addition to these guidelines, the UNIGE offers a practical guide that includes information on generative AI, its risks, advice on how to use it effectively (Guidebook for the University Community 2024) and a guide to citation standards for AI-generated texts (Referencing the use of Generative AI). However, Faculties are responsible for integrating AI according to their specific needs, particularly for teaching and skills assessment.

At the behest of the Rectorate, seven of the UNIGE's nine Faculties have thus issued recommendations and guidelines on the GenAI: Medicine, Humanities, Social Sciences, Theology, Psychology and Educational Sciences, Law, Translation and Interpretation (Geoffroy & Ortoleva 2024). Neither the Faculty of Science nor the Geneva School of Economics and Management has yet published anything. To summarise, Faculty guidelines aim to provide a framework for the use of generative AI by defining clear rules for its use. Lecturers are often advised to tell students explicitly whether these tools are permitted in their courses. In Medicine and Psychology, both students and lecturers are encouraged to use GenAI, and even to train proactively. In the Humanities, encouragement to train students in the GenAI is implied, but it is still recommended that writing assistance should be prohibited if it prevents students' personal language skills from being assessed. Social Sciences, Theology and Translation and Interpretation leave it up to the teaching staff to decide whether to allow the use of GenAI in their courses. The Faculty of Law has only issued guidelines on plagiarism and transparency of sources.

In addition to the issues of citation and declaration of sources, the Faculties guidelines also address the assessment of written work, particularly dissertations, proposing solutions such as the addition of a declaration of honour, the increased importance of an oral defence, or a higher weighting of the oral defence in the final assessment. Finally, the issues of GenAI reliability and ecology are also raised, as well as, to a lesser extent, accessibility.

Despite all these recommendations, it should be noted that the only course on AI available to date is an e-learning module from the Faculty of Medicine aimed at bachelor students, but also useful for teachers. The teaching support service has organised a few pedagogical lunches, for peer-to-peer experience sharing, but no specific training in the use of AI is available to teaching teams. What's more, no GenAI tool has yet been formally authorised by the UNIGE's DPO, a situation that is alienating, to say the least.

1.2. *The problematic*

As we can see, the UNIGE is taking a generally favourable and even partly proactive stance on the use of GenAI in teaching, by encouraging the training of students and teachers in their responsible use. It is therefore partly in response to these directives that the CCDE has begun to think about integrating GenAI into the training given to teaching teams in continuing education programmes. The main reason however is rather the realisation that these tools can indeed be of great help in our context, where teachers often have no training or are only employed part-time, by supporting and speeding up the process of creating interactive online courses. Furthermore, as the quality of our continuing education programmes is always at the heart of our concerns, it is important that our teachers be able not only to appropriate GenAI tools that are relevant in the context of online teaching, but also to pass on their experience and knowledge of GenAI to their learners. including ethical and critical issues.

2. The context

2.1. The context of the Centre for Continuing and Distance Education

The Centre for Continuing and Distance Education (CCDE) at the University of Geneva is pivotal in developing lifelong learning programs, working closely with the University's faculties. With a small team of fewer than 20 staff members, the centre oversees more than 400 training programmes. The main concern remains ensuring the quality of these programmes, a quality that obviously depends very much on the teaching teams, comprising some 350 persons. These teams often include people with administrative rather than academic profiles, in charge of placing content on Moodle. With limited resources and a heterogeneous public, training all the members of these teams in digital skills requires a tailored and scalable solution, and represents therefore a main challenge for the CCDE.

2.2. The "Three-Level" approach challenged by the arrival of AI

To address these challenges and enhance the digital skills of all staff, the CCDE has developed a "Three-Level" training approach (Wang Szilas & Birchler Emery, 2022) to support the digital transformation of continuing education programmes at the University of Geneva, with a particular focus on the use of the Moodle platform. This approach includes:

- A Threshold Level: an entry-level, self-paced online training course designed to build essential Moodle skills for all staff, with a final test to assess learning outcomes.
- A Standard Level: a series of hands-on workshops aimed at ensuring that the delivery of training programmes in Moodle meets the CCDE's quality standards.
- A Personalised Level: tailored workshops focused on developing specialised digital skills required for specific tasks or disciplines.

The "Three-Level" training model has undergone three design iterations, with learning analytics used after each cycle to identify key insights for improvement. In the latest analysis (Birchler Emery & Wang Szilas, 2023), three key findings emerged:

- Training needs to be adapted to the diversity of the teaching community, ensuring specific programmes address varying skill levels and requirements.
- The focus should shift from using advanced digital tools to enhancing learning design, prioritising pedagogical effectiveness.
- A progressive training framework should be developed to accommodate different teaching contexts, ranging from "emergency" responses to long-term "normalisation" of digital education.

The 3-level model has already evolved considerably since its creation in 2019. With the arrival of GenAI and the adaptation it requires, it is entering its fourth design cycle. But before embarking on a redesign of the model, it is important to consider the extent to which GenAI will significantly alter the digital competency requirements for university teaching staffs and to reconsider the goals and methods of the existing training model.

3. Integration of GenAI skills into digital training

The CCDE has initiated an exploratory project for the integration of AI in digital skills training. As a preliminary, several initiatives took place, such as workshops, experimentation and testing of GenAi tools, and ongoing monitoring of relevant resources and guidelines.

In October 2023 and February 2025 two workshops have been organised for continuing education teaching and coordination staff, the first one built on the UNIGE's position paper and focusing generally on the challenges and opportunities presented by the arrival of GenAI in higher education, the second one concentrating on presenting the available resources and exploring the use of GenAI. Among the numerous tools on offer for creating interactive online activities, two have been selected for testing. The results have been documented and presented on several occasions (Wang Szilas & Birchler Emery 2024; Wang Szilas & Birchler Emery 2025), providing a clearer picture of the contribution GenAI can bring to teaching, but also of its limitations. Finally, the CCDE has contributed to the ongoing monitoring of available resources on GenAI, guidelines and recommendations, frameworks and online courses, that could be useful for the continuing education teachers.

3.1 Pilot Project: analysing AI use in the continuing education community

A pilot project was launched to evaluate the use of AI within the continuing education community, collecting data through a questionnaire and workshop feedback to improve future AI skills training. The two questions are presented in the table below.

1. Have you ever used AI tools for the following tasks? (Tick all relevant options.)

- Course design and storyboarding
- Writing course texts
- Translation of texts, messages, or papers
- Designing course activities
- Evaluation design
- AI-powered plagiarism detection
- Communication with students
- Analysis of learning data (learning analytics)
- Customization of learning paths
- Administrative management (e.g., automated responses, task organization)
- Other (please specify): ____________
- I have never used any AI tools

2. Which AI tool(s) have you already used for your teaching or management? (Tick all relevant options.)

- ChatGPT (conversational assistant, text generation)
- Claude (AI assistant, ethical security)
- Grammarly (language correction)
- DeepL (translation)
- MidJourney (image generation)
- Compilatio (AI-powered plagiarism detection)
- Microsoft Copilot (AI tools integrated into Microsoft Office)
- Perplexity AI (AI-powered search assistant)
- ELSA Speak (AI-assisted language learning)
- Synthesia (AI-generated videos with avatars)
- Google Bard (AI assistant, conversational search)
- Other (please specify): ________________

The survey was sent to 347 personal email addresses within the continuing education community, yielding 57 responses, with a response rate of about 16%. During the workshop, around 30 participants shared their answers on a Padlet.

3.2 Questionnaire answers analysis

Summary of results for question 1

The most popular task for which AI tools are used is translating texts, messages and papers, with 78.95% of respondents saying they use AI for this purpose. Writing course texts is the second most popular task, with 28.07% of respondents using AI in this area. In addition, 22.81% of respondents use AI for course design and storyboarding, while the same percentage (22.81%) use it for administrative management tasks such as automated responses and task organisation. On the other hand, AI is least used for image creation, with only 3.51% of respondents reporting its use, and even fewer (1.75%) report using AI to analyse learning data.

Figure 1. Results for question 1 (questionnaire)

Translation and course text creation are the most common uses of AI, suggesting that respondents see AI as a useful tool for automating and assisting with routine tasks such as translating or creating course-related content. The low usage of image creation and learning data analysis suggests that the application of AI in these areas is not as essential or widespread in educational and administrative tasks. A significant 8.77% of respondents indicated that they had never used AI tools, which may indicate a lack of familiarity with AI or a reluctance to adopt it.

Summary of results for question 2

The most popular AI tools reported by respondents are ChatGPT and DeepL, with 84.21% and 77.19% of participants using them respectively. ChatGPT is widely favored for text generation and academic support, while DeepL is primarily used for translation. In addition, there are other tools with notable usage. Compilatio, used by 36.84% of respondents, highlights the importance of AI in plagiarism detection, although this may be because it is an institutional tool. Microsoft Copilot is also widely used, with 21.05% of respondents using it, often for productivity and organisational tasks. Among the less popular tools, Grammarly was used by 7.02% of respondents. Creative AI tools such as MidJourney, Synthesia and Google Bard were much less widely used, with only 1.75% of participants using them.

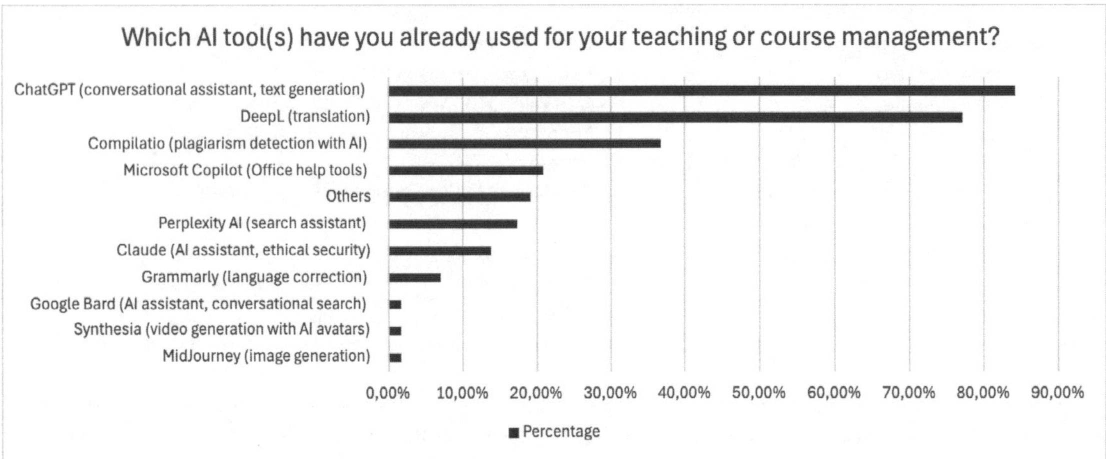

Figure 2. Results for question 2 (questionnaire)

The results indicate that ChatGPT and DeepL are the most widely used AI tools, suggesting that text generation, communication and translation are the most common applications for AI. The adoption of Compilatio suggests that plagiarism detection is an important concern, particularly in academic settings, highlighting the role of AI in maintaining academic integrity. Microsoft Copilot shows that productivity tools are being used, but their adoption is not as widespread as the language-focused tools.

Image and video creation tools, such as MidJourney and Synthesia, as well as Google Bard, are less widely used, suggesting that creative AI tools may have niche applications in education and administration.

In addition, other tools mentioned, such as Mistral, Canva, Infomaniak, Scribbr, etc., reflect the growing diversity of AI solutions that educators are turning to. These tools serve specific purposes that may not be universally recognised but can be valuable for specialised tasks.

3.3 Workshop responses analysis

As for the workshop, 42 participants shared their responses in a Padlet to answer the same two questions posed in the questionnaire.

Summary of results for question 1

Of the 42 workshop participants, 29 responses were collected, showing that AI is mainly used for content creation, communication, and translation. Common applications include social media posts (5), email writing (4), text enhancement (3), and image creation (5). Other uses include code generation, text summarization, exam question generation, podcast production, and medical queries.

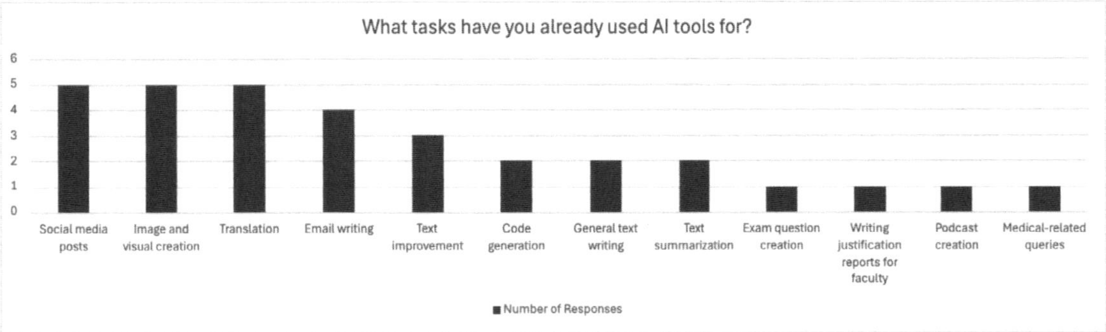

Figure 3. Results for question 1 (workshop)

The workshop and questionnaire results highlight writing, translation, and communication as the main AI use cases, with some differences:

- Image creation was more common in the workshop (5 mentions) than the questionnaire (2 mentions, 3.51%), indicating a stronger engagement with visual content creation among workshop participants.
- Exam question creation appeared in both groups but remains a niche use case, suggesting limited use in assessment design.
- Podcast production, medical question creation, and faculty report creation were only mentioned in the workshop, showing AI's diverse and unexpected applications based on individual needs.

These differences suggest that AI adoption varies by user familiarity and professional needs, which should be considered in AI skills training.

Summary of results for question 2

Of the 42 workshop participants, 22 responses were collected, with some respondents using multiple AI tools. The most frequently mentioned tools were ChatGPT (11), Copilot (4), DeepSeek (3), Claude (2), Poe (2), and general AI tools (2). Other tools mentioned once each included Photoshop, Adobe Acrobat Pro, Illustrator, Padlet AI, Canva AI, DeepL and Adobe Firefly.

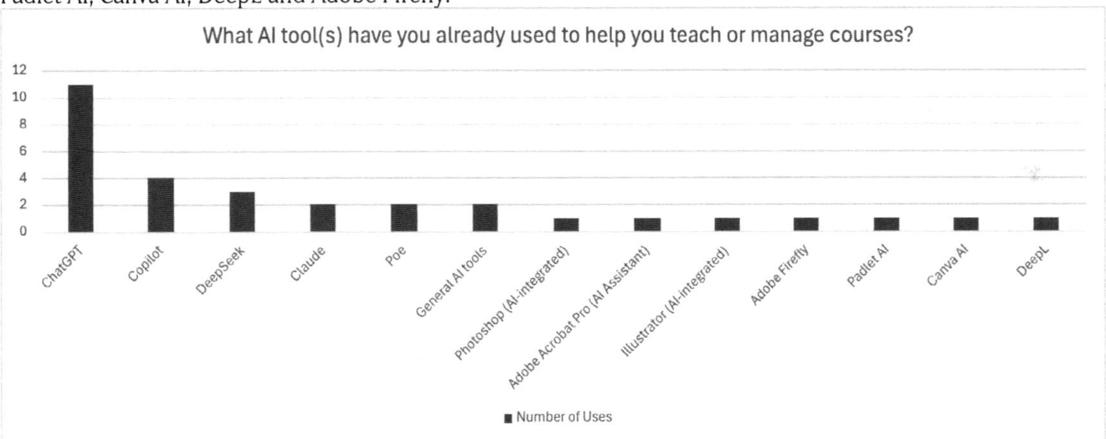

Figure 4. Results for question 2 (workshop)

Additional question: concerns about using AI tools

During the workshop, participants expressed several concerns about AI tools. The most common issue was reliability (16 participants), citing problems like lack of references, AI-generated inaccuracies, and inconsistencies in images. Privacy was the second concern (4 participants), highlighting risks when using AI tools. Other concerns included difficulty in creating effective prompts, ethical issues in student assessment, and the environmental impact of AI tools.

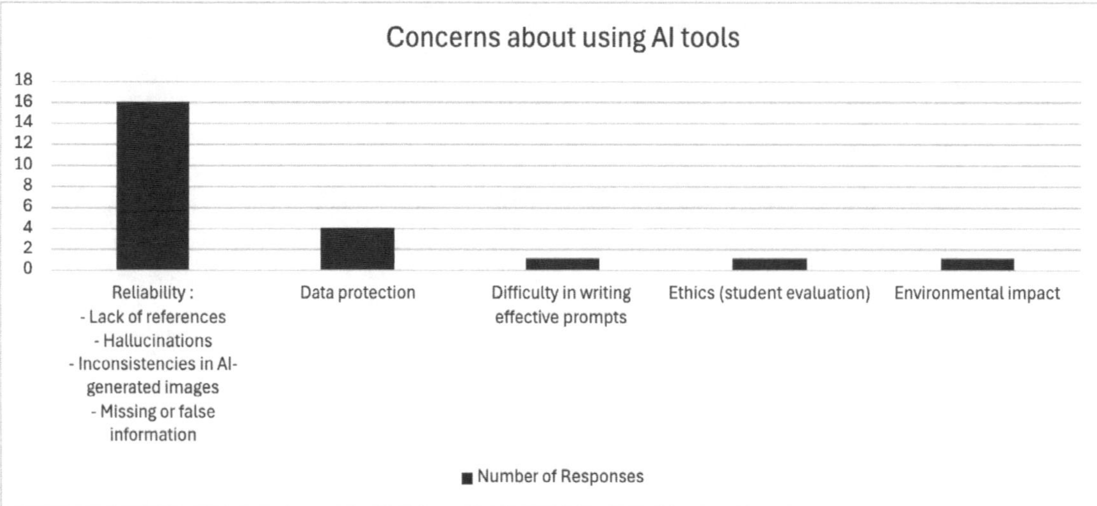

Figure 5. Results for additional question (workshop)

Our analysis of reliability issues suggests that users are cautious about inaccurate or misleading results. Concerns such as hallucinations and lack of transparency (e.g. no citations) highlight the need for more reliable AI models and a better understanding of their limitations. Data protection concerns highlight privacy risks, underscoring the importance of compliance with regulations. Prompting challenges suggest a need for better guidance on using AI tools effectively. Ethical concerns in assessments focus on fairness, accuracy, and integrity, while growing environmental impact concerns call for more sustainable AI solutions. Although participants recognize AI's benefits, they remain cautious about its limitations and ethical implications, particularly regarding reliability, privacy, and ethics.

3.4 Insights for the next steps concerning AI skills training

Based on the results and analysis of both the questionnaire and the workshop, and considering the context of our centre (a small unit serving a large number of training programmes with limited staff), we can make several suggestions to guide future AI skills training initiatives:

- Highlight language-related tools: Since ChatGPT and DeepL are the most widely used tools, future workshops should focus on their potential for content creation, translation and communication. A deeper exploration of their advanced features would be particularly valuable.
- Tailor training to different groups: AI skills training programmes should be tailored to the needs of different user groups, as their use of and familiarity with AI tools will vary. Teachers, administrators and other staff may require different approaches.
- Categorise AI skills according to need: Training should be broken down to address different needs.
    - General skills for all: ethical considerations, data security, and societal implications of AI.
    - Specific skills for different groups: practical applications of AI tools for generating educational content, creating quizzes, and developing teaching tools.
- Addressing AI hesitation: For those reluctant to adopt AI tools, workshops should include an introductory session to dispel misconceptions and highlight the practical benefits of AI in teaching and management.

These guiding principles provide a good foundation for structuring AI skills training initiatives that are both relevant and effective. By focusing on language-related tools, tailoring training to different user groups, categorising skills according to need, and addressing potential barriers to AI adoption, we ensure a more targeted and engaging learning experience, with specific methodologies and detailed training content provided at the end.

4. Implementation: a concise action plan

A concise action plan for AI skills training, based on insights from our data analysis, can enrich our established three-level training framework with AI skills training that remains meaningful, accessible and practical, and meets the evolving needs of educators and administrators.

- ***Expanding the foundation: the Threshold level***

Having already introduced basic digital literacy, we now suggest incorporating AI-specific elements. Self-paced learning modules could explore ethical considerations, data security and the societal impact of AI. Reliable institutional resources would provide guidance on best practices for integrating AI into education and government, ensuring that staff feel confident and informed.

- ***Improving practical applications: the Standard level***

Our existing workshops, designed for different professional groups, could be adapted to include AI tools that improve efficiency and engagement. Administrators could explore the role of AI in communication, documentation and workflow automation, while teachers could integrate AI into content creation, student engagement and assessment.

To support these efforts, frequently used tools like DeepL and ChatGPT would take centre stage together with institutional tools. This layer would emphasise critical reflection, exploring the importance of human agency in the use of AI, following UNESCO principles, and integrating Universal Design for Learning (UDL) to ensure inclusivity.

- ***Developing specialist expertise: the personalised level***

For those seeking a deeper understanding of AI applications, we suggest expanding specialised training to include the role of AI in content generation, personalised learning and, where relevant, image processing and visual content enhancement.

- ***Hands-on ideas: AI workshops for teaching staff***

To help teachers confidently incorporate AI into their classrooms, we can propose adapting our existing training to include hands-on practice with DeepL and ChatGPT. DeepL could be used for translation, text refinement and writing assistance, while ChatGPT could help educators process texts, generate quizzes and create interactive learning experiences. More than just technical skills, this workshop would encourage thoughtful engagement with AI and guide educators on how to adapt AI-generated content to different teaching contexts and design inclusive, accessible learning experiences using UDL principles.

5. Conclusion

In conclusion, integrating AI competencies into the three-level model for digital skills training at the University of Geneva's Centre for Continuing and Distance Education holds significant potential for enhancing the quality of lifelong learning. The challenges faced during the integration process provide valuable insights into how training can be tailored to meet both general and specific needs. As AI technologies continue to evolve, ongoing adaptation and the refinement of training models will be necessary to maintain the quality and relevance of continuing education programs.

References

Cukurova, M., & Miao, F. (2024). AI competency framework for teachers. UNESCO. https://unesdoc.unesco.org/ark:/48223/pf0000391105

Geoffroy, F., & Ortoleva, G., (2024, December 17). Tour d'horizon de recommandations des facultés UNIGE sur l'utilisation de l'IA générative dans l'enseignement [Blog post] https://ciel.unige.ch/2024/12/tour-dhorizon-de-recommandations-des-facultes-unige-sur-lutilisation-de-lia-generative-dans-lenseignement/)

Guidebook for the University Community (University of Geneva, v1.0, June 2024). https://www.unige.ch/numerique/files/5217/2587/8420/ENGLISH_-_Rapport_IA_Generatives_-_UNIGE_-_Fevrier_2024_-_vENG.pdf

Miao, F., & Holmes, W. (2021). International Forum on AI and the Futures of Education, developing competencies for the AI Era, 7-8 December 2020: synthesis report. UNESCO. https://unesdoc.unesco.org/ark:/48223/pf0000377251

Referencing the use of Generative AI (University of Geneva, December 2024). https://www.unige.ch/biblio/fr/actus/archive/archive-des-actualites-2024/guide-iag/

University of Geneva position paper on artificial intelligence (June 2024). http://www.unige.ch/files/7517/2900/5788/A4-PositionUNIGE-IA-062024-EN.pdf

Wang Szilas, J., & Birchler Emery, P. (2022). Training Digital Competences of Educators in Continuing Education: A Three-Level Approach. In Väljataga, T., & Laanpere, M. (Eds.): Shaping the Digital Transformation of the Education Ecosystem in Europe. EDEN 2022 (pp. 127-136): Springer International Publishing. 10.1007/978-3-031-20518-7_10

Wang Szilas, J., & Birchler Emery, P. (2023). A "Threshold" Self-Paced Online Training For Teaching Staff: What's New? Proceedings of the EDEN annual conference 2023 in Dublin: "Yes we can!"–Digital Education for Better Futures, 91-92. https://eden-europe.eu/wp-content/uploads/2023/07/EDEN-2023-Annual-Conference-Proceedings.pdf

Wang Szilas, J., & Birchler Emery, P. (2024). Can 'Smart Import' Create Smart Learning Content? Proceedings of the EDEN annual conference 2024 in Graz: Learning in the Age of AI: Towards Imaginative Futures, 37-38. https://eden-europe.eu/wp-content/uploads/2023/07/EDEN-2023-Annual-Conference-Proceedings.pdf

Wang Szilas, J., & Birchler Emery, P. (2025). Can Smart Import create Smart Learning content? Articles by our experts, University of Geneva Centre for Continuing and Distance Education. www.unige.ch/formcont/en/experts/smart-learning

The European Maturity Model for Blended Education: A Retrospective and an Outlook for the Future

Katie Goeman[1], Wiebe Dijkstra[2]

[1] KU Leuven, Teacher Training, Belgium; Katie.Goeman@kuleuven.be
[2] Marnix Academie Utrecht, The Netherlands; w.dijkstra@hsmarnix.nl

Correspondence: Katie Goeman: Katie.Goeman@kuleuven.be

Abstract:

The COVID-19 pandemic underscored the critical role of blended education and teaching in addressing challenges inherent in online learning environments. In May 2020, the European Maturity Model for Blended Education (EMBED) was launched, providing a structured framework for evaluating and enhancing blended practices across European higher education institutions. A mixed-method analysis, involving a survey, a literature review, and a force field analysis, was conducted to assess the impact and effectiveness of EMBED. The results show that the project's deliverables have been adopted across higher education institutions in Belgium, the Netherlands, and Turkey, driving institutional assessments, action plans, and staff training. EMBED proved particularly valuable during the pandemic, guiding institutions through the rapid shift to online learning and being integrated into various EU projects and professional development initiatives. Building on these findings, EMBED+ will be developed to address evolving educational needs and to integrate technological advancements. It will expand the original model by introducing updates and new features, focusing on four key pathways: the development of a contemporary model, the creation of an open-source resources hub, an EU-wide road tour to share outcomes, and the establishment of a transnational expert network. Through its comprehensive approach, EMBED+ aims to foster sustainable mature blended practices across Europe.

Keywords: Blended education, blended teaching, European Model for Blended Education (EMBED), maturity, EMBED+

Introduction

Human-centred digital education design connects learners and educators across both online and onsite environments (Selkrig et al., 2023). At the heart of this approach are blended learning (BL) and blended teaching (BT). BL is defined as "learning resulting from a purposeful, integrated combination of online and face-to-face learning activities," while BT refers to the "designing and facilitating of blended learning activities" that effectively combine both modes. The Covid-19 pandemic not only reinforced the lasting relevance of these blended formats but also demonstrated their essential role in addressing key challenges in online distance education, such as "transactional distance" (Moore, 2019) and social isolation (Rasheed et al., 2020). International research further highlights that blended practices enhance efficiency, effectiveness, and accessibility for both learners and educators in higher education (UNESCO, 2020; Valverde-Berrocoso et al., 2020).

Recognizing the need for specialized expertise among teaching staff, supportive services, and leadership in this regard, seven European project partners established a conceptual framework and operational tools for blended education and teaching. In May 2020, the European Maturity Model (EMM) was launched as part of the Erasmus+ project, the European Maturity Model for Blended Education (EMBED) (https://embed.eadtu.eu/). The project aimed to provide European higher education institutions with a systematic approach to evaluate and improve their blended learning practices, strategies, and policies.

EMBED's research and development process involved five key phases:

1. Development of the conceptual framework and model, based on mixed-method research;

2. Design of assessment tools to gauge maturity of blended practices at various decision-making levels;

3. 3-round Delphi study to validate the framework, model and its instruments;

4. Establishment of the final reference model, the European Maturity Model (EMM), together with a comprehensive set of implementation guidelines (Van Valkenburg et al., 2020);

5. Creation of a Massive Open Online Course (MOOC) 'Making Blended Education Work' (https://www.futurelearn.com/courses/making-blended-education-work) for professional development, aimed at instructional designers, institutional support services, and programme coordinators;

The EMM is a staged maturity model that assesses a higher education institution's (HEI) capabilities and growth across predefined dimensions. It focuses on tangible practices, with institutions advancing to higher levels as they demonstrate capability in previous phases. Stakeholders can evaluate the presence of dimensions by reviewing detailed descriptions of BT and BE practices at each maturity level. The model categorizes maturity at the course, programme, and institutional levels, using indicators to assess blended practices in HE settings. Higher maturity levels indicate a more comprehensive approach (Goeman et al., 2021; Goeman & Dijkstra, 2022).

Project Assessment

In education and technological innovation projects, it is crucial to assess outcomes not only after completion but also years later. Long-term evaluations provide insights into the sustainability and actual impact of changes, revealing long-term effects and potential improvements initially overlooked (Cox & Marshall, 2007). Reevaluating outcomes years later helps gauge the longevity of intended changes, which is critical in education to ensure sustained effectiveness. Evaluating sustainability ensures that immediate positive effects continue benefiting the target audience. Some impacts may only appear in the long term, and ongoing evaluation identifies and analyzes these delayed effects, offering a thorough understanding of the project's impact. Long-term evaluations also assess the flexibility and adaptability of outcomes in changing circumstances, ensuring continued relevance and effectiveness.

Such information helps policymakers make informed decisions and refine policies based on proven effectiveness, enhancing future project success and sustainability. Integrating insights from long-term evaluations allows stakeholders to understand nuanced project effects, adapt strategies to changing circumstances, and ensure that educational improvements endure beyond the initial implementation (Fanta et al., 2020). Therefore, evaluating the EMBED framework and its adaptation is essential for gaining insights into its impact. This evaluation provides valuable opportunities to implement improvements, ensuring a more sustainable and lasting impact on blended education.

Method

Between March 2022 and November 2023, an extensive data gathering process was undertaken to evaluate the status of affairs of EMBED through diverse sources. The ultimate objective was to identify the impact of EMBED in different ways and to comprehend the needs of EMBED's stakeholders, in order to develop future plans that would best meet their requirements. This involved disseminating a survey among the EMBED partners and by means of the snowball technique to a wider range of stakeholders. All responses were compiled and a narrative analysis was applied to elucidate all essential elements required to comprehend the effectiveness and usability of the original EMBED framework and related outputs. Furthermore, we conducted a comprehensive literature search and evaluation of articles, books, policy documents, and reports with the aim of gaining a deeper understanding of the citation of EMBED in various publications. Additionally, a force field analysis identified prevailing trends and challenges within the digital higher education landscape in Europe. This methodological tool is utilised to identify the driving and restraining forces that influence a particular decision, such as the implementation of digital technologies in higher education.

It entails examining the magnitude and direction of each force to determine the overall impact on the decision. By comprehending the force field analysis, decision-makers in higher education can address the challenges and capitalise on the opportunities presented.

Results

Embedment in higher education institutions since 2020

From 2020 and beyond, the EMM and its assessment tools and implementation guidelines have been adopted across HEIs in Belgium, The Netherlands and Turkey. Several Dutch institutions for tertiary education have implemented comprehensive institution-wide assessments and action plans. These aim to standardize and mature blended practices. In this regard, a policy advisor noted about the employment of the EMM, "It has been one of the pillars of our blended education policy." One example of such an initiative is "Moving BL 2 Maturity," which was implemented at the Delft University of Technology with the specific goal of enhancing the maturity of blended education. The Turkish Gaziantep University has created training materials based on the EMM to enhance the skills of educational staff in blended learning (see https://vu.nl/en/news/2022/next-steps-in-blended-education-at-gaziantep-university-turkiye). Belgian universities advanced blended education with focused initiatives. Thomas More University of Applied Sciences and KU Leuven emphasize professional support and course design improvements. The University of Antwerp has developed a comprehensive policy for blended learning and an online self-assessment tool to continuously refine their educational practices. At Howest University of Applied Sciences, a series of workshops designed for programme managers resulted in prototypes that aligned with the EMM. The institution also refined its guidelines for implementation, focusing on managers responsible for professional development in their respective domains.

Central to this achievement is that the EMBED framework enabled effective communication. In this regard, EMBED proved useful in workshops, guiding discussions on blended teaching. Action plans were developed, and changes were evaluated iteratively. According to a policy advisor, "EMBED has aided us in developing a language to discuss high-quality blended learning design. It serves as a handy tool that facilitates conversation." One individual stated, "EMBED provided a framework for a shared language (...)" Another added, "This clear and structured approach has proven beneficial not only for blended education but also for other themes within our educational strategy." This approach has fostered deeper understanding and collaboration among educators. As another policy advisor stated, the approach has been "productive because people realised that they were talking from different perspectives and had different interpretations of either maturity levels or specific measures. It raised awareness that blended education requires more than innovative lecturers." This observation highlighted the need for a comprehensive framework to address challenges at different levels: course and program design (micro level), strategic issues within institutions (meso level), and policy matters at the governmental level (macro level).

Utility during the Covid-19 pandemic

The Covid-19 pandemic has highlighted the necessity for higher education institutions (HEIs) to be prepared for digital education and to swiftly adapt their teaching and learning services. The global shift to (a)synchronous distance teaching exposed significant deficiencies, reinforcing the advantages of blending face-to-face and online instructional methods. Various authors describe the lasting changes this will have on post-covid education (Bloom et al., 2020; Zhao & Watterston, 2021).This requires a robust organizational framework, instructors and students with advanced skills and 'agency' (Elen, 2021), and updated support services, resources, and infrastructure (Porter et al., 2016). The pandemic also underscored the need for effective short-to-midterm strategies to tackle educational challenges. Numerous studies have noted the difficulties HEIs faced in implementing emergency remote teaching (Ashraf et al., 2021). The EMM, with its tools and guidelines, proved valuable, offering a framework for applying principles and making informed decisions. It facilitated the design and evaluation of both synchronous and asynchronous online learning environments, showcasing the EMBED framework's adaptability and practicality. Furthermore, during the pandemic, the EU DigiTel project (2020-2022) partners delivered three courses on online, blended, and hybrid education using the EMBED framework, demonstrating its application across various educational contexts.

Publications and projects

During the tenure of the EMBED project, various publications such as conference papers, journal articles, and other works were produced (https://embed.eadtu.eu). The project further gained recognition through publications by national and international professional alliances, such as the Organisation for Economic Cooperation and Development (OECD, see Staring et al., 2022). The EMBED framework was subsequently referenced in monographs by Last (2022), Last and Jong (2021, 2023), as well as in edited books by Zawacki-Richter and Jung (2022) and the publications series of the European Association of Distance Teaching Universities on digital teaching and learning and quality assurance (Henderikx et al., 2022). Last and Jong (2023) emphasized the framework's utility in course design and establishing conditions for blended teaching in their latest work on blended learning design.

EMBED has been seamlessly integrated into continuous professional development schemes, including EMPOWER webinars organised by the EADTU and the European Commission's Digital Education Hub (https://education.ec.europa.eu/focus-topics/digital-education/action-plan/european-digital-education-hub). EMBED has maintained close ties with a variety of European projects and initiatives, such as the EU DigiTel project and the European Bloom hub. These collaborations underscore EMBED's importance and relevance in the higher education sector.

Opportunities and challenges

The COVID-19 crisis catalyzed the adoption and enhancement of blended education in European HEIs, establishing these methods as essential. Leading universities have advanced in digital education maturity by developing policies, strategies, frameworks, and tools, equipping faculty with resources for course design, digital content creation, interaction, and inclusive education. The digitalizing societal context, including the rise of generative AI, further drives universities to invest in new pedagogies and digital education infrastructure. Recognizing the need for digital transformation, universities are implementing structural CPD programs at various levels, involving diverse stakeholders to foster an organizational culture supportive of digital education. In light of the increasing impact of digitalization on higher education, the need for mature decision-making processes has become even more critical, even in frontrunner universities.

A maturity model that supports iterative and deliberate decision-making at all levels of the university - encompassing teaching staff, course teams, program boards, support services, and leadership - addresses this need. Such a model should also be flexible enough to keep pace with emerging educational technologies and pedagogical opportunities across European universities. Despite these positive developments, the force field analysis also identified several negative forces and challenges that could impede progress. A significant number of European universities were not prepared to deliver a systematic response to the disruptions caused by COVID-19. These institutions still lack adequate digital education policies, strategies, and organizational structures to effectively support digital learning. Resistance to change remains a considerable barrier, with some leaders, teachers, and students reluctant to move away from traditional teaching methods. Additionally, many universities struggle to invest in professionalisation, support, and the technological infrastructure to keep pace with emerging technologies, such as artificial intelligence, augmented, virtual and extended reality. This lack of investment is compounded by the fact that equitable access to technology for students is not universally achieved. Moreover, many universities do not have the expertise needed for innovative course and curriculum design, leading to misconceptions about digital teaching and learning. The development of scalable, high-quality, and cost-effective digital education solutions is progressing too slowly and in a fragmented manner across institutions. Finally, the analysis highlights the lack of regular, deliberate decision-making on digital education within universities. Decisions are often made randomly rather than being based on valid information and evidence. This challenge is exacerbated by the absence of systemic funding and governmental policy support in many countries.

EMBED+: Advancing blended education and teaching in Europe

Objectives and expected outcomes

In summary, EMBED has garnered attention and recognition in recent years, proving successful in guiding the design and implementation of blended learning approaches. However, our insights have also highlighted valuable lessons and pressing needs. Therefore, a new consortium of HEI's initiated EMBED+. The project name incorporates a '+' symbol to indicate substantial improvements, namely:

- Update: EMBED+ enhances the original model with revisions based on user feedback, developments, and relevant research and professional literature, aligning with societal, educational, and technological changes since 2020.;
- Extend: EMBED+ introduces new features enhancing the integration of materials, procedures, and professional development with hybrid solutions;

- Upscale: EMBED+ broadens its European impact, addressing fragmented adoption of the EMM, improving practical understanding, and fostering collaboration across diverse HEIs.

The EMBED+ project is structured around four key pathways (see Figure 1):

1. Development of a contemporary, evidence-informed model to support decision-making for various stakeholders involved in blended education and teaching;
2. Creation of a hybrid open-access hub to provide HEIs a series of resources for improving blended education and teaching;
3. An EU road tour to share the project's outcomes across Europe to maximize its reach and impact;
4. Creation of an online, transnational community of experts to promote knowledge exchange among European HEIs.

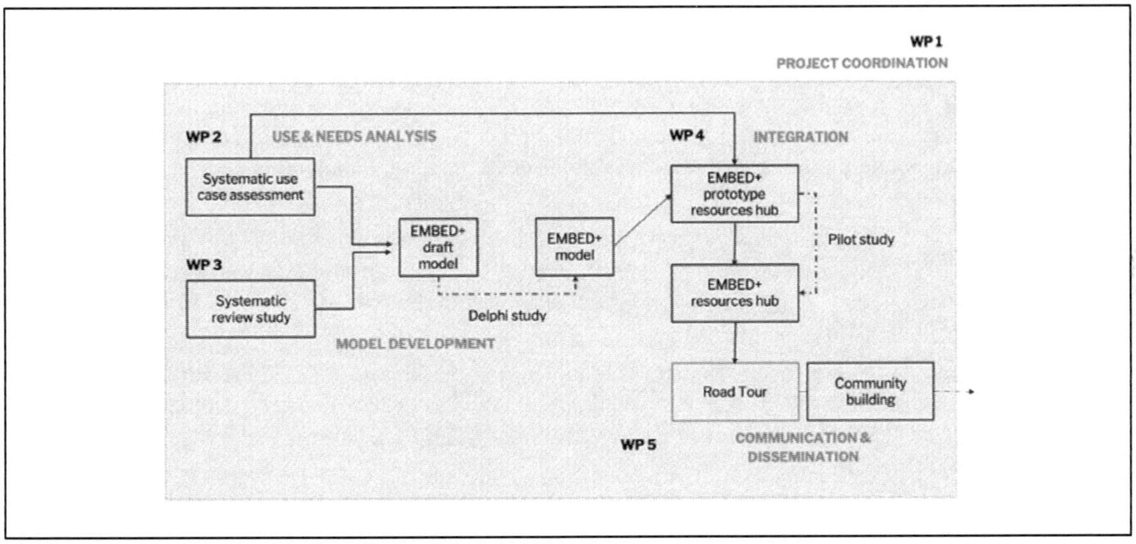

Figure 1: EMBED+ project work packages (2024-2027)

Aligning with technological and educational advancements

EMBED+ is designed to modernize the EMM framework, tools and resources, ensuring its relevance across diverse educational settings. Through rigorous mixed-method research and synthesis, the project integrates current technological advancements. This approach is aligned with the EU's broader strategies for digitalization, which advocate for using emerging technologies to improve teaching quality and equitable access to education.

The EMBED+ initiative will create a hybrid resources hub for blended education, featuring tools, materials, expert insights, and best practices to support CPD and community engagement.

By enhancing capacity and fostering collaboration among HEIs, EMBED+ strengthens Europe's leadership in digital education and supports transnational cooperation in line with key objectives of the European Digital Education Action Plan (https://education.ec.europa.eu/focus-topics/digital-education/action-plan).

Continuous professional development

The COVID-19 pandemic accelerated the digital transformation of education, revealing gaps in many HEIs' readiness for online and blended learning. EMBED+ aims to address these challenges by providing HEIs with the tools and strategies needed to build resilient digital education systems. Investing in CPD is critical to ensure that educators are equipped to sustain and adapt blended learning models and apply new educational technology (Vaughan, 2007).

One of the key objectives of EMBED+ is to support CPD in blended education, essential for helping HEIs navigate the growing digitalization of education. The project will offer a series of training sessions, conferences, and events, both in-person and virtual, organized through HE alliances and university networks across Europe.

Building an online community of experts and users

EMBED+ places a strong emphasis on community-building, aiming to create an online platform that supports the implementation of advanced blended learning practices, which is essential for knowledge management and innovation (Alwazae et al., 2015). By engaging a wide range of stakeholders, including government agencies, educational technology experts, and research centers, EMBED+ ensures its tools and resources remain relevant and widely accessible. The platform will allow for continuous feedback and collaboration, further enhancing the project's sustainability across the European higher education landscape.

Conclusion

The EMBED project has garnered significant recognition for its contributions to higher education initiatives and the professional development of blended teaching across Europe. Its deliverables, including tools, guidelines, and a MOOC, support the maturation of blended education by aiding decision-making at various stages of development. In 2023, an assessment of EMBED's effectiveness identified key challenges and set the stage for a follow-up project. EMBED+ aims to build on this foundation by creating an evidence-informed framework, driving institutional assessment and change, and accelerating the adoption of blended education through community-building and continuous professional development opportunities.

References

Alwazae, M., Perjons, E., & Johannesson, P. (2015). Applying a Template for Best Practice Documentation. The Third Information Systems International Conference 2015, 72, 252-260. https://doi.org/10.1016/j.procs.2015.12.138

Ashraf, M. A., Yang, M., Zhang, Y., Denden, M., Tlili, A., Liu, J., ... & Burgos, D. (2021). A systematic review of systematic reviews on blended learning: Trends, gaps and future directions. Psychology Research and Behavior Management, 1525-1541. DOI: 10.2147/PRBM.S331741

Bloom, D. A., Reid, J. R., & Cassady, C. I. (2020). Education in the time of COVID-19. Pediatric Radiology, 50(8), 1055-1058. https://doi.org/10.1007/s00247-020-04728-8

Cox, M. J., & Marshall, G. (2007). Effects of ICT: Do we know what we should know? Education and Information Technologies, 12(3), 59-70.

Elen, J. (2021). Context and agency: complementarity and interactivity. Educational Technology Research and Development, 69(1), 195-197.

European Maturity Model for Blended Education (EMBED) - project coordinated by EADTU, co-funded by DG Education and Culture of the European Commission, see https://embed.eadtu.eu

Fanta, P., Mynaříková, L., & Dobrucká, L. (2020). Educational projects evaluation. In Edulearn2020 Proceedings (pp. 3449-3454). 10.21125/edulearn.2020.0972

Gaebel, M., Zhang, T., Stoeber, H., & Morrisroe, A. (2021). Digitally enhanced learning and teaching in European higher education institutions. European University Association.

Goeman, K., & Dijkstra, W. (2022). Creating Mature Blended Education: The European Maturity Model Guidelines. Higher Education Studies, 12(3), 34-46.

Goeman, K., Dijkstra, W., Poelmans, S., Vemuri, P., & Van Valkenburg, W. (2021), Development of a Maturity Model for Blended Education: A Delphi Study. International Journal on E-Learning, 20(3), 229-258.

Henderikx, P., Ubachs, G., & Antonaci, A. (2022). Models and guidelines for the design and development of teaching and learning in digital higher education. Global Academic Press.

Last, B. & Jongen, S. (2021). Blended learning en onderwijsontwerp: Van theorie naar praktijk (1ste editie). Boom Lemma.

Last, B. (2002). Blended learning in de praktijk: Modellen, strategieën, voorbeelden en andere handvatten. Boom.

Moore, M. G. (2019). The theory of transactional distance. In Handbook of Distance Education: Second Edition (pp. 84-103). Routledge.

Porter, W. W., Graham, C. R., Bodily, R. G., & Sandberg, D. S. (2016). A Qualitative Analysis of Institutional Drivers and Barriers to Blended Learning Adoption in Higher Education. Internet and Higer Education, 28, 17-27. https://doi.org/10.1016/j.iheduc.2015.08.003.

Professional Development in Digital Teaching and Learning Professional Development (DigiTeL Pro) - project coordinated by EADTU, co-funded by DG Education and Culture of the European Commission, see https://Digitelpro.eadtu.eu/

Rasheed, R. A., Kamsin, A., & Abdullah, N. A. (2020). Challenges in the online component of blended learning: A systematic review. Computers & Education, 144, 103701.

Selkrig, M., Dulfer, N., Harrison, M., Smith, C., Cochrane, T., & McKernan, A. (2023). Keeping IT human: Learning design in the digital age. The University of Melbourne.

Staring, F., Brown, M., Bacsich, P., & Ifenthaler, D. (2022). Digital Higher Education: Emerging Quality Standards, Practices and Supports. OECD Education Working Papers. No. 281. OECD Publishing.

Ubachs, G., & Henderikx, P. (2023). Quality Assurance Systems for Digital Higher Education in Europe. In: Zawacki-Richter, O., Jung, I. (Eds.), Handbook of Open, Distance and Digital Education, 1-20. Springer.

UNESCO. (2020, 05 08). COVID-19 Educational Disruption and Response. Retrieved from www.unesco.org: https://en.unesco.org/covid19/educationresponse

Valverde-Berrocoso, J., Del Carmen Garrido-Arroyo, M., Burgos-Videla, C., & Morales-Cevallos, M. B. (2020). Trends in Educational Research about e-Learning: A Systematic Literature Review (2009–2018). MDPI, 12(12), 1-23. doi:10.3390/su12125153

Van Valkenburg, W., Dijkstra, W., de los Arcos, B., & Goeman, K. (2020). European Maturity Model for Blended Education. EADTU. Retrieved from https://embed.eadtu.eu/download/2470/European%20Maturity%20Model%20for%20Blended%20Education.pdf?inline=1

Vaughan, N. (2007). Perspectives on Blended Learning in Higher Education. International journal on e-learning, 6(1), 81-94.

Zhao, Y., & Watterston, J. (2021). The changes we need: Education post COVID-19. Journal of Educational Change, 22(1), 3-12. https://doi.org/10.1007/s10833-021-09417-3

Developing and Publishing Academic Profiles for EdTech Needs

Janika Leoste[1], Ugljesa Marjanovic[2], Slavko Rakic[3], Kristjan Kask[4], Luis Peña Sánchez[5], Piedad Tolmos Rodríguez-Piñero[6]

[1] School of Educational Sciences, Tallinn University, Estonia; leoste@tlu.ee
[2] Faculty of Technical Sciences, University of Novi Sad, Serbia; umarjano@uns.ac.rs
[3] Faculty of Technical Sciences, University of Novi Sad, Serbia; slavkorakic@uns.ac.rs
[4] School of Natural Sciences and Health, Tallinn University, Estonia; kristjan.kask@tlu.ee
[5] Lurtis Rules, Spain; luis.penya@lurtis.com
[6] Economía Financiera y Contabilidad, Universidad Rey Juan Carlos, Spain; piedad.tolmos@urjc.es

Correspondence: Janika Leoste: leoste@tlu.ee

Abstract:

Collaboration between academia and the EdTech industry is crucial for innovation. Academic profiles that reflect industry needs can facilitate collaboration. We examine the professional online profiles of educational researchers from the School of Educational Sciences of Tallinn University, focusing on the international LinkedIn, national ETIS and institutional TLU platforms. We aim to identify how researchers market their skills, relevant to the EdTech sector. Our findings indicate that some key areas, such as instructional design, project management and technical proficiency, that are vital for EdTech industry, remain often underrepresented in academic profiles. While LinkedIn facilitates networking, it may not necessarily reach the depth needed for comprehensive representation, whereas the Estonian national research database ETIS provides rich academic details with limited industry appeal. Our suggestions call for strategic improvements in how researchers can present their expertise online to improve industry-academia collaboration. By creating detail-rich and strategically targeted professional profiles, researchers will have better chances to attract the attention of the EdTech industry.

Keywords: EdTech industry; academic profiles; open innovation; professional development; academia-industry collaboration

1. Introduction

Technological advances continue to emerge at an unprecedented rate, a trend described by Kurzweil (Kurzweil, 2005) in his theory of accelerating returns. In the education sector, the rapid pace of innovation requires on-going integration of new technologies to ensure that education meets the continuously changing demands of the labor market. EdTech companies stand at the forefront of developing these technology-based education solutions. To remain competitive and responsive, companies increasingly rely on open innovation models that allow faster feedback, and the inclusion of real-world classroom needs in the development process (Cañibano, Otamendi & Andújar, 2008; Gaughan & Bozeman, 2008). One of the most effective open innovation strategies is the user innovation model, where end users, such as teachers or educational researchers, are actively involved in the development of new technologies. This approach ensures that the products developed remain both innovative as well as practical and adapted to the actual needs of teachers and students (von Hippel, 2005). However, many EdTech companies are hesitant to implement this model. A significant obstacle is the difficulty of identifying and engaging educational researchers who have the necessary skills and expertise to effectively contribute to the development of new products (Amador & González, 2023). Public platforms such as LinkedIn, national research databases like Estonia's www.etis.ee (ETIS), and institutional information systems, such as Tallinn University's www.tlu.ee (TLU), are often used to provide industry partners, including EdTech companies, with relevant information regarding researchers' skills and areas of expertise (Wang, Allouache & Joubert, 2021). These platforms allow educational researchers to demonstrate their expertise, facilitating connections with industry partners who can benefit from their knowledge (Woolley & Turpin,

2009). However, the effectiveness of these platforms varies. Although widely used and accessible, due to its focus on networking and broad visibility, LinkedIn seems to be lacking the depth and specificity necessary to adequately represent researchers' industry-relevant academic and practical expertise (Hadzic, 2023; Sun & Scott, 2005). National research databases represent a higher potential to offer a more comprehensive overview of researchers' academic contributions but may not appear as user-friendly or even be particularly known beyond the academic community of a specific country (Menekse Dalveren & Peker, 2021; Shaw & Gaines, 1987). Institutional databases maintained by universities can provide detailed and regularly updated information but are often difficult to access or navigate by professionals outside of academia (Li & Bozeman, 2006). Due to these challenges, researchers should present their skills and precisely defined areas of expertise in a manner that is clear, concise, and accessible to their industry partners. This article examines how educational researchers present their knowledge and skills on open platforms, by analyzing publicly accessible data from LinkedIn, ETIS and TLU. The research question that guides the study is formulated as follows:

> RQ: What skills and expertise relevant to EdTech companies are most acknowledged by the researchers of the Tallinn University School of Education in their public profiles?

The article is organized as follows: First, in the background section, we discuss the background of modern educational technologies (EdTechs), the importance of cross-sectoral collaboration between educational researchers and EdTech companies, the skills required by EdTech companies, and the platforms for educational researchers to present their technology-relevant skills and knowledge. Next, in the methodology section we outline the approach used to analyze researcher profiles across the LinkedIn, ETIS, and TLU platforms. Then, in the results section, we present our findings, the ramifications of which are examined in more detail in the discussion section. Finally, the article concludes with the study's limitations and suggestions for future research.

2. Background

2.1. Technologies in Education

Emerging digital technologies are putting enormous pressure on the educational sector as it struggles to respond to the rapidly changing needs of the 21st-century labor market, as well as those of civil society. These novel EdTechs offer tools that enhance learning experiences, improve accessibility, and facilitate personalized education. Kurzweil suggested already in 2005 that the rapid pace of technological advancement, characterized by accelerating returns, has made it essential for educational institutions to incorporate these innovations swiftly to stay relevant (Kurzweil, 2005). Emerging technologies such as artificial intelligence (AI), virtual reality (VR), and data analytics are increasingly being integrated into experimental educational frameworks, providing new methods for students to engage with content and for teachers to assess learning outcomes (Davé, 2023; Sun & Scott, 2005). AI-driven platforms seem to carry the potential to personalize learning experience by analyzing student data and adapting content to the individual needs of each learner. This enhanced data analytics provide teachers with insights into student performance, enabling better targeted interventions and improved educational outcomes. VR and AR tools provide immersive experiences that can simulate real-world environments, visualizing complex concepts and allowing students to safely explore historical sites or conduct experiments in a controlled virtual environment.

Despite these advancements, the implementation of emerging technologies has its own challenges. Educational institutions need to address issues such as the high cost of technology, resistance to change among teachers, and the need for ongoing professional development to effectively integrate new technologies into classroom practices (Leoste et al., 2020; Menekse Dalveren & Peker, 2021). One of the primary challenges in implementing new technologies in education is ensuring that these tools meet the practical needs of both teachers and students. The gap between the capabilities of emerging technologies and the realities of classroom environments can lead to the underutilization or misapplication of these tools. For instance, a highly sophisticated AI tool may not be used to its potential if teachers are not adequately trained to integrate it into their teaching practices. This is where user involvement in the development process becomes crucial. By engaging educational researchers in the development of EdTech solutions, companies can create products that are innovative and address the actual needs and workflows of teachers and students (Wang, Allouache & Joubert, 2021). Involvement of competent stakeholders allows for rapid and effective feedback, which can significantly enhance the usability and effectiveness of EdTechs, ensuring that these remain both practical and impactful in real-world educational settings. In this sense, researchers' engagement in knowledge transfer and exchange activities is crucial in the effective adoption of emerging EdTechs – essential for aligning these technologies with the diverse needs of users and maximizing their impact in educational contexts.

2.2. Innovation Models in Education Technology

Innovation in EdTechs can be understood through various models, each having its advantages and challenges. The traditional closed innovation model relies on internal resources and expertise within the organization that develops new products. This model can be effective in maintaining control over the development and the protection of intellectual property, as it limits external input and collaboration. However, the spread of diverse ideas is restricted and the innovation process can slow down due to its self-contained and insulating nature (Chesbrough, 2003). Closed innovation may also result in products that do not fully meet the needs of the users, as in this case development is primarily driven by internal perspectives rather than feedback from the actual external users. In contrast, in the educational context, the open innovation model encourages collaboration with external partners, such as researchers, teachers, students or even parents, to co-create technology-supported solutions. This model allows for a broader range of inputs and faster development cycles, making it particularly suitable for the dynamic field of educational technology (von Hippel, 2005). Open innovation can lead to more user-focused products that reflect better the actual market needs. However, the model also presents distinct challenges, such as managing intellectual property rights and coordinating contributions by multiple stakeholders.

A specific form of open innovation is user innovation where the actual end-users, such as teachers, are directly involved in the development process. This model is highly effective in the educational context, as it ensures that the newly developed products are fitted to the needs of teachers. For example, teachers can provide insights into how students interact with educational tools, which features are most useful, and what improvements are needed. In addition, as educational researchers are often higher education teachers, user innovation allows engagement of scientifically backed teacher experience, while providing EdTech companies with immediate feedback, enabling them to make iterative improvements to their products. And yet, many EdTech companies are still hesitant to fully embrace this model due to concerns about the complexity of coordinating with multiple stakeholders and the perceived risk of exposing their intellectual property to external parties (Amador & González, 2023). To overcome these fears, it is crucial for educational researchers to provide EdTech companies with easily graspable overviews of their skills' profiles and areas expertise. One mechanism to achieve this is for educational researchers to publish detailed profiles that highlight their skills and expertise relevant to the development of educational technologies. By demonstrating their expertise in areas such as curriculum design, educational psychology, and classroom management, researchers can build trust with EdTech companies and alleviate concerns regarding the risks of external collaboration (Gaughan & Bozeman, 2008). These detailed profiles could be viewed as a collaboration-supporting bridge between academic expertise and industry needs.

2.3. Essential Skills Required in the EdTech Industry

EdTech companies often require sets of skills and profiles of expertise from their academic partners that are distinctly different from those traditionally emphasized in academic research organizations. While educational researchers typically focus on theoretical and methodological rigor, EdTech companies are more concerned with practical applications that can be scaled across diverse educational settings (Li & Bozeman, 2006). Skills in instructional design, user experience research, and data analytics are particularly valuable in the EdTech industry, as they directly impact the usability and effectiveness of educational tools. In addition, knowledge of educational policies, standards, and compliance is essential for developing products that meet regulatory requirements and can be adopted by schools and institutions (Li & Bozeman, 2006). Kang and Ritzhaupt (2015) analyzed 400 EdTech-related job announcements published in five international online job search databases and identified the most important skills and expertise required in the field of educational technology. They suggest that EdTech companies value most highly professionals with a strong foundation in instructional design, project management, and technical skills to use software tools such as learning management systems and eLearning development platforms. In addition, soft skills such as communication, collaboration, and interpersonal skills are critical as these roles often require working closely with different teams and stakeholders. The ability to manage multiple projects and effectively prioritize tasks emerged as key competencies in the field. Together, these skills highlight the need for a balanced mix of technical expertise and interpersonal skills to succeed in the education technology industry.

2.4. Platforms for Publishing Researchers' Data

In the digital age, various platforms offer opportunities for researchers to publish and share their professional profiles. While platforms like Facebook and Twitter are popular for social networking, they are less suited for professional networking and collaboration (Jordan, 2019; Idoko, 2023). LinkedIn, on the other hand, stands out as one of the best suitable platforms for connecting researchers with EdTech companies. LinkedIn allows researchers to create detailed profiles that include their academic achievements, skills, and professional experiences, making it easier for EdTech companies to identify potential collaborators (Wang, Allouache & Joubert, 2021). LinkedIn has become an increasingly valuable platform for both researchers and professionals in the EdTech space, offering a powerful combination of professional networking and collaboration opportunities, and enhanced visibility within their respective communities. The platform's features, such as endorsements, recommendations, and the ability to present publications and projects, make it an essential tool for professionals seeking to highlight their achievements and engage with broader audiences. For researchers, LinkedIn provides a space to connect with peers across disciplines, stay informed regarding the latest developments in their respective fields, and engage with industry professionals, potentially leading to fruitful collaborations and career advancements (Van Noorden. 2014). Similarly, in the EdTech sector, LinkedIn facilitates networking within specific interest groups, allowing educational researchers to connect with industry professionals who share similar interests or goals. This network-oriented structure encourages the building of professional relationships and the sharing of insights within industry-specific groups, fostering a collaborative environment that can drive innovation. By bridging the gap between academic research and its industrial application, LinkedIn serves as a crucial tool for both researchers and EdTech professionals, enabling them to expand their reach, influence, and impact in their respective fields (Collins, Shiffman & Rock, 2016).

Despite the advantages of social media platforms such as LinkedIn, national research information systems (for example ETIS), and institutional information systems (for example TLU) remain relevant. These systems offer a level of validation and credibility that is critical in academic and professional contexts. Institutional information systems, typically managed by universities or research institutions, provide a controlled environment for presenting researchers' profiles, while national systems are often linked to government agencies, constituting a reliable source of information regarding researchers' qualifications and achievements. For example, ETIS is a comprehensive database that includes detailed records of publications, projects, and professional activities, which can be essential for establishing researchers' credibility (Menekse Dalveren & Peker, 2021; Shaw & Gaines, 1987). Furthermore, such platforms allow for the aggregation of research outputs and metrics, which can be useful for both academic evaluation and industry collaboration. These systems often include peer-reviewed publications, grant information, and other academic credentials that are crucial for validating a researcher's expertise. By maintaining profiles on both LinkedIn and national research systems, researchers can ensure that their skills and knowledge remain visible to a wide audience while also benefiting from the credibility associated with institutional affiliations. This dual presence can help researchers making their expertise accessible and appealing to a broader range of potential partners from both the academia and industry. Even though national and institutional databases like ETIS are comprehensive and credible, researchers should also maintain an active presence on LinkedIn, as these databases, while containing detailed academic records, peer-reviewed publications, and verified credentials, are often underutilized by industry professionals. The reasons for this include the limited accessibility and specialized interfaces of these databases, focusing more on academic audiences rather than industry representatives (Menekse Dalveren & Peker, 2021; Shaw & Gaines, 1987). In this sense, LinkedIn seems to be more accessible for industry professionals to discover and engage with researchers, as it functions as a widely recognized platform with the premise of effectively connecting academia and industry. Its user-friendly interface and networking capabilities make it easier for EdTech companies and other industry stakeholders to identify and connect with researchers who have the expertise they need (Wang, Allouache & Joubert, 2021). By maintaining active and detailed LinkedIn profiles, researchers can ensure that their expertise is more visible and easily discoverable by industry professionals, thereby enhancing their opportunities for collaboration on innovative projects. This dual strategy, taking advantage of both LinkedIn and academic databases, should allow researchers, as a matter of principle, to benefit from the credibility and depth of institutional records while also making use of the networking and visibility that LinkedIn offers. In this way the circulation of their academic profiles is broadened in support of more effective partnerships with industry, leading ultimately to more effective innovation in the EdTech sector.

3. Resources and Methods

3.1. Data Sources

Our objective was to identify the skills and knowledge most highlighted by education researchers on their public profiles, using the School of Educational Sciences of Tallinn University as a case study. To achieve this, we analyzed the public profiles of researchers from the Tallinn University School of Educational Sciences across three platforms: LinkedIn (www.linkedin.com), the Estonian Research Information System (ETIS, www.etis.ee), and the Tallinn University homepage (TLU, www.tlu.ee). These platforms were selected because they represent the most relevant and publicly accessible online meeting places where researchers in Estonia, particularly those affiliated with Tallinn University, demonstrate their professional skills and academic achievements. LinkedIn is widely used for the purposes of professional networking and contacting prospective partners (EATRIS-ERIC, 2019); ETIS is the primary research information system for researchers in Estonia; and the Tallinn University homepage provides verified staff profiles.

3.2. Specific Aspects of ETIS and TLU

We set limits to our examination of ETIS data due to the latter's focus on providing research-related information. ETIS is designed to hold the following aspects of a researcher's profile: (a) general information, which includes name, contact details, links to Google Scholar and ORCID profiles, fields of research, and freely fillable "Description" and "Specification" fields; (b) career, listing academic positions held; (c) education, detailing the researcher's academic background and degrees earned; (d) awards, listing any honors or recognitions received; (e) administrative work, detailing the researcher's administrative roles; (f) projects, providing a list of research projects the researcher is involved in; (g) publications, listing the researcher's scientific articles; and (h) supervision, indicating the researcher's involvement in mentoring early career researchers and students. These sections contain mostly information that is related to the individuals' research and offer only limited insight into their potential to collaborate with EdTech companies. Therefore, in our analysis of ETIS profiles, we focused on whether researchers had completed the "Description" and "Specification" fields in the General section, and whether these fields contained information relevant to EdTech companies, which falls outside the traditional academic context.

TLU profiles include the staff members' job titles, and their respective structural units of employment. In addition, the records include their contact information and a links to ETIS profiles. Finally, TLU profiles contain the "Introduction" field, where researchers can in a free form describe their relevant skills, knowledge, and expertise. For the purposes of our study, we focused primarily on the content of the "Introduction" field to determine whether researchers disclosed information that might be of interest to EdTech companies.

3.3. Sample and Data Analyses

We began by compiling a list of academic staff members from the School of Educational Sciences of Tallinn University, deliberately excluding junior researchers, understood as a rule as doctoral students, as they are less likely to have developed consistent professional profiles. In total, our selection included 40 researchers. Of these, 31 had LinkedIn accounts, and all had profiles on both the TLU and ETIS platforms. We then systematically recorded the content of the researchers' profiles across the selected platforms and anonymized the data to ensure confidentiality.

To analyze the gathered data, two researchers first employed the open coding method, a qualitative analysis technique commonly used in grounded theory research (Strauss & Corbin, 1998), to identify possible patterns and themes (Saldaña, 2016). This approach allowed us to identify the specific skills and knowledge highlighted in the profiles, facilitating a comprehensive understanding of the professional attributes that education researchers choose to emphasize in publicly accessible platforms. After examining the datasets, we located and counted the records that contained skills and expertise relevant to the EdTech industry, by comparing the identified data to the skills and expertise that Kang and Ritzhaupt (2015) had outlined as needed for EdTech jobs. We relied on the general meaning (as jointly defined by involved researchers) of a skill or expertise if a direct match was not found.

4. Results

Our sample consisted of 40 researchers from the School of Educational Sciences at Tallinn University. Of these, 31 had public LinkedIn profiles, and 28 had filled in their skills and expertise sections. While all researchers had ETIS accounts, 34 had provided more detailed information regarding their skills and expertise in their ETIS profiles' "Description" or "Specification" fields. Surprisingly enough, although all researchers had TLU accounts, only 12 of them had provided introductions of any sort about themselves, including their skills, and areas of expertise.

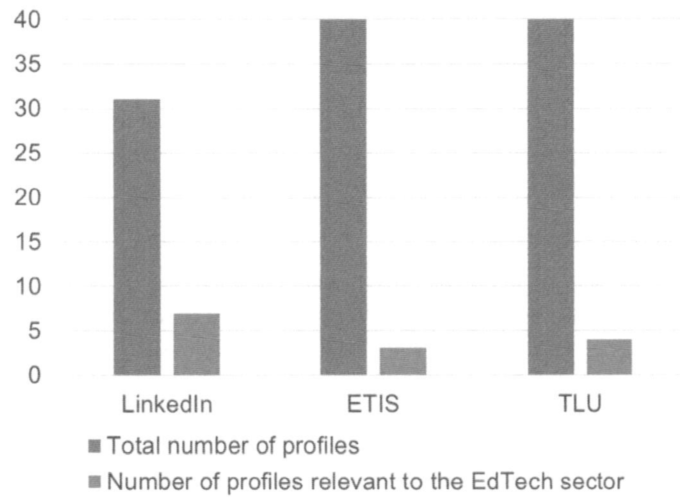

Figure 1: The number of profiles on a platform vs the number of profiles relevant to the EdTech sector.

We found that only 7 LinkedIn profiles, 3 ETIS profiles, and 4 TLU profiles referred to the skills and areas of expertise relevant to the EdTech industry (Figure 1). The identified skills and expertise are listed in Table 1.

Table 1: Skills and expertise identified in researchers' LinkedIn, ETIS and TLU profiles.

LinkedIn	ETIS	TLU
• Digital ecosystems • Digital transformation in education • EdTech Hackathon organization • Educational innovation • Educational robotics • E-learning • Hybrid and blended learning • Project management • Social robotics • STEAM education • Telepresence robotics	• Adult learning • Digital ecosystems • Educational innovation • Educational robotics • Educational technology • Hybrid and blended learning • Socio-technological learning systems • STEAM education • Technology-enhanced • workplace learning	• Digital transformation in education • Educational robotics • Educational technology • Hybrid and blended learning • STEAM education • Technology in supporting special needs education

Our analysis indicates (Table 1) that researchers' profiles usually miss several key skills and areas of expertise that are crucial from the perspective of the EdTech industry, as high-lighted by Kang and Ritzhaupt (2015). For example, the researchers, as a rule, do not report their expertise in instructional design, particularly related to principles of operations and the application of models required for the development of digital and online learning environments, which remain central to the development of a variety of effective EdTechs. Although some curriculum development experience has been usually mentioned, specific attention to instructional design for digital platforms remains weak. In addition, while project management skills have been occasionally noted, they are generally associated with academic projects rather than technology-based initiatives. This would leave the potential partners uninformed regarding the researchers' ability to manage multiple projects, meet tight deadlines, and lead technology-focused teams, although all these skills are indispensable in the fast-paced EdTech industry. Next, technical skills in the key areas such as learning management systems, authoring tools, and advanced multimedia production (such as video and audio editing or web development) remain underrepresented, despite being highly sought after by EdTech companies. In terms of soft skills, although communication and collaboration skills have been regularly mentioned, there is a lack of emphasis on the interpersonal and leadership skills required for effective teamwork in industry. The ability to lead teams, manage clients, and communicate with stakeholders is critical to successful EdTech collaborations, but it is insufficiently highlighted in the majority of the profiles. Finally, openness to new technologies, a trait highly valued in the EdTech sector, has not been sufficiently demonstrated. Addressing these gaps would allow better aligning researchers' skills with the industry's needs, greatly increasing their collaborative potential and impact in EdTech.

5. Discussion

Our aim in this study was to examine how well does educational researchers' presentation of their skills and the areas of expertise match with the needs of EdTech companies. To this end, we compared the online profiles from three different platforms: an international networking platform (LinkedIn), a national research database (ETIS), and an institutional database (TLU). These profiles were then compared to the skills and expertise needed by EdTech companies, as identified by Kang and Ritzhaupt (2015). The identified mismatch suggests that making available specific trainings and offering professional development opportunities could significantly increase the relevance of the researchers' professional profiles for the purposes of the EdTech industry. For instance, Kang and Ritzhaupt (2015) have highlighted instructional design, project management, and technical proficiency as essential skills required for the EdTech-related positions, yet these all remain often neglected describing academic profiles.

5.1. Platform Comparisons and Audience Considerations

Comparison of the three selected platforms (LinkedIn, ETIS and TLU) reveals that each of these offers distinct benefits that shape how researchers present their skills. First of all, as demonstrated in Figure 1, besides it being easily accessible for the EdTech professionals, LinkedIn is also the platform where the educational scientists show their EdTech-relevant skills and expertise most often. Researchers who effectively utilize LinkedIn (e.g., provide frequent updates, use strategically chosen keywords, and are engage actively) tend to emphasize their connections to industry and potential for collaboration, aligning their profiles with market demands. These approaches favor improvements in the visibility of their profiles to potential industry partners, as also suggested by (Van Noorden. 2014).

In contrast, ETIS profiles appear generally more detailed and academically oriented, focusing on documenting research outputs and academic achievements. These profiles are typically completed by researchers aiming to present their academic contributions, including detailed descriptions of projects and methodologies. However, the focus on academic rigor may not necessarily align with the practical needs of EdTech companies, which often prioritize skills that can be applied directly to product development and implementation.

TLU profiles that focus on internal university roles, tend to highlight teaching responsibilities and administrative duties. While these profiles provide a comprehensive view of a researcher's contributions within the academic context, they may not adequately emphasize skills relevant to the EdTech industry. This may be due to the profiles' intended audience, which is primarily university's employees and (prospective) students. However, due to the increasing importance of interdisciplinary collaboration, TLU profiles could benefit from a more strategic approach that also highlights industry-relevant expertise. As noted by (Woolley & Turpin, 2009), researchers should consider the diverse audiences of these platforms and tailor their profiles accordingly to maximize their professional opportunities.

5.2. Recommendations for Enhancing Profile Relevance

Educational researchers should make a more conscious effort to link their professional profiles to real-world applications in the interests of bridging the gap between academic research and industry needs, as similarly suggested also by (Gaughan & Bozeman, 2002; Hadzic, 2023). For this purpose, researchers should enhance the relevance of their profiles across these platforms, and consider providing more detailed descriptions of their work, particularly its practical applications in the EdTech field.

On LinkedIn, including examples of industry collaboration and utilizing keywords aligned with current educational technology trends have the potential to increase both visibility and appeal. Researchers would also benefit from engaging more actively with LinkedIn's professional groups and forums, which can further enhance their network and industry connections (Collins, Shiffman & Rock, 2016). For ETIS, researchers might focus on explicitly linking their research outcomes to potential industry applications. This could involve detailing how their academic findings can inform product development or improve educational practices, making their profiles more attractive to EdTech companies. In addition, researchers should ensure that their profiles on ETIS are comprehensive, including all relevant skills and experiences that could be of interest to industry partners. Regarding the TLU profiles, we would recommend that researchers emphasize how their academic roles contribute to broader educational technology initiatives. This may involve highlighting involvement in EdTech projects, curriculum development for digital learning, or collaborations with industry partners.

5.3. Support Mechanisms and the Role of Intermediaries

To address the mentioned challenges, it is essential for educational institutions to provide measures of support that would help researchers revising their profiles (Leoste et al., 2020; Llopis et al., 2018). For example, workshops can be used to discuss and practice profile development, the strategic use of keywords, and the integration of industry-relevant content. Also, institutions might use incentives to encourage researchers to maintain up-to-date profiles that reflect their full range of skills and experience. The role of intermediaries or knowledge brokers is also important in bridging the above-discussed gap between academia and industry. These professionals can help translating academic research into practical applications, making it more accessible and appealing to EdTech companies. Similarly to what is suggested by Chesbrough (Chesbrough, 2003), such intermediaries can play a pivotal role in fostering collaboration between the academia and industry, ultimately driving innovation and the development of more effective educational technologies.

5.4. Conclusions

From a theoretical perspective, this study contributes to the understanding about the gap between educational research and the EdTech industry. It highlights how researchers tend to overlook the EdTech industry's needs while presenting their skills and expertise in online platforms. From the practical perspective, the study offers actionable recommendations for researchers to better position themselves for industry collaboration. Educational researchers need to strategically refine their public profiles, particularly on LinkedIn, by incorporating skills directly relevant to EdTech companies, such as digital instructional design, project management, and technical capabilities. In addition, to provide relevant information in appropriate context, researchers should maintain unpretentious and clear, up to thousand character-long bios on platforms such as LinkedIn. These biographies should highlight skills and experiences directly related to the needs of the EdTech industry, making it easier for those companies to identify and partner with the suitable experts (Woolley & Turpin, 2009). Universities and research institutions should offer training and support mechanisms to help researchers optimize their profiles across platforms, ensuring that their academic expertise is presented in a manner attractive to industry partners. Moreover, involving intermediaries or knowledge brokers should be considered to make professional information available for the use fostering innovations, i.e., make researchers more accessible to the EdTech industry – thus improving collaboration between the academia and EdTech industry, facilitating innovation and supporting educational technology development.

5.5. Limitations and Future Perspectives

In this study, we examined how the skills and knowledge presented by educational researchers align with the needs of the EdTech industry, focusing only on the content of their profiles. A further study is needed to explore which EdTech-relevant skills do educational researchers actually possess and how their professional profiles meet the industry's needs, in order to offer recommendations regarding further trainings to be provided to researchers to better meet the EdTech companies' needs for academic expertise.

The focus on LinkedIn, ETIS, and TLU profiles may not necessarily fully capture the breadth of researchers' professional activities or their interactions with the EdTech industry. By excluding other platforms such as ResearchGate or Academia.edu, important aspects of researchers' visibility and engagement might have been overlooked. In addition, the study concentrated on the content and structure of profiles without considering contextual factors, such as institutional policies or individual motivation, which may influence how researchers present themselves online. Also, our analysis was based on the findings of Kang and Ritzhaupt (2015), who derived their results from 400 job offers. Including data from additional sources might yield different results and provide a broader perspective. To address these limitations, future research should include a wider range of platforms, examine the motivations behind profile creation, and quantify the impact of profile features on industry collaborations. Expanding the study to include multiple institutions and incorporating feedback from industry professionals would also enhance the robustness and applicability of the findings.

Finally, integrating social media analytics would provide further insights into how profiles are engaged with, particularly on LinkedIn, where content visibility plays a critical role in fostering collaborations.

Competing interests

The authors have no competing interests to declare.

Ethics and consent (if applicable)

The study does not involve human or animal subjects.

Authors' contributions (optional)

Conceptualization: JL, UM, LPS; methodology: JL, UM; validation: JL; formal analysis: JL, KK, SR; investigation: JL, UM, SR, KK; resources: JL; data curation: JL, SR; writing (original draft preparation): JL, PTRP; writing (review and editing): JL, UM, SR, KK, LPS, PTRP; visualization: JL; supervision: JL; project administration: JL. All authors have read and agreed to the published version of the manuscript.

References

Amador, F., & González, R. (2023). Sistemas de información curricular en Iberoamérica. Universidad de Pinar del Río. Available online: https://rc.upr.edu.cu/handle/DICT/3097 (accessed on September 12, 2024).

Cañibano, C., Otamendi, J., & Andújar, I. (2008). Measuring and assessing researcher mobility from CV analysis: The case of the Ramón y Cajal programme in Spain. Research Evaluation, 17(1), 17–31. https://doi.org/10.3152/095820208X292797

Chesbrough, H. W. (2003). Open innovation: The new imperative for creating and profiting from technology. Harvard Business Press.

Collins, K., Shiffman, D., & Rock, J. (2016). How are scientists using social media in the workplace? PLoS ONE, 11(10), e0162680. https://doi.org/10.1371/journal.pone.0162680

Davé, P. (2023). The revolutionary intersection of AI and immersive learning in higher education. Emerging Technologies, Columbia University. Available online: https://etc.cuit.columbia.edu/news/revolutionary-intersection-ai-and-immersive-learning-higher-education (accessed on September 12, 2024).

EATRIS-ERIC. (2019). CORBEL academia-industry collaboration: Best practices guide. EATRIS-ERIC. Available online: https://eatris.eu/wp-content/uploads/2019/12/CORBEL_Academia_Industry_Collaboration_Best_Practices_Guide.pdf (accessed on September 12, 2024).

Gaughan, M., & Bozeman, B. (2002). Using curriculum vitae to compare some impacts of NSF research center grants with research center funding. Research Evaluation, 11(1), 17–26.

Gaughan, M., & Bozeman, B. (2008). Faculty publication productivity, collaboration, and grants velocity: Impacts of grants and contracts. Research Evaluation, 17(2), 103–110.

Hadzic, A. (2023). Value and limitations of LinkedIn. NYSORA Journal. Available online: https://www.nysora.com/industry-news/value-and-limitations-of-linkedin-op-ed-by-dr-hadzic/ (accessed on September 12, 2024).

Idoko, N. (2023). Understanding the different social networking platforms. Available online: https://nicholasidoko.com/blog/2023/06/08/understanding-the-different-social-networking-platforms/ (accessed on September 12, 2024).

Jordan, K. (2019). Separating and merging professional and personal selves online: The structure and processes that shape academics' ego-networks on academic social networking sites and Twitter. Journal of the Association for Information Science and Technology, 70(8), 830–842. https://doi.org/10.1002/asi.24170

Kang, Y., & Ritzhaupt, A. D. (2015). A job announcement analysis of educational technology professional positions: Knowledge, skills, and abilities. Journal of Educational Technology Systems, 43(3), 231–256. https://doi.org/10.1177/0047239515570572

Katz, R., & Allen, T. J. (1982). Investigating the not invented here (NIH) syndrome: A look at the performance, tenure, and communication patterns of 50 R&D project groups. R&D Management, 12(1), 7–19. https://doi.org/10.1111/j.1467-9310.1982.tb00478.x

Kurzweil, R. (2005). The singularity is near: When humans transcend biology. Viking.

Leoste, J., Heidmets, M., Ley, T. T., & Stepanova, J. (2020). Classroom innovation becoming sustainable: A study of technological innovation adoption by Estonian primary school teachers. Interaction Design and Architecture(s) Journal, 47, 144–166. https://doi.org/10.55612/s-5002-047-007

Lin, M. W., & Bozeman, B. (2006). Researchers' industry experience and productivity in university–industry research centers: A scientific and technical human capital explanation. Journal of Technology Transfer, 31(2), 269–290. https://doi.org/10.1007/s10961-005-6111-2

Llopis, O., Sánchez-Barrioluengo, M., Olmos-Peñuela, J., & Castro-Martínez, E. (2018). Scientists' engagement in knowledge transfer and exchange: Individual factors, variety of mechanisms and users. Science and Public Policy, 45(2), 249–263. https://doi.org/10.1093/scipol/scy020

Menekse Dalveren, G. G., & Peker, S. (2021). Accessibility and usability evaluation of digital library article pages. In App and Website Accessibility Developments and Compliance Strategies (pp. 58–76). IGI Global. https://doi.org/10.4018/978-1-7998-7848-3.ch003

Saldaña, J. (2016). The coding manual for qualitative researchers (3rd ed.). Sage Publications.

Shaw, M. L., & Gaines, B. R. (1987). KITTEN: Knowledge initiation and transfer tools for experts and novices. International Journal of Man-Machine Studies, 27, 251–280. https://doi.org/10.1016/S0020-7373(87)80055-X

Strauss, A., & Corbin, J. (1998). Basics of qualitative research techniques and procedures for developing grounded theory (2nd ed.). Sage Publications.

Sun, P. Y., & Scott, J. L. (2005). An investigation of barriers to knowledge transfer. Journal of Knowledge Management, 9(2), 75–90. https://doi.org/10.1108/13673270510590236

Van Noorden, R. (2014). Online collaboration: Scientists and the social network. Nature, 512(7513), 126–129. https://doi.org/10.1038/512126a

von Hippel, E. (2005). Democratizing innovation. MIT Press.

Wang, Y., Allouache, Y., & Joubert, C. (2021). Analysing CV corpus for finding suitable candidates using knowledge graph and BERT. In Proceedings of the Thirteenth International Conference on Advances in Databases, Knowledge, and Data Applications (DBKDA 2021), Valencia, Spain (pp. 16–21).

Woolley, R., & Turpin, T. (2009). CV analysis as a complementary methodological approach: Investigating the mobility of Australian scientists. Research Evaluation, 18(2), 143–151. https://doi.org/10.3152/095820209X441808

Teacher Digital Competences in Online Higher Education: A Systematic Literature Review

Renato Moraes[1], Cassio Santos[2], Neuza Pedro[3]

[1] Unidade de Investigação e Desenvolvimento em Educação e Formação (UIDEF), Instituto de Educação, Universidade de Lisboa, Portugal; renatomoraes@edu.ulisboa.pt
[2] Unidade de Investigação e Desenvolvimento em Educação e Formação (UIDEF), Instituto de Educação, Universidade de Lisboa, Portugal; cassiosantos@ie.ulisboa.pt
[3] Unidade de Investigação e Desenvolvimento em Educação e Formação (UIDEF), Instituto de Educação, Universidade de Lisboa, Portugal; nspedro@ie.ulisboa.pt

Correspondence: Renato Moraes: renatomoraes@edu.ulisboa.pt

Abstract:

This systematic literature review (SLR) examines the latest advancements in educational digital competences in higher education from 2020 to 2025, identifying methodologies, tools, and frameworks used to assess instructors' digital competences. Following suggested procedure, 29 studies were selected through a structured search and analysed using textual, thematic, and interpretative methods. Findings highlight the prevalence of quantitative approaches, the role of frameworks like DigCompEdu, TPACK, and others, and the impact of the COVID-19 pandemic in accelerating digital adoption while exposing gaps in teacher readiness and student access. Tools such as DigCompEdu Checkin and flipped classrooms proved effective for engagement and digital competence assessment. Addressing digital competency challenges requires investment in infrastructure, teacher training, and inclusive policies to foster an innovative, equitable, and future-ready education system.

Keywords: digital competences, systematic literature review (SLR), higher education, online teaching, teacher training, digital literacy

Introduction

In an era characterised by rapid digital transformation, the evolution and understanding of digital competences have become a critical area for educators and policymakers alike.

According to Santos (2023), digital competences extend far beyond sheer technical proficiency; they encompass a holistic set of skills that enable individuals to navigate, evaluate, and create content within digital environments effectively. This broader understanding aligns with global frameworks such as the European DigCompEdu Framework (Redecker, 2017), which emphasises technical skills and cognitive, social, and ethical dimensions of digital literacy.

Considering the unprecedented challenges posed by the COVID-19 pandemic, the need for flexible and resilient approaches to teaching and learning became evident. Educators were compelled to adopt digital tools rapidly, more often with inadequate preparation or support, highlighting gaps in their digital readiness. However, this period also catalysed innovation, encouraging educators to rethink traditional pedagogical practices and integrate technology meaningfully into their teaching strategies.

Moreover, the evolution of digital competences reflects broader shifts in educational policies and frameworks designed to address the nowadays demands (European Commission. Joint Research Centre., 2016). Santos (2023) highlights the significance of aligning teachers training programs with contemporary technological advancements, ensuring that future educators are prepared to leverage digital resources effectively. Such alignment fosters a culture of continuous professional development, enabling educators to stay abreast of emerging trends and technologies while addressing the unique needs of diverse learners.

To gain a comprehensive understanding of how recent academic papers address digital competences, including the methodologies and frameworks employed by researchers, as well as their perspectives on the subject, a Systematic Literature Review (SLR) was conducted.

Methodology

SLR is a structured approach to reviewing literature that aims to minimise bias by using explicit methods to perform a comprehensive literature search and critical appraisal of individual studies (Munn et al., 2018; Sarmento, 2024). This process allows researchers to collect, critically evaluate, integrate, and present findings from multiple studies on a specific research question or topic of interest (Smela et al., 2023; Xiao & Watson, 2019). This SLR sought to examine the topic from multiple perspectives and highlight its recent advancements, considering a 5 year-time-scope (between 2020 and 2025).

This study adopts a descriptive approach. This methodological choice aligns with the theoretical perspectives of Creswell and Creswell (2021) and Flick (2023), who emphasise the value of detailed descriptions in achieving a comprehensive and contextualised understanding of the phenomenon being analysed.

Protocol

To ensure greater rigour and transparency in the research process, the Preferred Reporting Items for Systematic Reviews and Meta-Analyses (PRISMA 2020) protocol was adopted. This framework is widely recognised for providing clear guidelines for conducting systematic reviews and meta-analyses (Galvão & Ricarte, 2019; Galvão et al., 2022; Higgins et al., 2024; Page et al., 2021, 2022, 2024).

The PRISMA protocol outlines three key stages in its workflow: Identification, Screening, and Inclusion. During the identification stage, searches can be conducted across one or more databases using Boolean equations (Table 1), supplemented by additional sources such as article bibliographies, to identify potential studies for inclusion in the review. The screening stage consists of two steps. First, the titles and abstracts of identified records were reviewed, and studies deemed irrelevant based on predefined inclusion and exclusion criteria were excluded. In the second step, full texts of the remaining studies were evaluated to determine their eligibility according to the inclusion criteria, with their exclusions documented and justified. At the final stage, studies that met all inclusion criteria were included in the systematic review, and relevant data were extracted for subsequent analysis.

To follow the PRISMA protocol, the identification stage was carried out by searching both Web of Science (WoS) and Scopus databases, on February 24, 2025. Due to each platform's syntax restrictions, two search strategies employed, as table 1 shows.

Table 1: Query strings and fields used for searching different databases

Database: Scopus Fields: Topic (Article, Abstract and Keywords) String: ("digital literacy" OR "computer literacy" OR "technological literacy" OR "digital skills" OR "competências digitais" OR "literacia digital" OR "digital competence" OR "digital competences") AND ("higher education" OR college OR university OR "post-secondary" OR postsecondary OR undergraduate OR graduate) AND ("distance learning" OR "distance education" OR "online learning" OR "on-line learning" OR "online education" OR "online education" OR "on line learning" OR "on line education" OR e-learning) AND (educator OR instructor OR teacher OR lecturer OR academic OR professor) AND (instruments OR tools OR measures OR questionnaires OR scales OR framework) AND NOT (review OR meta-analysis OR revisão)
Database: Web of Science Fields: Topic (Article, Abstract, Keywords plus and author Keywords) String: ("digital literacy" OR "computer literacy" OR "technological literacy" OR "digital skills" OR "competências digitais" OR "literacia digital" OR "digital competence" OR "digital competences") AND ("higher education" OR college OR university OR "post-secondary" OR postsecondary OR undergraduate OR

graduate) AND ("distance learning" OR "distance education" OR "online learning" OR "on-line learning" OR "online education" OR "online education" OR "on line learning" OR "on line education" OR e-learning) AND (educator OR instructor OR teacher OR lecturer OR academic OR professor) AND (instruments OR tools OR measures OR questionnaires OR scales OR framework) NOT (review OR meta-analysis OR revisão)

The selection criteria were determined according to the predefined objective of the SLR, alongside the reasons for excluding each article, ensuring that the research's comprehensiveness was not compromised. Tables 2 and 3 illustrate the inclusion and exclusion criteria developed beforehand and applied during the screening phase.

Table 2: Inclusion Criteria

Code	Criterion	Parameter	Justification
CI-1	Publication Period	After February 24, 2020, and before February 24, 2025	Focuses on recent studies within a 5-year timeframe.
CI-2	Article Type	Scientific Journals	Ensures quality by including only peer-reviewed journal articles.
CI-3	Access	Full Text	Excludes restricted access or oral presentation summaries to ensure completeness of data.
CI-4	Language	Portuguese, English and Spanish	Aligns with EU scientific communication and researcher proficiency.
CI-5	Uniqueness	Unique Articles	Removes duplicates.

Table 3: Exclusion Criteria

Code	Criterion	Justification
CE-1	No focus on teacher participation	Studies not addressing teacher involvement are excluded as the review focuses on teachers' digital competences.
CE-2	No focus on higher education	Only studies within the higher education context are relevant.
CE-3	No focus on online teaching	The review specifically targets online higher education, so unrelated studies are excluded.
CE-4	No assessments conducted	Studies without empirical data are excluded, as the review aims to prioritize investigations with concrete data over theoretical reviews.
CE-5	Not related to digital competences measurement	Studies without any relation to digital competences evaluations are excluded since the review aims to analyse ways of digital competences measurement.

Results

The search strategy in the information source initially identified 800 articles, 262 in WoS and 538 in Scopus. After the initial filtering based on the inclusion criteria (Table 2), this number was reduced to 403 articles (172 in WoS and 231 in Scopus). Next, at the screening stage, both record sets were concatenated to a single set of records to verify and exclude duplicates and further filtering. At this time each article was downloaded and broadly analysed, with the same inclusion criteria applied manually to ensure accuracy, resulting in 287 eligible articles. Subsequently, the exclusion criteria (Table 3) were applied, refining to 29 articles included in this review, as illustrated in Figure 1.

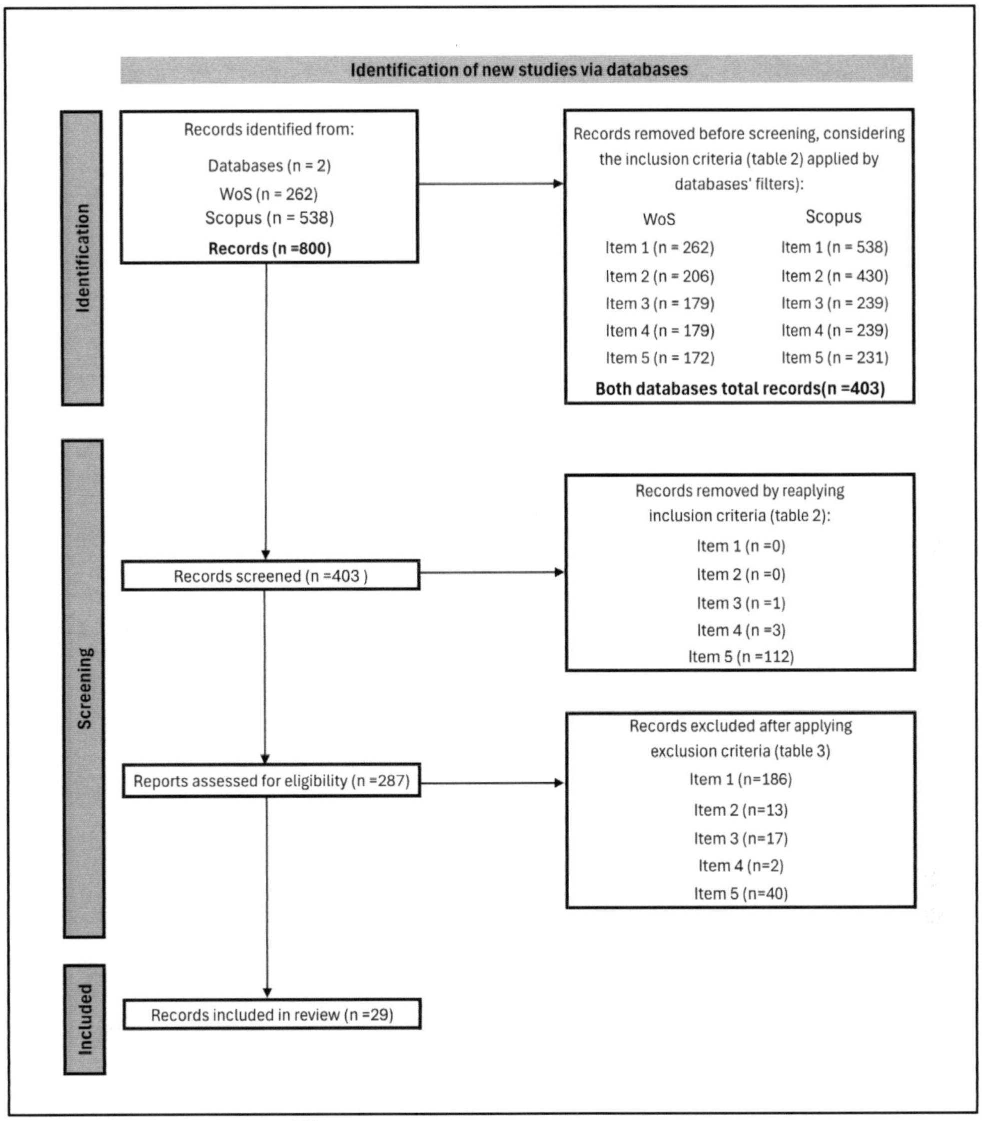

Figure 1: PRISMA 2020 workflow.

After identifying the studies to be included, the relevant data were systematically extracted. Table 4 lists each included article, providing title, authors, language, year of publication, and journal in which it was published.

Table 4: SLR Document Corpus

Code	Title	Author(s)	Journal	Language
1	An investigation of EAP teachers' views and experiences of E-learning technology	Dhillon & Murray (2021)	Education Sciences	English
2	Assessment of digital teaching competences of university professors	Mendez Gijon (2022)	Conrado	English
3	Competências digitais de docentes universitários em tempos de pandemia: análise da autoavaliação Digcompedu	Trindade & Santo (2021)	Práxis Educacional	Portuguese
4	COVID-19 accelerating academic teachers' digital competence in distance teaching	Myyry et al. (2022)	Frontiers in Education	English
5	Currículo FIPAD-TCD: diretrizes iniciais para a reestruturação curricular da formação inicial de professores a distância com base na transversalidade das competências digitais	Silva & Ramos (2024)	Revista Iberoamericana de Educación	Portuguese
6	Digital competence of higher education teachers at a distance learning university in portugal	Moreira et al. (2023)	Computers	English
7	Digital literacy and online course design: Study of Indonesian educators	Stefany & Helmi (2024)	Jurnal Cakrawala Pendidikan	English
8	Digital literacy of teachers within Covid-19	Ibatova & Gromova (2021)	Revista Tempos e Espaços em Educação	English
9	Digital teaching competence of university teachers: levels and teaching typologies	Esteve-Mon et al. (2022)	International Journal of Emerging Technologies in Learning	English
10	Evaluation of digital competence level among educators in UAE Higher education institutions using Digital competence of educators (DigComEdu) framework	Muammar et al. (2023)	Education and Information Technologies	English
11	Examining teachers' satisfaction with the new normal in a disruptive online hospitality, travel, and tourism education system	Chakraborty et al. (2024)	Global Knowledge, Memory and Communication	English
12	Experiences of virtual teaching during COVID-19 in medical institutes of Karachi, Pakistan: teachers' perspective	Azim et al. (2022)	Journal of the Pakistan Medical Association	English
13	Faculty readiness for a digital education model: A self-assessment from health sciences educators	Olivares et al. (2021)	Australasian Journal of Educational Technology	English
14	Influence of knowledge area on the use of digital tools during the COVID-19 pandemic among latin american professors	Antón-Sancho & Sánchez-Calvo (2022)	Education Sciences	English

15	Influence of organizational suport and digital literacy on lecturer acceptance of E-learning in indonesia: a modification of technologi acceptance model	Feriady et al. (2020)	International Journal of Scientific & Technology Research	English
16	La competencia digital del profesorado universitario durante la transición a la enseñanza remota de emergencia	Pérez López & Yuste Tosina (2023)	Revista de Educación a Distancia	Spanish
17	Moderating effects of academic position and computer literacy skills on E-learning portal usage: SEM application on theory of planned behaviour	Mashroofa et al. (2020)	Rupkatha Journal on Interdisciplinary Studies in Humanities	English
18	New challenges in higher education: a study of the digital competence of educators in covid times	Núñez-Canal et al. (2022)	Technological Forecasting and Social Change	English
19	On powerpointers, clickerers, and digital pros: Investigating the initiation of digital learning activities by teachers in higher education	Lohr et al. (2021)	Computers in Human Behavior	English
20	Online education in hungary and armenia during the pandemic and its aftermath	Varga et al. (2024)	International Journal of Instruction	English
21	Perceptions of novice and experienced instructors of translation at selected saudi universities toward technological pedagogical content knowledge for teaching professional development	Alian & Alhaj (2024)	Theory and Practice in Language Studies	English
22	Production of polimedia by university professors and degree of acceptance in the dominican republic	Palacios-Rodríguez et al. (2022)	Revista Electrónica de Investigación Educativa	English
23	Qual a aplicabilidade do Referencial DigCompEdu para o ensino superior online? Um estudo com professores portugueses	Santos & Pedro (2024)	Revista Digital de Investigación en Docencia Universitaria	Portuguese
24	Station rotation model of blended learning in higher education: achieving a balance between online and in-person instruction	Yukhymenko et al. (2024)	Conhecimento & Diversidade	English
25	The impact of gender and years of teaching experience on college teachers' digital competence: an empirical study on teachers in gansu agricultural university	Zhao et al. (2021)	Sustainability	English
26	The massive implementation of ICT in universities and its implications for ensuring SDG 4: challenges and difficulties for professors	Rangel-Pérez et al. (2021)	Sustainability	English
27	The scale of digital competence and utilization of open educational resources (CD-REA): factors associated with competence in bimodal university teachers	Sarango-Lapo et al. (2020)	Revista Ibérica de Sistemas e Tecnologias de Informação	Spanish

28	The use of virtual reality in the countries of the central american bank for economic integration (CABEI)	Antón-Sancho et al., (2024)	Future Internet	English
29	Veterinary teaching in COVID-19 times: perspectives of university teaching staff	Kanwischer et al., (2024)	Frontiers in Veterinary Science	English

As illustrated in Table 4, the 29 studies included were distributed across 27 distinct journals. Notably, 24 articles were written in English, 3 in Portuguese and 2 in Spanish.

Bibliometric analysis

This study employed descriptive statistics to summarise quantitative data, while it used textual, thematic and interpretative analysis (Lakatos & Marconi, 2022; Severino, 2021) to identify emerging themes from qualitative data. This multi-method approach facilitated a deeper understanding of the phenomenon under investigation.

The publication years of the studies presented in Table 4 were reorganised visually in Figure 2 to highlight that the peak number of publications (9 articles) occurred in 2024.

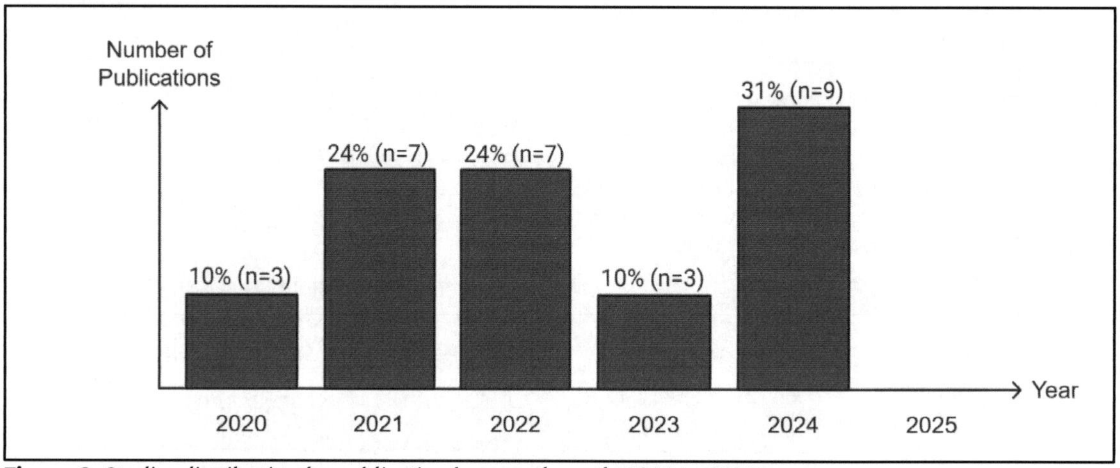

Figure 2: Studies distribution by publication by year, through 2020 to 2025.

The articles included in the review offer a multifaceted view of educators' digital competence in higher education, exploring their experiences with e-learning technologies across diverse contexts and fields. They analyse how factors like institutional support, digital literacy, age, and teaching experience impact the adoption and satisfaction with online teaching. Overall, the articles examine the digital transformation landscape in higher education and the challenges educators face, as clearly shown in Table 5. Note that several authors do not always explicitly differentiate the terms used and "digital skills", "digital competences" or "digital literacy" as well as other similar terms are often taken as synonyms. This study presents the terms used as they are found in the articles.

Table 5: Main objectives and arguments about relevancy of digital competences

Code	General objective	Online education gist
1	To explore the use of technology in English for Academic Purposes teaching and learning, examining specific tools and their impact.	E-learning is a staple of modern education, requiring both teachers and students to have digital literacy skills, while also acknowledging associated benefits and limitations.
2	To evaluate the use of digital tools and teaching strategies in a university setting, focusing on curriculum, assessment, and teacher competence.	Online education integrates theoretical and technological elements to promote teachers' techno-pedagogical knowledge, facilitating flexible and community-based learning.
3	To assess the digital competences of university teachers and inform tailored teacher training, especially in light of the shift to online education during the COVID-19 pandemic.	Online education as both a democratising force, expanding access, and a source of inequality, requiring careful design to address the digital divide and ensure effective learning outcomes.
4	To examine the digital competence of academic teachers during the shift to digital distance learning at the start of the COVID-19 pandemic.	Online education became essential during the COVID-19 pandemic, highlighting the need for teacher training in digital competences to effectively adapt teaching practices and assessment methods to the digital environment.
5	To develop guidelines for distance teacher training emphasising digital competences transversality.	Online education requires a restructuring of teacher training curricula to integrate digital competences, ensuring educators are equipped to effectively use technology in their pedagogical practices.
6	To present the results of a study on the digital competences of teachers at Universidade Aberta in Portugal and to propose a training plan to develop these competences further.	Online education at Universidade Aberta in Portugal requires targeted training to enhance teachers' digital competence in areas like digital resources and assessment to fully leverage the potential of virtual learning environments..
7	To explore the relationship between Indonesian educators' digital literacy and their competence in online course design in higher education.	Online education faces challenges in terms of technological infrastructure and digital literacy skills, with many educators using social media tools instead of more structured online learning platforms, impacting the quality of education.
8	To study the digital competence of teachers and their opinions on integrating ICT into student education, identifying ICT usage, and the level of digitalization in the educational process.	Online education is discussed in the context of the digital literacy of teachers and the implementation of ICT, highlighting the need to modernise the learning process and the importance of digital competence for educators.

9	To explore university teachers' digital teaching competence using a new self-perception assessment questionnaire.	Online education requires teachers to develop digital teaching competence, focusing on aspects like professional engagement, digital resources, teaching and learning, assessment, empowering learners, and facilitating their digital competence, while also acknowledging the diverse digital profiles of university teachers and the need for contextualized training
10	To investigate the digital competences of educators in United Arab Emirates universities.	Online education has become crucial due to the COVID-19 pandemic, which has accelerated the use of technology and digital literacy, forcing educators to adapt and develop new skills to meet the demands of online teaching, including communication, delivery of lectures, and exam preparation.
11	The source examines factors influencing teacher satisfaction with online teaching, particularly during the COVID-19 pandemic, and aims to investigate the relationship between perceived organisational support and online teaching satisfaction.	Online education became ubiquitous as a consequence of the COVID-19 pandemic, leading to an abrupt transition with challenges for both teachers and students, and requiring adaptation to digital platforms.
12	To evaluate the experiences of medical faculty with virtual teaching during COVID-19.	Online education has been restructured from asynchronous to almost complete synchronization, with faculty members using online platforms to deliver lectures.
13	To assess educators' digital skills and adapt training programs in response to the COVID-19 pandemic, with the long-term potential to inform recruitment and development in higher education.	The source argues that online education offers flexibility and affordability but requires significant resources to replicate face-to-face tasks and address challenges like motivation and technical support.
14	The objectives are to analyse the pandemic's impact on Latin American professors' ICT usage, identify specific ICT tools with increased usage, and study gaps in ICT usage frequency among professors of different knowledge areas.	The sources discuss online education in terms of its rapid digitisation, impact during the COVID-19 pandemic, and use of ICT to enhance learning, including teachers' digital competences and students' self-regulated learning, with some focusing on specific tools and methodologies.
15	To explore the factors influencing lecturers' acceptance of E-learning in Indonesian universities by modifying the Technology Acceptance Model (TAM) with organizational support and digital literacy.	Online education is seen as a key effort to improve the quality of higher education, particularly through blended learning, and is growing rapidly in Indonesia.
16	To assess the digital competence of university teaching staff during the transition to emergency remote teaching.	The source argues that the transition to Emergency Remote Teaching due to the pandemic highlighted deficits in university systems, particularly regarding digital competence of teaching staff.

17	The objective is to investigate the moderating effect of academic position and computer literacy on E-learning portal usage among academics, using the Theory of Planned Behaviour.	Online learning usage is influenced by behavioural intention and perceived behavioural control, with attitude and subjective norm also playing a role, but pedagogy, cultural factors, and user-friendliness of the systems need more attention.
18	To analyse the geographical dispersion of teaching staff, assess digital competence in higher education and explore the impact of ICT in pedagogy.	Online education encompasses various models like web-based and blended learning, with a shift to online accelerated by the COVID-19 crisis but now evolving into hybrid models combining remote and in-person learning.
19	To investigate factors related to digital learning activities in higher education, including institutional, personal, and teaching setting variables.	Online courses might be a setting for a high level of digital learning activities, but variability in teaching settings exists.
20	To present higher education from the instructors' point of view, focusing on online education, digital competences, platforms, and experience, detailing advantages, disadvantages, and difficulties.	Online education is presented as a response to the pandemic, utilising digital technology to deliver content, with benefits like increased participation, but also challenges such as educators' inexperience and the need for digital skills.
21	To investigate translation instructors' perceptions of their technological, pedagogical, and content knowledge (TPACK) in Saudi Arabian universities.	Integrating technology into education, specifically for translation instructors in Saudi universities, enhances professional development by improving teaching methods and techniques.
22	To explore the uses and acceptance of Polimedia productions in university education, particularly in the Dominican Republic.	Online education, particularly through videos in MOOCs and flipped classrooms, is seen as a valuable tool for delivering content, assessing students, and teaching practical skills.
23	To validate the DigCompEdu's core competences in the context of online higher education teaching.	DigCompEdu framework is generally applicable to online higher education, though some specific digital competence areas for learners receive less emphasis from Portuguese instructors.
24	To empirically test the effectiveness of the station rotation model in a blended learning format, based on a survey of university teachers in Ukraine.	Online education is seen as increasingly relevant due to digitalisation, with digital technologies playing an important role in ensuring the effectiveness of innovative learning environments.
25	To describe in-service teachers' self-perceptions of digital competence and analyse the impact of gender and age on this.	Online education is experiencing a fast transition with technical support, but teacher training shortcomings have emerged, especially regarding digital competence.

26	To demonstrate how Spanish professors are working towards Sustainable Development Goal 4 (quality education), identifying opportunities for ICT implementation in higher education.	Online education has presented challenges and opportunities, including increased effort and exhaustion, but also the development of new skills and greater understanding, while highlighting the digital divide's impact on equal access.
27	To identify factors associated with digital competence in university teachers using open educational resources.	Digital competence is an important factor in the use of open educational resources among bimodal university teachers.
28	To analyse Latin American university professors' assessments of Virtual Reality (VR) technology for didactic use.	Supranational economic alliances like Central American Bank for Economic Integration positively impact digitisation in higher education, but that the impact on specific VR technology use is minimal, creating inequalities between private and public universities.
29	To investigate the implementation and impact of digital teaching in veterinary medicine at the University of Veterinary Medicine Hannover.	Blended learning, combining online and in-person teaching, is seen as offering advantages like flexibility and increased student engagement, potentially improving motivation and learning outcomes.

Final remarks

This analysis examines the evolution of digital competence among educators, focusing on three key phases: pre-pandemic, pandemic, and post-pandemic.

Before the pandemic, the significance of digital skills for educators was already established in academic literature. Studies highlighted the need to integrate digital competencies into teaching (Myyry et al., 2022; Núñez-Canal et al., 2022; Rangel-Pérez et al., 2021). This period saw the development of frameworks and assessment tools such as DigCompEdu, which provided a background for identifying educators' level of digital proficiency (Moreira et al., 2023; Santos & Pedro, 2024). Self-assessment instruments like DigCompEdu CheckIn further supported professional growth by allowing educators to evaluate and enhance their digital skills (Santos & Pedro, 2024).

The COVID-19 pandemic marked a turning point, accelerating digital adoption in higher education. Institutions worldwide shifted abruptly to remote teaching, forcing educators to rapidly enhance their digital competencies (Myyry et al., 2022; Núñez-Canal et al., 2022). While some adapted effectively, others struggled with insufficient training, inadequate digital literacy, and inequitable access to technology (Azim et al., 2022). Virtual classrooms, assessment platforms, and collaborative tools became essential teaching resources (Gijon, 2022; Muammar et al., 2023). However, disparities emerged, with disciplinary differences influencing digital tool adoption (Antón-Sancho & Sánchez-Calvo, 2022; Esteve-Mon et al., 2022). Geographical and institutional variations further shaped digital adaptation, as highlighted by comparative studies across Portugal, Finland, Spain, Indonesia, the UAE, Pakistan, Latin America, and Saudi Arabia (Azim et al., 2022; Myyry et al., 2022; Stefany & Helmi, 2024; Trindade & Santo, 2021).

Post-pandemic, the focus has shifted to evaluating and refining digital competencies. Studies continue to assess proficiency levels, identifying areas for improvement (Gijon, 2022; Moreira et al., 2023). Autonomy in digital learning environments has become a key theme, with methodologies such as gamification and problem-based learning gaining traction (Muammar et al., 2023; Silva & Ramos, 2024). Researchers are also exploring innovative assessment models suited to online education (Gijon, 2022; Muammar et al., 2023). Emerging technologies, particularly virtual reality (VR), are now being examined for their potential applications in higher education (Antón-Sancho et al., 2024).

A dominant theme across studies is the evaluation and development of educators' digital competence, frequently assessed through self-perception measures and structured frameworks such as DigCompEdu (Santos

& Pedro, 2024; Trindade & Santo, 2021). Researchers have explored how digital competence varies across disciplines/subjects, geographical locations, and academic hierarchies, revealing persistent gaps in ICT proficiency and pedagogical integration (López & Tosina, 2023; Moreira et al., 2023). The need for contextualised and discipline-specific training has emerged as a crucial insight, particularly in highly specialised fields such as veterinary medicine (Kanwischer et al., 2024) and medical education (Azim et al., 2022).

Recent research highlights that digital competence extends beyond technical skills to include strategic technology integration, contextual adaptation of Open Educational Resources (OERs), and critical information literacy development (Mendez Gijon; Sarango-Lapo et al.). Self-assessment plays a crucial role in identifying areas for ongoing professional development, reinforcing lifelong learning among educators (Moreira et al., 2023; Muammar et al., 2023; Trindade & Santo, 2021).

The shift towards online and hybrid models has necessitated significant curricular reconfiguration to embed digital literacy and ensure pedagogical effectiveness (Silva & Ramos, 2024; Yukhymenko et al., 2024). Studies advocate for a transversal integration of digital competences across teacher training programmes, moving beyond isolated workshops towards a systemic reorganisation of instructional methodologies (Santos & Pedro, 2024). Moreover, research underscores the importance of aligning digital tools with pedagogical objectives, facilitating student engagement and adaptive learning pathways (Muammar et al., 2023; Silva & Ramos, 2024).

Beyond individual competence, institutional and organisational structures play a pivotal role in facilitating digital transformation. Studies indicate that educators' acceptance of e-learning is significantly influenced by organisational support, professional development opportunities, and digital infrastructure (Feriady et al., 2020; Muammar et al., 2023).

Research also highlights that faculty members with prior experience in distance learning demonstrate greater proficiency in digital integration (Myyry et al., 2022), while those with limited exposure require substantial institutional support. Additionally, age and experience influence digital competency levels, with younger faculty members and those in technology-intensive disciplines exhibiting higher proficiency levels (Moreira et al., 2023; Trindade & Santo, 2021; Zhao et al., 2021).

The implementation of ICT in higher education has been framed both as a catalyst for innovation and a source of inequality (Rangel-Pérez et al., 2021; Sarango-Lapo et al., 2020). While online education has expanded access to learning opportunities, it has also exacerbated disparities in digital access, competence, and engagement (Dhillon & Murray, 2021; Trindade & Santo, 2021). Studies on gender, age, and academic position indicate that younger faculty members and those with prior exposure to technology tend to adapt more readily to digital environments (Zhao et al., 2021).

The literature brought by the SLR on digital competence and online education reveals a multifaceted landscape, shaped by institutional structures, pedagogical strategies, technological access, and disciplinary variations.

In short, integrating digital competences has improved educational practices, aligning them with contemporary demands. Continued research into digital methodologies and educational models is essential for reducing inequalities and fostering a more innovative, inclusive, and future-ready education system.

Funding Information

This work was supported by National Funds through FCT-Portuguese Foundation for Science and Technology, I.P., under the scope of UIDEF - Unidade de Investigação e Desenvolvimento em Educação e Formação, UIDB/04107/2020, https://doi.org/10.54499/UIDB/04107/2020.

References

Alian, E. M. I., & Alhaj, A. A. M. (2024). Perceptions of novice and experienced instructors of translation at selected saudi universities toward technological pedagogical content knowledge for teaching professional development. Theory and Practice in Language Studies, 14(3), 844–853. https://doi.org/10.17507/tpls.1403.27

Antón-Sancho, Á., Fernández-Arias, P., Ariza, E. A., & Vergara, D. (2024). The use of virtual reality in the countries of the central american bank for economic integration (CABEI). Future Internet, 16(7), 249. https://doi.org/10.3390/fi16070249

Antón-Sancho, Á., & Sánchez-Calvo, M. (2022). Influence of knowledge area on the use of digital tools during the COVID-19 pandemic among latin american professors. Education Sciences, 12(9), 635. https://doi.org/10.3390/educsci12090635

Azim, S. R., Nisar, M., Baig, M., Azfar, S. M., Azim, S. N., & Anwar, A. (2022). Experiences of virtual teaching during COVID-19 in medical institutes of Karachi, Pakistan: Teachers' perspective. Journal of the Pakistan Medical Association. https://doi.org/10.47391/JPMA.4849

Chakraborty, T., Bhandari, H., & Mittal, A. (2024). Examining teachers' satisfaction with the new normal in a disruptive online hospitality, travel, and tourism education system. Global Knowledge, Memory and Communication, 73(6/7), 720–737. https://doi.org/10.1108/GKMC-04-2022-0095

Creswell, J., & Creswell, J. D. (2021). Projeto de pesquisa: Métodos qualitativo, quantitativo e misto (5ª, Issue 5). Penso.

Dhillon, S., & Murray, N. (2021). An Investigation of EAP Teachers' Views and Experiences of E-Learning Technology. Education Sciences, 11(2), 54. https://doi.org/10.3390/educsci11020054

Esteve-Mon, F. M., Llopis-Nebot, M. Á., Viñoles-Cosentino, V., & Adell-Segura, J. (2022). Digital teaching competence of university teachers: Levels and teaching typologies. International Journal of Emerging Technologies in Learning (iJET), 17(13), 200–216. https://doi.org/10.3991/ijet.v17i13.24345

European Commission. Joint Research Centre. (2016). DigComp 2.0: The digital competence framework for citizens. Publications Office. https://data.europa.eu/doi/10.2791/11517

Feriady, M., Nurkhin, A., Mahmud, N., Setiani, R., & Astuti, D. P. (2020). Influence of organizational suport and digital literacy on lecturer acceptance of E-learning in indonesia: A modification of technologi acceptance model. INTERNATIONAL JOURNAL OF SCIENTIFIC & TECHNOLOGY RESEARCH, 9(1), 2229. https://www.ijstr.org/final-print/jan2020/Influence-Of-Organizational-Suport-And-Digital-Literacy-On-Lecturer-Acceptance-Of-E-learning-In-Indonesia-A-Modification-Of-Technologi-Acceptance-Model.pdf

Flick, U. (2023). An introduction to qualitative research (7th edition). SAGE.

Galvão, & Ricarte, I. L. M. (2019). Revisão sistemática da literatura: Conceituação, produção e publicação. Logeion: Filosofia Da Informação, 6(1), 57–73. https://doi.org/10.21728/logeion.2019v6n1.p57-73

Galvão, T. F., Tiguman, G. M. B., & Sarkis-Onofre, R. (2022). A declaração PRISMA 2020 em português: Recomendações atualizadas para o relato de revisões sistemáticas. Epidemiologia e Serviços de Saúde, 31(2), e2022364. https://doi.org/10.1590/ss2237-9622202200011

Gijon, F. M. (2022). Assessment of digital teaching competencies of university professors. Conrado, 18(89), 289–298. http://scielo.sld.cu/scielo.php?script=sci_abstract&pid=S1990-86442022000600289&lng=es&nrm=iso&tlng=es

Higgins, J., Thomas, J., Chandler J, Cumpston, M., Li, T., Page, M., & Welch VA (Eds.). (2024). Cochrane handbook for systematic reviews of interventions version 6.5 (updated august 2024). Cochrane. https://training.cochrane.org/handbook/current

Ibatova, A. Z., & Gromova, A. V. (2021). Digital literacy of teachers within Covid-19. Revista Tempos e Espaços Em Educação, 14(33), e16853. https://doi.org/10.20952/revtee.v14i33.16853

Kanwischer, M., Tipold, A., & Schaper, E. (2024). Veterinary teaching in COVID-19 times: Perspectives of university teaching staff. Frontiers in Veterinary Science, 11, 1386978. https://doi.org/10.3389/fvets.2024.1386978

Lakatos, E. M., & Marconi, M. (2022). Fundamentos de Metodologia Científica (9th ed.). Editora Atlas Ltda.

Lohr, A., Stadler, M., Schultz-Pernice, F., Chernikova, O., Sailer, M., Fischer, F., & Sailer, M. (2021). On powerpointers, clickerers, and digital pros: Investigating the initiation of digital learning activities by teachers in higher education. Computers in Human Behavior, 119, 106715. https://doi.org/10.1016/j.chb.2021.106715

López, E. P., & Tosina, R. Y. (2023). La competencia digital del profesorado universitario durante la transición a la enseñanza remota de emergencia. Revista de Educación a Distancia (RED), 23(72). https://doi.org/10.6018/red.540121

Mashroofa, M. M., Haleem, A., & Jahufer, A. (2020). Moderating effects of academic position and computer literacy skills on E-learning portal usage: SEM application on theory of planned behaviour. Rupkatha Journal on Interdisciplinary Studies in Humanities, 12(4). https://doi.org/10.21659/rupkatha.v12n4.18

Moreira, J. A., Nunes, C. S., & Casanova, D. (2023). Digital competence of higher education teachers at a distance learning university in portugal. Computers, 12(9), 169. https://doi.org/10.3390/computers12090169

Muammar, S., Hashim, K. F. B., & Panthakkan, A. (2023). Evaluation of digital competence level among educators in UAE higher education institutions using digital competence of educators (DigComEdu) framework. Education and Information Technologies, 28(3), 2485–2508. https://doi.org/10.1007/s10639-022-11296-x

Munn, Z., Peters, M. D. J., Stern, C., Tufanaru, C., McArthur, A., & Aromataris, E. (2018). Systematic review or scoping review? Guidance for authors when choosing between a systematic or scoping review approach. BMC Medical Research Methodology, 18(1), 143. https://doi.org/10.1186/s12874-018-0611-x

Myyry, L., Kallunki, V., Katajavuori, N., Repo, S., Tuononen, T., Anttila, H., Kinnunen, P., Haarala-Muhonen, A., & Pyörälä, E. (2022). COVID-19 accelerating academic teachers' digital competence in distance teaching. Frontiers in Education, 7, 770094. https://doi.org/10.3389/feduc.2022.770094

Núñez-Canal, M., De Obesso, M. D. L. M., & Pérez-Rivero, C. A. (2022). New challenges in higher education: A study of the digital competence of educators in covid times. Technological Forecasting and Social Change, 174, 121270. https://doi.org/10.1016/j.techfore.2021.121270

Olivares, S. L. O., Lopez, M., Martinez, R., Nigenda Alvarez, J. P., & Valdez-García, J. E. (2021). Faculty readiness for a digital education model: A self-assessment from health sciences educators. Australasian Journal of Educational Technology, 37(5), 116–127. https://doi.org/10.14742/ajet.7105

Page, M. J., McKenzie, J., Bossuyt, P., Boutron, I., Hoffman, T., Mulrow, C., Shamseer, L., Tetzlaff, L., Akl, E., Brennan, S., Chou, R., Glanville, J., Grimshaw, J., Hrobjartsson, A., Lalu, M., Li, T., Loder, E., Mayo-Wilson, E., McDonald, S., ... Moher, D. (2024). Declaração PRISMA 2020: Uma diretriz atualizada para publicação de revisões sistemáticas. https://doi.org/10.5281/ZENODO.13271469

Page, M. J., McKenzie, J. E., Bossuyt, P. M., Boutron, I., Hoffmann, T. C., Mulrow, C. D., Shamseer, L., Tetzlaff, J. M., Akl, E. A., Brennan, S. E., Chou, R., Glanville, J., Grimshaw, J. M., Hróbjartsson, A., Lalu, M. M., Li, T., Loder, E. W., Mayo-Wilson, E., McDonald, S., ... Moher, D. (2021). The PRISMA 2020 statement: An updated guideline for reporting systematic reviews. BMJ, n71. https://doi.org/10.1136/bmj.n71

Page, M. J., McKenzie, J. E., Bossuyt, P. M., Boutron, I., Hoffmann, T. C., Mulrow, C. D., Shamseer, L., Tetzlaff, J. M., Akl, E. A., Brennan, S. E., Chou, R., Glanville, J., Grimshaw, J. M., Hróbjartsson, A., Lalu, M. M., Li, T., Loder, E. W., Mayo-Wilson, E., McDonald, S., ... Moher, D. (2022). A declaração PRISMA 2020: Diretriz atualizada para relatar revisões sistemáticas. Revista Panamericana de Salud Pública, 46, 1. https://doi.org/10.26633/RPSP.2022.112

Palacios-Rodríguez, A., Cabero-Almenara, J., & Puentes-Puente, Á. (2022). Production of Polimedia by University Professors and Degree of Acceptance in the Dominican Republic. Revista Electrónica de Investigación Educativa, 24, 1–17. https://doi.org/10.24320/redie.2021.24.e11.4366

Rangel-Pérez, C., Gato-Bermúdez, M.-J., Musicco-Nombela, D., & Ruiz-Alberdi, C. (2021). The massive implementation of ICT in universities and its implications for ensuring SDG 4: Challenges and difficulties for professors. Sustainability, 13(22), 12871. https://doi.org/10.3390/su132212871

Redecker, C. (2017). European framework for the digital competence of educators: DigCompEdu. https://www.doi.org/10.2760/159770

Santos, C. (2023). Desenvolvimento do E-DigCompEdu: Quadro de referência das competências digitais docentes do ensino superior online [Tese de Doutoramento, Universidade de Lisboa]. https://repositorio.ul.pt/handle/10451/58016

Santos, C., & Pedro, N. (2024). Qual a aplicabilidade do Referencial DigCompEdu para o ensino superior online? Um estudo com professores portugueses. Revista Digital de Investigación en Docencia Universitaria, 18(1), e1816. https://doi.org/10.19083/ridu.2024.1816

Sarango-Lapo, C. P., Mena, J., Ramírez-Montoya, M.-S., & Real, E. (2020). The scale of digital competence and utilization of open educational resources (CD-REA): Factors associated with competence in bimodal university teachers; [La escala de competencia digital y uso de recursos educativos abiertos (CD-REA): Factores asociados a la competencia de los docentes universitarios bimodales]. In RISTI - Revista Iberica de Sistemas e Tecnologias de Informacao (566; Vol. 2020, Issue E28, pp. 545–558). https://www.scopus.com/inward/record.uri?eid=2-s2.0-85080998464&partnerID=40&md5=a7521486594f23636b9ef33d1e18d103

Sarmento, H. (with Saavedra, N. O., & Rosado, A.). (2024). Revisão Sistemática da Literatura. Universidade do Estado do Rio Grande do Norte - Edições UERN.

Severino, A. (2021). Metodologia do trabalho científico (24th ed.). Cortez Editora.

Silva, G. A. D., & Ramos, D. K. (2024). Currículo FIPAD-TCD: Diretrizes iniciais para a reestruturação curricular da formação inicial de professores a distância com base na transversalidade das competências digitais. Revista Iberoamericana de Educación, 95(1), 73–91. https://doi.org/10.35362/rie9516297

Smela, B., Toumi, M., Świerk, K., Francois, C., Biernikiewicz, M., Clay, E., & Boyer, L. (2023). Rapid literature review: Definition and methodology. Journal of Market Access & Health Policy, 11(1), 2241234. https://doi.org/10.1080/20016689.2023.2241234

Stefany, S., & Helmi, J. (2024). Digital literacy and online course design: Study of Indonesian educators. Jurnal Cakrawala Pendidikan, 43(3), Article 3. https://doi.org/10.21831/cp.v43i3.71403

Trindade, S. D., & Santo, E. D. E. (2021). Competências digitais de docentes universitários em tempos de pandemia: Análise da autoavaliação Digcompedu. Práxis Educacional, 17(45), 1–17. https://doi.org/10.22481/praxisedu.v17i45.8336

Varga, E., Hambardzumyan, G., & Juhász, T. (2024). Online education in hungary and armenia during the pandemic and its aftermath. International Journal of Instruction, 17(4), 289–306. https://doi.org/10.29333/iji.2024.17417a

Xiao, Y., & Watson, M. (2019). Guidance on Conducting a Systematic Literature Review. Journal of Planning Education and Research, 39(1), 93–112. https://doi.org/10.1177/0739456X17723971

Yukhymenko, V., Borysova, S., Bazyl, O., Hubal, H., & Barkar, U. (2024). Station rotation model of blended learning in higher education: Achieving a balance between online and in-person instruction [Modelo de rotação de estações de aprendizagem em banda no ensino superior: Alcançar um equilíbrio entre o ensino em linha e presencial]. Conhecimento & Diversidade, 16(41), 182–202. https://doi.org/10.18316/rcd.v16i41.11434

Zhao, Y., Pinto Llorente, A. M., Sánchez Gómez, M. C., & Zhao, L. (2021). The impact of gender and years of teaching experience on college teachers' digital competence: An empirical study on teachers in gansu agricultural university. Sustainability, 13(8), 4163. https://doi.org/10.3390/su13084163

Transforming Assessment Mindsets: Professional development in early English language education through a blended MOOC and an online community of practice

António Moreira Teixeira[1], João Paz[2], Sandie Mourão[3], Maria João Spilker[4], Paula Cardoso[5], Ana Paula Rocha[6]

[1] Laboratório de Educação a Distância e eLearning, Universidade Aberta, Portugal: Antonio.Teixeira@uab.pt
[2] Laboratório de Educação a Distância e eLearning, Universidade Aberta, Portugal: joao.paz@uab.pt
[3] Centre for English, Translation, and Anglo-Portuguese Studies, Nova University of Lisbon, Portugal; sandramourao@fcsh.unl.pt
[4] Laboratório de Educação a Distância e eLearning, Universidade Aberta, Portugal: maria.spilker@uab.pt
[5] Laboratório de Educação a Distância e eLearning, Universidade Aberta & Polytechnic University of Leiria, Portugal: paula.cardoso@ipleiria.pt
[6] Laboratório de Educação a Distância e eLearning, Universidade Aberta, Portugal: ana.rocha@uab.pt

Correspondence: António Moreira Teixeira: Antonio.Teixeira@uab.pt

Abstract:

The Transforming Assessment Mindsets (TAM) project aims both to research and support teacher training in the real-world context of professional development (PD) in early English language education using a blended Massive Open Online Course (bMOOC). The use of technology in teachers' PD is recognised as being effective and meaningful and bMOOCs have the potential to widen participation and disseminate innovation. Additionally, bMOOCs associated with online or virtual communities of practice (vCoPs) have been shown to reduce professional isolation, foster engagement and result in higher rates of course completion. The bMOOC Classroom-based assessment in primary English education has been developed with a learning environment design that follows adult learning theories, combining cognitivist and social learning with socio-constructivism and is directed to Portuguese Primary English Teachers. This paper presents the results of the first iteration cycle analysing the pre-bMOOC survey and post-bMOOC survey replies with a focus on the content and structure of the bMOOC. These show general satisfaction with the course but also point out some dimensions that should be enhanced in further iterations, as the navigation and orientation through the different online spaces of the online environment. One major additional finding is that participants reported using regularly Gen AI-supported tools for fine tuning their writings, finding further information and summarising responses

Keywords: Blended Massive Open Online Course, Community of Practice, Assessment on Primary English Teaching, Teacher Training

Introduction

The Transforming Assessment Mindsets (TAM) project explores a holistic approach to professional development (PD) in early English language education by combining research with teacher education in a real-world context. This is conducted through the development of a blended Massive Open Online Course (bMOOC) integrated with an online or virtual community of practice (vCoP). The use of technology in teachers' PD is recognised as being effective and meaningful and bMOOCs have the potential to widen participation and disseminate innovation. When associated with vCoPs, bMOOCs have been shown to reduce professional isolation, foster engagement and result in higher rates of course completion. The bMOOC Classroom-based assessment in primary English education has been developed with a learning environment design that follows adult learning theories, combining cognitivist and social learning with socio-constructivism and is directed at Primary English Teachers (PETs) in Portugal. The rationale supporting its structure and content is the assumption that teacher education works best by focusing on practice supported by meta-cognition, so the bMOOC alternates modules of theory and practice for PETs to engage with theory then plan for, implement, and reflect on mini-classroom-based interventions. The bMOOC includes features typical of a formal online learning experience, e.g. videos of good practice, examples of resources, peer assessment and e-portfolios and task structures are interactive, practical and exploratory and supported by reflection.

The TAM-bMOOC project responds to an identified need in PE teachers' PD. The planned educational innovation using a bMOOC and follow-up facilitated CoP will contribute to transforming teaching and learning cultures and contribute to improved knowledge around PETs' classroom-based assessment practices, PD MOOCs and CoPs in language education. The bMOOC thus creates novel conditions for learning that theory suggests might be productive but presently are not common or well understood. The project aims to investigate the effectiveness of the instructional design features of the bMOOC to stimulate a change in mindsets and classroom practices and to foster the development of a community of practice. The project has the following main Research Questions:

- RQ1: How does the participation in the bMOOC and follow-up CoPs influence teachers' CbA practices and combat their professional isolation?
- RQ2: What is an optimal design for a bMOOC to support PE teachers' professional development in assessment literacy and how can the follow-up CoP also contribute to combating professional isolation?

In this paper we present the theoretical background for the research, describe the development and structure of the course, as well as the methods used to collect data, and discuss the main results related to the content and structure of the bMOOC so far.

Theoretical Background

Classroom-based assessment (CbA) is seen as "principled ways of collecting and using evidence on the quality and quantity of people's learning" (Rixon & Prošić-Santovac 2019, p. 1). Regarding early language learning (ELL), traditional assessment methods associated with tests are considered problematic because they do not contemplate attitudinal and motivation goals, oral skills, or intercultural communicative competence. Assessment practices have not accompanied the introduction of English at earlier ages, and assessment remains troublesome (Rixon & Prošić-Santovac 2019). This is due to inadequate planning during policy implementation, assessment being at odds with the playful, oral-based approaches of ELL programmes and the influence of general education which overlooks the specificities of ELL (Mourão, et al.,2021). Teachers play a crucial role in the decision-making process which impacts on CbA, and improved assessment literacy can overcome negative mindsets towards assessment amongst teachers and stakeholders (Papp, 2019). Despite being one of the most relevant aspects of teacher education, it has been a pressing issue for decades and teachers continue to require a deeper understanding of "the purposes of and social role of assessment in education" and to grasp "the link between various assessment purposes, tools or instruments, methods and the curriculum" (Papp, 2019, p. 400). Research in Portugal (Mourão et al., 2025) has identified an incongruence between teaching and learning goals in PETs' CbA practices, which is confounded by an absence of training in assessment, misunderstanding learning outcomes, traditional cultures of assessment and professional isolation (Mourão et al., 2021). Recommendations highlight the need for an effective, nationwide intervention to upgrade the assessment literacy of Portuguese PETs that changes mindsets and CbA practices and counters professional isolation.

Effective professional development in ELL should combine practice-related tasks and reflection, experimentation and dialogue to increase awareness of the theory-practice nexus and support the development of action plans for future practice (Rich 2019). Effective PD is content focused; incorporates active learning; supports collaboration; uses models of effective practice; provides coaching and expert support; offers feedback and reflection and is of sustained duration (Darling-Hammond et al., 2019).

Massive Open Online Courses (MOOCs) have the potential to widen participation and disseminate pedagogical innovation (Teixeira et al., 2015). Richer MOOC design approaches, such as the iMOOC (Teixeira et al., 2013) which is inspired by the connectivist theory approach, make full use of networking and task-based approaches together with other features typical of a formal online learning experience, and consider many of the above-mentioned effective PD features in their equitable learning environments. These MOOCs combine "autonomous and self-directed learning with a strong social dimension and the interaction that make learning experiences richer and more rewarding" (Teixeira et al., 2015, p. 146). MOOCs are relatively under-researched for PD (Orsini-Jones et al., 2018), yet they have proven to enhance pedagogical knowledge, improve classroom practices, promote collaborative learning and contribute to continuous PD (Teixeira et al., 2018). They facilitate peer exchange, contribute to building a community, involve peer review activities, use content as a trigger for learning through reflection, sharing and exchange, facilitate transfer to practice and are flexible (Herz et al., 2021). Of particular interest to the development of the TAM-bMOOC are the short videos, with demonstrations of assessment practices which develop capacities of noticing and reflection in teacher participants (Marsh & Mitchell, 2014). Additionally, as approaches to assessment in MOOCs are formative and involve peer-assessment this allows for "a reverberation between process and content" (Woodward, 2003, p. 303) in PD that targets assessment literacy. In hybrid or blended MOOCs, their association with communities of practice (CoPs) (Wenger et al., 2002), have been shown to combat professional isolation, foster engagement and result in higher rates of course completion (Hertz et al., 2021).

CoPs are communities of practitioners who support each other in learning to develop their craft – they involve the establishment of mutual engagement, a joint enterprise and the building of a shared repertoire (Wenger et al, 2002). The technological affordances of a MOOC can sow the seeds for the start of such a community (Jones et al., 2016), which can further develop and grow once the MOOC has been completed. Trust and Horrocks (2019) make recommendations for the sustainability of (blended) CoPs, that start with organizational support, and include leadership roles, personalized learning, guiding principles, social learning and purpose. A clear structure that facilitates the move from sensemaking towards critical reflective learning with the support of administrators, teacher educators and or researchers has shown to be influential in educational contexts (Ng & Tan, 2009). Fostering a safe environment for 'sharing, daring and support' (Hadar & Brody, 2010, p. 1649) in CoPs contributes to breaking isolation and reinforcing professional identity, which is central to teacher development.

Development and Structure of the bMOOC

The bMOOC Classroom-Based Assessment in Primary English Education was developed in response to challenges identified in a nationwide study about assessment practices in primary English teaching in Portuguese schools (Moreira et al, 2021). English became part of the primary curriculum in 2015, but most primary English teachers are requalified secondary teachers with limited training in age-appropriate pedagogy. Their classroom practices rely heavily on summative assessment and focus primarily on reading and writing, disregarding national guidelines that emphasize formative approaches and the development of listening and speaking skills. The fact that many of these teachers are professionally isolated, lacking opportunities for collaborative learning or professional dialogue, is also a relevant factor.

To address these issues, the bMOOC was designed as a real-world intervention to support teachers' professional development in a scalable and flexible way. As a closed 50-hour course each edition is planned for the participation of 150 primary English teachers accompanied by 10 teacher educators as online facilitators. Grounded in adult learning theory, the bMOOC integrates cognitivist, social, and socio-constructivist principles. Its aim is to enhance formative assessment literacy among primary English teachers while fostering reflective, practice-oriented learning in a supportive online community.

Consisting of nine modules, it begins with an introductory Bootcamp, followed by a foundational module on classroom-based assessment. The next six modules are grouped into three pairs, each focusing on a different oral skill: listening, spoken production, or spoken interaction. Each pair includes a theory module—where teachers explore relevant pedagogical and assessment concepts—and a practice module—where they plan, implement, and reflect on a classroom-based activity. Interactive tasks, good-practice videos, activity and assessment tool models, peer feedback, guided reflection, and collaborative discussions are integral to each phase (Darling-Hammond et al., 2019). The final module supports participants in preparing for future changes through action planning (Rich 2019).

The course is delivered via two integrated platforms: a traditional xMOOC platform (Open Edx) on NAU and a Community Platform (developed in WordPress). This dual structure supports both content delivery through the NAU platform and the development of an online community of practice, enabling sustained professional engagement beyond the course itself on the Community Platform – where the forums were placed. A third platform, Padlet, ensures that teachers have a structured space for their e-portfolios which are part of the assessment process, necessary for the course to be accredited for career progression.

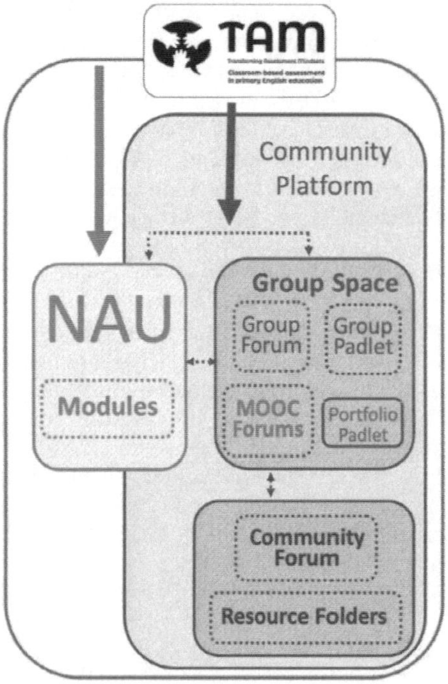

Figure 1: The TAM bMOOC ecosystem (https://www.tambmooc.com/the-tam-bmooc-ecosystem)

Method

Applying a design-based research (DBR) methodology that is highly relevant in an educational context where authentic, real-world interventions aim at changing practice, the TAM-bMOOC project encompasses the inter-relationships of theory, designed artifacts, and practice. The iterative DBR cycle, that includes i) enactment in context, ii) analysis and iii) redesign, will take place in 3 iterative intervention cycles over approximately 2 years. Each cycle is an 8 week-long enactment in context (the bMOOC intervention) and 16 weeks of analysis and redesign (total 6 months). The TAM-bMOOC project integrates the iterative approach of DBR following the cycles of analysis/exploration, design/construction and evaluation/reflection recommended by McKenney and Reeves (2012) and the two main RQs are structured around these cycles. Although the project intends to use several data collection methods (e.g., surveys and focus groups) and data analysis techniques (e.g., social network analysis, content analysis, statistical analysis), in this paper we only address the bMOOC surveys (data collected using SurveyMonkey) from the course first edition and analyse their results statistically and through content analysis (analysed using MAXQDA).

Results and Discussion

Two surveys were designed and integrated into the bMOOC for all course participants to complete, in the Bootcamp and immediately after the completion of the course.

Pre-bMOOC Survey

The pre-bMOOC survey had the following objectives:

- To characterize the participants' professional situation.
- To gather information about participants' online professional development experience.
- To identify the participants' views about teaching and assessing listening and speaking in primary English classes.

A total of 107 participants answered the pre-bMOOC survey, of which 90 (84%) completed the course. The respondents were 96% women and 4% men. Most of them (69%) were in the 41-50 age group and 21% were between 51-60 years old. As for their education, 69% declared having a master's degree or equivalent, and 30% a bachelor's degree or equivalent.

Main objectives for enrolling in the course

Regarding this item, the three most chosen options were: 1st: To learn more about the topic for my professional development (34,6%), 2nd: To connect and interact with other primary English teachers (24,2%) and 3rd: To get accreditation for my professional development (23,9%). The main objectives of the participants for enrolling in the online course align therefore with the project objectives, namely, expanding knowledge for professional development and connect and interact with other teachers. Of course, getting accreditation for professional development and progression is a main drive, but not the top one.

Prior experience with open and online education

The participants' experience as online students is not substantial and even very low regarding MOOCs. The majority of the participants Low (fewer than 5 courses, 43%) to Medium (between 5-10 courses, 45%) experience as online students. Most participants' experience was both in e-learning and b-learning formats (52%), with 41% having experience only in e-learning format, and 65% had already participated in a course with official accreditation for professional purposes. Nevertheless, 69% of the participants replied that they had no experience as a MOOC participant, and only 22% registered participating in, at least three MOOCs.

Experience with platform and software

In what regards the **experience as a user of the NAU courses' platform (Open EdX)**, where the course was delivered, 71% replied they had no experience with the platform, with only 24% reporting they had some experience due to participation in some courses provided by NAU. By the contrary, 60% of the participants reported having some **experience using Padlet** and 26% reported being very experienced users of the app. Interestingly, about 80% of the participants reported having no **experience with the WordPress platform**, with only 19% reporting they had some experience with WordPress.

What participants value most about MOOCs

Regarding **what participants valued most about MOOCs**, the most referred items were 1st: Course available online (16,2%), 2nd: Self-paced course (15%), 3rd: Focusing on developing specific skills (14,3%), 4th: Course with no fixed schedule (12,1%). In what refers to the form of professional development preferred, 59% of the participants chose e-learning format, 19% b-learning format and 14% face to face.

Post-bMOOC Survey

The post-bMOOC survey had the following objectives:

- To gather information about participants' perceptions about the bMOOC online environment (course and vCoP).
- To collect information about the impact of the course on participants' teaching practice. The data collected corresponding to this objective is not analysed in this paper, which focus mostly on the course content and structure rather than the perceived learning.

A total of 71 participants answered the post-bMOOC survey out of the 88 that completed it. The age and gender demographics were similar to the pre-bMOOC survey. Concurring with the MOOC experience reported by the participants, 68% reported this was their first experience participating in a MOOC.

Satisfaction with the online platforms

The global satisfaction about the use of the three platforms of the bMOOC concurred with the users' previous experience of using them, with Padlet having the highest scores followed by NAU Platform. The **Padlet Platform** had averages between 4,62 and 4,73. The evaluation of the quality of the **NAU Platform** and its content was also rather positive (the averages ranging from 4,48 to 4,75), in particular the videos. Some participants remarked minor problems with the videos' captions.

Although still positive, the **WordPress Community Platform** had the lowest scores (averages between 3,75 and 4,52). Asked to explain their evaluation, a relevant number of responses referred to difficulties in navigating the WordPress Community Platform at least in the beginning. The participants referred to navigation not being intuitive and difficulties using the message system (only one file as attachment). In the forums, they mentioned navigation issues when there were a lot of messages. Some mentioned also that using three platforms was too many spaces to manage.

Course evaluation

Regarding the **quality of the pre-course preparations**, the TAM-bMOOC website and the pre-course information sent by email were rated positively, with averages of 4,3 and 4,6. The same happened with the **Introductory Bootcamp Module**, rated with an average of 4,6. The **theory modules** had excellent scores (between 4,7 and 4,8), and the same happened with the **practice modules** (averages between 4,70 and 4,75). Asked to explain their evaluation, the participants offered some suggestions in particular needing more time/too much workload in the Practice Modules weeks. The **satisfaction with the alternation between theory and practice** was also positively rated (average of 4,7), with some more mentions to needing more time in the explaining options question.

The **quality of course support** was also positive (averages ranging from 4,29 to 4,48). Nevertheless, some participants remarked they would have liked more feedback. Regarding **interaction with peers**, the forums that the participants used more for interacting were the Module Forums and the MOOC Group Forum all housed in the WordPress Community Platform. Asked if they used **other channels of communication** (like WhatsApp or email) most of the participants stated that they did not, having used mainly the communication spaces provided in the course.

Use of Gen AI Tools

Respondents indicated having used Gen AI-supported tools to conduct several tasks. Mostly they reported making use of these tools for three types of tasks: ***fine tuning something you had written*** (32,0%), ***finding further information about a topic*** (28,0%), and ***summarising a response*** (26,0%). Significantly, course participants who responded the survey didn't value the use of Gen AI tools for **check your response to a question prompt** (2,0%) and even less so to ask for **help to complete a course task** (0%). This indicates that the use of these tools, which was neither banned nor suggested, has clearly to become mainstream within the PETs community.

What participants valued most and least in the bMOOC

The features participants considered more positive in the bMOOC were the development of specific skills/knowledge on English Teaching (21,7%) and the opportunity to learn more and rethink about assessment (21,1%), two of the main course objectives. In third place, they reported interaction and sharing with peers (14,3%), even with the reported difficulties by some on using the learning environment(s). The participants also referred the course flexibility (8%), enabling them to work at their own pace and time, and being online as positive aspects.

On the opposite, the main aspect that participants considered negative was the course high workload for the time available (47%). The fact that there were too many platforms and spaces (12,8%) and they found, at least in the beginning, some difficulty navigating throughout the various platforms (6,8), were referred as the next negative aspect. There were also some references to Feedback and Peer assessment issues.

Recommendations for improvement

The main recommendations of the course participants were to adjust workload and course structure to time to take course (25,9%), and to reduce number of platforms or interaction spaces (19,6%). Some suggestions were also made to Improve the course structure and to Improve moderators support and feedback.

Conclusions

The TAM-bMOOC project was designed in response to the need for improving PETs' PD opportunities, especially in what concerns learning assessment methodologies. The approach used intended to ensure a more effective link between research, pedagogical innovation and the transformation of teacher practices. To achieve this, it is critical to support immersive teacher training in real contexts of educational practice. Literature shows that the development and use of a bMOOC associated to vCoP could reduce professional isolation, foster engagement and result in higher rates of participation and course completion. The results of the 1st iteration cycle of the TAM bMOOC, seem to prove this assertion. The participants report general satisfaction with the course and the impact of the training in the transformation of their teaching practices. Nevertheless, there are some dimensions which need to be improved in further iterations of the bMOOC, such as the navigation and orientation through the different spaces of the online environment and the adequation of the course structure and participants' expected workload to its pace and duration. One major additional finding is that participants who at first expressed low levels of digital literacy reported after completing the course the use of digital technologies to conduct their professional tasks. The survey shows that PETs regularly use Gen AI-supported tools for fine tuning their writings, find further information and summarise responses. The next iterations of the bMOOC will be fundamental to assess if the vCoP is sustainable in the long run and if it is able to promote a continuous reflective PD of PETs as aimed by the project.

Competing interests

The authors have no competing interests to declare.

Ethics and consent

The research was conducted and published according to recognised international standards, e.g. the Declaration of Helsinki. The identity of the research subjects was anonymised. Free, prior and informed consent to participate in the study was obtained from the respondents to the study. The research received the approval of the Ethics Committees of both the NOVA University of Lisbon and the Laboratory of Distance Education and eLearning – LE@D.

Acknowledgements

The authors acknowledge the CETAPS research centre for the funding of the research and LE@D for the support to the TAM project.

References

Darling-Hammond, L., Hyler, M. E., & Gardner, M. (2017). Efective teacher professional development. Learning Policy Institute.

Fortunato, M., Moreira, A., & Simões, A.R. (2021). Práticas dos docentes de inglês no 1° CEB: O que dizem os relatórios do Inspeção Geral da Educação e Ciência. Indagatio Didactica, 13(5), 45-72. https://doi.org/10.34624/id.v13i5.27160

Hadar, L. & Brody, D. (2010). From isolation to symphonic harmony: Building a professional development community among teacher educators. Teaching and Teacher Education, 26(8), 1641-1651. https://doi.org/10.1016/j.tate.2010.06.015

Hertz, B. & Engelhardt, K. (2021). Using personalized support & school-based study groups to increase teachers' participation in MOOCs – findings from two European pilot projects. IUL Research, 2(3), 3-20.

Jones, K. L. M., Stephens, M., Branch-Mueller, J. & de Groot, J. (2016). Community of practice or affinity space: A case study of a professional development MOOC. Education for Information, 32 (1) 101–119.

Kennedy, E. (2021). Blended learning in teacher education & training: Findings from research & practice. European Schoolnet.

Marsh, B., & Mitchell, N. (2014). The role of video in teacher professional development. Teacher Development 18(3), 403-417. https://doi.org/10.1080/13664530.2014.938106

McKenney, S., & Reeves, T. C. (2012). Conducting Educational Design Research. Routledge.

Moreira, M.A., Mourão, S., Leslie, C., & Monteiro, E. (2021). Avaliação das aprendizagens de Inglês no 1° CEB: Um estudo em Portugal continental. CETAPS, NOVA FCSH. https://run.unl.pt/handle/10362/127374

Mourão, S., Leslie, C., Moreira, M., & Monteiro, E. (2021). Battling against a traditional assessment culture: The case of early English learning in Portugal. In C. Bongartz & J. Rymarczyk (Eds.), Current research into young FL and EAL learners' literacy skills. (pp. 141-164). Peter Lang.

Mourão, S., Leslie, C., Moreira, M.A., & Monteiro, E. (2025). From (mis)perceptions to (mis)practices: The assessment of oral skills in primary English education in Portugal. In D. Karoulla-Vrikki, & L. Lopriore, L. (Eds.), Oracy acquisition and development in early second language learning: Voices from diverse international contexts. Multilingual Matters.

Ng, P.T., & Tan, C. (2009). Community of practice for teachers: Sensemaking or critical reflective learning? Reflective Practice, 10 (1), 37-44. https://doi.org/10.1080/14623940802652730

Orsini-Jones, M., Conde, B., Borthwick, K., Zou, B. & Ma, W. (2018). B-MELTT: Blending MOOCs for English language teacher training. British Council. https://www.teachingenglish.org.uk/sites/teacheng/files/Pub_J121_Blending%20MOOCs%20for%20English%20language%20teacher%20training_FINAL_Web.pdf

Papp, S. (2019). Assessment and young English language learners. In S. Garton & F. Copland (Eds.), Routledge handbook of teaching English to young learners. (pp.389-407). Routledge.

Reeves, T. C., & Amiel, T. (2008). Design-Based Research and Educational Technology: Rethinking Technology and the Research Agenda. Educational Technology & Society, 11(4), 29–40. https://doi.org/10.1590/S0325-00752011000100012

Rixon, S., & Prošić-Santovac, D. (2019). Introduction: Assessment and early language learning. In D. Prošić-Santovac & S. Rixon (Eds.), Integrating assessment in early language learning and teaching practice (pp. 1-18). Multilingual Matters.

Rich, S. (2019). Early language learner teacher education. In S. Garton & F. Copland (Eds.), Routledge handbook of teaching English to young learners. (pp. 44-59). Routledge.

Teixeira, A. M., Correia, C. J., Afonso, F., Maina, M., Cabot, A. G., López, E. G., Tortosa, S. O., Piedra, N., Canuti, L., Guzmán, J., Solís, M. A. C. (2013). Inclusive Open Educational Practices: How the uses and reuse of OER can support virtual higher education for all. Eurodl. Best of EDEN 2012. 78-91.

Teixeira, A., Mota, J., García-Cabot, A., García Lopéz, E. & y de-Marcos, L. (2015). A new competence-based approach for personalizing MOOCs in a mobile collaborative and networked environment. RIED Revista Iberoamericana de Educación a Distancia, 19(1), 143-160.

Teixeira, A., Miranda, B., Oliveira, I & Pinto, M. (2018). MOOC "Competências para Professores": uma prática formativa inovadora. RIED Revista Iberoamericana de Educación a Distancia, 21(2), 143-160. doi:10.5944/ried.21.2.19784

Trust, T., & Horrocks, B. (2019). Six key elements identified in an active and thriving blended community of practice. TechTrends, 63(2), 108-115.

Wenger, E., McDermott, R., & Snyder, W.M. (2002). Cultivating communities of practice: A guide to managing knowledge. Harvard Business School Press.

Woodward, T. (2003). Loop input. ELT Journal, 57(3), 301-304. https://doi.org/10.1093/elt/57.3.301

AUTHOR INDEX